VMware vSphere 6.7 Cookbook
Fourth Edition

Practical recipes to deploy, configure, and manage VMware vSphere 6.7 components

Abhilash G B

BIRMINGHAM - MUMBAI

VMware vSphere 6.7 Cookbook
Fourth Edition

Commissioning Editor: Vijin Boricha
Acquisition Editor: Heramb Bhavsar
Content Development Editor: Drashti Panchal
Senior Editor: Rahul Dsouza
Technical Editor: Prachi Sawant
Copy Editor: Safis Editing
Project Coordinator: Vaidehi Sawant
Proofreader: Safis Editing
Indexer: Pratik Shirodkar
Production Designer: Jyoti Chauhan

First published: July 2013
Second edition: February 2015
Third edition: January 2018
Fourth edition: August 2019

Production reference: 1300819

Published by Packt Publishing Ltd.
Livery Place
35 Livery Street
Birmingham
B3 2PB, UK.

ISBN 978-1-78995-300-8

www.packt.com

This book is dedicated to the memory of my father, who very subtly instilled diligence as my second nature. Furthermore, it is impossible to adequately thank my wife and my little six-year-old princess, without whose support this book would not have been possible.

Packt.com

Subscribe to our online digital library for full access to over 7,000 books and videos, as well as industry leading tools to help you plan your personal development and advance your career. For more information, please visit our website.

Why subscribe?

- Spend less time learning and more time coding with practical eBooks and Videos from over 4,000 industry professionals

- Improve your learning with Skill Plans built especially for you

- Get a free eBook or video every month

- Fully searchable for easy access to vital information

- Copy and paste, print, and bookmark content

Did you know that Packt offers eBook versions of every book published, with PDF and ePub files available? You can upgrade to the eBook version at www.packt.com and as a print book customer, you are entitled to a discount on the eBook copy. Get in touch with us at customercare@packtpub.com for more details.

At www.packt.com, you can also read a collection of free technical articles, sign up for a range of free newsletters, and receive exclusive discounts and offers on Packt books and eBooks.

Contributors

About the author

Abhilash G B is a virtualization specialist, author, and a VMware vExpert (2014-2019). His primary focus is in the areas of data center virtualization and cloud computing. He has been in the IT industry for more than a decade and has been working on VMware products and technologies since the beginning of 2007. He holds several VMware certifications, including VCIX6-DCV, VCAP-DCA/DCD, VCP-DCV, VCP-Cloud, and VCP-NV. He is also the author of six other publications.

Thanks to the technical reviewer, Mario Russo, for his valuable input. Special thanks to the entire Packt team for their support during the course of writing this book.

About the reviewer

Mario Russo is a senior solution architect at Atos Italy, and a solution leader expert – TTS – RFP – RFQ – Presales. He has worked as an IT architect, as a senior technical VMware trainer, and in the presales department, and has been involved with VMware technology since 2004. He is a VCI-certified instructor level 2s of VMware, and is certified in VCAP5-DCA - VCP-Cloud – VMware Certified Professional 6 – Data Center Virtualization, VMware Certified Professional 6 – Network Virtualization (NSX v6.2), VCP7-CMA VMware Certified Professional 7, and many other technologies. He has also been the technical reviewer of many other Packt books.

Thanks to my Wife, Lina, and my daughter, Gaia, for supporting me in any experience and in every challenge that life puts me in front of.

Packt is searching for authors like you

If you're interested in becoming an author for Packt, please visit authors.packtpub.com and apply today. We have worked with thousands of developers and tech professionals, just like you, to help them share their insight with the global tech community. You can make a general application, apply for a specific hot topic that we are recruiting an author for, or submit your own idea.

Table of Contents

Preface

With more and more data centers being virtualized using its technologies, VMware is still the undisputed leader in providing virtualization solutions ranging from server virtualization to storage and network virtualization. Despite the efforts from Citrix and Microsoft, VMware's vSphere product line is still the most feature-rich and futuristic in the virtualization industry. Knowing how to install and configure the latest vSphere components is important if you want to give yourself a head start in virtualization using VMware. This book covers the installation and upgrade of the vSphere environment and also the administration tasks that one would commonly need to handle when managing a VMware infrastructure.

VMware vSphere 6.7 Cookbook is a task-oriented, fast-paced, practical guide to installing and configuring vSphere 6.7 components. It will take you through all of the steps required to accomplish various configuration tasks with less reading. Most of the tasks are accompanied by relevant screenshots and flowcharts with the intention of providing visual guidance as well. The book concentrates more on the actual task at hand, rather than the theory around it, making it easier to understand what is really needed to achieve the task. However, most of the concepts have been thoroughly described to help you understand the background and how they work.

Who this book is for

This book is for anyone who wants to learn how to install and configure VMware vSphere components. It is an excellent handbook for administrators, along with anyone else looking for a head start in learning how to upgrade, install, and configure vSphere 6.7 components. It is also a useful, task-oriented reference guide for consultants who design and deploy with vSphere.

What this book covers

Chapter 1, *Deploying a New vSphere 6.7 Infrastructure*, walks you through the procedures involved in deploying a new vSphere 6.7 infrastructure. It covers the installation of ESXi and the deployment of the vCenter Server virtual appliance.

Chapter 2, *Planning and Executing the Upgrade of vSphere*, discusses the procedures involved in upgrading an existing vSphere infrastructure to vSphere 6.7. It covers upgrading vCenter Server and the ESXi hosts.

`Chapter 3`, *Configuring Network Access Using vSphere Standard Switches*, explains how to set up and configure vSphere networking using vSphere Standard Switches.

`Chapter 4`, *Configuring Network Access Using vSphere Distributed Switches*, explains how to set up and configure vSphere networking using vSphere Distributed Switches. It covers advanced network configurations such as port mirroring, NetFlow, and the use of PVLANs.

`Chapter 5`, *Configuring Storage Access for Your vSphere Environment*, walks you through the procedures involved in configuring access to Fiber Channel, iSCSI and NFS storage for the ESXi hosts.

`Chapter 6`, *Creating and Managing VMFS Datastores*, walks you through the procedures involved in creating and managing VMFS datastores.

`Chapter 7`, *SIOC, Storage DRS, and Profile-Driven Storage*, covers the use of storage policies to ensure that the **virtual machines** (**VMs**) are placed in datastores categorized into different capability tiers, using SIOC to enable balanced I/O between VMs running on different hosts, and using Storage DRS to cluster datastores for I/O load balancing.

`Chapter 8`, *Configuring vSphere DRS, DPM, and VMware EVC*, covers the configuration of vSphere Distributed Resource Scheduler, Distributed Power Management, and VMware Enhanced vMotion Compatibility on an ESXi cluster.

`Chapter 9`, *Achieving High Availability in a vSphere Environment*, covers the concepts and configuration of high availability for vSphere components – the ESXi host (vSphere HA), the VM (VMware FT), and vCenter Server (VCHA).

`Chapter 10`, *Achieving Configuration Compliance Using vSphere Host Profiles*, covers the use of host profiles to create, manage, and use ESXi host configuration templates.

`Chapter 11`, *Building Custom ESXi Images Using Image Builder*, covers using Image Profiles to customize ESXi images.

`Chapter 12`, *Auto-Deploying Stateless and Stateful ESXi Hosts*, covers the procedures involved in standing up a vSphere Auto Deploy infrastructure to enable faster provisioning of stateless or stateful ESXi hosts.

`Chapter 13`, *Creating and Managing Virtual Machines*, covers essential virtual machine administration tasks.

`Chapter 14`, *Upgrading and Patching Using vSphere Update Manager*, covers the configuration of vSphere Update Manager and the Update Manager Download Service to update/patch ESXi hosts.

Chapter 15, *Securing vSphere Using SSL Certificates*, teaches you how to secure communication between the vSphere components and its endpoints using SSL certificates.

Chapter 16, *Monitoring the vSphere Infrastructure*, covers a high-level overview of the essential tools used to monitor the performance of ESXi and VMs in a vSphere infrastructure.

To get the most out of this book

You will learn about the software requirements for every vSphere component covered in this book in their respective chapters, but to start with a basic lab setup, you will need at least two ESXi hosts, a vCenter Server, a Domain Controller, a DHCP server, a DNS server, and a TFTP Server. For learning purposes, you don't really need to run ESXi on physical machines. You can use VMware Workstation to set up a hosted lab on your desktop PC or laptop, provided the machine has adequate compute and storage resources.

For shared storage, you can use any of the following free virtual storage appliances:

- OpenFiler can be downloaded from https://www.openfiler.com.
- HP StoreVirtual VSA can be downloaded from http://www8.hp.com/in/en/products/data-storage/storevirtual.html.

Download the color images

We also provide a PDF file that has color images of the screenshots/diagrams used in this book. You can download it here: https://static.packt-cdn.com/downloads/9781789953008_ColorImages.pdf.

Conventions used

There are a number of text conventions used throughout this book.

CodeInText: Indicates code words in text, database table names, folder names, filenames, file extensions, pathnames, dummy URLs, user input, and Twitter handles. Here is an example: "Browse the ISO contents and navigate to the migration-assistant folder."

Any command-line input or output is written as follows:

```
esxtop -b -a -d 10 -n 50 > /tmp/perf_statistics.csv
```

Bold: Indicates a new term, an important word, or words that you see onscreen. For example, words in menus or dialog boxes appear in the text like this. Here is an example: "Specify an optional **Name and Description** and click **Finish** to create the Host Profile."

 Warnings or important notes appear like this.

 Tips and tricks appear like this.

Sections

In this book, you will find several headings that appear frequently (*Getting ready*, *How to do it...*, *How it works...*, *There's more...*, and *See also*).

To give clear instructions on how to complete a recipe, use these sections as follows:

Getting ready

This section tells you what to expect in the recipe and describes how to set up any software or any preliminary settings required for the recipe.

How to do it...

This section contains the steps required to follow the recipe.

How it works...

This section usually consists of a detailed explanation of what happened in the previous section.

There's more...

This section consists of additional information about the recipe in order to make you more knowledgeable about the recipe.

See also

This section provides helpful links to other useful information for the recipe.

Get in touch

Feedback from our readers is always welcome.

General feedback: If you have questions about any aspect of this book, mention the book title in the subject of your message and email us at customercare@packtpub.com.

Errata: Although we have taken every care to ensure the accuracy of our content, mistakes do happen. If you have found a mistake in this book, we would be grateful if you would report this to us. Please visit www.packtpub.com/support/errata, selecting your book, clicking on the Errata Submission Form link, and entering the details.

Piracy: If you come across any illegal copies of our works in any form on the Internet, we would be grateful if you would provide us with the location address or website name. Please contact us at copyright@packt.com with a link to the material.

If you are interested in becoming an author: If there is a topic that you have expertise in and you are interested in either writing or contributing to a book, please visit authors.packtpub.com.

Reviews

Please leave a review. Once you have read and used this book, why not leave a review on the site that you purchased it from? Potential readers can then see and use your unbiased opinion to make purchase decisions, we at Packt can understand what you think about our products, and our authors can see your feedback on their book. Thank you!

For more information about Packt, please visit packt.com.

Deploying a New vSphere 6.7 Infrastructure

vSphere is a suite of core infrastructure solutions that form the foundation of any modern data center that is virtualized using VMware. Planning the deployment of these components and their implementation is important as it forms the basis for any other solution.

vSphere essentially includes the hypervisor (ESXi), vCenter Server and its plugins, supporting databases and host management agents. These hypervisors create a platform to run **virtual machines** (**VMs**), and vCenter forms the management layer. vCenter enables the creation of virtual data centers. Every other solution interfaces and interacts with vCenter to manage or utilize the virtual data center. For example, vRealize Automation, NSX, and vRealize Operations interact with vCenter.

Having said that, VMware does offer APIs that allow third-party software developers to build tools that help to manage platforms or leverage the management layer formed by the vCenter servers in an environment. For example, your backup software interacts with vCenter to manage virtual machine backups.

The following software components form the foundation of a vSphere environment:

- **Hypervisor**: VMware ESXi 6.7
- **Core management software**: VMware vCenter 6.7 server and its components
- **Patch management software**: VMware Update Manager 6.7

ESXi Hypervisor is the abstraction layer that allows you to run multiple instances of traditional operating systems as VMs sharing the same physical resources. With every major release, 6.7 enhances the ability of the hypervisor to scale up, as well as other new features. One of the notable new features is **Quick Boot**. Unlike the previous versions, a reboot does not power cycle the host; instead, it restarts just the hypervisor, reducing a considerable amount of the time that is otherwise required during server initialization.

Read the *WHAT'S NEW IN VMWARE vSPHERE 6.7* whitepaper for a brief insight into all the new features of vSphere 6.7 at `https://www.vmware.com/content/dam/digitalmarketing/vmware/en/pdf/products/vsphere/vmware-whats-new-in-vsphere-whitepaper.pdf`.

Although the book was based on vSphere 6.7 U1, VMware did release two additional updates post that. Read the release notes of vSphere 6.7 U2 and U3 for details.

vSphere 6.7 U2: `https://docs.vmware.com/en/VMware-vSphere/6.7/rn/vsphere-esxi-67u2-release-notes.html` and `https://docs.vmware.com/en/VMware-vSphere/6.7/rn/vsphere-vcenter-server-67u2-release-notes.html`

vSphere 6.7U3: `https://docs.vmware.com/en/VMware-vSphere/6.7/rn/vsphere-esxi-67u3-release-notes.html` and `https://docs.vmware.com/en/VMware-vSphere/6.7/rn/vsphere-vcenter-server-67u3-release-notes.html`

Core management software – VMware vCenter Server 6.7 and its components:

The vCenter Appliance with vSphere 6.5 was a significant improvement and saw a substantial shift in the adoption of **vCenter Server Appliance (VCSA)**. VCSA 6.5/6.7 is equally scalable, as the Windows version of the vCenter, needless to say, is more stable and easier to troubleshoot as all the software components are packaged to run on a lightweight Linux operating system called **PHOTON OS** (`https://vmware.github.io/photon/`). Also, VMware is gradually shifting away from its dependence on Microsoft SQL and Oracle Database systems by using a PostgreSQL-based (`https://www.postgresql.org/`) database called **vPostgres.**

 vSphere 6.7 will be the last release that includes a Windows installable version of vCenter. All future versions of vCenter will only be as an appliance (VCSA).

VMware began bundling essential services, such as SSO, Inventory Service, and certificate management, into a single manageable component called the **Platform Services Controller (PSC)**, starting with vSphere 6.0. With versions prior to vCenter 6.0 for Windows, all of these components had individual installers, making it possible for them to be either installed on the same machine as the vCenter or installed onto separate machines. Therefore, it became necessary to protect and manage more than one virtual or physical machine running Windows. It also made upgrading and troubleshooting cumbersome. Bundling them together onto the same Windows machine or deploying as an appliance made management and the upgrade of these components a breeze.

PSC can be deployed as a separate virtual machine (Windows/VCSA) or remain as an embedded component of the VCSA. Starting with vSphere 6.7, the need for an external PSC has been deprecated.

SSO is an authentication server component that's embedded into the PSC. It acts as an authentication gateway and accepts authentication requests from registered components and validates the credential pair against identity sources that are added to the SSO server. Once successfully authenticated, they are provided with security tokens for authentication exchanges going forward.

vCenter Update Manager (**VUM**) is used to upgrade or patch a vSphere environment. It is predominantly used to install patches or perform ESXi upgrades. It can perform additional tasks, such as upgrading VMware tools and upgrading virtual machine hardware. The solution is fully integrated into the vCenter Appliance and is enabled by default.

vSphere Certificate Manager is a built-in certificate manager that uses **VMware Certificate Authority** (**VMCA**) as the issuing authority by default.

VMware Licensing Service is a repository for the licensing information of all VMware products that work with the PSC/vCenter. License information is replicated between PSCs that are in the same SSO domain.

The **vCenter database** is the source of truth for vCenter. vCenter will not function without an active connection to the database.

In this chapter, we will cover the following recipes:

- Installing ESXi – the interactive method
- Configuring the ESXi Management Network
- Scripted deployment of ESXi
- Deploying the vCenter Server Appliance (VCSA)
- Deploying vCenters in a Linked Mode configuration
- Configuring Single Sign-On (SSO) identity sources
- Configuring vCenter Roles and Permissions
- Joining ESXi to an Active Directory domain

Installing ESXi – the interactive method

VMware ESXi can be installed in more than one way. The traditional approach is to use the ESXi CD/DVD-ROM image to perform an interactive installation. In this recipe, we will learn how to install ESXi using the bootable installer image.

Getting ready

Before you begin, it is recommended that you refer to the VMware Compatibility Guide to verify whether the server hardware is compatible with VMware ESXi 6.7.

 The VMware Compatibility Guide can be found at `http://www.vmware.com/resources/compatibility/search.php`.

Hardware requirements

Once you have made sure that the server hardware is compatible, the next step is to make sure that the server meets the hardware capacity requirements, which are as follows:

- The physical server should have at least two 64-bit x86 CPU cores.
- AMD **No Execute** (**NX**) and Intel **Execute Disable** (**XD**) processor functions should be enabled in the server BIOS.
- To be able to run 64-bit operating systems on VMs, you will need to allow the use of hardware virtualization (Intel VT-x or AMD RVI) in the server BIOS.
- A minimum of 4 GB of physical memory for the hypervisor alone, and an additional 4 GB to start hosting VMs.

Software required for the installation

The VMware ESXi 6.7 hypervisor ISO image can be downloaded from VMware's downloads page, at `https://my.vmware.com/web/vmware/downloads`.

 Server vendors provide customized images of ESXi so that it can include the drivers and other components, such as CIM providers. Always contact the vendor to download the OEM ESXi image.

Using the ESXi image

You need a way to present the ISO to the physical machine so that it can boot from it.

Of course, you could burn the ISO to a physical DVD and then insert it into the DVD drive of the physical machine. However, most modern servers will have a method to present the ISO image to the server as a virtual drive via its IPMI interface. If you are an administrator, you may already be aware of terms such as ILO (HP), DRAC (Dell), and KVM manager (Cisco). These are web-based tools that will connect to a **Remote Access Card** (**RAC**) on the server and enable remote access to the server's console through the web interface.

How to do it...

The following procedure will guide you through the steps involved in deploying ESXi 6.7 using the interactive installer:

1. Mount the ISO to the server via its IPMI interface.
2. Boot the server of the ISO. Unlike the older version of the installers, it no longer presents you with the installer boot menu. Instead, it starts loading the installer into the memory and subsequently shows the following `Welcome to the VMware ESXi 6.7.0 Installation` screen:

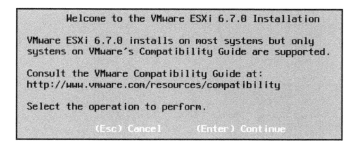

3. Once you hit *Enter* to continue, on the next screen, hit *F11* to accept the license agreement and continue.

4. On the next screen, you will be prompted to choose a storage device to install ESXi on, which could be a local SSD, a local hard disk, or a LUN from remote storage (in a boot from a SAN scenario). Use the keyboard to make a selection and hit *Enter* to confirm. Alternatively, to make a cautious effort to ensure that you have selected the correct disk, and before you confirm the selection by hitting *Enter*, hit *F1* to fetch more details regarding the storage device that you've selected. *Step 5* covers this process:

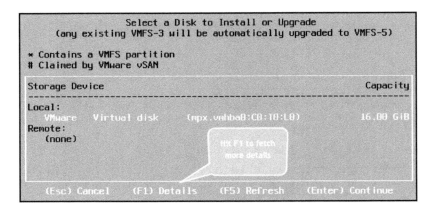

5. An optional step: select the storage device and hit *F1*. You will now be presented with unique details, such as the CTL path to the device, LUN ID, Target ID (if using iSCSI), and the capacity of the disk, along with other general information. It will also tell you if an existing installation of ESXi is present on the storage device:

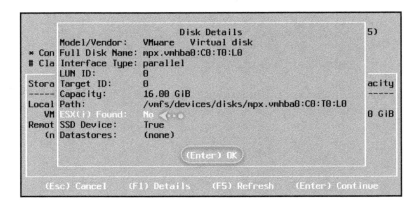

General Disk details

6. Once you are done with the verification process, hit *Enter*. You will be taken back to the `Select a Disk to Install or Upgrade` screen. Hit *Enter* to confirm the device selection.

7. On the next screen, select a keyboard layout. The US default is preselected. Make a different selection if necessary and hit *Enter* to continue.

8. You will be prompted to set a password for the ESXi `root` account. Once you type in the password, hit *Enter* to continue.

 At this stage, the installer will scan the server hardware for additional information or prerequisites that it would need to proceed further. If any of the prechecks fail, you will be warned accordingly. For instance, if you do not have Intel VT-x or AMD-V enabled in the BIOS, then it will warn you about that. It can also warn you about unsupported devices that are detected during the scan. Most warnings will not stop you from proceeding further, and will only indicate what will not be configured or supported. Hit *Enter* to continue.

9. At the `Confirm Install` screen, review the storage device name that's displayed. If that is the correct device, hit *F11* to start the installation. If you are unsure, use *F9* to go back and make the necessary changes:

10. The `Install ESXi 6.7.0` screen will show the progress of the installation. It could take a few minutes to complete.

11. When the installation completes, you will be advised to remove the installation media (unmount the ISO) before you restart the server. Once done, hit *Enter* to reboot:

12. After a reboot, you will be at the main screen for ESXi 6.7.0.

This completes the process of installing ESXi on a bare-metal server using the ESXi installer ISO.

How it works...

The ESXi installer loads all the necessary modules into the memory, detects hardware resources, and then lets you perform the installation on a storage device that's been specified. Once installed, ESXi runs in a 60-day evaluation mode and needs to be licensed for production use. The first post-installation step is to make the ESXi host available on the network by configuring its management TCP/IP stack. Read the following *Configuring the ESXi management network* recipe to learn more.

Configuring the ESXi Management Network

After installing ESXi, it is essential to configure its management network. The management network configuration is associated with a VMkernel interface. Think of it as a virtual network interface for VMkernel. We will learn more about these in the Chapter 3, *Configuring Network Access Using vSphere Standard Switches*. ESXi hypervisor runs a DHCP client, so it procures a DHCP address if there is a DHCP server on its network; however, in most cases, this is not enough. For instance, if your management network is on a VLAN, then you will need to configure a VLAN ID. Also, it is recommended to assign a static IP address for ESXi's management network.

In this recipe, we will use the **Direct Console User Interface** (**DCUI**) to achieve this.

Getting ready

You will need the following information to proceed with the steps:

- You will need access to the server's remote console via its IPMI interface (Dell DRAC, HPE ILO, Cisco KVM).
- The password for the root account.
- TCP/IP configuration - IP address, subnet mask, IP gateway address, VLAN ID, DNS server addresses, and hostname.

How to do it...

The following procedure will guide you through the steps that are required to set up the TCP/IP configuration for ESXi's management network:

1. At the main screen of ESXi, hit *F2* to log in to the DCUI by supplying the root password.
2. Navigate to **Configure Management Network** and hit *Enter*:

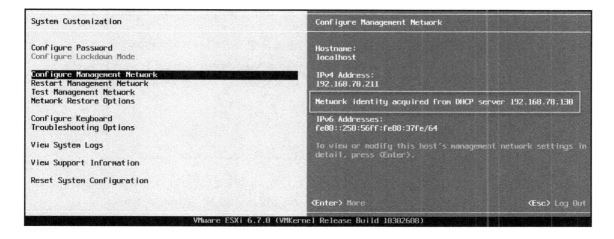

3. The **Configure Management Network** screen will present you with options to select the **Network Adapters**, assign a VLAN ID if necessary, and configure the IPv4/IPv6 settings and DNS configuration. Each of these sections can be selected by hitting *Enter* and then using the onscreen instructions to select/modify/confirm the settings:

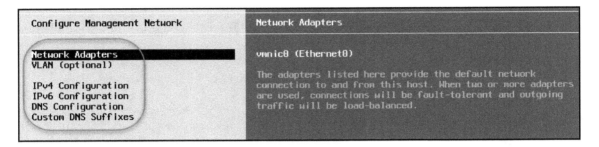

4. The **Network Adapters** section can be used to assign/unassign adapters to the Management Network Port Group. Use the onscreen instructions to make selections and confirm them:

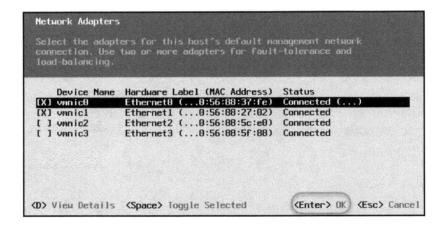

5. The **VLAN (optional)** section is used to supply a VLAN ID for the interface. The **IPv4 Configuration** section is used supply an **IP Address/Subnet Mask/Default Gateway**:

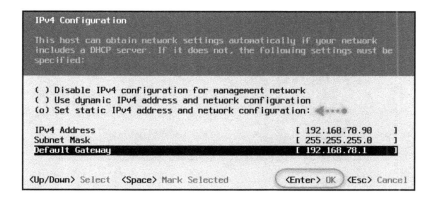

6. The **IPv6 Configuration** section is used to supply IPv6 addresses. IPv6 is enabled by default. If IPv6 is not required for your environment, select the **Disable IPv6 (restart required)** option and hit *Enter*.

7. The **DNS Configuration** section can be used to supply primary/alternate DNS server addresses and hostnames:

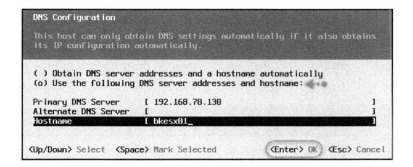

 If you do not supply an FDQN when setting the hostname, then ensure that you configure a Custom DNS Suffix.

8. **Custom DNS Suffixes** are optional if you used an FQDN as a hostname in the previous step:

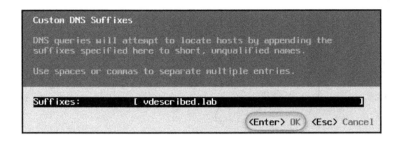

9. Once you are done with all the network configuration, while on the **Configure Management Network: Confirm** screen, hit *Esc*. You will be prompted to apply the changes by restarting the management network. Hit *Y* to apply the settings and reboot the hosts:

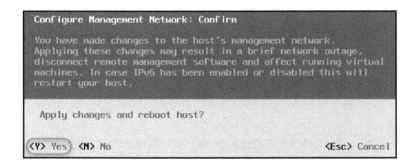

10. Once the reboot is complete, you should be able to reach the ESXi host over the network. From here, the ESXi host can be managed directly using the host client or can be added to vCenter Server.

How it works...

Much like the VMs that would run on the ESXi hosts, the VMkernel would also need to interface with the network for a variety of purposes. These interfaces act as network node points for the VMkernel. The very first VMkernel interface – vmk0 is created during the installation of ESXi. This interface is the management interface for the ESXi host. VMware allows you to create a maximum of 256 (vmk0 – vmk255) VMkernel interfaces on an ESXi host.

The use cases include interfaces for Management traffic, VMotion traffic, FT traffic, Virtual SAN traffic, iSCSI, and NAS interfaces. Since each interface is a network node point, it will need an IP configuration and a MAC address.

The first VMkernel interface (vmk0) will procure the MAC address of the physical NIC it is connected to. The remaining interfaces pick up the VMware OUI MAC address that's generated by the ESXi host.

OUI MAC addresses

Every physical network interface will have a burned-in **48-bit MAC address** whose numbering is organizationally unique. This is because every vendor that makes the card will have a set of **organizationally unique identifiers** (**OUI**) assigned to them by the **Institute of Electrical and Electronics Engineers** (**IEEE**).

 VMware also has a set of OUIs assigned to it, that is, `00:50:56` and `00:0C:29`. Although both OUIs are used differently, they can be assigned to virtual machine NICs and the VMkernel interface.

All VMkernel interfaces except for vmk0 will receive a MAC address with a OUI of `00:56:54`.

Scripted deployment of ESXi

When you have a large number of ESXi hosts to deploy, any method to automate and reduce the amount of manual work is considered gold. The main benefit of automating installation is that it helps standardize multiple installations without having to carefully audit each installation. VMware has always supported the scripted installation of ESXi hosts, and that has not changed with vSphere 6.7.

Like with any automated task, the scripted installation of an ESXi host requires the use of a configuration file that contains the intended host configuration that's stored at a location that's accessible to the ESXi host. The configuration file is referred to as a kickstart file (`.cfg`).

A kickstart file can be stored at any of the following supported locations:

- A webserver (access over HTTP or HTTPS)
- A network file server (FTP/NFS)
- A local storage medium that's accessible to the host (CD-ROM/USB)

In this recipe, we will learn how to perform an unattended installation of ESXi using the installer medium, a local USB device, and a network location.

Getting ready

Before you begin, prepare a script for the installation. A default script is available on every ESXi host at /etc/vmware/weasel/ks.cfg. Although the extension is .cfg, the filename doesn't need to be the same. It should be a plain text file with the .cfg extension.

Here is a sample script:

```
# Sample scripted installation file for vdescribed.lab
# Accept the VMware End User License Agreement
vmaccepteula
# Clear/format existing partitions
clearpart --firstdisk --overwritevmfs
# Set the root password for the DCUI and Tech Support Mode
rootpw password@123
# The install media is in the CD-ROM drive
install --firstdisk --overwritevmfs
# Set a static IP Configuration
network --bootproto=static --device=vmnic0 --ip=192.168.78.91 --
netmask=255.255.255.0 --gateway=192.168.78.1 --nameserver=192.168.78.130 --
hostname=bkesx02
reboot
# Post Installation Tasks
%firstboot --interpreter=busybox
#Create vSwitch
esxcli network vswitch standard add --vswitch-name=vSwitch2
# Disable ipv6
esxcli network ip set --ipv6-enabled=false
sleep 30
reboot
```

Once the script has been prepared, store it in one of the support locations. For this recipe, I have stored it on an NFS server.

How to do it...

The following procedure will guide you through the steps that are required to perform a scripted installation of the ESXi host:

1. Boot the server using the ESXi ISO. The ISO can be mounted to the server via its IPMI interface (DRAC, ILO, and so on).

2. At the **Loading ESXi Installer** screen, before it automatically boots, hit *Shift + O* to edit the boot options. This is indicated in the bottom right-hand corner of the screen:

3. On the next screen, enter the location of the kickstart file and hit *Enter* to begin the installation:

4. Once the installation is complete, if the kickstart script includes a `reboot` command, like it does in our script, the server will be rebooted; otherwise, you will be prompted for confirmation.

How it works...

When using a kickstart file, the ESXi installation requires no user intervention. The kickstart file can be configured to run a variety of tasks. It can also be configured to run Python scripts after the installation.

Let's examine the sample script that was used in this recipe. This script is available in the *Getting ready* section:

Script command	Purpose
vmaccepteula	Accepts the ESXi End User License Agreement.
clearpart --firstdisk --overwritevmfs	Used to format the selected disk and overwrite any VMFS volume. This is a destructive process and cannot be reversed.
install --firstdisk --overwritevmfs	Used to indicate that this is a fresh installation, and the installation will be informed on the first disk in the list by overwriting any VMFS volume.
rootpw password@123	Sets the root password as password@123.
network --bootproto=static --device=vmnic0 --ip=192.168.78.91 --netmask=255.255.255.0 --gateway=192.168.78.1 --nameserver=192.168.78.130 --hostname=bkesx02	Configures a static IP address, a DNS server address, and a hostname for ESXi.
reboot	Reboots the ESXi host.
%firstboot --interpreter=busybox	This is used to indicate that the commands following this line will be executed on first boot. Setting the interpreter to busybox will let you execute the CLI command. Setting it to Python will let you run Python scripts.
esxcli network vswitch standard add -v=vSwitch2	Creates a second standard switch with the name vSwitch2.
esxcli network ip set --ipv6-enabled=false	Disables IPv6.
sleep 30	Will not execute any commands for 30 seconds.

For a list of all supported commands in the kickstart file, refer to the *Installation and Upgrade Script Commands* section on page 78 of the *VMware ESXi Installation and Setup* guide, which can be found at https://docs.vmware.com/en/VMware-vSphere/6.7/vsphere-esxi-67-installation-setup-guide.pdf.

There's more...

Although scripted installation automates the process to some extent, it still requires you to log in to each ESXi host and supply a location for the script file. An unattended deployment should not require any user intervention other than just booting up the server. This is achieved by PXE booting the hosts and using the kickstart script from a network location to run the installation. However, if unattended deployment has been considered, then the recommendation is to use vSphere Auto Deploy, which offers more control and manageability. vSphere Auto Deploy will be covered in a later chapter.

Deploying the vCenter Server Appliance (VCSA)

Deployment of the VCSA is done with an installer, which deploys the VCSA VM onto a chosen ESXi host. The installer GUI collects all the information that's required to configure the vCenter server.

There are two types of deployment:

- Embedded Appliance
- Separate vCenter and PSC Appliance (deprecated)

An external PSC was a requirement in the past if you chose to configure Enhanced Linked Mode for your vCenters. This is no longer the case in vSphere 6.7. With vCenter 6.7, the concept of an external PSC is deprecated, and Enhanced Linked Mode between vCenters with embedded PSCs is now fully supported. We will learn more about Enhanced Linked Mode in the *Deploying vCenter Servers in a Linked Mode configuration* recipe.

Getting ready

Here is what you will need before you install vCenter Server:

- Download the VMware VCSA 6.7 ISO from `https://my.vmware.com/web/vmware/downloads`
- Access to a machine (Windows/Linux/macOS) to run the vCenter installer from
- IP address/FQDN of the ESXi host or the vCeter the VCSA will be deployed on

- IP configuration (static IP address, subnet mask, gateway address, and DNS server addresses)
- A DNS host record for the VCSA

How to do it...

The following procedure will walk you through the steps involved in deploying VCSA 6.7 with an embedded PSC:

1. Mount the VCSA ISO to a machine to run the installer from.
2. Navigate to the `CDROM:\\VMware VCSA\vcsa-ui-installer\win32` directory and run `installer.exe` to bring up the VCSA installer wizard.

Stage 1 of the deployment starts here:

1. On the **Stage 1: Deploy appliance** screen, click **Install**.
2. On the **Introduction** screen, click **Next** to continue.
3. Accept the **End user license agreement** and click **Next**.
4. On the **Select deployment type** screen, choose **Embedded Platform Services Controller**:

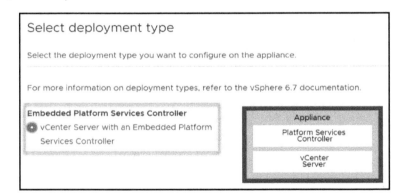

5. On the **Appliance deployment target** screen, supply the IP address of the ESXi host or vCenter the VCSA will be deployed on and provide its credentials. Click **Next** to continue.
6. Accept the vCenter/ESXi certificate by clicking **Yes**.

7. On the **Set up appliance VM** screen, specify a VM name for the VCSA and set its root password. The **VM name** doesn't need to be the same as the hostname or FQDN for the appliance:

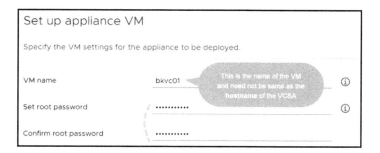

8. On the **Select deployment size** screen, specify a **Deployment size** and **Storage size** for the appliance. There is a default storage size for each deployment size. However, this can be overridden by selecting a larger storage size (**Large** or **X-Large**) if you want a larger disk (vmdk) for the /storage/seat partition that stores the stats, tasks, events, and alarms:

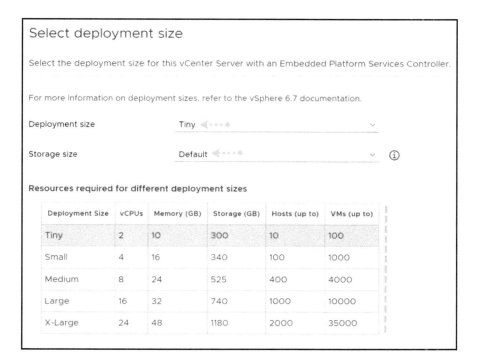

9. On the **Select datastore** screen, choose a datastore for the VCSA and click **Next** to continue. **Enable Thin Disk Mode** is selected by default.

10. On the **Configure network settings** screen, choose a VM port group for the VCSA VM, the IP version, and set the IP address type to **static**. Specify the FQDN, IP address/netmask, gateway, and DNS server addresses. Don't change the **Common Ports** (HTTP/HTTPS) from 80/443 unless absolutely necessary:

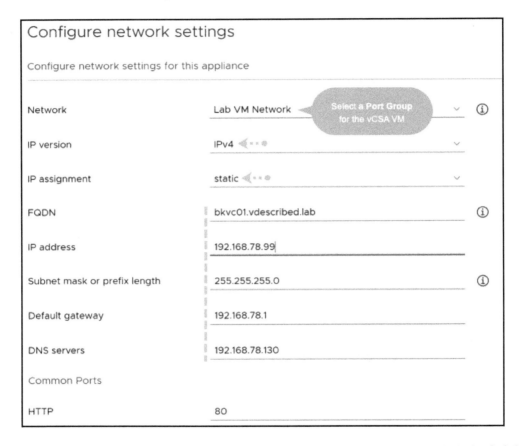

11. On the **Ready to complete stage 1** screen, review the settings and click **Finish** to start deploying the VM.

12. Once the deployment completes, you will be presented with a screen confirming this. Click **Continue**:

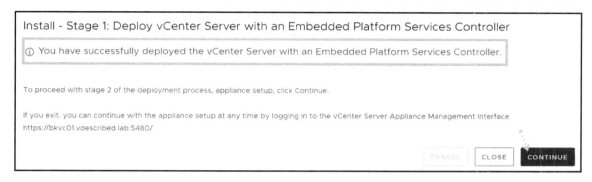

If you accidentally close the wizard or choose to continue at a later time, then the stage 2 installer can be started by connecting to the appliance administration URL, that is, `https://VCSA IP or FQDN:5480`, and using the **Set up vCenter Server Appliance** option.

Stage 2 of the deployment starts here:

1. On the **Install - Stage 2: Set up vCenter Server Appliance with an Embedded PSC** screen, click **Next**.

2. On the **Appliance Configuration** screen, specify a **Time synchronization mode** and enable **SSH access** (disabled by default).

3. On the **SSO configuration** screen, choose to **Create a new SSO domain**. Specify a domain name (the default is `vsphere.local`) and set the password for the SSO administrator:

4. On the **Configure CEIP** screen, choose to uncheck the **Join VMware Customer Experience Improvement Program** (CIEP).

5. On the **Ready to complete** screen, review the settings and click **FINISH** to initiate the configuration:

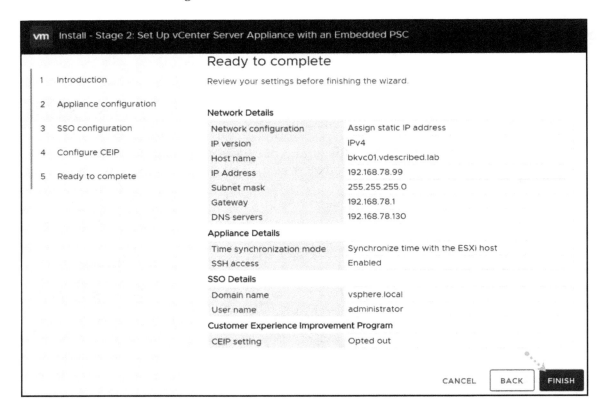

6. You will be prompted with a warning indicating that once you choose to continue, the operation cannot be stopped. Click **OK** to continue.

7. Once the setup/configuration is complete, you will be presented with a confirmation screen and the URL (`https://FQDN of vCSA:443`) to vCenter's **Getting Started** page. Click **Close** to exit the installer.

This finishes the installation, and you will now be able to get to vCenter's **Getting Started** page:

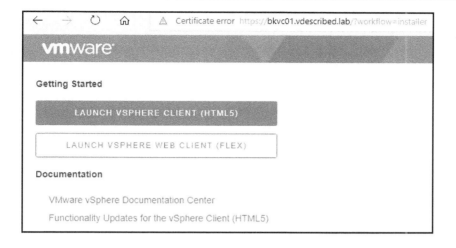

How it works...

The process of deploying a VCSA is split into two phases. In **phase 1**, the installer deploys a vCenter appliance virtual machine based on the sizing requirements specified, while in **phase 2**, you need to specify the SSO configuration. It is a general practice to take a snapshot of the newly deployed VCSA after phase 1 so that it can be reused if phase 2 of the installation were to fail for any reason.

Deploying vCenters in a Linked Mode configuration

When you have more than one vCenter to manage in your environment, being able to manage them under a single view is always beneficial. This is achieved by configuring the PSCs to become part of the same SSO domain, thereby putting them in an Enhanced Linked Mode configuration. vCenters in a Linked Mode will replicate roles and permissions, licenses, and other details, letting the administrator perform a single login into the vSphere Web Client to view and manage the inventory objects of all the linked vCenter Servers.

vCenter 6.7 now fully supports configuring embedded PSCs in a Linked Mode configuration, thereby eliminating the need to protect the PSC nodes when configuring high availability for vCenter.

Getting ready

You will need the following information at hand before you proceed:

- The VMware VCSA 6.7 ISO from `https://my.vmware.com/web/vmware/downloads`
- Access to a machine (Windows/Linux/macOS) to run the vCenter installer from
- The IP address/FQDN of the ESXi host or the vCenter the VCSA will be deployed on
- The IP configuration (including the static IP address, subnet mask, gateway address, and DNS server addresses)
- A DNS host record created for the new VCSA
- The IP address/FQDN of the peer PSC
- The SSO domain name of the peer PSC
- SSO administrator credentials for the chosen domain

How to do it...

The following procedure will guide you through the steps that are required to configure vCenters in a Linked Mode configuration:

1. Go through with **Stage 1** of the installation by deploying a new VCSA.
2. On the **Install - Stage 2: Set up vCenter Server Appliance with an Embedded PSC** screen, click **Next**.
3. On the **Appliance Configuration** screen, specify a **Time synchronization mode** and enable SSH access (disabled by default).
4. On the **SSO configuration** screen, choose to **Join an existing SSO domain**. Specify the FQDN/IP of the peer PSC, its SSO domain, and the administrator credentials:

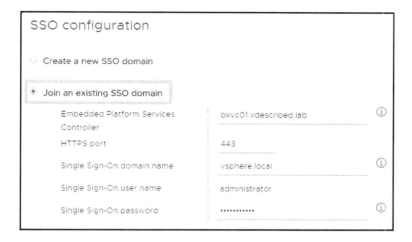

5. On the **Configure CEIP** screen, choose to uncheck the **Join VMware Customer Experience Improvement Program (CIEP)**.

6. On the **Ready to complete** screen, review the settings and click **FINISH** to initiate the configuration:

7. Once the setup/configuration is complete, you will be presented with a confirmation screen, as well as the URL (`https://FQDN of VCSA:443`) to vCenter's **Getting Started** page. Click **Close** to exit the installer.

This finishes the Linked Mode configuration:

Now, when you log in to the web client, it should list all the vCenter servers in the same PSC domain.

How it works...

Once the vCenters are in ELM, they replicate the VMDir contents, license keys, global permissions, tags, and categories.

The replication status can be checked from each node by running the following commands:

```
root@bkvc01 [ ~ ]# /usr/lib/vmware-vmdir/bin/vdcrepadmin -f showservers -h localhost -u administrator -w Password@123
cn=bkvc01.vdescribed.lab,cn=Servers,cn=default-site,cn=Sites,cn=Configuration,dc=vsphere,dc=local
cn=bkvc02.vdescribed.lab,cn=Servers,cn=Default-First-Site,cn=Sites,cn=Configuration,dc=vsphere,dc=local
root@bkvc01 [ ~ ]#
root@bkvc01 [ ~ ]# /usr/lib/vmware-vmdir/bin/vdcrepadmin -f showpartnerstatus -h localhost -u administrator -w Password@123
Partner: bkvc02.vdescribed.lab
Host available:    Yes
Status available: Yes
My last change number:          6961
Partner has seen my change number: 6961
Partner is 0 changes behind.
root@bkvc01 [ ~ ]#
```

The same commands, when executed on the peer vCenter/PSC, should report similar data:

```
root@bkvc02 [ ~ ]# /usr/lib/vmware-vmdir/bin/vdcrepadmin -f showservers -h localhost -u administrator -w Password@123
cn=bkvc01.vdescribed.lab,cn=Servers,cn=default-site,cn=Sites,cn=Configuration,dc=vsphere,dc=local
cn=bkvc02.vdescribed.lab,cn=Servers,cn=Default-First-Site,cn=Sites,cn=Configuration,dc=vsphere,dc=local
root@bkvc02 [ ~ ]#
root@bkvc02 [ ~ ]# /usr/lib/vmware-vmdir/bin/vdcrepadmin -f showpartnerstatus -h localhost -u administrator -w Password@123
Partner: bkvc01.vdescribed.lab
Host available:   Yes
Status available: Yes
My last change number:         6239
Partner has seen my change number: 6239
Partner is 0 changes behind.
root@bkvc02 [ ~ ]#
```

There's more...

You can still deploy external PSCs in vSphere 6.7, although there is no strong use case for doing so. If your 6.5.x or older environment had externalized PSC or SSO servers, they will be migrated/upgraded to become external PSCs by default. These can, however, be converted into embedded VCSAs during the upgrade. We will learn more about this in the next chapter.

Configuring Single Sign-On (SSO) identity sources

An SSO identity source is a repository of users or groups. It can be a repository of local OS users, Active Directory or OpenLDAP and VMDir. Adding an identity source allows you to assign vCenter permissions to users from such a repository.

The VCSA Photon OS (local OS) and SSO domain (vsphere.local) are pre-recognized identity sources. However, when you try to add identity sources, you are allowed to add three different types:

- Active Directory (Windows Integrated Authentication)
- Active Directory over LDAP
- Open LDAP

In this recipe, we will learn how to add an Active Directory identity source.

How to do it...

The following two-part procedure will allow you to join the PSC to Active Directory and add an Active Directory identity source.

Part 1 – Joining the PSC to Active Directory

 Joining the PSC to Active Directory needs to be done only once during the life cycle of the PSC.

1. Log in to the vCenter Server/PSC as the SSO administrator (`administrator@vsphere.local`).
2. Use the **Menu** to navigate to **Administration**:

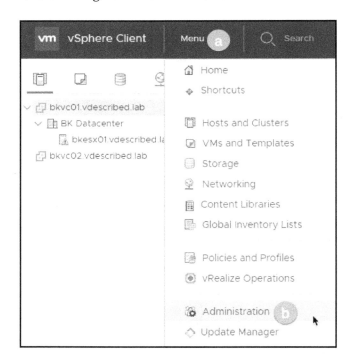

Menu | Administration

3. On the **Administration** page, navigate to **Single Sign On** | **Configuration** | **Active Directory Domain** and click on **JOIN AD**:

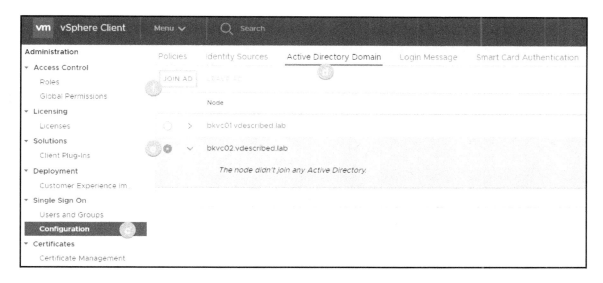

4. On the Join Active Directory Domain window, specify the name of the domain, OU (optional), and the credentials of a domain user that has permission to join the machine to the domain. Click **Join**.

5. Once done, the host has to be rebooted for the changes to take effect.

6. Once the reboot is complete, it should show the vCenter/PSC as joined to the domain:

Part 2 – Adding the identity source

Use the following process to add an identity source:

1. Go to the **Administration** page, navigate to **Single Sign On** | **Configuration** | **Identity Sources**, and click on **ADD IDENTITY SOURCE**:

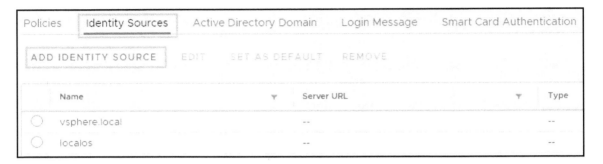

2. On the **Add Identity Source** window, set the **Identity Source Type** to **Active Directory (Windows Integrated Authentication)**. The **Domain name** will be prepopulated with the FQDN of the domain the PSC is joined to. Use the machine account to authenticate:

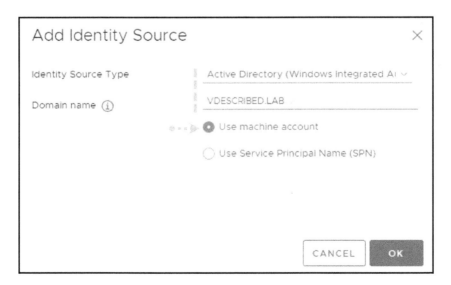

3. Once done, the Active Directory domain will be listed among the other identity sources:

This completes the process of configuring SSO identity sources on a vCenter Server.

How it works...

VMware SSO is an authentication server that was made available starting with vSphere 5.1. With version 5.5, it has been rearchitected so that it is simple to plan and deploy, as well as easier to manage. With vSphere 6.0 and 6.5, it is now embedded into the PSC.

SSO acts as an authentication gateway, which takes the authentication requests from various registered components and validates the credential pair against the identity sources that are added to the SSO server. The components are registered to the SSO server during their installation.

Once authenticated, the SSO clients are provided with a token for further exchanges. The advantage here is that the user or administrator of the client service is not prompted for a credential pair (username and password) every time it needs to authenticate.

SSO supports authenticating against the following identity sources:

- Active Directory
- Active Directory as an LDAP server
- Open LDAP
- Local OS

Here are some of the components that can be registered with the VMware SSO and leverage its functionality. These components, in SSO terms, are referred to as SSO clients:

- VMware vCenter Server
- VMware vCenter Orchestrator
- VMware NSX
- VMware vCloud Director
- VMware vRealize Automation
- VMware vSphere Web Client
- VMware vSphere Data Protection
- VMware log browser

Configuring vCenter Roles and Permissions

By default, the SSO-Domain\Administrators (`vsphere.local\Administrators`) group is assigned an Administrator role on the vCenter and is defined as a **Global Permission**. This means that if there were to be more than one vCenter in an Enhanced Linked Mode configuration, then the `vsphere\Administrators` group will have Administrator role permissions on all the connected vCenters.

The only member of the `vsphere.local\Administators` group is the SSO administrator (`administator@vsphere.local`). Users from other identity sources can be added as members of this group if you so desire.

However, in most environments, although multiple vCenters will be managed under a single ELM umbrella, you will sometimes need to provide vCenter-specific permissions. For instance, if you manage multiple vCenters belonging to different customers, then assigning global permissions is not considered ideal. In such cases, you will need to provide user access to specific vCenters only.

In this recipe, we will learn how to assign vCenter permissions to an Active Directory user/group.

Getting ready

Before you set off and assign vCenter permissions, ensure that the domain hosting the intended user/group is added as an identity source. To learn how to add identity sources, read the *Configuring SSO identity sources* recipe in this chapter.

How to do it...

The following procedure will guide you through the steps required to configure vCenter permissions to a domain user or group:

1. Log in to the vSphere Client (HTML 5) interface as the SSO administrator.
2. Select the vCenter object from the inventory, navigate to its **Permissions** tab, and click + to bring up the **Add Permission** window:

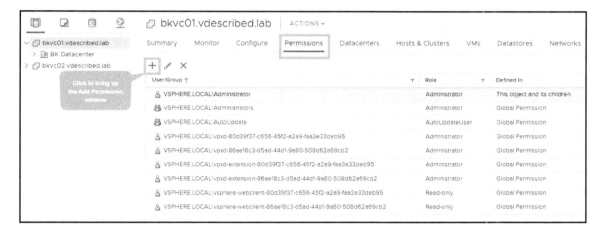

3. On the **Add Permission** window, select a domain user or group using the search box, and then specify a role. You can also choose to propagate the permissions to waterfall down to other inventory objects. Click **OK** to confirm:

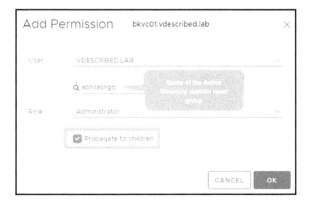

4. Once done, the user/group should be listed under **Permissions**.

How it works...

Any user account that is used to log in to the vSphere Web Client needs permission on the vCenter to be able to view and manage its inventory. When configuring global permissions, it is important to ensure that it is propagated to the child objects so that the permissions are set on the vCenter Server(s) as well. Permissions can be configured for both local and Active Directory users, provided that the required identity sources are added to SSO.

Joining ESXi to an Active Directory domain

As an administrator managing a vSphere environment, the last thing that you would want to do is share the root password. Remember, a forgotten root password cannot be recovered/reset and will require a reinstallation of ESXi.

Joining an ESXi host to an Active Directory domain will allows users from a particular domain user group to log in to the ESXi host without needing to know the root password. This not only eliminates the need to periodically change the root password, but also enables better auditing.

Getting ready

Here is what you will need before you join the ESXi host to the domain and configure access to it:

- The name of the domain
- The username and password of a domain user that has permissions to join the machine to the domain
- The name of the domain user group that selected users will be a part of

How to do it...

The following procedure will guide you through the steps that are required to join the ESXi host to the domain and allow a domain user group access to it:

1. Connect to the vCenter Server's HTML 5 interface, that is, `https://FQDN of vCenter/ui`.
2. Select the ESXi host from the **Inventory** and navigate to **Configure | System | Authentication Services**. From here, click on **Join Domain**.
3. On the **Join Domain** screen, specify a domain name and domain credentials and click **OK**:

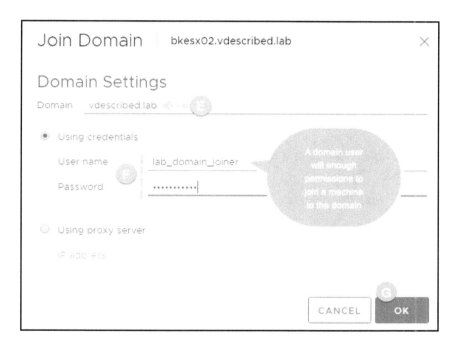

4. You should see a **Join Windows Domain task complete successfully** message in the **Recent Tasks** pane.

   Now that the host is joined to the domain, we can configure it to allow access for a domain user group.

5. With the host selected, navigate to **Configure** | **System** | **Advanced System Settings** and click **Edit**.

6. On the **Edit Advanced System Settings** screen, type `esxadmin` into the search box to filter the settings.

7. Click on the **Value** field corresponding to the `Config.HostAgent.plugins.hostsvc.esxAdminsGroup` setting and enter the name of the domain user group:

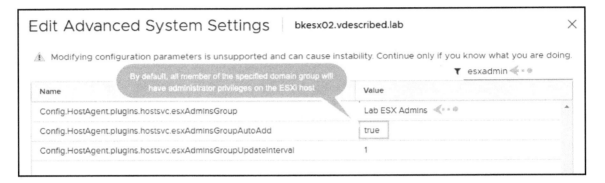

You should now be able to log in as a domain user to the console (direct/SSH) and DCUI using the following formats:

- `user@domain`: For example, `abhilashgb@vdescribed`
- `domain\user`: For example, `vdescribed\abhilashgb`

How it works...

Once the ESXi host has been joined to the Active Directory domain, a domain user group can be allowed to log in to the ESXi host. This access is enabled by specifying the name of the user group using the advanced system setting, that is, `Config.HostAgent.plugins.hostsvc.esxAdminsGroup`.

By default, this user group is granted administrator privileges. This behavior can, however, be changed by using the advanced system setting, that is, `Config.HostAgent.plugins.hostsvc.esxAdminsGroupAutoAdd`.

Planning and Executing the Upgrade of vSphere

2

The goal of this chapter is to help you to understand, plan, and execute the process of upgrading your core vSphere infrastructure to VMware vSphere 6.7. The core includes your ESXi hypervisor, vCenter Server, and the vCenter Server's components. The upgrade of the third-layer products that leverage the core vSphere infrastructure, such as vRealize Automation, NSX, and VMware Horizon View, are not covered in this chapter as they are beyond the scope and purpose of this book.

Let me introduce you to the core infrastructure components that will be upgraded:

- **VMware vCenter Server**: The viability of an upgrade or the need for a new build will depend on the current version of vCenter and the supported upgrade path.
- **vCenter Inventory Service**: This is no longer a separate service in vCenter 6.5/6.7.
- **vSphere Web Client**: The Web Client component will be upgraded as part of vCenter Upgrade.
- **vSphere Platform Services Controller (PSC)**: If you are upgrading from vSphere 6.0 to 6.7, you will need to review the current deployment model and apply an apt strategy to upgrade the PSC. Once the PSCs have been upgraded to 6.7 Update 1, they can be converged into the vCenter Appliance and then decommissioned.
- **vSphere Update Manager (VUM)**: VUM should be updated to the latest version before it can be used to upgrade ESXi hosts that are managed by the vCenter VUM it is integrated with. VUM components are now built into the vCenter Appliance.
- **VMware ESXi**: The hypervisor can be upgraded by booting the server using the ISO image, using vSphere Update Manager, or updating the image profile if the existing servers are auto-deployed.

It is important to note that there is no direct upgrade path from **vSphere 5.5** to **vSphere 6.7**. You will need to upgrade to vSphere 6.0/6.5 before you can upgrade the environment to vSphere 6.7.

In this chapter, we will be covering the following recipes:

- Planning the upgrade of your vSphere infrastructure
- Running VMware Migration Assistant
- Upgrading Platform Services Controllers (PSCs)
- Upgrading vCenter Servers
- Using the vCenter Convergence Tool
- Upgrading ESXi hosts using the interactive installer
- Upgrading ESXi using the command-line interface

Planning the upgrade of your vSphere infrastructure

Before you embark upon the journey of upgrading all of the various components of your vSphere infrastructure, it is essential to prepare and layout the effects of upgrading the components, which include accounting for any necessary downtime. So, where do we begin? The answer depends on the components/solutions in our environment and the effects of their compatibility once upgraded.

We start by using reference works such as the VMware Product Interoperability Matrices and VMware Compatibility Guides. The same applies to other products/solutions in our environment. For example, if we have a third-party backup solution, then it is critical to ensure that the backup solution is compatible with the version of vSphere we are upgrading to.

Another critical aspect is failure mitigation. What if the upgrade fails? It is essential to include a rollback procedure when you prepare a runbook.

In this recipe, you will learn how to plan the upgrade of your vSphere environment.

Getting ready

You will need the following tools to plan the upgrade:

- VMware Compatibility Guide
  (`www.vmware.com/resources/compatibility/search.php`)
- VMware Product Interoperability Matrices
  (`www.vmware.com/resources/compatibility/sim/interop_matrix.php`)
- Access to vendor documentation for third-party products that integrate with vSphere

How to do it...

The following high-level procedures can be used to plan the upgrade of a vSphere environment:

- Determine the version and compatibility of the vSphere components.
- Verify the upgrade path and ensure that it is supported.
- Plan the upgrade sequence of the vSphere components.
- Plan for the downtime of the vSphere components.
- Plan for upgrade failure mitigation.

How it works...

Let's go over these steps, one by one:

Part 1: Determine version and compatibility:

- Gather the current version and build numbers of the vCenter Server and ESXi hosts.
- Verify whether the server hardware is compatible with VMware ESXi 6.7.x using the VMware Compatibility Guide.
- Make a list of all of the vCenter Server Plugins that are currently installed.
- For VMware plugins, use the VMware Product Interoperability Matrices to confirm their compatibility with vSphere 6.7.
- For third-party plugins, use the corresponding vendor documentation to confirm their compatibility with vSphere 6.7.

Part 2: Verify the upgrade path:

- Every product, be it VMware or a third-party solution that integrates with vSphere, needs to follow an upgrade path. For instance, a vSphere 5.5 environment cannot be directly upgraded to 6.7. It needs to be upgraded to 6.0 or later for vCenter and ESXi 6.0 U3 or later before it can be upgraded to vSphere 6.7.

 Use the **Upgrade Path** section of the VMware Product Interoperability Matrices to do this.

- Some third-party products will also need to make a jump to a particular version (build) before they can be upgraded to a version that's compatible with vSphere 6.7. Refer to the vendor documentation to verify the upgrade path.

Part 3: Plan the upgrade sequence of the vSphere components:

- Once the product versions and their compatibility have been confirmed, you will need to arrive at an order (sequence) in which the components will be upgraded.
- For VMware products, use **VMware KB#53710** (kb.vmware.com/kb/53710) to understand the sequence in which the solutions should be upgraded. If your vSphere infrastructure has other VMware products, such as vROPS, vRA, SRM, NSX, and so on, it is essential to use the KB to understand the sequence.
- Once vCenter has been upgraded, you can then upgrade the ESXi hosts.
- Upgrading vCenter components doesn't change the deployment model/topology. This means that, if there are external PSCs in the environment, they will have to be upgraded first.
- **vCenter 6.7 Update 1** includes a **Convergence Tool**, which can be employed to transform external PSCs as embedded components of VCSA 6.7 Update 1.
- With every major ESXi version, VMware includes a new virtual hardware version that brings in new features and enhancements. vSphere 6.7 has hardware version 14. We will learn how to upgrade VMware tools and virtual hardware on individual **virtual machines** (**VMs**) in Chapter 13, *Creating and Managing Virtual Machines*. This process can be orchestrated using VMware Update Manager in order to handle the upgrades of multiple VMs. We will learn more about this in a separate chapter that covers VMware Update Manager.

Part 4: Plan for the downtime of the vSphere components:

- Most of the upgrade can be performed without any downtime for the VM workloads. However, the solutions that are being upgraded will incur a temporary downtime. The amount of downtime that's required will depend on how long an upgrade would take to complete. For instance, if you were to migrate from vCenter (Windows) to vCSA, during the upgrade, the database is transferred to the vCSA over the network. The amount of data and network congestion could play a part in determining the time that's required for the import and upgrade.
- The upgrade of ESXi hosts will require a reboot.
- When accounting for the downtime that's required, you will need to consider the time that's required to troubleshoot an upgrade or the time that's required to perform a rollback in case the upgrade fails.

Part 5: Plan for failure mitigation:

- Upgrading the current version of Windows/Appliance to 6.7, Appliances always deploys a new VCSA with the data transferred to it, which means it wouldn't make any modifications to the source VCSA. However, it is still recommended to take snapshots of the source VMs before the upgrade so that you can roll back if required. A rollback without a snapshot is also possible by simply powering off the target appliance and powering on the source VMs.
- An ESXi upgrade is non-destructive in most cases. If the upgrade fails for any reason, the host just needs to be rebooted. However, in rare cases, you will need to perform a fresh installation.
- It is recommended to take snapshots on the VM before a VMware tools or virtual hardware upgrade. The process of upgrading tools and virtual hardware will be covered in `Chapter 14`, *Upgrading and Patching Using vSphere Update Manager*.

Once you have arrived at a verified plan and documented it, you can proceed with the execution of the upgrade. If your existing environment includes Windows-based vCenter components, then you will need to start with learning how to use the migration assistant. Please refer to the *Running VMware Migration Assistant* recipe for more information.

Running VMware Migration Assistant

VMware Migration Assistant is used as a proxy agent so that you can gather configuration information about the vCenter components running on Microsoft Windows and run pre-upgrade checks, and it aids in the transfer of data from the Windows machine to the vCenter appliance.

 The migration assistant is bundled with the vCenter Server Appliance Installer ISO.

In this recipe, you will learn how to run VMware Migration Assistant on Windows machines by running the PSC, vCenter, and Update Manager vCenter components.

Getting ready

Before you begin, download the vCenter Server Appliance 6.7 Installer ISO and mount it to the Windows machine that's running the PSC or vCenter.

How to do it...

The following procedure will guide you through the steps involved in running the vCenter 6.7 Migration Assistant on a source vCenter component machine:

1. Copy the `migration-assistant` folder from the root of the VCSA 6.7 Installer ISO to the source PSC that needs to be upgraded:

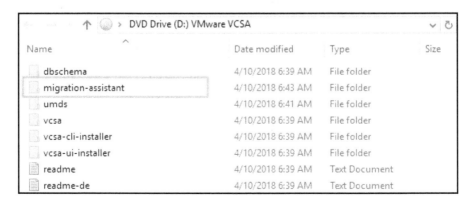

2. Run `VMware-Migration-Assistant` from the `migration-assistant` folder on the hard drive:

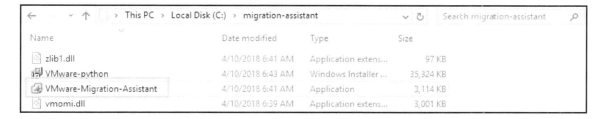

3. During its initialization, you will be prompted for the SSO administrator password. Type in the password and hit *Enter*; it will start running pre-checks.

4. Once it's done running the pre-checks, it will display the source configuration and confirm that it's ready to start the migration process:

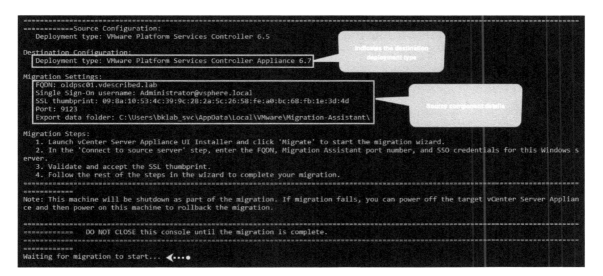

5. The migration assistant should continue to run until the upgrade completes. Don't close the window until it's finished doing so.

During the upgrade of vCenter Server, if you have Update Manager running on a different Windows machine, then the migration assistant needs to be running on it as well.

How it works...

`migration-assistant` should be run on the machines hosting vCenter/PSC/Update Manager services separately before initiating the vCenter migration/upgrade. The migration/upgrade process will only migrate data from all of the components servers with an **active migration-assistant session**.

If the installer detects an Update Manager plugin registered to vCenter and if the migration assistant is not active on the Windows machine running the Update Manager service, then the installation could fail by indicating the same.

Upgrading Platform Services Controllers (PSCs)

In an environment where the PSCs are externalized, you will need to upgrade all of the PSCs in an SSO domain first before the corresponding vCenter Servers can be upgraded. During the upgrade, the PSCs will be of a later version compared to their corresponding vCenters. Such a mixed version configuration is only supported during the course of the upgrade.

In this recipe, we will learn how to upgrade or migrate PSCs.

Getting ready

You will need the following before you proceed with the upgrade:

- An understanding of the current topology: You will need to identify all of the PSCs in a single SSO domain. vCenters corresponding to these PSCs will be in an **Enhanced Linked Mode (ELM)** configuration.
- Temporary IP addresses for the PSC appliances that will be deployed: A temporary IP is assigned to the appliance during its installation so that the data/configuration can be transferred from the source PSC to the appliance. The new appliance will take the identity of the source PSC during the final stage of the upgrade (after the data transfer is complete).
- Create a snapshot of the source PSC (*Optional*).

How to do it...

The following procedure will guide you through the steps involved in upgrading PSCs (Windows/Appliance) to PSC 6.7.

Migrating PSC (Windows) to PSC (Appliance) 6.7

1. Run the migration assistant on the source PSC. For instructions, read the *Running VMware Migration Assistant* recipe.
2. Run the VCSA 6.7 installer from a machine other than the source PSC.

> The installer location for Windows is CDROM:\vcsa-ui-installer\win32\installer.exe.

Migrate – Stage 1: Deploy appliance:

3. On the **vCenter Server Appliance 6.7 Installer - Stage 1: Deploy Appliance** screen, click **Migrate**.
4. On the **Introduction** screen, click **Next** to continue.
5. Accept the **End user license agreement** and click **Next** to continue.
6. On the **Connect to source server** screen, supply the FQDN/IP address of the source Windows machine running the PSC and the SSO Administrator credentials. Click **Next** to continue:

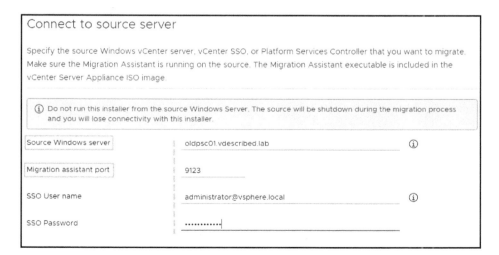

7. On the **Verify Thumbprint** screen, compare the thumbprint with the source configuration captured by the migration assistant (under **Migration Settings** in the Migration Assistant window on the source) and click **Yes** to continue.

8. On the **Appliance deployment target** screen, supply the IP address/FQDN of the ESXi host the appliance will be deployed to and supply the ESXi root credentials. Click **Next** to continue:

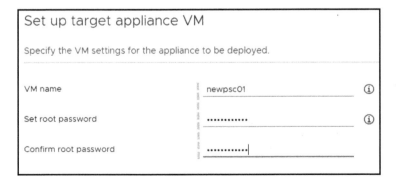

9. On the **Certificate Warning** screen, verify the thumbprint of the ESXi host and click **Yes**.

10. On the **Set up target appliance VM** screen, specify a name for the PSC appliance VM and set the root password. When you're done, click **Next** to continue:

11. On the **Select datastore** screen, choose the desired datastore to place the VM. Optionally, you can choose to thin provision its VMDKs by selecting the **Enable Thin Disk Mode** checkbox. Click **Next** to continue.

12. On the **Configure network settings** screen, select the port group for the PSC appliance VM to connect to a temporary IP address configuration. Click **Next** to continue:

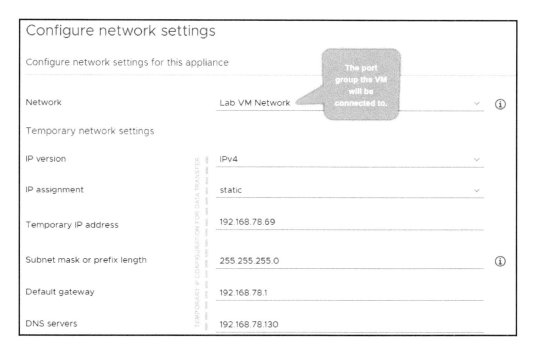

13. On the **Ready to Complete stage 1** screen, review the settings and click **Finish**.
14. Once the PSC appliance has been successfully deployed, it will confirm the same and suggest continuing to Stage 2. This can be done by clicking **CONTINUE** or using the `https://Temp-IP:5480` page:

Migrate – Stage 2: Platform Service Controller Appliance:

15. On the **Introduction** screen of the **Migrate – Stage 2: Platform Service Controller Appliance** wizard, click **Next** to continue.

16. On the **Connect to source SSO or PSC** screen, most of the information is prepopulated (including the SSO password). Click **Next** to continue:

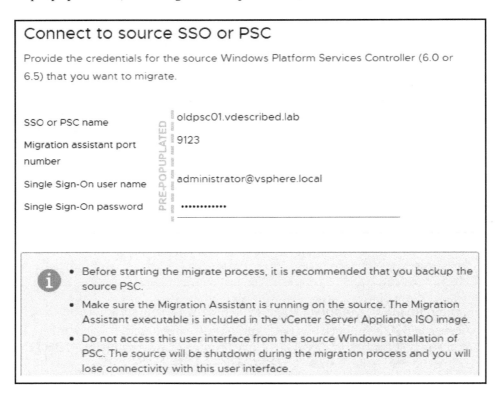

Connect to source SSO or PSC

Provide the credentials for the source Windows Platform Services Controller (6.0 or 6.5) that you want to migrate.

SSO or PSC name	oldpsc01.vdescribed.lab
Migration assistant port number	9123
Single Sign-On user name	administrator@vsphere.local
Single Sign-On password	••••••••••••

PRE-POPUPLATED

- Before starting the migrate process, it is recommended that you backup the source PSC.
- Make sure the Migration Assistant is running on the source. The Migration Assistant executable is included in the vCenter Server Appliance ISO image.
- Do not access this user interface from the source Windows installation of PSC. The source will be shutdown during the migration process and you will lose connectivity with this user interface.

17. It then performs a premigration check and moves to the **Join AD Domain** screen. Supply AD credentials to join the PSC appliance to the domain and click **Next** to continue:

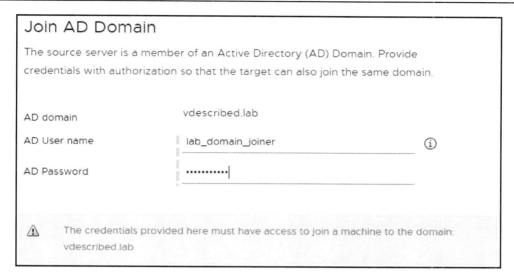

18. On the **Configure CIEP** screen, you can choose to join or not join the CIEP. Make a choice and click **Next** to continue.

19. On the **Ready to complete** screen, select the checkbox that confirms that you have backed up the source PSC, review the settings, and click **FINISH**:

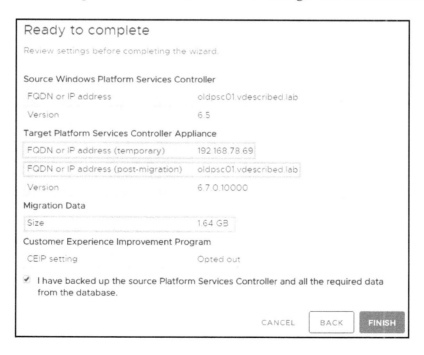

20. On the **Shutdown Warning** screen, click **OK**.

21. The installer will start copying the data from the source PSC to the target PSC, shut down the source PSC, then configure the target PSC to take up the identity of the source PSC, start the services, and import the data/configuration that was copied from the source PSC.

22. Once the deployment is complete, you will be presented with a **Migrate – Stage 2: Complete** screen. Click **CLOSE** to exit the installer:

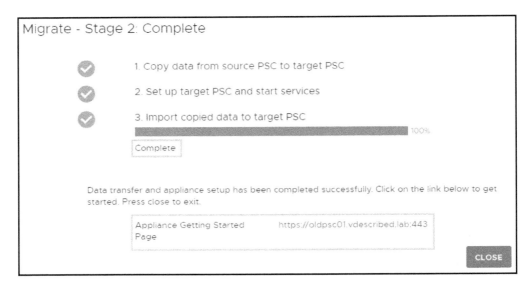

This finishes the migration of the PSC (Windows) to PSC 6.7 (Appliance).

Upgrading PSC Appliance to PSC 6.7

Unlike migrating from PSC (Windows), upgrading an appliance does not require the use of a migration assistant. Let's get started:

Upgrade – Stage 1: Deploy the target PSC Appliance:

1. Run the VCSA installer from a machine that has network access to the source PSC and the destination ESXi host the target PSC will be placed on.

2. On the **vCenter Server Appliance 6.7 Installer - Stage 1: Deploy Appliance** screen, click **Upgrade**.

3. On the **Introduction** screen, click **Next** to continue.

4. Accept the **End user license agreement** and click **Next** to continue.

5. On the **Connect to source appliance** screen, supply the FQDN/IP address of the source PSC appliance and click **CONNECT TO SOURCE**:

6. If the installer can connect to the source PSC appliance, then the same screen is automatically expanded to prompt for additional details, such as the PSC appliance's root password, FQDN/IP address of the ESXi/vCenter that manages the source PSC appliance VM, and the username/password (root if ESXi or SSO credentials if vCenter). Supply the requested details and click **Next** to continue:

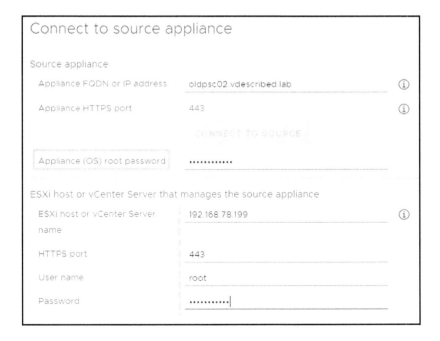

7. The **Certificate Warning** displays the thumbprints for both the source PSC and for managing ESXi/vCenter. Click **Yes** to confirm.

8. On the **Appliance deployment target** screen, specify a target ESXi/vCenter and its credentials:

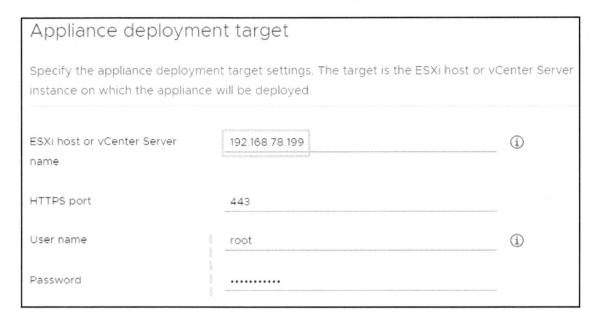

9. The **Certificate Warning** displays the thumbprint for the target ESXi/vCenter. Click **Yes** to confirm.

10. On the **Set up target appliance VM** screen, specify a name for the target PSC VM and set a root password for the appliance:

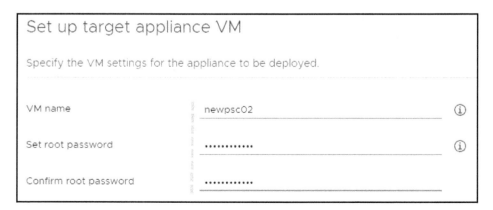

11. On the **Select datastore** screen, choose the desired datastore to place the VM. Optionally, you can choose to thin provision its VMDKs by selecting the **Enable Think Disk Mode** checkbox. Click **Next** to continue.

12. On the **Configure network settings** screen, select a port group for the target PSC appliance VM and specify a temporary IP address configuration. Click **Next** to continue:

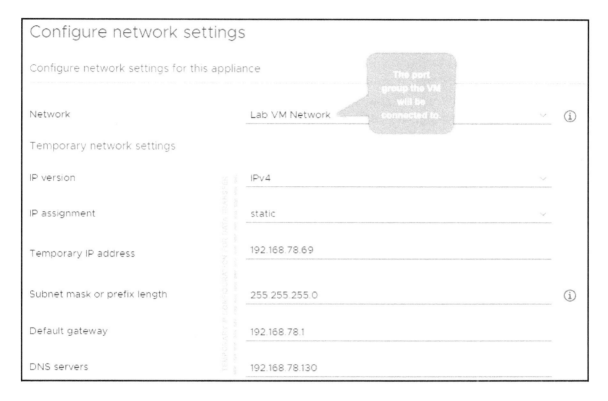

13. On the **Ready to complete stage 1** screen, review the settings and click **Finish**.

14. Once the target PSC appliance has been successfully deployed, it will confirm the same and suggest that you continue to Stage 2, which can be done by clicking **Continue** or using the `https://Temp-IP:5480` page.

Upgrade – Stage 2: Use the Platform Services Controller Appliance wizard:

15. On the **Upgrade - Stage 2: Introduction** screen, click **Next** to continue.

16. On the **Connect to source PSC** screen, supply the source PSC and the managing ESXi/vCenter details. Click **Next** to continue.

17. It will now perform a pre-upgrade check and proceed to the next screen.

18. On the **Configure CEIP** screen, choose to join or not join the VMware CEIP and click **Next** to continue.

19. On the **Ready to complete** screen, review the settings and use the checkbox to confirm that the source PSC appliance has been backed up. Then, click **Finish**.

20. On the **Shutdown Warning** screen, click **OK**.

21. Once the upgrade is complete, you will be presented with an **Upgrade – Stage 2: Complete** screen. Click **Close** to exit the installer.

This completes the upgrade of the Platform Service Controller.

How it works...

The migration process deploys a vCSA Appliance and imports the data from the vCenter windows installation. It retains the vCenter Server's IP address, UUID, hostname, SSL certificates, and management object reference IDs; therefore, once the installation is complete, the vCenter Server Windows machine is shut down. If, for any reason, the upgrade fails and the vCenter Windows machine is shut down, all you need to do is to power off the VCSA VM and power on the vCenter Windows machine. The upgrade and migrate process will not make any changes to the source Windows machine.

All of the PSCs in your vCenter infrastructure should be upgraded before you upgrade the vCenter Server. Therefore, you should repeat the same procedure on other PSCs in the same SSO domain. Once all of the PSCs have been migrated/upgraded, you can proceed with the migration/upgrade of the vCenter Server.

Upgrading vCenter Servers

vSphere 6.7 is the last release to include or support the installation of vCenter on Windows. Going forward, all vCenter versions will be Appliances. Therefore, it makes sense to adopt the appliance model. A Windows-based vCenter can be migrated (during the upgrade process) to become an appliance.

In this recipe, we will cover the steps involved in upgrading vCenter, assuming that their corresponding PSCs have already been upgraded.

Getting ready

You will need the following to be able to complete this recipe:

- VCSA 6.7 Installer ISO
- FQDN or IP address of the source vCenter
- Temporary IPs for the VCSA

How to do it...

The following procedure will guide you through the steps involved in upgrading a vCenter and PSC Windows pair to VCSA 6.7 and PSC 6.7 appliances:

Upgrade – Stage 1: Deploy vCenter Server: Deploy the target appliance:

1. Mount the vCSA 6.7 Installer ISO onto a Windows machine.
2. Run the installer from the source, that is, `CDROM:\vcsa-ui-installer\win32\installer.exe`.
3. On the **vCenter Server Appliance 6.7 Installer – Stage 1: Deploy Appliance** screen, click **Migrate**.
4. On the **Introduction** screen, click **Next** to continue.
5. Accept the **End user license agreement** and click **Next** to continue.

6. On the **Connect to source appliance** screen, supply the **Source appliance** details (Source FQDN/IP, SSO credentials, source appliance root password) and the managing ESXi/vCenterFQDN/IP and its credentials:

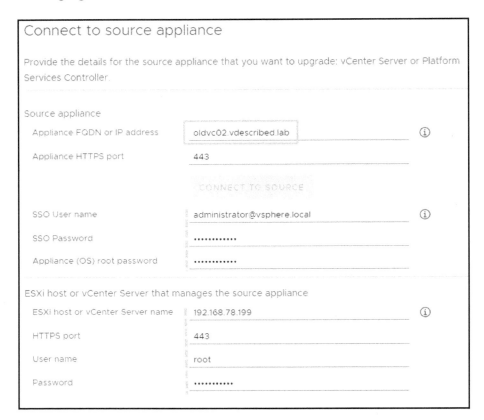

 Accept the certificate warning, if prompted.

7. On the **Appliance deployment target** screen, specify the details of the vCenter/ESXi the target appliance will be deployed on and click **Next** to continue.

8. On the **Set up target appliance VM** screen, specify a name for the target appliance VM and set the target appliance's root password.

9. On the **Select deployment size** screen, choose a deployment size (tiny, small, medium, large, or X-large). A default storage size is chosen based on the deployment type selected, but you could choose a non-default storage size if you so desire. Make a choice and click **Next** to continue.

10. On the **Select datastore** screen, chose a location for the target VM, choose to thin provision if desired, and click **Next** to continue.

11. On the **Configure network settings** screen, select a port group to connect the target VM to and specify the **Temporary IP** configuration. This will be used during the data transfer. Click **Next** to continue.

12. On the **Ready to complete stage 1** screen, review the settings and click **Finish**.

13. Once the VCSA appliance has been successfully deployed, it will confirm the same and suggest that you continue to Stage 2. This can be done by clicking **Continue** or using the `https://Temp-IP:5480` page.

Upgrade – Stage 2 vCenter Appliance:

14. On clicking **Continue**, you will be taken to the **Upgrade – Stage 2: vCenter Appliance** wizard.

15. On the **Introduction** screen, click **Next**.

16. The **Connect to Source** screen will use prepopulated details to automatically start the pre-upgrade check. If it doesn't, enter the details when prompted and click **Next**.

17. Once the pre-upgrade checks are complete, you may be presented with a **Pre-upgrade check result** screen. If you are, click **CLOSE** to continue:

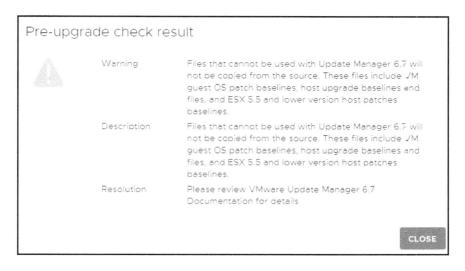

18. On the **Select Upgrade data** screen, you can choose to transfer only the configuration or include historical data and performance metrics. By default, only the configuration is selected. Make the desired selection and click **Next** to continue:

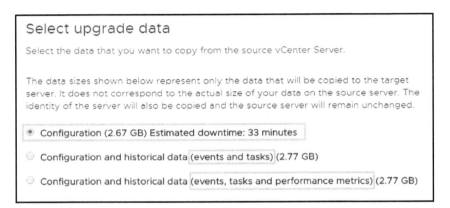

19. On the **Ready to complete** screen, review the settings and use the checkbox to confirm that you have backed up the source appliance. Then, click **Finish**:

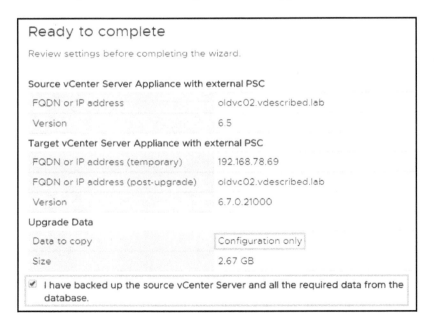

Click OK on the **Shutdown Warning** indicating that the source appliance will eventually be shut down.

20. Once the upgrade is complete, you will be presented with an **Upgrade - Stage 2: Complete** screen. Click **Close** to exit the installer.

This completes the upgrade of the vCSA.

How it works...

The procedure to migrate a vCenter from Windows is similar, with the exception of running the VMware Migration Assistant on the source Windows machines running vCenter Server and Update Manager.

Using the vCenter Convergence Tool

Starting with vSphere 6.7, there is no need to externalize the PSC for ELM, thereby making it simpler to protect vCenter Servers using **vCenter High Availability** (**vCHA**). However, if your existing environment has external PSCs, then upgrading them to vCenter 6.7 will retain the same topology.

With vCenter 6.7 Update 1, VMware includes a Convergence Tool, which can be used to install PSC components into existing VCSA 6.7U1 nodes and migrate the PSC configuration from the external PSCs into it, thereby getting rid of the external PSC nodes.

PSC 6.7 U1 (Windows) cannot be converted into embedded components of an existing vCenter. The Convergence Tools only work with vCenter and PSC Appliances.

At the time of the release of this book, the most recent version is vCenter 6.7 U2. Update 2 includes a GUI version of the Convergence Tool. However, the catch is that the source PSCs should also be running 6.7U2. For more details refer to VMware Tech Pubs demonstration - `https:// youtu.be/HlL4KzAPx0c`

Getting ready

The following conditions have to be met before you can use the vCenter Convergence Tool:

- vCenter and PSC should be appliances running version 6.7 Update 1 or later.
- vCHA should be disabled. Note that this is not vSphere HA.
- Create snapshots on the vCSAs and the PSCs.
- Alternatively, you could create vCSA file-based backups of the VCSA and PSCs.
- Review the vCenter for all plugin/solutions that are currently registered and authenticate them with PSC. This is necessary because the IP address and the FQDN for the PSC will change after they are converged into the vCSA.
- Set the vSphere **Distributed Resource Scheduler** (**DRS**) automation level to **Manual** on the destination cluster to avoid the migration of the target vCSA or the source PSC during convergence.

How to do it...

The following procedure will guide you through the steps involved in migrating the PSC components and their configuration into an existing vCSA:

1. Ensure that the prerequisites mentioned in the *Getting ready* section have been met.
2. Note the **Type** of the vCenter in the **Summary** tab of the vCenter's VAMI. It should read **vCenter Server with an external Platform Services Controller**:

3. Mount the VCSA 6.7U1 Installer ISO onto a Windows machine.
4. Locate the `converge.json` file on the **DVD Drive**. It should be in `vcsa-converge-cli\templates\converge`:

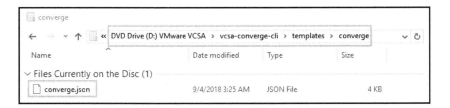

5. Copy the `converge.json` file to a read/write location, such as `C:\Converge\converge.json`. Open the file in a rich text editor such as WordPad and specify the requested details. Then, **Save** the changes:

```
{
    "__version": "2.11.0",
    "__comments": "Template for VCSA with external Platform Services Controller converge".
    "vcenter": {
        "description": {
            "__comments": [
                "This section describes the vCenter appliance which you want to",
                "converge and the ESXi host on which the appliance is running. "
            ]
        },
        "managing esxi or vc": {
            "hostname": "192.168.78.199",        Details of the vCenter/ESXi
            "username": "root",                   managing the target vCSA
            "password": "letmein_321"
        },
        "vc_appliance": {
            "hostname": "oldvc02.vdescribed.lab",    Target VCSA to which
            "username": "administrator@vsphere.local",  the PSC will be
            "password": "Password@123",                 converged into
            "root_password": "Password@123"
        },
        "ad_domain_info": {
            "__comments": [
                "Important Note: This section is needed only when PSC (Platform Services Controller)
                appliance is joined to a domain.",
                "Remove this section if PSC appliance is not joined to a domain.",
                "Keeping this section without valid values results in JSON validation errors."
            ],
            "domain_name": "vdescribed.lab",
            "username": "lab_domain_joiner",
            "password": "letmein_321",
            "dns_ip": "192.168.78.130"
        }
    },
    "replication": {
        "description": {
            "__comments": [
                "Important Note: Make sure you provide the information in this section very carefully, as
                this changes the replication topology.",
                "Refer to the documentation for complete details. Remove this section if this is first
                converge operation in your setup.",
                "This section provides details of the PSC node which will be set up as a replicated node
                for a new PSC on the target VCSA node."
            ]
        },
        "partner": {
            "hostname": "oldpsc02.vdescribed.lab"       Source PSC that you want to
        }                                                 converge
    }
}
```

6. Start Windows Command Prompt as an Administrator and navigate to the DVD ROM:`\vcsa-converge-cli\win32` directory. Then, issue the following command:

```
vcsa-util.exe converge --no-ssl-certificate-verification --backup-
taken --verbose <Ptch to converge.json>
```

Following is the output of the preceding command:

```
Administrator: Command Prompt - vcsa-util.exe converge --no-ssl-certificate-verification --backup-taken --verbose C:\Converge\converge.json    —    □    ×

D:\vcsa-converge-cli\win32>vcsa-util.exe converge --no-ssl-certificate-verification --backup-taken --verbose C:\Converge\converge.json
Updating log file location, copying 'C:\Users\ADMINI~1\AppData\Local\Temp\vcsaCliInstaller-2019-02-04-11-34-e439trdt\vcsa-converge-cli.log'
 to desired location as a backup: 'C:\Users\ADMINI~1\AppData\Local\Temp\vcsaCliInstaller-2019-02-04-11-34-e439trdt\workflow_1549280074213\v
csa-converge-cli.log.bak'
Adding the following cli arguments to blackboard {'cli_arg_pause_on_warnings':
False, 'cli_arg_template_help': False, 'cli_arg_terse': False,
'cli_arg_verbose': True, 'cli_arg_sub_command': 'converge',
'cli_arg_verify_template_only': False, 'cli_arg_skip_domain_handling': False,
'cli_arg_backup_taken': True, 'cli_arg_silent': False,
'cli_arg_no_ssl_certificate_verification': True, 'cli_arg_precheck_only': False,
'cli_arg_template': ['C:\\Converge\\converge.json'], 'cli_arg_skip_reboot':
False, 'cli_arg_log_dir': None}
Workflow log-dir
C:\Users\ADMINI~1\AppData\Local\Temp\vcsaCliInstaller-2019-02-04-11-34-e439trdt\workflow_1549280074213
SyntaxValidationTask: Executing Template Syntax Validation task
 [START] Start executing Task: To validate the syntax of the template. at
11:34:34
Template syntax validation for template 'C:\Converge\converge.json' succeeded.
Syntax validation for all templates succeeded.
 [SUCCEEDED] Successfully executed Task 'SyntaxValidationTask: Executing
Template Syntax Validation task' in TaskFlow 'template_validation' at 11:34:34
VersionProcessingTask: Executing Template Version Processing task
 [START] Start executing Task: To check the version of each template, convert
it to the latest template format, and save it to the Template Blackboard at
```

7. Once the convergence is complete, it will indicate the same and recommend a reboot. Press *Y* to proceed:

```
[17/18] [SUCCEEDED] Starting all services on converged VCSA node
[18/18] [SUCCEEDED] Cleanup after converge
Converged to VCSA with embedded PSC successfully!

 Converged to VCSA with embedded PSC successfully!

You may proceed with next step according to the documentation at https://docs.vmware.com/en/VMware-vSphere/index.html for your topology or
PSC HA configuration
Downloading /var/log/vmware/converge/converge.log from appliance to local file
C:\Users\ADMINI~1\AppData\Local\Temp\vcsaCliInstaller-2019-02-04-11-34-e439trdt\workflow_1549280074213\converge\converge_mgmt.log
Proceed with certificate thumbprint check...
 [SUCCEEDED] Successfully executed Task 'MonitorPSCDeployTask: Running
MonitorPSCDeployTask' in TaskFlow 'converge' at 11:50:28
VCJoinADDomainTask: Running VCJoinADDomainTask
= [START] Start executing Task: Post converge, join the AD Domain at 11:50:28 =
Proceed with certificate thumbprint check...
Cannot produce a normalized IP address from the given string:
'oldvc02.vdescribed.lab'. If this string is an FQDN, this warning can be
disregarded.
Running command on vm newvc02: /bin/bash --login -c
'/opt/vmware/share/vami/vami_set_dns -d vdescribed.lab 192.168.78.130'
Running command on vm newvc02: /bin/bash --login -c
'/opt/likewise/bin/domainjoin-cli join vdescribed.lab lab_domain_joiner *****'
VC joined to AD Domain.
Running command on vm newvc02: /bin/bash --login -c
'/opt/vmware/share/vami/vami_set_dns -d vdescribed.lab 127.0.0.1 192.168.78.130'
DNS list updated to have local caching ip 127.0.0.1

This machine has to be rebooted to finish the operation. Reboot now?Press (Y|y)es to proceed:
y
Machine reboot started. vCenter should be available in few minutes
Running command on vm newvc02: /bin/bash --login -c 'reboot'
 [SUCCEEDED] Successfully executed Task 'VCJoinADDomainTask: Running
VCJoinADDomainTask' in TaskFlow 'converge' at 12:16:23
vcsa-util execution successfully completed, workflow log dir:
C:\Users\ADMINI~1\AppData\Local\Temp\vcsaCliInstaller-2019-02-04-11-34-e439trdt\workflow_1549280074213
================================= 12:16:23 =================================
Result and log file information...
WorkFlow log directory:
C:\Users\ADMINI~1\AppData\Local\Temp\vcsaCliInstaller-2019-02-04-11-34-e439trdt\workflow_1549280074213

D:\vcsa-converge-cli\win32>
```

8. Once completed, the **Summary** tab of vCenter will indicate that it is now a **vCenter with an embedded Platform Services Controller**:

9. Once convergence is complete, the next step is to decommission the source PSC that was successfully converged.

A general rule of thumb is to ensure that all of the vCenter Servers registered to the PSCs have been converged before you proceed with decommissioning the external PSCs. Move on to the next section to learn how to decommission external PSCs.

Decommissioning external PSCs

At this stage, the external PSC is still in partnership with the newly formed embedded PSC. This can be determined by verifying the replication agreements by using the vdcrepadmin utility on the PSC at /usr/lib/vmware-vmdir/bin/vdcrepadmin.

The syntax is vdcrepadmin -f showpartnerstatus -h localhost -u administrator -w <SSO password> and is shown in the following screenshot:

```
root@oldpsc02 [ ~ ]#
root@oldpsc02 [ ~ ]# /usr/lib/vmware-vmdir/bin/vdcrepadmin -f showservers -h localhost -u administrator -w Password@123
cn=oldpsc02.vdescribed.lab,cn=Servers,cn=Site-B,cn=Sites,cn=Configuration,dc=vsphere,dc=local
cn=oldvc02.vdescribed.lab,cn=Servers,cn=Site-B,cn=Sites,cn=Configuration,dc=vsphere,dc=local
root@oldpsc02 [ ~ ]#
root@oldpsc02 [ ~ ]# /usr/lib/vmware-vmdir/bin/vdcrepadmin -f showpartners -h localhost -u administrator -w Password@123
ldap://oldvc02.vdescribed.lab
root@oldpsc02 [ ~ ]#
root@oldpsc02 [ ~ ]# /usr/lib/vmware-vmdir/bin/vdcrepadmin -f showpartnerstatus -h localhost -u administrator -w Password@123
Partner: oldvc02.vdescribed.lab
Host available:   Yes
Status available: Yes
My last change number:          4439
Partner has seen my change number: 4439
Partner is 0 changes behind.
root@oldpsc02 [ ~ ]#
root@oldpsc02 [ ~ ]#
```

The following procedure will guide you through the steps involved in decommissioning already converged PSCs:

1. Locate the decommission_psc.json file on the DVD drive at vcsa-converge-cli\templates\decommission\.

2. Copy the `decommission_psc.json` file to a read/write location, such as `C:\Converge\decommission_psc.json`.

3. Open the file in a rich text editor such as WordPad and specify the requested details. Then, **Save** the changes:

```json
{
    "__comments": "Template for decommissioning PSC node with converge CLI tool.",
    "__version": "2.11.0",
    "psc": {
        "description": {
            "__comments": [
                "This section describes the PSC appliance which you want to",
                "decommission and the ESXi host on which the appliance is running. "
            ]
        },
        "managing esxi or vc": {
            "hostname": "192.168.78.199",
            "username": "root",
            "password": "password@123",
        },
        "psc_appliance": {
            "hostname": "oldpsc02.vdescribed.lab",
            "username": "administrator@vsphere.local",
            "password": "Password@123",
            "root_password": "Password@123"
        }
    },
    "vcenter": {
        "description": {
            "__comments": [
                "This section describes the embedded vCenter appliance which is in ",
                "replication with the provided PSC"
            ]
        },
        "managing esxi or vc": {
            "hostname": "192.168.78.199",
            "username": "root",
            "password": "password@123",
        },
        "vc_appliance": {
            "hostname": "oldvc02.vdescribed.lab",
            "username": "administrator@vsphere.local",
            "password": "Password@123",
            "root_password": "Password@123"
        }
    }
}
```

ESXi/vCenter managing the external PSC

External PSC details

ESXi/vCenter managing the vCSA with the new embedded PSC

vCSA with the new embedded PSC

4. Start Windows Command Prompt as an Administrator and navigate to the DVD ROM:\vcsa-converge-cli\win32 directory. Then, issue the vcsa-util.exe decommission --no-ssl-certificate-verification --verbose <Path to decommission_psc.json> command:

```
Administrator: Command Prompt - vcsa-util.exe  decommission --no-ssl-certificate-verification --verbose C:\Converge\decommission_psc.json       —   □   ×
d:\vcsa-converge-cli\win32>
d:\vcsa-converge-cli\win32>vcsa-util.exe decommission --no-ssl-certificate-verification --verbose C:\Converge\decommission_psc.json
Updating log file location, copying 'C:\Users\ADMINI~1\AppData\Local\Temp\vcsaCliInstaller-2019-02-04-13-25-e2j3lj7s\vcsa-converge-cli.log'
 to desired location as a backup: 'C:\Users\ADMINI~1\AppData\Local\Temp\vcsaCliInstaller-2019-02-04-13-25-e2j3lj7s\workflow_1549286712932\v
csa-converge-cli.log.bak'
Adding the following cli arguments to blackboard
{'cli_arg_verify_template_only': False, 'cli_arg_pause_on_warnings': False,
'cli_arg_log_dir': None, 'cli_arg_precheck_only': False,
'cli_arg_template_help': False, 'cli_arg_terse': False, 'cli_arg_template':
['C:\\Converge\\decommission_psc.json'],
'cli_arg_no_ssl_certificate_verification': True, 'cli_arg_sub_command':
'decommission', 'cli_arg_verbose': True}
Workflow log-dir
C:\Users\ADMINI~1\AppData\Local\Temp\vcsaCliInstaller-2019-02-04-13-25-e2j3lj7s\workflow_1549286712932
SyntaxValidationTask: Executing Template Syntax Validation task
 [START] Start executing Task: To validate the syntax of the template. at
13:25:13
```

5. The decommissioning process might take a while to complete:

```
 [SUCCEEDED] Successfully executed Task 'PrecheckVCDecommissionTask: Running
PrecheckVCDecommissionTask' in TaskFlow 'decommission_psc' at 13:25:21
DecommissionTask: Running DecommissionTask
========= [START] Start executing Task: Decommission task at 13:25:22 =========
Proceed with certificate thumbprint check...
Cannot produce a normalized IP address from the given string:
'oldpsc02.vdescribed.lab'. If this string is an FQDN, this warning can be
disregarded.
Powering off PSC machine...
PSC machine powered off successfully.
Proceed with certificate thumbprint check...
Cannot produce a normalized IP address from the given string:
'oldvc02.vdescribed.lab'. If this string is an FQDN, this warning can be
disregarded.
Decommissioning PSC node. This may take some time. Please wait.
Running command on vm newvc02: /bin/bash --login -c '/usr/bin/cmsso-util
unregister --node-pnid oldpsc02.vdescribed.lab --username
administrator@vsphere.local --passwd *** --debug'
```

6. Once done, the vdcrepadmin -f showpartners or showpartnerstatus commands should not list the decommissioned external PSC:

```
root@oldvc02 [ ~ ]# /usr/lib/vmware-vmdir/bin/vdcrepadmin -f showpartners -h localhost -u administrator -w Password@123
root@oldvc02 [ ~ ]#
root@oldvc02 [ ~ ]# /usr/lib/vmware-vmdir/bin/vdcrepadmin -f showpartnerstatus -h localhost -u administrator -w Password@123
root@oldvc02 [ ~ ]#
root@oldvc02 [ ~ ]#
```

This completes the process of decommissioning a Platform Services Controller.

How it works...

During convergence, PSC components are installed on the target vCenter Appliance, and then the embedded PSC is joined to the same SSO domain as the external PSC, thereby establishing a replication agreement with it. Once done, the vCenter is automatically repointed to the embedded PSC.

When decommissioning the already converged external PSCs, the PSC node is shut down, and it is unregistered from the SSO domain. The unregistration task is automatically executed from the vCenter with the newly embedded PSC.

Converging PSCs into embedded appliances reduces the complexity of your vCenter topology and eliminates the need for the availability of PSC nodes using network load balancers.

Upgrading ESXi using the interactive installer

Once you are done upgrading the management layer (vCenters/PSCs), the ESXi hosts in the environment can be upgraded. There is more than one way to upgrade ESXi hosts, and the way you do so also depends on how they were deployed previously. For instance, if the hosts are running stateless/stateful auto-deployed ESXi hosts, then it wouldn't make sense to use the interactive installer to upgrade the hosts. The ESXi host can be upgraded without needing to console into each of them using VMware Update Manager. We will learn how to use Update Manager in Chapter 14, *Upgrading and Patching Using vSphere Update Manager*.

Other methods include using the ESXi CLI or a kickstart script.

In this recipe, we will learn how to use the interactive installer to upgrade ESXi.

Getting ready

Here is what you will need to do before you can upgrade ESXi to ESXi 6.7:

- Ensure that the hardware is compatible with ESXi 6.
- Ensure that the version running is ESXi 6.0 U3 or later.

- Download the ESXi 6.7 OEM ISO image for installation.
- Ensure that you have access to the servers console by using the IPMI remote access interfaces (DRAC, ILO, KVM, and so on).

How to do it...

The following procedure will guide you through the steps involved in upgrading ESXi to ESXi 6.7:

1. Mount the ISO to the server via its IPMI interface.
2. Boot the server of the ISO. Unlike the older version of the installers, it no longer presents you with the installer boot menu. Instead, it starts loading the installer into memory and subsequently shows a **Welcome to ESXi Installation** screen. Hit *Enter* to continue.
3. On the EULA screen, hit *F11* to **Accept and continue**.
4. On the **Select a Disk to Install or Upgrade** screen, you will need to select the device that contains the previous installation. If you are unsure, select a device and hit *F1* to find its details.
5. If the **Disk Details** screen indicates that it has a previous installation of ESXi on it, then you have the correct device:

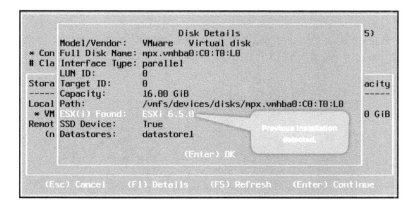

Disk Details screen with the previous installation detected

6. Hit *Enter* to return to the **Select a Disk to Install or Upgrade** screen. Hit *Enter* again to confirm the selection and continue.

7. On the **ESXi and VMFS found** screen, choose to **Upgrade ESXi, preserve the VMFS datastore** and hit *Enter* key to continue:

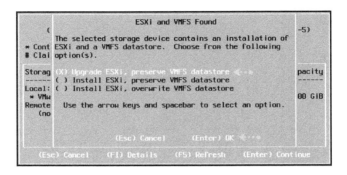

Installation options

8. On the **Confirm Upgrade** screen, review the details and hit *F11* to initiate the upgrade:

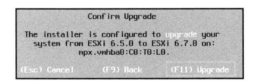

9. If the upgrade completes successfully, you will be presented with an **Upgrade Complete** screen. Unmount the ISO from the server's console and hit *Enter* to reboot:

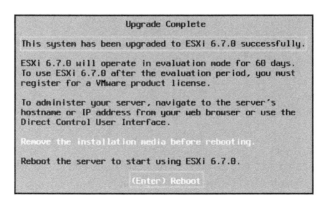

This finishes the ESXi upgrade using the ESXi 6.7 interactive installer.

How it works...

The ESXi interactive installer detects an existing installation and lets you upgrade it if you choose to. The upgrade can be performed by either preserving the local VMFS volume or by simply overwriting it. In most cases, you preserve any data that's available.

Upgrading ESXi using the command-line interface

ESXi can be upgraded from the CLI. Unlike the interactive method, the CLI requires the use of an offline ZIP bundle.

Here is what you will need to perform an ESXi upgrade using the CLI:

- Ensure that the hardware is compatible with ESXi 6.7.
- Ensure that the version running is ESXi 6.0 U3 or later.
- Download the ESXi 6.7 OEM offline bundle's `.zip` file .
- SSH access to the ESXi host and the root password.

How to do it...

The following procedure will guide you through the steps involved in upgrading an ESXi host from its command-line interface:

1. Upload the ESXi Offline ZIP bundle to any of the datastores that are accessible by the ESXi host. This can be done by using the **Upload** function of the vCenter/ESXi datastore browser.
2. SSH into the ESXi host as the `root` user.
3. Run the `esxcli software sources profile list` command against the offline bundle to list all of the image profiles included in the bundle:
    - **Syntax**: `esxcli software sources profile list -d /vmfs/volumes/oldesx02_local/<Full Path to the Offline Bundle>`
    - **Example**: `esxcli software sources profile list -d /vmfs/volumes/oldesx02_local/update-from-esxi6.7-6.7_update01.zip`

4. Run the `esxcli software profile update` command to upgrade using a desired image profile from the offline bundle:
   - **Syntax:** `esxcli software profile update -p <Image Profile>-d <Full Path to the Offline Bundle>`
   - **Example:** `esxcli software profile update -p ESXi-6.7.0-20181002001-standard -d /vmfs/volumes/oldesx02_local/update-from-esxi6.7-6.7_update01.zip`

```
[root@oldesx02:~]
[root@oldesx02    ] esxcli software sources profile list -d /vmfs/volumes/oldesx02_local/update-from-esxi6.7-6.7_update01.zip
Name                                Vendor        Acceptance Level
----------------------------------  ------------  ----------------
ESXi-6.7.0-20181002001-no-tools     VMware, Inc.  PartnerSupported
ESXi-6.7.0-20181001001s-no-tools    VMware, Inc.  PartnerSupported
ESXi-6.7.0-20181001001s-standard    VMware, Inc.  PartnerSupported
ESXi-6.7.0-20181002001-standard     VMware, Inc.  PartnerSupported
[root@oldesx02:~]
[root@oldesx02    ] esxcli software profile update -p ESXi-6.7.0-20181002001-standard -d /vmfs/volumes/oldesx02_local/update-from-esxi6.7-6.7_update01.zip
Update Result
   Message: The update completed successfully, but the system needs to be rebooted for the changes to be effective.
   Reboot Required: true
```

esxcli software profile update output screen

5. Reboot the ESXi host.

This finishes the CLI method of upgrading ESX.

How it works...

The ESXi CLI upgrade method is an alternative to the interactive installer. With the interactive installer method, the ESXi needs to boot off the ISO image to performing the upgrade, meaning that you would need physical access to the server or access to its IPMI interface.

However, with the CLI method, the upgrade can be performed while the ESXi is up and running. This is done via an SSH session to the host and only requires a single reboot. You cannot use an ESXi Installer ISO image to perform the CLI installation – this can only be achieved using an offline bundle. An offline bundle can have multiple image profiles, and one of them needs to be specified to perform the upgrade. You will learn more about image profiles in `Chapter 11`, *Building Custom ESXi Images Using Image Builder*.

3
Configuring Network Access Using vSphere Standard Switches

Networking is the backbone of any infrastructure, be it virtual or physical. It enables connections between various infrastructure components. When it comes to traditional server-side networking components, we often talk about one or more physical adapters cabled to a physical switch. But things would slightly change when you install a hypervisor on a server and run a virtual machine a top. So why and what should change?

First, now that we can create virtual machines on the hypervisor, each of the virtual machines would need a network identity to enable it to become part of a network. Therefore, we create **vNICs** on the virtual machine, which will appear as network adapters to the guest operating system (Windows/Linux) that runs inside the virtual machine.

Now that we have taken care of the network connection for the virtual machine, the second hurdle is to let the virtual machines communicate over the network. On a server, since there would be a limited number of physical NICs, it is a challenge to present these NICs to individual virtual machines. For instance, if you were to run 20 virtual machines on a host with four physical NICs, then there should be a way to effectively allow all of the virtual machines to share the physical NIC resources. The sharing of physical network interface hardware is achieved by enabling a layer of abstraction called the vSphere virtual switch.

Virtual switch (or simply **vSwitch**) is a software switching construct which provides network infrastructure for the virtual machines running on a host. It allows you to aggregate network connections from multiple vNICs, applies network configuration policies on them, and also pins them to the physical network adapters on the ESXi hosts for traffic flow. Unlike a physical switch, a vSwitch is not a managed switch. It doesn't learn MAC addresses and build a **Content Addressable Memory** (**CAM**) table like a physical switch, but it has just enough intelligence built into it to become aware of the MAC addresses of the virtual machine vNICs connected to it.

There are two other layers of abstraction, called the **virtual machine port groups** and the **VMkernel port group**. A port group, in general, is a method for grouping a set of virtual ports on a vSwitch under a common configuration umbrella. A **virtual machine port group** can only be used for connecting virtual machine network interfaces to it. A **VMkernel port group** is formed when a VMkernel interface is created. We will learn more about this later on in this chapter.

vSphere Standard Switch is a software switching construct that is created and managed per ESXi host. On the other hand, the **vSphere Distributed Switch** is managed by the vCenter Server, eliminating the need to manage local virtual switches on each ESXi hosts. We will learn more about distributed switches in the next chapter.

In this chapter, we will cover the following recipes:

- Creating vSphere Standard Switches
- Creating Virtual Machine Port Groups on vSphere Standard Switches
- Creating additional VMkernel interfaces on vSphere Standard Switches
- Creating additional VMkernel TCP/IP stacks
- Managing the Physical Uplinks of a vSphere Standard Switch
- Configuring Security, Traffic Shaping, Teaming and Failover

Creating vSphere Standard Switches

A vSwitch is local to each ESXi host. A default standard switch, **vSwitch0**, with a **Management Portgroup** and a **Virtual Machine Port Group** is created during ESXi installation. In this recipe, we will learn how to create new vSphere Standard Switches using both the HTML5 client and the ESXi CLI.

Getting ready

Before you begin, it is important to identify the correct uplinks. Not all physical uplinks on a host can pass all traffic. For instance, only a certain number of VLANs would be trunked to the physical switch port(s) the uplink(s) are cabled to.

How to do it...

The following procedure will guide you through the steps involved in creating a vSphere Standard Switch (vSwitch) using the HTML5 client. We will be using the **Add Networking** wizard to accomplish this task. This wizard can be initiated from various vantage points in the inventory. In this recipe, we will be using the **Networking configuration** section of the host. We will start by learning how to create a vSwitch using the HTML5 client, and then learn how to use the ESXi CLI.

Creating a vSwitch using the HTML5 client

The following are the steps for creating vSwitches:

1. Log in to the vCenter Server using the HTML5 client.
2. From the **Hosts and Clusters** inventory view, select the ESXi host to create the vSwitch on.
3. Navigate to **Configure** | **Networking** | **Virtual switches** and click **Add Networking...** to start the wizard:

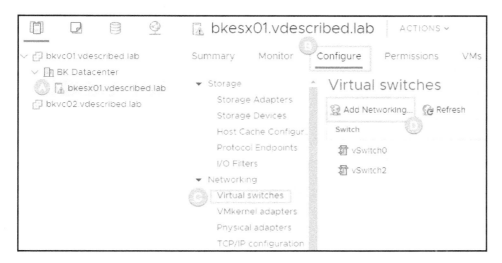

4. In the **Add Networking** wizard, set the **connection type** to **Physical Network Adapter** and click **Next**:

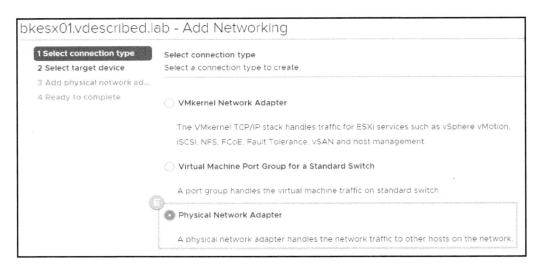

5. On the **Select target device** screen, choose to create a **New standard switch**, and leave the **MTU (Bytes)** at the default of **1500** bytes unless there is a specific need to increase it. Click **Next** to continue:

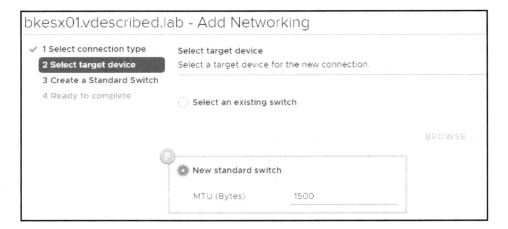

6. On the **Create a Standard Switch – Assigned adapters** screen, you will need to assign network adapters (vmnic) to the vSwitch. Click the + icon to bring up the **Add Physical Adapters to the Switch** window:

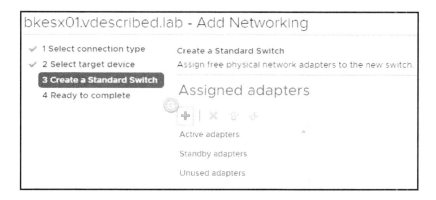

7. On the **Add Physical Adapters to the Switch** screen, select the vmnics to add and click **OK**:

8. Once you are back on the **Create a Standard Switch – Assigned adapters** screen, you will see the selected adapters list as **Active adapters**. You can use this to delete or change the order of the vmnics:

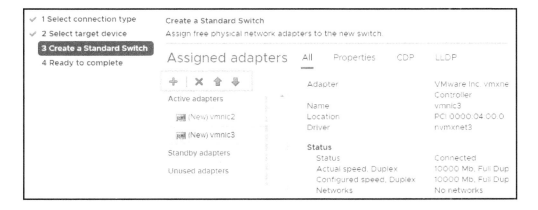

9. On the **Ready to complete** screen, review the settings and click **Finish**:

10. The **Recent Tasks** pane should show that an **Update network configuration** task was completed successfully.
11. Once done, the newly created vSwitch should be listed as one of the virtual switches under **Configure | Networking | Virtual switches**.

Creating a vSwitch using the ESXi command-line interface

vSphere Standard Switches can be created using the ESXi CLI as well. The procedure requires you to either access the command-line console of the ESXi host via an IPMI console (HPE ILO, Dell DRAC, KVM, and so on) or SSH into the ESXi host using tools such as PuTTY or SecureCRT. Let's get started:

1. SSH (PuTTY) into the ESXi host as the root user.
2. Run the esxcfg-nics -l command to list all of the physical network adapters on the host.
3. Create a vSphere Standard switch using the following command syntax:

```
# esxcli network vswitch standard add -v <Name of the vSwitch>
```

4. Add an uplink to the newly created vSwitch using the following command syntax:

```
# esxcli network vswitch standard uplink add -u <Name of the vmnic>-v <Name of the vSwitch created>
```

5. Run the following command (syntax) to view the details of the newly created vSwitch:

```
# esxcli network vswitch standard list -v <Name of the vSwitch created>
```

The following is the output of the preceding commands:

```
[root@bkesx01:~] esxcfg-nics -l
Name    PCI          Driver      Link Speed      Duplex MAC Address        MTU   Description
vmnic0  0000:0b:00.0 nvmxnet3    Up   10000Mbps  Full   00:50:56:88:37:fe  1500  VMware Inc. vmxnet3 Virtual Ethernet Controller
vmnic1  0000:13:00.0 nvmxnet3    Up   10000Mbps  Full   00:50:56:88:27:02  1500  VMware Inc. vmxnet3 Virtual Ethernet Controller
vmnic2  0000:1b:00.0 nvmxnet3    Up   10000Mbps  Full   00:50:56:88:5c:e0  1500  VMware Inc. vmxnet3 Virtual Ethernet Controller
vmnic3  0000:04:00.0 nvmxnet3    Up   10000Mbps  Full   00:50:56:88:5f:88  1500  VMware Inc. vmxnet3 Virtual Ethernet Controller
[root@bkesx01:~]
[root@bkesx01:~] esxcli network vswitch standard add -v BKDevSwitch
[root@bkesx01:~]
[root@bkesx01:~] esxcli network vswitch standard uplink add -u vmnic3 -v BKDevSwitch
[root@bkesx01:~]
[root@bkesx01:~] esxcli network vswitch standard list -v BKDevSwitch
BKDevSwitch
   Name: BKDevSwitch
   Class: cswitch
   Num Ports: 2560
   Used Ports: 3
   Configured Ports: 128
   MTU: 1500
   CDP Status: listen
   Beacon Enabled: false
   Beacon Interval: 1
   Beacon Threshold: 3
   Beacon Required By:
   Uplinks: vmnic3
   Portgroups:
[root@bkesx01:~]
```

This completes the process of creating a standard vSwitch using the ESXi CLI.

> One of the benefits of using the command-line interface is that it will let you create a vSwitch with a user-defined name. The GUI method that's using the HTML5 client uses the vSwitchX naming convention.

How it works...

The standard vSwitch is a core networking construct of the ESXi hypervisor. The following diagram is a logical representation of a vSphere Standard Switch. It shows a single vSwitch with port groups using two physical NICs connected to two stacked switches.

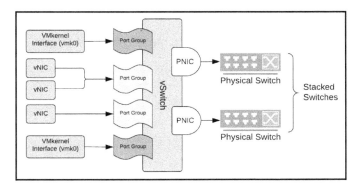

A vSwitch—**vSwitch0**—is created during the installation to configure the management **VMkernel interface (vmk0)** on it.

To understand how a virtual switch works, it is essential to compare its functions to a physical switch.

When a frame enters a physical switch, its destination is determined by the switch port number corresponding to its destination MAC address in the physical switch's MAC table. If it can't find an entry in the MAC table, it floods the frame via every port other than the source port. Much like the physical switch, a virtual switch also maintains a MAC table, but there is no learning process for a virtual switch. A virtual switch will already have a list of MAC addresses and their virtual port numbers. If a frame with a destination MAC that isn't present in the virtual switch's MAC table enters a virtual switch, then it is sent out via physical NICs (active uplinks) that are connected to the virtual switch. This holds true only if a virtual machine or a VMkernel interface is the source of the flow, that is, only if that frame enters via a virtual port. If a frame with an unknown MAC enters the virtual switch via its physical uplinks, then that frame will be dropped by the virtual switch.

Physical switches will have a fixed number of ports; however, a virtual switch will have a maximum limit but a large number of configurable ports. The third difference is that, unlike some, or most, physical switches; it is not a manageable switch, per se, meaning that it doesn't have it is own management IP address or an operating system such as the Cisco IOS. Instead, the virtual switches are managed at the hypervisor or the vCenter, depending on the type of virtual switch (standard vSwitch or VDS) in use.

Creating Virtual Machine Port Groups on vSphere Standard Switches

Port groups are logical containers that are created on a virtual switch. Think of them as port aggregators to which configuration and traffic management policies can be applied; for instance, a VLAN ID can be set on a port group. Virtual machines are provided network access when you connect their virtual NIC(s) to a port group.

In this recipe, we will learn how to create a virtual machine port group.

Getting ready

Before you begin, you will need the following information at hand:

- The desired name (network label) for the port group. It is important to note that the name is *case-sensitive.*
- Physical uplinks (vmics) to use for the port group (optional).
- An optional VLAN ID. If a VLAN ID is used, then it is essential to identify the physical uplinks to use with the port group. This is because not all of the uplinks are configured to pass all traffic.

How to do it...

The following procedures will help you to create virtual machine port groups. Much like other networking tasks, we could use the **Add Networking** wizard or the ESXi CLI method.

Creating a standard port group using the HTML5 interface

Follow these steps to create a standard port group:

1. Log in to the vCenter Server using the HTML5 client.
2. From the **Hosts and Clusters** inventory view, select the ESXi host to create the vSwitch on.
3. Navigate to **Configure** | **Networking** | **Virtual switches** and click **Add Networking** to start the wizard.

4. In the **Add Networking** wizard, select **Virtual Machine Port Group for a Standard Switch** and click **Next** to continue:

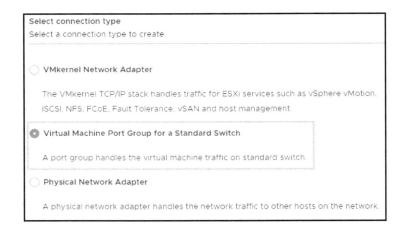

5. On the **Select target device** screen, browse and select an existing standard vSwitch and click **Next** to continue:

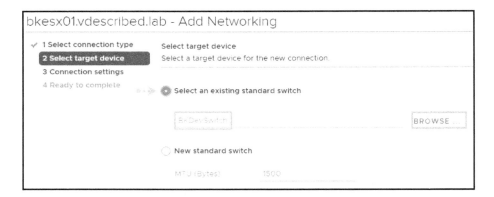

 You could also choose to create a new standard vSwitch for the port group to be formed on.

6. On the **Connection settings** screen, specify a name (**Network label**) for the port group and an optional **VLAN ID**. Click **Next** to continue:

7. On the **Ready to complete** screen, review the settings and click **Finish**:

8. The **Port Groups** tab of the vSwitch should now list the newly created port group:

This completes the process of creating a port group on a standard vSwitch using the HTML5 client.

Creating a standard port group using the ESXi CLI

A standard port group can be created using the ESX CLI as well. This method comes in handy when you don't have access to the graphical user interface. The procedure requires you to either access the command-line console of the ESXi host via an IPMI console (HPE ILO, Dell DRAC, KVM, and so on) or SSH into the ESXi host using tools such as PuTTY or SecureCRT. Let's get started:

1. SSH (PuTTY) into the ESXi host as the `root` user.

2. Create a port group on an existing vSwitch using the following command syntax:

   `# esxcli network vswitch standard portgroup add -p` `<Network Label for the port group> -v <Name of the existing vSwitch>`

3. (Optional) Assign a VLAN ID to the port group using the command syntax:

   `# esxcli network vswitch standard portgroup set -p` `<Network Label for the port group> -v <VLAN Number>`

4. Run the following command to list all of the available port groups on the ESXi host. The newly created port group should be listed in the output:

   `# esxcli network vswitch standard portgroup list`

   The following is the output of the preceding commands:

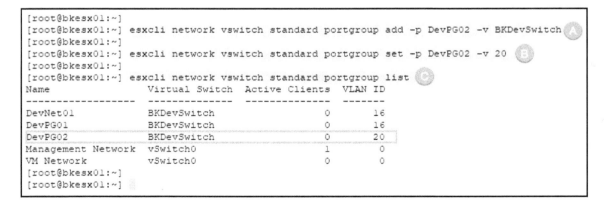

```
[root@bkesx01:~]
[root@bkesx01:~] esxcli network vswitch standard portgroup add -p DevPG02 -v BKDevSwitch
[root@bkesx01:~]
[root@bkesx01:~] esxcli network vswitch standard portgroup set -p DevPG02 -v 20
[root@bkesx01:~]
[root@bkesx01:~] esxcli network vswitch standard portgroup list
Name                  Virtual Switch  Active Clients  VLAN ID
--------------------  --------------  --------------  -------
DevNet01              BKDevSwitch                  0       16
DevPG01               BKDevSwitch                  0       16
DevPG02               BKDevSwitch                  0       20
Management Network    vSwitch0                     1        0
VM Network            vSwitch0                     0        0
[root@bkesx01:~]
[root@bkesx01:~]
```

This completes the process of creating a port group on a standard vSwitch using the ESXi CLI.

How it works...

Port groups are logical constructs that are used for grouping virtual ports on a vSwitch. The standard vSwitch does not expose individual ports in the user interface to apply policies on. Instead, we are allowed to use a port group to achieve the same. It is interesting to note that there is no set number or limit on the number of virtual ports that a port group can encompass. However, there are per vSwitch and per host limits. The *Configuration Maximums* guide is the absolute reference to understand these configuration limits and can be found at `https://configmax.vmware.com`.

The ports are added under the umbrella of a port group as you connect more and more vNICs to it. Since vSphere 5.5, there is no set number of ports on a vSwitch. If you were to view the same vSwitch properties, then the number of ports value will be shown as elastic, meaning that the virtual ports are added/used on a vSwitch when you connect vNICs to a port group.

A **virtual machine port group** can only be used to connect a virtual machines' vNICs to it. There can be more than one virtual machine port group on a standard vSwitch.

A **VMkernel port group** can only be used to connect a VMkernel interface. A number of virtual machines can connect to a single virtual machine port group, but each VMkernel port group requires a separate port group on a standard vSwitch. This behavior is slightly different on a distributed vSwitch - which will be covered in `Chapter 4`, *Configuring Network Access Using vSphere Distributed Switches*.

Creating additional VMkernel interfaces on vSphere Standard Switches

VMkernel interfaces (vmks) are network interfaces for VMkernel. The default management network interface of an ESXi host is a VMkernel interface that is created during the installation process. VMware allows you to create up to 256 VMkernel interfaces (vmk0 – vmk255) per ESXi host.

In this recipe, we will learn how to create VMkernel interfaces on a standard vSwitch.

Getting ready

Before you proceed with creating VMkernel interfaces, you will need the following information at hand:

- You need the desired name of the port group for the VMkernel interface.
- You need to identify the vSwitch that the interface will be formed on.
- You need uplinks if you are going to create a new vSwitch for the interface.

How to do it...

This section will cover both the HTML5 and CLI methods of creating VMkernel interfaces on a Standard Switch.

Creating a VMkernel interface using the HTML5 client

The following are the steps for creating a VMkernel interface:

1. Log in to the vCenter Server using the HTML5 client.
2. From the **Hosts and Clusters** inventory view, select the ESXi host to create the vSwitch on.
3. Navigate to **Configure | Networking | Virtual switches** and click **Add Networking** to start the wizard.
4. In the **Add Networking** wizard, select **VMkernel Network Adapter** and click **Next** to continue:

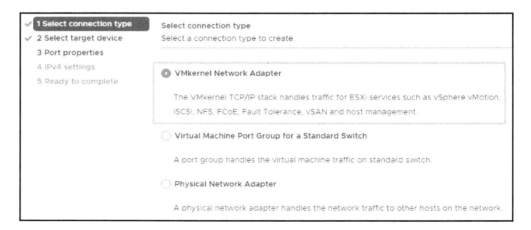

5. On the **Select target device** screen, browse and select a standard switch to form the VMkernel interface on. Then, click **Next** to continue:

 You could choose a create a separate vSwitch for the VMkernel interface if desired. This, however, will depend on the availability of unused physical uplinks (vmnics) that can pass the intended traffic.

6. On the **Port properties** screen, specify a network label for the port group, an optional VLAN ID, MTU, a TCP/IP Stack to use, and the services enabled on it. Click **Next** to continue:

VMkernel has three default TCP/IP stacks: a default stack, a provisioning stack, and a vMotion stack. Using different stacks enables the use of different gateways, allowing for better traffic isolation.

7. In the **IPv4 settings** screen, supply a static IP for the VMkernel interface, specify a different gateway if desired, and click **Next** to continue:

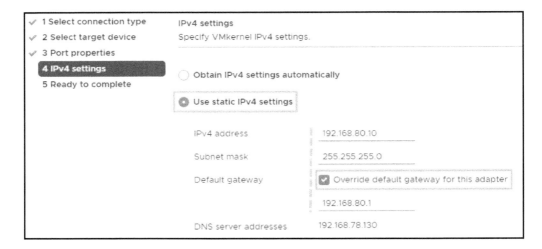

8. On the **Ready to complete** screen, review the settings and click **Finish**:

9. Once you're done, you should see the newly created interface under **Configure** |
Networking | **VMkernel adapters**:

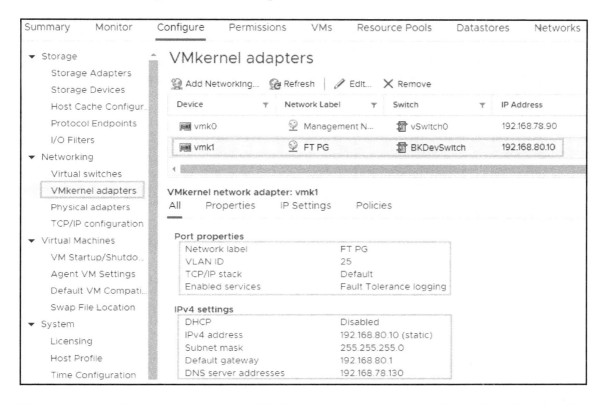

This completes the process of creating VMkernel interfaces on a standard vSwitch using the
HTML5 client.

Creating VMkernel interfaces using the ESXi CLI

This procedure requires you to either access the command-line console of the ESXi host via
an IPMI console (HPE ILO, Dell DRAC, KVM, and so on) or SSH into the ESXi host using
tools such as PuTTY or SecureCRT. Let's get started:

1. SSH (PuTTY) into the ESXi host as the `root` user.
2. Create a port group on a standard vSwitch using the following command syntax:

```
# esxcli network vswitch standard portgroup add -p <Network Label
for the port group> -v <Name of the existing vSwitch>
```

3. Once you're done, create a VMkernel interface on the port group using the following command syntax:

   # **esxcli network ip interface add -p** <Network Label for the port group>

   Since we did not specify an interface name (vmkx) using the -i option, a new sequentially numbered vmk interface is created on the port group that's specified.

4. To find the newly created VMkernel interface, run esxcfg-vmknic -l.

5. Once the new interface (vmkx) is identified, issue the following commands to assign a TCP/IP configuration and associate a traffic type tag with the interface:

   # **esxcli network ip interface ipv4 set -t**=<static/dhcp> -I=<IP Address> -N=<Subnet Mask> -g=<Gateway > -i <vmkx>

The following command is used to associate a traffic type tag with the interface:

   # **esxcli network ip interface tag add** -i vmk2 -t vSphereProvisioning

The following screenshot shows the preceding commands in action:

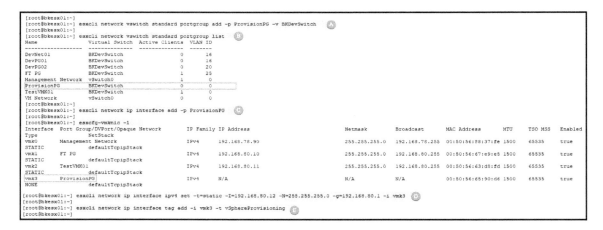

This completes the process of creating VMkernel interfaces using the ESXi CLI.

How it works...

Much like the virtual machines that run on the ESXi hosts, the VMkernel also needs to interface with the network for a variety of purposes. These interfaces act as network node points for the VMkernel.

The following traffic types require the use of a VMkernel interface:

- ESXi management traffic
- vMotion traffic
- VMware **Fault Tolerance** (**FT**) traffic
- vSAN traffic
- iSCSI
- NFS

Each VMkernel interface requires a unique network identifier, that is, a MAC and IP address. The default (first) VMkernel interface—vmk0—will use the MAC of the first active physical uplink (vmnic).

The vmk should be connected to a port group on a vSwitch. On a standard vSwitch, each VMkernel interface needs its own port group, and the port group cannot be shared with other VMkernel interfaces or virtual machines.

The first VMkernel interface (vmk0) will procure the MAC address of the physical NIC it is connected to. The remaining interfaces pick up the **VMware OUI MAC** address that's generated by the ESXi host.

Creating additional VMkernel TCP/IP stacks

VMkernel includes more than one TCP/IP stack. There are three system stacks: vMotion, provisioning, and the default. However, you are also allowed to create custom TCP/IP stacks. In this recipe, we will learn how to set up and use custom TCP/IP stacks.

Getting ready

This procedure requires you to either access the command-line console of the ESXi host via an IPMI console (HPE ILO, Dell DRAC, KVM, and so on) or SSH into the ESXi host using tools such as PuTTY or SecureCRT.

How to do it...

The following procedure will guide you through the steps involved in creating custom/additional TCP/IP stacks:

1. SSH (PuTTY) into the ESXi host as the `root` user.

2. Issue the following command to create a TCP/IP stack:

   # esxcli network ip netstack add -N <Name of the custom stack>

   List all of the stacks on the host to verify them, as follows:

   # esxcli network ip netstack list

   The following is a screenshot showing the preceding commands:

```
[root@bkesx01:~]
[root@bkesx01:~] esxcli network ip netstack add -N DevStack Ⓐ
[root@bkesx01:~]
[root@bkesx01:~] esxcli network ip netstack list Ⓑ
defaultTcpipStack
    Key: defaultTcpipStack
    Name: defaultTcpipStack
    State: 4660

ProdNetwork
    Key: ProdNetwork
    Name: ProdNetwork
    State: 4660

DevStack
    Key: DevStack
    Name: DevStack
    State: 4660
[root@bkesx01:~]
```

3. Create a VMkernel interface and map it to the newly created custom TCP/IP stack:

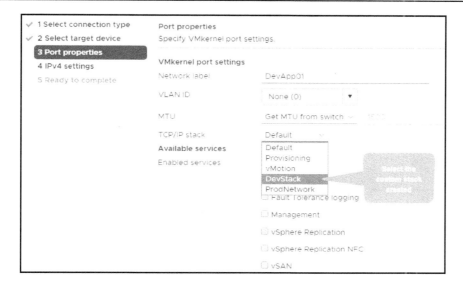

 To learn how to create VMkernel interfaces, read the *Creating additional VMkernel interfaces on a Standard Switch* recipe of this chapter.

4. Use the HTML5 client to navigate to the host's **Configure** | **Networking** | **TCP/IP Configuration** section, select the newly created TCP/IP stack, and click **Edit...**:

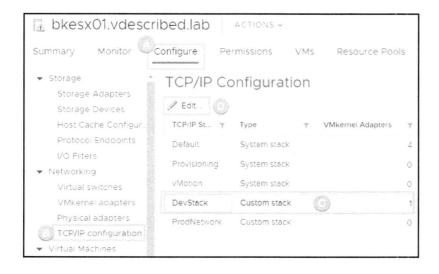

5. On the **Routing** section of the **Edit TCP/IP Stack Configuration** screen, specify a default gateway address for the stack and click **OK**:

6. Unfortunately, like vCenter 6.7 U1, the DNS settings are not available via the HTML5 client. Edit the stack using the web client and specify a DNS server address for the stack's subnet:

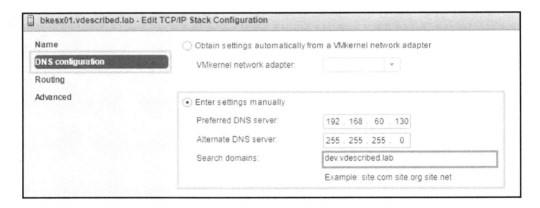

7. In the **Advanced** section, you can choose a desired **Congestion control algorithm** and the **Max. number of connections**. You are not required to make any changes to the default configuration under normal circumstances:

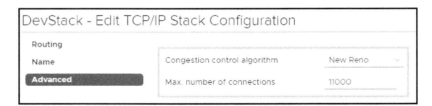

8. Once you're done, the new **Custom stack** will be listed with all of the specified configurations:

This completes the process of creating additional (custom) TCP/IP stacks for the VMkernel.

How it works...

The concept of multiple TCP/IP stacks for VMkernel was introduced with vSphere 5.5. Using the TCP/IP stack means that VMkernel interfaces cannot be on separate network segments, but they can maintain separate memory heap, ARP tables, routing tables, and default gateways. This allows for better traffic isolation and security.

There are three predefined TCP/IP stacks, as follows:

- **Default stack**: This will be the only stack that's used if you do not specify a stack for an interface while creating it
- **vMotion stack**: This can be used to isolate all vMotion traffic away from the default stack
- **Provisioning stack**: This is used to isolate virtual machine cloning, cold migration, and long-distance NFC traffic

Custom stacks can be used to isolate traffic on separate VMkernel gateways if required.

Managing the Physical Uplinks of a vSphere Standard Switch

Uplink is a vSphere term for a physical network adapter. There can be scenarios wherein there is a need to map additional uplinks to a vSwitch for teaming and load balancing purposes. Such an addition is generally done with the intention of enabling the use of teaming and load balancing features. There are different GUI methods to achieve this: you could either use the **Add Networking** wizard or manage the physical network.

In this recipe, we will learn how to accomplish this via the HTML5 client and the ESXi CLI.

How to do it...

The following procedure will walk you through the steps involved in mapping a physical NIC to a vSwitch and then managing them using the HTML5 client:

1. Log in to the vCenter Server using the HTML5 client.
2. From the **Hosts and Clusters** inventory view, select the ESXi host to create the vSwitch on.
3. Navigate to **Configure** | **Networking** | **Virtual switches**, select the desired vSwitch, and click **Manage Physical Adapters...**:

4. On the **Manage Physical Network Adapters** window, click + to add physical adapters. Once they've been added, use the **x** ↑↓ icons to remove or change the order of the adapters. Once you're done, click **OK** to save the changes:

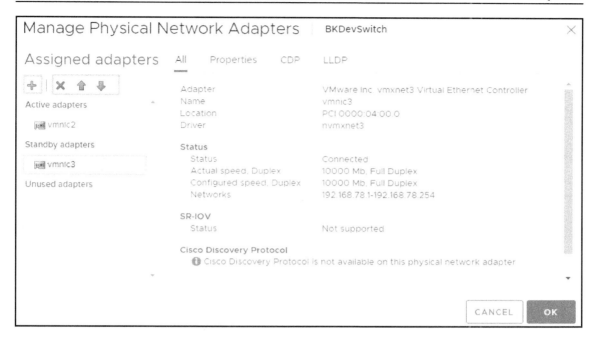

This completes the process of mapping a physical NIC to a vSwitch and then managing them using the HTML5 client.

How it works...

Every physical NIC port that's detected by the ESXi host is enumerated as a vmnic. Each vmnic corresponds to an Ethernet port.

You can enable up to a maximum of 32 1-Gbps, 16 10-Gbps Ethernet ports, and 16 20-Gbps Ethernet ports on an ESXi 6.7 host. The maximums are governed by the make/model/driver/feature of the NIC cards and their combinations. For instance, you may have up to 32 Broadcom 1-GB Ethernet ports using a tg3 driver and NetQueue disabled, but the same NIC with NetQueue enabled can only present 16 ports. If you were to use a combination of 10 GB and 1 GB Ethernet ports, then only 16 10-GB and 4 1-GB ports could be enabled.

Now that ESXi is capable of managing a large number of physical NICs, there should be a method to logically present these NICs so that we can apply configuration policies on them. This is achieved by enumerating the physical NIC with a vmnicX pattern (vmnic0...vmnic32). There is also a logic behind the enumeration. The NICs are sequentially enumerated during the ESXi boot process by scanning the PCI bus, slot, and port number. The PCI-ID to vmnic mapping can be found in the /etc/vmware/esx.conf configuration of an ESXi host.

The following is a screenshot of the configuration of an ESXi host:

```
[root@bkesx01:~] grep vmkname /etc/vmware/esx.conf
/device/00000:027:00.0/vmkname = "vmnic2"
/device/00000:019:00.0/vmkname = "vmnic1"
/device/00000:004:00.0/vmkname = "vmnic3"
/device/00000:011:00.0/vmkname = "vmnic0"
/device/00000:003:00.0/vmkname = "vmhba0"
/device/00000:000:07.1/vmkname = "vmhba1"
[root@bkesx01:~]
```

There's more...

Although the order of the adapters cannot be changed using the ESXi CLI, there are CLI methods available so that you can add and remove physical adapters. Let's go through these now:

1. SSH into the ESXi host as the root user.
2. To add an uplink to a physical vSwitch, use the following command syntax:

   # esxcli network vswitch standard uplink add -u <Physical Uplink>
   -v <Name of the vSwitch>

3. Issue the following command to fetch the details of the vSwitch and verify whether the physical uplink has been successfully added:

   # esxcli network vswitch standard list -v <Name of the vSwitch>

The following is a screenshot showing the preceding commands:

```
[root@bkesx01:~]
[root@bkesx01:~] esxcli network vswitch standard list -v BKDevSwitch
BKDevSwitch
   Name: BKDevSwitch
   Class: cswitch
   Num Ports: 2560
   Used Ports: 7
   Configured Ports: 128
   MTU: 1500
   CDP Status: listen
   Beacon Enabled: false
   Beacon Interval: 1                        Before adding the
   Beacon Threshold: 3                           uplink
   Beacon Required By:
   Uplinks: vmnic2
   Portgroups: DevPG02, DevPG01, DevNet01, DevApp01, ProvisionPG, TestVMK01, FT PG
[root@bkesx01:~]
[root@bkesx01:~] esxcli network vswitch standard uplink add -u vmnic3 -v BKDevSwitch
[root@bkesx01:~]
[root@bkesx01:~] esxcli network vswitch standard list -v BKDevSwitch
BKDevSwitch
   Name: BKDevSwitch
   Class: cswitch
   Num Ports: 2560
   Used Ports: 9
   Configured Ports: 128
   MTU: 1500
   CDP Status: listen
   Beacon Enabled: false
   Beacon Interval: 1                        After adding the
   Beacon Threshold: 3                           uplink
   Beacon Required By:
   Uplinks: vmnic3, vmnic2
   Portgroups: DevPG02, DevPG01, DevNet01, DevApp01, ProvisionPG, TestVMK01, FT PG
[root@bkesx01:~]
```

This completes the process of mapping physical NIC/uplinks to a standard vSwitch using the ESXi CLI.

Configuring Security, Traffic Shaping, Teaming and Failover

The Security, Traffic Shaping, Teaming and Failover mechanisms are identical for a standard vSwitch and a Distributed vSwitch (dvSwitch or VDS), with VDS offering slightly more functionality.

VDS can be configured to handle both ingress and egress traffic shaping, and it supports load balancing based on the load on a physical NIC.

Although we will look at how to configure these settings, we will be discussing the underlying concepts in detail in the next chapter.

How to do it...

The following procedure will guide you through the steps involved in Configuring Security, Traffic Shaping, Teaming, and Failover on a vSphere Standard Switch:

1. Log in to the vCenter Server by using either of the following methods:
   - Use the HTML5 client.
   - From the **Hosts and Clusters** inventory view, select the ESXi host to create the vSwitch on.

2. Navigate to **Configure** | **Networking** | **Virtual switches**, select the desired vSwitch, and click **Edit...**:

3. Use the **Security** section of the **Edit Settings** window to configure the desired **Promiscuous mode**, **MAC address changes**, and **Forged transmits** policies for the vSwitch:

4. Use the **Traffic shaping** section to control the **Average/Peak** bandwidth and the burst size of the Egress traffic:

5. Use the **Teaming and failover** section to specify load balancing and other desired configuration:

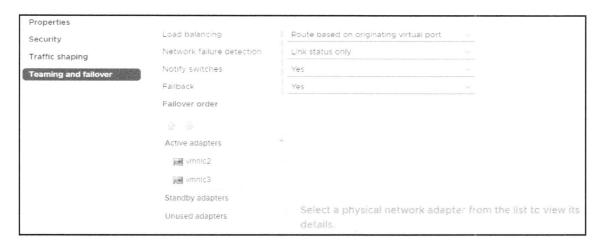

This completes the process of Configuring Security, Traffic Shaping, Teaming, and Failover on vSphere Standard Switches.

We will deep dive into each of these settings in Chapter 4, *Configuring Network Access Using vSphere Distributed Switches*, where we will compare them with the vSphere Distributed Switch.

4
Configuring Network Access Using vSphere Distributed Switches

A **vSphere Distributed Switch** (**dvSwitch** or **vDS**) is the second type of software switching construct that can be used in a vSphere environment. Unlike a **vSphere Standard Switch** (**vSS**), which needs to be managed on a per-host basis, the vDS is managed at the vCenter layer. This, however, doesn't change the way ESXi handles network I/O.

A vDS is often misconceived as a single virtual switch spanning multiple ESXi hosts. One of the reasons for this misconception is that it is commonly documented as a data center-wide vSwitch. In essence, it is only the management plane of the vDS that creates this illusion. VMware still uses an individual data plane (hidden virtual switches) on each ESXi host. It is called a distributed switch since the management plane and the data planes that are distributed on the ESXi hosts are treated as a single manageable entity.

dvSwitch provides advanced functionalities, such as native MAC learning, ingress/egress traffic shaping, link aggregation groups, port mirroring, and NetFlow. The following logical diagram depicts the concept of a dvSwitch:

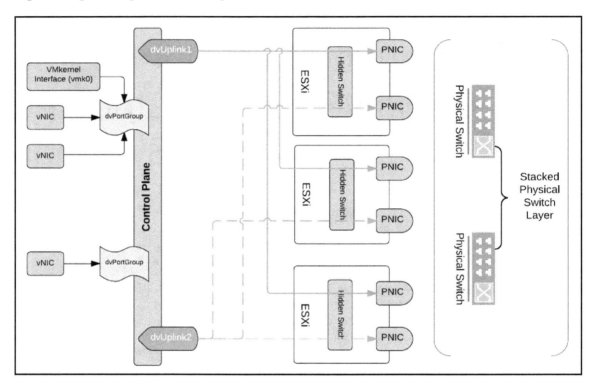

A **Distributed Port Group** (**dvPortGroup**) is much like a standard port group but can span across ESXi hosts. However, the standout difference is that, unlike the need for VMkernel port groups and virtual machine port groups with standard switches, a dvPortGroup can serve both Virtual Machine and VMkernel traffic types.

A **dvUplink** is a layer of abstraction that is used to manage and apply teaming, load balancing and failover policies for physical NICs on an ESXi host. Each dvUplink has a one-to-many relationship with the physical uplinks from different hosts. The number of dvUplinks dictates the number of physical uplinks (*from each ESXi host*) that can participate in the network configuration.

You can configure up to a maximum of 32 dvUplinks on a dvSwitch. This maximum is dictated by the 32 physical adapters limit on an ESXi host.

All dvUplinks are managed under a single **dvUplink port group**.

In this chapter, we will cover the following topics:

- Creating a vSphere Distributed Switch (vDS)
- Connecting ESXi hosts to a vDS
- Creating Distributed Port Groups (dvPortGroup)
- Configuring Security, Traffic Shaping, Teaming, and Failover
- Configuring VLANs on vDS
- Configuring Private VLANs on a vDS
- Configuring a Link Aggregation Group (LAG) on a vDS
- Configuring user-defined network pools—NIOC
- Migrating Virtual Machine Network from vSS to vDS
- Migrating VMkernel interfaces from vSS to vDS
- Configuring port mirroring on vDS
- Configuring NetFlow on vDS
- Upgrading vDS
- Backing up and restoring a vDS

Creating a vSphere Distributed Switch (vDS)

Unlike the vSphere Standard Switch(vSS), which is created on an ESXi host, the vDS needs to be created at the vCenter's data center object level. Therefore, it goes without saying that you will need access to a vCenter that has permission to create and manage vDS.

How to do it...

The following procedure will guide you through the steps involved in creating a vDS:

1. Connect to vCenter Server using the HTML5 client.
2. Navigate to the **Networking inventory** view, right-click on the **BK Datacenter**, and then go to **Distributed Switch** | **New Distributed Switch...**:

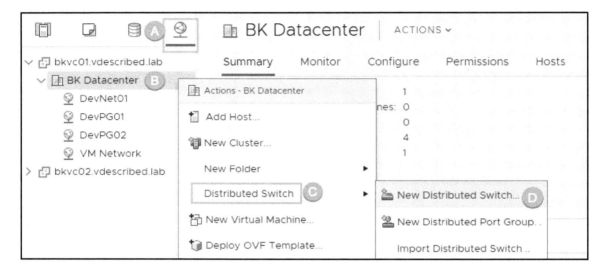

Start New Distributed Switch wizard

3. On the **New Distributed Switch** wizard, specify a **Name** for the vDS and click **Next** to continue:

4. On the **Select version** screen, choose a version for the vDS. Note the version and its compatibility before you proceed. For instance, if the vDS is being created for a mixed data center environment with older versions of ESXi hosts, then you will need to choose a vDS version that's compatible with the oldest ESXi version:

5. On the **Configure settings** screen, you can specify the **Number of uplinks** per host (the default is **4**) and **Network I/O Control** (**Enabled** by default) and then choose to create or not create a **Default port group** and **Port group name**:

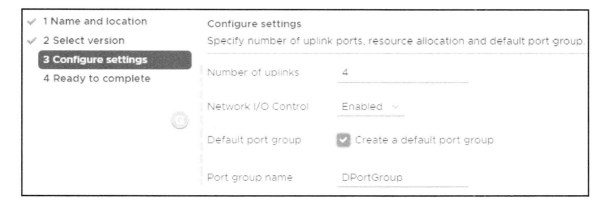

6. On the **Ready to complete** screen, review the settings and click **Finish**:

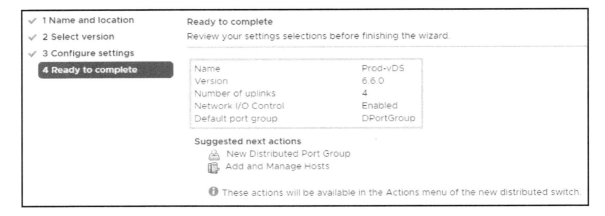

7. The **Recent Tasks** pane should show tasks that are related to creating the vDS, enabling NIOC, and creating the default dvPortGroup complete successfully:

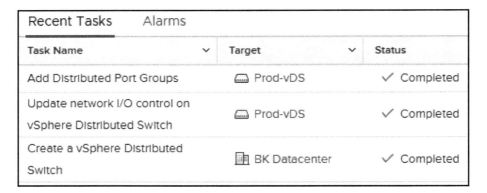

This completes the process of creating a vDS.

How it works...

The dvSwitch configuration is saved in the vCenter database, and a local copy of the configuration is saved on each of the participating ESXi hosts in the `/etc/vmware/dvsdata.db` file. `dvsdata.db` is synced with the vCenter database every 300 seconds.

Connecting ESXi hosts to a vDS

Once you have created a vDS, the next step is to add ESXi hosts to it. This process essentially associates the desired ESXi hosts with the vDS. However, mapping just the ESXi hosts to the vDS doesn't make them usable. You will need to map physical uplinks from the ESXi hosts to the dvSwitch. The number of physical adapters that can be mapped to a dvSwitch depends on the number of dvUplinks that were configured on the vDS. The default is 4 (the maximum is 32).

How to do it...

The following procedure will walk you through the steps involved in mapping ESXi hosts to a vDS:

1. Connect to vCenter Server using the HTML5 client and go to the **Networking inventory** view.
2. Right-click on the desired vDS and click **Add and Manage Hosts...**:

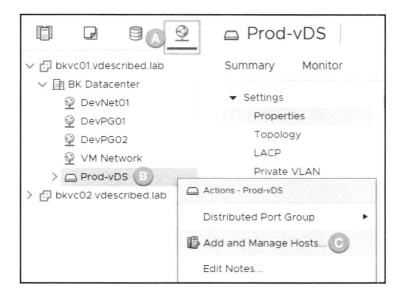

3. In the **Add and Manage Hosts** wizard, select **Add hosts** and click **Next** to continue:

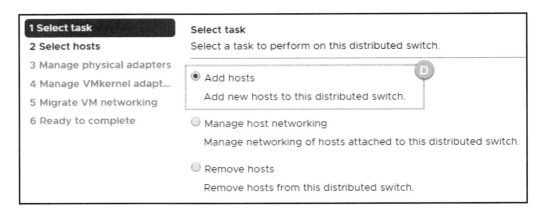

4. On the **Select hosts** screen, click on **New hosts...** to add the desired ESXi hosts. Once you're done, click **Next** to continue:

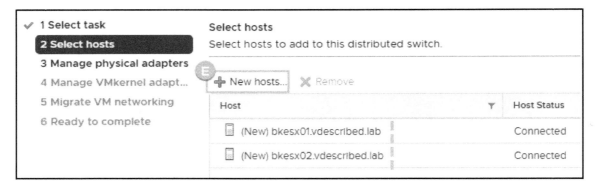

5. On the **Manage physical adapters** screen, select the desired physical adapter (vmnic) to map and click **Assign uplink**:

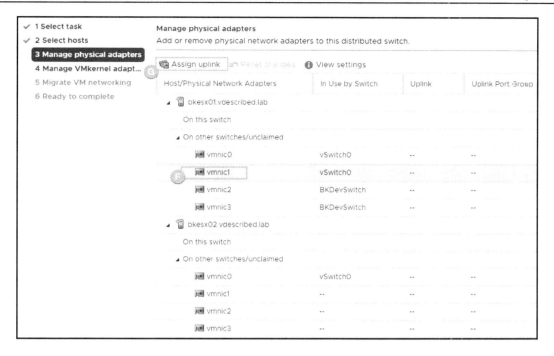

6. On the **Select an Uplink** screen, choose a desired dvUplink for the vmnic and select the **Apply this uplink assignment to all other hosts** checkbox to keep the uplink assignments uniform across the ESXi hosts that are being added. Click **OK** to confirm the selection:

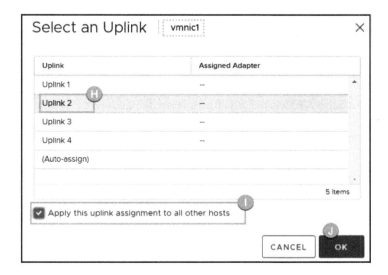

7. Once you're done, you will be back at the **Manage physical adapters** screen.
    Review the assignments and click **Next** to continue:

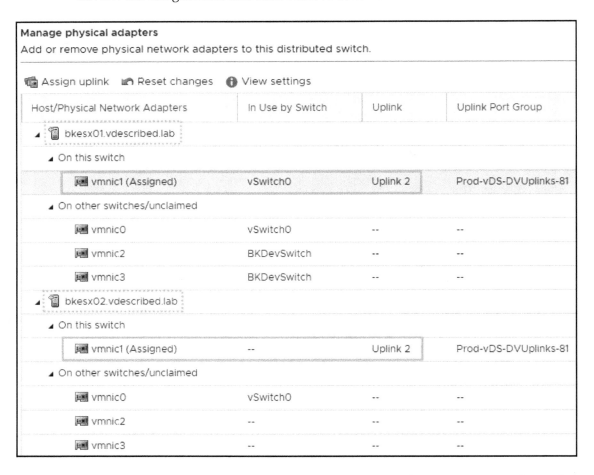

8. On the **Manage VMkernel adapters** screen, you can choose to migrate the vmk
    interfaces to dvPortGroups on the vDS. Since we are just adding the hosts to the
    vDS, we don't have to make any changes on this screen. Click **Next** to continue.

9. On the **Migrate VM networking** screen, you can choose to migrate virtual interfaces to the dvPortGroups on the vDS. Again, since we are just adding the hosts to the vDS, we don't have to make any changes on this screen. Click **Next** to continue.

10. On the **Ready to complete** screen, review the summary and click **Finish**:

11. The **Recent Tasks** pane should indicate successful completion of all of the related tasks:

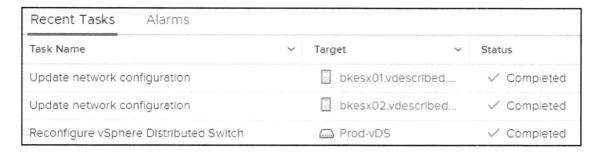

How it works...

Once a host is added to the vDS, running the `net-dvs` command on the ESXi host should show the host's copy of the vDS:

```
[root@bkesx01:~] net-dvs
switch 50 3a ff 0e fe df 9d f3-a4 e7 0d ee e3 7e a2 6b (cswitch)
        max ports: 2560
        global properties:
                com.vmware.common.alias = Prod-vDS ,    propType = CONFIG
                com.vmware.common.version = 0x 6. 0. 0. 0
                        propType = CONFIG
                com.vmware.common.opaqueDvs = false ,   propType = CONFIG
                com.vmware.etherswitch.ipfix:
                        idle timeout = 15 seconds
                        active timeout = 60 seconds
                        sampling rate = 0
                        collector = 0.0.0.0:0
                        internal flows only = false
                        obsDomainID = 0
                        propType = CONFIG
                com.vmware.common.portset.mtu = 1500 ,  propType = CONFIG
                com.vmware.etherswitch.cdp = CDP, listen
                        propType = CONFIG
                com.vmware.vswitch.multicastFilter = legacyFiltering ,  propType = CONFIG
                com.vmware.vrdma.uuid = 52 fb 9d c2 15 e6 27 e8-9e 42 e9 db la da dd be ,        propType = CONFIG
                com.vmware.common.uplinkPorts:
                        Uplink 1, Uplink 2, Uplink 3, Uplink 4
                        propType = CONFIG
                com.vmware.common.respools.version = version3 ,        propType = CONFIG
                com.vmware.common.resv.threshold = 0x4b. 0. 0. 0
```

This information is stored on the host in the `/etc/vmware/dvsdata.db` file.

Once the hosts have been added to the vDS, any changes to the vmnic-to-dvUplink mapping can be done from each ESXi host or by using the **Manage host networking** workflow of the **Prod-vDS - Add and Manage Hosts** wizard. The following is a screenshot of the **Prod-vDS - Add and Manage Hosts** wizard:

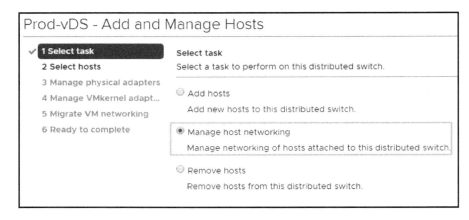

The workflow is identical to **Add hosts**, with additional options to manage the uplinks, as follows:

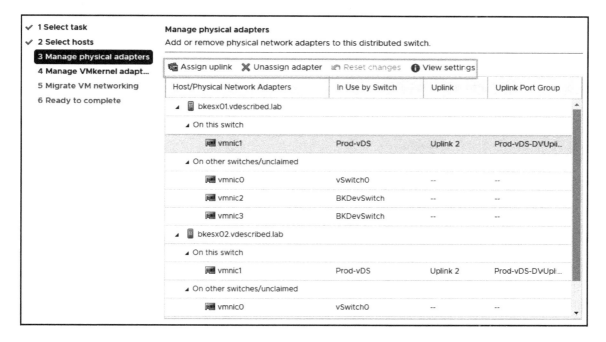

Now that we learned how to connect ESXi hosts to a vDS, in the next section we will learn how to create dvPortGroups.

Creating Distributed Port Groups (dvPortGroup)

When creating a vDS using the **New Distributed Switch** wizard, a dvPortGroup is created by default. However, there are several use cases for more than one dvPortGroup; for instance, a separate dvPortGroup for VMs needing a VLAN. Like vSphere 6.7, vDS can have about **10000** static/elastic dvPortGroups and about **1016** ephemeral port groups.

Refer to *VMware Configuration Maximums* at https://configmax.vmware.com to understand configuration limits.

How to do it...

The following procedure will help you to create a vSphere dvPortGroup:

1. Connect to the vCenter Server using the HTML5 client and go to the **Networking inventory** view.

2. Right-click on the desired vDS and go to **Distributed Port Group** | **New Distributed Port Group...**:

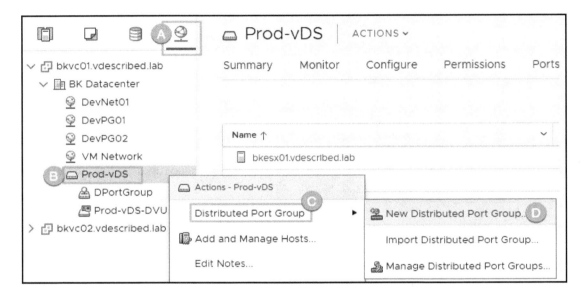

3. On the **New Distributed Port Group** wizard, specify a name for the dvPortGroup and click **Next** to continue:

4. On the **Configure settings** screen, do the following:
   - Specify the desired **Port binding (Static/Ephermeral)** and **Port allocation (Static-Elastic/Static-Fixed)** methods.
   - Specify the **Number of ports** for the dvPortGroup.
   - Provide a **Network resource** pool.
   - Provide a **VLAN type (VLAN/VLAN Trunking/Private VLAN)**.

5. Select **Customize default policies configuration** under **Advanced** to enable security, traffic shaping, teaming and failover, NetFlow, and port blocking:

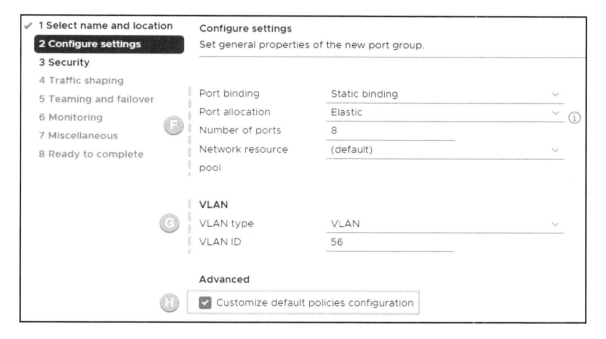

6. On the **Security** screen, you can change how the dvPortGroup handles **Security** and **MAC address changes**:

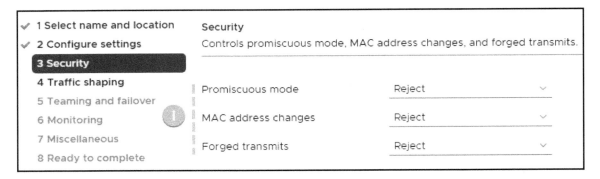

7. On the **Traffic shaping** screen, choose to configure **Ingress/Egress traffic shaping**:

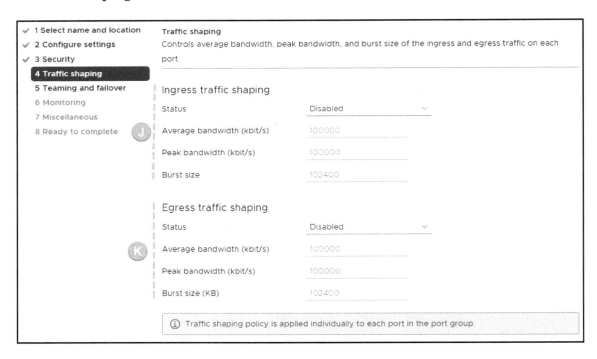

8. On the **Teaming and failover** screen, configure how the network is load
   balanced and how the uplinks are teamed to handle failure:

9. On the **Monitoring** screen, you can choose to enable **NetFlow**:

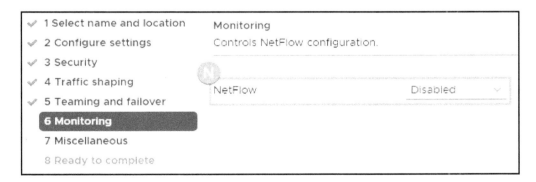

10. On the **Miscellaneous** screen, you can choose to **Block All Ports** if required. The default is **No**:

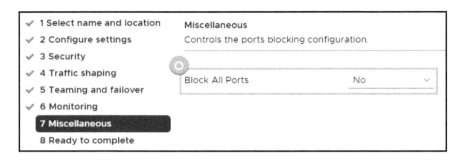

11. On the **Read to complete** screen, review the summary and click **Finish**:

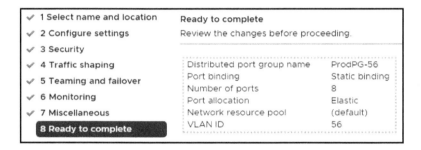

12. You should see an **Add Distributed Port Groups** task complete successfully in the **Recent Tasks** pane.

13. The newly created dvPortGroup will be listed under the **Networks** tab of the vDS:

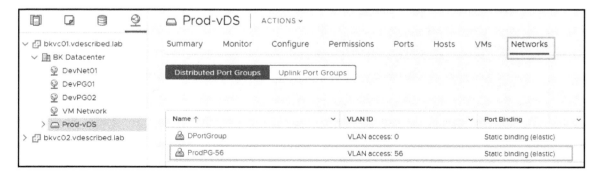

This completes the process of creating dvPortGroups.

How it works...

Every port group that you create on a vDS is referred to as a network. Every vDS will have a port group for dvUplinks, which makes the network count on the vDS a default of 1. Every other port group that you create on the vDS increases the network's work.

In the following screenshot, we can see **3 Networks** and **24 Ports**. We have three networks because we have one dvUplink port group and two dvPortGroups. The port count is **24** because all three port groups have a default port count of **8**:

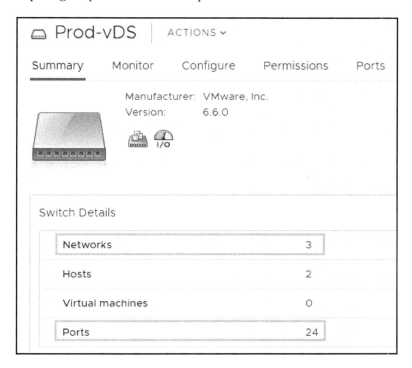

Port binding and port allocation

When you connect a virtual machine to a dvPortGroup, the VM's vNIC is connected to a **dvSwitch port** (**dvPort**). dvPorts are associated with vNICs using two methods:

- Static binding
- Ephemeral (no binding)

Static binding is the default method, wherein vCenter assigns and reserves a dvPort for a vNIC when it is connected to a dvPortGroup for the first time. The reservation is held until the vNIC is disassociated from the dvPortGroup. It is important to note that disconnecting the vNIC will not remove the reservation. The static method of binding retains port statistics, which enable monitoring of the VM's traffic.

The Ephemeral method doesn't involve reserving a dvPort for a vNIC. dvPorts are created and deleted on demand. A dvPort is created and associated with a vNIC when a VM connected to the dvPortGroup is powered on. The dvPort is deleted if the vNIC is disconnected or if the VM is migrated or powered off.

 Static binding requires vCenter's availability, whereas Ephermeral allocation doesn't rely on vCenter.

Port allocation refers to the concept of allocating ports to a dvPortGroup when the static binding method is used. There are two types of port allocation method:

- **Elastic method**: As the name suggests, the port group expands and contracts in terms of the number of dvPorts. By default, every port group has 8 dvPorts (unless configured with a different number). More dvPorts are made available to the dvPortGroup on demand and when the ports are no longer in use, the dvPorts are unallocated. However, it is important to note that the dvPort count will not drop below the configured number.
- **Fixed method**: The number of dvPorts remains fixed at the configured number of ports. The default is **8**. This means that you can only connect up to n number of vNICs to the dvPortGroup, n being the configured number of ports.

Network resource pool

The network resource pool option that's available in the dvPortGroup creation wizard will allow you to select a user-defined network resource pool. If no user-defined resource pools are available, it will default to the system network resource pool called **Virtual Machine Traffic**, although this is not explicitly indicated in the user interface.

VLAN type

The dvPortGroup allows you to specify a VLAN number for all network traffic, trunk all VLAN traffic, or use a private VLAN:

- **VLAN type - VLAN**: You can set a VLAN number for the port group. All traffic will be tagged at the port group with the configured VLAN number.
- **VLAN type - VLAN trunking**: You can specify a comma-separated list and/or a range of VLAN numbers to trunk. This method is used for **Virtual Guest Tagging** (**VGT**).

The following screenshot depicts the VLAN type and trunk range:

We will learn more about VLANs in the *Configuring VLANs on a vDS* recipe of this chapter.

Configuring Security, Traffic Shaping, Teaming, and Failover

As indicated in the previous chapter, the S*ecurity, Traffic Shaping, Teaming and Failover* mechanisms function identically on both standard and distributed switches, with vDS offering additional features and enhancements. You should have already had a glimpse of these settings if you read the *Creating Distributed Port Groups* recipe. In this recipe, we will see where we can configure these settings on a vDS—or more precisely, on a dvPortGroup that has already been created.

It is important to note that these settings cannot be configured on the vDS itself but only on the dvPortGroups.

The *How it works...* section of this recipe explains the impact of each of these settings on the network traffic.

How to do it...

The following procedure will help you to configure the security, traffic shaping, teaming, and failover settings on a dvPortGroup:

1. Connect to vCenter Server using the HTML5 client and go to the **Networking inventory** view.

2. Right-click on the desired dvPortGroup and click **Edit Settings...**:

3. On the **Edit Settings** window, use the **Security** screen to accept/reject **Promiscuous mode**, **MAC address changes**, and **Forged transmits**. Note that all three settings are set to **Reject** by default:

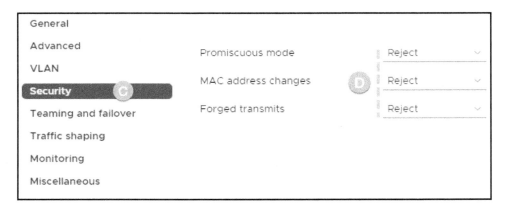

4. On the **Teaming and failover** screen, configure **Load balancing**, **Network failure detection**, **Notify switches**, and **Failback**. Also, configure the **Failover order** of the uplinks, if necessary:

5. On the **Traffic shaping** screen, enable and configure **Ingress/Egress traffic shaping**:

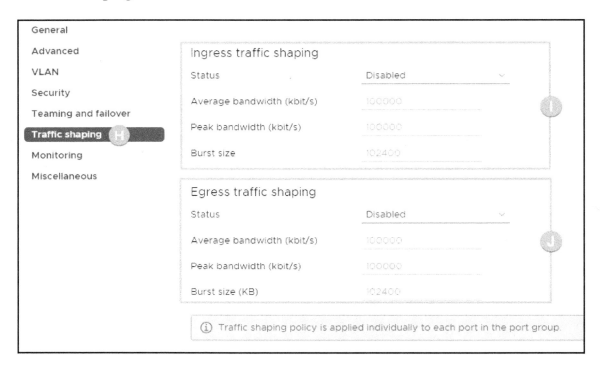

6. Once the desired settings have been configured, click **OK** to confirm.

This completes the process of Configuring Security, Traffic Shaping, Teaming, and Failover on a vDS.

How it works...

Before we delve deeper into each of these settings, let's compare the settings that are available on both vSS and vDS.

Security, Traffic Shaping, Teaming and Failover – vSS versus vDS:

Category	vSphere Standard Switch (vSS)	vSphere Distributed Switch(vDS)
Security	Promiscuous mode MAC Address changes Forged Transmits	Promiscuous mode MAC Address changes Forged Transmits
Traffic shaping	Egress Traffic Shaping Average Bandwidth Burst Size Peak Bandwidth	Egress and Ingress Traffic Shaping Average Bandwidth Burst Size Peak Bandwidth
Teaming and failover	Route based on originating virtual port Route based on IP hash Route based on source MAC hash Use explicit failover order Failover detection Failover order	Route based on originating virtual port Route based on IP hash Route based on source MAC hash Route based on physical NIC load Use explicit failover order Failover detection Failover order

Let's deep dive into each category.

Security

The network security settings have the same impact on traffic, regardless of the switch type it is configured on:

- A vDS allows for an additional level of granularity by making the same settings configurable at the dvPort level. For this to work, the dvPortGroup should be configured to allow dvPort-level policy overrides.
- With a vSS, security settings can only be applied at the port group level.

The three network security settings that can be set to either Accept/Reject are as follows:

- Promiscuous mode
- MAC address changes
- Forged transmits

Promiscuous mode

When promiscuous mode is enabled (`Accept`) on a port group, all of the virtual machine vNICs connected to the port group can see all of the traffic on the virtual switch. This is why it is always disabled (`Reject`) by default. When set to `Reject`, a vNIC will only see traffic destined for its MAC address. Promiscuous mode is particularly useful if you need to let VMs running Network Monitoring tools analyze traffic on the virtual switch. As a best practice, on a vSS, such VMs are placed into a separate port group with Promiscuous Mode set to `Accept`. By doing so, you are enabling only those VMs to see the desired traffic. However, on a vDS, these setting can be configured for each of the dvPorts the monitoring VM's vNICs are connected to.

MAC address changes and forged transmits

Every virtual machine has two MAC addresses by definition. The MAC address that is assigned to the vNIC of a virtual machine when the vNIC is created is called the initial MAC address. The MAC address that a guest operating system configures for the network interface it detects is called the **effective MAC address**. The effective MAC address should generally match the initial MAC address (which is the actual MAC on the NIC).

MAC address changes (Default: Reject): This applies to the traffic *entering a virtual machine from the virtual switch*. If MAC address' changes are set to `Accept`, then it means that you allow the virtual machine to receive traffic that was originally intended for another VM by impersonating the other VM's MAC address.

For example, if VM-A wanted to receive traffic intended for VM-B, then VM-A will need to present itself with a MAC address belonging to VM-B. This is usually achieved by changing the effective MAC address (OS level). Such a VM's initial MAC address will remain unchanged. With MAC address changes set to `Accept`, the virtual switch will allow the effective MAC address to be different from the initial MAC address. With MAC address changes set to `Reject`, the port/dvPort to which the vNIC is connected will be blocked if the effective MAC doesn't match the initial MAC address. Consequently, the VM will stop receiving any traffic.

Forged transmits (Default: Reject): This applies to traffic exiting a virtual machine and entering the virtual switch. If forged transmits are set to `Accept`, it allows for MAC address spoofing. This means that a virtual machine will be allowed to send out Ethernet frames with a source MAC address that is different from the effective/initial MAC address. When set to `Reject`, the virtual switch will drop the Ethernet frame with a source MAC address that is different from the effective/initial MAC.

Traffic shaping

Virtual switches (vSS/vDS) include a traffic shaper that enables control of network transfer rates. The only difference is that the traffic shaper on the vSS can only handle the egress traffic, though the vSphere Distributed Switch can handle both ingress and egress.

Anything that leaves a virtual switch (vSS or vDS) is **Egress Traffic**, and anything that enters a virtual switch (vSwitch or dvSwitch) is **Ingress Traffic**. The ingress source can either be a vNIC or a VMkernel interface.

VMware cannot control what happens beyond the host's physical network adapter boundaries. Therefore, the traffic flow that the traffic shaper can control is the flow (ingress/egress) between the virtual machines/VMkernel interfaces and the virtual switch. The following diagram illustrates the Ingress/Egress Traffic Direction.

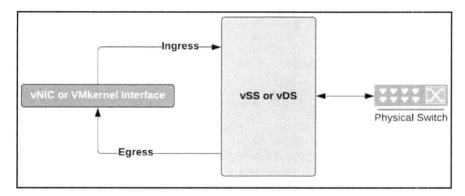

The traffic shaper does its job by controlling three parameters:

- Average bandwidth
- Peak bandwidth
- Burst size

Average bandwidth is the average transfer rate at which the virtual switch can send traffic. It is measured in kilobits per second (kbps). The value is normalized over time.

Peak bandwidth is the maximum transfer rate that the virtual switch is allowed to perform at. It is measured in kilobits per second (kbps). This limit cannot be breached.

Burst size is a tricky concept to understand. Although specified in kilobytes (KB), it is actually the effective amount of time (measured in seconds) that the virtual switch is allowed to perform at the maximum transfer rate.

The effective amount of burst time is calculated using the following formula: *Effective burst time = (Burst size in kilobits)/(Peak bandwidth value in kbps).*

Let's review a scenario so that we can understand how the effective burst time is arrived at.

If you were to set the peak bandwidth value to 4,000 kbps, the average bandwidth to 2,000 kbps, and the burst size to 2,000 KB, then you are allowing the virtual switch to perform at the maximum transfer rate of 4,000 kbps, which lasts no more than 4 seconds.

Here is how the value was arrived at:

1. The burst size in KB needs to be converted into kbits by multiplying the value by 8. In this case, it is *2,000 KB * 8 = 16,000 kbits.*
2. Now, we apply the formula, that is, *16,000 kbits/4,000 kbps = 4 seconds.*

Teaming and failover

Virtual machine workloads share not just compute and storage resources on an ESXi server, but the physical network interfaces as well. There are physical limits on how well these network interfaces can serve the bandwidth needs of the virtual machines. More importantly, not every virtual machine has the same network workload characteristics. Therefore, it becomes extremely critical for the virtual switches to have network load distribution, load balancing, and failover capabilities.

Let's begin by comparing the teaming and failover capabilities of both switch types:

Teaming methods	vSS	vDS
Route based on the originating virtual port ID	Yes	Yes
Route based on source MAC hash	Yes	Yes
Load-based teaming	No	Yes
Use explicit failover order	Yes	Yes

Let's go over the various teaming and failover methods, one by one.

Route based on the originating virtual port ID

This is the default load balancing mechanism for both vSS and vDS. With this mechanism, every virtual switch port to which a vNIC/VMkernel interface connects to is associated with an uplink (vmnic/dvUplink) in a round-robin fashion. Once associated, the corresponding uplinks are always used for traffic unless there is an uplink failure, a VMotion, or a power cycle of a VM.

The following diagram depicts the round-robin distribution of ports - where-in port 1 and 3 are assigned to uplink-A and ports 2 and 3 to uplink B :

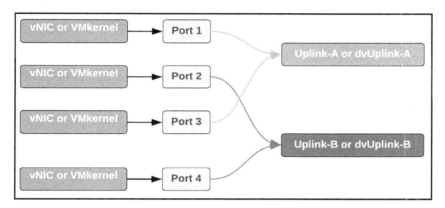

Route based on source MAC hash

This is a deprecated method of load balancing wherein an uplink is chosen based on the source MAC address of the frame that enters the virtual switch.

Route based on IP hash

This method uses a combined hash value of the source and destination IP addresses to choose an uplink. However, for this mechanism to function, the physical NICs must be in the same link aggregation group. If the physical NICs are cabled to different physical switches, then those switches should be stacked. The IP hash mechanism is particularly beneficial when the traffic includes multiple sources and destination IP addresses—for instance, a web server with multiple clients connecting from a number of subnets is an ideal candidate.

Route based on physical NIC load

Load-based teaming is only available on a dvSwitch. Unlike the other methods, this offers a true network load balancing method. The other methods that we've discussed so far only offer a load distribution mechanism, which is done by handling physical adapter assignments based on the chosen algorithm. With load-based teaming, the initial assignment is done in a round-robin fashion, but from then on, the physical adapters are monitored for load saturation. If any of the physical adapters hit a saturation threshold of 75% that persists for over 30 seconds, then some of the traffic is relocated to an unsaturated physical adapter.

Use explicit failover order

Although presented as an option under teaming and failover, using explicit failover order is not a load balancing or distribution method. Instead, it uses a predefined failover order to use the active, available physical adapters in the event of a failure. When you set load balancing to use explicit failover order, all of the traffic is traversed through a single physical adapter at any point in time. If there is more than one active physical adapter, then it will choose the adapter that has been up and active for the longest time. For instance, if vmnic1, vmnic2, and vmnic3 are the three active uplinks, and they have an uptime of 48 hours, 32 hours, and 5 minutes, respectively, then vmnic1 with 48 hours of uptime is chosen. The logic behind such a choice is to select the most stable/reliable among the available adapters.

Network failure detection

Network failure detection is used to determine the liveliness of a physical uplink using one of two mechanisms—link status only or beacon probing:

- Link status only is used to determine the connectivity status of the physical uplink, which could have encountered a NIC failure, a cable disconnect, and so on.
- Beacon probing is used to determine an upstream network failure. For more information on beacon probing, read *VMware Knowledge Base article* 100577 at https://kb.vmware.com/kb/1005577.

Notify switches

Layer 2 physical switches have the ability to maintain a MAC address table. The table maps MAC addresses to a physical switch's port numbers. If there is no corresponding entry for a frame's destination MAC address in the lookup table, the switch will flood the frame via every switch port, other than the source port. To reduce the occurrence of such flooding, the switch has a mechanism to learn the MAC addresses and maintain a mapping table. It does so by reading the source MAC address' information from the frames that enter the switch.

Now, when you cable the physical NICs of an ESXi host to the physical switch ports, the switch is expected to see the MAC addresses of a number of vNICs. The switch will only be able to add an entry to the lookup table if the VMs start to communicate. VMware ESXi, however, can proactively notify the physical switch of the virtual machine's MAC addresses so that its MAC table is up to date even before a VM begins to communicate. It achieves this by sending a gratuitous ARP (seen as a RARP frame by the switch) with a vNIC's effective MAC address as the source MAC of the RARP frame. The RARP will have the destination MAC address set to the broadcast address, which is in the form of FF:FF:FF:FF:FF:FF.

ESXi sends out a RARP under the following circumstances:

- **When a virtual machine is powered on**: The VM's vNIC has to be bound to a physical NIC. The physical uplink that's chosen would depend on the load balancing policy that's used. To learn more about these load balancing policies, read the *Teaming and failover* section. When vSwitch associates a physical NIC to a vNIC, ESXi will need to send a RARP frame to enable the **physical switch** to update its lookup table with a new physical port number mapping for the vNIC's MAC address. This is necessary because, every time a virtual machine is powered on, it isn't guaranteed that the same vNIC to PNIC mapping will be used.

- **When a virtual machine is vMotioned from one host to another**: After a vMotion, the vNIC of VM will now be associated with the physical uplink on the destination ESXi host. Therefore, it becomes a proactive necessity to make the physical switch aware of the fact that the VM's MAC address is now on a different physical switch port so that the MAC table can be updated accordingly.

- **When a physical uplink fails over**: After an uplink failure, the virtual ports are failed over to other available physical uplinks, thereby creating a new association. Therefore, it becomes necessary to notify the physical switch of the new physical port number that the MAC addresses are on.
- **When load-based teaming rebinds a vNIC to a different uplink**: Load-based teaming can automatically relocate VM traffic based on the load on the physical uplinks. When such a relocation occurs, the physical switch needs to be notified of the new physical port that the virtual machine's MAC addresses are on.

Failback

When set to `Yes` (default), it enables a recovered uplink to resume its active role. In other words, a failed active uplink, when returned to normalcy, will be redesignated as the active uplink. The impact of this configuration is dependent on the failover order that's been configured.

Failover order

Physical uplinks on an ESXi host can be teamed up to provide failover, performance, and redundancy.

With both types of virtual switches, we can control the participation of the uplinks in different teaming configurations. This is done by grouping the available uplinks into three categories:

- Active
- Standby
- Unused

Active adapters are available for use in any configuration and will carry traffic.

Standy adapters act as a backup to the active adapters and will be made active only if any of the active adapters fail.

Unused adapters cannot participate in any of the configurations on the virtual switch. In essence, they won't be used to carry traffic.

There's more...

By default, all of the network settings are managed at the dvPortGroup level, and we are not allowed to configure network settings on a dvPort. However, this behavior can be changed by enabling overrides for port policies. This can be done in the **Advanced** section of the **Edit Settings** screen of a dvPortGroup, as follows:

For instance, in this case, we have allowed VLAN and NetFlow to be overridden, which means that we can override the configuration at the dvPort level:

Configuring VLANs on vDS

VLAN is a method that you can use to subdivide a network subnet into separate broadcast domains. In a modern-day infrastructure, it is very common to host your business workloads or other components in different VLANs. Both vSS and vDS support the use of VLANs.

How to do it...

The following procedure will help you to configure VLAN on a dvPort group:

1. Connect to vCenter Server using the HTML5 client and go to the **Networking inventory** view.
2. Right-click on the desired dvPortGroup and click **Edit Settings...**.
3. On the **Edit Settings** window, go to **VLAN** and set the desired **VLAN type** (**VLAN**, **VLAN trunking**, **Private VLAN**). Then, click **OK**:

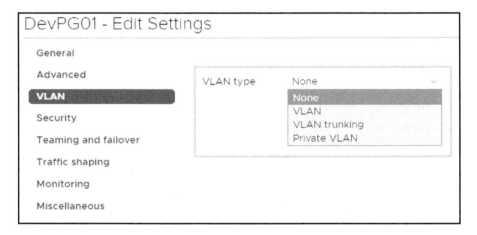

4. Setting the **VLAN type** to **VLAN** will be required to specify a VLAN number (the default is **1**):

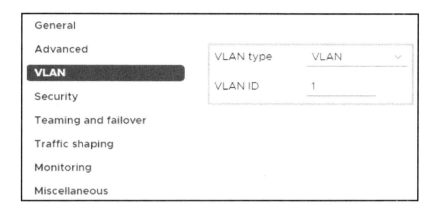

5. Setting the **VLAN type** to **VLAN trunking** will require you to specify the VLANs to be trunked by the dvPortGroup. The default is **0-4094**, which is all VLANs:

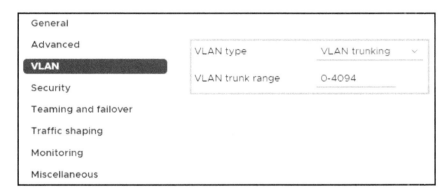

Frames with the VLAN number specified by this range will not be tagged/untagged by the vDS. Unlike the vSS, wherein you need to specify 4095 to enable trunking, with vDS, you can specify a range or comma-separated VLAN number to trunk.

6. Setting the **VLAN type** to **Private VLAN** requires it be already configured on the vDS. We will learn how to do this in the *Configuring private VLANs on vDS* recipe:

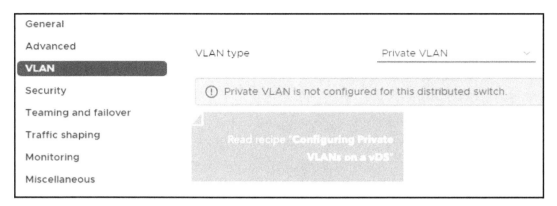

This completes the process of configuring VLANs on a vDS.

How it works...

vDS supports four types of VLAN tagging:

- External switch tagging
- **Virtual Switch Tagging (VST)**
- **Virtual Guest Tagging (VGT)**
- **Private VLANs (PVLANs)**—only supported on a vDS

External switch tagging

With external switch tagging, it will be the physical switch that the ESXi host is connected to that does the tagging or untagging of the Ethernet frames. The physical switch ports, in this case, are access ports. Therefore, there is no need to configure VLANs on the port groups of the virtual switch. Frames enter and leave the virtual switch untagged.

One of the major drawbacks of this type of implementation is that the entire virtual switch (all of the port groups on it) will only handle traffic from a single layer-2 subnet. This is because an access port on a physical switch cannot be configured to carry traffic from more than one VLAN. The following diagram illustrates the Frame Flow in EST Mode.

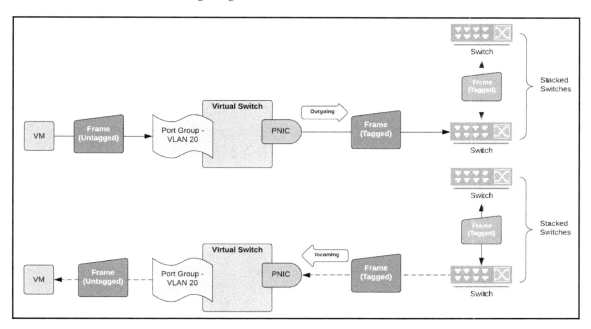

VST

With **VST**, Ethernet layer-2 frames are tagged at the virtual switch layer.

For this implementation to work, the physical NIC carrying the traffic should be connected to a physical switch port, which is configured to trunk the necessary VLANs. The port groups on the vSwitch have to be configured with the VLAN IDs of their respective subnets.

VST is the most common and favored implementation in most large/medium/small environments, not just because of the flexibility it offers but also because of the fact that most modern-day blade system environments have reduced the number of physical NIC ports on the server hardware, owing to the advent of 10 Gbps Ethernet. The following diagram illustrates the Frame flow in VST Mode:

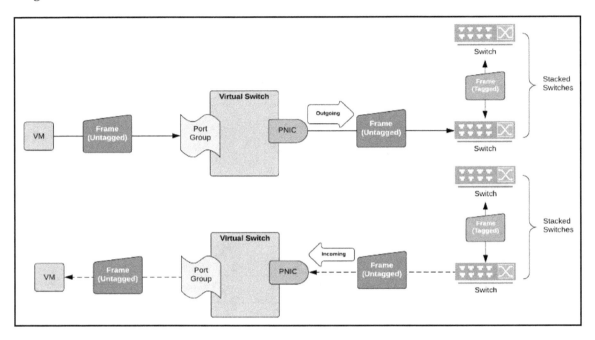

In VST mode, a frame from a VM enters the virtual switch untagged. The virtual switch then assigns a VLAN tag to the frame based on the VLAN number that's configured on the port group. The tagged frame will then be carried over the active physical NIC to the trunk port on the physical switch.

When a tagged frame enters a virtual switch from the physical switch, the virtual switch layer will remove the tag before it is sent to the virtual machine.

VGT

With VGT, the frames aren't tagged by either the physical switch or the virtual switch. Both of the switching layers will trunk the traffic from the virtual machines. The guest operating system running on the VM is solely responsible for tagging and untagging frames. The following is a diagram of frame flow in VGT mode:

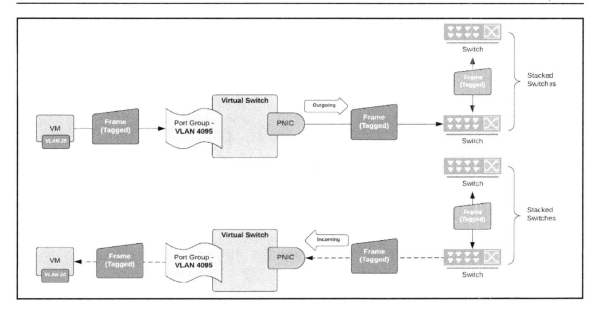

For VGT to work, the port group on the virtual switch should be configured to trunk VLANs.

On a vSphere Distributed Switch, the **VLAN type** on the dvPortGroup should be set to **VLAN trunking** and specify a range or comma-separated VLAN numbers to trunk:

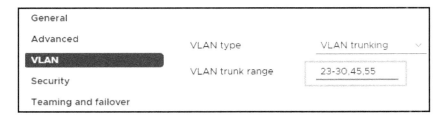

On a vSphere Standard vSwitch, you specify a **VLAN ID** of **4095** to enable trunking. By doing this, all of the VLANs will be trunked:

It is essential to be aware that VLANs cannot be configured on virtual switches—they can only be configured on port groups (standard/dvPortGroup) and dvPorts.

Configuring Private VLANs on a vDS

VLANs provide the logical segmentation of a network in order to different broadcast domains. PVLANs provide a method to further segment a VLAN into different private groups. We can add and configure PVLANs on a vSphere Distributed Switch. For PVLANs to work, the physical switches backing your environment should be PVLAN-aware.

PVLANs should be configured on the physical switches for the configuration to work. Contact your network administrator for the primary, community, and isolated VLAN numbers.

How to do it...

The following procedure will help you to configure PVLANs on a vDS:

1. Connect to vCenter Server using the HTML5 client and go to the **Networking inventory** view.
2. Right-click on the desired vDS and go to **Settings** | **Edit Private VLAN...**:

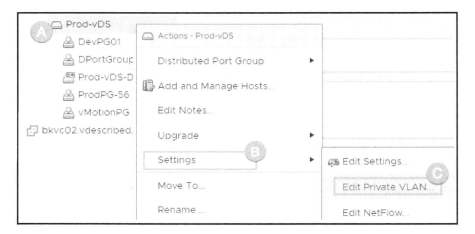

3. On the **Edit Private VLAN Settings** window, add the **Primary VLAN ID** and then the desired secondary VLAN IDs. Once you're done, click **OK**:

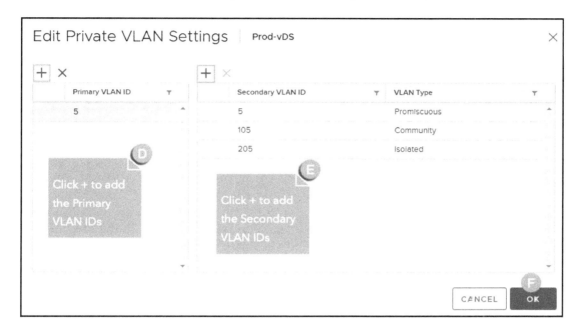

4. Now, you should be able to set a **Private VLAN ID** to a dvPortGroup:

This completes the process of configuring PVLANs on a vDS.

How it works...

As we mentioned at the beginning of this recipe, for PVLANs to work, primary and secondary VLANs should be created on the physical switch. The primary VLAN is a VLAN that's been configured as a private VLAN on the physical switch interface in **Promiscuous Mode**. Secondary VLANs are VLANs that are associated with a primary VLAN.

There are three types of secondary PVLANs:

- **Promiscuous PVLAN**: VMs in a promiscuous private VLAN can communicate with any VM belonging to any of its secondary PVLANs. The promiscuous PVLAN acts as a gateway for other secondary PVLANs.
- **Community PVLAN**: VMs in a community private VLAN can only talk among the VMs in the same community PVLAN or the promiscuous PVLAN. They cannot communicate with VMs in any other secondary PVLANs.
- **Isolated PVLAN**: VMs in an isolated PVLAN and isolated from every other VM in the same isolated PVLAN. They can only communicate with the VMs in a promiscuous PVLAN. There can only be one single isolated PVLAN per primary PVLAN.

These PVLANs are shown in the following diagram:

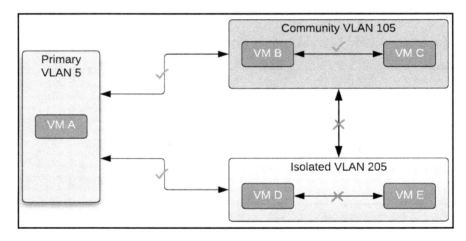

As we mentioned previously, private VLAN support allows for further segregation of VLAN subnets. It offers a level of flexibility with its intrinsic access boundary definitions. PVLAN is not a VMware concept, but a network concept that VMware supports on VDS.

Configuring a Link Aggregation Group (LAG) on a vDS

The **Link Aggregation Control Protocol** (**LACP**) allows you to group host physical adapters and the ports on a physical switch to form a bigger communication pipeline, thereby increasing availability and bandwidth. Such a pipeline is referred to as **Ether Channel**. The following diagram illustrates the LAG Configuration Workflow:

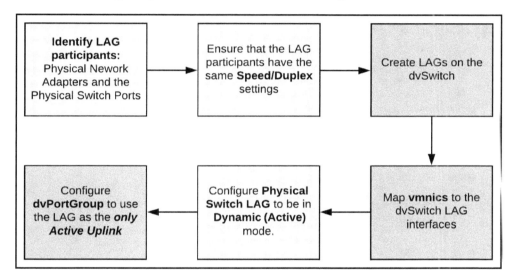

The physical network adapters and physical switch port groups are called **LAG**.

How to do it...

The following procedure will help you to configure LAG on a vDS:

1. Connect to vCenter Server using the HTML5 client and go to the **Networking inventory** view.

2. Select the vDS, navigate to **Configure** | **Settings** | **LACP**, and click **+ NEW**:

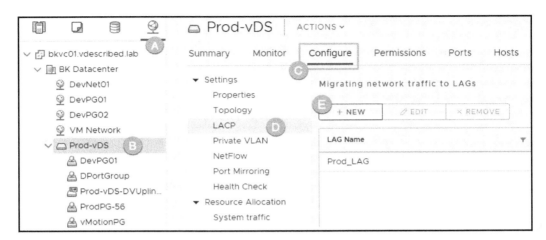

3. On the **New Link Aggregation Group** window, supply a **Name** for the LAG, **Number of ports**, **Mode**, and **Load balancing mode**. Once the settings have been specified, click **OK** to create the LAG:

4. Now, use the **Migrating network traffic to LAGs** workflow to migrate the desired traffic to the newly created LAB without losing network connectivity:

As you could see from the screenshot above, migrating traffic to the LAG is a three-step process and the following subsections cover them.

Setting LAG as a standby uplink on distributed port groups

The first step in migrating the network traffic is to make the LAG a standby uplink on the desired dvPortGroup. Let's get started:

1. On the **Migrating Network Traffic to Link Aggregation Groups** window, click on **Manage Distributed Port Groups**.

2. On the **Select port group policies** screen, select **Teaming and failover**. Click **Next** to continue:

3. On the **Select port groups** screen, select a dvPortGroup and click **Next**:

4. On the **Teaming and failover** screen, move the LAG from **Unused uplinks** to **Standby uplinks**:

5. On the **Confirm Teaming and Failover Settings** window, click **OK**:

6. On the **Ready to complete** screen, click **Finish**.

Once you have added the LAG as a standby uplink for the dvPortGroup, the next step is to start reassigning physical NICs to the LAG ports.

Reassigning the physical network adapters of hosts to the LAG ports

The following procedure will help you map vmnics to the LAG ports:

1. On the **Migrating Network Traffic to Link Aggregation Groups** window, click **Add and Manage Hosts.**
2. On the **Add and Manage Hosts** wizard, select **Manage host networking**. Click **Next** to continue.
3. On the **Select hosts** screen, click **Attached hosts...** to add the desired hosts. Click **Next** to continue:

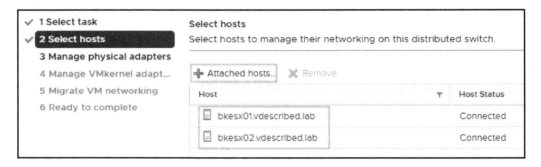

4. On the **Manage physical adapters**, click **Assign uplink** to map the **LAG ports** to the vmnics. Then, click **Next** to continue:

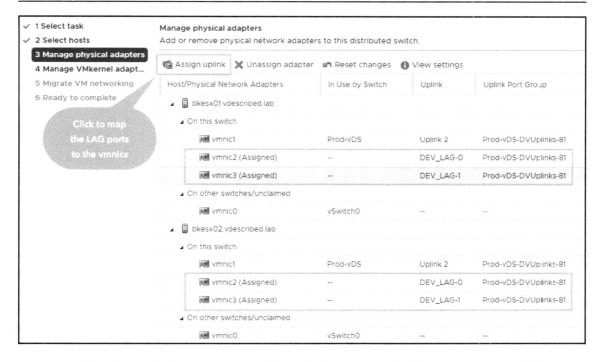

5. Skip through the **Manage VMkernel adapters** and **Migrate VM networking** screens by clicking **Next**.

6. On the **Ready to complete** screen, click **Finish**.

Once the physical NICs are assigned to the LAGs, the next step is to reconfigure the dvPortGroup with LAG as the only active uplink.

Setting the LAG to be the only active uplink on the distributed port groups

The following procedure will help you configure the dvPortGroup's NIC failover order to make the LAG as the active uplink:

1. On the **Migrating Network Traffic to Link Aggregation Groups** window, click on **Manage Distributed Port Groups**.

2. On the **Manage Distributed Port Groups** screen, select **Teaming and failover**. Click **Next** to continue.

3. On the **Select port groups** screen, select the desired dvPortGroup and click **Next**.

4. On the **Teaming and failover** screen, move the LAG from **Standby uplinks** to **Active uplinks** and ensure that it is the only active uplink for the dvPortGroup. Then, move all of the other uplinks to **Unused uplinks**:

5. On the **Ready to complete** screen, click **Finish**.

You have now successfully configured the dvSwitch and the desired port group to use link aggregation groups.

How it works...

Although the LAGs are created on the vDS, they are associated directly with the ESXi host from which the uplinks are used. You can configure up to a maximum of 64 LAGs per ESXi host, and so the total number of LAGs on a vDS is also 64. Each LAG can have up to 32 LAG ports, meaning that each host can contribute up to 32 vmnics to a LAG.

For the LAGs that are created on the vDS to work, it's important to ensure that the vmnics that are mapped to the LAG ports that have been created are members of an Ether Channel group on the physical switch. The following diagram illustrates the LACP - Infrastructure Wide configuration Layout:

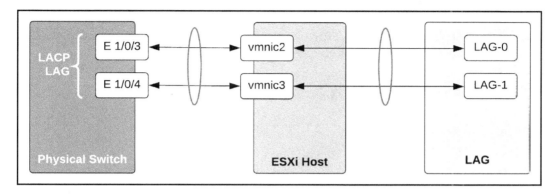

LACP LAGs operate in two modes: active (dynamic) and passive (static). In **dynamic** mode, the LAG is in active mode, whereby it can send LACP PDUs in order to negotiate LACP status and configuration. In **static** mode, the LAG is in passive mode, waiting on LACP PDUs from the active LAG. At least one of the LAGs in an Ether Channel group should be in active mode for LACP to work.

Configuring user-defined network pools—NIOC

The **Network I/O Control** (**NIOC**) is a vDS functionality that can manage the network bandwidth usage of system traffic types based on shares, reservation, and limits. NIOC is currently at version 3 and was released with vSphere 6.0. There are different types of system traffic management: FT, vMotion, VM, iSCSI, NFS, vSphere replication, vSAN, and vSphere data protection. The following is a screenshot of the different types of system traffic management:

Traffic Type	Shares	Shares Value	Reservation	Limit
Management Traffic	Normal	50	0 Mbit/s	Unlimited
Fault Tolerance (FT) Traffic	Normal	50	0 Mbit/s	Unlimited
vMotion Traffic	Normal	50	0 Mbit/s	Unlimited
Virtual Machine Traffic	High	100	0 Mbit/s	Unlimited
iSCSI Traffic	Normal	50	0 Mbit/s	Unlimited
NFS Traffic	Normal	50	0 Mbit/s	Unlimited
vSphere Replication (VR) Traffic	Normal	50	0 Mbit/s	Unlimited
vSAN Traffic	Normal	50	0 Mbit/s	Unlimited
vSphere Data Protection Backup Traffic	Normal	50	0 Mbit/s	Unlimited

By default, system traffic has no reservation. However, you can set a reservation on the virtual machine traffic type and then further segregate the bandwidth by creating network resource pools. These user-defined network resource pools are then mapped to dvPortGroups.

In this recipe, we will learn how to create user-defined network resource pools.

Getting ready

NIOC is an Enterprise Plus license feature and is enabled by default on a vDS:

If you chose to disable the NIOC that created the vDS, you will need to enable the NIOC before you proceed.

How to do it...

The following procedure will help you to create user-defined network resource pools:

1. Connect to vCenter Server using the HTML5 client and go to the **Networking inventory** view.
2. Select the vDS and navigate to **Configure| Resource Allocation | Network resource pools**. Then, click on **Reserve bandwidth for virtual machine traffic**:

3. In the **Edit Resource Settings** window, set a **Reservation** in Mbps or Gbps and click **OK**:

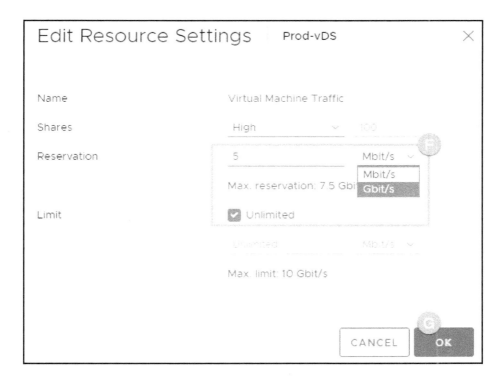

4. Once you're done, click + **ADD** to create a network resource pool:

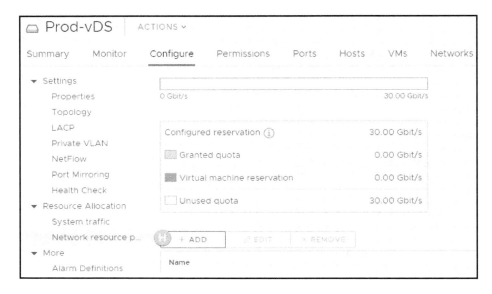

5. In the **New Network Resource Pool** window, specify a **Name**, set a bandwidth reservation in Gbps or Mbps, and click **OK**:

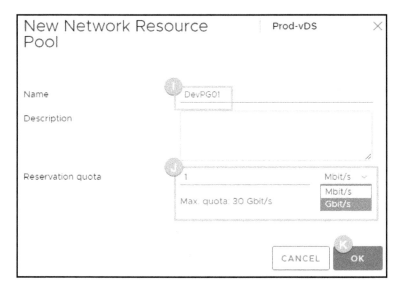

You have now successfully created a network resource pool.

How it works...

The reservation we configured for the virtual machine network on the vDS is a bandwidth reservation per physical NIC (vmnic). The total reservation is equivalent to the total number of physical NICs participating in vDS, multiplied by the bandwidth that's been reserved per NIC.

For instance, *5 Gbps reservation x 6 vmnics = 30 Gbps*. There are six vmnics because there are three participating vmnics from two hosts:

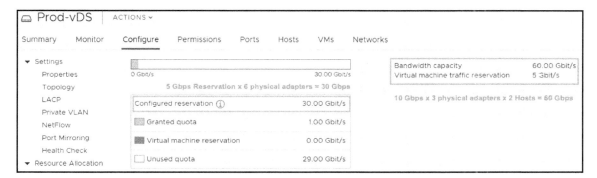

> *Bandwidth Capacity = (Physical Adapter's Bandwidth) x (Number of vmnics from each participating ESXi) x (Number of ESXi hosts).*
>
> *Configured Reservation = (Bandwidth Reservation) x (Number of vmnics from each participating ESXi) x (Number of ESXi hosts).*

The newly created network resource pool can be mapped to a dvPortGroup. Doing so will ensure that the VMs in the dvPortGroup are guaranteed to receive the reserved bandwidth during contention:

Unlike reservations, shares allocate unreserved bandwidth among contenting traffic types or VMs based on their relative share value. Check out the following instances:

- The default share value of 50 for the vMotion, management, and vSphere replication traffic types.
- The uplinks that are used should have the same bandwidth capacity, which, in this case, is 10 Gbps.
- Since each traffic type has a share value of 50, the cumulative share value is 150.
- During contention, each of the traffic types will get *(50/150) x 100 = 33%* of the total bandwidth. This is 33% of 30 Gbps, which is approximately 9.9 Gbps for each traffic type.

Migrating Virtual Machine Network from vSS to vDS

Once you have created and configured the vDS and its dvPortGroup, then one of the next steps is to migrate the virtual machine network from vSS to vDS. This is done by changing the network label (port group) that's used by the vNICs to the desired dvPortGroup. Although this can be done using various UI methods, the most intuitive and user-friendly method is to use the **Migrate VMs to Another Network** wizard as it allows you to selectively orchestrate this process for a large number of VMs across hosts.

Getting ready

Before you begin, it is essential to ensure that the dvPortGroups are configured to use the same VLAN, MTU, teaming, and security settings.

To ensure that the VMs don't lose network connectivity, the dvPortGroup should be configured with an uplink that supports the virtual machine's traffic.

How to do it...

The following procedure will help you to migrate virtual machines that are currently connected to port groups on a vSS to dvPortGroups on a vDS:

1. Connect to vCenter Server using the HTML5 client and go to the **Networking inventory** view.

2. Right-click on the vSphere Standard Port Group you would like to migrate the VM from and click **Migrate VMs to Another Network**:

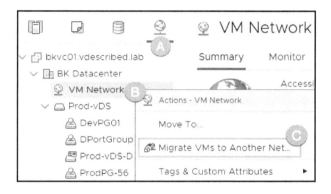

Start Migration Wizard

3. On the **Select source and destination networks** screen, browse and set the desired dvPortGroup as the **Destination network**. Once you're done, click **Next** to continue:

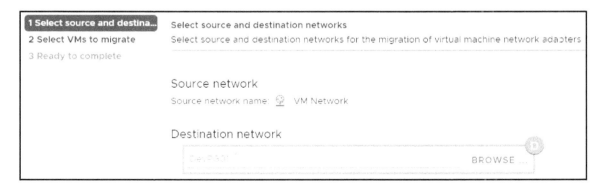

4. On the **Select VMs to migrate** screen, select **All virtual machines** or select only the VMs that you intend to migrate. Then, click **Next** to continue:

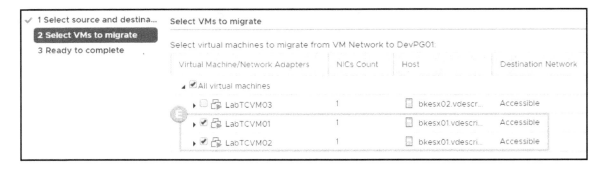

5. On the **Ready to complete** screen, review the summary and click **Finish**:

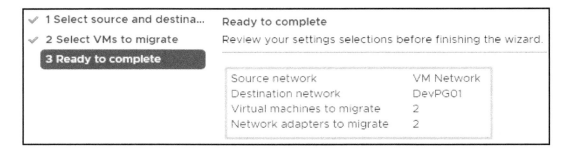

6. The **Recent Tasks** pane should list that the **Reconfigure virtual machine** tasks have been completed successfully:

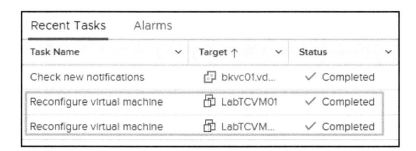

This completes the process of migrating a virtual machine network from vSS to vDS.

How it works...

When you migrate a virtual machine network from a vSS to a vDS, it changes the network label (port group) mapping for the selected vNICs to match the dvPortGroup's name. As long as the destination dvPortGroup has uplinks that support the virtual machine network traffic (for example, it is on the same VLAN), the network connectivity for the VMs will remain unaffected.

Migrating VMkernel interfaces from vSS to vDS

One of the next steps after creating a vDS and its dvPorts is to migrate the VMkernel interfaces on the ESXi host to the VDS. Since the VMkernel interfaces are specific to each host, the best method is to use the **Migrate networking** wizard from the ESXi host.

Getting ready

Before you migrate the VMkernel interfaces (which may include the management interface), it is essential that the dvPortGroup is configured with at least one uplink that supports the traffic. Also, ensure that VLAN, MTU, teaming, and security settings are replicated from the vSS port group.

How to do it...

The following procedure will help you to migrate VMkernel interfaces from vSS to vDS:

1. Connect to vCenter Server using the HTML5 client and go to the **Host and Cluster** view.

2. Select the desired ESXi host, navigate to **Configure** | **Virtual switches**, select the vDS you intend to migrate the VMkernel interfaces to, and click **Migrate Networking...**:

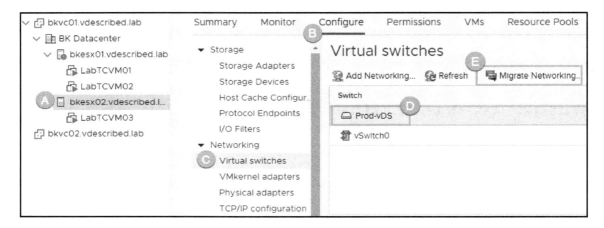

3. On the **Migrate Networking** wizard's **Manage physical adapters** screen, map uplinks to the VDS if you haven't done so already. Then, click **Next** to continue:

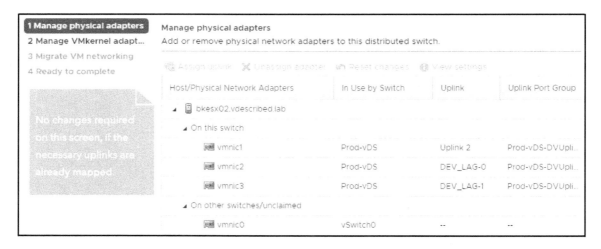

4. On the **Manage VMkernel adapters** screen, select the VMkernel interface and click **Assign port group** to map a dvPortGroup to it. Once you're done, click **Next** to continue:

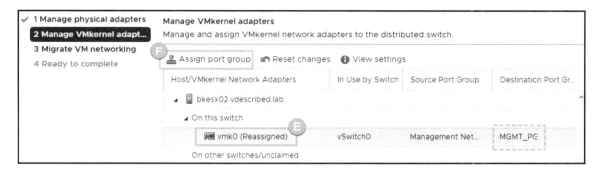

5. Skip the **Migrate VM networking** screen by clicking **Next** since it is irrelevant for this procedure.

6. Review the summary on the **Ready to complete** screen and click **Finish**:

7. Once done, the VMkernel interface should now be on the vDS:

This completes the process of migrating VMkernel interfaces from vSS to vDS.

How it works...

During the migration of the VMkernel interface, the communication over these resources will remain unaffected. However, if for any reason you end up migrating the management VMkernel interface to a dvPortGroup without the necessary configuration to support the traffic for the interfaces, then you will lose connectivity to the ESXi host. To recover from this, you will need to get to the console of the ESXi host via the host's IPMI console, such as the DRAC, ILO, or KVM, and use the DCUI to restore the standard vSwitch or use the CLI to modify the configuration of the dvPortGroup.

There's more...

More information on migrating a VMkernel interface that's used for the management network between standard vSwitches (*VMware Knowledge Base article* 2037654) is available at `http://kb.vmware.com/kb/2037654`.

Configuring port mirroring on vDS

Port mirroring is a functionality that allows you to clone network traffic on a dvPort to another port or uplink (destination) on the same dvSwitch. This is particularly useful when you have a packet analyzer or **Intrusion Detection System** (**IDS**) deployed on the network. Port mirroring can only be enabled on a vDS and not on a vSS.

Getting ready

Before you learn how to configure port mirroring, it's important that you have a good understanding of mirroring methods and the supported source/destinations.

The following table compares the **select sources/destinations** options that are available based on the mirror session types, which will help you to decide on the correct type of mirror session that's required:

Session type	Supported source types	Supported destination types
Distributed port mirroring	dvPorts	dvPorts
Remote mirroring source	dvPorts	Uplinks
Remote mirroring destination	VLAN	dvPorts
Encapsulated remote mirroring (L3) source	dvPorts	IP address

How to do it...

The following procedure will help you to configure port mirroring on a vDS:

1. Connect to vCenter Server using the HTML5 client and go to the **Networking inventory** view.
2. Select the desired vDS and go to **Configure** | **Port Mirroring**. Then, click **New**...:

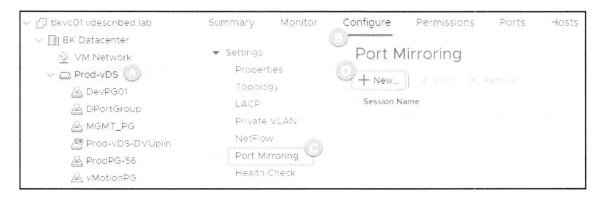

3. On the **Select session type** screen, select the desired session type and click **Next** to continue.

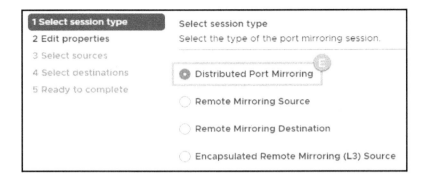

To learn more about the different session types read the *How it works...* section of this recipe.

4. On the **Edit properties** screen, settings for the session can be configured as shown in the following screenshot:

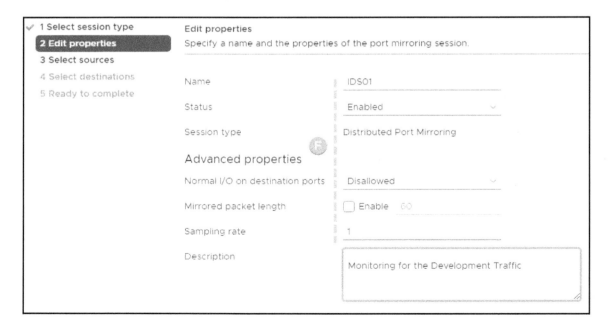

Let's review the mirroring session settings:

- **Name**: This is a unique name for the session.
- **Status**: The status should be set to **Enabled**.
- **Normal I/O on destination ports**: **Disallowed/Allowed** – this is used to allow/disallow regular traffic, along with the mirrored traffic on the destination port.
- **Mirrored packet length**: This is used to set a limit on the mirrored packet length in bytes. The default is **60** bytes. The remainder of the packet is truncated. There is no need to configure this unless the destination monitoring tool is configured to break down/combine packets per its requirement.
- **Sampling rate**: This is used to define the nth packet that needs to be mirrored. The default is **1**, which mirrors every packet. For instance, if you set it to **4**, it mirrors every 4th packet.
- **Description**: This is an optional description.
- **Encapsulation VLAN ID**: This is made available only when the **Session type** is **Remote Mirroring Source**. Since the destination for the *Remote Mirroring Source* session type is an uplink(s), it is possible that the uplinks are trunked for multiple VLANs. Therefore, it may become necessary to encapsulate the frames using a VLAN. If the source dvPorts are on a different VLAN themselves, then you could choose to preserve the original VLAN option to double-encapsulate the frames that are being mirrored.

5. The options that are presented in the **Select sources** and **Select destinations** screens depend on the mirroring type that's selected.
6. On the **Ready to complete** screen, review the settings and click **Finish**:

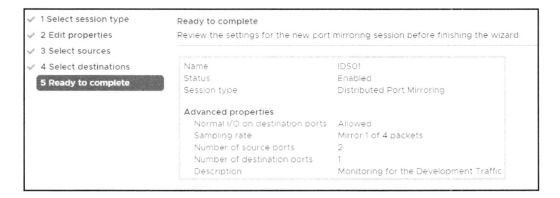

This completes the process of configuring port mirroring on a vDS.

How it works...

Once a port mirroring session has been created, all of the traffic from the selected source is mirrored to the desired destination. These can be dvPorts or VLANs. The destination can be dvPorts, uplinks, or the IP addresses of machines running the traffic monitoring application.

There are four types of mirroring:

- **Distributed Port Mirroring**: This replicates traffic from one or more dvPorts to other dvPorts to which the vNICs of the VM running the monitoring software are connected. This session type will work only if the source and destination VMs are on the same ESXi host.
- **Remote Mirroring Source**: This replicates traffic from one or more dvPorts to uplinks. This is used when a traffic analyzer is a machine connected to one of the ports on the physical switch. This would require a configuration change on the physical switch to mirror the traffic that's received on a physical port to another physical port on the same switch to which the packet analyzer machine is connected or to a port on a different switch (with the help of RSPAN VLAN).
- **Remote Mirroring Destination**: This replicates traffic from a VLAN to dvPorts. This is used when you want to monitor traffic from a particular VLAN by mirroring traffic to a dvPort that a monitoring VM is connected to.
- **Encapsulated Remote Mirroring (L3) Source**: This replicates traffic from one or more dvPorts to a remote IP address. This is used when the packet analyzer is running on a machine on a different subnet.
- **Distributed Port Mirroring(Legacy)**: This replicates traffic from one or more dvPorts to other dvPorts or uplink ports on the host.

Configuring NetFlow on vDS

NetFlow is an industry-standard for network traffic monitoring. Originally developed by Cisco, it has since become an industry standard. VMware supports **IP Flow Information Export** (**IPFIX**), which is similar to NetFlow and was originally based on NetFlow version 9. Although VMware refers to it as NetFlow version 10, it's basically IPFIX.

Once enabled, it can be used to capture IP traffic statistics from all of the interfaces where NetFlow is enabled, and send them as records to the NetFlow collector software.

How to do it...

The following procedure will help you to configure IPFIX on a vDS and enable it on a dvPortGroup:

1. Connect to vCenter Server using the HTML5 client and go to the **Networking inventory** view.

2. Select the desired vDS, go to **Configure** | **NetFlow**, and click **EDIT...**:

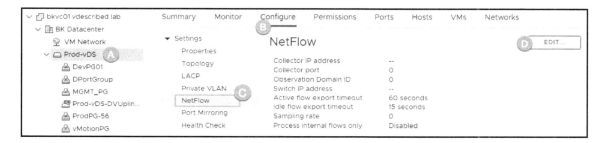

3. On the **Edit NetFlow Settings** screen, specify the details request and click **OK**:

4. Once you're done, you can now enable NetFlow on the desired dvPortGroups:

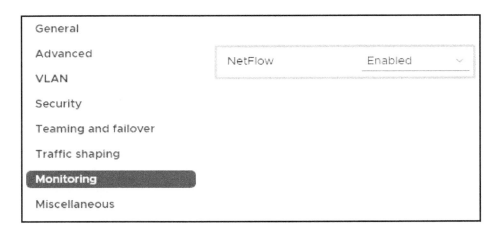

This completes the process of enabling NetFlow on a vDS.

How it works...

NetFlow, once configured on the dvSwitch, will allow the NetFlow collector software to capture and analyze statistics for the dvSwitch. The dvSwitch is identified by the NetFlow collector software using the IP address that we assigned to the dvSwitch while configuring NetFlow on it. The IP that's assigned to the dvSwitch doesn't give it a network identity. It is only used by the NetFlow collector to uniquely identify the dvSwitch. If you don't specify an IP, then you will see a separate session for the ESXi host that is a member of the dvSwitch.Collector IP address. This is the IP address of the NetFlow collector machine in your environment.

Let's review all the Net Flow Settings:

- **Collector IP address**: This is the IP address of the NetFlow collector machine in your environment.
- **Collector port**: UDP port 2055 is the most widely used NetFlow collector port number.
- **Observation domain ID**: This is the observation ID of the NetFlow collector. This information can be obtained from the NetFlow collector machine.
- **Switch IP address**: This is just a representative IP address and not the real one. This doesn't make up the VDS part of any network. It only provides a unique ID to the VDS in the NetFlow monitoring software.
- **Active flow export timeout**: This is the amount of time, measured in seconds, that the VDS will wait before it begins to fragment an active traffic flow and send the data to the NetFlow monitor.
- **Idle flow export timeout**: This is the amount of time, measured in seconds, that the VDS will wait before it begins to fragment an idle flow and send the data to the NetFlow monitor.
- **Sampling rate**: This value determines the number and frequency of the packet's collection. The default value of **1** will collect every packet. If the value is set to **5**, then it collects every fifth packet.
- **Process internal flows only**: This is used to collect data from traffic that never leaves an ESXi host. For instance, traffic between two VMs in the same VLAN and the same host doesn't have to leave the host.

Upgrading a vDS

During the process of upgrading a vSphere environment, once the vCenter and the ESXi hosts have been upgraded, one of the next steps will be to upgrade the vSphere Distributed Switches, if any.

How to do it...

The following procedure will help you to upgrade a vDS:

1. Connect to vCenter Server using the HTML5 client and go to the **Networking inventory** view.
2. Right-click on the desired vDS and go to **Upgrade** | **Upgrade Distributed Switch...**:

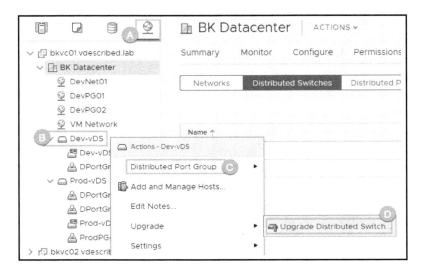

Start Upgrade Distributed Switch wizard

3. In the wizard's **Configure upgrade** screen, choose a version to upgrade to and click **Next** to continue:

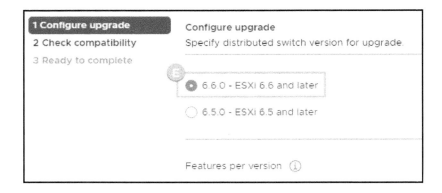

4. The **Check compatibility** screen will show the results of the host compatibility check. Review these settings and click **Next** to continue:

5. On the **Ready to complete** screen, review the summary and click **Next** to continue:

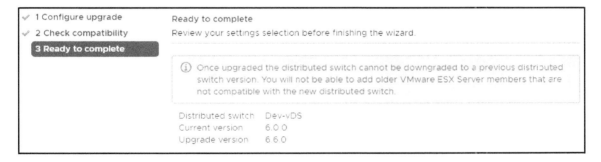

6. You should see a completed related task in the **Recent Tasks** pane:

This completes the process of upgrading vSphere Distributed Switches.

How it works...

Upgrading the vDS is a non-disruptive process, but cannot be reversed.

Backing up and restoring a vDS

vDS configuration can be backed up and then restored from, if necessary. In this recipe, we will learn how to export vDS configuration and then restore from an exported configuration.

How to do it...

The following procedure will help you to back up and restore vDS using the HTML5 client.

Exporting vDS configuration

Let's look at the following steps:

1. Connect to vCenter Server using the HTML5 client and go to the **Networking inventory** view.
2. Right-click on the desired vDS and go to **Settings | Export Configuration...**:

3. On the **Export Configuration** screen, choose either the entire vDS or just the vDS excluding dvPortGroups, supply an optional description, and click **OK**:

4. This will export a file called `backup.zip`.

Restoring from a backup

Let's look at the following steps:

1. Connect to vCenter Server using the HTML5 client and go to the **Networking inventory** view.
2. Right-click on the desired vDS and go to **Settings | Restore Configuration..**:

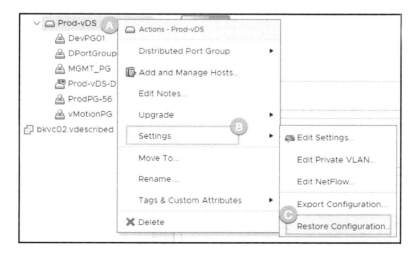

3. On the **Restore switch configuration** screen, browse and select the backup file and choose to either restore the entire vDS or just the vDS without dvPortGroups. Then, click **Next** to continue:

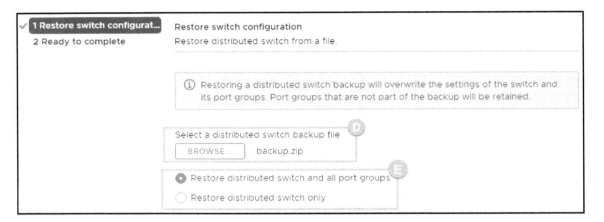

4. On the **Ready to complete** screen, review the settings and click **Finish**:

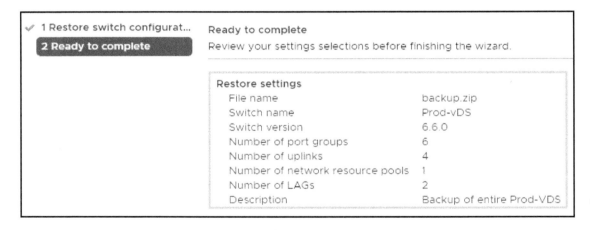

This completes the process of backing up and restoring a vDS.

How it works...

The export that's created is a snapshot of the current vDS configuration. The ZIP archive contains the vDS data files in binary format and a `data.xml` file with the dvSwitch metadata:

The `data` folder maintains a separate `.bak` file for each dvPortGroup and one for the vDS:

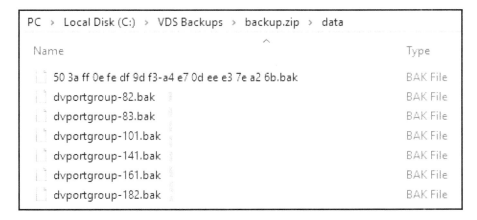

The backup ZIP file can be used to restore configuration or even form a new vDS via the **Import Distributed Switch** wizard.

5

Configuring Storage Access for Your vSphere Environment

Storage is an integral part of any vSphere infrastructure as it is required to store your **virtual machines** (**VMs**). Different types of storage can be incorporated into a vSphere infrastructure, and these types are determined based on a variety of factors, such as the type of disks used, the storage protocol, and the type of connectivity. The most common way of referring to the types of storage presented to a vSphere infrastructure is based on the storage protocol used, their connection type, and their locality (directly attached or remote storage).

ESXi supports both local and remote storage. Local storage refers to storage accessible from within the server or directly connected to the server using point-to-point connectivity. Remote storage, on the contrary, is accessed via a network infrastructure, be it **Fiber Channel** (**FC**) or Ethernet. The following diagram shows supported disk types, initiators, and storage protocols:

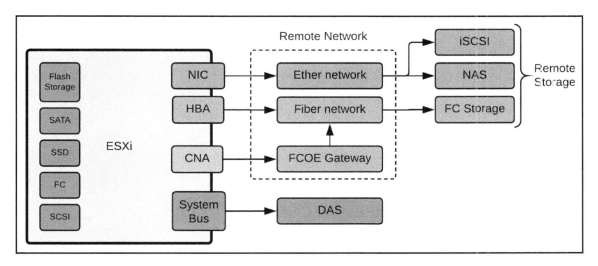

Let's review each of the storage protocols supported in a vSphere environment:

- **Fiber Channel (FC)**: This type of storage is accessed over a Fiber Channel Network made up of fabric switches and the FC array. The FC protocol is used to encapsulate and transmit SCSI commands between the hosts and the array. Hosts connect to the FC network using an **FC Host Bus Adapter (FC-HBA)**. The storage array connects to the FC network using the ports on their endpoints called the Storage Processor, Storage Controller, or Service Processor.

- **FC over Ethernet (FCoE)**: This type of storage connects over an Ethernet network made up of FCoE-capable switches and the FC array. FC frames are encapsulated in FCoE frames. It is important to note that FCoE does not use TCP/IP for transporting frames. Hosts connect to the FCoE network using an FCoE-capable converged network adapter.

- **Network-Attached Storage (NAS)**: This type of storage connects over the existing TCP/IP network, making it easier to implement. Unlike FC and FCoE, this is not a lossless implementation. As the SCSI commands are sent over the TCP/IP network, they are prone to experience packet loss due to various factors. Although packet loss does not break anything, it will have a significant impact compared to FC and FCoE. ESXi supports two types of NAS—**Internet SCSI (iSCSI)** and **Network File System (NFS)**:

  - **iSCSI**: This allows you to send SCSI commands over an IP network to a storage system that supports the use of this protocol.

  - **NFS**: This is a distributed filesystem protocol that allows you to share access to files over the IP network. Unlike iSCSI, FC, FCoE, or **Direct Attached Storage (DAS)**, this not a block storage protocol. The critical difference here is that the block storage can be presented in a raw format with no filesystem on it. On the contrary, NFS storage is nothing but a shared-folder (mount) on an already existing filesystem. VMware supports NFS version 3 and NFS 4.1.

- **Direct Attached Storage (DAS)**: This is a storage pod that is directly connected to the host.

There are four other common terms that we use when dealing with storage in a vSphere environment: **Logical Unit Number** (**LUN**), **Virtual Machine File System** (**VMFS**), NFS mounts, and datastores:

- **LUN**: Storage from an array is presented in the form of logical containers. The container is nothing but a collection of storage blocks carved up from the entire pool of the free space available on the array. Each such logical container is assigned a logical unit number or LUN. These logical units are seen as storage devices by an ESXi host.

  vSphere 6.7 supports up to 1,024 LUN per host. However, VMware only supports up to 1,024 shared datastores in a cluster.

- **VMFS**: A LUN presented from FC/iSCSI/DAS storage can be formed using VMware's proprietary filesystem, called VMFS. The most recent version of VMFS is VMFS6. VMFS allows more than one ESXi host to perform read/write on the same volume. This is achieved by employing an on-disk locking mechanism called distributed locking, which prevents a file from being simultaneously accessed by more than one host process. The locks are implemented by either using SCSI-2 reservations or VAAI's ATS primitive:
  - VMFSv6 supports a maximum volume size of 64 TB, a uniform block size of 1 MB, and smaller sub-blocks of 8 KB.
  - VMFS6 also supports automatic space reclamation using VAAI UNMAP.
- **NFS mounts**: Unlike VMFS volumes, NFS mounts are shared mounts on a remote filesystem. The underlying filesystem can vary depending on the type of NFS server.

  You can configure up to 256 NFS version-specific mounts on an ESXi host. This means that we can mount 256 NFSv3 along with 256NFS4.1 mounts.

- **Datastores**: This is a common term used to refer to storage containers created on an ESXi host. The containers could be VMFS volumes or NFS mounts. All files that make up a VM are stored in a datastore.

In this chapter, we will cover the following recipes:

- Connecting ESXi hosts to a Fabric Storage
- Connecting ESXi to iSCSI Storage
- iSCSI multipathing using Port Binding
- Connecting ESXi hosts to NFS Storage
- Viewing storage devices and datastores on ESXi hosts
- Masking paths to a storage device
- Unmasking paths to a storage device

Connecting ESXi hosts to a Fabric Storage

ESXi hosts can be configured to access LUNs from a Fabric Storage. This is achieved by connecting the ESXi hosts to the FC switches to which the Fiber Channel array is attached. The following diagram is a common infrastructure configuration:

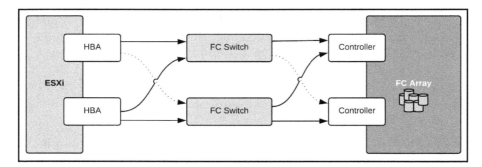

How to do it...

In this recipe, we will cover a very high-level overview of what needs to be done to present LUNs to ESXi hosts:

1. Plan and implement the fabric infrastructure to avoid single points of failure:
   - **At the host**: Every **Host Bus Adapter** (**HBA**) on a host is a single point of failure.
   - **At the fabric**: Each fabric switch is a single point of failure.
   - **At the array**: Each storage controller, RAID controller, and disk is a single point of failure.

2. Once the hosts have been connected (cabled) to the FC switches, create FC zones to provide access to the storage array controllers. Zoning is used to configure logical segments within a fabric. Only the nodes within a zone can communicate with each other. Zoning is usually done by using the **World Wide Names** (**WWNs**) of the nodes that log on to the fabric.

3. Once the hosts have been granted access to the storage controllers, use masking to further restrict access to LUNs, if necessary.

4. At the storage array, assign LUNs to the host initiators. The method varies with every storage vendor, but the concept of mapping LUNs remains the same.

5. Issue a rescan on the HBAs on the ESXi hosts to detect the LUNs presented to it.

6. You can then create VMFS volumes on these LUNs or use the LUNs as raw device mappings.

 We will learn more about creating and managing VMFS volumes in later recipes of this chapter.

How it works...

Modern-day data centers are filled with so many components that it is very easy to overlook single points of failure. Component failures are relatively common when you have a large infrastructure. Hence, it is necessary to design the infrastructure to survive such failures. Storage access is an integral part of any VMware infrastructure. Hence, it is imperative to ensure that the storage infrastructure is designed and implemented in a manner that not only achieves the desired level of performance but also makes it resilient to failures. Resiliency can be achieved by designing the infrastructure for redundancy. We will learn more about this in the following sections.

Designing for redundancy

Modern-day data centers are filled with so many components that it is very easy to overlook single points of failure. Component failures are relatively common when you have a large infrastructure. Hence, it is necessary to design the infrastructure to survive such failures. Storage access is an integral part of any VMware infrastructure. It is mainly for this reason that it is critical to make sure that it is designed and implemented in a manner that not only achieves the desired level of performance but also makes it resilient to failures.

The most common types of failures that you will encounter include the following:

- Faulty fabric cables
- HBA/port failures
- Fabric switch/port failures
- Storage array controller/port failures
- Hard disk failures

Now, let's review the proactive measures that can be considered to avoid single points of failure in storage infrastructure. We will cover the following measures:

- Avoiding single points of failure at the ESXi host
- Avoiding single points of failure at the fabric
- Avoiding single points of failure at the storage array

Avoiding single points of failure at the ESXi host

ESXi hosts that need to access FC storage will need to be equipped with FC initiators or HBAs. Some servers come with onboard adapters, some with an option to install cards, and some with a combination of both. HBAs are made with either single or multiple ports per card. Regardless of the number of ports, every single HBA is a point of failure, so it is important to make sure that you have at least two HBAs per server on which ESXi will be installed.

Avoiding single points of failure at the fabric

The FC network is formed using a set of fabric switches. Such networks are referred to as **fabrics**. It is recommended to use more than one fabric switch in order to support your fabric to eliminate single points of failure.

Avoiding single points of failure at the storage array

The storage array is the heart and soul of any data center and it stores most of the business' data. It is of prime importance to ensure that there are different levels of redundancy within a storage array in order to avoid single points of failure. To start with, all the LUNs that are created in the storage array are backed by multiple **Hard Disk Drives (HDDs)** in a RAID group to support the performance and recovery envisioned. If there are no RAID groups and if the LUNs are backed by a single large HDD, then the hard disk's components, such as the HDD controller, will become a single point of failure. Most arrays today will have more than one storage controller providing access to all the LUNs and eliminating single points of failure.

Fabric Zoning and Masking

When you implement an infrastructure with FC storage, it is imperative to make sure that when presenting the storage to the ESXi hosts, you make sure that only the intended ESXi hosts see the required LUNs. This is achieved by using two methods, called zoning and masking.

Zoning is configured on the fabric switch that the ESXi HBAs and the storage controllers are cabled to. The zoning function is used to create logical segments within a fabric. Only the nodes within a zone can communicate with each other, with initiators (HBAs) and targets (controllers) in it. There are two types of zoning: Hard Zoning and Soft Zoning:

- **Hard Zoning** is done by grouping the F-ports into a zone. An F-port is a physical port on a fabric switch. Any device that connects to an F-port in the zone will have access to the other devices in the zone. Every F-port will have a dynamically assigned FC address assigned to it when the port logs onto the fabric. This is considered to be the most secure type of zoning, but since the FC addresses can be affected by configuration changes on the fabric, such events will require you to redo the zoning with the newly assigned FC addresses of the F-ports. The following diagram illustrates Fabric Hard Zoning:

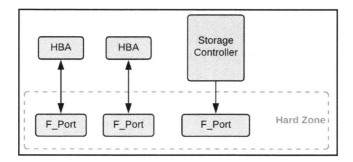

- **Soft Zoning** is done by using the WWNs of the nodes that log onto the fabric. Since the WWNs are static and not bound to change, this is considered to be the most flexible type of zoning. You could even redo the cabling of the nodes to different F-ports on a fabric switch without affecting the zone configuration. The following diagram illustrates Fabric Soft (WWN) Zoning:

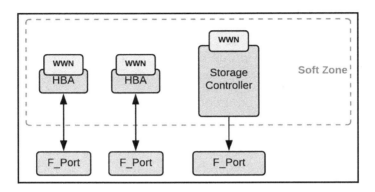

WWNs: Much like what MAC addresses are meant for in an Ethernet infrastructure, in an FC infrastructure, every device is assigned a 64-bit unique identifier called a WWN. WWNs can be of two types: a **World Wide Node Name** (**WWNN**) or a **World Wide Port Name** (**WWPN**). WWPNs are also referred to as *Node Port IDs*. For example, a dual-port HBA adapter will have a WWPN assigned to each of its ports and a single WWNN for the HBA itself.

Masking can be done at either the storage array or the ESXi host. Zoning cannot go beyond the boundaries of the node ports that log on to the fabric. Masking is done to add a deeper level of security within a zone. When you zone HBAs and storage controllers into a zone, the HBAs have access to all the LUNs presented to the storage controllers. In a large environment, a storage array will host a number of LUNs and not all of them should be visible to every initiator node that is in the zone. This is where masking comes into the picture. Masking further segments a zone into access control lists by only allowing the intended hosts to see the required LUNs.

Let's consider the following example:

- With the zoning complete, we have two hosts, [H1] and [H2], zoned to access storage controllers [A] and [B].
- Controller [A] has LUNs [L1] and [L2] mapped to it and controller [B] has LUNs [L2] and [L3] mapped to it. The following diagram illustrates LUN access post zoning:

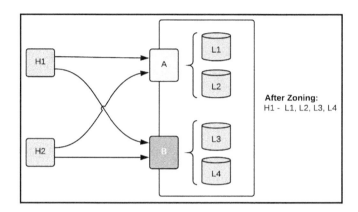

Now, let's assume that not all the ESXi hosts in the zone should access all the zoned LUNs. In this case, [H1] needs access to LUNs [L1] and [L4] only and [H2] needs access to LUNs [L2] and [L3] only. This can be achieved by creating **Access Control Lists** (**ACLs**) at controllers [A] and [B]. The following diagram illustrates LUN access after masking at the Storage Array Zoning:

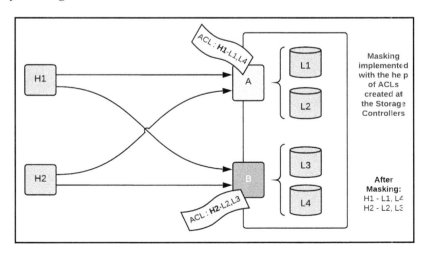

Therefore, Controller[A] will have an ACL entry for [H1] and LUNs [L1] and [L4], and Controller[B] will have an ACL entry for [H2] and LUNs [L2] and [L3].

Connecting ESXi to iSCSI Storage

iSCSI is a protocol used to transport SCSI commands over a TCP/IP network. In an iSCSI environment, the client machine (in this case, an ESXi host) uses iSCSI initiators (hardware/software) to connect to iSCSI targets on an iSCSI storage system (array).

In this recipe, we will learn how to configure and connect to the array using the most widely used type: the software iSCSI initiator.

Getting ready

Before you begin, you will need to have the following information handy:

- A discoverable IP address of the iSCSI target server and the port number to use
- **Challenge Handshake Authentication Protocol (CHAP)** authentication details (if any)

How to do it...

The following procedure will help you to enable software iSCSI and configure access to the iSCSI storage:

1. Connect to vCenter Server using the HTML5 client.
2. Select the ESXi host, navigate to **Configure | Storage Adapters**, and click **Add Software Adapter**:

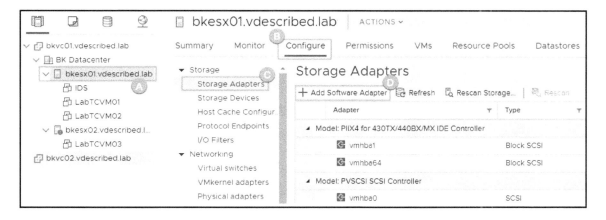

3. In the **Add Software Adapter** window, click **Add software iSCSI adapter** and click **OK**:

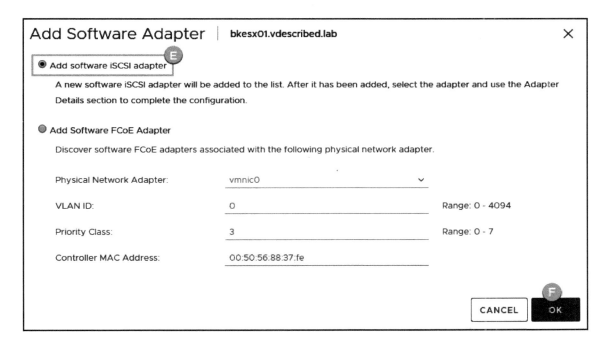

To configure access to the array, follow these steps:

1. Select the iSCSI adapter and make a note of its **iSCSI Qualified Name** (**IQN**) in the **Properties** tab. The IQN is used to add the host initiator at the array and map LUNs to it:

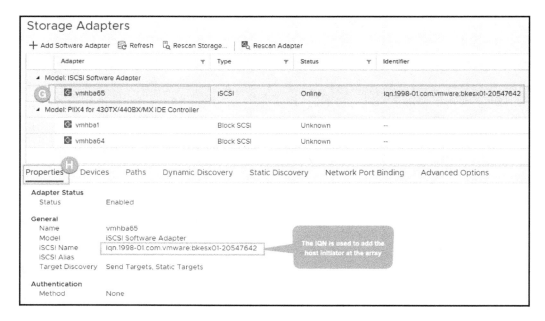

2. Go to the **Dynamic Discovery** tab and click **Add...** to specify the details of the iSCSI server/array:

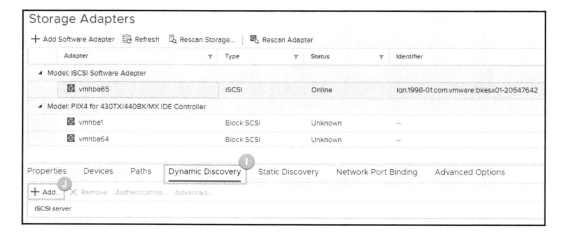

3. In the **Add Send Target Server** window, specify the FQDN or IP address of the iSCSI server and click **OK**:

4. Rescan the software iSCSI adapter in order to discover the devices mapped tc it:

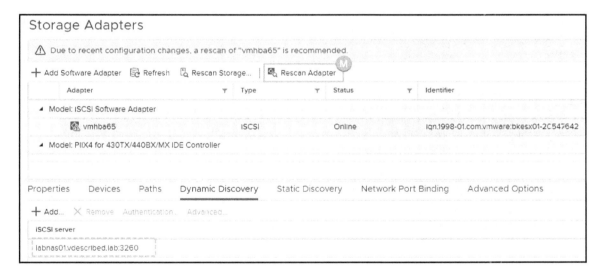

5. When the rescan is complete, the **Devices** tab will list the LUNs mapped to the host:

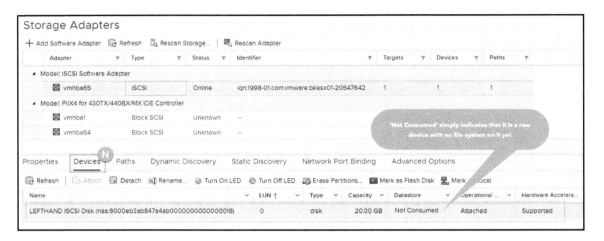

This completes the process of configuring iSCSI access for ESXi using a software iSCSI adapter.

How it works...

Let's review some of the essential iSCSI concepts that would help you learn about how iSCSI works in a vSphere environment:

- **iSCSI initiator**: This is a software/hardware adapter that resides on an ESXi host and can connect to an iSCSI target. The software iSCSI adapter is built into the VMkernel and can be enabled when intended. The hardware iSCSI adapter can be of two types: *dependent* and *independent*. While the dependent iSCSI adapter handles the packet processing, it is still reliant on ESXi for its network configuration and management. The independent iSCSI adapter provides for both configuration and packet processing.
- **iSCSI target**: This is a *network interface on the iSCSI array* or *simply a reference to a LUN*. Some arrays, such as Dell EqualLogic and HP StoreVirtual, present each LUN as a target.

Starting with vSphere 6.5, the iSCSI initiator and the iSCSI target can now be on two different layer-2 subnets.

- **iSCSI portal**: This is a combination of the iSCSI target's IP address and the listening port (default: 3260). An iSCSI portal at the initiator is the IP address of the VMkernel interface and a random port number.
- **iSCSI session**: This is a TCP/IP session established between an iSCSI initiator and an iSCSI target. Each session can have one or more connections to the same target. In the case of a software iSCSI, a session is established between each bounded (*port binding*) VMkernel interface and an iSCSI target. For example, if there are two VMkernel interfaces bound to the iSCSI initiator, then the initiator will establish two separate sessions for each target it discovers.
- **iSCSI connection**: Each iSCSI session can have multiple connections to the iSCSI target portal. The following diagram illustrates a single iSCSI session with two connections:

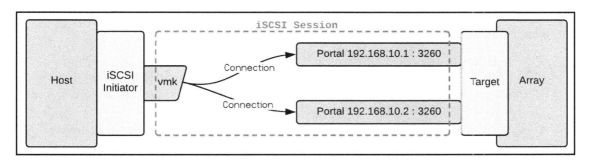

- **CHAP**: This is used by iSCSI to make sure that the initiator and target establish a trusted and secure connection.
- **Dynamic Discovery**: This is the most commonly used target discovery mechanism, which comes in handy when the iSCSI server exposes a large number of LUNs/targets via its target portal.
- **Static Discovery**: Unlike the Dynamic Discovery mechanism, Static Discovery does not see every LUN/target exposed via the target portal. Instead, it only sees the specified targets.

- **IQN**: This is a unique identifier associated with each iSCSI initiator or iSCSI Target. The identifier starts with the string IQN followed by the year and month when the naming authority was established, the domain of the naming authority in reverse, and a unique name for the storage node. Each of these strings is separated by a period (.). The following diagram illustrates the iSCSI Qualified Name Format:

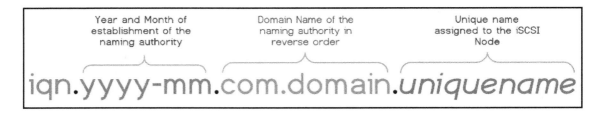

iSCSI multipathing using Port Binding

iSCSI multipathing will depend on the type of storage and the network topology in use. There are two methods for this:

- **Multipathing for iSCSI using port binding**: This is achieved by having two VMkernel interfaces configured with an active adapter each, but no standby adapters. Once done, these VMkernel (vmk) interfaces should be bound to the software iSCSI adapter.
- **Multipathing for iSCSI without port binding**: Read the *When not to use port binding* section of *VMware KB: 2038869* for more details (`http://kb.vmware.com/kb/2038869`).

In this recipe, we will learn about how to prepare the vSphere network for iSCSI multipathing by creating multiple VMkernel interfaces, which we will do by using the same set of physical NICs in alternating active/unused pairs. This method is used to achieve iSCSI multipathing by using the port binding method.

Getting ready

Create two VMkernel interfaces on two separate port groups (standard or distributed), with IP addresses in the same subnet as the iSCSI storage system (target portal). Use the following screenshot as an example:

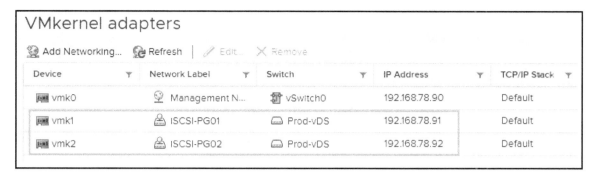

Once done, modify the failover order in such a way that only one of the uplinks is active and the other is unused. Use the following screenshot as an example:

For port binding to work, the VMkernel interfaces and the iSCSI target portals cannot be on disparate network subnets. In other words, they should be in the same broadcast domain (VLAN). This is only a limitation with port binding; *iSCSI otherwise supports routing.*

There are cases when port binding should not be used to achieve multipathing. The *When not to use port binding* section of *VMware Knowledge Base article* 2038869 (`https://kb.vmware.com/kb/2038869`) has more details.

How to do it...

The following procedure will help you to bind VMkernel adapters to the software iSCSI adapter:

1. Ensure that the VMkernel adapters have been prepared by using the instructions in the *Getting ready* section of this recipe.
2. Go to the ESXi host and navigate to **Configure** | **Storage Adapters**, select the iSCSI adapter, go to its **Network Port Binding** tab, and click **+ Add...**:

3. In the **Bind vmhba65 with VMkernel Adapter** window, select both of the port groups corresponding to the VMkernel interfaces and click **OK**:

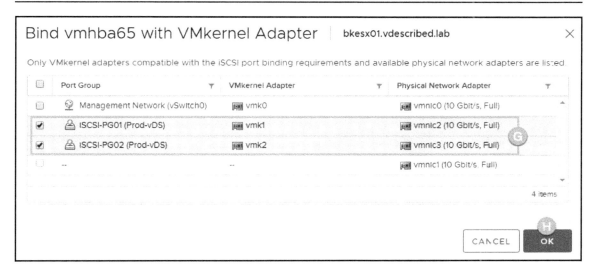

4. Once done, the VMkernel adapters will be listed under **Network Port Binding**. The **Path Status** is **Not used** because the targets have not been associated with the interfaces yet. Issue a rescan to associate the targets to the VMkernel interface:

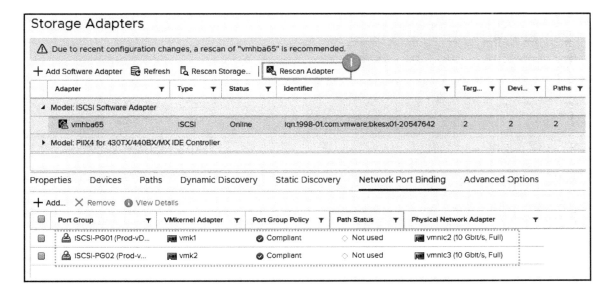

5. After a rescan, the **Path Status** for both bound interfaces are set to **Active**:

	Port Group		VMkernel Adapter		Port Group Policy		Path Status		Physical Network Adapter	
	ISCSI-PG01 (Prod-vDS)	▼	vmk1	▼	✓ Compliant	▼	◆ Active	▼	vmnic2 (10 Gbit/s, Full)	▼
	ISCSI-PG02 (Prod-vDS)		vmk2		✓ Compliant		◆ Active		vmnic3 (10 Gbit/s, Full)	

6. You should now see two paths per target from the iSCSI initiator:

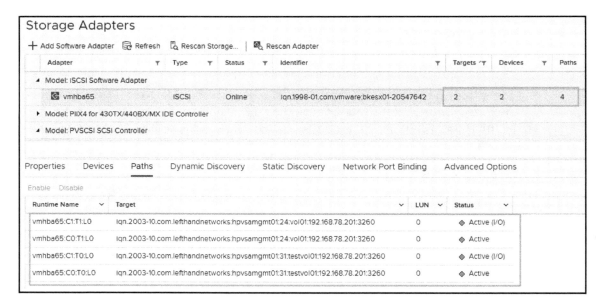

Storage Adapters

+ Add Software Adapter   Refresh   Rescan Storage... | Rescan Adapter

Adapter	▼	Type	▼	Status	▼	Identifier	▼	Targets	Devices	▼	Paths
▲ Model: ISCSI Software Adapter											
vmhba65		ISCSI		Online		Iqn.1998-01.com.vmware:bkesx01-20547642		2	2		4
▶ Model: PIIX4 for 430TX/440BX/MX IDE Controller											
▲ Model: PVSCSI SCSI Controller											

Properties   Devices   **Paths**   Dynamic Discovery   Static Discovery   Network Port Binding   Advanced Options

Enable Disable

Runtime Name	✓	Target	✓	LUN	✓	Status	✓
vmhba65:C1:T1:L0		Iqn.2003-10.com.lefthandnetworks:hpvsamgmt01:24:vol01:192.168.78.201:3260		0		◆ Active (I/O)	
vmhba65:C0:T1:L0		Iqn.2003-10.com.lefthandnetworks:hpvsamgmt01:24:vol01:192.168.78.201:3260		0		◆ Active	
vmhba65:C1:T0:L0		Iqn.2003-10.com.lefthandnetworks:hpvsamgmt01:31:testvol01:192.168.78.201:3260		0		◆ Active (I/O)	
vmhba65:C0:T0:L0		Iqn.2003-10.com.lefthandnetworks:hpvsamgmt01:31:testvol01:192.168.78.201:3260		0		◆ Active	

This completes the process of binding VMkernel ports to the software iSCSI adapter to achieve multipathing.

How it works...

By default, only a single egress path exists between the software iSCSI adapter and an iSCSI target:

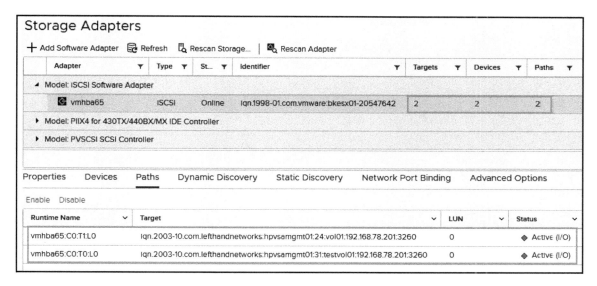

To enable load balancing or redundancy for iSCSI traffic regressing an ESXi host, we use *port binding*. With port binding, you bind multiple VMkernel interfaces (vmk) to the software iSCSI adapter, as shown in the following diagram:

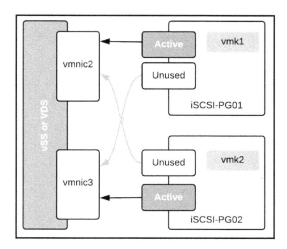

The number of paths made available to the iSCSI initiator will depend on the type of the iSCSI storage system (array).

The type of an iSCSI array is based on the *number of targets or target portals* it exposes. The key difference between a target and target portal is that *an iSCSI target will have a unique IQN associated with it*, whereas *a target portal is identified with an IP Address: Port Number combination*.

There are three types of iSCSI array, as follows:

- Single-portal array
- Multi-portal array
- Multi-target array

With a **single-portal array**, the storage system exposes a single portal to be discovered by the source (initiator). Hence, the number of paths to such an array will depend on the number of VMkernel interfaces associated with the iSCSI initiator. The process of associating VMkernel interfaces with an iSCSI initiator is called **port binding**. We will learn more about port binding in this recipe.

With a **multi-portal array**, the storage system exposes multiple portals to be discovered by the iSCSI initiator. Therefore, the number of paths to the array will not only depend on the number of VMkernel ports bound to the iSCSI initiator but also the number of portals exposed. For instance, if two VMkernel ports are bound to the iSCSI initiator discovering four target portals, then the number of paths to the iSCSI target is eight.

With a **multi-target array**, the storage system exposes more than one iSCSI target interface (hence different IQNs) with one or more portals associated with each interface. It is important to understand that this is different from the storage system exposing LUNs as targets to the initiator.

The formula to calculate the number of possible paths is dependent on the number of source portals (VMkernel ports) and target portals, and not the number of targets:

- *The total number of paths = (Number of Source Portals) x (Number of Target Portals).*
- Here, the source portal is nothing but the VMkernel interfaces bound to the iSCSI initiator.

When you view the multipathing information for single/multi-portal arrays from the vCenter GUI, every discovery portal will be listed as a target. These targets will have the same IQN, but different portal IP addresses associated with them. However, for multi-target arrays, you will see targets with different IQNs as well.

Connecting ESXi hosts to NFS Storage

NFS storage is also a NAS, like iSCSI. Therefore, it can be easily integrated into the existing TCP/IP network. Unlike, iSCSI, NFS is not a block storage system, meaning NFS maintains its filesystem. Hence, ESXi cannot format or form a new filesystem on the volumes presented to it from an NFS array. Instead, the NFS volumes (also called **exports**) are configured as mount points to remote shares on an NFS storage array.

VMware introduced support for NFS 4.1 starting with vSphere 6.0:

- It now supports AES encryption.
- It supports for IPv6.
- It supports for Kerberos' integrity checking mechanism.

You can create both NFS 3 and NFS 4.1 datastores on ESXi.

Getting ready

You will need the following details handy before you proceed:

- The FQDN/IP address of the NFS server
- A full path to the share on the NFS server
- A VMkernel interface on the ESXi host that can connect to the NFS server
- Allow root access to the shares on the NFS server, which is commonly referred to as `no_rootsquash`

How to do it...

The following procedure will help you to create an NFS datastore:

1. Connect to vCenter Server using the HTML5 client.
2. Navigate to the **Storage** inventory, right-click on the datacenter object, and go to **Storage | New Datastore...**:

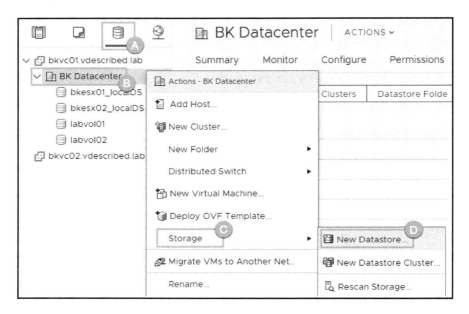

3. In the **New Datastore** wizard, select **Type** as **NFS** and click **Next** to continue:

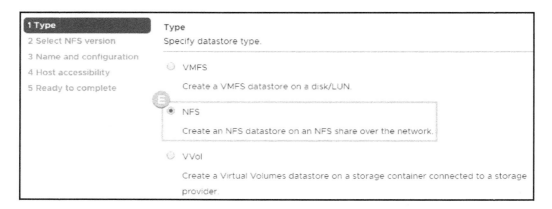

4. On the **Select NFS version** screen, choose the NFS version supported by the NFS server and click **Next**:

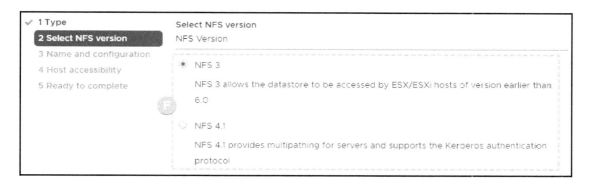

5. On the **Name and configuration** screen, specify a name for the datastore, the folder path of the NFS share (as it is at the NFS server), and the FQDN/IP address of the NFS server. Also, you could optionally choose to **Mount NFS as read-only**. Once done, click **Next** to continue:

6. On the **Host accessibility** screen, select the desired ESXi host(s) and click **Next** to continue:

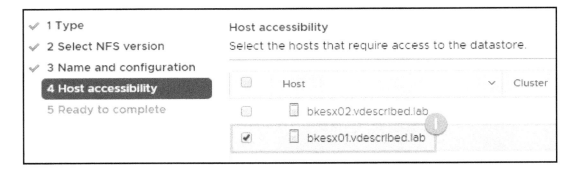

7. On the **Ready to complete** screen, review the settings and click **Finish**:

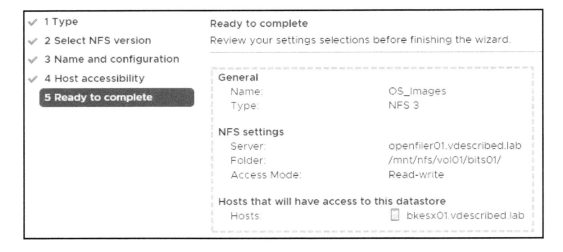

8. **Recent Tasks** should show a **Create NAS datastore** task that has completed successfully:

This completes the process of mapping NFS storage mounts to ESXi hosts.

How it works...

By default, you can only create *eight* NFS mounts per ESXi server. Although this limit can be increased up to **256** by using the advanced **NFS.MaxVolumes** setting, increasing this limit would generally require an increase in the minimum amount of VMkernel TCP/IP heap memory. The minimum heap memory value can be specified using the advanced **Net.TcpipHeapSize** setting. You can also set the maximum amount of heap size by using the advanced **Net.TcpipHeapMax** setting.

 For more information regarding the TCP/IP heap size value, read the *VMware Knowledge Base article* 2239 (`https://kb.vmware.com/kb/2239`).

Viewing storage devices and datastores on ESXi hosts

VMware ESXi uses logical storage containers called **datastores** for storing files that back a VM. A datastore can be a VMFS volume or an NFS mount. Each ESXi host maintains a list of devices and datastores that it has access to.

In this recipe, we will learn how to view the available devices and datastores on an ESXi host.

How to do it...

The following procedure will help you to view storage devices and datastores available on an ESXi host:

1. Connect to vCenter Server using the HTML5 client.
2. Select the host from the inventory and navigate to **Configure** | **Storage Devices** in order to view all the LUN devices seen by the ESXi host:

3. Navigate to the **Datastores** tab to view all the datastores seen by the ESXi host:

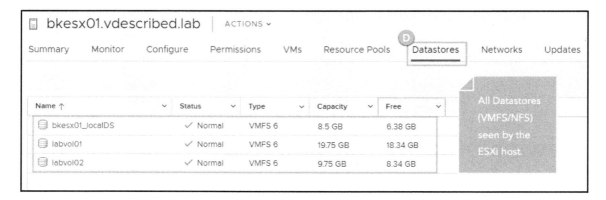

This completes the process of viewing information regarding storage devices and datastores accessible to the ESXi hosts.

How it works...

Although it is fairly simple, it is essential to know how to review information regarding accessible storage while auditing your environment or troubleshooting an issue.

You could also use the ESXi **command-line interface** (**CLI**) to view the devices and the datastores:

```
[root@bkesx01:~]
[root@bkesx01:~]
[root@bkesx01:~] esxcli storage core device capacity list ◄---- Device List
Device                                 Physical Blocksize  Logical Blocksize  Logical Block Count     Size   Format Type
-------------------------------------  ------------------  -----------------  -------------------  --------   -----------
naa.6000eb3ab847a4ab000000000000001f                  512                512             20971520  10240 MiB  512n
mpx.vmhba1:C0:T0:L0                                   2048               2048               162494    317 MiB  Unknown
mpx.vmhba0:C0:T0:L0                                    512                512             33554432  16384 MiB  512n
naa.6000eb3ab847a4ab0000000000000018                  512                512             41943040  20480 MiB  512n
[root@bkesx01:~]
[root@bkesx01:~] esxcli storage vmfs extent list ◄---- Datastore list
Volume Name       VMFS UUID                              Extent Number   Device Name                            Partition
----------------  -------------------------------------  -------------   -------------------------------------  ---------
bkesx01_localDS   5c35bf45-267aea32-7894-0050568837fe                0   mpx.vmhba0:C0:T0:L0                             3
labvol01          5c8dd9de-72194e3a-0564-005056885f88                0   naa.6000eb3ab847a4ab0000000000000018           1
labvol02          5c8dda01-a96a23cb-dbb8-005056885f88                0   naa.6000eb3ab847a4ab000000000000001f           1
[root@bkesx01:~]
```

Some of the other commands include the following:

- `esxcli storage filesystem list`
- `esxcli storage nfs list`
- `esxcli storage vmfs extent list`
- `esxcli storage san iscsi list`
- `esxcli storage san fc list`

Masking paths to a storage device

While troubleshooting storage access issues, you can remove access via individual paths to a storage device. This is achieved by using PSA's `MASK_PATH` plugin to claim the desired paths corresponding to the device.

The following flowchart depicts a high-level overview of the process:

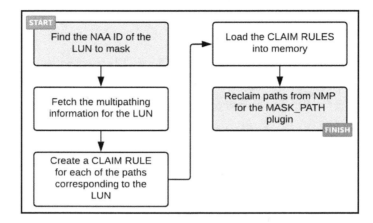

Getting ready

Before you mask paths to a LUN, it is important to ensure that the VMFS volumes corresponding to them are no longer hosting any running VMs. Also, if the LUNs are **Raw Device Mappings** (**RDMs**), then they should not be mapped to any of the running VMs.

How to do it...

The following procedure will help you to mask individual paths to a LUN device:

1. SSH into the desired ESXi host.
2. Get the NAA ID of the device for which the path needs to be masked, by issuing the following command:

   ```
   esxcli storage vmfs extent  list
   ```

   Once you run the preceding command, you will see the following output:

```
[root@bkesx01:~] esxcli storage vmfs extent list
Volume Name     VMFS UUID                            Extent Number  Device Name                               Partition
--------------  -----------------------------------  -------------  ----------------------------------------  ---------
bkesx01_localDS 5c35bf45-267aea32-7894-0050568837fe             0   mpx.vmhba0:C0:T0:L0                               3
labvol01        5c8f50d4-986a3073-2d9c-005056885f88             0   naa.6000eb3ab847a4ab0000000000000018             1
labvol01        5c8f50d4-986a3073-2d9c-005056885f88             0   naa.6000eb3ab847a4ab0000000000000042             1
labvol02        5c96d7c4-742eed2f-0d46-005056885f88             0   naa.6000eb3ab847a4ab0000000000000076             1
[root@bkesx01:~]
```

3. Get the current multipathing information of the device by using the following command syntax:

```
esxcfg-mpath -l -d <naa-id of the LUN>
```

Once you run the preceding command, you will see the following output:

```
[root@bkesx01:~] esxcfg-mpath -l -d naa.6000eb3ab847a4ab0000000000000076
iqn.1998-01.com.vmware:bkesx01-20547642-00023d000002,iqn.2003-10.com.lefthandnetworks:hpvsamgmt01:118:vol02,t,1-naa.6000eb3ab847a4ab000000000C000076
   Runtime Name: vmhba65:C1:T3:L0
   Device: naa.6000eb3ab847a4ab0000000000000076
   Device Display Name: LEFTHAND iSCSI Disk (naa.6000eb3ab847a4ab0000000000000076)
   Adapter: vmhba65 Channel: 1 Target: 3 LUN: 0
   Adapter Identifier: iqn.1998-01.com.vmware:bkesx01-20547642
   Target Identifier: 00023d000002,iqn.2003-10.com.lefthandnetworks:hpvsamgmt01:118:vol02,t,1
   Plugin: NMP
   State: active
   Transport: iscsi
   Adapter Transport Details: iqn.1998-01.com.vmware:bkesx01-20547642
   Target Transport Details: IQN=iqn.2003-10.com.lefthandnetworks:hpvsamgmt01:118:vol02 Alias= Session=00023d000002 PortalTag=1

iqn.1998-01.com.vmware:bkesx01-20547642-00023d000001,iqn.2003-10.com.lefthandnetworks:hpvsamgmt01:118:vol02,t,1-naa.6000eb3ab847a4ab000000000C000076
   Runtime Name: vmhba65:C0:T3:L0
   Device: naa.6000eb3ab847a4ab0000000000000076
   Device Display Name: LEFTHAND iSCSI Disk (naa.6000eb3ab847a4ab0000000000000076)
   Adapter: vmhba65 Channel: 0 Target: 3 LUN: 0
   Adapter Identifier: iqn.1998-01.com.vmware:bkesx01-20547642
   Target Identifier: 00023d000001,iqn.2003-10.com.lefthandnetworks:hpvsamgmt01:118:vol02,t,1
   Plugin: NMP
   State: active
   Transport: iscsi
   Adapter Transport Details: iqn.1998-01.com.vmware:bkesx01-20547642
   Target Transport Details: IQN=iqn.2003-10.com.lefthandnetworks:hpvsamgmt01:118:vol02 Alias= Session=00023d000001 PortalTag=1
```

> vmhba65:C1:T3:L0 will be masked in this exercise

In this instance, there are two paths to the LUN device and we will mask one of the paths (`vmhba65:C1:T3:L0`).

4. Create a claim rule to mask the desired path by using the following command syntax:

```
esxcli storage core claimrule add -r <rule_number> -t location -A
<vmhba> -C <channel number> -L <LUN Number> -P MASK_PATH
```

Once you run the preceding command, you will see the following output:

```
[root@bkesx01:~] esxcli storage core claimrule add -r 130 -t location -A vmhba65 -C 1 -L 0 -P MASK_PATH
[root@bkesx01:~]
[root@bkesx01:~] esxcli storage core claimrule list
Rule Class   Rule   Class    Type        Plugin      Matches
----------   -----  -------  ---------   ---------   ----------------------------------------
MP              50   runtime  transport   NMP         transport=usb
MP              51   runtime  transport   NMP         transport=sata
MP              52   runtime  transport   NMP         transport=ide
MP              53   runtime  transport   NMP         transport=block
MP              54   runtime  transport   NMP         transport=unknown
MP             101   runtime  vendor      MASK_PATH   vendor=DELL model=Universal Xport
MP             101   file     vendor      MASK_PATH   vendor=DELL model=Universal Xport
MP             130   file     location    MASK_PATH   adapter=vmhba65 channel=1 target=* lun=0
MP           65535   runtime  vendor      NMP         vendor=* model=*
[root@bkesx01:~]
[root@bkesx01:~]
```

> Rule created is now on file. It needs to be loaded to the memory to be active.

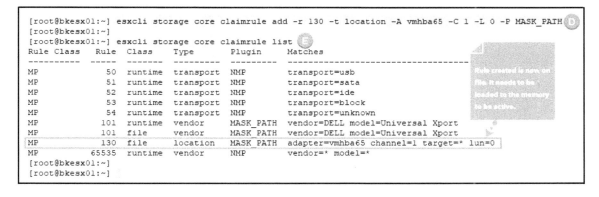

5. A claim rule created, has to be loaded into the memory for it to be in effect. This is achieved by running the following command:

```
esxcli storage core claimrule load
```

Once you run the preceding command, you will see the following output:

```
[root@bkesx01:~] esxcli storage core claimrule load
[root@bkesx01:~] esxcli storage core claimrule list
Rule Class   Rule   Class     Type        Plugin      Matches
----------   -----  -------   ---------   ---------   --------------------------
MP             50   runtime   transport   NMP         transport=usb
MP             51   runtime   transport   NMP         transport=sata
MP             52   runtime   transport   NMP         transport=ide
MP             53   runtime   transport   NMP         transport=block
MP             54   runtime   transport   NMP         transport=unknown
MP            101   runtime   vendor      MASK_PATH   vendor=DELL model=Universal Xport
MP            101   file      vendor      MASK_PATH   vendor=DELL model=Universal Xport
MP            130   runtime   location    MASK_PATH   adapter=vmhba65 channel=1 target=* lun=0
MP            130   file      location    MASK_PATH   adapter=vmhba65 channel=1 target=* lun=0
MP          65535   runtime   vendor      NMP         vendor=* model=*
[root@bkesx01:~]
```

Rule created is now loaded into the memory, hence the classified as runtime"

6. Now that the rule is active, the path can be claimed by the MASK_PATH plugin, by using the following command syntax:

```
esxcli storage core claiming reclaim -d <naa.id of the device>
```

Once you run the preceding command, you will see the following output:

This completes the process of masking paths to a storage device presented to an ESXi host.

How it works...

Once you have masked the paths to a LUN device, the ESXi host will not have access to the LUN. The access can be restored only by unmasking the paths to the LUN.

Unmasking paths to a storage device

It is possible to unmask paths to a storage device. Deleting the claim rules and unclaiming the paths from the MASK_PATH plugin achieves this. Understanding how the paths to a LUN are masked will be a good starting point for this task. Read the *Masking paths to a storage device* recipe before you begin this recipe.

The following flowchart provides a high-level overview of the unmasking procedure:

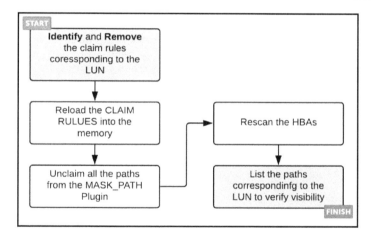

How to do it...

The following procedure will help you to unmask paths to a storage device:

1. SSH into the ESXi host.
2. Identify the claim rule corresponding to the device. The claim rules on the host can be listed by using the following command syntax:

```
esxcli storage core claimrule list
```

Once you run the preceding command, you will see the following output:

```
[root@bkesx01:~] esxcli storage core claimrule list  Ⓐ
Rule Class   Rule  Class    Type       Plugin      Matches
----------   ----- -------  ---------  ---------   -----------------------------------
MP            50   runtime  transport  NMP         transport=usb
MP            51   runtime  transport  NMP         transport=sata
MP            52   runtime  transport  NMP         transport=ide
MP            53   runtime  transport  NMP         transport=block
MP            54   runtime  transport  NMP         transport=unknown
MP           101   runtime  vendor     MASK_PATH   vendor=DELL model=Universal Xport
MP           101   file     vendor     MASK_PATH   vendor=DELL model=Universal Xport    Ⓑ
MP           130   runtime  location   MASK_PATH   adapter=vmhba65 channel=1 target=* lun=0
MP           130   file     location   MASK_PATH   adapter=vmhba65 channel=1 target=* lun=0
MP         65535   runtime  vendor     NMP         vendor=* model=*
[root@bkesx01:~]
[root@bkesx01:~]
```

3. Remove the rule identified by using the following command syntax:

   `esxcli storage core claimrule remove -r <Rule ID>`

   Doing so will remove the file entry corresponding to the rule specified. As shown in the following screenshot, the file entry corresponding to the runtime entry gets removed.

```
[root@bkesx01:~] esxcli storage core claimrule remove -r 130  Ⓒ
[root@bkesx01:~]
[root@bkesx01:~] esxcli storage core claimrule list  Ⓓ
Rule Class   Rule  Class    Type       Plugin      Matches
----------   ----- -------  ---------  ---------   --------------------
MP            50   runtime  transport  NMP         transport=usb               The file entry corresponding
MP            51   runtime  transport  NMP         transport=sata              to the rule entry gets
MP            52   runtime  transport  NMP         transport=ide               removed, leaving just the
MP            53   runtime  transport  NMP         transport=block             runtime entry. A reload will
MP            54   runtime  transport  NMP         transport=unknown           clear the runtime entry
MP           101   runtime  vendor     MASK_PATH   vendor=DELL model=Universal Xport
MP           101   file     vendor     MASK_PATH   vendor=DELL model=Universal Xport
MP           130   runtime  location   MASK_PATH   adapter=vmhba65 channel=1 target=* lun=0
MP         65535   runtime  vendor     NMP         vendor=* model=*
[root@bkesx01:~]
```

4. Reload the claim rules for the changes to take effect by running the following command:

   esxcli storage core claimrule load.

   Doing so will remove the rule's runtime entry since the rule's file entry has already been removed, thereby deactivating the claim rule. The following screenshot shows that the runtime has also been removed.

```
[root@bkesx01:~] esxcli storage core claimrule load      E
[root@bkesx01:~]
[root@bkesx01:~] esxcli storage core claimrule list      F
Rule Class    Rule   Class    Type       Plugin      Matches
----------    ----   -------  ---------  ---------   ------------
MP              50   runtime  transport  NMP         transport=usb
MP              51   runtime  transport  NMP         transport=sat
MP              52   runtime  transport  NMP         transport=ide
MP              53   runtime  transport  NMP         transport=blc
MP              54   runtime  transport  NMP         transport=unknown
MP             101   runtime  vendor     MASK_PATH   vendor=DELL model=Universal Xport
MP             101   file     vendor     MASK_PATH   vendor=DELL model=Universal Xport
MP           65535   runtime  vendor     NMP         vendor=* model=*
[root@bkesx01:~]
```

Both file and run time entries corresponding to Rule-130 are now gone - thereby deactivating the rule.

5. Once the claim rule has been deactivated, the paths can be claimed back from the MASK_PATH plugin by using the following command syntax:

   esxcli storage core claiming unclaim -t location -A <vmhba number>-**C** <channel number> **-L** <LUN ID> **-P MASK_PATH**

6. Now, issue a rescan on the adapter by using the following command syntax:

   esxcfg-rescan <vmhba number>

7. Verify the outcome of the unmasking operation by listing all the paths corresponding to the device. Do so by using the following command syntax:

   esxcfg-mpath -l -d <naa.id of the LUN>

Once you run the preceding command syntax, you will see the following output:

```
[root@bkesx01:~] esxcli storage core claiming unclaim -t location -A vmhba65 -C 1 -L 0 -P MASK_PATH  G
[root@bkesx01:~]
[root@bkesx01:~] esxcfg-rescan vmhba65 H
[root@bkesx01:~]
[root@bkesx01:~] esxcfg-mpath -l -d naa.6000eb3ab847a4ab0000000000000076 I
iqn.1998-01.com.vmware:bkesx01-20547642-00023d000002,iqn.2003-10.com.lefthandnetworks:hpvsamgmt01:118:vol02,t,1-naa.6000eb3ab847a4ab0000000000000076
   Runtime Name: vmhba65:C1:T3:L0
   Device: naa.6000eb3ab847a4ab0000000000000076
   Device Display Name: LEFTHAND iSCSI Disk (naa.6000eb3ab847a4ab0000000000000076)
   Adapter: vmhba65 Channel: 1 Target: 3 LUN: 0
   Adapter Identifier: iqn.1998-01.com.vmware:bkesx01-20547642
   Target Identifier: 00023d000002,iqn.2003-10.com.lefthandnetworks:hpvsamgmt01:118:vol02,t,1
   Plugin: NMP
   State: active
   Transport: iscsi
   Adapter Transport Details: iqn.1998-01.com.vmware:bkesx01-20547642
   Target Transport Details: IQN=iqn.2003-10.com.lefthandnetworks:hpvsamgmt01:118:vol02 Alias= Session=00023d000002 PortalTag=1

iqn.1998-01.com.vmware:bkesx01-20547642-00023d000001,iqn.2003-10.com.lefthandnetworks:hpvsamgmt01:118:vol02,t,1-naa.6000eb3ab847a4ab0000000000000076
   Runtime Name: vmhba65:C0:T3:L0
   Device: naa.6000eb3ab847a4ab0000000000000076
   Device Display Name: LEFTHAND iSCSI Disk (naa.6000eb3ab847a4ab0000000000000076)
   Adapter: vmhba65 Channel: 0 Target: 3 LUN: 0
   Adapter Identifier: iqn.1998-01.com.vmware:bkesx01-20547642
   Target Identifier: 00023d000001,iqn.2003-10.com.lefthandnetworks:hpvsamgmt01:118:vol02,t,1
   Plugin: NMP
   State: active
   Transport: iscsi
   Adapter Transport Details: iqn.1998-01.com.vmware:bkesx01-20547642
   Target Transport Details: IQN=iqn.2003-10.com.lefthandnetworks:hpvsamgmt01:118:vol02 Alias= Session=00023d000001 PortalTag=1

[root@bkesx01:~]
```

How it works...

Unmasking paths to a LUN restores access to the LUNs on the ESXi host. This activity is usually performed once the intended storage maintenance or troubleshooting activity has been completed.

Creating and Managing VMFS Datastores

6

In the previous chapter, we learned how to configure ESXi hosts to access iSCSI and Fiber Channel storage devices or LUNs.

LUNs presented from the array, would not have any filesystem on it. VMware allows you to create a proprietary filesystem called the **Virtual Machine File System** (**VMFS**). The most recent version of VMFS is version 6. vSphere 6.7 enables the creation of either a VMFS5 or VMFS6 filesystem on the storage device.

In this chapter, we will cover the following recipes:

- Creating VMFS datastores
- Upgrading VMFS datastores
- Managing Storage Multipathing
- Expanding or growing a VMFS datastore
- Extending a VMFS datastore
- Unmounting VMFS datastores and detaching storage devices
- Attaching storage devices and remounting VMFS datastores
- Managing VMFS snapshots

Creating VMFS datastores

The storage devices (LUNs) presented to the ESXi host can be formatted with the **Virtual Machine File System** (**VMFS**) to create datastores that can be used to store virtual machines. The datastore can be created by *either* directly connecting to the ESXi host *or* from the vCenter.

In this recipe, we will learn about how to create VMFS datastores using the vCenter Server.

How to do it...

The following procedure will help you to create a VMFS datastore:

1. Connect to vCenter Server using the HTML5 client.
2. In the **Storage** inventory view, right-click on the desired **Datacenter** and navigate to **Storage** | **New Datastore...**:

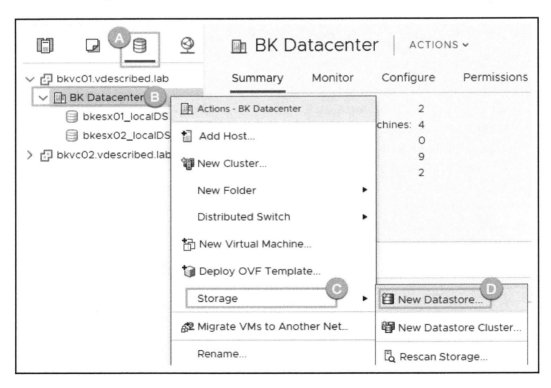

3. In the **New Datastore** wizard, select **Type** as **VMFS** and click **Next** to continue:

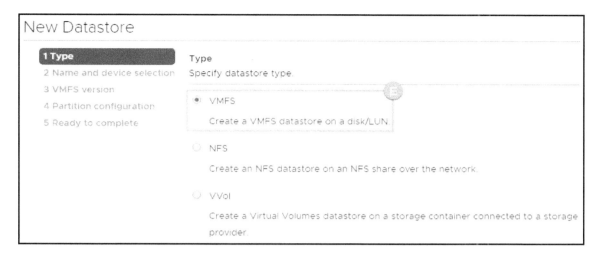

4. On the **Name and device selection** screen, specify a name for the datastore, select an ESXi host to which the LUNs have been presented, and then select the desired LUN device. Once done, click **Next** to continue:

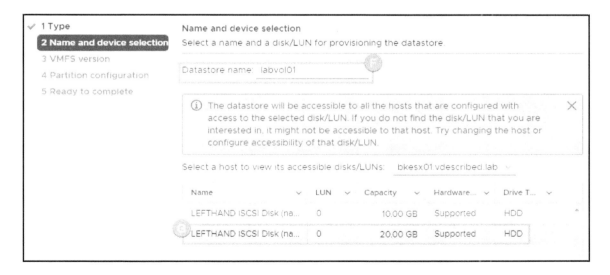

5. On the next screen, select the desired **VMFS version** and click **Next** to continue:

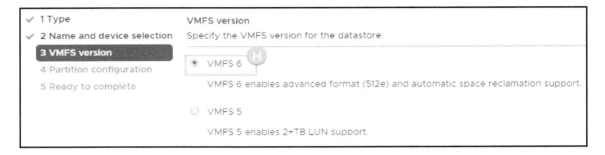

6. On the **Partition configuration** screen, choose **Use all available partitions**, and then specify **Datastore Size** and **Space Reclamation Priority** (none/low). **Block size** and **Space Reclamation Granularity** will be set to **1 MB** and cannot be changed:

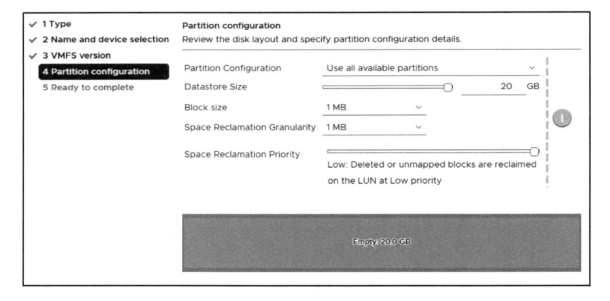

7. On the **Ready to complete** screen, review the summary and click **Finish** to create the datastore:

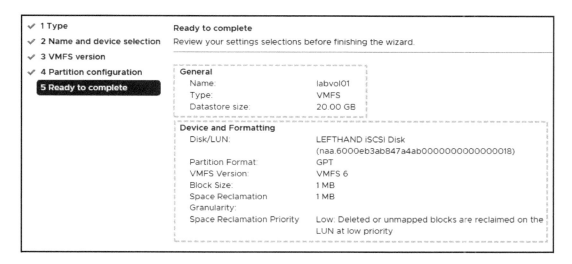

8. Once done, the newly created datastore will be listed under the datacenter object, which is in the **Storage** inventory. Select the datastore and go to the **Hosts** tab to see a list of ESXi hosts that the datastore is connected to:

This completes the process of creating VMFS datastores.

How it works...

Creating a VMFS datastore essentially erases the LUN selected and writes the VMFS onto it. The operation has to be performed only once from any of the ESXi hosts that can access the LUN. Once done, all the other ESXi hosts can see the VMFS volume created on the LUN.

Upgrading VMFS datastores

If there are existing VMFS5 datastores in your environment, then it is important to note that there is no method to perform an in-place upgrade of VMFS5 to VMFS6. This is due to the changes made to the structure of VMFS6 metadata to make it compatible with 4K alignment.

This recipe will provide you with a very high-level overview of how to plan the migration of your workloads to VMFS 6.

How to do it...

The following procedure provides general guidance on how VM workloads on VMFS5 can be migrated to VMFS6:

1. Make a list of all VMFS5 datastores and their current storage utilization.
2. Depending on the amount of free capacity available in the storage system, you can choose to either create VMFS6 datastores of similar sizes or create a set of larger datastores for temporary storage.
3. If similarly sized VMFS6 datastores are created, then Storage vMotion the VM's storage onto the new datastore.
4. If you have created larger temporary LUNs, then you need to perform the following steps:
   1. Select VMs from more than one VMFS5 datastore and migrate the VMs onto a larger LUN.
   2. Once done, delete the now empty VMFS5 datastores.
   3. Create VMFS6 datastores on the same LUNs.
   4. Migrate the VMs from the larger LUNs to the VMFS6 datastores.

How it works...

Since every environment is different, there are several factors that would affect the methodology chosen. Refer to *VMware KB article* 2147824 – `https://kb.vmware.com/kb/2147824` – for different use cases and methods.

Managing Storage Multipathing

The availability of storage presented to the ESXi hosts is essential for the functioning of a vSphere environment. One of the factors that increases storage availability is maintaining resilient connectivity to the storage system. Resiliency is achieved by forming redundant paths to the storage presented to the ESXi hosts. The paths can either be used for failover or load balancing.

In this recipe, we will learn about how to review the current multipathing configuration for each storage device.

How to do it...

The following procedure will help you to view and manage multipathing configuration:

1. Connect to vCenter Server using the HTML5 client and navigate to the **Hosts and Clusters** inventory view:

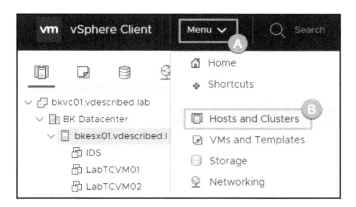

2. Select the desired ESXi host and navigate to **Configure | Storage Devices**.

3. On the **Storage Devices** screen, select a storage device and its **Paths** tab to review the configured paths for the device. On the same screen, you could even choose to **Enable/Disable** a path if required:

Storage Device Paths

4. If you intend to change the device's **Multipathing Policy** (**Path Selection Policy** (**PSP**)), then go to the device's **Properties** tab and click **Edit Multipathing...**:

5. On the **Edit Multipathing Policies** tab, select the preferred **Path selection policy** and click **OK** to save the changes:

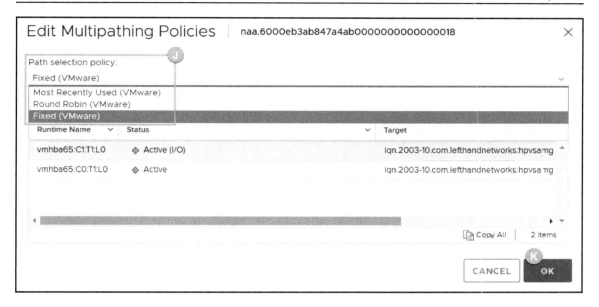

6. For instance, here we have two paths to the device, with one marked **Active (I/O)** since the policy is set to **Fixed (VMware)**. Therefore, you are allowed to select a preferred path by highlighting it.

7. Now, if we change **Path selection policy** to **Round Robin (VMware)**, then both patches will be marked for **Active (I/O)**, as shown in the following screenshot:

This completes the procedure involved in viewing and managing paths to storage devices.

How it works...

A path to a LUN includes the HBA or initiator, the fabric/network switches, and the storage controllers in the array. The availability of a path will be affected if any of these hardware components along the path fail or stop functioning. Multipathing is a method for configuring and maintaining multiple paths between the host and the storage array. Although redundant fabric switches will be used to achieve this, the multipathing information available at ESXi will not show the switches that are involved.

Storage multipathing on an ESXi host is achieved with the help of a framework of APIs called **Pluggable Storage Architecture** (**PSA**). The APIs can be used by the storage vendors to develop **Multipathing Plugins** (**MPPs**), thus enabling a closer integration of their storage devices. Some examples of available third-party MPPs are as follows:

- EMC PowerPath
- Dell EqualLogic MEM for iSCSI multipathing
- VERITAS dynamic multipathing for VMware

 The default multipathing plugin on an ESXi host is called a **Native Multipathing Plugin** (**NMP**). The NMP adds support for all the supported storage arrays in the VMware compatibility list.

The following sections will help you to understand how the NMP works and the different storage types supported in a vSphere environment.

NMP

The NMP has two sub-plugins known as the **Storage Array Type Plugin** (**SATP**) and **Path Selection Plugin** (**PSP**). VMware includes the SATP and PSP associations for all tested and supported storage arrays in the form of claim rules. The SATP detects the path state and handles path failover, whereas PSP determines which available physical path should be used to send the I/O.

VMware NMP uses both the SATP and PSP to maintain access to the storage devices presented to the ESXi host. Let's review what happens during an I/O operation, as handled by NMP:

- When an I/O is issued to a storage device, the NMP will instruct the PSP corresponding to the LUN to place the I/O on a path based on the policy (**Most Recently Used (MRU)/Fixed/Round Robin (RR)**) chosen.
- If, for some reason, the I/O operation fails to complete, then it is reported back to the NMP.
- The NMP, in turn, instructs the SATP to determine the cause of the failure and take appropriate action.
- If the I/O had failed due to a path failure, then the SATP will mark that path as dead and make another path active.
- The NMP will then call the PSP again to retry the I/O.
- This time, the PSP can choose to use the new active path.

VMware supports the following PSPs:

- **Most Recently Used (MRU)**: In the event of a path failover, this would continue to use the path even if the original path becomes accessible again. Its initial path selection happens during the bootup of ESXi, where it selects the first path it discovers as the active path. MRU is the preferred PSP for active/passive arrays and **Asymmetric Logical Unit Access** (**ALUA**)-based arrays.
- **Fixed**: One of the multiple paths is marked as the preferred path. So, in the event of a preferred path becoming accessible again, it will fail back to the preferred path. This is most commonly used with active/active arrays and ALUA-based arrays.
- **Round Robin (RR)**: This distributes I/O to all the active paths. By default, it distributes 1,000 I/O operations on an active path before it sends the next 1,000 I/Os down the next active path.

Multipathing – array types

It is also important to understand different array types from the multipathing perspective. The array type is determined by the mode in which it operates. There are three such types from a multipathing perspective:

- Active/active arrays
- Active/passive arrays
- ALUA arrays

Active/active arrays

An **active/active** or **symmetric active/active** array will have all the ports on its storage controllers configured to in order to allow simultaneous processing of the I/O, thereby offering the same levels of performance and access to all LUNs. Hence, they essentially support the simultaneous ownership of a LUN by more than one storage processor. There is no concept of a standby controller on an active/active array:

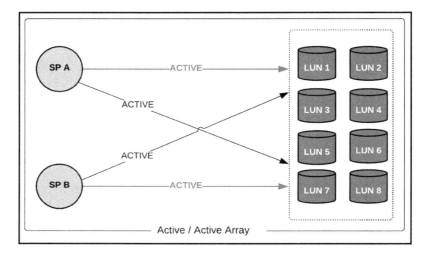

> When configuring multipathing to storage presented from such an array, you choose the different preferred paths on different sets of ESXi hosts in a cluster/data center.

For instance, if you have an eight-host cluster, then you could set four hosts to use a preferred path via Storage Controller-A, and the remaining four hosts to use a preferred path via Storage Controller-B. This is done to achieve I/O load distribution across controllers.

Active/passive arrays

Active/passive arrays have active and standby storage controllers. A controller is referred to as active or passive in relation to the LUNs they own. An active/passive array supports only one storage processor owning a particular LUN.

In an active/passive array, an I/O to a set of LUNs can only be processed by a storage controller that owns them. The controller that owns a set of LUNs is referred to as an active controller for those LUNs. The very same controller can act as a standby controller for another set of LUNs. Hence, during failover, the standby controller can assume ownership of the LUNs corresponding to the failed controller, thereby becoming the new active controller for those LUNs. The following diagram illustrates the Active/Passive Array:

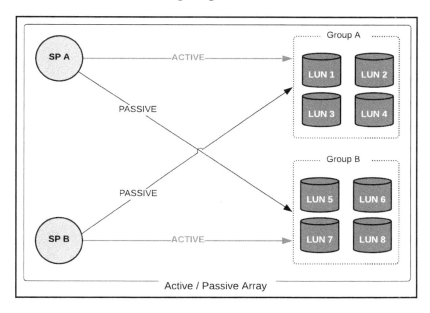

In this example, there are two LUN groups, **Group A** and **Group B**, on an Active/Passive Array with the storage controllers SP A and SP B:

- SP A has been configured to own LUNs from Group A, and SP B has been configured to own LUNs from Group B.
- SP A becomes an Active controller, and SP B becomes a Passive controller, for LUNs in Group A.
- SP B becomes an Active controller, and SP A becomes a Passive controller, for LUNs in Group B.

When designing an environment with active/passive arrays, ensure that all ESXi hosts are configured to see the LUNs via their *owning* controllers. A misconfiguration will cause the array to trespass the LUN ownership, which may lead to *path thrashing*.

Asymmetric Logical Unit Access (ALUA) Arrays

The ALUA array is a type of *active/active* array, which can concurrently use all its controllers to process I/O and also stand in as failover partners of each other.

Much like in an *active/passive* array, a LUN, or a set of LUNs, can only be owned by a single controller. The owning controller will have symmetric (direct) access to the LUN, hence offering the best performance. The non-owning controller can process the I/O indirectly (asymmetric) for the LUN by transferring the I/O via the interconnect to the owning controller. Hence, there is a performance hit owing to the time required to transfer the I/O to the owning controller via the interconnect.

Since the array presents a way to—optimally and suboptimally—the process I/O for the LUNs, there has to be a way to let ESXi know about the direct and indirect (via interconnect) paths to the LUN. This is achieved by an array feature called **Target Port Groups** (**TPGS**). TPGS is a method to group direct and indirect paths to a LUN separately. ESXi sees them as active (optimized) and active (non-optimized) paths to the LUN. The active (non-optimized) storage controller ports could be active (optimized) ports for another set of LUNs. ESXi will always place I/O on the active (optimized) paths.

The storage administrator should evenly distribute the LUNs among the controllers as necessary to achieve effective utilization of an ALUA array, as shown in the following diagram.

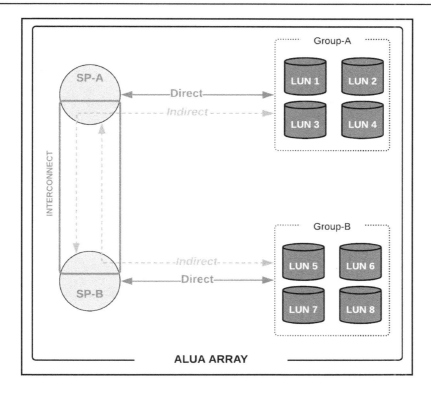

If you were to have an array configured as shown in the preceding diagram, then an I/O for **Group A**, if issued via the **SP B** controller, would result in SP B passing the traffic via the interconnect to controller SP A, which would then process the I/O. This alternative path will be referred to as an **active non-optimized** path.

Expanding or growing a VMFS datastore

As you deploy more and more VMs in your environment, you can run into a situation wherein the amount of free space in a datastore may not be sufficient for daily operations, such as backups, which involve taking snapshots. Free space can be added to the VMFS datastore if the storage device backing the VMFS volume can be increased in size as well. Alternatively, you could use another LUN to extend the VMFS volume onto it. The procedure to extend the datastore will be covered in the next recipe, *Extending a VMFS Datastore*.

The decision to choose either method would depend on whether or not the storage administrator can increase the size of the LUN device backing the VMFS volume.

The procedure to resize/expand the LUN in the storage array differs from vendor to vendor, and, as this is beyond the scope of this book, we assume that the LUN either has free space on it or has already been expanded.

The following flowchart provides a high-level overview of the procedure:

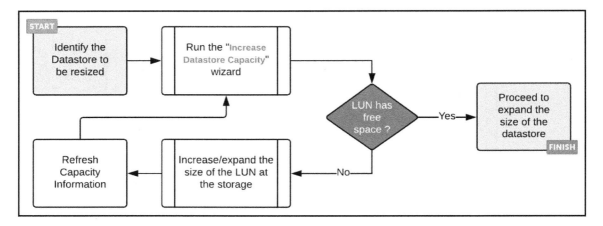

How to do it...

The following procedure will help you to expand the size of a datastore by using the free space on the backing storage device:

1. Connect to vCenter Server using the HTML5 client.
2. Select the desired datastore from the **Storage** inventory, and then navigate to its **Configure** tab in order to identify the LUN device backing the VMFS volume:

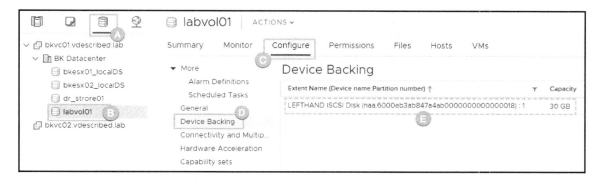

3. Contact your storage administrator to increase the size of the LUN device backing the datastore that you are about to expand.

4. Now, right-click on the datastore again and click on **Increase Datastore Capacity...**:

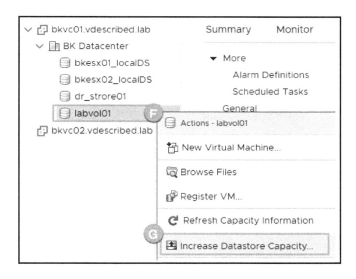

5. Select the LUN device that corresponds to the datastore and click **Next** to continue:

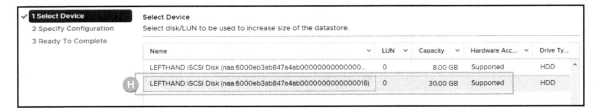

6. The **Specify Configuration** screen will show the amount of free space on the LUN. There is no need to make any changes on this screen. Click **Next** to continue:

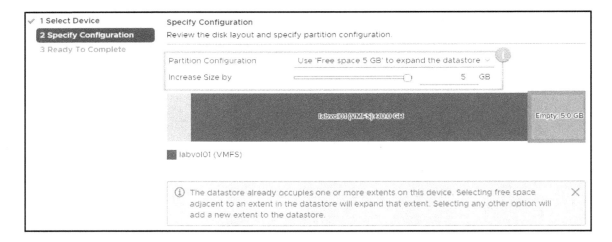

7. On the **Ready To Complete** screen, review the summary and click **Finish**:

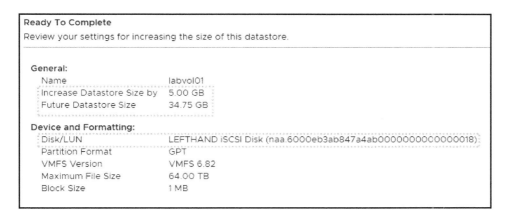

8. You should see related tasks complete successfully in the **Recent Tasks** pane:

This completes the process of increasing/expanding the size of a datastore by utilizing existing or newly created free capacity on the LUN backing the VMFS volume.

How it works...

Expanding a VMFS datastore refers to the act of increasing its size within its own extent. This is only possible if there is free space available immediately after the extent. The maximum size of a LUN is 64 TB, so the maximum size of a VMFS volume is also 64 TB. The VMs hosted on this VMFS datastore can continue to be in the power-on state while this task is being completed.

Extending a VMFS datastore

In the *Expanding or growing a VMFS datastore* recipe, we learned about how to increase the size of a datastore by utilizing the unused space on the same LUN backing the datastore.

You can run into a situation wherein there is no unused space on the LUN that is backing the VMFS volume, and the storage administrator is unable to expand the LUN any further. Fortunately, vSphere supports the spanning of a VMFS volume onto multiple LUNs. This means you can span the VMFS volume onto a new LUN so that it can use the free space on it. This process of **spanning** a VMFS volume onto another LUN is called **extending** a VMFS datastore.

Getting ready

Before you begin,

- Present an unused LUN of the desired size to all the ESXi hosts that share the VMFS datastore.
- Make a note of the NAA ID, LUN ID, and the size of the blank LUN.
- Issue a rescan of the storage adapters on all the ESXi hosts that share the datastore.

How to do it...

The following procedure will help you to increase the size of a VMFS datastore by extending/spanning the volume onto an additional unused LUN with free capacity:

1. Connect to vCenter Server using the HTML5 client.
2. Navigate to the **Storage** inventory, right-click on the datastore again, and click on **Increase Datastore Capacity...**:

Start Increase Datastore Capacity wizard

3. On the **Increase Datastore Capacity** wizard, in the **Select Device** screen, select the device that corresponds to the details (NAA ID, LUN ID, and size) provided by the storage administrator, and then click **Next** to continue:

4. On the **Specify Configuration** screen, you can choose to specify a size lower than the free capacity, if desired. Otherwise, no changes are required on this screen. Click **Next** to continue:

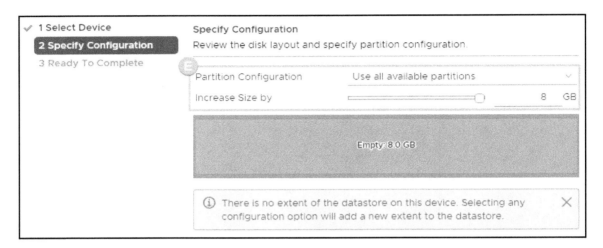

5. On the **Ready To Complete** screen, review the summary and click **Finish**:

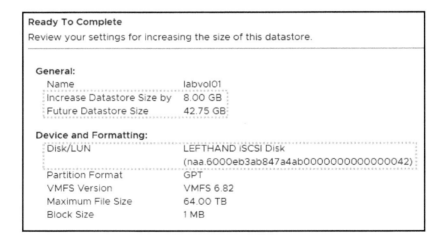

6. You should see the related tasks complete successfully in the **Recent Tasks** pane:

This completes the process of increasing the size of a datastore by extending the VMFS volume onto an additional LUN device.

How it works...

Unlike expanding/growing a VMFS volume, extending a volume will make the volume span across multiple LUNs, and this is done by adding further extents to the VMFS volume. When I say *adding further extents*, the contextual meaning refers to the primary partition on the new LUN, which will be used to extend the VMFS volume onto it.

A VMFS datastore can span across a maximum of 32 LUN extents. The size of the extent can be greater than 2 TB, with the limit being the maximum VMFS volume size of 64 TB.

The first extent on the VMFS volume contains the metadata for the entire set of extents. If the LUN with the first extent was lost, then you would end up losing data on all the other dependent extents.

Here is what an extended VMFS volume would look like. The volume was initially 4 TB in size and was backed by LUN-A, which was of the same size. The volume was then extended onto a new LUN (LUN-B), which was 2 TB in size, thus increasing the effective size on the VMFS volume to 6 TB. The following diagram illustrates extended VMFS volumes:

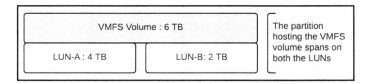

A common misconception is that if either of these LUNs (LUN-A or LUN-B) goes offline or is inaccessible, then the VMFS volume (datastore) will become inaccessible as well. This is not true. When you add extents to a datastore, the very first LUN that originally backed the datastore will become the head extent because it holds all the information regarding the other extents. If, for any reason, you lose the head extent, then that would make the entire VMFS datastore go offline. However, if you lose an extent that is not a head extent, then the datastore will still remain accessible, but only the VMs whose virtual disks depend on the lost extent will become inaccessible.

Unmounting VMFS datastores and detaching storage devices

Unmounting a datastore is done when you intend to preserve the data on a VMFS volume, but remove access to the volume. Detaching is performed on a LUN device and is performed to make sure that the access to the LUN is gracefully removed. It is recommended that you **unmount** a VMFS datastore and detach its corresponding **storage device** entry before the LUN backing the datastore is unmapped from an ESXi host.

Getting ready

Before you begin, make sure that the following steps have been performed:

- Migrate all the VMs on the datastore that you intend to unmount to another datastore.
- The datastore should be removed from a datastore cluster.
- The datastore should remain unmanaged by **Storage DRS (SDRS)**.
- The **Storage I/O Control (SIOC)** should be disabled for the datastore.
- The datastore should not be in use as a vSphere **High Availability (HA)** heartbeat datastore.

- Make a note of the NAA ID of the storage device backing the VMFS datastore. This can be done by selecting the datastore and navigating to **Configure** | **Device backing**:

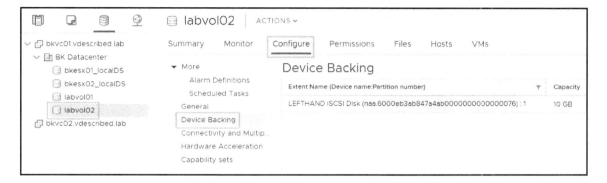

- Alternatively, you can run the `esxcli storage vmfs extent list` command to see the following list:

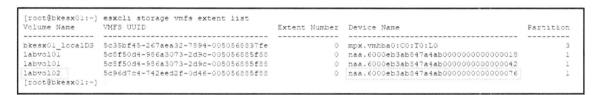

Regardless of the method used, it is important to unmount the VMFS volume from all the hosts before you detach the storage device and unpresent the LUN.

How to do it...

The following procedure will help you to unmount and detach a VMFS datastore:

1. Connect to vCenter Server using the HTML5 client and navigate to the **Storage** inventory.

2. Right-click on the desired datastore and select **Unmount Datastore...**:

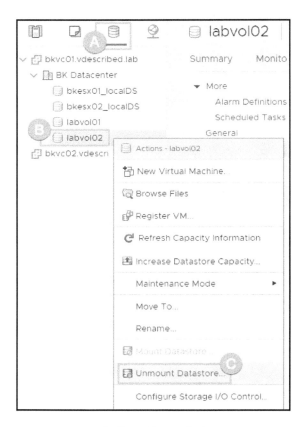

Start Unmount Datastore wizard.

3. In the **Unmount Datastore** window, select the ESXi host to unmount the datastore from and click **OK**:

4. The **Recent Tasks** pane will show the successful completion of **Unmount VMFS volume**:

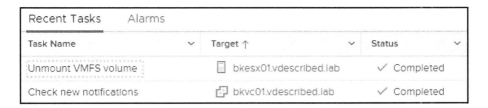

5. Once done, go to the **Configure | Storage Devices** tab of the ESXi host the datastore was unmounted from, select the device corresponding to the VMFS datastore, and then click **Detach**:

6. On the **Detach Device** window, click **YES**:

7. The **Recent Tasks** pane will show that the **Detach SCSI LUN** task has completed successfully:

8. Once done, the storage device should be listed as **Detached**:

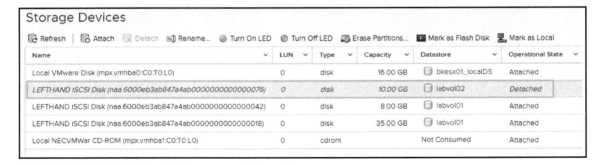

This completes the process of unmounting a datastore and detaching the storage device from the ESXi. You can now safely unmap the LUN from the ESXi host by using the array's storage management system.

How it works...

Unmounting a datastore is a way of telling the ESXi host that the LUN will no longer be available for any I/O operation until it is remounted. It is recommended to unmount a VMFS datastore before the LUN backing it is unpresented from an ESXi host.

The `esxcli` command can also be used to unmount the VMFS datastore, but keep in mind that as this is done via the command line, it is done at a per-host level. If you need to unmount the datastore this way on more than one ESXi host, then you will have to SSH/console into each of those ESXi hosts and issue the `unmount` command.

Attaching storage devices and remounting VMFS datastores

A previously detached storage device can be re-attached and the VMFS volume on it can be mounted again. If the LUN was unmapped using the storage system, then it needs to be mapped to the host before you proceed.

How to do it...

The following procedure will help you to mount a VMFS datastore from a reattached device on the ESXi host:

1. Connect to vCenter Server using the HTML5 client.
2. Go to the **Configure** | **Storage** devices tab of the ESXi host that the datastore was unmounted from.
3. Select the detached device and click **Attach**:

4. The **Recent Tasks** pane should show that an **Attach SCSI LUN** task has completed successfully:

5. Once done, switch to the **Storage** inventory, right-click on the datastore, and click on **Mount Datastore...**:

Start Mount Datastore wizard

6. The **Mount Datastore** window will only list hosts to which the datastore is not currently mounted. Use the checkbox to select the ESXi host and click **Next**:

7. The **Recent Tasks** pane should show that **Mount VMFS volume** has completed successfully:

This completes the process of attaching LUN devices to ESXi hosts and mounting the VMFS volumes on it.

How it works...

The mount operation can only be performed on a LUN device that is no longer detached. Doing so will make the VMFS datastore available for I/O operations.

Managing VMFS snapshots

A business can decide to maintain backups of their production workloads by periodically *replicating* or *snapshotting* the LUNs backing their datastores. If, for any reason, a replicated LUN or its snapshot is presented to an ESXi host, then the host will not mount the VMFS volume on the LUN. This is a precaution to prevent data corruption.

ESXi identifies each VMFS volume by using its signature denoted by a **Universally Unique Identifier** (**UUID**). The UUID is generated when the volume is first *created or resignatured* and is stored in the LVM header of the VMFS volume.

When an ESXi host scans for new storage devices, it compares the physical device ID (NAA ID) of the LUN with the device ID (NAA ID) value stored in the LVM header of the VMFS volume on the device. If it finds a mismatch, then it flags the volume as *snapshot volume*. Such volumes can be mounted by either assigning a new signature or keeping the existing signature.

Getting ready

Before you begin, ensure that the original VMFS datastore is unmounted and that the LUN backing is detached from the ESXi host that the snapshot LUN is being presented to. Also, procure the details of the LUN from the storage administrator. The details include NAA ID, LUN capacity, and LUN ID.

The following screenshot shows the NAA-IDs of both the original and snapshot LUNs:

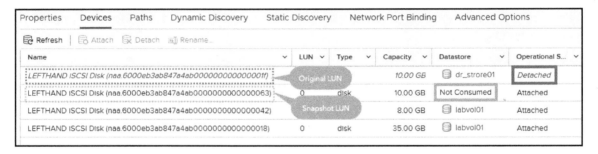

How to do it...

The following procedure will help you to mount VMFS volumes from storage devices that are detected as snapshots:

1. Connect to vCenter Server using the HTML5 client and navigate to the **Hosts and Clusters** inventory.
2. Right-click on the ESXi host to which the snapshot LUN has been mapped and go to **Storage | Rescan Storage...**:

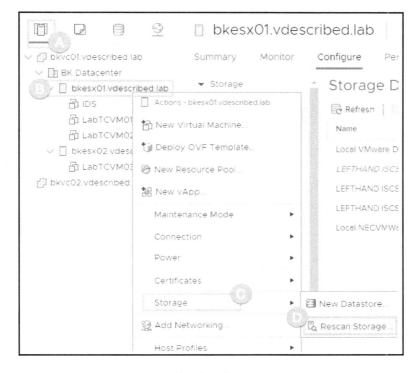

Initiate Storage Rescan

3. On the **Rescan Storage** window, click **OK**:

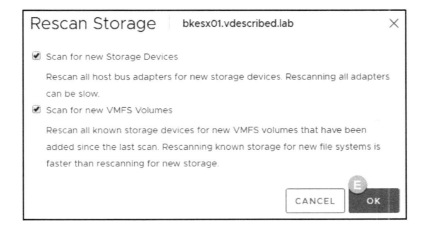

4. Right-click on the ESXi host again and go to **Storage** | **New Datastore...**:

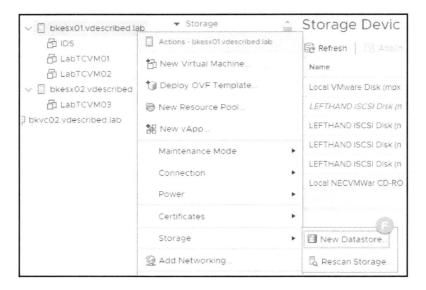

5. On the **New Datastore** wizard's **Type** screen, select the datastore type as **VMFS** and click **Next**:

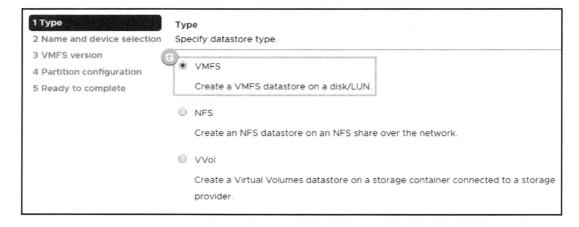

6. On the **Name and device selection** screen, select the correct storage device and click **Next**:

7. On the **Mount option** screen, choose to either **Assign a new signature** or **Keep the existing signature** and click **Next**:

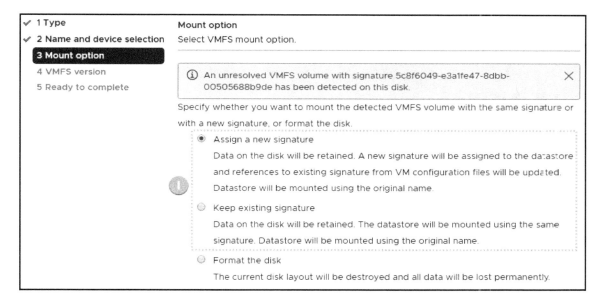

8. Select the desired **VMFS version** and click **Next** to continue:

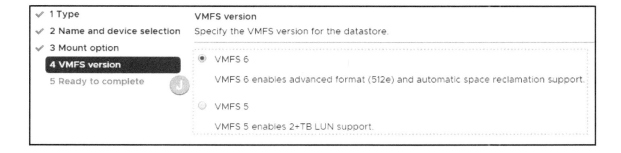

9. The **Ready To complete** screen provides a summary of the expected outcome. Review it and click **Finish**:

> **Ready to complete**
> Review your settings selections before finishing the wizard.
>
> | | |
> |---|---|
> | Type: | VMFS |
> | Disk/LUN: | LEFTHAND iSCSI Disk |
> | | (naa.6000eb3ab847a4ab0000000000000070) |
> | Mount Option: | Assign a new signature |

This completes the process of managing VMFS volumes detected as snapshots.

How it works...

VMFS volumes on storage devices detected as snapshots are not mounted by default. There are two ways to mount such volumes/datastores:

- **Mount them by keeping the existing signature intact**: This is used when you are attempting to temporarily mount the snapshot volume on an ESXi that does not see the original volume. If you were to attempt to mount the VMFS volume by keeping the existing signature, and if the host were to see the original volume, then the VMFS volume on the snapshot LUN would not be mounted.
- **Mount them by assigning a new signature**: This has to be used if you are mounting a clone or a snapshot of an existing VMFS datastore to the same host(s). The process of assigning a new signature will not only update the LVM header with the newly generated UUID, but also with the physical device ID (NAA ID) of the snapshot LUN. Here, the VMFS volume/datastore will be renamed by prefixing the word snap-, followed by a random alphanumeric string and the name of the original datastore.

7
SIOC, Storage DRS, and Profile-Driven Storage

In the previous chapter, we learned how to configure and manage access to **Fiber Channel (FC)**, **Internet Small Computer System Interface (iSCSI)**, and **Network File System (NFS)** storage devices. Once we present storage devices to the ESXi host or a cluster of ESXi hosts, the business will start using the provisioned storage by hosting **virtual machine (VM)** data on them.

As time progresses, more and more VMs are added to the mix and consume storage capacity in terms of space and throughput. Hence, it becomes important to not only fine-tune the process of placing the VMs on datastores backed by the correct type of storage tier, but to also control the space and bandwidth utilization between the VMs.

Storage I/O Control (SIOC) is one of the mechanisms to use to ensure a fair share of storage bandwidth allocation to all VMs running on shared storage, regardless of the ESXi host the VMs are running on.

Storage Distributed Resource Scheduler (Storage DRS) monitors datastore space utilization and SIOC metrics to redistribute VM files among datastores in a datastore cluster. It also provides initial placement recommendations when deploying VMs on the datastore cluster.

Storage Policy-Based Management (**SPBM**) helps a vSphere administrator to create the VM storage policies to enable the selection of datastores based on their storage characteristics, which are either user-defined or learned using a **vStorage APIs for Storage Awareness** (**VASA**) provider.

In this chapter, we will cover the following topics:

- Configuring Disk Shares on VM storage
- Enabling SIOC
- Balancing storage utilization using Storage DRS (SDRS)
- Defining storage capabilities using vCenter Tags
- Creating VM storage policies

Configuring Disk Shares on VM storage

Setting custom disk shares is particularly useful when you want to make sure that a VM receives a larger chunk of the disk bandwidth during contention for storage I/O bandwidth. By default, the disk share is set to **Normal** (**1000**). The other presets available to set custom shares are **Low** (**500**) and **High** (**2000**). In this recipe, we will learn how to configure disk shares on **Virtual Machine Disks** (**VMDKs**).

How to do it...

The following procedure will help you to configure/modify disk shares on a VMDK:

1. Connect to vCenter Server using the HTML5 client.

2. Right-click on the desired VM and go to **Edit Settings...**:

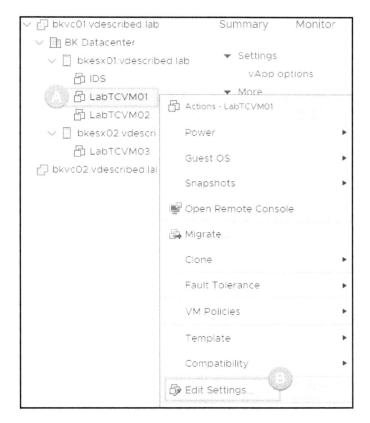

Bring-up Edit Settings screen

3. In the **Edit Settings** window, expand the desired **Hard disk 1** and use the **Shares** setting to set a share value equal to **Low** (**500**), **Normal** (**1000**), or **High** (**2000**), or set a **Custom** share value. Once done, click **OK** to save the settings:

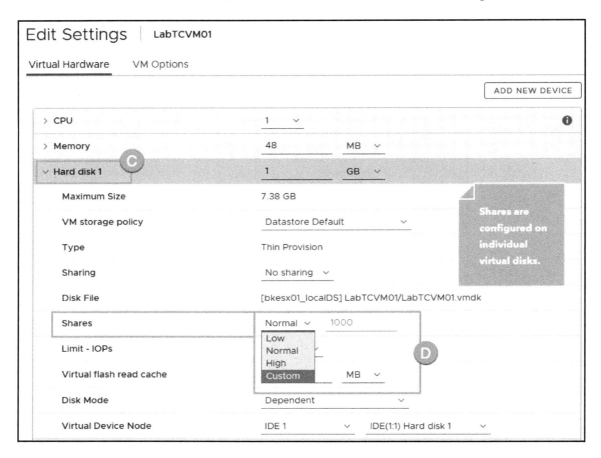

How it works...

Every ESXi host runs a *local scheduler* to monitor and balance the I/O between the VMs.

If there are VMs generating a considerable amount of I/O (more than normal), then it is important to ensure that the other VMs running on the same datastore remain unaffected, in that they should be allowed to issue I/O to the device with the expected performance. This can be achieved by setting per-disk (VMDK) shares, thereby controlling the volume of I/O that each participating VM can generate during contention.

Disk shares work pretty much like the CPU/memory shares and kick in only during contention:

- The default virtual disk share value is 1,000, with high being 2,000 and low being 500.
- The disk with a relatively higher share value will get to issue a larger volume of I/O to the device.

 SIOC will take into account the custom share value when throttling the VMkernel device queue.

Enabling SIOC

The use of disk shares will work just fine as long as the datastore is seen by a single ESXi host. Unfortunately, that is not a common case. Datastores are often shared among multiple ESXi hosts. When datastores are shared, you bring more than one localhost scheduler into the process of balancing the I/O among the VMs. However, these lost host schedulers cannot talk to each other and their visibility is limited to the ESXi hosts they are running on. This easily contributes to a serious problem called the *noisy neighbor situation*.

In the following example, since **VM-C** is the only VM on **ESX-02**, it gets to consume the entire queue depth, which could starve VMs on the other two hosts. If VM-C does indeed do a lot of I/O consuming of the **LUN's queue depth**, then it will be referred to as a noisy neighbor:

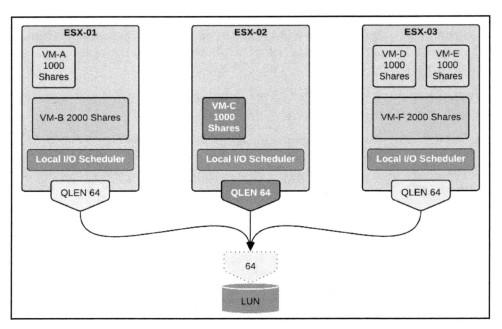

The job of SIOC is to enable some form of communication between localhost schedulers so that I/O can be balanced between VMs running on separate hosts. We will learn more about how SIOC betters the situation in the *How it works...* section of this recipe. But before that, we will learn how to enable SIOC.

Getting ready

Before you begin, it is important to understand the following prerequisites:

- SIOC cannot be enabled on datastores with multiple extents.
- The datastore should only be managed by a single vCenter. This means that were you to share the datastore across host clusters managed by different vCenters, then enabling SIOC on such a datastore would not be supported.
- If your array supports storage tiering, consult your storage vendor before enabling SIOC on your datastores.

How to do it...

The following procedure will help you to enable SIOC on a datastore:

1. Connect to vCenter Server using the HTML5 client and go to the storage inventory.
2. Right-click on the desired datastore and click on **Configure Storage I/O Control...**:

Bring-up SIOC configuration screen.

3. On the **Configure Storage I/O Control** screen, check **Enable Storage I/O Control and statistics collection**. Review the **Congestion Threshold** value and ensure that it is ideal for your environment. By default, SIOC dynamically sets the latency value learned while the datastore is operating a peak throughput of 90%. The I/O statistics collected will be for Storage DRS by default. This can be changed by unchecking the **Include I/O statistics for SDRS** checkbox:

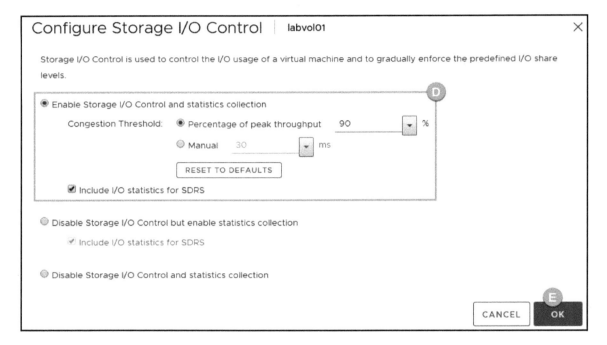

4. Once done, navigate to the datastore's **Configure** | **General** | **Datastore Capabilities** page to confirm:

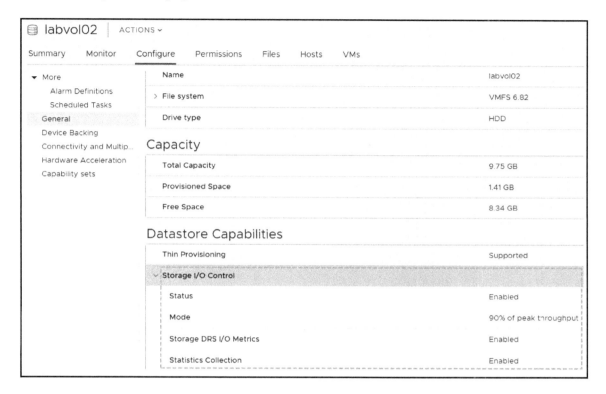

This completes the process of enabling SIOC on a datastore.

How it works...

SIOC enables communication between the localhost schedulers so that I/O can be balanced between VMs running on separate hosts. It does so by maintaining a shared `iostats` file in the datastore that all hosts can read/write/update.

The local scheduler on each of the ESXi hosts maintains an `iostats` file to keep its companion hosts aware of the device I/O statistics observed on the LUN. The file is placed in a directory (`naa.xxxxxxxxx`) on the same datastore:

When SIOC is enabled on a datastore, it starts monitoring the device latency on the LUN backing the datastore. If the latency crosses the threshold, it throttles the LUN's queue depth on each of the ESXi hosts in an attempt to distribute a fair share of access to the LUN for all of the VMs issuing the I/O operations.

Let's review the scenario introduced at the beginning of this recipe and see how SIOC helps to resolve a noisy neighbor situation.

As per the scenario, there are *six* VMs running on *three* different ESXi hosts, accessing a shared LUN. Among the 6 VMs, four of them have a normal share value of 1,000 and the remaining 2 have high (2,000) disk share value set on them. These VMs have only a single VMDK attached to them.

VM-C on host **ESX-02** is issuing a large number of I/O operations. Since that is the only VM accessing the shared LUN from that host, it gets the entire queue's bandwidth. This can induce latency on the I/O operations performed by the other VMs: **ESX-01** and **ESX-03**. If SIOC detects that the latency value is greater than the dynamic threshold, then it will start throttling the queue depth.

The following table will help you to understand how the fair share percentage is calculated by SIOC:

Hosts	ESX-01		ESX-02	ESX-03			How to arrive at the ratio (portion value) ?	
VMs	VM-A	VM-B	VM-C	VM-D	VM-E	VM-F		
Disk Shares	1000	2000	1000	1000	1000	2000	Ratio	(VM Share Value) / (Total Share Value)
VM's portion of the shares	1/8	1/4	1/8	1/4	1/8	1/8	1/8	1000/8000
							1/4	2000/8000
VM's Percent of Shares	12.5	25	12.5	25	12.5	12.5		
DQLEN for the VM	8	16	8	16	8	8		
DQLEN for the Host	24		8	32				

The throttled DQLEN for a VM is calculated as follows:

DQLEN for the VM = (VM's Percent of Shares) of (Queue Depth)

See the following example of this:

*12.5 % of 64 -> (12.5 * 64)/100 = 8.*

The throttled DQLEN per host is calculated as follows:

DQLEN of the Host = Sum of the DQLEN of the VMs on it

See the following example of this:

VM-A (8) + VM-B(16) = 24.

The following diagram shows the effect of SIOC throttling the queue depth:

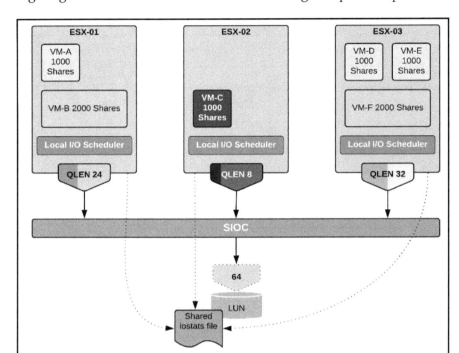

Balancing storage utilization using Storage DRS (SDRS)

Storage DRS is a mechanism to balance Space Utilization and I/O load across Datastores in a *Datastore Cluster. The balancing is achieved by* migrating Virtual Machines between datastores using Storage vMotion.

Storage DRS can only be enabled on a datastore cluster.

Datastores (VMFS/NFS) can be grouped to form a datastore cluster. Storage DRS monitors the datastore space utilization and SIOC metrics to redistribute VM files among datastores in a datastore cluster. It also provides initial placement recommendations when deploying VMs into the datastore cluster.

In this recipe, we will learn how to create a datastore cluster and enable Storage DRS on it.

Getting ready

Before you begin, it is essential to understand the following requirements:

- The datastores in a datastore cluster should only be accessible to ESXi hosts from a single datacenter (vCenter datacenter inventory object).
- A datastore cluster cannot contain both VMFS and NFS datastores.

For Storage DRS FAQs, check out the *VMware Knowledge Base article* 2149938 at `https://kb.vmware.com/kb/2149938`.

How to do it...

The following procedure will help you to create a datastore cluster with SDRS enabled on it:

1. Connect to vCenter Server using the HTML5 client and go to the storage inventory.

2. Right-click on the datacenter object and go to **Storage** | **New Datastore Cluster...**:

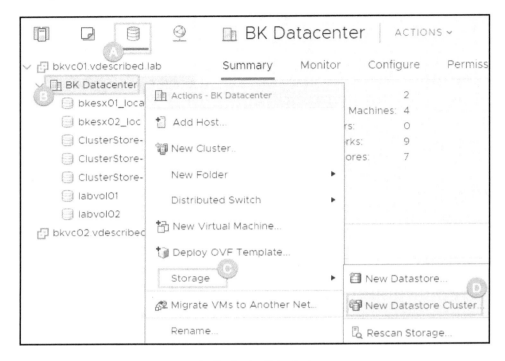

Start New Datastore Cluster wizard.

3. In the **New Datastore Cluster** wizard's **Name and Location** screen, specify a name for the datastore cluster, ensure that the **Turn ON Storage DRS** is selected, and click **Next** to continue:

4. On the **Storage DRS Automation** screen, configure the desired automation levels. There are two automation levels:

   - **No Automation (Manual Mode)**
   - **Fully Automated** (this is the default mode)

   You can also configure space, I/O balance, affinity rules' enforcement, storage/VM policy enforcement, and VM evacuation automation levels. By default, all of these parameters inherit the automation level configured on the cluster:

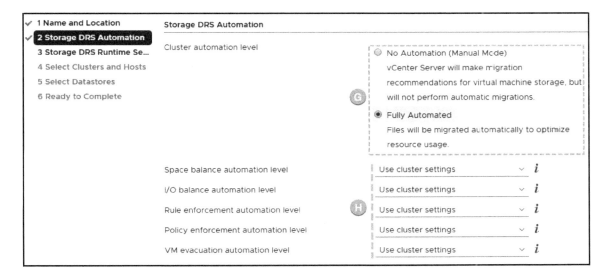

5. On the **Storage DRS Runtime Settings** screen, specify whether or not the I/O metric is used for SDRS recommendations. The default threshold is 15 milliseconds. Also, specify the space utilization threshold based on a usage percentile (this is the default method) or a minimum amount of free space:

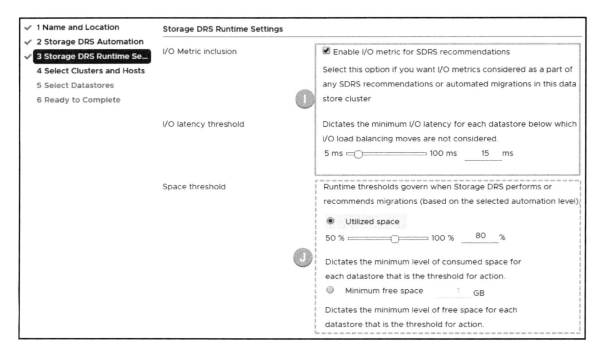

6. On the **Select Clusters and Hosts** screen, choose the desired hosts and click **Next** to continue:

7. On the **Select Datastores** screen, select all of the datastores to be included in the datastore cluster and click **Next** to continue:

8. On the **Ready to Complete** screen, review the summary of the cluster configuration and click **Finish**:

9. The **Recent Tasks** pane should show the related tasks complete successfully:

This completes the process of enabling Storage DRS on a datastore cluster.

How it works...

Once Storage DRS is enabled, it runs periodically every 8 hours and generates storage migration recommendations based on the space utilization and latency thresholds. It operates based on the **Runtime Settings** configured. The runtime setting determined whether or not to consider I/O metrics when generating recommendations, the I/O latency and Space threshold.

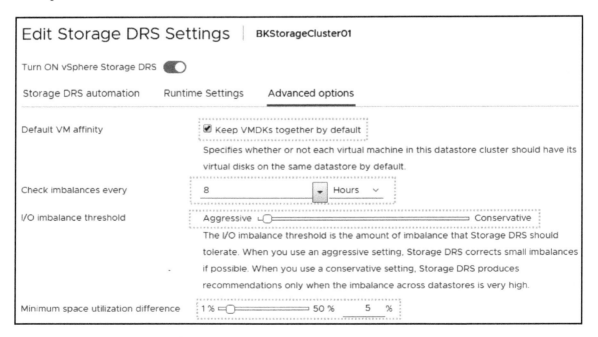

When you deploy a VM onto a datastore cluster with SDRS enabled, SDRS will provide placement recommendations based on the space utilization and I/O load on the datastores. This reduces the complexity in decision-making when you have a large number of datastores in the environment, and of course, they must be part of a datastore cluster for this to work.

SDRS provides placement recommendations and chooses one of the recommended datastores. However, the user can opt to select another recommended datastore. Although I/O load balancing can be disabled, the SDRS will still have access to the I/O statistics of the datastores. If SDRS finds more than one datastore suitable to place the VM, then it will choose the datastore with the lowest I/O load.

Without Storage DRS, it is quite possible that, over time, as you deploy more and more VMs, you end up saturating the free space on a particular set of datastores while leaving a few other datastores underutilized. This could eventually cause *out-of-space* conditions, affecting the VMs running on those datastores.

With Storage DRS enabled on a datastore cluster, the space utilization on the datastores and the growth rate of the VMDKs (if thinly provisioned) are monitored. The default threshold for space utilization is 80 percent. Storage DRS will start generating Storage vMotion recommendations when this threshold is exceeded. However, when doing so, it considers the **Minimum space utilization difference** percentile configured in the Advanced Options on the cluster. The default value is set to 5% - meaning if the difference in space utilization between two database does not exceed 5% then SDRS will not generate migration recommendations for moving VM data between those two datastores.

The I/O load on a datastore is measured based on the current I/O latency, as seen by the VMs running on the given datastore. The default threshold for the latency is 15 milliseconds (15,000 microseconds). If I/O load balancing is enabled, then the I/O latency statistics are evaluated every eight hours. SDRS uses 16 hours' worth of data to generate Storage vMotion recommendations. The migrations based on I/O load imbalance occur only once a day.

 By default, when generating SDRS recommendations, the virtual disks corresponding to a VM are always kept together.

Here are some of the configurable **Advanced options**, changed by editing the datastore cluster settings:

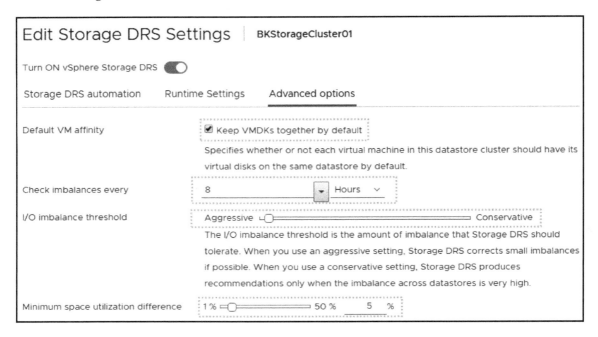

Since all of the advanced options are self-explanatory, we will not be discussing them separately in this recipe.

Defining storage capabilities using vCenter Tags

The **Storage Policy-Based Management** (SPBM) helps a vSphere administrator to create VM storage policies to enable the selection of datastores based on their storage characteristics, which are either user-defined or learned using a VASA provider.

If you have a VASA-capable array, then you can add a VASA provider to vCenter Server so that it can generate array capabilities for each LUN or datastore. A capability generated by the provider is called a system storage capability.

Refer to the storage vendor's documentation for instructions on how to configure vCenter to connect with the VASA provider.

Since configuring a VASA provider is beyond the scope of this book, we will concentrate on defining storage capabilities using vCenter tags.

How to do it...

The following procedure will help you to define storage capabilities using vCenter tags:

1. Connect to vCenter Server using the HTML5 client and go to **Menu** | **Tags Custom Attributes**:

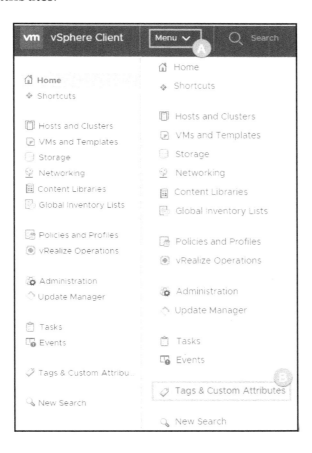

We will create four tags—Gold, Silver, Bronze, and Local Storage—and then associate them with the datastores.

2. On the **Tags & Customer Attributes** page, go to **Categories** and click on + to create a category:

3. Use the **Add Category** window to create a **Storage Tiers** category, with **Tags Per Object** set to **One tag**, and allow associations with **Datastores** and **Datastore Clusters**:

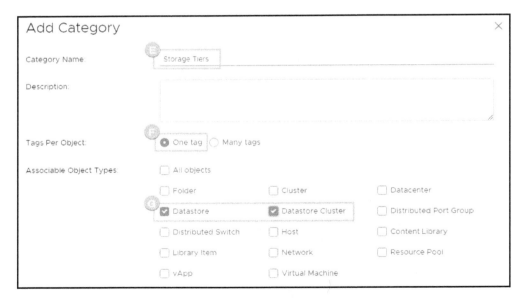

4. On the **Tags & Customer Attributes** page, go to **Tags** and click on + to create tags:

5. In the **Add Tag** window, specify a **Name**, a **Description**, and a **Category** for the new tag. Each tag should be associated with a category. Hence, if there are no desired categories available to choose from, a new category should be created using *steps 2* and *3*:

6. Use *step 5* to create additional tags if necessary. In this case, we will be creating Gold Tier, Silver Tier, and Bronze Tier tags:

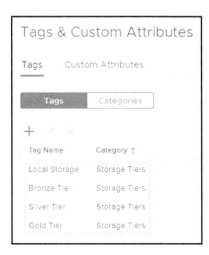

Now that we have created our tags, we associate them with a datastore/datastore clusters:

1. Right-click on a datastore/datastore cluster and go to **Tags & Custom Attributes | Assign Tag...**:

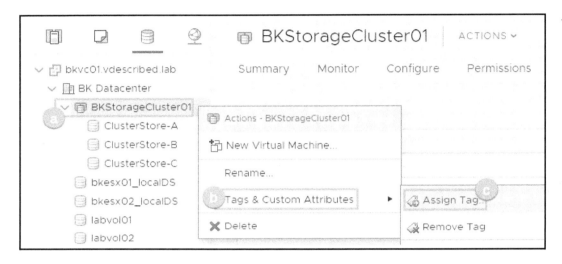

2. Select a tag from the **Assign Tag** window to be associated with the datastore/datastore cluster:

This completes the process of defining storage capabilities using vCenter tags and associating them with datastores.

How it works...

As our virtual datacenters continue to host diverse VM workloads, it becomes important to segregate, isolate, and allocate storage resources to optimize performance and reliability. To achieve this, the VMs should be placed on the datastores with the relevant characteristics to aid in the optimal functioning of these workloads. Unfortunately, most VMware administrators wouldn't necessarily have visibility of the underlying storage characteristics, largely because, in most organizations, a different team manages the storage. A VMware administrator would generally request for a LUN of a particular size, then the storage administrator carves a LUN from an available storage pool and presents it to the ESXi host. This would mean that the administrator would only be able to distribute the workloads across multiple datastores based on space utilization.

So, how can the administrator get around this problem? There are three ways:

- Use a worksheet, or any form of record-keeping method, to maintain a list of all of the LUNs presented to the ESXi hosts and their storage characteristics. The storage characteristics information has to be collected from the storage team.
- If the array is capable of VMware VASA, then a VASA provider from the storage vendor can be deployed and configured to fetch the storage characteristics.
- If VASA is not configured, then we could use vCenter's tagging mechanism to create and associate tags with datastores. The tags are *user-defined* and can have any name and category. The tags can then be included in a storage policy to aid in the placement of VMs on them.

Creating VM Storage Policies

VM Storage Policies will allow an administrator to group datastores under policies based on the datastore's capability. These capabilities can be related to capacity, performance, or redundancy characteristics. The capabilities can either be learned via VASA if the storage array supports the API, or via user-defined capability tags.

For example, if you have categorized your storage into different tiers based on their performance characteristics, then you can create VM storage policies for easier decision-making when creating or migrating VMs.

In this recipe, we will learn how to create VM storage policies using the user-defined vCenter tag-based storage capabilities.

Getting ready

Before you begin, you will need storage capabilities; either user-defined using vCenter tags, or learned via a VASA provider. Also, most importantly, using storage profiles requires the *vSphere Enterprise Plus* license.

How to do it...

The following procedure will help you to create VM storage policies:

1. Connect to vCenter Server using the HTML5 client.
2. Go to the **Shortcuts** inventory and click on **VM Storage Policies**:

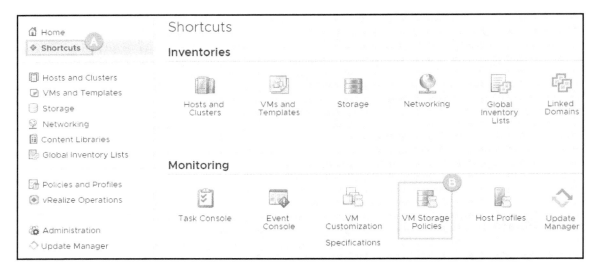

3. On the **VM Storage Policies** page, click on **Create VM Storage Policy**:

4. In the **Create VM Storage Policy** screen, select the vCenter server on which the policy is being created and supply a name and an optional description for the policy:

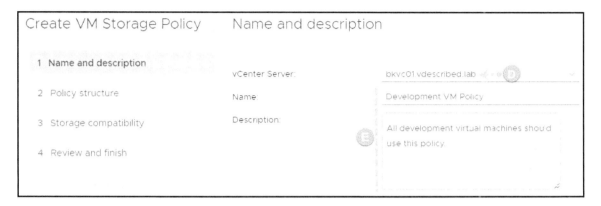

5. On the **Policy structure** screen, select **Enable tag-based placement rules** and click **Next** to continue:

6. On the **Tab based placement** screen, do the following:
   - Select the desired **Tag category.**
   - Set the **Usage option** to **Use storage tagged with.**
   - Browse and select the desired tag:

7. The **Storage compatibility** screen should now list all tag-compatible datastore/datastore clusters. Click **Next** to continue:

8. On the **Review and finish** screen, review the summary and click **Finish**:

This completes the process of creating VM storage policies.

How it works...

Once VM storage policies are assigned to a VM and its VMDKs, its profile compliance status will remain non-compliant unless they are moved to a datastore matching the VM storage policy. The VM can be moved using the migration wizard. In the migration wizard, the intended VM storage policy can be selected to list the compliant datastores so that the VM and its files can be moved to one of them.

Once created, VM storage policies can also be used to filter and choose the desired datastore during various VMDK placement scenarios. For instance, if you were to create a new VM, then you can choose to place its VMDKs on a datastore that matches the VM storage policy. The following screenshot shows the datastore list being filtered based on the VMware storage policy selected:

VM storage policies can also be applied to existing VMs and remediated for compliance.

With VM storage policies, every storage characteristic will have an impact on either the performance or reliability a LUN can offer. Before we proceed further, it is important to know what some of these storage characteristics could be and what role they play in decision-making regarding the placement of the VMs. Here is a common list of storage characteristics and their impact on performance and reliability:

Characteristics	Performance	Reliability
RAID level	Yes	Yes
Underlying disk technology	Yes	Yes
Spindle speed	Yes	No
Capacity	No	No
Storage tiers	Yes	Yes

In vSphere terms, these characteristics are referred to as storage capabilities, which can either be system-learned (via VASA) or user-defined. Regardless of whether they are learned or defined, there should be a way to associate the VMs with the datastores that have the desired capability. Such an association is created using **VM storage policies**. Once the policies are defined, the VM disks can then be associated with these policies. This will allow vSphere to make VM placement decisions.

8
Configuring vSphere DRS, DPM, and VMware EVC

vSphere **Distributed Resource Scheduler** (**DRS**) is probably the most underrated VMware technology. It is enabled/configured on a cluster of ESXi hosts. An ESXi cluster is a vCenter functionality that allows you to pool the compute resources (CPU and memory) from more than one ESXi host under a single manageable resource-umbrella. Compute resources are not contiguous beyond the physical boundaries of the hosts. Therefore pooling compute resources allow for the efficient placement of Virtual Machine workloads across ESXi hosts to ensure optimal resource utilization within the cluster.

During the lifecycle of the cluster, DRS periodically monitors the cluster's utilization and redistributes the VMs within the cluster. This is done to ensure that no single ESXi host in the cluster is overburdened with the resource demands of the VMs. Doing so, in turn, guarantees that the VMs themselves get the resources they need.

In this chapter, we will cover the following recipes:

- Enabling vSphere DRS on a cluster
- Changing the default DRS behavior
- Configuring VM Automation
- Creating DRS Groups
- Creating DRS VMs to Host Affinity Rules
- Creating DRS inter-VM Affinity Rules
- Configuring Predictive DRS
- Configuring DPM
- Using VMware Enhanced vMotion Compatibility (EVC)

Enabling vSphere DRS on a cluster

As introduced, at the start of the chapter, vSphere DRS is enabled on a cluster of ESXi hosts. DRS uses vSphere vMotion to migrate VMs between hosts in the cluster to balance resource utilization within the cluster.

Let's go over some of the benefits of DRS:

- DRS is flexible when it comes to allowing rules/conditions to be configured by the administrator when placing VMs or reorganizing the cluster. You can create DRS host affinity rules and/or VM anti-affinity rules, which allows for the conditional placement of VMs.
- DRS is also used by vCenter when you are entering hosts into maintenance mode. When you put an ESXi host into maintenance mode, vCenter leverages DRS to migrate VMs running on the host to other suitable hosts in the cluster.
- DRS extends its capabilities to reduce the energy consumption of the cluster by evacuating underutilized hosts and powering them off with the help of **Distributed Power Management** (**DPM**).

Getting ready

DRS can only be enabled on a cluster of vMotion-enabled ESXi hosts, and so the prerequisites for vMotion have to be met for DRS to function:

- VMotion enabled VMkernel interfaces should be configured on each participating host.
- The hosts in the cluster should have CPUs with the same make and family. If they don't, you should consider enabling **Enhanced vMotion Compatibility** (**EVC**) on the cluster.
- The cluster should share storage.
- vSphere DRS is an Enterprise Plus license feature. Therefore, you need to ensure that the hosts are licensed accordingly.

How to do it...

The following procedure will help you to enable DRS on a cluster:

1. Connect to vCenter Server using the HTML5 client and go to the host and cluster inventory.

2. Select the ESXi cluster, navigate to **Configure** | **vSphere DRS**, and click **EDIT...**:

3. In the **Edit Cluster Setting** window, enable DRS and click **OK**. On this screen, you could also choose the default **Automation Level** and **Migration Threshold**, enable **Predictive DRS** (*disabled by default*), or disable **Virtual Machine Automation**, though all of this is optional:

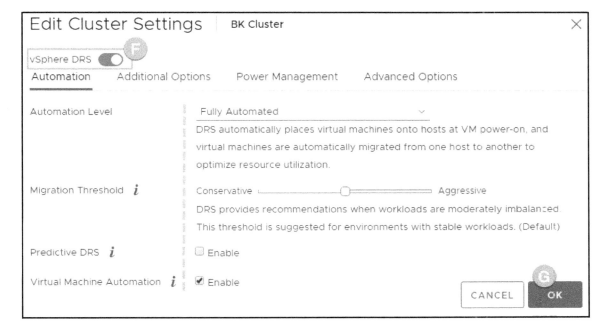

4. You should see a **Reconfigure cluster** task complete successfully in the **Recent Tasks** pane.

How it works...

DRS, once enabled, will have a holistic view of the cluster's compute resources, and so it will have the ability to migrate VMs as per their changing runtime compute workload requirements. The cluster's compute resources are aggregated under a root resource pool. It becomes the parent resource pool for administrator-created DRS resource pools.

DRS uses vMotion to migrate VMs between the hosts in order to balance the workload on the hosts.

Balancing the compute resources will ensure that the VMs in the cluster get the resources when they need it, thereby increasing service levels.

vCenter runs a DRS thread per cluster. Its job is to load balance the DRS cluster for better utilization of the cluster resources. It does so by migrating or generating migration recommendations for VMs whenever they're needed. It also provides initial placement for the VMs. Migration recommendations will be generated by vSphere DRS, but only when it identifies a resource imbalance in the cluster.

A resource imbalance is determined on a per-ESXi-host basis. It does so by considering the resource reservations for all of the VMs on the ESXi host, comparing these against the total capacity of the host, and then checking whether the host can or cannot meet the cumulative resource reservations of the VMs. The result will become a deviation metric, which is then compared against the migration threshold that's set on the cluster. DRS does this imbalance check on every ESXi host in the DRS cluster every 300 seconds (5 minutes). When DRS detects a cluster imbalance, it will check the migration threshold value that's set on the cluster. If the deviation that's calculated is more than the migration threshold, then DRS will generate a **migration recommendation**. DRS generates migration recommendations by simulating the migration of each VM on the ESXi host in order to recalculate cluster imbalance metrics. It will then choose to generate a migration recommendation for a VM whose migration would best serve in reducing the resource crunch on the ESXi host.

The behavior of vSphere DRS can be tuned by configuring an ideal automation level and a migration threshold. We will delve deeper into these in the following sections.

DRS automation levels

DRS automation levels can be configured when/after enabling DRS on a cluster.

DRS automation levels define how DRS reacts to compute resource imbalances in a cluster and whether it requires little or no manual intervention. DRS can choose to apply the generated migration and initial placement recommendations or present them on the vCenter GUI for the administrator to take action on them.

By default, DRS works in **Fully Automated** mode. You can, however, set it to **Manual** or **Partially Automated** mode:

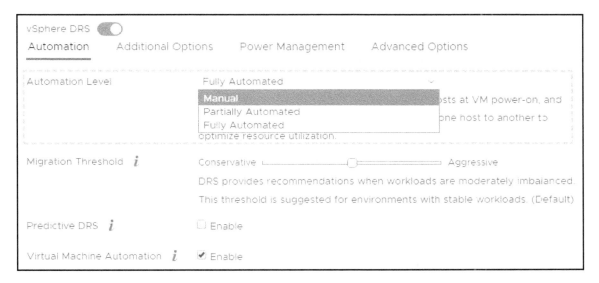

Let's describe the use of these automation levels:

- **Manual mode**: This generates and presents the initial placement and migration recommendations. This requires the administrator to action them.
- **Partially automated mode**: This generates and executes the initial placement recommendations. The migration recommendations that are generated need to be actioned by the administrator.
- **Fully automated mode**: This automatically carries out both initial placements and migrations.

If there is more than one migration recommendation, then the administrator is given a prioritized list of recommendations to choose from.

Initial placement refers to the process of choosing an ESXi host from a DRS cluster to power on or resume a VM. DRS generates these recommendations by choosing an ESXi host that has enough resources to run the VM that is being powered on or resumed.

The following table compares how migration recommendations and initial placements are dealt with, based on the DRS automation level that's been configured on the cluster:

DRS automation level	VM migrations (vMotion)	VM initial placements
Fully automated	VMs are automatically migrated.	VMs are automatically powered on or resumed on a suitable ESXi host.
Partially automated	Migration recommendations are presented. The administrator has to manually apply one of the migration recommendations.	VMs are automatically powered-on or resumed on a suitable ESXi host.
Manual	Migration recommendations are presented. The administrator has to manually apply one of the migration recommendations.	Placement recommendations are presented. The administrator has to manually apply one of the recommendations.

Migration threshold

The migration threshold can be configured when/after enabling DRS on a cluster:

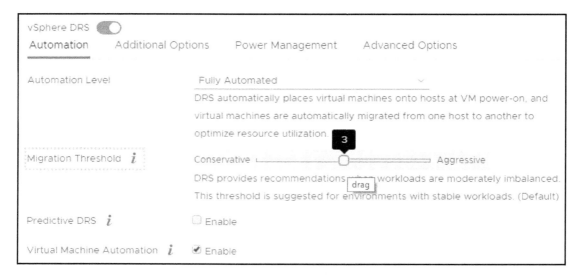

Setting migration thresholds is a way to tell DRS what priority level recommendations should be actioned or displayed. However, doing so doesn't stop DRS from working on generating recommendations.

Based on the level of compute load imbalance that's detected in a cluster, every migration recommendation that's generated by DRS will have a priority level (1-5) associated with it. But before they are displayed (if manual/partially automated) or applied (if fully automated), the priority level associated with the generated recommendation will be compared against the migration threshold set on the cluster:

- The recommendations with a priority level that is **lower** or **equal** to the migration threshold value will be applied.
- If the priority level of the recommendation is higher than the migration threshold, then it is ignored.

The following table will help you to understand how migration recommendations are applied/displayed based on their priority values:

Migration Threshold	Priority Levels of the Recommendations that will be Applied or Displayed				
	Priority 1	Priority 2	Priority 3	Priority 4	Priority 5
Level 1 - Conservative	Yes	No	No	No	No
Level 2	Yes	Yes	No	No	No
Level 3 - Default	Yes	Yes	Yes	No	No
Level 4	Yes	Yes	Yes	Yes	No
Level 5 - Aggressive	Yes	Yes	Yes	Yes	Yes

Changing the default DRS behavior

The default DRS behavior can be further altered based on what is ideal for the environment. This can be achieved via the **Additional Options** section in the DRS cluster settings.

How to do it...

The following procedure will help you further tune DRS behavior using additional options available:

1. Connect to vCenter Server using the HTML5 client and go to the host and cluster inventory.
2. Select the ESXi cluster, navigate to **Configure | vSphere DRS**, and click **EDIT...**
3. Navigate to the **Additional Options** tab and configure the available options as desired. The options available are - **VM Distribution, Memory Metric for Load Balancing** and **CPU Over-Commitment**.

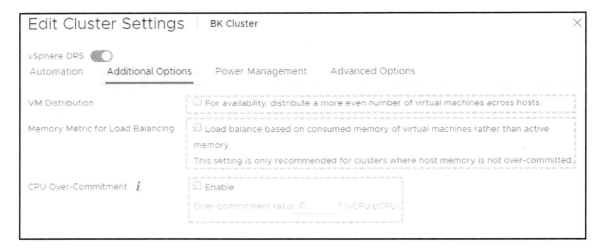

4. Once you have set the desired configuration, click **OK** to save the settings and close the window.

This completes the workflows for configuring additional DRS options.

How it works...

Once enabled, each of the additional options will have a corresponding **Configuration Parameter** under **Advanced Options**, as shown in the following screenshot:

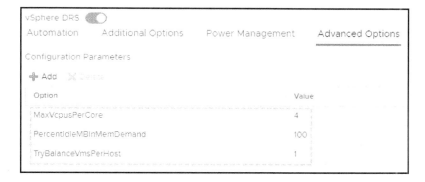

Now, let's delve a bit deeper into how each of these options impacts the DRS behavior.

VM distribution

With VM distribution enabled, DRS will attempt to evenly distribute the number of VMs onto the hosts in the cluster. This is done to ensure that, during a host failure, only a lower than usual number of VMs are affected. For instance, if there were 40 VMs in a four-host cluster, then DRS will try to distribute `40 / 4 = 10` VMs per ESXi host.

However, if an even distribution of the VMs leads to a resource imbalance in the cluster, then DRS will generate migration recommendations to mitigate that.

Once enabled, it is represented by an advanced configuration parameter: **TryBalanceVmsPerHost**, which is set to **1**.

Memory metric for load balancing

By default, DRS looks into the active memory resource utilization/demand when reviewing the cluster for a memory resource imbalance. Unfortunately, that wouldn't make any impactful difference if the cluster isn't overcommitted.

If your cluster isn't overcommitted for memory resources, then you can choose to use the consumed memory metric instead of the active memory metric for DRS calculations. The consumption metric accounts for the amount of memory the VM has used during its uptime. For instance, if an 8 GB VM had its memory utilization spike up to 7 GB since it was powered on, then 7 GB is the consumed memory. If it's currently using only 4 GB of memory, then 4 GB is the active memory.

By choosing to load balance based on the consumed memory, you are usually accounting for peak memory utilization of the VM.

Once enabled, it is represented by an advanced configuration parameter: **PercentIdleMBInMemDemand**, which is set to **100**.

CPU over-commitment

You can configure a vCPU:pCPU limit that is enforced on all ESXi hosts in the cluster. This option will come in handy if you are running CPU latency-sensitive workloads in your cluster. The over-commitment value can range from 0 to 500 vCPUs per pCPU. However, since you can only have a maximum of 32 vCPUs per core, that ratio is also limited to 32 vCPUs per pCPU.

Once enabled, it is represented by an advanced configuration parameter: **MaxVcpusPerCore**.

Configuring VM Automation

VM automation refers to the method of overriding DRS cluster automation levels for individual VMs. It is achieved by configuring VM overrides.

Getting ready

Ensure that **Virtual Machine Automation** is enabled in the DRS cluster settings:

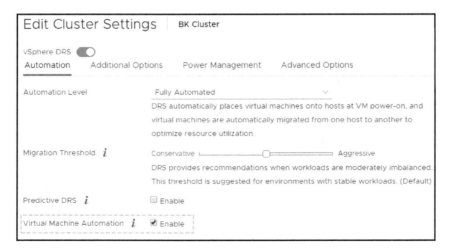

Make a list of VMs that you need to create overrides for and the desired automation levels.

How to do it...

The following procedure will help you to configure the virtual machine's automation:

1. Connect to vCenter Server using the HTML5 client.
2. Select the DRS cluster, navigate to **Configure** | **Configuration** | **VM Overrides**, and click **Add...**:

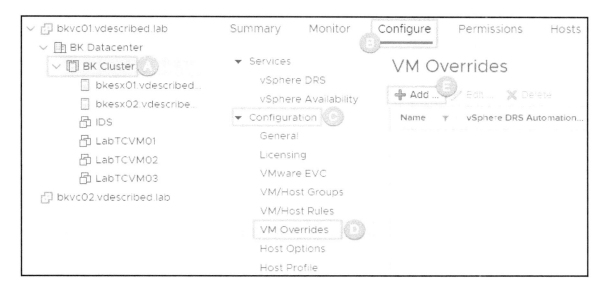

3. In the **Add VM Override** wizard, select the desired VMs and click on **Next**:

4. Enable the **Override** checkbox against the **DRS automation level** and select the desired automation level for the VMs. Once done, click **Finish**:

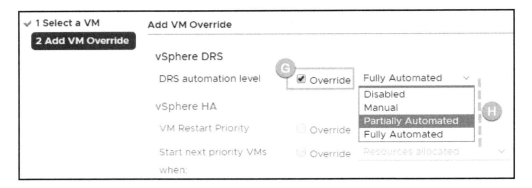

5. You should see a **Reconfigure cluster** task complete successfully in the **Recent Tasks** pane.
6. The **VM Overrides** page should now show the VMs and their configuration automation levels:

How it works...

An override that has been created for a VM will allow that VM to have an automation level that is different from the cluster-level settings. A possible use case would be the need to have more control and awareness over the initial placement and migration activities that correspond to a VM running a business-critical service or application.

For instance, you can create a VM override for a VM and set the automation level to manual. By doing this, all placement and migration recommendations that are specific to that VM will be displayed in the vCenter GUI for the administrator's approval.

Creating DRS Groups

DRS lets you define affinity rules for hosts and VMs that are managed by it. These rules affect the migration and placement recommendations that are generated by DRS. The VM-Host affinity rules, however, require the administrator to segregate ESXi hosts and VMs into DRS hosts and VM groups before the rules can be applied.

In this recipe, we will learn how to create **DRS host groups** and **DRS VM groups.**

Getting ready

Make a list of Virtual Machines and Hosts that have to be grouped and arrive at desired group naming conventions before you proceed with creating the groups.

How to do it...

The following procedure will help you to create DRS groups, which is a prerequisite for creating VM to Host affinity rules:

1. Connect to vCenter Server using the HTML5 client.
2. Select the DRS cluster, navigate to **Configure** | **Configuration** | **VM/Host Groups** and click **Add...**:

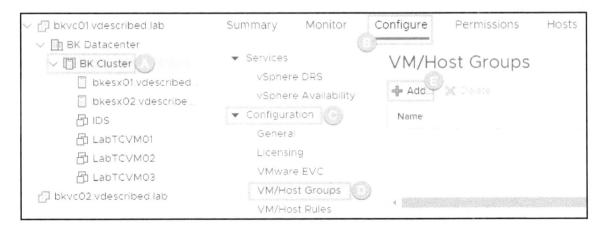

3. On the **Create VM/Host Group** window, supply a name for the group, set the **Type** to **VM Group**, and click **Add...** to add the desired VMs to the group. Once you're done, click **OK**:

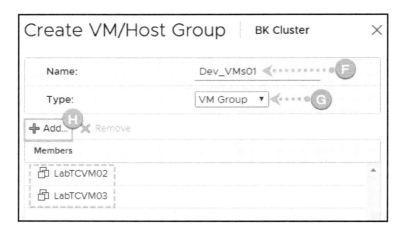

4. In the **Create VM/Host Group** window, supply a name for the group, set the **Type** to **Host Group**, and click **Add...** to add the desired ESXi hosts to the group. Once you're done, click **OK**:

5. Use *steps 3 and 4* to create additional host and VM groups, as necessary. Once you're done, the **VM/Host Groups** screen should list all of the DRS groups that were created, along with their members:

How it works...

Once the DRS groups have been created, we can create VM to host affinity rules. Read the *Creating DRS VMs to Host Affinity Rules* recipe to learn more.

The other types of DRS affinity rules are as follows:

- Inter-VM affinity rules
- Inter-VM anti-affinity rules

We will learn more about these later in this chapter.

Creating DRS VMs to Host Affinity Rules

We can create DRS affinity rules that will affect the VM migration or initial placement recommendations based on the virtual machine's affinity or anti-affinity relationship with a group of ESXi hosts.

The VM to Host affinity rules is generally used to meet specific requirements, such as licensing and access to hardware resources. For instance, let's say you have a set of VMs that need access to a directly attached tape library. Here, you can create a *Must Rule* to ensure that the VMs are always placed on the hosts that have access to the tape library.

Getting ready

The VMs to hosts DRS affinity rules cannot be applied to individual hosts or VMs. Therefore, we will need to group them into their respective types. Read the *Creating DRS groups* recipe for instructions on how to do this.

How to do it...

The following procedure will help you to create DRS VMs to host affinity rules:

1. Connect to vCenter Server using the HTML5 client.
2. Select the DRS cluster, navigate to **Configure** | **Configuration** | **VM/Host Rules**, and click **Add...**:

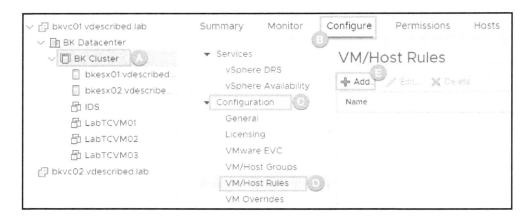

3. On the **Create VM/Host Rule** window, supply a name for the rule, set the **Type** to **Virtual Machines to Hosts**, and specify the desired rule. Once you're done, click **OK**:

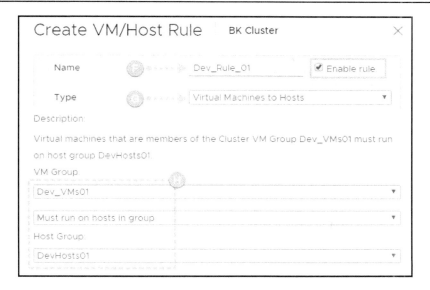

4. Use *step 3* to create additional rules if necessary. Once you're done, the **VM/Host Rules** page will list the DRS rules that have been created:

This completes the process of defining VM to host affinity rules.

How it works...

VM to host affinity rules can either indicate a preference or a requirement. The requirements are classified as *'Must Rules'*, while the preferences are classified as *'Should Rules'*:

Must Rules	Should Rules
Must run on hosts in a group	Should run in hosts in a group
Must *not run* on hosts in a group	Should *not run* on hosts in a group

'Should Rules' just state just a preference, hence the virtual machines can run on other ESXi hosts if the *'Should Rules'* cannot be met. However, *'Must Rules'* should be mandatorily satisfied. vSphere HA, DRS, and DPM will not violate the *'Must Rules'*. Hence, *'Must Rules'* should be defined very cautiously as they could even prevent vSphere HA from restarting virtual machines, thus affecting the availability of those virtual machines.

Creating DRS Inter-VM Affinity Rules

We can create DRS Inter-VM affinity rules that determine whether the VMs participating in the rule should or shouldn't run on the same ESXi hosts. DRS always tries to satisfy inter-VM affinity rules.

Getting ready

Make a list of Virtual Machines and their relationship affinities before you proceed with creating the rules.

How to do it...

The following procedure will help you configure inter-VM affinity rules:

1. Connect to the vCenter Server using the HTML5 client.
2. Select the DRS cluster, navigate to **Configure** I **Configuration** I **VM/Host Rules**, and click **Add...**:

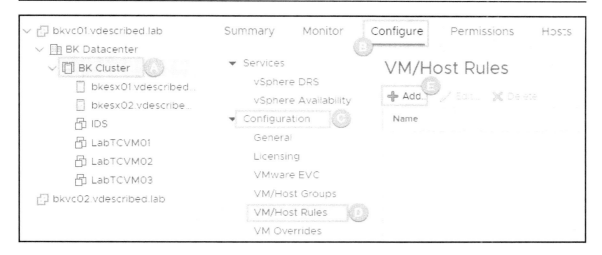

3. In the **Create VM/Host Rule** window, supply a name for the rule, choose the desired type, and click **Add...** to add the VMs to the rule. Once you're done, click **OK** to confirm:

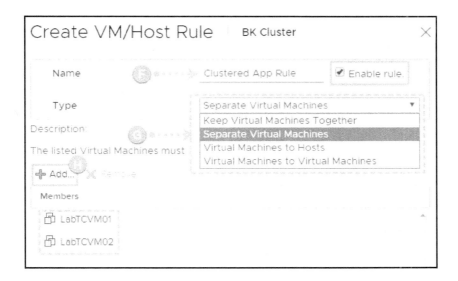

4. Once done, the **VM/Host Rules** screen should list the rule and its members:

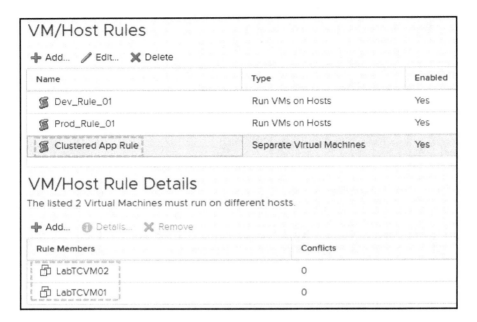

This completes the process of defining inter-VM affinity rules.

How it works...

When there is a conflict between the rules, the oldest rule takes precedence, and the others will be disabled by DRS.

There are two DRS inter-VM rules:

- **Keep VMs together**: VMs that are members of this rule will always run together on the same host.
- **Separate VMs**: VMs that are members of this rule will never be allowed to run together on the same host.

A sample use case for the inter-VM affinity rule is as follows: a two-VM application cluster requires both VMs to always run on different hosts in order to avoid cluster downtime due to a host failure.

Configuring Predictive DRS

The idea behind Predictive DRS is to use the analytics capability of vRealize Operations Manager to predict the resource demands of VMs and generate migration recommendations accordingly.

Getting ready

You will need access to vRealize Operations Manager with permissions to make changes to the vCenter adapter.

How to do it...

The procedure to configure Predictive DRS is two-phased:

- Configuring vROPS for Predictive DRS
- Enabling Predictive DRS

Configuring vROPS for Predictive DRS

The following procedure will help you to configure vROPS to send data to Predictive DRS:

1. Connect to the vROPs instance that's collecting data from the vCenter.

2. Navigate to **Administration** | **Solutions** | **VMware vSphere**, select the vCenter adapter corresponding to your vCenter, and click on the settings icon to configure the adapter settings:

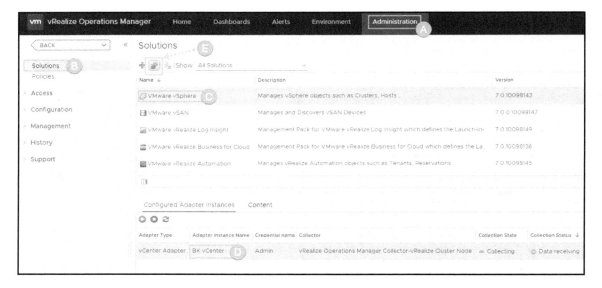

3. On the **Manage Solution – VMware vSphere** window, ensure that the correct vCenter instance is selected and click on **Advanced Settings**. Set **Provide data to vSphere Predictive DRS** to **true** and click **SAVE SETTINGS**:

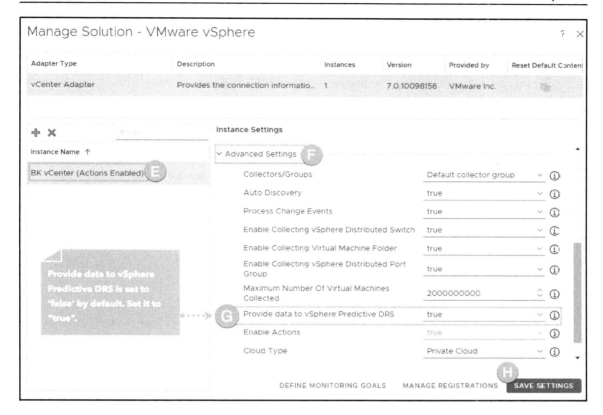

4. Click **OK** on the **Adapter instance successfully saved** message and close the **Manage Solution – VMware vSphere** window.

Now that vROPS has been configured to send data to Predictive DRS, the next step is to enable Predictive DRS on the cluster.

Enabling Predictive DRS

The following procedure will help you to enable Predictive DRS on the cluster:

1. Connect to vCenter Server using the HTML5 client.
2. Select the DRS cluster, navigate to **Configure | vSphere DRS**, and click **EDIT**...:

3. On the **Edit Cluster Settings** window, use the checkbox to enable **Predictive DRS** and click **OK**:

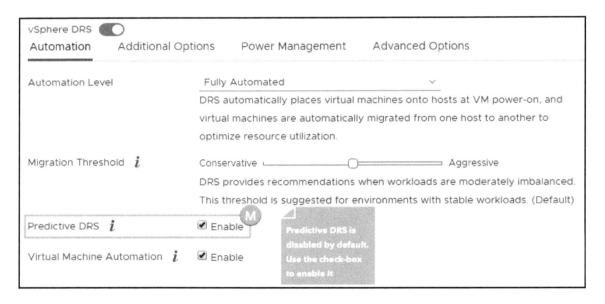

DRS should now generate predictive (proactive) migration recommendations based on the data provided by vROPS.

How it works...

Although vROPS isn't a real-time monitoring solution, it learns about the rescurce demands of the VM workloads over time. For instance, if vROPS has learned that a VM requires more CPU/memory at the start of each day, then Predictive DRS can generate migration recommendations ahead of time so that the VM is placed on a host with enough resources to satisfy the demand.

Configuring DPM

DPM is a DRS capability, and so it can only be enabled on a DRS cluster. DRS uses DPM to change the power state of underutilized ESXi hosts to reduce the energy consumption by the cluster. DPM is disabled by default. It uses the **Intelligent Platform Management Interface (IPMI)** for power management.

Getting ready

ESXi hosts that are managed by DPM should have their corresponding **Baseboard Management Controller (BMC)** settings configured correctly using **DPM Host Options**.

Cluster Host Options need to be configured with the details of the BMC card on each host. The following procedure will help you to configure host options with the details of the BMC card on each host:

1. Connect to vCenter Server using the HTML5 client.
2. Select the DRS cluster and navigate to **Configure** | **Configuration** | **Host Options**.

3. Select each ESXi host and click **Edit...**:

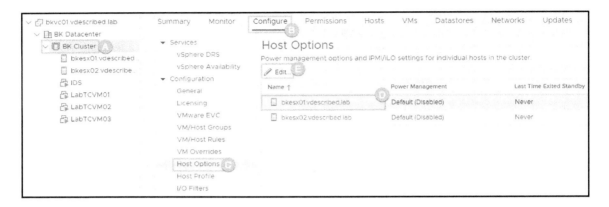

4. On the **Edit Host Options** screen, supply the BMC interface's details and click **OK**. You can choose to override the cluster's automation level if desired:

How to do it...

The following procedure will help you to enable DPM on the cluster:

1. Select the DRS cluster, navigate to **Configure** | **vSphere DRS**, and click **EDIT...** button.

2. On the **Edit Cluster Settings** window, go to **Power Management** and use the checkbox to enable DPM. Then, choose the desired **Automation Level** (**Manual/Automatic**) and **DPM Threshold**. Once you're done, click **OK** to confirm the settings:

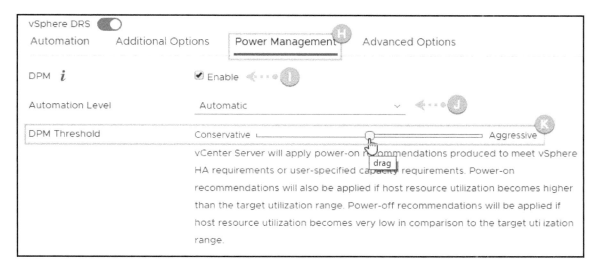

3. In the **Turn ON DPM** window, click **OK** to confirm that you have tested the host's ability to enter or exit DPM standby mode:

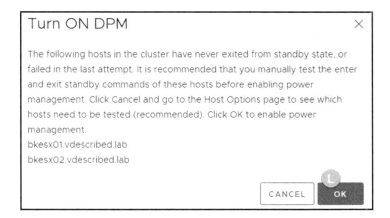

4. You should see a **Reconfigure cluster** task complete successfully in the **Recent Tasks** pane.

How it works...

Once DPM is enabled on a DRS cluster, it will analyze the cumulative resource requirements (current usage plus reservations), verify vSphere HA requirements, and determine the number of ESXi hosts that are required to meet them. DPM will then selectively put ESXi hosts into DPM standby mode (the host will actually be powered off). Prior to putting an ESXi host into standby mode, DPM will leverage DRS to migrate all of the VMs from the selected host onto other ESXi hosts in the cluster.

vSphere DPM allows for two automation levels:

- **Manual**: In this mode, the DPM recommendations are displayed in the vCenter GUI for an administrator to apply them.
- **Automatic**: In this mode, the DPM generated recommendations are automatically applied.

DPM can power on the hosts that are in DPM standby mode if the resource demands in the cluster increase.

Using VMware Enhanced vMotion Compatibility (EVC)

As your ESXi clusters scale-out, *though* it is imperative to have CPUs of the same make and model, you could end up having newer servers in the cluster with uncommon processor feature sets. To be able to migrate VMs between hosts in the cluster, it is necessary to guarantee that the CPU feature sets of all the ESXi hosts in the cluster are identical. This is achieved by enabling EVC on an ESXi cluster.

The following diagram will help you with decision-making when you're planning to use EVC:

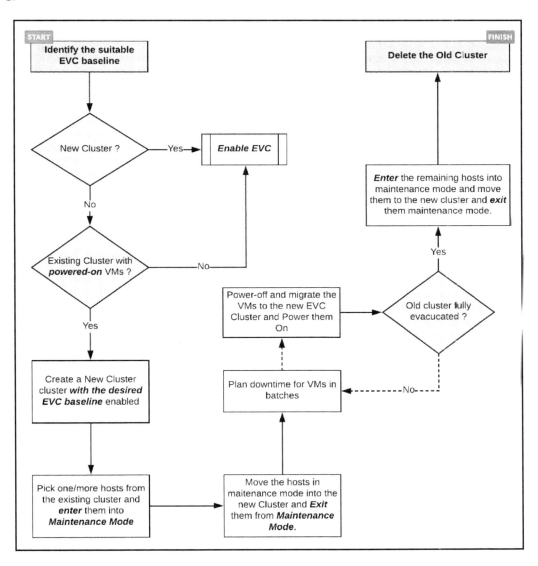

How to do it...

The following procedure will help you to enable EVC on a cluster with no running VMs:

1. Connect to vCenter Server using the HTML5 client.
2. Select the DRS cluster, navigate to **Configure** | **Configuration** | **VMware EVC**, and click **EDIT**...:

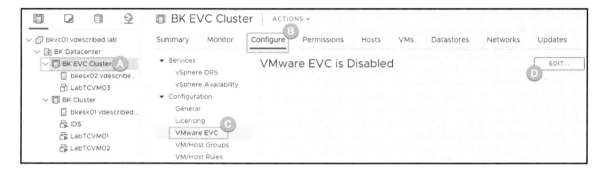

3. On the **Change EVC Mode** screen, choose the desired EVC mode and a baseline. Click **OK** to confirm the settings:

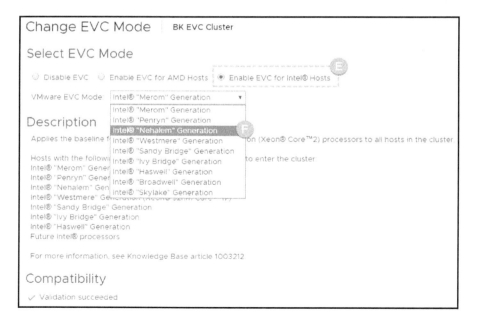

Change EVC Mode screen

4. You should see related tasks complete successfully in the **Recent Tasks** pane:

Recent Tasks	Alarms			
Task Name	⌄	Target ↑	⌄	Status
Enable/reconfigure EVC		🗗 BK EVC Cluster		✓ Completed
Retrieve EVC		🗗 BK EVC Cluster		✓ Completed
Validate EVC configuration		🗗 BK EVC Cluster		✓ Completed

This completes the process of configuring/creating an EVC cluster.

How it works...

With EVC, you can present a common feature set to all of the VMs in the cluster. VMware has made several baselines available that you can choose from for both AMD and Intel processors.

Here is a list of EVC baselines that are available with vSphere 6.7 Update 1:

Intel baselines [9 baselines]	AMD baselines [8 baselines]
Intel® Merom Generation	AMD Opteron™ Generation 1
Intel® Penryn Generation	AMD Opteron™ Generation 2
Intel® Nehalem Generation	AMD Opteron™ Generation 3 (no 3DNow!™)
Intel® Westmere Generation	AMD Opteron™ Generation 3
Intel® Sandy Bridge Generation	AMD Opteron™ Generation 4
Intel® Ivy Bridge Generation	AMD Opteron™ Piledriver Generation
Intel® Haswell Generation	AMD Opteron™ Steamroller Generation
Intel® Broadwell Generation	AMD Zen Generation
Intel® Skylake Generation	N/A

The baselines are generally categorized by make and processor generations. Refer to *VMware Knowledge Base article number* 1003212 (`https://kb.vmware.com/s/article/1003212`) for more details regarding these baselines.

9
Achieving High Availability in a vSphere Environment

It is essential to ensure the availability of not just your virtual machine workloads but also your vSphere infrastructure components. VMware offers three availability solutions—vSphere HA, vCenter HA, and VMware FT.

vSphere HA, when configured on a cluster, enables the cluster to respond to an unplanned downtime event and ensures the availability of the virtual machines that were running on them, with the minimal amount of downtime possible. There is much more to what vSphere HA can do in terms of providing high availability to the virtual machines that run on the HA protected hosts. It can monitor the guest operating systems and applications running inside a virtual machine and then decide to restart the affected virtual machine in an effort to reduce the downtime of service due to an affected guest operating system hosting the service or an unresponsive application corresponding to the service. It can also access events such as **All Paths Down (APD)** and **Permanent Device Loss (PDL)** and choose to reset the virtual machines if necessary.

 It is important to understand that, even though HA is configured on a cluster of ESXi hosts, it can only restart VMs that were running on a failed host. It cannot restart affected ESXi hosts.

VMware Fault Tolerance offers true high availability for virtual machines—however, it comes with certain limitations. A virtual machine with FT enabled will have a secondary virtual machine in lock-step mode, so that, in the event of a host failure, a reboot of the VM is not necessary. Instead, the secondary VM continues to operate from where the primary VM left off before the host failure.

vCenter HA is a quorum-based service availability solution that ensures that the vCenter service continues to run if the vCenter active node goes down for any reason.

In this chapter, we will cover the following topics:

- Enabling vSphere High Availability
- Configuring vCenter Admission Control
- Configuring Heartbeat Datastores
- Overriding Restart Priority for Virtual Machines
- Creating VM to VM Dependency Rules
- Disabling Host Monitoring
- Enabling Virtual Machine Monitoring
- Enabling Virtual Machine Component Protection (VMCP)
- Configuring VMware Fault Tolerance (FT)
- Configuring vCenter Native High Availability (VCHA)

Enabling vSphere High Availability

vSphere HA can only be enabled via the vCenter Server that is managing the ESXi cluster. Since HA restarts virtual machines that were running on a failed host, it is essential to ensure that all of the ESXi hosts in the cluster have access to the same storage and the same virtual machine networks and that they have CPUs from the same family and feature set. If these factors are not considered before enabling HA on a cluster, then it could increase the chances of unplanned downtime.

In this recipe, we will learn how to enable HA on a host cluster.

How to do it...

The following procedure will help you to enable and configure HA on an ESXi cluster:

1. Connect to vCenter Server using the HTML5 client.
2. Select the cluster from the inventory, navigate to **Configure** | **vSphere Availability**, and click **EDIT...**:

3. On the **Edit Cluster Settings** window, enable HA by using the toggle switch, and ensure **Host Monitoring** is enabled. The **Host Failure Response** is to restart VMs. The **Response for Host Isolation** is **Disabled** by default (which means the VMs on the isolated host will be left powered-on). Once done, click **OK**:

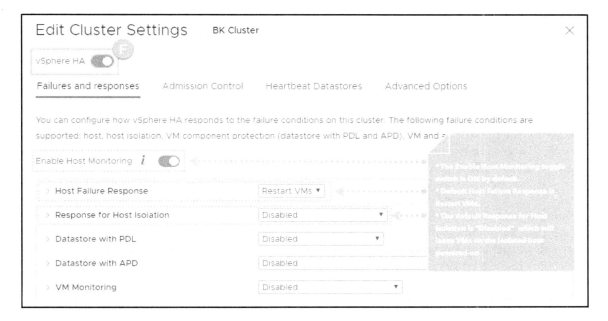

4. In the **Recent Tasks** pane, you should see the **Configuring vSphere HA** task complete successfully on the ESXi hosts in the cluster:

Recent Tasks	Alarms		
Task Name ⌄	Target ↑ ⌄	Status	
Reconfigure cluster	▢ BK Cluster	✓ Completed	
Configuring vSphere HA	▢ bkesx01.vdescribed.lab	✓ Completed	
Configuring vSphere HA	▢ bkesx02.vdescribed.lab	✓ Completed	
Configuring vSphere HA	▢ bkesx03.vdescribed.lab	✓ Completed	

This completes the process of enabling vSphere HA on an ESXi cluster. Read the *How it works...* section for more information regarding the settings involved in configuring the *Host Failure Response* and the *Host Isolation Response*.

How it works...

When HA is enabled on a cluster of ESXi hosts, the **Fault Domain Manager** (**FDM**) will install its agents on every host in the cluster. Once done, one of the ESXi hosts in the cluster is elected as a **master**, and the remainder as **slaves**. During the election process, an ESXi host with access to the largest number of datastores will be chosen as the master, and the remainder of the hosts are flagged as slaves. The master node is responsible for restarting virtual machines, updating state information to vCenter, and monitoring its slave nodes. Every set of slave nodes will have a master node to exchange information with. If, for any reason, there is a network partition in an HA cluster, which means that a set of nodes in an HA cluster stop communicating with another set of nodes in the same cluster, then a network partition is said to have formed between the two sets of nodes. Now, if the nodes in each of those partitioned sets can talk to each other, then they would participate in an HA election process again in order to choose a master node for that particular partition.

An election process is initiated if the current master node fails. The election process will take approximately 15 seconds, and it will choose a host with the largest number of connected datastores. In the case that there is a tie between hosts, then the host with the highest **Management Object ID** (**MOB ID**) is chosen as the master. The MOB IDs are compared lexically, which means that 9 will be higher than 10.

vSphere HA will remain functional only if every set of HA-enabled hosts has a master node elected. One of the roles of the master is to monitor the slaves for their liveliness, which is done by sending and receiving network heartbeats between the master and the slaves over their management VMkernel interfaces. The network heartbeats are exchanged every second. If any of the slave hosts stop receiving heartbeats from the master, then it will begin determining whether it is network isolated with the master. This entire process can take up to a minute before it decides to execute the isolation response.

The following sections delve deeper into how the *host failure* and *isolation response* configurations impact vSphere HA's decision making.

Host Failure Response

Host Failure Response determines the action that needs to be taken by vSphere HA when it detects that a host has failed. It can be either set to **Disabled** or **Restart VMs**. Setting it to disabled will essentially disable HA on the cluster, as shown in the following screenshot:

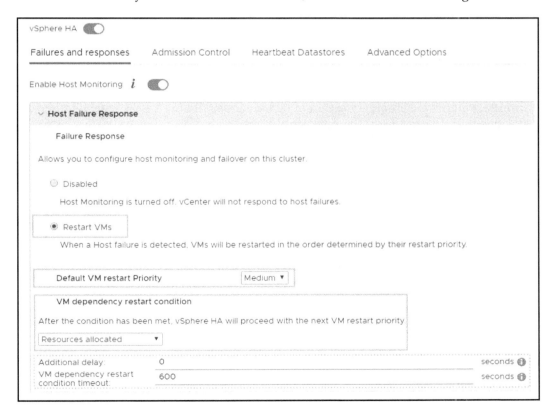

Furthermore, you can configure the VM restart priority and the VM dependency restart condition. Continue reading the following sub-sections for details on those.

VM restart priority

The default VM restart priority for all VMs that will be restarted by HA is **Medium**. We will learn more about the VM restart priority in the *Overriding Restart Priority for Virtual Machines* recipe.

You can configure additional delay and restart condition timeout values, as shown in the following screenshot:

For example, when the default condition of 600 seconds (10 minutes) is reached, then HA will continue with the restart of the next set of VMs.

 The **VM dependency restart condition timeout** value does not affect the VM dependency restart condition; it only affects the VM restart priority.

VM dependency restart condition

The function of the VM dependency restart condition is to specify a condition that, if met, then the restart attempt is deemed successful before HA can initiate the restart of the dependent VMs. We will learn how to create VM to VM dependency in the *Configuring VM to VM Dependency Rules* recipe.

There are four restart conditions, which are as follows:

- Resource allocated
- Powered-on
- Guest heartbeats detected
- App heartbeats detected

All of the preceding restart conditions are *mandatory;* meaning, the *VM to VM Dependency Rules* are *Must Rules*. Hence, if the condition is not met, then the dependent VMs will not be restarted.

Response for Host Isolation

The **Response for Host Isolation** setting is used by the ESXi host, which detects itself as being network isolated from the heartbeat network, in order to decide whether or not to change the power state of the running virtual machines. The vSphere HA Host Isolation response can be modified when/after enabling vSphere HA on a cluster. It is disabled by default, as shown in the following screenshot:

If the HA master node is network isolated, it pings its isolation address, and then within 5 seconds of the network being isolated, it will execute the configured isolation response.

If a slave node stops receiving heartbeats from the master, it elects itself as the master (this is because it doesn't receive any election traffic), pings the isolation address to determine the network isolation, and then actions the isolation response approximately 60 seconds after it stops receiving the heartbeats from the master.

There are three different host isolation responses:

- **Disabled**: This setting will not change the power state of the virtual machines that are running on the isolated host. This is generally used in cases where you are aware that they could be network disconnected, and if they are, then it won't affect the iSCSI/NFS or the virtual machine network.
- **Power-off and restart VMs**: This setting will power-off the virtual machines that are running on the isolated host. It is used in cases where the management network and the NFS or iSCSI storage are using the same physical NICs on the host, hence, increasing the chances of the host losing access to storage when there is a network isolation. Powering off the virtual machines in response to network isolation will reduce the chances of more than one instance of the virtual machine running in the cluster. Also, if the virtual machines were to lose access to the storage, then a graceful shutdown of the guest operating system will not be possible.
- **Shutdown and restart VMs**: This will gracefully shutdown the virtual machines. This is useful in a case where both the management and virtual machine network could be affected, but the storage connection will remain active. If the graceful shutdown doesn't complete within 300 seconds, then a power-off is issued.

Configuring vCenter Admission Control

A well-designed HA cluster should have enough free resources to restart all of the business-critical virtual machines in the cluster, in the event of a host(s) failure. For this to be possible, it is essential for the cluster to maintain enough free CPU and memory resources, which are referred to as **failover capacity**. The failover capacity enables the restarting of the VMs while the cluster capacity is reduced, owing to the host failure.

A failover capacity that has been configured on a cluster determines the number of host failures that the cluster can sustain and still leave enough usable resources to support all the running and restarted virtual machines in the cluster. vCenter ensures that the configured failover capacity is maintained by using a mechanism called **vCenter Admission Control**.

We will cover more about this in the *How it works...* section of this recipe.

How to do it...

Admission control policies can be modified when/after enabling vSphere HA on a cluster. It defaults to tolerating a single host failure and uses the **cluster resource percentage** as the default method to calculate cluster capacity:

1. Navigate to the **Admission Control** tab in the **Edit Cluster Settings** window of the desired cluster.
2. Set the number of host failures that the cluster should tolerate, and choose the desired failover capacity calculation method. You could also specify the **Performance degradation VMs tolerate**:

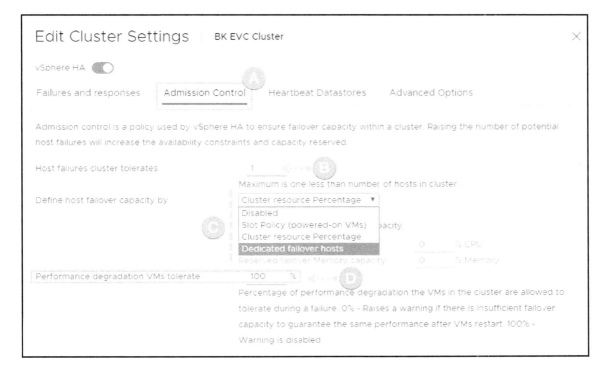

3. Once done, click **OK** to save the settings and close the **Edit Cluster Settings** window.

This completes the process of enabling Admission Control on an HA cluster.

How it works...

vCenter Admission Control is a measure that is used to monitor and maintain the configured failover capacity in an HA cluster. It does so by restricting the number of operations that, if allowed, will reduce the failover capacity. Any operation that violates the resource constraints that are imposed by the admission control policy will not be permitted. Some of these operations include a virtual machine power-on operation, a vMotion operation, and a change in the CPU/memory reservation of the VM.

There are two aspects to configuring the failover capacity on a cluster:

- Host Failures Cluster Tolerates
- Failover Capacity Calculation Method

Host Failures Cluster Tolerates defaults to **one**, and it defines the number of hosts that can fail while still allowing the cluster to restart VMs and provide resources for the workloads.

Failover capacity is calculated using any of the following methods and the number of host failures to tolerate:

- Cluster resource percentage
- Slot policy (powered-on VMs)
- Dedicated failover hosts

Let's delve a bit deeper into how each of the preceding options affects the failover capacity.

Cluster resource percentage

This method calculates the amount of cluster resources that have to be reserved as failover capacity, based on the number of host failures that the cluster can tolerate. You can also choose to manually specify the percentage of CPU and memory resources—however, this is no longer necessary. Letting the cluster automatically calculate the failover percentage is the most efficient method, since you do not have to redo the calculations manually when increasing/decreasing the host count of a cluster.

HA uses a different formula to calculate the percentage of free resources in the cluster. It does so by using the following parameters:

- **Total available resources**: The actual capacity of the hosts
- **The cumulative amount of reserved resources**: The sum of all vCPU/memory reservations

The formula is as follows:

$$[(Total\ Available\ resources) - (Cumulative\ CPU/Memory\ Reservations)] / [Total\ Available\ resources] = \%\ of\ free\ resources$$

You can also choose to override and specify the percentiles manually:

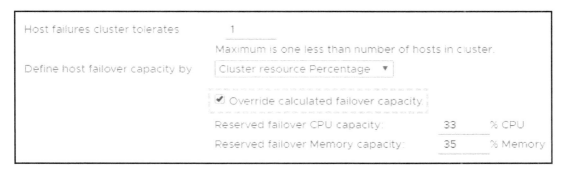

Let's consider the following example. Assume that you have reserved 25% CPU and 40% memory as failover resources, as shown in the following diagram:

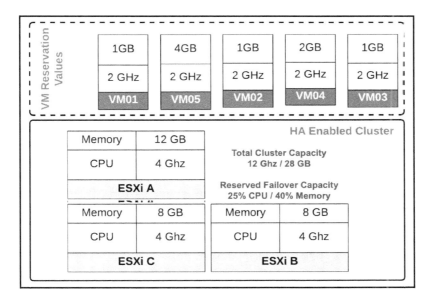

Here are the parameters for the cluster configuration:

- **Total available CPU resources**: 12 GHz
- **Total available memory resources**: 28 GB
- **The cumulative amount of reserved CPU resources**: 10 Ghz
- **The cumulative amount of reserved memory resources**: 9 GB

The percentage of free capacity (available resources) is as follows:

- **CPU**: (12 Ghz - 10 Ghz) or 12 Ghz: 16%
- **Memory**: (28 GB - 9GB) or 28 GB: 67%

In this case, it violates the CPU reservation for failover, but meets the memory reservation for failover. Since the failover requirement for one of the resources hasn't been met, it is considered to violate admission control.

The slot policy (power-on VMs)

This method calculates the amount of cluster resources that have to be reserved as failover capacity, based on the number of host failures that the cluster can tolerate. However, unlike the *cluster resource percentage* method, here, admission control uses *slot sizes* to calculate the current failover capacity. A *slot* represents a combination of the CPU and memory resources that are to be allocated to virtual machines. The number of slots that a virtual machine will require depends on its resource requirements.

Now that we know what slots are, let's review how HA determines *slot sizes*. HA picks the largest CPU and memory reservation values as slot sizes. If no reservations are used, a value of **32 MHz** and **100 MB** is used. Once the slot sizes are determined, the number of slots that each of the ESXi hosts in the cluster can hold is also determined. It then picks the hosts with the largest number of slots as failover hosts and starts determining the current failover capacity of the cluster. If the current failover capacity of the cluster is less than the configured failover capacity, then it is considered an admission control violation. This will be better understood with an example.

For instance, let's assume that your current cluster status, in terms of the number of hosts, virtual machines, and their resource reservations, are as shown in the following diagram:

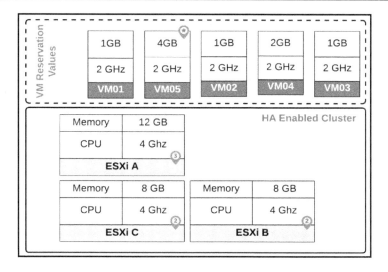

Here, the largest memory reservation by a virtual machine is 4 GB, and the vCPU is 2 GHz. The slot size is (**4 GB, 2 Ghz**).

Now, let's calculate the slot capacity per host:

- Host A: Three memory slots and two vCPU slots
- Host B: Two memory slots and two vCPU slots
- Host C: Two memory slots and two vCPU slots

Since **ESXi A** has the largest set of slots, it is taken out of the equation. So, with just **ESXi B** and **ESXi C,** we only have *four* slots in total.

Now, let's take a look at the slot sizes that are required by the virtual machines:

- VM01: One slot
- VM02: One slot
- VM03: One slot
- VM04: One slot
- VM05: One slot

We need a total of *five* slots to power-on all of the VMs, but we have only four. Hence, the current failover capacity is less than the configured failover capacity of one. Therefore, you will need to power-off one of the VMs in order to enable admission control. Once admission control is enabled, if you try to power-on the VM, then it won't let you, since it violates the failover capacity requirement.

When you define the slot policy, it is recommended that you *cover all powered-on virtual machines* in almost all cases. The following screenshot shows the options that are available with the powered-on VMs slot policy:

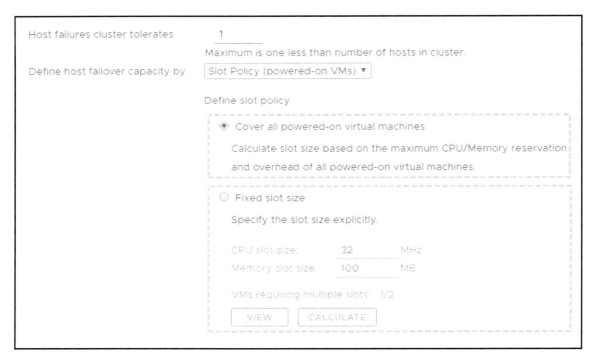

The *fixed slot size* method can come in handy when, for instance, you have a VM with a very large reservation value, which can affect the slot size.

Dedicated failover hosts

You can define a set of ESXi hosts that are to be used as failover hosts. These hosts will not be permitted to run any virtual machines on them unless there is an HA event. The following screenshot shows how to add failover hosts:

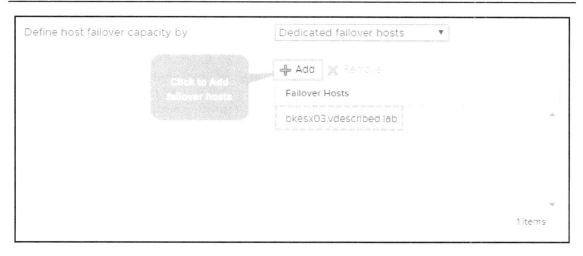

However, it is essential to ensure that the failover host has enough capacity to run all business-critical VMs in case there is a host failure in the cluster. If, for any reason, the failover host is not online *or* runs out of free compute capacity, then HA will try to place the VMs from the failed host(s) onto other available hosts in the cluster.

Performance degradation VMs tolerate

The default value of 100% is never an ideal value since, if that is the amount of degradation a VM suffers, then it defeats the purpose of high availability. The value should be modified depending on the type of workload that you run in your environment. The following screenshot shows the performance degradation tolerance when it is set to 50% by default:

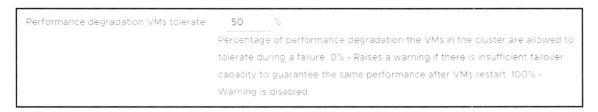

Now that you have learned how admission control works, you have equipped yourself with enough knowledge to optimally configure an HA cluster.

Configuring Heartbeat Datastores

The HA master uses network heartbeats to monitor the liveliness of the slave nodes. It is, however, sometimes possible that a slave node, though isolated from the heartbeat (management) network, could still be running and providing all of the necessary resources to the virtual machines that are running on them. To verify the existence of such a scenario, HA has another type of heartbeat method, called **datastore heartbeating**.

In this recipe, we will learn how to configure heartbeat datastores.

How to do it...

Heartbeat datastores can be selected when/after enabling vSphere HA on a cluster. The following procedure will help you to configure datastore heartbeating on the cluster:

1. Navigate to the **Heartbeat Datastores** tab in the **Edit Cluster Settings** window of the desired cluster.
2. Specify the desired **Heartbeat datastore selection policy**:

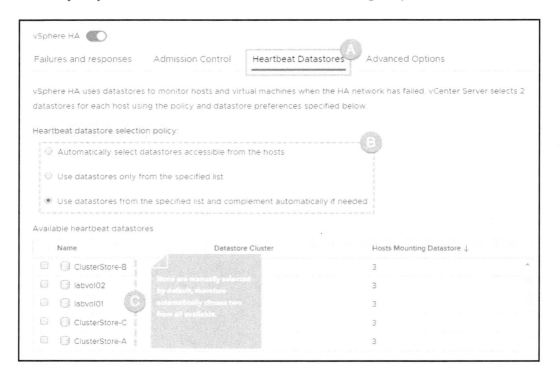

3. Once done, click **OK** to save the settings, and close the **Edit Cluster Settings** window.

4. Select the cluster from the inventory and navigate to **Monitor | vSphere HA | Heartbeat** to verify/review the selection:

This completes the process of configuring heartbeat datastores.

How it works...

Datastore heartbeating is enabled by default and chooses *two heartbeat datastores per host*. It does so by making sure that it selects the datastores that are not backed by the same NFS server or storage, and are mapped to at least two ESXi hosts. Datastore heartbeating works by using VMFS's filesystem locking mechanism. It creates files—what VMware calls heartbeat files, which are kept open in order to keep a filesystem lock active on that file. Every host in the HA cluster gets a corresponding heartbeat file. In the event of network isolation, the master checks the liveliness of the isolated host by checking whether there is an active lock on its heartbeat file. The heartbeat files are stored in a directory called **.vSphere-HA**, which can be located on the root of the heartbeat datastore, as you can see in the following screenshot:

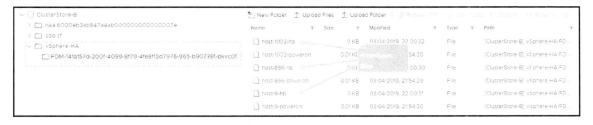

Heartbeat Files

There are three different heartbeat datastore selection policies:

- **Automatically select datastores that are accessible from the hosts**: This selects two heartbeat datastores from all of the datastores that can be seen by the ESXi host in the cluster.
- **Use datastores only from the specified list**: This selects only the datastores that you specify as the heartbeat datastores. In other words, you can manually assign two desired heartbeat datastores from the entire list. It is important to note that, with this setting, you also set just one datastore as the heartbeat datastore. If you select more than one datastore, then HA will automatically select any two from the specified datastores.
- **Use datastores from the specified list and complement automatically if needed**: This selects two heartbeat datastores from the specified list, but it can also automatically select datastores if you specify less than two or more than two datastores. For instance, if you were to select just one datastore from the list, then HA will use the specified datastore and automatically select the second datastore. If you were to select more than two datastores, then HA will automatically select two of the three specified datastores as heartbeat datastores.

Overriding Restart Priority for Virtual Machines

Setting VM restart priorities for individual virtual machines will assist vSphere HA to determine which VM should be restarted first when a host fails. It is common practice to leave the cluster's restart priority at medium and set the required priorities on individual virtual machines. In this recipe, we will learn how to override restart priorities for virtual machines.

How to do it...

The following procedure will help you to override restart priorities on VMs:

1. Connect to the vCenter Server using the HTML5 client.
2. Select the HA-enabled cluster from the inventory and navigate to **Configure** | **Configuration** | **VM Overrides**:

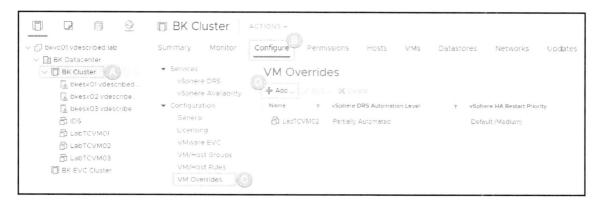

3. Click **Add** to bring up the **Add VM Override** wizard, select the desired VM(s), and click **NEXT**:

4. On the **Add VM Override** screen, use the **Override** checkbox corresponding to **VM Restart Priority** to enable the override, and select the desired restart priority (**Lowest/Low/Medium/High/Highest/Disabled**). Click **FINISH**:

5. Repeat *steps 3* and *4* if you have additional VMs to set priorities on.

This completes the procedure of how to create overrides for VM restart priorities.

How it works...

The VM restart priorities that are configured are relative. vSphere HA will restart virtual machines with the highest priority first. If the priority is set to **Disabled** for a VM, then in the event of a host failure, that particular VM will not be restarted:

VM Overrides

+ Add ...　／ Edit　✕ Delete

Name	▼	vSphere DRS Automation Level	▼	vSphere HA Restart Priority ↑	▼
⊡ LabTCVM02		Partially Automated		Default (Medium)	
⊡ LabTCVM03		Default (Fully Automated)		High	
⊡ LabTCVM01		Default (Fully Automated)		Highest	

For example, in this case, the order of restart will be `LabTCVM01`, `LabTCVM03`, and `LabTCVM02`, the priorities being **Highest**, **High**, and **Medium**.

The priorities set are only for HA to determine the restart order; they don't affect VM Monitoring.

Now, let's assume that we have set the failover capacity of an HA cluster to one host and the default cluster-wide restart priority as **Medium**. With this configuration in place, if more than one ESXi host fails, then you would want to make sure that, even though your cluster capacity is reduced as compared to what the cluster was originally prepared for, the high-priority VMs are started first. This can be achieved by setting restart priorities for the VMs by overriding the cluster settings.

Creating VM to VM Dependency Rules

Virtual machines host business applications, and these applications, in most cases, have service dependencies. During an HA-initiated restart of such VMs, if such service dependencies are not taken into account, even though the VMs will be restarted, the business applications will not be in a functional state. Services dependencies are time-sensitive, meaning if service-A is dependant on service-D, starting service-A prior to a full startup of service-D may either cause service-A not to start, or to run in a non-functional state. HA will not restart services in a guest OS once the VM has been started.

For instance, if an application is dependent on its database being hosted in a different VM, then it is important to ensure that the database VM and its services start up first, before the application VM is started. In this recipe, we will learn how to create virtual machines to virtual machines dependency rules.

Getting ready

Virtual machines for which the dependency rules will be created should be grouped respectively. Read the recipe, *Creating DRS Groups*, in `Chapter 8`, *Configuring vSphere DRS, DPM, and VMware EVC*, to learn how to create VM groups.

How to do it...

The following procedure will help you to create a VM to VM dependency rule:

1. Connect to vCenter Server using the HTML5 client.
2. Select the HA cluster and navigate to **Configure** | **VM/Host Rules** and click **Add...**:

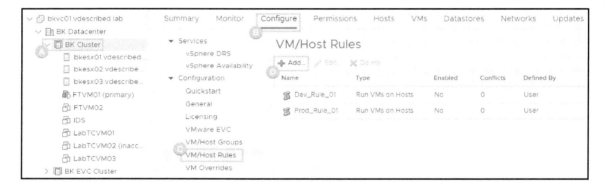

3. On the **Create VM/Host Rule** window, specify a **Name** for the rule, and set the **Type** to **Virtual Machines to Virtual Machines**. Specify the dependency relationship between the groups and click **OK**:

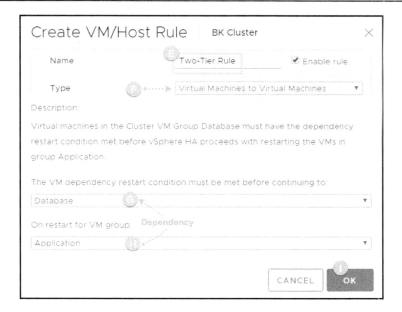

4. The **VM/Host Rules** page will list the newly created rule and the participating VMs. You can choose to add VMs to the groups from this screen by using the **Add...** button:

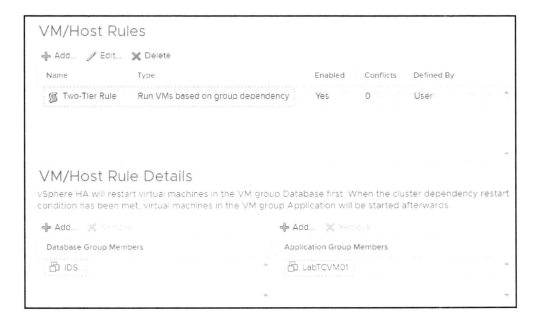

This completes the process of creating VM to VM dependency rules.

How it works...

VM to VM Dependency Rules will be validated and actioned by vSphere HA's VM dependency restart condition. As discussed in the *Enabling vSphere HA* recipe, the *VM to VM Dependency Rules* is a *Must Rules*, which needs to mandatorily satisfy the condition configured before the dependent VMs can be restarted.

To reiterate, any of the following four mandatory conditions can be specified:

- Resource allocated
- Powered-on
- Guest heartbeats detected
- App heartbeats detected

Disabling Host Monitoring

During the maintenance of your cluster, it may make sense to temporarily disable HA in order to prevent unnecessary HA events. This can be done by modifying the HA settings on this cluster to disable host monitoring.

How to do it...

The following procedure will help you to disable host monitoring on a cluster:

1. Connect to vCenter server using the HTML5 client.
2. Select the cluster from the inventory, navigate to **Configure | vSphere Availability**, and click **Edit...**
3. On the **Edit Cluster Settings** window, flip the toggle switch next to **Enable Host Monitoring** from *green* to *gray* to turn off host monitoring, and click **OK**:

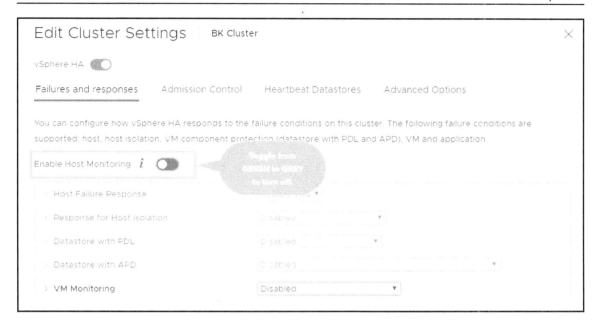

4. You should see a **Reconfigure Cluster** task complete successfully in the **Recent Tasks** pane.

This completes the process of temporarily disabling host monitoring in a vSphere HA cluster.

How it works...

Unlike disabling HA on the cluster, which will, in turn, unconfigure the HA agents on every host in the cluster, disabling host monitoring temporarily stops HA from monitoring the ESXi hosts. This avoids the need for a cluster-wide reconfiguration of vSphere HA.

Enabling Virtual Machine Monitoring

vSphere HA can be configured to monitor virtual machines so that unresponsive VMs can be restarted (reset). This can be achieved by enabling VM Monitoring on the HA cluster. HA can further monitor the applications running inside the VM if application monitoring is enabled. However, this would mean that the application should be coded to use the necessary APIs. VM Monitoring is very handy when you have VMs hosting services for which you can't afford longer downtime.

How to do it...

The following procedure will help you to configure Virtual Machine Monitoring on a vSphere HA-enabled cluster:

1. Connect to vCenter Server using the HTML5 client.
2. Select the cluster from the inventory, navigate to **Configure | vSphere Availability**, and click **EDIT...**:

3. On the **Edit Cluster Settings** window, go to **Failures and responses** and click on **VM Monitoring** to expand its settings:

4. On the **VM Monitoring Settings** screen, you can choose to enable either **VM Monitoring Only** or **VM and Application Monitoring**. The VM Monitoring sensitivity has a default preset of high, which translates to the following configuration, as shown in the following screenshot:

- Failure interval set to 30 seconds
- Minimum uptime set to 120 seconds
- Maximum per-VM resets to 3
- No maximum reset time window

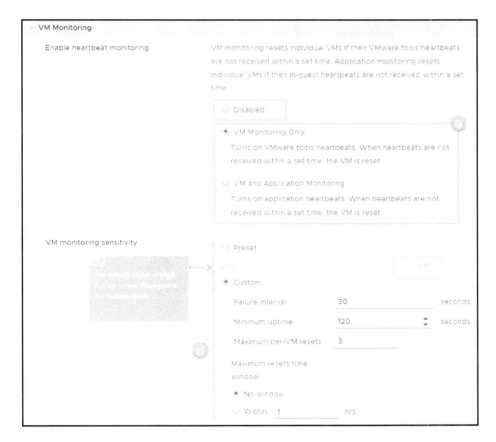

5. Once done, click **OK** to save the settings.

This completes the process of enabling VM Monitoring.

How it works...

Once enabled, VM Monitoring, with the help of the VMware tools that are installed in the VMs, will monitor the heartbeats from the VMs. The intervals are governed by the monitoring sensitivity that is configured for the VM. The default monitoring sensitivity is set to high, in which case, HA expects a heartbeat from the virtual machine every 30 seconds. If the heartbeat is not received, then VM Monitoring will look for any storage or network I/O activity in the past 120 seconds (this is the default `das.iostatsInterval` value). If there are none, then the VM is reset, and more importantly, it is reset only three times during an hour's reset-time window.

Prior to issuing a reset, a screenshot of the virtual machine's console will be captured.

Enabling Virtual Machine Component Protection (VMCP)

Unlike an ESXi host going down, taking all of the virtual machines with it, it is quite possible that the storage access issues can render the virtual machine unusable. The **VMware Component Protection** (**VMCP**) feature of vSphere HA can recover VMs that have been affected by storage access issues. VMCP enables protection against two types of storage access issues, ADP and PDL, as previously mentioned.

In this recipe, we will learn how to enable protection against such storage events.

How to do it...

The following procedure will help you to enable VMCP on an HA cluster:

1. Connect to vCenter Server using the HTML5 client.
2. Select the cluster from the inventory, navigate to **Configure** | **vSphere Availability**, and click **EDIT...**:

3. On the **Edit Cluster Settings** window, go to **Failures and Responses**, click on **Datastore with PDL** to expand its settings, and specify the desired response for a PDL situation. It will be **Disabled** by default:

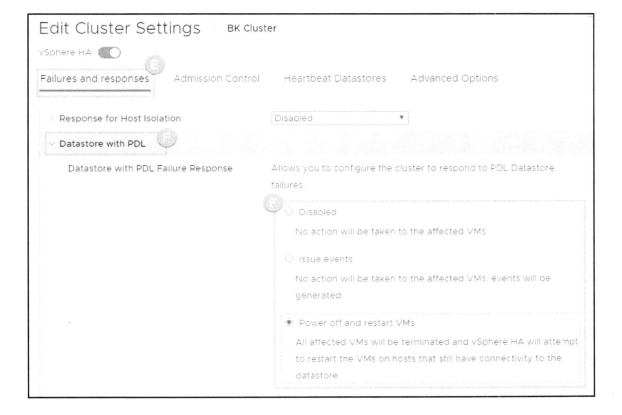

4. Click on **Datastore with APD** to expand its settings and specify the desired response for an APD situation. It will be **Disabled** by default:

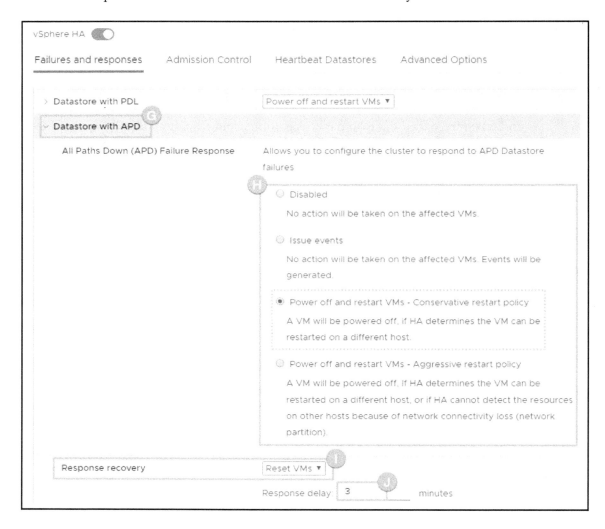

5. Once done, click **OK** to save the settings.

This completes the process of configuring VMCP, APD, and PDL responses for an HA cluster.

How it works...

HA monitors the datastores for PDL and APD events on a VMCP-enabled cluster and recovers (restarts) VMs on the affected datastores.

The first question to answer is: *Why do we need HA to recover these VMs?*

The answer to the question is the fact that APD/PDL events may not affect all of the ESXi hosts in the cluster. There can be hosts in the cluster that might still have access to the affected LUN device. Hence, HA can be used to restart the affected VMs onto ESXi hosts that have access to the LUN. This is an additional effort to meet the uptime SLAs for virtual machines.

 For more details on the SCSI sense codes and log events that indicate PDL or APD, refer to *VMware Knowledge Base Article number* 2004684 at `https:/ /kb.vmware.com/kb/2004684`.

Let's delve a bit deeper into understanding the differences between APD and PDL events.

Datastore with PDL

A PDL occurs when an ESXi is notified about the fact that a LUN device is permanently unavailable. A PDL event can occur only when the ESXi can still communicate with the array. The array notifies the host by issuing a SCSI sense code to the ESXi host. On detecting a PDL state for a LUN, the ESXi hosts will stop sending I/O requests to the LUN device.

We can configure *three* responses for PDL events:

- **Disabled (default)**: HA will not respond to PDL events.
- **Issue events**: HA will notify the administrator of such events.
- **Power-off and restart VMs**: HA will power-off the virtual machines on the affected datastores and attempt to restart them on another ESXi host in the same cluster that has access to the datastore in question.

Datastore with APD

An APD occurs when an ESXi host loses access to a LUN device but has not received a PDL SCSI sense code from the array. This could happen if there is a failure at the fabric or at the initiators. Since the ESXi host is unsure about the state of the LUN, except for the fact that it has lost access to it, it assumes the condition to be transient in nature and continues to retry the commands until it reaches the APD timeout value of *140 seconds*. On reaching the timeout value, ESXi will start failing the outstanding I/O to the device.

We can configure *four* responses for APD events:

- **Disabled (default)**: HA will not respond to APD events.
- **Issue events**: HA will notify the administrator of such events.
- **Power-off and restart VMs—conservative restart policy**: HA will attempt to power-off and to restart the affected virtual machines on a host that has access to the affected datastore. However, it won't attempt the restart unless it finds a host that has access to the datastore. It also verifies whether the HA-enabled cluster has enough resources to power-on the virtual machine/s. If the affected host is unable to reach the master HA node to determine the same, then the restart will not be attempted.
- **Power-off and restart VMs—aggressive restart policy**: Unlike the conservative approach, with this option selected, HA will not wait to find an ESXi host that has access to the affected datastore. It will simply power-off the VMs so that they can be restarted. It would, however, attempt to determine whether there is enough free capacity in the cluster to power-on the virtual machines. But, in case it is unable to reach the master HA node, it would still attempt the restart. In this case, it is quite possible that vSphere HA might not be able to power-on all of the affected virtual machines on another host.

APD response recovery and response delay

Response recovery and **response delay** options are enabled only if you choose the power-off or restart action for the APD events. As explained at the start of this topic, since APD is considered a transient condition, the ESXi host will retry the I/O commands to the LUN until the APD timeout of *140 (default) seconds* is reached. The delay for VM failover for the APD option will make VMCP wait for an additional *180 (default) seconds* before the VMs are powered-off.

Keep in mind that the APD default timeout value is *140 seconds* and that the VMCP timeout is *180 seconds*. Hence, it waits for a cumulative of *320 seconds* before it actions the configured response.

Response recovery has two options:

- Reset VMs
- Disabled

Since VMCP waits for another *180 seconds* after the APD timeout, it is possible that the host might recover from the transient APD conditions, thereby restoring the connection to the affected LUN, before the VMCP timeout is reached. In such a scenario, you can choose to either reset the VMs, or not to restart them by disabling the response.

Configuring vSphere Fault Tolerance (FT)

vSphere HA monitors a cluster of ESXi hosts and, in the event of a host(s) failure, it attempts to restart virtual machines that were running on the failed host(s) onto other available hosts in the cluster. This is more of a *fault-recovery* solution, and the virtual machines do incur a downtime, which translates to application/service downtime. There can be mission-critical applications in your environment that cannot tolerate such a downtime. Virtual machines hosting such applications require **continuous availability**—which can be achieved by enabling FT.

With vSphere FT enabled on a virtual machine, the guest operating system or the application will never incur downtime due to an ESXi host failure.

In this recipe, we will learn how to configure Fault Tolerance on VMs.

Getting ready

Before you begin, it is essential that you understand the following requirements:

- Fault Tolerance can only be enabled on VMs running in a vSphere HA-enabled cluster.
- Hosts in the cluster should support Fault Tolerance. Use the VMware compatibility guide to verify whether the feature is compatible with your hosts.
- Hosts in the cluster should have hardware virtualization enabled in the BIOS.

- Hosts in the cluster should be licensed for Fault Tolerance. vSphere *Standard* and above include support for Fault Tolerance:
    - *Standard* and *Enterprise* licenses allow you to enable FT on **2-vCPU** SMP VMs.
    - Starting with vSphere 6.7, the *Enterprise Plus* license allows you to enable FT on **8-vCPU** SMP VMs. vSphere 6.5 only allows up to 4-vCPU SMP VMs.
- FT logging-enabled VMkernel interfaces should be configured on every host on the cluster, as shown in the following screenshot:

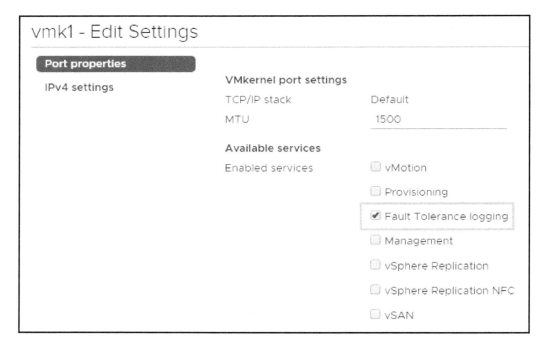

- If it is enabled on selective hosts, then you will need to configure VM-host affinity rules for your FT-enabled VM.
- VMotion-enabled VMkernel interfaces should be configured over every host in the cluster.
- It is recommended that you use a 10 GBps dedicated FT logging network.

How to do it...

The following procedure will help you to enable FT on a virtual machine:

1. Connect to vCenter Server using the HTML5 client.
2. Right-click on the desired VM and go to **Fault Tolerance** | **Turn On Fault Tolerance**:

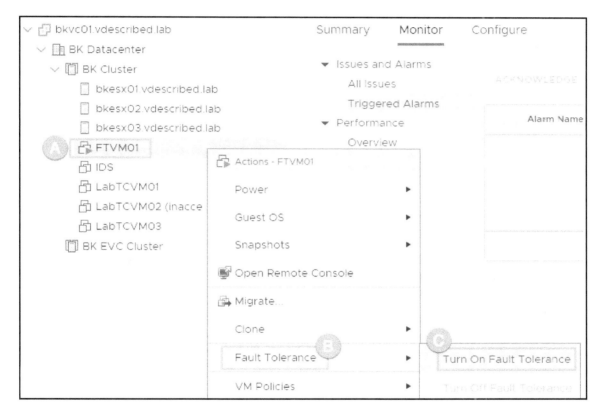

Start Fault Tolerance wizard

3. On the **Turn On Fault Tolerance** wizard, select the datastore for the secondary VM and click **Next** to continue. You are only allowed to select a datastore that is different from the one that the original VM is hosted on:

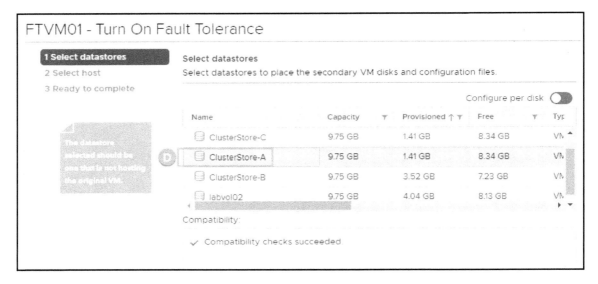

Select datastore for Secondary VM

4. On the **Select host** screen, select a desired host for the secondary VM and click **Next** to continue. Only hosts other than the one hosting the original VM will be listed:

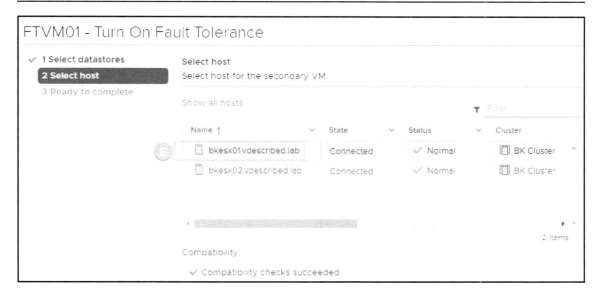

5. On the **Ready to complete** screen, review the placement details of the secondary VM and click **Finish**:

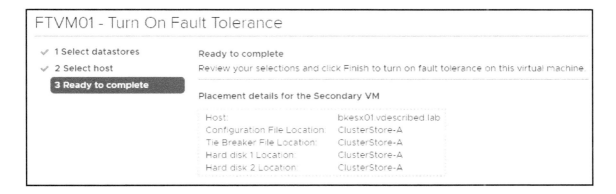

6. The **Recent Tasks** pane should show a **Turn On Fault Tolerance** and **Start Fault Tolerance Secondary VM** task complete successfully:

7. Once done, you should see two listed VMs running on the cluster. However, only the primary VM will be listed in the vCenter inventory tree:

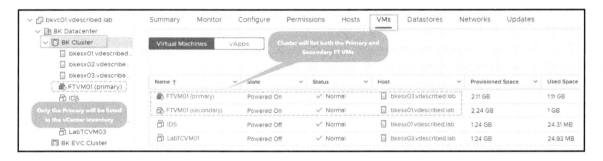

This completes the process of enabling vSphere Fault Tolerance on a VM.

How it works...

When you enable VMware FT on a VM, it effectively creates another copy of the same VM on a different host and a different datastore. This duplicate copy of the VM is referred to as the **secondary VM** and the FT-protected VM as the **primary VM**. Both of the VMs are fully synchronous. Events occurring on the primary VM are recorded and replayed on the secondary VM—meaning that they are kept in a lock-step mode.

VMware uses a method called atomic file locking to ensure that only one of the VMs will be the active (primary) VM. This is achieved by using two files that are created and maintained by the secondary VM's home directory.

The following screenshot shows the home directory contents of the secondary VM:

```
[root@bkesx02:/vmfs/volumes/5c98391d-e9d0fd24-5061-005056885f88/FTVM01] ls -alh
total 1278080
drwxr-xr-x    1 root     root        76.0K Apr  6 04:55 .
drwxr-xr-t    1 root     root        72.0K Apr  6 02:11 ..
-rw-rw-rw-    1 root     root            0 Apr  6 01:47 .ft-generation2
-rw-r--r--    1 root     root           95 Apr  6 04:55 FTVM01-37efdc72.hlog
-rw-------    1 root     root            0 Apr  6 01:47 FTVM01-5d3dd070.vswp
-rw-------    1 root     root         1.0G Apr  6 04:55 FTVM01-flat.vmdk
-rw-------    1 root     root         8.5K Apr  6 04:55 FTVM01.nvram
-rw-------    1 root     root          493 Apr  6 04:55 FTVM01.vmdk
-rw-r--r--    1 root     root            0 Apr  6 01:47 FTVM01.vmsd
-rwxr-xr-x    1 root     root         3.3K Apr  6 04:55 FTVM01.vmx
-rw-------    1 root     root            0 Apr  6 04:55 FTVM01.vmx.lck
-rwxr-xr-x    1 root     root         3.3K Apr  6 04:55 FTVM01.vmx~
-rw-------    1 root     root         1.0G Apr  6 04:55 FTVM01_1-flat.vmdk
-rw-------    1 root     root          469 Apr  6 04:55 FTVM01_1.vmdk
-rw-------    1 root     root          485 Apr  6 01:47 shared.vmft
-rw-r--r--    1 root     root        90.3K Apr  6 04:10 vmware-1.log
-rw-r--r--    1 root     root        89.7K Apr  6 04:57 vmware.log
-rw-------    1 root     root       110.0M Apr  6 01:47 vmx-FTVM01-1564332144-1.vswp
-rw-------    1 root     root       110.0M Apr  6 04:55 vmx-FTVM01-1564332144-2.vswp
[root@bkesx02:/vmfs/volumes/5c98391d-e9d0fd24-5061-005056885f88/FTVM01]
```

Let's review the files created by FT, as follows:

- A ".ftgenerationX" file is a zero-byte file, which is maintained to avoid a split-brain scenario if the host that is running any of the VMs goes down.
- A "shared.vmft" file contains the VMX file paths of both primary and secondary VMs and their UUIDs. The following screenshot shows the contents of the file:

```
[root@bkesx02:/vmfs/volumes/5c98391d-e9d0fd24-5061-005056885f88/FTVM01] cat shared.vmft
.encoding = "UTF-8"
uuid = "50 3a 80 68 9e 77 04 c7-6c 85 d5 44 ae c7 e9 53"
primary.uuid = "50 3a 57 ff 36 21 51 7f-46 17 23 25 0b 4b a1 08"   ◄···• Primary UUID
primary.vmxFilePath = "/vmfs/volumes/5c983940-4c4eec27-8d7b-00505688b9de/FTVM01/FTVM01.vmx"
secondary.secondary0.uuid = "50 3a 80 68 9e 77 04 c7-6c 85 d5 44 ae c7 e9 53"   ◄···• Secondary UUID
secondary.secondary0.vmxFilePath = "/vmfs/volumes/5c98391d-e9d0fd24-5061-005056885f88/FTVM01/FTVM01.vmx"
secondary.secondary0.enabled = "1"
secondary.secondary0.valid = "1"
[root@bkesx02:/vmfs/volumes/5c98391d-e9d0fd24-5061-005056885f88/FTVM01] cat .ft-generation2
[root@bkesx02:/vmfs/volumes/5c98391d-e9d0fd24-5061-005056885f88/FTVM01]
```

If the ESXi host that is running the primary VM fails, then the secondary VM is made the primary VM, and a new secondary VM is spawned. If the host that is running the secondary VM fails, then a new secondary VM is spawned.

In the event that the host that is running the FT VMs experiences a storage PDL/APD situation, the FT VM will be restarted by HA on another available host that has access to the storage. However, this would work only if vSphere HA is configured to react to APD/PDL events:

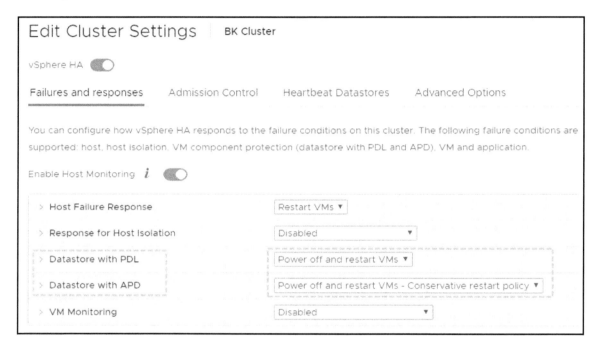

Now that we have learned how Fault Tolerance works, let's review some of its limitations in the next section.

Limitations

It is essential to be mindful of the following limitation before you plan to use vSphere Fault Tolerance in your environments:

- By default, you can run up to *four* FT-enabled (*including primary and secondary*) virtual machines on an ESXi host. And you can have up to *eight* FT-enabled vCPUs (*including primary and secondary*) on an ESXi host. This includes vCPUs on primary and secondary VMs.

    Consider the following example:

    If a host has a 2-vCPU FT (primary/secondary) VM running on it, then it can only host three more 2-vCPU FT (primary/secondary) VMs on it.

    If a host has a 4-vCPU FT (primary/secondary) VM running on it, then it can only host one additional 4-vCPU FT (primary/secondary) or two more 2-vCPU FT (primary/secondary) VMs.

    If a host has an 8-vCPU FT (primary/secondary) VM running on it, then you cannot host any more FT VMs on the same host.

- FT cannot be enabled on VMs with VMDKs that are 2TB or larger in size.
- FT cannot be enabled on VMs with RDM mapped to them.
- If the VM is configured to use a CD-ROM device, then it cannot be backed by a physical device or a remote device. You can, however, map an ISO image from a shared datastore.
- FT does not support creating snapshots. However, it supports a disk-only snapshot created by backup software.
- You cannot store vMotion FT-enabled VMs.
- FT cannot be enabled on VMs that are backed by virtual volumes.

Refer to *vSphere 6.7 Availability Guide for Best Practices*: `https://docs.vmware.com/en/VMware-vSphere/6.7/vsphere-esxi-vcenter-server-67-availability-guide.pdf`.

Configuring vCenter Native High Availability (VCHA)

While vSphere HA can cover for host failures and restart the vCenter VM onto a different host, up until the release of VCHA with vSphere 6.5, there was no method to cover for vCenter service outages since the discontinuation of vCenter heartbeat.

vCenter HA is a quorum-based distributed application cluster, which maintains a passive clone of the vCenter, and a witness node, which acts as a quorum.

 In vSphere 6.7, the VCHA workflow has been further simplified, and with vCenter 6.7 Update 1, the VCHA workflow is now available in the HTML5 client.

In this recipe, we will learn how to configure VCHA.

Getting ready

Before you begin, it is essential that you understand the following requirements:

- You will need a DRS cluster with at least three ESXi hosts.
- If the Active node is hosted in a different management cluster that is managed by a different vCenter, then you will need the single sign-on credentials to that vCenter.
- You will need three IP addresses for the VCHA interfaces. These should be from a subnet other than the vCenter's primary (management) network.
- License requirements: You do not need three vCenter licenses. Only the Active node needs to be licensed with vCenter standard.

How to do it...

The following procedure will help you to configure VHCA on a vCenter:

1. Connect to vCenter Server using the HTML5 client.
2. Select the vCenter Server object and navigate to **Configure** | **Settings** | **vCenter HA**, then click on **SET UP VCENTER HA**:

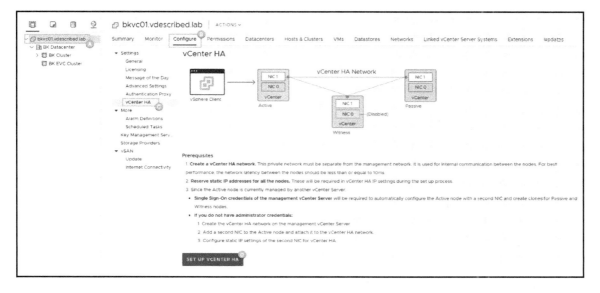

vCHA configuration page before set-up

3. The **Set Up vCenter HA** screen has three sections with which to supply
   settings—**Management vCenter Server Credentials**, **Resource Settings**, and **IP
   settings**:

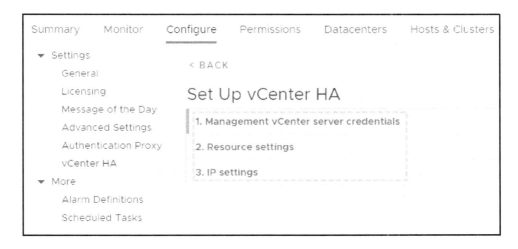

4. In the **Management vCenter server credentials** section, specify the SSO credentials of the vCenter that is managing the active node vCenter VM, and click **Next** to continue:

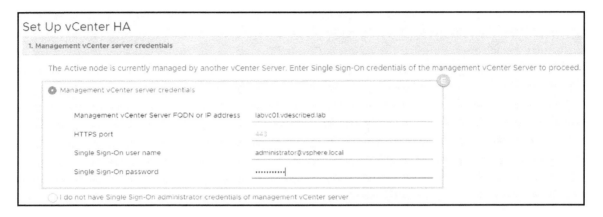

Set Up vCenter HA

1. Management vCenter server credentials

The Active node is currently managed by another vCenter Server. Enter Single Sign-On credentials of the management vCenter Server to proceed.

Management vCenter server credentials

Management vCenter Server FQDN or IP address	labvc01.vdescribed.lab
HTTPS port	443
Single Sign-On user name	administrator@vsphere.local
Single Sign-On password	•••••••••••

○ I do not have Single Sign-On administrator credentials of management vCenter server

5. Click **Yes** to accept the **Certificate Warning** and move on to the **Resource Settings** screen.
6. In the **Resource Settings** section, click **Browse** and select the port group for the VCHA network.
7. Use the **Edit** buttons corresponding to **Passive** and **Witness Node** to bring up their corresponding node resource settings wizard.
8. The **Resource settings** wizard is reasonably straightforward. Use it to specify the following details:
   - Specify the vCenter inventory location (data center or virtual machine folder) for the Passive node.
   - Specify the compute resource (cluster/ESXi host) for the Passive node.
   - Specify the datastore for the Passive node.
   - Specify the port groups corresponding to the vCenter management network and the VCHA network. For the Witness node, you will be prompted to select the VCHA network:

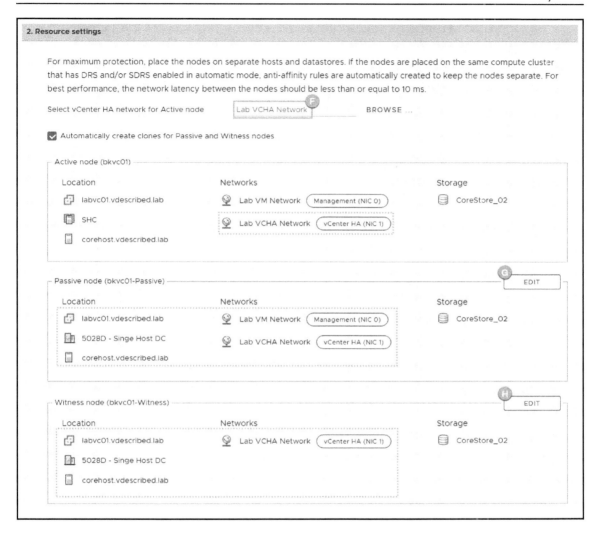

2. Resource settings

For maximum protection, place the nodes on separate hosts and datastores. If the nodes are placed on the same compute cluster that has DRS and/or SDRS enabled in automatic mode, anti-affinity rules are automatically created to keep the nodes separate. For best performance, the network latency between the nodes should be less than or equal to 10 ms.

Select vCenter HA network for Active node   Lab VCHA Network   BROWSE ...

☑ Automatically create clones for Passive and Witness nodes

Active node (bkvc01)

Location	Networks	Storage
labvc01.vdescribed.lab	Lab VM Network (Management (NIC 0))	CoreStore_02
SHC	Lab VCHA Network (vCenter HA (NIC 1))	
corehost.vdescribed.lab		

Passive node (bkvc01-Passive)   EDIT

Location	Networks	Storage
labvc01.vdescribed.lab	Lab VM Network (Management (NIC 0))	CoreStore_02
5028D - Singe Host DC	Lab VCHA Network (vCenter HA (NIC 1))	
corehost.vdescribed.lab		

Witness node (bkvc01-Witness)   EDIT

Location	Networks	Storage
labvc01.vdescribed.lab	Lab VCHA Network (vCenter HA (NIC 1))	CoreStore_02
5028D - Singe Host DC		
corehost.vdescribed.lab		

9. Once done, click **Next** to move to the **IP Settings** section.

10. In the **IP Settings** section, specify the IP addresses for the VCHA network's subnet for the second NICs of all three nodes and click **Finish** to begin the VCHA configuration:

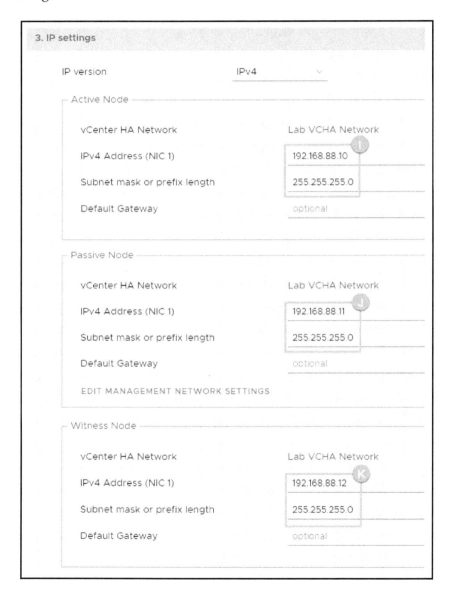

11. You should see the clone and power-on tasks complete successfully in the **Recent Tasks** pane of the management vCenter:

12. Once the VCHA configuration completes successfully, the cluster status should indicate health and all three nodes will be reported as up and running:

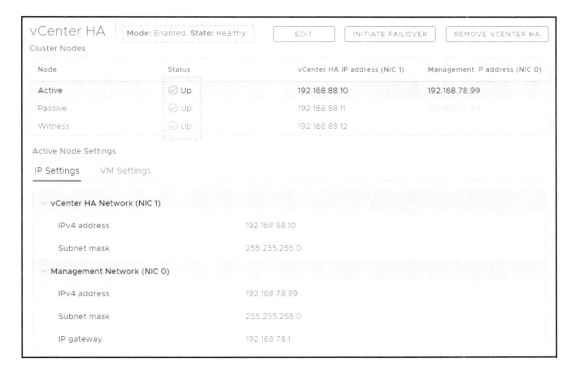

This completes the process of configuring VCHA.

How it works...

Enabling VCHA will configure a second network adapter for the *Active* node and configures it to connect to the VCHA network. The VCHA network should be a different subnet than the primary (management) network of the vCenter. It then clones two copies of the active node. One of the clones is configured as the *Passive* node and the other as the *Witness* node.

The following screenshot depicts the architecture of VCHA. The *Active* node synchronously replicates the **vPostGres Database** (**VCDB**) to the *Passive* node using Native PostgreSQL replication. The changes to the configuration files are *asynchronously* replicated to the passive node using Linux **Remote Sync** (**Rsync**). See the following diagram, vCenter Native HA Architecture:

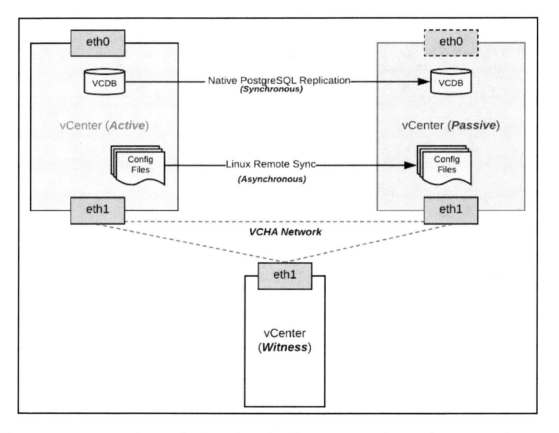

It is important to note that *no data is replicated* to the *Witness* node. It only acts as a **tie-breaker (quorum)** for the VCHA cluster.

If the **Active** node fails, then the cluster fails over, and the Passive node takes the identity (FQDN/IP address) of the vCenter Server. It does so by sending a gratuitous ARP, which notifies the network of the new MAC address.

If the **Passive** node fails for any reason, the cluster will be in a degraded state, therefore preventing automatic/manual failovers. You will need to either repair or redeploy the node. The following screenshot shows the **REDEPLOY** option being made available on an affected cluster:

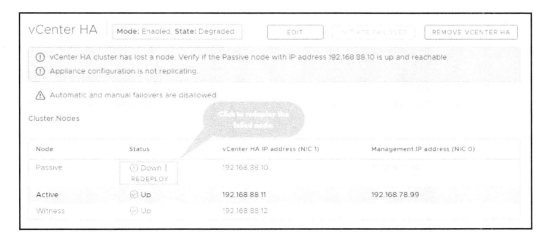

If the **Witness** node fails, then the cluster enters a degraded state, therefore preventing automatic/manual failovers. You will need to either repair or redeploy the node.

Externalizing the PSCs is a deprecated concept in vCenter 6.7. Hence, there is no real need to deploy external PSCs and then place them behind a network load balancer.

10
Achieving Configuration Compliance Using vSphere Host Profiles

It is of prime importance to ensure that every ESXi host in a cluster is configured identically to achieve operational efficiency at the cluster level. There is a lot of configuration that goes into an ESXi host after it is deployed. This includes the general/advanced settings, storage, and networking configuration, as well as licensing and much more. With the number of ESXi hosts that can be part of a cluster and vCenter increasing with every release of vSphere, the amount of work to be done manually will also increase.

Starting with vSphere 4.1, VMware introduced a method to extract the configuration from an ESXi host and form a configuration template, often referred to as a blueprint or golden image. Such a configuration template is called a **vSphere Host Profile**.

 It is important to note that Host Profiles require Enterprise Plus licenses to be applied to ESXi hosts.

Host Profiles help a vSphere administrator to maintain compliance with configuration standards on the desired set of ESXi hosts. They can also be used to make a configuration change that will be pushed to the hosts without having to implement the change on the ESXi host.

For instance, if the NTP time source for the environment changes, then there is a need to make this change on every host using the time source. Such a change can be pushed through a Host Profile. Another example would be a change in the VLAN ID for the virtual machine network on a cluster of ESXi hosts that have been configured with standard vSwitches. Since the hosts are using standard vSwitches, the VLAN ID should be manually specified on the virtual machine port group on each of the hosts in the cluster. This manual work can be avoided by editing the Host Profile and then pushing the VLAN ID change to the entire cluster.

In this chapter, we will cover the following topics:

- Creating Host Profiles
- Associating Host Profiles with ESXi hosts or clusters
- Checking Host Profile Compliance
- Scheduling Host Profile Compliance Checks
- Performing Host Customizations
- Remediating non-compliant Hosts
- Using Host Profiles to push a configuration change
- Copying settings between Host Profiles
- Exporting Host Profiles
- Importing Host Profiles
- Duplicating Host Profiles

Creating Host Profiles

Host Profiles are created by extracting the host configuration from a reference ESXi host. Once created, it will be listed as an object of the Host Profile type in the **Host Profiles Objects** tab.

Host Profiles contain configuration policies that are either fetched from the reference host or added to the Host Profile at a later stage.

A Host Profile can contain the following information:

- Advanced configuration settings
- General system settings
- Networking configuration
- Security and services
- Storage configuration

Not all advanced configuration settings can be configured using a Host Profile. VMware *Knowledge Base article* 2001994 provides more details: https://kb.vmware.com/kb/2001994.

Keep in mind that you will need access to a vCenter Server to create Host Profiles. This is because the object data corresponding to the Host Profiles is saved in the vCenter Server database.

Getting ready

Before you begin, make sure that you have identified a reference host so that you can extract the configuration to form a template. A reference host is prepared so that its configuration can be extracted and saved to a Host Profile, which becomes the golden image.

The following diagram provides an overview of the procedure that's involved in preparing a reference host:

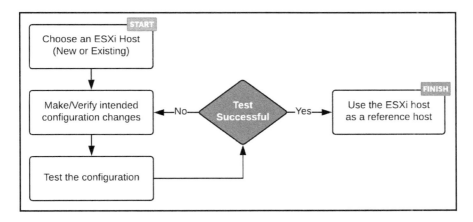

It is important that you take extra care in configuring the reference host since this configuration will be applied to the rest of the hosts in the cluster/environment.

How to do it...

The following steps will help you to create a host profile using a reference host:

1. Connect to vCenter Server using the HTML5 client.
2. Navigate to **Menu** | **Policies and Profiles**:

Policies and Profile Menu

3. On the **Policies and Profiles** screen, go to **Host Profile** and click on **EXTRACT HOST PROFILE**:

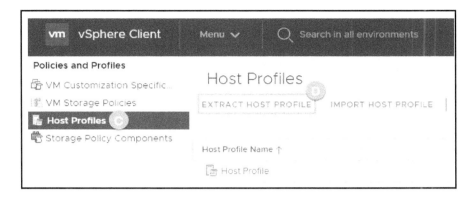

4. In the **Extract Host Profile** wizard, select the reference host and click **Next**:

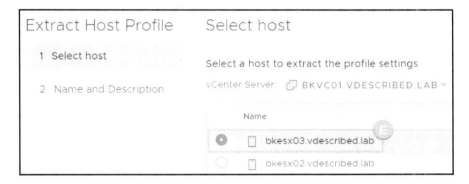

5. Specify an optional **Name and Description** and click **Finish** to create the Host Profile:

6. Once done, the newly created profile should be listed on the **Host Profiles** page:

This completes the process of creating/extracting Host Profiles.

Associating Host Profiles with ESXi hosts or clusters

The whole purpose of creating Host Profiles is to automate the large-scale configuration of ESXi hosts. However, before you can apply a host profile, there should be a way to associate the host(s) with it, which is done by attaching the ESXi hosts to the Host Profile.

How to do it...

The following steps will help you attach/detach hosts to/from Host Profiles:

1. Connect to the vCenter Server using the HTML5 client.
2. Navigate to **Menu | Policies and Profiles**.
3. On the **Policies and Profiles** screen, go to **Host Profiles**.

4. Right-click on the desired Host Profile and click on **Attach/Detach Hosts and Clusters...**:

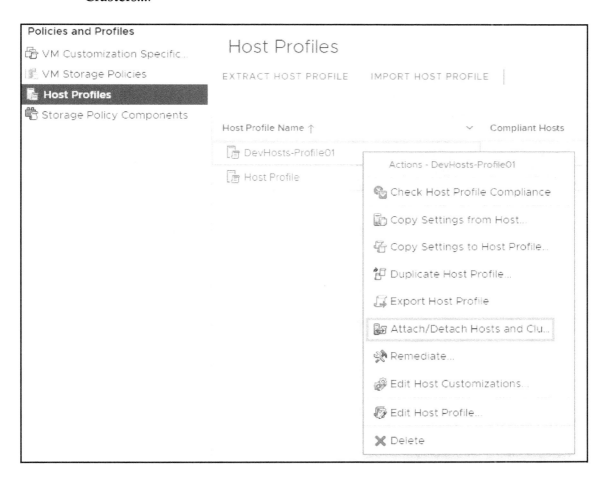

5. In the **Attach/Detach** window, use the checkbox to select (attach) or deselect (detach) Hosts/Clusters. Then, click **SAVE**:

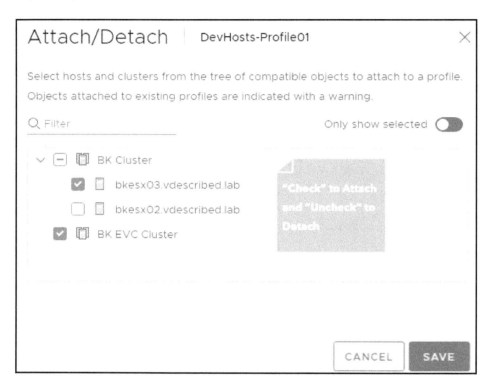

This completes the process of attaching/detaching Host Profiles to a set of ESXi hosts or a cluster. Such an association is subsequently used for compliance checks and remediating new configuration changes. If you decide not to associate a host with a particular Host Profile for some reason, then you could choose to detach the host from the Host Profile. Both the Attach/Detach operations are performed using the same workflow wizard.

Checking Host Profile Compliance

To ascertain whether the ESXi Hosts in a vSphere environment adhere to the necessary configuration policies/requirements, they can be verified for compliance against an associated Host Profile.

Getting ready

Before you can check the profile compliance of an ESXi Host, it should be attached to the Host Profile. For instructions on this, read the *Associating Host Profiles with ESXi hosts or clusters* recipe.

How to do it...

The following steps will help you to check whether a host/cluster is compliant with the host profile attached to it:

1. Connect to vCenter Server using the HTML5 client.
2. Navigate to **Menu | Policies and Profiles**:

Policies and Profile Menu

3. On the **Policies and Profiles** screen, go to **Host Profiles** and click on the desired Host Profile:

4. On the **Monitor** tab of the host profile, select the desired host(s) and click **Check Compliance**:

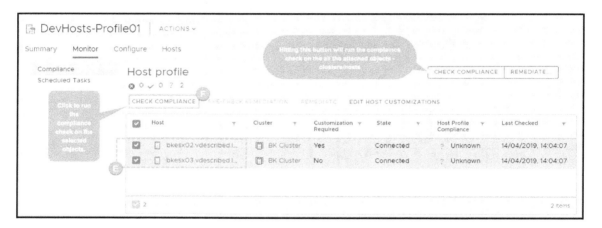

5. The **Recent Tasks** pane should show that the compliance check on the selected objects completed successfully.
6. Once the compliance checks are complete, the host will show a **Compliant/Non-Compliant** status:

This completes the process of running a Host Profile compliance check on a set of hosts or clusters. The compliance check verifies the configuration of the ESXi hosts against the settings of the Host Profile they are attached to. Host(s) with a configuration that differs from the Host Profile will be marked as non-compliant. Such hosts can be remediated to make them compliant. We will learn how to perform Host Profile remediation in a separate recipe.

Scheduling Host Profile Compliance Checks

We can create scheduled tasks to periodically run Host Profile compliance checks on the attached hosts. This is an effective method to ensure that the hosts remain compliant to the configuration standards of the infrastructure.

Compliance checks can only be scheduled to run on ESXi hosts that are attached to the Host Profile. For instructions on how to attach hosts to a profile, read the *Associating Host Profiles with ESXi hosts or clusters* recipe.

How to do it...

The following steps will help you to schedule compliance checks on hosts attached to a Host Profile:

1. Connect to vCenter Server using the HTML5 client.
2. Navigate to **Menu | Policies and Profiles**.
3. On the **Policies and Profiles** screen, go to **Host Profiles** and click on the desired Host Profile.
4. On the **Monitor** tab of the Host Profile, go to **Scheduled Tasks**.

5. On the **Scheduled Tasks** screen, go to **NEW SCHEDULED TASK** | **Check Compliance**:

6. On the **Schedule New Tasks** (**Check Compliance**) window, supply a **Task Name** and optional description, and choose the desired frequency. You could also specify email addresses to notify the administrators of the results of the compliance check. Once done, click **SCHEDULE THE TASK** to confirm the task configuration:

7. The **Recent Tasks** pane should show that a **Create scheduled task** has completed successfully.

This completes the process of creating scheduled Host Profile compliance checks.

How it works...

Compliance check schedules are created on each Host Profile. As shown in the following screenshot, the checks can be configured to run on a specific date and time or after each startup of vCenter Server:

It can also be configured to run periodically at a defined frequency—**Hourly**, **Daily**, **Weekly**, or **Monthly**.

The **Hourly** schedule defaults to every hour but can be configured to recur at the desired hourly frequency. It can be set to start on a specific date/time and configured to be either a perpetual task by setting **End** to **Never** or specifying an end date/time:

The **Daily** schedule defaults to *every day* but can be configured to recur at the desired daily frequency. Much like the hourly/daily schedule, it can be set to start on a specific date/time and configured to be either a perpetual task by setting **End** to **Never** or specifying an end date/time:

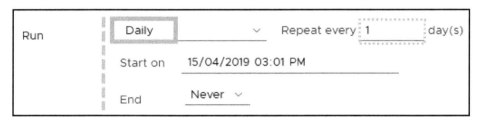

The **Weekly** schedule defaults to *every week* but can be configured to recur at the desired weekly frequency. You could also specify the day(s) in the week the compliance check will be executed. Much like the hourly/daily schedule, it can be set to start on a specific date/time and configured to be a perpetual task by setting **End** to **Never** or specifying an end date/time:

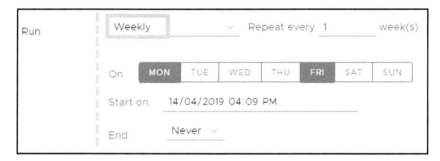

The **Monthly** schedule defaults to *every month* but can be configured to recur at the desired monthly frequency. The task can be configured to run on the nth day of the month or a specific day in any of the four weeks in a month. Much like the other scheduling methods, it can be set to start on a specific date/time and configured to be either a perpetual task by setting **End** to **Never** or specifying an end date/time:

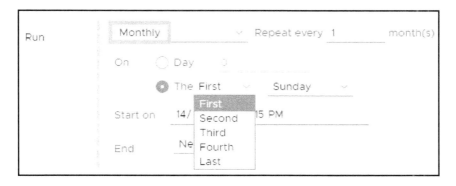

Expanding a scheduled task displays its configuration and the history of the last five runs:

Performing Host Customizations

vSphere Host Profiles can be used to maintain a standard configuration across clusters of ESXi hosts. However, every host will have a set of unique settings—for instance, the IP addresses of the VMkernel interfaces. You can modify such unique settings by launching the **Edit Host Customizations** wizard for each object (cluster/host). However, it is understandably an error-prone and cumbersome process to edit the setting of each host using the wizard interface.

An alternative and efficient method would be to prepare a customizations (`.csv`) file with the host-specific values and use it to perform the host customization.

In this recipe, we will learn how to export and prepare a customization file and then use it for remediating customizations to the attached objects.

The following diagram depicts a high-level overview of this process:

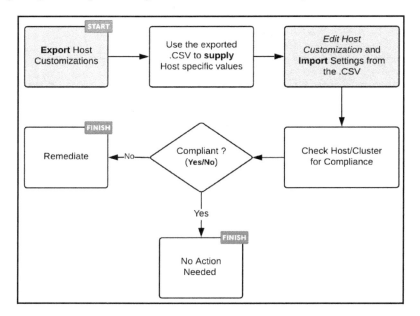

Getting ready

Before you begin, it is essential to ensure that all of the ESXi hosts that need to be customized are attached to the Host Profile you will be generating the customization file for. To learn how to attach hosts to Host Profiles, read the *Associating Host Profiles with ESXi hosts or clusters* recipe.

How to do it...

The following steps will help you to perform host customization on a host(s) or a cluster(s) by using Host Profiles:

1. Connect to vCenter Server using the HTML5 client and switch to the host and clusters view (the keyboard shortcut is *Ctrl + Alt + 2*).

2. Right-click on the desired cluster and navigate to **Host Profiles** | **Export Host Customizations...**:

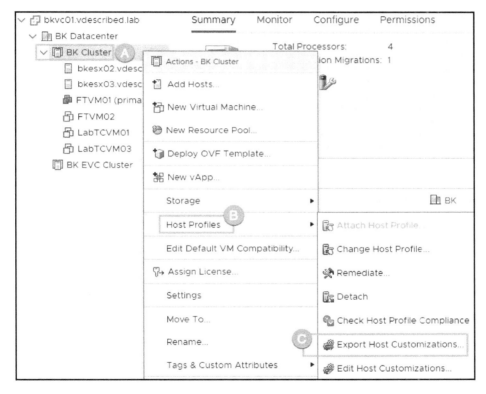

Export Host Customizations option

3. On the **Export Host Customizations** window, click **SAVE** to download and save the `<ObjectName_customizations>.csv` file:

4. Edit the `.csv` file and supply the required settings. Then, save the changes:

Host Customizations CSV File Contents

5. Now, right-click on the cluster again and navigate to **Host Profiles | Edit Host Customizations...**:

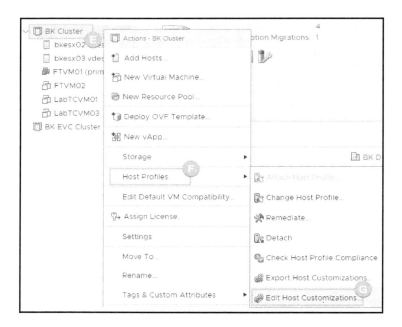

Edit Host Customization option

6. On the **Edit Host Customizations** wizard, select the ESXi hosts and click **Next**:

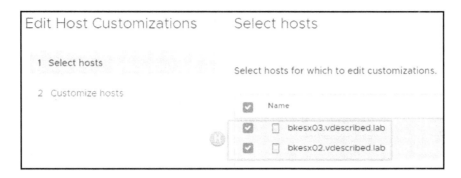

7. On the **Customize Hosts** screen, click **Import Host Customizations** to browse and select the `.csv` file. You should now see that the desired settings have been imported into the wizard interface. Click **FINISH** to apply these settings:

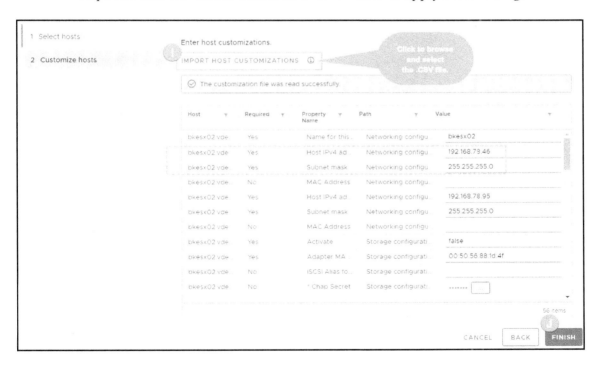

8. The **Recent Tasks** pane should show an **Update Host Customizations** task complete successfully.

9. Now, if you run a check on the cluster for compliance, the hosts that do not match the customization will be listed as non-compliant:

10. You can then proceed with the remediation of the ESXi hosts. To learn how to remediate them, read the *Remediating non-compliant hosts* recipe.

This completes the process of performing host customization on a set of ESXi hosts, without having to edit each host manually. Once the host customizations have been imported, they can be modified by either editing the host customizations or simply re-importing a modified .csv file. It is good practice to run a remediate pre-check to understand the changes that will be made to the hosts before remediating. You will learn more about this in the next recipe.

Remediating non-compliant Hosts

ESXi host(s) that are found to be non-compliant with a Host Profile need a configuration change to be made compliant. Such changes are automated with the help of the remediate operation. The remediate operation will modify the configuration of the host to match the profile.

The following diagram depicts a high-level overview of the remediation process:

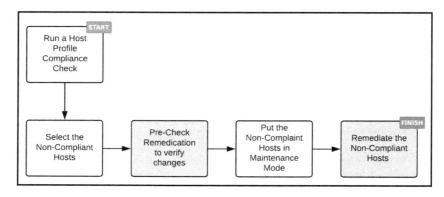

Getting ready

Before you begin, it is important to run a compliance check to identify the non-compliant hosts. To learn how to perform a host profile compliance check, read the *Checking Host Profile compliance* recipe.

The following is a screenshot from one such pre-check:

Once identified, it is a good practice to run a remediation pre-check on the host to verify the changes.

How to do it...

The following steps will help you to remediate a non-compliant ESXi host(s):

1. Connect to vCenter Server using the HTML5 client.
2. Navigate to **Menu | Policies and Profiles**.
3. On the **Policies and Profiles** screen, go to **Host Profiles** and click on the desired Host Profile.

4. On the **Monitor** tab of the Host Profile, go to **Compliance**, select the non-compliant ESXi host, and click on **PRE-CHECK REMEDIATION**:

5. Once the precheck is complete, it will indicate the availability of the results. Click **View results**:

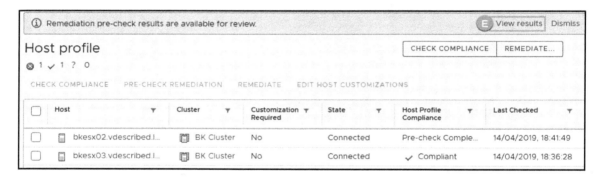

6. Review the results of the pre-check and choose to remediate if the host is already in maintenance mode. If not, the pre-check will indicate the same:

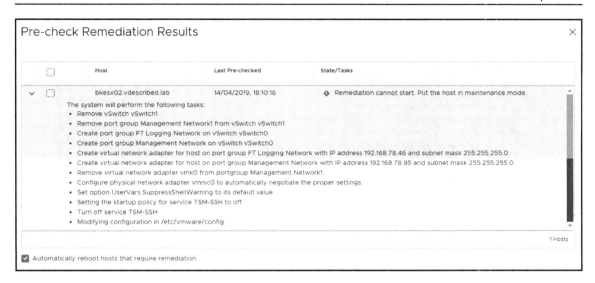

7. Right-click on the host and enter the host into **Maintenance Mode**:

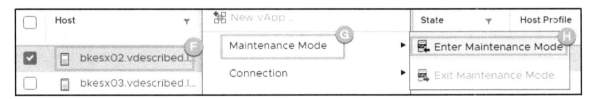

Maintenance Mode option

8. With the non-compliant host selected, click **REMEDIATE**:

9. On the **Remediate** window, click **OK** to start the remediation:

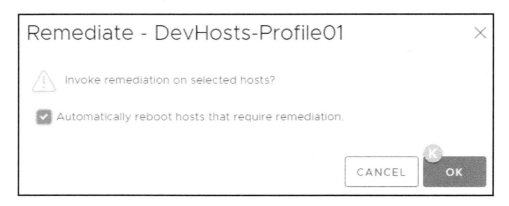

10. You should see another **Pre-check Remediation** and a **Batch apply host configuration** task completed successfully in the **Recent Tasks** pane:

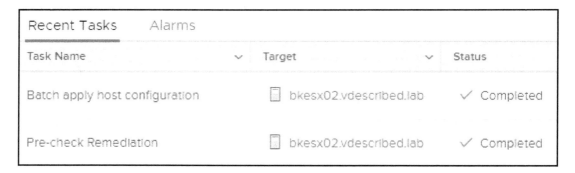

11. Once done, the host should now be shown as **Compliant**:

This completes the process of remediating non-compliant ESXi hosts.

How it works...

During the remediation process, the host configuration is modified in accordance with the settings in the Host Profile. Some changes may require a reboot to take effect. If the **Automatically reboot hosts that require remediation** option was selected, then the host will be rebooted; otherwise, the administrator will be notified about the need for a reboot.

Using Host Profiles to push a configuration change

The whole purpose of using Host Profiles is to effortlessly push the required configuration onto the ESXi hosts without the need for a manual configuration activity per ESXi host. This won't just come in handy when you need to deploy a new infrastructure, but also when you want to push a new configuration to all of the ESXi hosts.

The following diagram shows a high-level overview of the whole procedure:

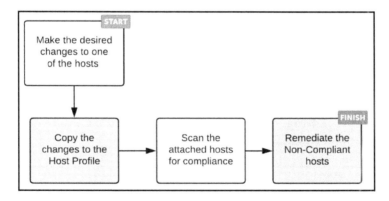

How to do it...

The following steps will help you to push configuration changes to a set of ESXi hosts:

1. Use one of the hosts attached to the profile to make the necessary configuration changes.
2. Navigate to **Menu | Policies and Profiles**.
3. On the **Policies and Profiles** screen, go to **Host Profiles**.

4. Right-click on the desired Host Profile and click on **Copy Settings from Host...**:

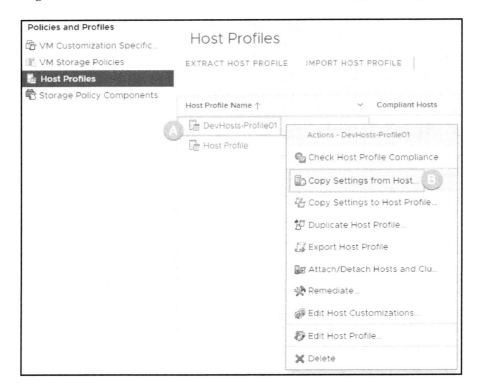

5. On the **Copy Settings from host** window, select the ESXi host the changes were made to and click **OK**:

6. You should see an **Update host profile** task complete successfully in the **Recent Tasks** pane.

7. Now, if you run a compliance check on the host, you will see the hosts without the new configuration marked as non-compliant. You should now be able to set the host customizations and remediate the non-compliant host.

This completes the process of pushing configuration changes using Host Profiles.

How it works...

Updating Host Profiles involves orchestrating a copy of all of the new or updated settings from the desired reference host. This process does not make any changes to the host; instead, it simply modifies the Host Profile with the configuration that's required for it to be compliant with the reference host. Once done, the configuration can then be pushed to other desired hosts the Host Profile is attached to.

Copying settings between Host Profiles

In a large environment, it is entirely possible that you arrive at a configuration change that needs to be published across different sets of hosts or, let's say, host clusters. Since a host or a cluster can only be attached to a single Host Profile at any point in time, there should be a way to publish configuration changes across clusters. It wouldn't make any sense to duplicate Host Profiles whenever such a need arises. Starting with vSphere 6.5, Host Profiles we can now copy settings from one Host Profile to one or more other Host Profiles. The following diagram shows a high—level overview of the logical steps involved in copying settings to host profiles:

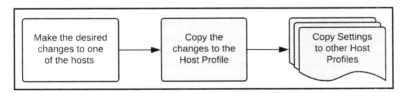

How to do it...

The following steps will help you to copy settings between Host Profiles:

1. Connect to vCenter Server using the HTML5 client.
2. Navigate to **Menu | Policies and Profiles**.
3. On the **Policies and Profiles** screen, go to **Host Profiles**.
4. Right-click on the desired source Host Profile and click on **Copy Settings to Host Profile...**:

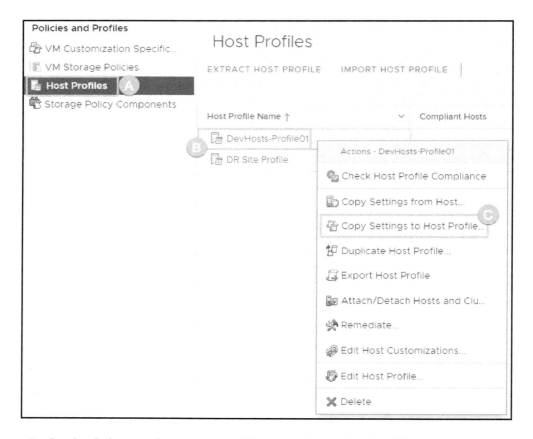

5. On the **Select settings** screen of the wizard, use the checkboxes to select the settings that need to be copied. Then, click **Next** to continue:

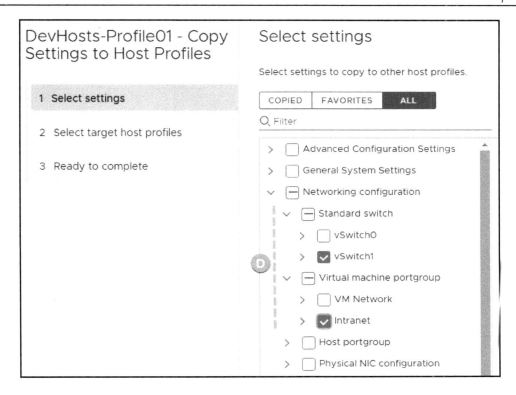

6. On the **Select target host profiles** screen, select the destination Host Profile and click **Next** to continue:

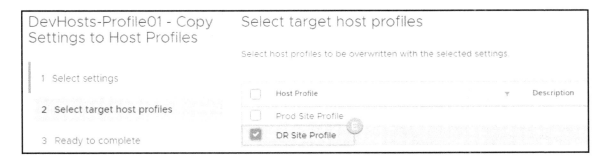

7. On the **Ready to complete** screen, you can click through the settings to review the changes that will be made to the destination/target Host Profile. Click **FINISH** to confirm:

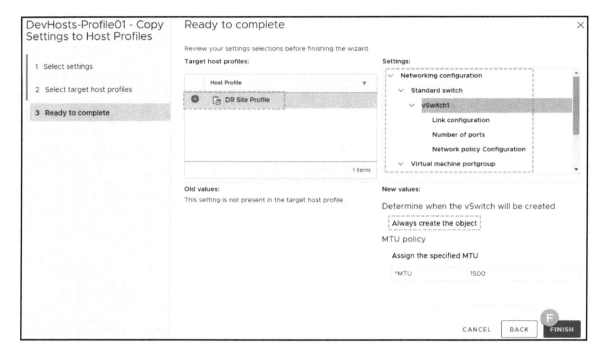

8. You should see a **Copy settings to host profiles** task completed successfully in the **Recent Tasks** pane.

This completes the process of copying settings between Host Profiles.

How it works...

When copying settings between Host Profiles, only the selected settings from the source profile are copied to the destination Host Profile. This process does not make any changes to the source Host Profile. The destination Host Profile to which the settings were copied to becomes non-complaint with the ESXi hosts attached to the profile. You will need to remediate the ESXi hosts to make them compliant again.

Exporting Host Profiles

vSphere Host Profiles can be exported in order to back up or transport the configuration. The exported data is stored in an XML data file with the `.vpf` extension. Since this is an XML file, the contents of the file can be viewed using any text editor, so the passwords are not exported into this file. This file can then be imported into vCenter Server as a Host Profile object. Host Profiles can also be duplicated for the purposes of cloning a copy of the Host Profile.

How to do it...

The following steps will help you to export host profiles:

1. Connect to vCenter Server using the HTML5 client.
2. Navigate to **Menu | Policies and Profiles**.
3. On the **Policies and Profiles** screen, go to **Host Profiles.**
4. Right-click on the desired Host Profile and click **Export Host Profile**:

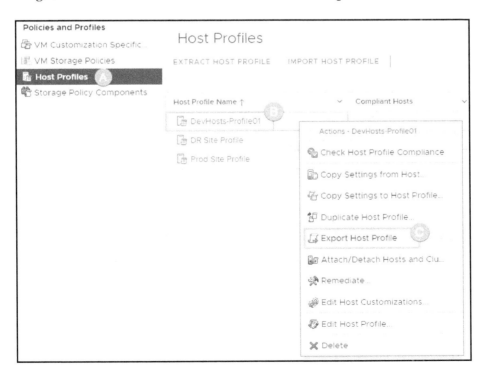

5. After the retrieval of the profile data, you will be prompted to acknowledge that the passwords will not be exported. Click **SAVE**:

 Depending on your browser's download settings, the `HostProfileName.vpf` file will either be automatically downloaded or will prompt for a filename and download location.

6. You should see an **Export Host Profile** task completed successfully in the **Recent Tasks** pane.

This completes the process of exporting Host Profiles. The exported .vpf files can be easily transported to the desired infrastructure locations and then used to create Host Profiles if you import their settings.

Importing Host Profiles

Exported .vpf files can be imported as Host Profile objects. For instance, if you were to build a new data center in your environment that will be managed by a new vCenter, and if the hosts in the new data center should be configured identically to an existing data center host, then a Host Profile from the existing data center can be exported and then imported into the new vCenter so that it can be applied to the new hosts.

How to do it...

The following steps will help you to import Host Profiles:

1. Connect to vCenter Server using the HTML5 client.
2. Navigate to **Menu** I **Policies and Profiles**.

3. On the **Policies and Profiles** screen, go to **Host Profiles** and click on **IMPORT HOST PROFILE**:

4. On the **Import Host Profile** window, click **Choose file** to browse and select a .vpf file. Specify a name for the Host Profile and an optional description. Then, click **OK**:

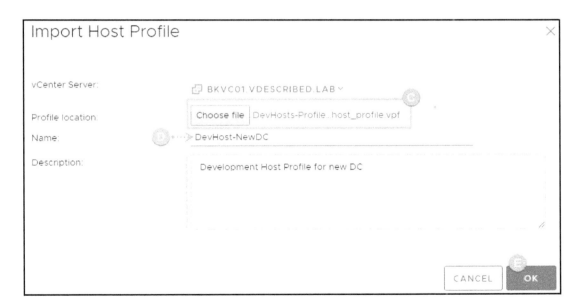

5. You should see a **Create a Host Profile** task completed successfully in the **Recent Tasks** pane.

This completes the process of importing Host Profiles. Since the exported `.vpf` files do not include the passwords, you will be prompted to supply the host credentials (root password) while remediating ESXi hosts using the imported Host Profile.

Duplicating Host Profiles

An existing Host Profile can be cloned to create a duplicate of the same. This can be achieved by using the duplicate Host Profile operation.

How to do it...

The following steps will help you to duplicate Host Profiles:

1. Connect to vCenter Server using the HTML5 client.
2. Navigate to **Menu | Policies and Profiles**.
3. On the **Policies and Profiles** screen, go to **Host Profiles**.
4. Right-click on the desired Host Profile and click **Duplicate Host Profile...**:

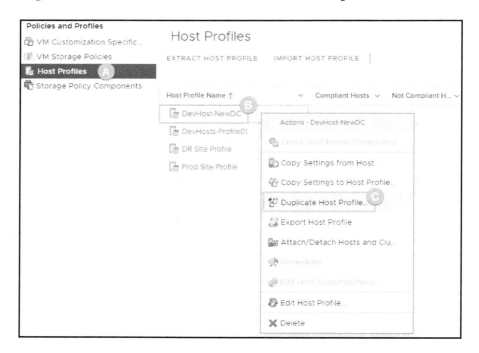

5. On the **Duplicate Host Profile** window, specify a **Name** for the Host Profile and an optional **Description**. Then, click **OK**:

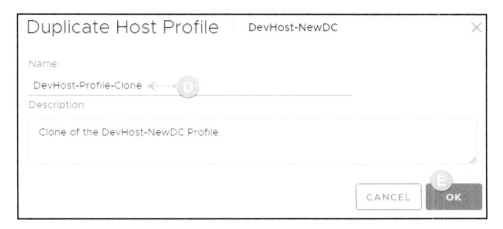

6. The **Recent Tasks** pane should show a **Create a host profile** task complete successfully.

This completes the process of duplicating Host Profiles. The duplicate operation creates a new Host Profile using the settings of the source profile. Duplicating a Host Profile will not retain the host's associations with the source profile.

Building Custom ESXi Images Using Image Builder

11

ESXi Image Builder is used to custom-build ESXi bootable images. There are several use cases, but the most prominent one is - *a server hardware vendor using ESXi Image Builder to package required device drivers, along with the ESXi image.* Image Builder is, in fact, used to create ESXi Image Profiles, which can then be exported as ISO images that contain bootable ESXi images. Before vSphere 6.5, all the Image Builder actions were performed using its PowerCLI plugin. Starting with vSphere 6.5, VMware introduced a vSphere Web Client GUI that makes it much easier to use the Image Builder service.

With vSphere 6.7, the Image Builder user interface is much more streamlined and easier to use, thereby removing the need to rely on the PowerShell plugin.

Before we delve into the details of how Image Builder can be used, it is essential to understand all the constructs and how they are related to each other:

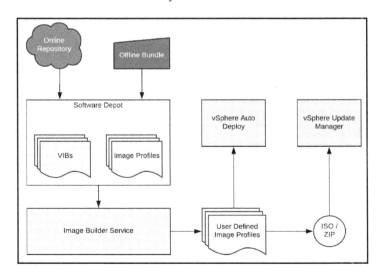

An **offline bundle** is an archive that can either be the entire ESXi image or a driver bundle. It is a collection of **vSphere Installation Bundles** (**VIBs**), their corresponding metadata, and the Image Profiles. All VMware ESXi offline bundles will have more than one VMware-defined Image Profile. It is the first thing that the ESXi Image Builder will need to perform any of its tasks. It is presented as a software depot to the Image Builder service. Therefore, a software depot is nothing but a collection of Image Profiles and VIBs.

An **Image Profile** is a predefined *or* custom-defined set of VIBs and ESXi boot images that can be addressed as a single package. Image Profiles are primarily used to deploy, upgrade, and patch auto-deployed ESXi hosts. To learn more about vSphere Auto Deploy, please read `Chapter 12`, *Auto Deploying Stateless and Stateful ESXi Hosts*.

A **VIB** is a packaged archive that contains a file archive, an XML configuration file, and a signature file. Most OEM hardware vendors bundle their drivers as VIBs.

In this chapter, we will cover the following recipes:

- Enabling ESXi Image Builder
- Importing a Software Depot
- Creating an Online Software Depot
- Creating a Custom Software Depot
- Cloning Image Profiles
- Creating Image Profiles using Software Packages
- Comparing Image Profiles
- Moving Image Profiles between Software Depots
- Exporting Image Profiles

Enabling ESXi Image Builder

ESXi Image Builder runs as a separate service and is disabled by default. It can be enabled either from the vCenter Server's HTML5 interface or by simply starting the service from the command-line interface.

How to do it...

The following procedure will help you enable the ESXi Image Builder service on a vCenter Server:

1. Connect to the vCenter Server using the HTML5 client.
2. Navigate to **Menu** | **Auto Deploy**:

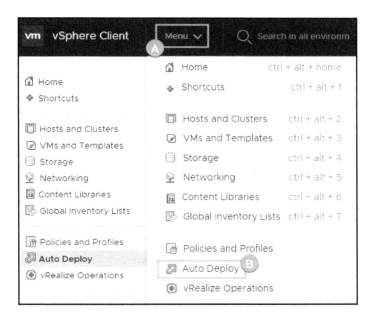

3. Click on **ENABLE IMAGE BUILDER** to enable just the Image Builder component:

4. Once you're done, you will be presented with the Image Builder interface, which will help you create/import and manage software depots:

This completes the process of enabling Image Builder.

How it works...

Enabling Image Builder doesn't install anything—it simply starts the Image Builder service on the vCenter Server. The status of the service can be verified by running the following command on the VCSA appliance CLI:

```
service-control --status vmware-imagebuilder
```

As indicated at the beginning of this recipe, Image Builder can also be enabled by simply starting the vmware-imagebuilder service on the vCenter Server using the following command:

```
service-control --start vmware-imagebuilder
```

The Image Builder server can also be stopped by using the `service-control --stop` command.

Importing a Software Depot

Image Builder requires a software depot to be imported first before you can create, clone, or manage Image Profiles.

An offline bundle is nothing but a `.zip` archive containing VIBs and Image Profiles. Image Builder refers to an offline bundle as a **software depot**. In this recipe, we will learn how to import an offline bundle into the Image Builder.

Getting ready

We cannot use the traditional ESXi installer ISO image with Image Builder. Offline bundles can be downloaded separately, either from the VMware **Downloads** page or from the server vendors repository. Most vendors make their ESXi images (installer ISOs and offline bundles) available for download via VMware's download portal. Here is VMware's downloads page showing both the ISO and offline bundle version of the ESXi 6.7 U2:

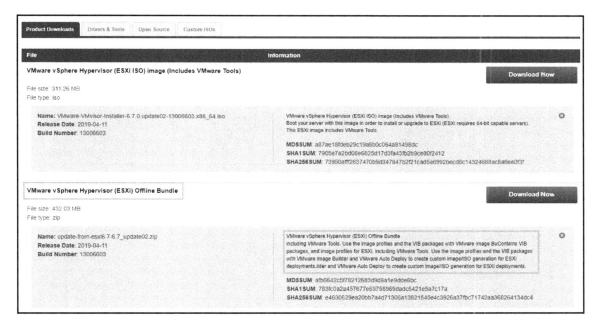

Once you have the offline bundle downloaded, you can then import it as a software depot for the Image Builder service.

How to do it...

The following procedure will help you import an offline bundle as a software depot into the Image Builder:

1. Connect to the vCenter Server using the HTML5 client.
2. Navigate to **Menu** | **Auto Deploy.**

3. On the **Auto Deploy** screen, under the **Software Depots** tab, click **IMPORT**:

4. On the **Import Software Depot** window, specify a **Name** for the depot, browse and select the offline bundle (.zip), and click **UPLOAD**:

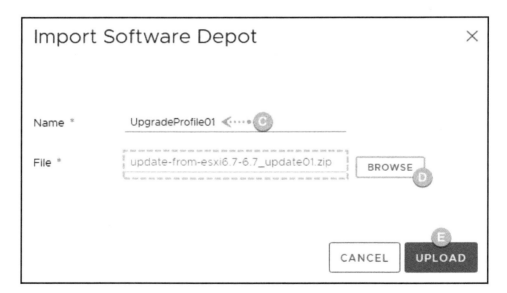

5. You should see the software depot being imported into the vCSA.

6. Once the import is complete, it will automatically close the window and take you back to the **Auto Deploy** screen, showing the Image Profiles that are available within the imported software depot:

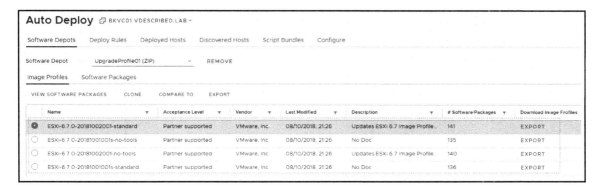

This completes the process of importing an offline bundle as a software depot for Image Builder.

How it works...

The import basically copies the offline bundle into the `/storage/imagebuilder/depot` directory of the vCenter Appliance:

```
root@bkvc01 [ /storage/imagebuilder/depot ]#
root@bkvc01 [ /storage/imagebuilder/depot ]# ls -lth
total 430M
-rw------- 1 root root 430M Apr 19 12:18 82f08b84c992d8805d81b5c54b68b33k6bdc6ddd.zip
root@bkvc01 [ /storage/imagebuilder/depot ]#
```

Now, let's review the contents of the offline bundle.

The bundle contains a `vib20` folder that stores all the VIBs:

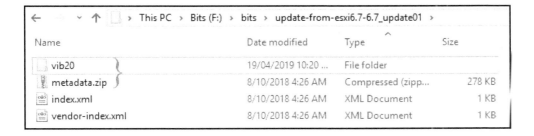

The `metadata.zip` folder contains the image profile definitions in the `profiles` folder, vibs metadata, and bulletins.

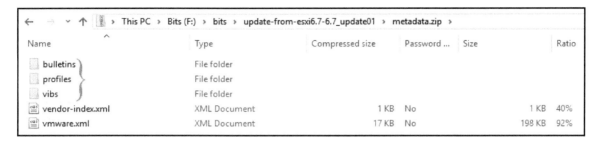

Bulletins are nothing but patch metadata. It is an XML file describing the list of vibs being updated by the patch, release date, release notes URL and a bulletin ID (which is usually the patch number - for instance, *ESXi670-201810234*).

Creating an Online Software Depot

Software depots can be sourced from online repositories as well. The repository can be VMware hosted or vendor-hosted. These depots may or may not contain Image Profiles. Some depots will only contain software packages.

Getting ready

To be able to create an online software depot, you will need to have the depot URLs handy.

Here are some sample URLs:

- **VMware:** https://hostupdate.vmware.com/software/VUM/PRODUCTION/main/vmw-depot-index.xml
- **HPE:** http://vibsdepot.hpe.com/index.xml
- **Dell:** http://vmwaredepot.dell.com/index.xml

How to do it...

The following procedure will help you create an online software depot:

1. Connect to the vCenter Server using the HTML5 client.
2. Navigate to **Menu** | **Auto Deploy.**
3. On the **Auto Deploy** screen, under the **Software Depots** tab, click **NEW**:

4. On the **Add Software Depot** window, select **Online depot**, specify a **Name**, the depot **URL**, and click **ADD**:

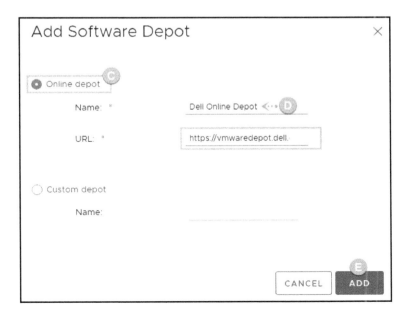

5. You should see a **Connect Depot** task complete successfully in the **Recent Tasks** pane.

This completes the process of adding online software depot.

How it works...

Once Image Builder is connected to an online depot, you can create/customize Image Profiles using the most recent VIBs from the online repository. This removes the need to manually download the driver *or* offline bundles.

Creating a Custom Software Depot

The Image Builder GUI will require you to create a custom depot to allow the cloning or creation of new Image Profiles.

Image Profiles can only be cloned to a custom depot. This applies to predefined Image Profiles as well.

 You can think of a custom depot as a work-desk for customizing new images.

Getting ready

There are no prerequisites for this task, except for the fact that you will need access to the vCenter Server.

How to do it...

The following procedure will help you create a custom depot:

1. Connect to the vCenter Server using the HTML5 client.
2. Navigate to **Menu** | **Auto Deploy.**

3. On the **Auto Deploy** screen, under the **Software Depots** tab, click **NEW**:

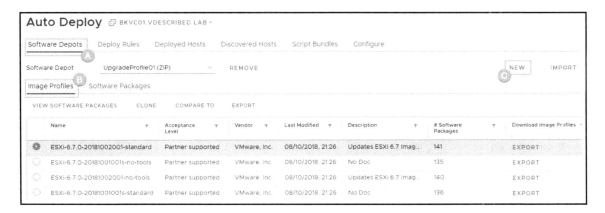

4. On the **Add Software Depot** window, select **Custom depot**, specify a **Name** for the depot, and click **ADD**:

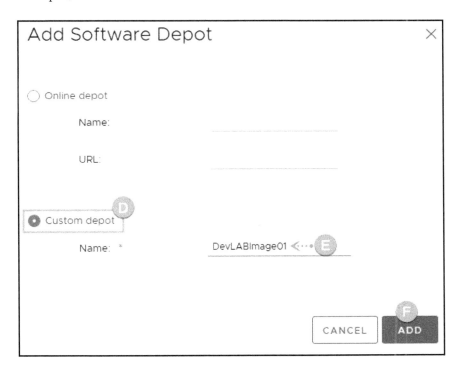

5. Once done, it should then show a software depot with no Image Profiles/Software Packages in it:

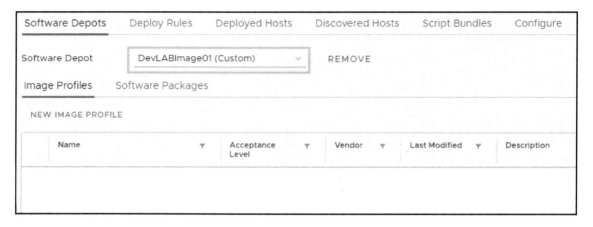

This completes the process of creating a custom software depot.

How it works...

A custom software depot, when created, is a blank container. You can then choose to either clone Image Profiles into it or create a new Image Profile using software packages that were imported from other software depots. Read the *Cloning Image Profiles* and *Creating Image Profiles using software packages* recipes for the next steps in this process.

Cloning Image Profiles

Predefined Image Profiles are read-only, and so they cannot be modified. Cloning will let you create an exact copy of the Image Profile with the read-only property set to false, thereby letting you modify the profile.

Getting ready

Before you begin it is important to be aware of the following aspects:

- Image Profiles can only be cloned to a custom depot, and so the required custom depots should be pre-created. Read the *Creating custom software depots* recipe for instructions.

- If there are no existing Image Profiles, then you will have import an offline bundle with Image Profiles before you proceed. Read the *Importing a software depot* recipe for instructions.

How to do it...

The following procedure will help you clone an existing Image Profile:

1. Connect to the vCenter Server using the HTML5 client.
2. Navigate to **Menu | Auto Deploy.**
3. On the **Auto Deploy** screen, under the **Software Depots** tab, select the desired depot.
4. Select a desired profile from the **Image Profiles** tab and click **CLONE**:

5. In the **Clone Image Profile** wizard, specify a **Name**, a **Vendor**, an optional **Description**, and the desired custom depot. Once you're done, click **Next** to continue:

6. On the **Select software packages** screen, set the desired **Acceptance level**, use the filter to find and select the desired packages, and click **Next** to continue:

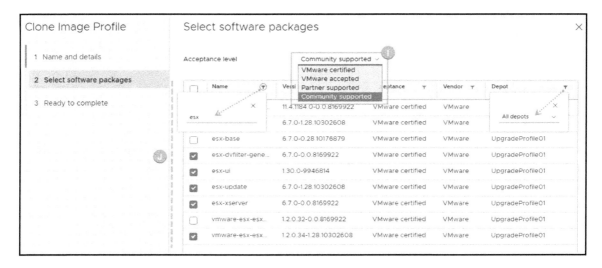

7. You may be presented with a **Validation Results** screen if problems were detected with the software package's selection (this will usually indicate dependency errors). Review the details and modify the software package's selection if required. If the warning was expected, click **Yes** to ignore it and continue.

8. On the **Ready to complete** screen, review the information and click **Finish**:

9. Once you're done, the custom depot should now list the cloned Image Profile:

This completes the process of cloning an existing Image Profile to make a new one with the desired changes.

How it works...

The acceptance level and the software packages that are included can be further modified on a cloned Image Profile. This is because the cloned Image Profiles don't have the read-only flag enabled on them. Once the necessary modifications have been made, the Image Profile can be exported as offline bundles or installer ISOs. Read the *Exporting Image Profiles* recipe for more information.

Creating Image Profiles using Software Packages

Image Profiles can be created from scratch, without the need to clone a predefined Image Profile. However, it is important to make sure that you include at least one ESXi base image and a bootable kernel module.

Getting ready

To be able to create Image Profiles from scratch, you will need offline or online software depot(s) with the required software packages that are already present to the Image Builder Service. Read the *Importing a software depot* and *Creating an online software depot* recipes to learn how to present offline and online depots to the Image Builder. You will also need to create a *Custom depot* before you proceed. Read the *Creating a custom software depot* recipe for instructions.

How to do it...

The following procedure will help you create an Image Profile from scratch:

1. Connect to the vCenter Server using the HTML5 client.
2. Navigate to **Menu | Auto Deploy.**
3. On the **Auto Deploy** screen, under the **Software Depots** tab, select the desired custom depot:

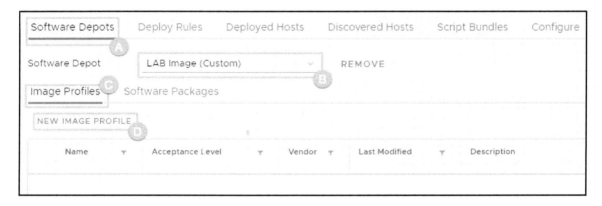

4. On the **New Image Profile** wizard screen, specify a **Name**, **Vendor**, and an optional **Description**. Click **Next** to continue:

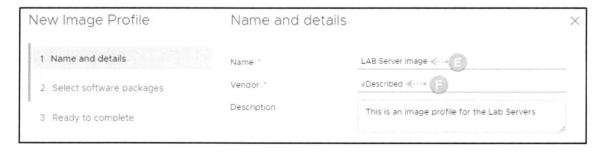

5. On the **Select software packages** screen, filter the software package list by choosing the desired **Acceptance level**. Then, use the column-filter to find and select the desired packages. Click **Next** to continue:

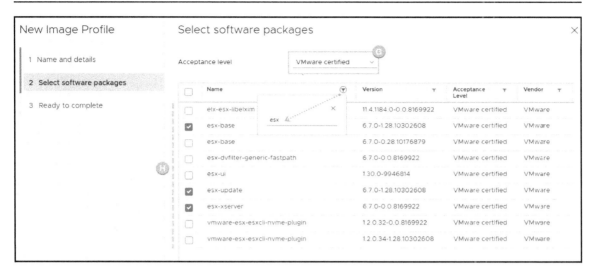

6. You may be presented with a **Validation Results** screen if problems were detected with the software package's selection (this will usually indicate dependency errors). Review the details and modify the software package's selection if required. If the warning was expected, click **Yes** to ignore it and continue.

7. On the **Ready to complete** screen, review the summary and click **Finish**:

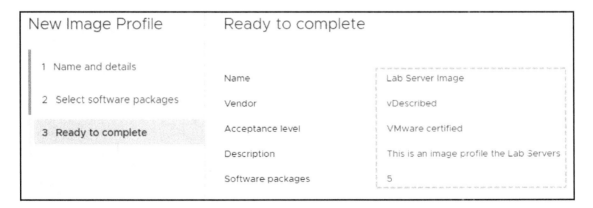

8. Once you're done, the custom depot should list the newly created Image Profile:

This completes the process of creating an Image Profile from scratch using the software packages that are presented to the Image Builder service.

How it works...

The Image Profiles that are created from scratch are no different from other types. They only differ because they're not based on a predefined (vendor defined) Image Profile.

Comparing Image Profiles

Sometimes, it becomes necessary to compare the differences between two Image Profiles. For instance, you can compare two different releases of ESXi to find out what's been upgraded or changed. The Image Builder GUI provides a very intuitive workflow to do this.

Getting ready

For you to be able to compare two Image Profiles, the offline bundle containing them should be presented as software depots to the Image Builder server. Read the *Importing a software depot* recipe for instructions.

How to do it...

The following procedure will help you compare two Image Profiles:

1. Connect to the vCenter Server using the HTML5 client.
2. Navigate to **Menu** | **Auto Deploy.**
3. On the **Auto Deploy** screen, under the **Software Depots** tab, select the desired software depot.
4. Go to the **Image Profiles** tab and select the desired Image Profile. Then, click **COMPARE TO**:

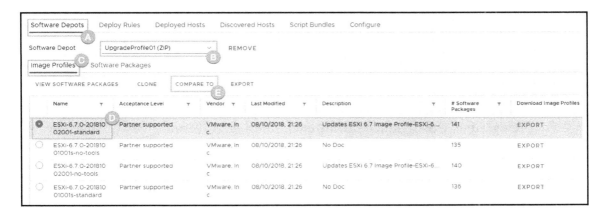

5. On the **Compare Image Profile** window, click on **CHANGE** to select an Image Profile to compare it to:

6. On the **Select Image Profile** window, choose a software depot, select the desired Image Profile, and click **OK**:

7. The **Compare Image Profile** window will now highlight the differences (**Upgraded**, **Downgraded**, **Additional**, **Missing**, and **Same**) between the two selected Image Profiles. Once you're done, you can choose to **CLOSE** the window:

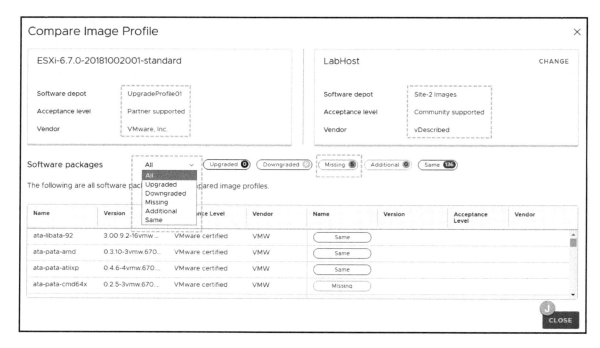

This completes the process of comparing two Image Profiles.

How it works...

The process of comparing two Image Profiles doesn't make any changes to the Image Profiles themselves. It is simply an intuitive method to compare the differences between the two profiles and make customization choices if necessary.

Moving Image Profiles between Software Depots

You can move Image Profiles between two *custom software* depots. A common use case is to use a single software depot as a staging area to prepare an Image Profile, and then move the desired ones to a separate software depot.

Getting ready

Getting ready for this task is fairly straightforward, as there are no specific prerequisites. All you need to know is the name of the Image Profile that needs to be moved and the name of the destination software depot.

How to do it...

The following procedure will help you move Image Profiles:

1. Connect to the vCenter Server using the HTML5 client.
2. Navigate to **Menu | Auto Deploy.**
3. On the **Auto Deploy** screen, under the **Software Depots** tab, select the custom depot which contains the desired Image Profile.

4. Go to the **Image Profiles** tab, select the desired Image Profile, click the ellipsis (**...**), and select **Move To**:

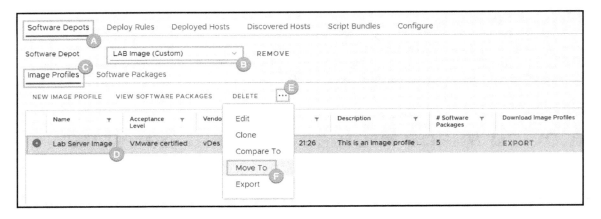

5. On the **Move Image Profile** window, select the destination Image Profile and click **OK**:

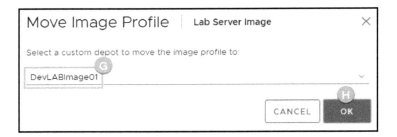

6. Once you're done, the Image Profile should be listed under the destination custom depot:

This completes the process of moving (relocating) Image Profiles between custom depots.

How it works...

Once an Image Profile has been moved to a different software depot, all the references to the Image Profile from the original depot are removed.

Exporting Image Profiles

The whole purpose of using ESXi Image Builder is to create custom ESXi images. Customization is achieved by modifying ESXi Image Profiles. This procedure reaches fruition only when you can generate a bootable ISO or a usable Offline Bundle. The Image Builder GUI can be used to export Image Profiles as ISOs or offline bundles (.zip files).

How to do it...

The following procedure will help you export Image Profiles:

1. Connect to the vCenter Server using the HTML5 client.
2. Navigate to **Menu | Auto Deploy.**
3. On the **Auto Deploy** screen, under the **Software Depots** tab, select the *custom depot* which contains the desired Image Profile.
4. Go to the **Image Profiles** tab, select the desired *Image Profile*, click the ellipsis (...), and select **Export**:

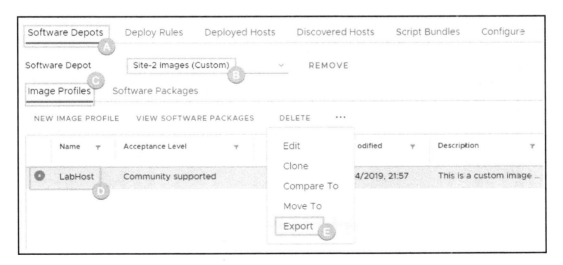

5. On the **Export Image Profile** window, choose to export as an ISO (with/without an installer) or as an offline bundle (`.zip`). Click **OK** to export:

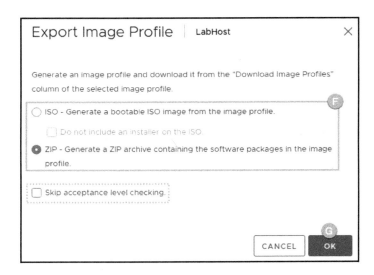

6. The **Recent Tasks** pane should show that an **Image Profile export** task has completed successfully:

7. Once you're done, you will be presented with an option to download the exported image. Click **DOWNLOAD** to download the image onto the client machine:

This completes the process of exporting Image Profiles as ISOs or offline bundles.

How it works...

All the exported images are cached in the /storage/imagebuilder/exports directory of the vCSA:

```
root@bkvc01 [ /storage/imagebuilder/exports ]#
root@bkvc01 [ /storage/imagebuilder/exports ]# ls -lh
total 923M
-rw------- 1 imagebuilder users 315M Apr 20 12:56 LabHost.iso
-rw------- 1 imagebuilder users 307M Apr 20 13:07 LabHost_noinstaller.iso
-rw------- 1 imagebuilder users 303M Apr 20 13:10 LabHost.zip
root@bkvc01 [ /storage/imagebuilder/exports ]#
```

The files in the exports directory are cleared periodically.

12
Auto-Deploying Stateless and Stateful ESXi Hosts

In a large environment, deploying ESXi hosts is an activity that requires a lot of planning and work. For instance, if you were to deploy a set of 25 ESXi hosts in an environment, then you might need more than one engineer to perform this task. The same would be the case if you were to upgrade or patch ESXi hosts. The upgrade or the patching operation should be done on each host. Of course, you have the vSphere Update Manager, which can be configured to schedule, stage, and remediate hosts, but, again, the process of remediation would consume a considerable amount of time, depending on the type and the size of the patch. VMware has a way to reduce the amount of manual work and time required for deploying, patching, and upgrading ESXi hosts. It's called **vSphere Auto Deploy**. In this chapter, you will learn how to not only design, install, and configure the vSphere Auto Deploy solution, but also how to provision ESXi hosts using it.

In this chapter, we will cover the following topics:

- Enabling vSphere Auto Deploy
- Configuring the Trivial File Transfer Protocol (TFTP) server for an ESXi PXE boot environment
- Configuring the DHCP server for a PXE boot
- Creating vSphere Auto Deploy rules
- Configuring Stateless Caching
- Deploying Stateful ESXi hosts

Enabling vSphere Auto Deploy

VMware vSphere Auto Deploy as a solution is not available as a separate download. It is packaged as a service with **vCenter Server Appliance** (**VCSA**). The service, however, is not enabled or started by default. You will need to manually enable it if your environment requires the use of Auto Deploy.

In this recipe, we will learn how to enable vSphere Auto Deploy on the vCenter Server.

Getting ready

You will need access to the vCenter Server as the SSO administrator (`administrator@vsphere.local`) to be able to enable or disable services.

How to do it...

The following steps will help you enable vSphere Auto Deploy:

1. Connect to the vCenter Server as the SSO administrator (`administrator@vsphere.local`).
2. Click on **Auto Deploy** from the left-hand pane or from the menu:

3. Click on **ENABLE AUTO DEPLOY AND IMAGE BUILDER** to enable the service:

4. Once this is done, the **Configure** tab should show the runtime summary for the service:

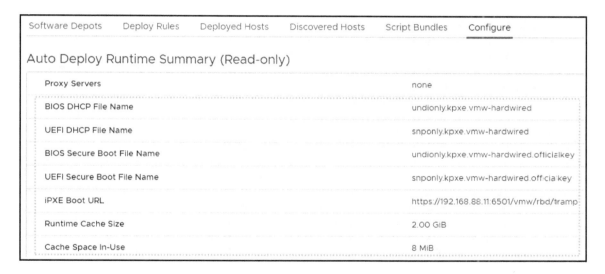

This completes the process of enabling vSphere Auto Deploy on a vCenter Server.

How it works...

Using vSphere Auto Deploy requires both the Auto Deploy and Image Builder services to be up and running. The services can be manually stopped and restarted from the VCSA CLI or the vCSA's VAMI (`https://IP address or FQDN of VCSA:5480`), if required.

Let's delve a bit deeper into this and understand the architecture of vSphere Auto Deploy.

vSphere Auto Deploy, once configured, can be used to quickly provision a large number of ESXi hosts without the need to use the ESXi installation image to perform an installation on the physical machine. It can also be used to perform upgrades or patch ESXi hosts without the need for the vSphere update manager.

So, how is this achieved? vSphere Auto Deploy is a centralized web server component that lets you define rules that govern how the ESXi servers are provisioned. However, it cannot work on its own. There are a few other components that play a supporting role for Auto Deploy to do its magic. These are as follows:

- DHCP server (with scope options 66 and 67 configured)
- TFTP server
- Auto Deploy server
- Hosts with a network boot (PXE) enabled in the BIOS

Now, let's examine how each of these components interact. The following diagram depicts the order of the execution of tasks involved in Auto Deploying ESXi hosts:

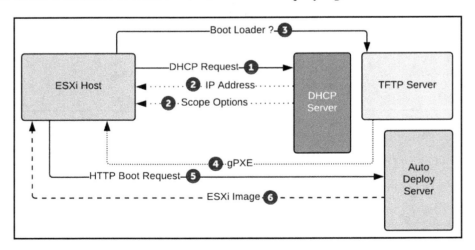

First, the ESXi host begins to network boot by requesting an IP address from the **DHCP Server**. The DHCP Server responds with an IP address; the DHCP scope options provide the details of the **TFTP Server**. The ESXi host then loads the gPXE boot image from the TFTP server to bootstrap the machine and subsequently sends an **HTTP Boot Request** to the **Auto Deploy Server** to load an ESXi image to the host's memory. The diagram is chosen based on the **Auto Deploy rules** that were created in the Auto Deploy server.

Configuring the Trivial File Transfer Protocol (TFTP) server for an ESXi PXE boot environment

TFTP is primarily used to exchange configuration or boot files between machines in an environment. It is relatively simple and nether provides nor requires authentication. The TFTP server component can be installed and configured on a Windows or Linux machine.

In this recipe, we will learn how to configure a TFTP server so that we can PXE boot ESXi hosts.

Getting ready

Before you begin, you will need to install and configure a TFTP server. There are many freeware TFTP servers on the internet to choose from, such as the **WinAgents** TFTP server manager and the **SolarWinds** TFTP server. The installation for all of them is generally straightforward.

 Ensure that the TFTP server is installed on a machine that is in the same subnet as the management network for the ESXi hosts.

You will need access to the vCenter Server as the SSO administrator (`administrator@vsphere.local`).

How to do it...

The following steps will help you configure a TFTP server with the files required to PXE boot an ESXi host:

1. Connect to the vCenter Server as the SSO administrator and navigate to **Auto Deploy** | **Configure**.

2. In the **Configure** tab, under **Auto Deploy Runtime Summary (Read-only)**, click **DOWNLOAD TFTP ZIP FILE**:

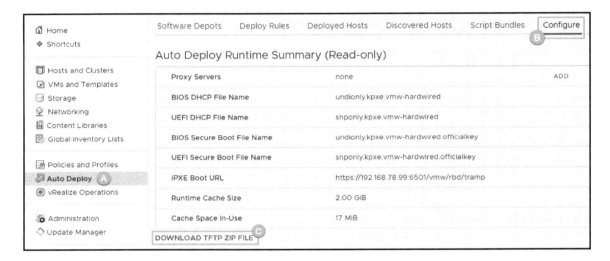

In some cases, your browser settings might prevent the download. Ensure that the browser's security settings allow file downloads.

3. Extract the contents of the `deploy-tftp.zip` file into the `root` folder of the TFTP server. Refer to your TFTP server's user guide for the location of the `root` folder. In this example, SolarWinds TFTP maintains a directory in the `C:` drive (`C:\TFTP-Root`):

Name ^	Date modified	Type	Size
snponly64.efi	23/05/2019 8:11 PM	EFI File	262 KB
snponly64.efi.officialkey	23/05/2019 8:11 PM	OFFICIALKEY File	266 KE
snponly64.efi.testkey	23/05/2019 8:11 PM	TESTKEY File	263 KE
snponly64.efi.vmw-hardwired	23/05/2019 8:11 PM	VMW-HARDWIRE...	262 KE
snponly64.efi.vmw-hardwired.officialkey	23/05/2019 8:11 PM	OFFICIALKEY File	266 KB
snponly64.efi.vmw-hardwired.testkey	23/05/2019 8:11 PM	TESTKEY File	263 KB
tramp	23/05/2019 8:11 PM	File	1 KB
undionly.0	23/05/2019 8:11 PM	0 File	122 KB
undionly.kpxe	23/05/2019 8:11 PM	KPXE File	122 KB
undionly.kpxe.debug	23/05/2019 8:11 PM	DEBUG File	92 KB
undionly.kpxe.debugmore	23/05/2019 8:11 PM	DEBUGMORE File	96 KB
undionly.kpxe.nomcast	23/05/2019 8:11 PM	NOMCAST File	122 K3
undionly.kpxe.vmw-hardwired	23/05/2019 8:11 PM	VMW-HARDWIRE...	122 K3
undionly.kpxe.vmw-hardwired-nomcast	23/05/2019 8:11 PM	VMW-HARDWIRE...	122 KB

This completes the process of configuring a TFTP server to facilitate the PXE booting of ESXi hosts. Next, we will configure the DHCP server for a PXE boot.

How it works...

Auto Deploy uses the TFTP server as remote storage to store configuration or boot files that are required to PXE boot the ESXi hosts. The TFTP server will be contacted during the Auto Deploy process for PXE-booting the server on which the ESXi hypervisor will be deployed. Hence, it is essential to deploy a TFTP server and configure it with a gPXE boot image and the necessary configuration files.

In the next recipe, we will learn how to configure the DHCP server for a PXE boot.

See also

More details on TFTP and a protocol walkthrough are available in the RFC 1350, which is available at `https://www.ietf.org/rfc/rfc1350.txt`.

Configuring the DHCP server for a PXE boot

Once you have the TFTP server configured, the next step is to configure the DHCP server with scope options 66 and 67. You will need access to the DHCP server that is available on the same subnet as the ESXi's management network.

Getting ready

Before you begin, you will need to install and configure a TFTP server for PXE booting ESXi hosts. Read the *Configuring the Trivial File Transfer Protocol (TFTP) server for an ESXi PXE boot environment* recipe. Also, make a note of the **BIOS DHCP file name** from the **Auto Deploy Runtime Summary**. As of vCenter 6.7, it is `undionly.kpxe.vmware-hardwired`.

How to do it...

The following steps will help you modify the DHCP scope settings to help PXE boot the ESXi hosts:

1. On your DHCP server, bring up the DHCP snap-in.
2. Expand the **Scope** corresponding to the ESXi management network's subnet.
3. Right-click on **Scope Options** and click on **Configure Options...**:

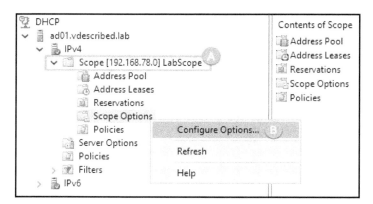

4. Under the **General** tab of the **Scope Options** window, scroll down and use the checkbox against **066 Boot Server Host Name** to enable the option, and set the **String value** to the `FQDN/IP address` of the TFTP server:

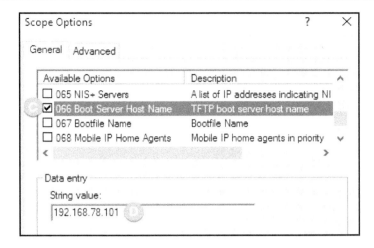

5. Next, enable the checkbox for **067 Bootfile Name**, and set the **String value** to match the BIOS DHCP file name (for example, `undionly.kpxe.vmware-hardwired`):

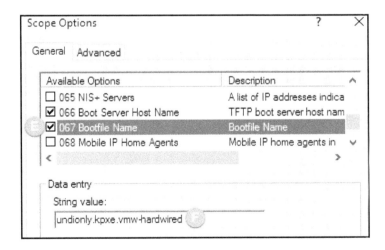

6. Click **Apply** and then **OK** to save and close the window.

This completes the process of configuring the DHCP server to facilitate the PXE boot of the ESXi hosts in an Auto Deploy environment.

How it works...

When a machine is chosen to be provisioned with ESXi and is powered on, it does a PXE boot by fetching an IP address from the DHCP server. DHCP scope configuration options 66 and 67 will direct the server to contact the TFTP server and load the bootable gPXE image and an accompanying configuration file.

There are three different ways in which you can configure the DHCP server for the PXE boot:

- Create a DHCP scope for the subnet to which the ESXi hosts will be connected to. Configure scope options 66 and 67.
- If there is an existing DHCP scope for the subnet, then edit scope options 66 and 67 accordingly.
- Create a reservation under an existing or newly created DHCP scope using the MAC address of the ESXi host.

For large-scale deployments, avoid creating reservations based on the MAC addresses because that creates a lot of extra work. Use of the DHCP scope without any reservations is the preferred method.

Creating vSphere Auto Deploy rules

Once the environment has been prepared to PXE boot, the next step is to configure vSphere Auto Deploy to install ESXi on the hosts. This is achieved by associating ESXi images with specific hosts or groups of hosts. Such an association is achieved by creating Auto Deploy rules, which uses supported patterns such as a MAC address, asset tag, serial number, vendor, domain, gateway address, and so on.

In this recipe, we will learn how to create and activate deploy rules.

Getting ready

Before you begin, you will need to prepare the image profiles that need to be used for deploying the hosts. You will also need the host profiles to be created/imported and placed in vCenter in order to configure the hosts.

How to do it...

The following steps will help you create and activate deploy rules:

1. Connect to the vCenter Server with a user with the Administrator role.
2. Navigate to **Menu** | **Auto Deploy** | **Deploy Rules**.
3. On the **Deploy Rules** screen, click on **NEW DEPLOY RULE**:

4. In the **New Deploy Rule** wizard, supply a **Name** for the rule, and select the **Hosts that match the following pattern** option, to choose the desired pattern to detect matching hosts:

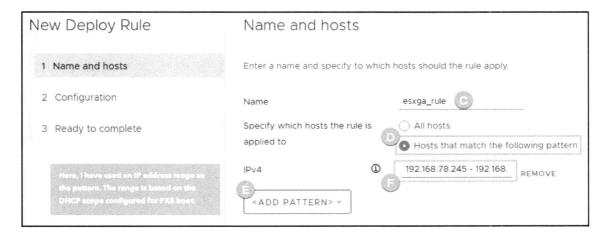

5. On the **Configuration** screen, include **Image Profile**, **Host Profile**, **Host Location**, or **Script Bundle** in the rule. In this case, we have selected **Image Profile**, **Host Profile**, and **Host Location**:

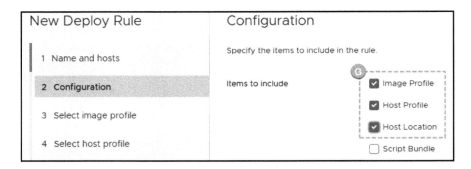

6. On the **Select image profile** screen, select a **Software depot** and then the desired ESXi image profile. Then, click **Next** to continue:

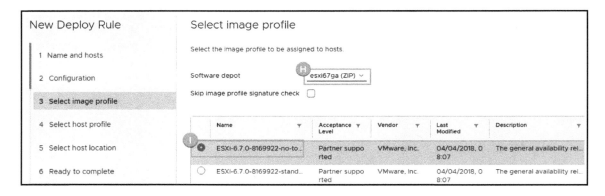

7. On the **Select host profile** screen, select the desired host profile and click **Next** to continue:

8. On the **Select host location** screen, select the vCenter inventory location for the host, and click **Next** to continue:

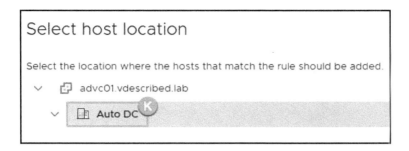

9. On the **Ready to complete** screen, review the settings and click **Finish**:

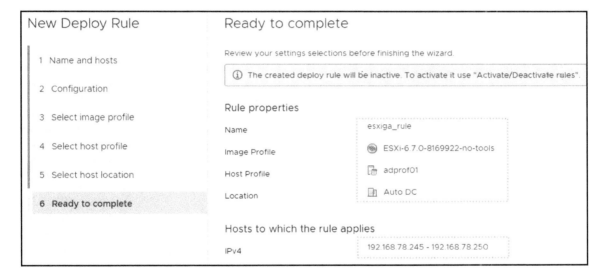

At this stage, you should see the **Create Deploy Rule** task progressing in the **Recent Tasks** pane. This can take a while to complete since the VIBs from the image are copied to the auto-deploy cache location: `/storage/autodeploy/cache`.

10. Once the deploy rule has been created, click **ACTIVATE/DEACTIVATE RULES** to bring up the **Activate and Reorder** window:

11. In the **Activate and Reorder** window, select the deploy rule from the bottom pane and click **ACTIVATE**. Click **OK** once this has been done:

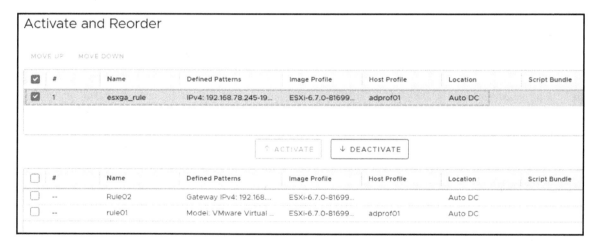

This completes the process of creating and activating the vSphere Auto Deploy rules.

How it works...

The Auto Deploy rules that are created are not activated by default. They have to be manually added to the active set. Only rules in the active ruleset are referenced by the Auto Deploy server when it receives an HTTP boot request. When a machine boots for the first time, the Auto Deploy servers select the image profile based on the lowest number deploy rule in the active ruleset. Once the image profile has been identified, it will be cached at the Auto Deploy server and reused during future reboots.

Now that we know how to prepare the environment for a PXE boot and then Auto Deploy the ESXi hosts, let's dive a bit deeper into what happens in the background during the first and subsequent boot-up operations:

- **First boot**: When a machine has been chosen to be provisioned with ESXi on, it does a PXE boot by fetching an IP address from the DHCP server. DHCP scope configuration options 66 and 67 will direct the server to contact the TFTP server and load the bootable gPXE image and an accompanying configuration file. The configuration will direct the server to send an HTTP boot request to the Auto Deploy server. The HTTP boot request will contain server attributes such as the IP address, MAC address, vendor details, and so on. On receipt of the HTTP boot request, the Auto Deploy server will check its rule engine to see whether there are any rules that match the host attributes. If it finds a corresponding rule, then it will use that rule from the active ruleset to load an appropriate ESXi image from an image profile.

- **Subsequent boot**: After the host has been provisioned and added to the vCenter Server, the vCenter Server holds the details of the image profile and the host profile associated with the host object in its database. Hence, during a subsequent reboot, the Auto Deploy server does not have to leverage its rule engine again. Instead, it uses the information from the vCenter database. If, for whatever reason, the vCenter service/database becomes unavailable, then the Auto Deploy rule engine is engaged to determine the image profile and the host profile to be used. However, the host profile cannot be applied to the host since vCenter is unavailable.

Configuring Stateless Caching

ESXi hosts that are deployed using Auto Deploy require the Auto Deploy server to be available and reachable every time the host reboots. However, if the network boot fails, the server will not have a source to continue the boot process. Enabling stateless caching adds a level of resiliency covering for situations where-in the network boot (PXE boot) fails. The stateless caching mode can be enabled by editing the host profile associated with the ESXi host.

In this recipe, we will learn how to enable stateless caching.

Getting ready

For stateless caching to work, the ESXi hosts should have access to some sort of local storage or USB storage.

How to do it...

The following steps will help you to enable stateless caching for Auto Deployed ESXi hosts:

1. Connect to the vCenter Server as a user with the Administrator role.
2. Navigate to **Menu** | **Policies and Profiles** | **Host Profiles**.
3. Right-click on the desired host profile and click **Edit host profile**.
4. In the **Edit host profile** window, filter through the settings by searching for `System Image Cache`, selecting **System Image Cache Configuration**, and then selecting **Enable stateless caching on the host**:

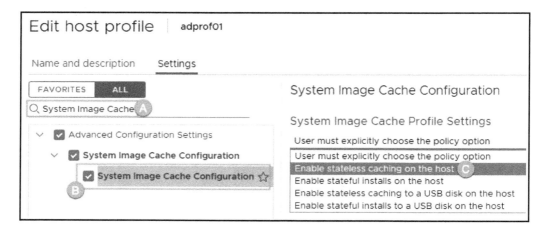

5. Modify the disk order if necessary. The default of **localesx,local** will require Auto Deploy to check whether there is a local disk that currently contains an ESXi image. If none is found, it will then use the first local empty disk that does not have a VMFS filesystem partition on it. The **Check to overwrite any VMFS volumes on the selected disk** option should be left unchecked to ensure that you do not overwrite any VMFS volumes. The **Check to ignore any SSD device connected to the host** option is useful when the local SSDs have been employed for a different purpose, such as reading the cache:

System Image Cache Configuration

System Image Cache Profile Settings

Enable stateless caching on the host **D**

| *Arguments for first disk: | localesx.local **E** |

| *Check to overwrite any VMFS volumes on the selected disk | ☐ |
| *Check to ignore any SSD devices connected to the host | ☐ |

6. Once this is done, click **Save** to apply the changes to the host profile.

This completes the process of enabling stateless caching for Auto Deployed ESXi hosts.

How it works...

Once you have enabled stateless caching on the associated host profile and configured the host to always do a network boot first then, during the next reboot of the ESXi machine, it performs a network boot and loads the ESXi image from the Auto Deploy server. The server finishes booting and applies (remediates) the host profile. Remediation will dump the ESXi image running in memory to the first disk (the local disk, by default) that's selected during the stateless configuration.

After this, if an attempt to network boot the ESXi host fails, it will load the image that was cached to the local disk during the previous successful network boot.

Deploying Stateful ESXi hosts

An auto-deployed ESXi server will always have to perform a network boot and engage the Auto Deploy server or the vCenter database (if it has the information of the image profile and the host profile). This is because the ESXi image is not stored on the host's storage but is loaded directly into the host's volatile memory during every boot.

vSphere Auto Deploy can also be used to install the ESXi image onto the local disk of the chosen host. This process is referred to as a **stateful install**, which allows you to automate the bulk installation of ESXi hosts in a data center.

In this recipe, we will learn how to configure Auto Deploy to perform a stateful installation of ESXi.

Getting ready

For the stateful installation to work, the ESXi hosts should have access to some sort of local storage or USB storage. More importantly, the hosts should be configured to boot from local storage first and then perform a network boot, if necessary.

How to do it...

The following procedure will help you enable a stateful installation of ESXi hosts using Auto Deploy:

1. Connect to the vCenter Server as a user with the Administrator role.
2. Navigate to **Menu** | **Policies and Profiles** | **Host Profiles.**
3. Right-click on the desired host profile and click **Edit host profile**.
4. In the **Edit host profile** window, filter the settings by searching for System Image Cache, selecting **System Image Cache Configuration**, and choosing to **Enable stateful installs on the host**.
5. The disk order and other settings function exactly the same as they do when enabling stateless caching. Refer to the *How to do it...* section of the previous recipe for details:

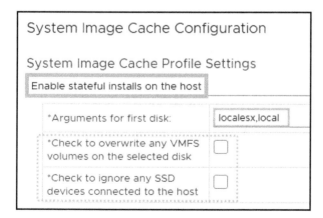

6. Once this has been done, click **Save** to apply the changes to the host profile.
7. Create a new deploy rule so that you can use the host profile with the stateful installation enabled.
8. Change the boot order on the host's BIOS/Firmware in such a way that the host attempts to boot from the local hard drive first and then perform a network boot if that fails.
9. Boot up the host. Once the host has loaded ESXi successfully, it will be automatically placed in maintenance mode.
10. Remediate the hosts with the host profile. Supply the necessary details if prompted for host customization and finish the remediation.
11. Once this has been done, reboot the server to load the ESXi image from the hard disk.

This completes the process of enabling a stateful installation of ESXi using vSphere Auto Deploy.

How it works...

Hosts intended for stateful installations are not configured to perform a network boot first. Instead, they are configured to boot from the hard disk first and then perform a network boot if necessary.

With a stateful install configured correctly, when you boot an ESXi host for the first time, it attempts to boot from the hard drive. Since there is no image on the local disk on the first attempt, it does a network boot and loads the ESXi image from the Auto Deploy server. The rule that's configured on the Auto Deploy server will attach the host profile to the ESXi server. The ESXi server that's deployed will be automatically put in maintenance mode.

Then, you have to manually remediate the hosts in order to apply the changes that are made to the host profile. Remediation will save the ESXi image from memory to the local hard disk of the ESXi machine. Bear in mind that, even though remediation dumps the image to the local hard drive, the server is still running an image loaded from memory. The server will have to be rebooted so that a boot from the local hard disk succeeds.

13
Creating and Managing Virtual Machines

All of the features or solutions that make up a software-defined datacenter aim to provide infrastructure for virtual machines. A virtual machine emulates a physical machine with well-known hardware on which traditional operating systems such as Microsoft Windows and Linux can be installed and operated. As of vSphere 6.7, it is based on the Intel 440BX chipset. This can change with any new release. It also emulates other hardware, such as the VGA controller, SCSI controllers, network cards, and various other devices.

In this chapter, we will cover the following topics:

- Creating a Virtual Machine
- Creating Virtual Machine Snapshots
- Deleting Virtual Machine Snapshots
- Reverting to the current Virtual Machine Snapshot
- Switching to an Arbitrary Virtual Machine Snapshot
- Consolidating Snapshots
- Exporting a Virtual Machine

Creating a Virtual Machine

A virtual machine can be created using vCenter. There are many GUI locations from where the wizard can be started. In this recipe, however, we will be using the VMs and templates inventory view.

Getting ready

Before you begin, it is essential to have the following information at hand:

- The desired name for the virtual machine
- Operating system type
- Number of vCPUs and the amount of memory required
- Number of hard disks and their sizes
- The amount of network interface cards you have and the networks (port groups) they need to connect to
- The name of the datastore(s) the virtual machine will be placed on

How to do it...

The following steps will help you to create a virtual machine:

1. Connect to vCenter Server using the HTML5 client.
2. Right-click on a datacenter or virtual machine folder and click **New Virtual Machine....**
3. In the **New Virtual Machine** wizard, select **Create a new virtual machine** and click **Next** to continue.
4. On the **Select a name and folder** screen, supply the desired name for the virtual machine and select an inventory location (datacenter or virtual machine folder). Notice that the inventory location the wizard was initiated from will be pre-selected.
5. On the **Select a compute resource** screen, select a DRS-enabled cluster or the desired ESXi host and click **Next** to continue. Notice that you are not allowed to select the desired host from a DRS-enabled cluster. This is intentional in order to let DRS perform an optimal placement of the VM.
6. On the **Select storage** screen, select a datastore cluster or datastore to place the VM in. You can use the VM storage policy to filter down a large list of datastores, if necessary.
7. On the **Select compatibility** screen, set the desired compatibility. Make a decision based on the backward compatibility requirements of the virtual machine. The virtual machine hardware version is different for each compatibility selection.

8. On the **Select a guest OS** screen, set the correct guest OS type based on the traditional operating system that will be installed on the virtual machine. On the **Customize hardware** screen, use the **Virtual Hardware** tab to review and modify the virtual hardware configuration:

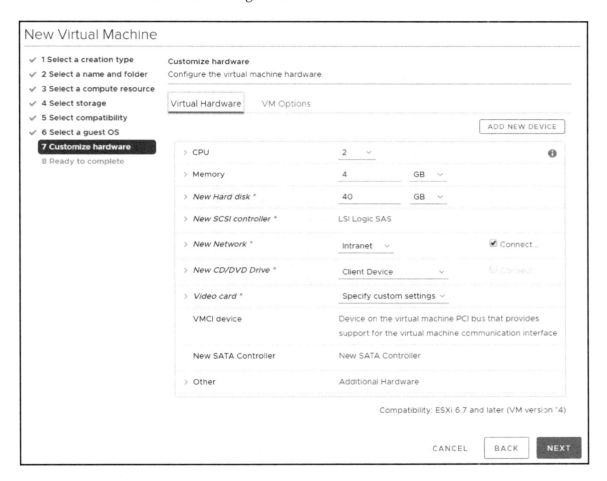

9. Use the **VM Options** tab to configure additional options, such as the boot firmware type (BIOS/UEFI):

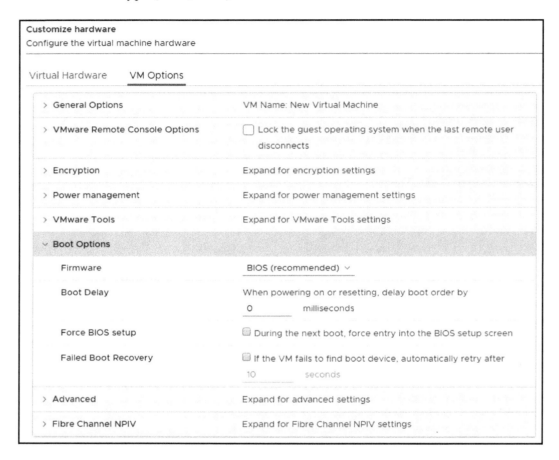

10. On the **Ready to complete** screen, review the summary of the options that you've selected and click **Finish** to create the VM.

This completes the process of creating a brand new virtual machine.

How it works...

Now that we know how to create virtual machines, let's review the components that make up a virtual machine.

Virtual machine components

A virtual machine will have the following default virtual hardware components:

- Memory, CPUs, a SCSI controller, hard disks, and network adapters
- Video card, VMCI device, SATA controller, and a CD/DVD drive

Additional components can be added using the **ADD NEW DEVICE** option:

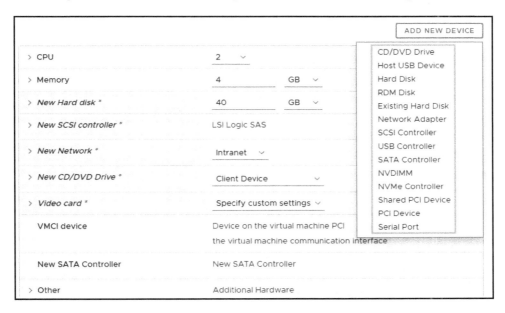

Files that back a virtual machine

Every virtual machine is backed by a set of files. The virtual machine configuration file with the .vmx extension holds all of the virtual machine's configuration information. For files associated with a virtual machine, refer to the following table:

Configuration file	File extension
Virtual machine configuration file	*.vmx
Virtual disk descriptor file	*.vmdk
Virtual disk data file	*-flat.vmdk
RDM mapping file (physical compatibility mode)	*-rdmp.vmdk
RDM mapping file (virtual compatibility mode)	*-rdm.vmdk

Virtual machine snapshot database	`*.vmsd`
Virtual machine snapshot state file	`*.vmsn`
Virtual machine snapshot delta file	`*-delata.vmdk`
Virtual machine team information file	`*.vmxf`
Virtual machine swap file	`*.vwsp`
Virtual machine BIOS file	`*.nvram`

The **virtual machine configuration (.vmx)** file holds all of the configuration information about the virtual machine, which includes the following:

- The virtual hardware version (14, 15 with vSphere 6.7 update 2)
- The CPU configuration (numvcpus, cpuid.coresPerSocket)
- Memory configuration (memSize)
- Virtual disk drives (scsix.virtualDev/present/deviceType/filename)
- Virtual network cards (ethernetx.virtualDev/present/networkName/addressType/generatedAddress)
- Guest OS type (guestOS)
- BIOS UUID of the virtual machine (uuid.bios)
- vCenter assigned UUID of the virtual machine (vc.uuid)

The **Virtual Machine BIOS** (`.nvram`) file holds the virtual BIOS (Phoenix BIOS) for a virtual machine. It can be accessed by pressing the *F2* function key during the VM's boot up. This file is created when the virtual machine is powered on for the first time. All of the BIOS changes are saved to this file. If the file is manually deleted, you will lose the previous BIOS configuration, but the file will be regenerated with the defaults during the next power on. For instance, if you were to forget the BIOS password, then a neat way to reset it is to turn off the VM, delete the NVRAM file, and power on the VM to regenerate a new NVRAM file with a fresh BIOS.

The **virtual machine disk** (**VMDK**) can be provisioned using two different methods: thick provisioning and thin provisioning. Thick provisioning can be further categorized into lazy zeroed thick provisioning and eager zeroed thick provisioning:

- **Eager zeroed thick provisioning**: An eager zeroed thick disk, when created, will get all of the space allocation it needs, and all of the disk blocks allocated to it are zeroed out. The creation time of an eager zeroed disk is longer compared to a lazy zeroed or thin-provisioned disk. An eager zeroed thick disk offers better first write performance. This is due to the fact that the disk blocks corresponding to an eager zeroed disk are already zeroed out during its creation.

- **Lazy zeroed thick provisioning**: A lazy zeroed thick disk will also get all of the space allocation it needs at the time of creation, but unlike an eager zeroed disk, it does not zero out all of the disk blocks. Each disk block is zeroed out during the first write. Although it doesn't offer the first write performance that an eager zeroed disk does, all of the subsequent writes to the zeroed blocks will have the same performance.

> A first write occurs when a disk block corresponding to a VMDK is accessed for the first time so that you can store data.

- **Thin provisioning**: A thin-provisioned disk will not use all of the disk space assigned to it during creation. It will only consume the disk space that's needed by the data on the disk. For instance, if you create a thin VMDK of 10 GB, then the initial size of the VMDK will not be 10 GB. When data is added to it, the VMDK will grow in size to store the added data. If a 100 MB file is added to the VMDK, then the VMDK will grow by 100 MB.

A virtual machine disk can also be in two different disk modes. These modes determine what operations can be performed on the VMDK:

- **Dependent disk mode**: This is the default disk mode for all of the virtual machine disks that you create. All VMDK-related operations can be performed while it is in *dependent* mode.
- **Independent disk mode**: When a virtual disk is in independent mode, no snapshot operations are allowed on it. These types of virtual disks are particularly useful with virtual machines in testing and development environments when you need to make changes and test the results, and want to revert to a standard baseline after the tests. It is also useful when you are using virtual machines to perform tests that can yield unpredictable results. These kinds of VMs are generally not backed up. An independent disk can have two fundamental behavioral modes:
  - **Persistent mode**: In this mode, all of the changes that are made to the files on disk are written to the disk. Because these changes are immediately written to the disk, they are retained across reboots. In a test/development environment, this mode is used to save changes to the test baseline.

- **Nonpersistent mode**: In this mode, changes that are made are not immediately written to the disk and are lost when you reboot or shut down the virtual machine. This mode is generally used in test environments, where changes can yield unpredictable results.

Creating Virtual Machine Snapshots

There are times when you need to save the current state of an application or operating system's configuration before you experiment with a change. A real-life example would be during a system development life cycle where changes are inevitable, and you need the ability to undo a change. vSphere allows you to save the state of a virtual machine, regardless of its power state.

A virtual machine snapshot can capture the following data:

- The contents of the virtual machine's memory
- The virtual machine's configuration
- The state of the virtual disks

Getting ready

To be able to perform snapshot operations on a virtual machine, you need to be connected to the vCenter Server either by using the vSphere HTML5 client or the web client or by directly connecting to the host using the host client. Also, keep in mind that snapshots cannot be created on virtual disks in independent mode or on RDMs in physical compatibility mode.

How to do it...

The following steps will help you to create a virtual machine snapshot:

1. Connect to vCenter Server using the HTML5 client.
2. Find the desired VM, right-click on it, and navigate to **Snapshots** | **Take a Snapshot**:

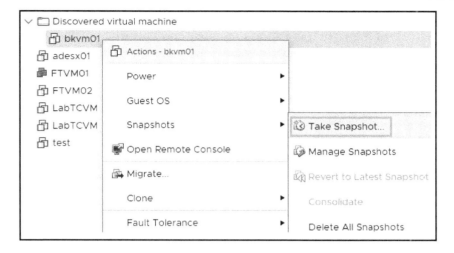

3. On the **Take Snapshot** window, supply a name and optional description, and use the checkboxes to include a virtual machine memory snapshot and/or quiesce on the guest filesystem.
4. With the desired options selected, click **OK**.

This completes the process of creating virtual machine snapshots.

How it works...

When creating a snapshot, you can opt to snapshot the virtual machine's memory and/or to quiesce the guest filesystem. Quiescing the filesystem means bringing the data that is on the disk to a state that would enable backups. This would flush the buffers onto the disk and wait for in-flight IO to complete and/or pause the running applications. For quiescing to work, you will need VMware tools to be installed. The VMware tools installation includes a version of Microsoft **Volume Shadow Service** (**VSS**) that's automatically installed/enabled if the operating system does not have VSS installed.

> While, in most cases, quiescing will create application-consistent snapshots, there can be old applications in the environment that may not work with the VSS API. Such an application would need additional scripts to quiesce its services.

If the virtual machine's memory was chosen to be included in the snapshot, then the ESXi server will flush all of the virtual machine's memory contents to disk. The flushed memory contents are stored in the **virtual machine state file** (`.vmsn`). While this is taking place, the virtual machine will temporarily remain frozen or unresponsive.

 The VMSN will hold the memory, VMX, and BIOS information.

The amount of time for which the virtual machine will continue to be in an unresponsive state depends on the amount of time that is needed to dump the memory to disk. The amount of memory that needs to be flushed and the disk's performance are also contributing factors.

Once the memory has been dumped to disk, the subsequent disk I/O will be redirected to a snapshot difference file called the delta file (`-delta.vmdk` or `-sesparse.vmdk`). The delta file is also a virtual disk data file and is referenced by using a virtual disk descriptor file.

 SEsparse is the default disk format for snapshot deltas on a VMFS6. VMFS5 uses the SEsparse format for delta disks larger than 2 TB.

The delta file will continue to hold all of the disk I/O changes from the time when the snapshot was taken. For the server to do the I/O to the delta file, the virtual machine should be configured to access the delta files instead of the base virtual disk. This happens automatically when you create a snapshot.

 The snapshot difference file (`-delta.vmdk`) cannot grow beyond the size of the original base disk. For instance, if the base disk is 40 G, then the delta can only grow up to 40 G in size.

Information regarding the snapshots is stored in a virtual machine snapshot database file called the **VMSD**. The snapshot manager GUI reads the VMSD file in order to display the snapshot's information.

When you create more than one snapshot on a VM, the snapshot chain is also updated. It does this by modifying the descriptors of the child disks.

There's more...

If left unattended, snapshots can double a VM's disk footprint on the datastore. This is because a snapshot can grow to be as large as the base-original disk. It can also affect the performance of the VM since every write would need ESXi to allocate disk blocks and grow the delta file. It is important to periodically monitor the VMs for leftover snapshots and delete them.

See also

- For best practices on creating virtual machine snapshots, read the *VMware Knowledge Base* article, 1025279. It is available at `https://kb.vmware.com/kb/1025279`.
- The *VMware Knowledge Base* article, *Working with snapshots* (1009402), should be a good read. It is available at `http://kb.vmware.com/kb/1009402`.

Deleting Virtual Machine Snapshots

To delete a virtual machine snapshot, you will need to use the snapshot manager. There are two types of delete operations:

- **Delete**: This operation will let you choose a snapshot to delete. When this is done, the data is held by its VMSN, the changes are recorded by the VMX, and the delta file is committed (written) to its immediate parent VMDK.
- **Delete All**: When this operation is performed, only the contents of the current snapshot and its delta file are committed to the base disk. The rest will be discarded; the VMSN and the delta files will be deleted as well.

Getting ready

Snapshots are deleted when you are certain that the changes that you've made to the virtual machine have yielded the desired result. Deleting snapshots will retain these changes; note that this operation is irreversible.

 The **guest OS** (**GOS**) remains completely unaware of the fact that its disks are backed by snapshots at any stage.

How to do it...

The following steps will help you to delete snapshots on a virtual machine:

1. Connect to vCenter Server using the HTML5 client.
2. Find the desired VM, right-click on it, and navigate to **Snapshots** | **Manage Snapshots.**
3. Select the snapshot to be deleted and hit **DELETE**. Use the **DELETE ALL** function if you wish to delete all of the snapshots:

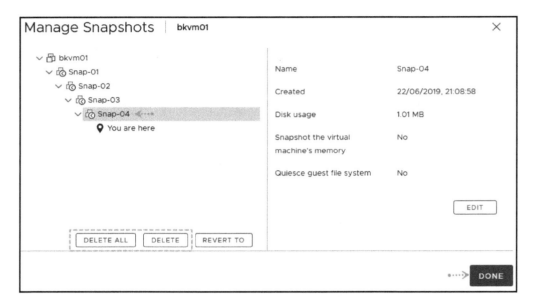

4. You will be prompted to confirm the operation. Click **OK** to confirm.
5. Once you are done using the desired delete function, click **DONE** to close the snapshot manager.

This completes the process of deleting virtual machine snapshots.

How it works...

To explain how the snapshot delete operation works, I have created four snapshots on a VM. We will go through the effects on the VM and the snapshot tree after the delete operations.

Here is what the snapshot manager looks like with all four snapshots created:

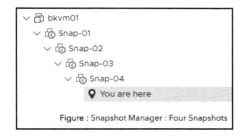

Figure : Snapshot Manager : Four Snapshots

The following table provides a correlation between snapshots, deltas, and GOS files for this example:

Disk/Snapshot	Files inside the GOS	Snapshot File Name	Snapshot Delta File Name	GOS File in Snapshot Delta
Base Disk (*No Snapshots*)	TestDoc		bkvm01-flat.vmdk	
Snap-01	TesDoc	bkvm01-Snapshot1.vmsn	bkvm01-000001-sesparse.vmdk	
When a new file (DevDoc1) is created at this stage, it is stored in the snapshot delta file - bkvm01-000001-sesparse.vmdk.				DevDoc1
Snap-02	TestDoc, DevDoc1	bkvm01-Snapshot2.vmsn	bkvm01-000002-sesparse.vmdk	
When a second new file (DevDoc2) is created at this stage, it is stored in the sapshot delta file - bkvm01-000002-sesparse.vmdk.				DevDoc2
Snap-03	TestDoc, DevDoc1, DevDoc2	bkvm01-Snapshot3.vmsn	bkvm01-000003-sesparse.vmdk	
When a third new file (DevDoc3) is created at this stage, it is stored in the snapshot delta file - bkvm01-000003-sesparse.vmdk.				DevDoc3
Snap-04	TestDoc, DevDoc1, DevDoc2, DevDoc3	bkvm01-Snapshot4.vmsn	bkvm01-000004-sesparse.vmdk	
When additional files (ProDoc1, ProdDoc2)are created at this stage, it is stored in the snapshot delta file - bkvm01-000004-sesparse.vmdk				ProDoc1, ProdDoc2

Now that we can use the table as a reference, let's go through a few scenarios:

- **Scenario 1 – deleting the current snapshot**: If we delete the current snapshot (Snap-04), then the contents of its delta (ProdDoc1 and ProdDoc2) are committed to the delta of the immediate parent snapshot, which is Snap-03. Now, Snap-03 becomes the last snapshot in the chain. Due to this, the delta (bkvm01-000003-sesparse.vmdk) will hold the DevDoc3, ProdDoc1, and ProdDoc2 files. However, keep in mind that, at this stage, the GOS will still have access to all of the files—TestDoc, DevDoc1, DevDoc2, DevDoc3, ProdDoc1, and ProdDoc2. The only difference when using the snapshots is the fact the changes that were made at different stages (snapshots) are held in different delta files.

- **Scenario 2 – deleting an arbitrary snapshot**: If we delete an arbitrary snapshot (Snap-03), then the contents of its delta (DevDoc3) is committed to the delta of its immediate parent snapshot, which is Snap-02. Once done, Snap-03 is deleted and the snapshot chain is modified so that Snap-02 becomes the parent of Snap-04:

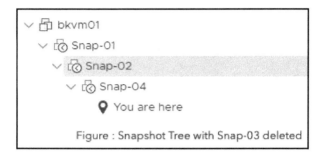

Figure : Snapshot Tree with Snap-03 deleted

- **Scenario 3 – delete all snapshots**: When a **DELETE ALL** operation is issued, the contents of the current snapshot and its delta are committed to the base disk. The rest will be discarded; the VMSN and the delta files will be deleted as well. If the current snapshot is Snap-04, then after a **DELETE ALL** operation, the base disk will have the TestDoc, DevDoc1, DevDoc2, DevDoc3, ProdDoc1, and ProdDoc2 files.

 During the remove operations, the snapshot manager will remove the entry corresponding to the chosen snapshot from the snapshot database. This is done prior to updating the child VMDK's descriptor file with the new parent disk's **Content ID** (**CID**) value.

See also

- Refer to the *Unable to delete the virtual machine snapshots* (2017072) due to locked files VMware Knowledge Base article at https://kb.vmware.com/kb/2017072.

Reverting to the current Virtual Machine Snapshot

The whole idea behind taking a snapshot is to save the current state of the virtual machine so that it will remain unaffected by the changes you intend to make. In a situation where you want to discard the changes you just made and return to the saved state of the virtual machine, the revert to latest snapshot operation is performed.

Getting ready

Reverting to the current snapshot will discard the most recent changes and is an irreversible operation, and so it is important to gather your thoughts before you proceed. This process does not require the use of the snapshot manager for the virtual machine.

How to do it...

The following steps will help you to revert to the latest/current snapshot:

1. Connect to vCenter Server using the HTML5 client.
2. Find the desired VM, right-click on it, and navigate to **Snapshots** | **Revert to Latest Snapshot**:

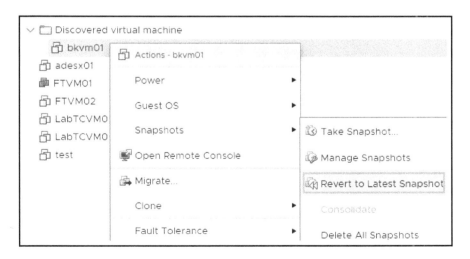

3. You will be prompted to confirm the operation. Click **Yes** to do so.
4. The **Recent Tasks** pane should show a **Revert to Current Snapshot** task completed successfully.

This completes the process of reverting a virtual machine's state to the most recent (latest/current) snapshot.

How it works...

Reverting to a current/latest snapshot will discard its delta contents. The contents of the delta file are permanently lost unless it is saved in a subsequent snapshot. That is, if the current snapshot isn't parenting a child snapshot, then its delta data is lost forever.

In our example (refer to the table from the previous recipe), the current snapshot was Snap-04, and its delta was saved to the Test4 file. After the **Revert to Current Snapshot** operation, the contents of its delta file, bkvm01-000004-sesparse.vmdk, is discarded and Snap-04 will only have TestDoc, DevDoc1, DevDoc2, and DevDoc3.

Switching to an Arbitrary Virtual Machine Snapshot

The **REVERT TO** option lets you revert to a selected snapshot. This is particularly useful if you want to discard all of the changes that you have made to the virtual machine and return to a snapshot that's older than the most recent state of the virtual machine.

Getting ready

This process requires the use of the snapshot manager for the virtual machine. It is important to keep in mind that, if we revert to a virtual machine snapshot that doesn't have the memory content captured, it will result in the virtual machine being powered off.

How to do it...

The following steps will help you to revert to an arbitrary snapshot:

1. Connect to vCenter Server using the HTML5 client.
2. Find the desired VM, right-click on it, and navigate to **Snapshots** | **Manage Snapshots**.
3. Select the desired snapshot from the chain and click on **REVERT TO**:

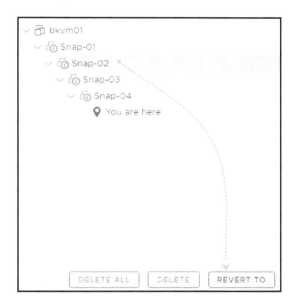

4. You will be prompted to confirm the operation. Click **Yes** to do so.
5. The **Recent Tasks** pane should state that a **Revert snapshot** operation has completed successfully.

How it works...

When you revert to a particular snapshot, the process will discard all of the contents of its difference file (delta) and all of the subsequent snapshots. Reverting to a snapshot will result in the selected snapshot's state, minus the contents of its delta.

For example, while the VM is currently running on the delta of Snap-04, if we revert to Snap-02, this will discard the contents of the delta file, bkvm01-000002-sesparse.vmdk (which holds the DevDoc2 file), as well as the contents of all of the other snapshots that were subsequently created. So, after reverting to Snap-02, the OS will only have the TestDoc and DevDoc1 files available:

Even though it discards the contents of its delta, it does not delete the delta file because the snapshots that were taken subsequent to that depend on the delta of its parent. That is, Snap-03 depends on the delta of Snap-02. Therefore, Snap-03 will have the state of Snap-02 and the changes recorded in the delta of Snap-02. So, after reverting to Snap-02, if we go back to Snap-03, GOS will see the TestDoc, DevDoc1, and DevDox2 files. If we go back to Snap-04, you will see the TestDoc, DevDoc1, DevDoc2, and DevDoc3 files.

There is a caveat that you should keep in mind when you choose to revert to snapshots. When you revert from a snapshot to an older one, the delta of the current snapshot (if it is the last snapshot in the chain) will be deleted.

That is, if Snap-04 is the last snapshot in the chain, and if you revert from Snap-04 to an older snapshot in the chain, this will result in the permanent loss of the contents of its delta file, bkvm01-000004-sesparse.vmdk, which contains the ProdDoc1 and ProdDoc2 files.

Consolidating Snapshots

Snapshot consolidation is the process of merging the content of all of the snapshots to the base disk. We have seen snapshot consolidations fail for various reasons. For instance, a backup appliance that hot adds the VMDK to its proxy server to back up its content should ideally remove the hot-added VMDK and issue a delete operation on the snapshot it created. If, for some reason, it fails to remove the hot-added VMDK, then all subsequent snapshot delete operations that it issues will also fail. This is because the file is in use.

If this goes undetected, then you will be left with a lot of snapshot delta files, all of which will eventually use up a lot/all of the free space on the datastore. Things get worse when the snapshot manager does not show all of the leftover snapshots, leaving the user/administrator with no GUI control over the situation.

 During a delete operation, the snapshot database (`.vmsd`) entries are removed prior to merging the deltas or updating the child VMDK's descriptor file with the new parent disk's CID value.

Getting ready

The **Consolidate** option is only made available if there is a mismatch between the information in the snapshot database (`.vmsd`) and the actual snapshot chain. Hence, it is important to identify and fix the cause of the failed snapshot-delete operation and resolve any file lock issues before you proceed, otherwise, the Consolidate operation will also fail.

How to do it...

The following steps will help you to Consolidate snapshots:

1. Connect to vCenter Server using the HTML5 client.
2. Find the desired VM, right-click on it, and navigate to **Snapshots** | **Consolidate**:

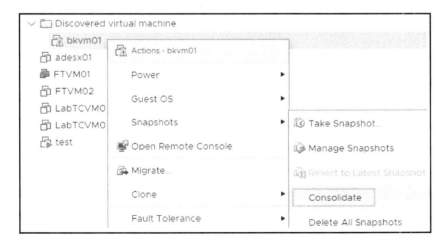

3. You will be prompted to confirm the operation. Click **Yes** to continue.

4. The **Recent Tasks** pane should show the **Consolidate virtual machine disk files** task completed successfully.

This completes the process of consolidating snapshots.

How it works...

The Consolidate operation is performed when a snapshot delete/delete all operation fails, but it also removes the snapshot information from the snapshot database. If this happens, the VM's home folder will still have the snapshot files (deltas), and the virtual machine will also be running on the snapshots.

Prior to the addition of the **Consolidate** option, the administrator had to rely on other methods to Consolidate snapshots. For instance, you could go through a tedious task of verifying the snapshot chain to make sure it is not broken, and then issue `vmkfstools -i` on the current snapshot (most recent) to clone and Consolidate the delta.

Exporting a Virtual Machine

A virtual machine can be packaged for transport. vSphere provides a method to do so by exporting a virtual machine in an open virtual machine format (OVF), which is an open standard that was developed by the **Distributed Management Task Force** (**DMTF**) with cooperation from VMware, Citrix, IBM, Microsoft, Sun, and other companies.

Getting ready

To be able to export a virtual machine to OVF, it needs to be in a **Powered Off** state. Starting with vSphere 6.5.x and 6.7, you can no longer export VMs to OVA using the web/HTML5 clients.

 You can convert an OVF package into OVA format using the VMware OVF tool (`https://www.vmware.com/support/developer/ovf/`).

How to do it...

The following steps can be followed to export a virtual machine as an OVF:

1. Connect to vCenter Server using the HTML5 client.
2. Find the desired VM, ensure that it is powered off, right-click on it, and navigate to **Template | Export OVF Template**.
3. In the **Export OVF Template**, supply a name and an optional annotation, choose to **Enable advanced options**, select the desired options, and click **OK**:

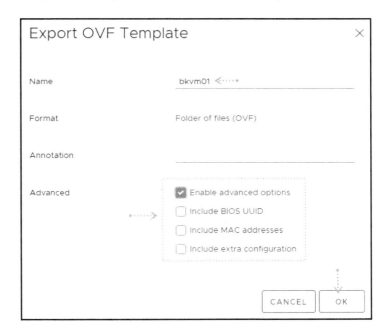

4. You should see the **Export OVF template** and **Export OVF Package** tasks completed successfully in the **Recent Tasks** pane.

This completes the process of exporting virtual machines as OVF packages.

How it works...

The OVF will package all of the virtual machine files into a single folder. It will have an OVF descriptor file, which will have an extension, `.ovf`; a manifest (`.mf`) file; the virtual disks; and certificates, if any.

The manifest file contains the SHA1 digest of all of the files in the package. The OVA is simply a TAR file with the OVF folder packaged inside it. The `.ova` extension can even be changed to TAR and have its content extracted by an un-archiver such as 7-Zip.

14
Upgrading and Patching Using vSphere Update Manager

Updating and patching your vSphere environment is part of a periodic maintenance routine. Although the update/upgrade/patch can be done manually, it becomes a tedious process when you're dealing with a large environment. **vSphere Update Manager** (**VUM**) allows you to manage patching and the upgrade process with ease.

VMware fully integrated Update Manager into its appliance with vSphere 6.5. It runs as a service and uses the vPostGres database. No changes have been made to this model in vSphere 6.7, but it has a much-improved workflow and HTML5 client integration.

In this chapter, we will cover the following topics:

- Downloading Patch Definitions
- Creating Patch Baselines
- Creating Host Upgrade Baselines
- Creating Baseline Groups
- Configuring Update Manager's Remediation Settings
- Patching/upgrading ESXi hosts using Update Manager
- Upgrading VMware Tools and virtual hardware using Update Manager
- Installing the Update Manager Download Service on Linux
- Configuring UMDS to download patches
- Configuring a Web Server on UMDS (Linux)

Downloading Patch Definitions

Patch definitions are metadata about patches that are made available by the patch source. These definitions allow you to download all of the available patch information, without needing to download all of the patch bundles. Like the patches, the definitions are downloaded from an internet source—VMware or the hardware vendor.

Getting ready

Before you begin, it is essential to ensure that the desired patch sources have been configured. By default, Update Manager includes a patch source from VMware, which you can access by going to `https://hostupdate.vmware.com/software/VUM/PRODUCTION/main/vmw-depot-index.xml`.

The configuration for patch sources is available under the **Settings** | **Patch Setup** tab of Update Manager:

The non-default patch sources in the preceding screenshot are the ones that were manually added. It's essential that all of the sources that you want to fetch patches from are **Enabled** and **Connected** before you proceed.

How to do it...

The following steps will help you to download the latest patch definitions:

1. Connect to vCenter Server using the HTML5 client as an administrator.
2. Use the left-hand pane or the inventory **Menu** to bring up the **Update Manager** page:

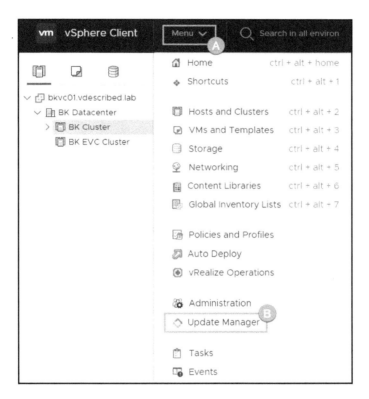

3. On the **Update Manager** screen, navigate to **Settings** | **Patch Downloads** and click **DOWNLOAD NOW**:

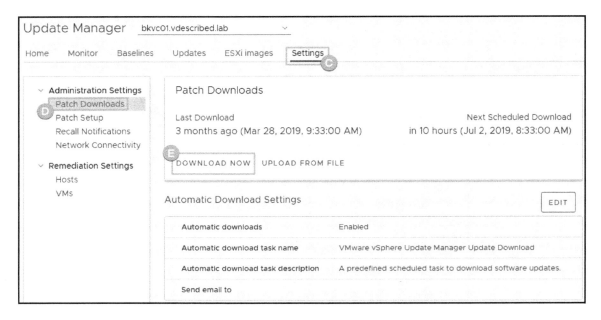

4. You should see a **Download patch definitions** task completed successfully in the **Recent Tasks** pane.

This completes the process of downloading the patch definitions.

How it works...

By default, patch definitions are downloaded every 24 hours. The download frequency can, however, be modified as per your requirements. Patches can also to be manually uploaded to the Update Manager's cache by using the **Upload From File** option.

Once the patch definitions have been downloaded, you can then use them to create the desired baselines.

Creating Patch Baselines

A baseline is a list of patches that can be used to check the ESXi hosts for compliance. By default, there are two sets of baselines that are predefined:

- Non-Critical Host Patches
- Critical Host Patches

In this recipe, we will learn how to create new patch baselines.

Getting ready

Before you begin, it is essential to ensure that you have the latest patch definitions downloaded. Read the *Downloading patch definitions* recipe for instructions.

How to do it...

The following steps will help you to create an Update Manager baseline:

1. Connect to vCenter Server using the HTML5 client as an administrator.
2. Use the left-hand pane or the inventory **Menu** to navigate to Update Manager.
3. On the **Update Manager** screen, go the **Baselines** tab and click **NEW | Baseline**:

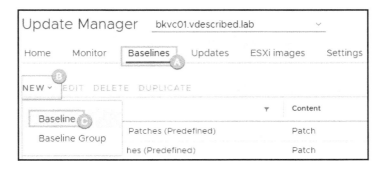

4. On the **Create Baseline** wizard screen, supply a **Name** for the baseline, and an optional **Description**, set the **Content** to **Patch**, and click **Next** to continue:

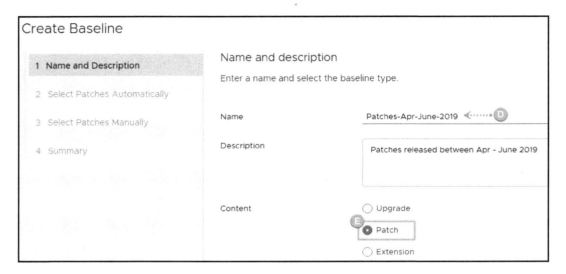

5. Set **Criteria** (for instance, before/after date) to filter the desired patches and click **Next** to continue:

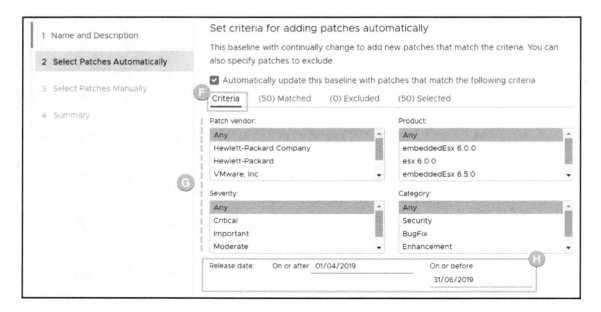

6. Select any additional patches to be included and click **Next**:

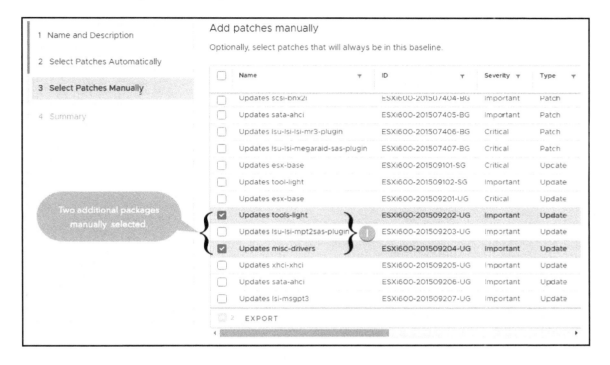

7. On the **Summary** screen, review the baseline configuration and click **Finish**:

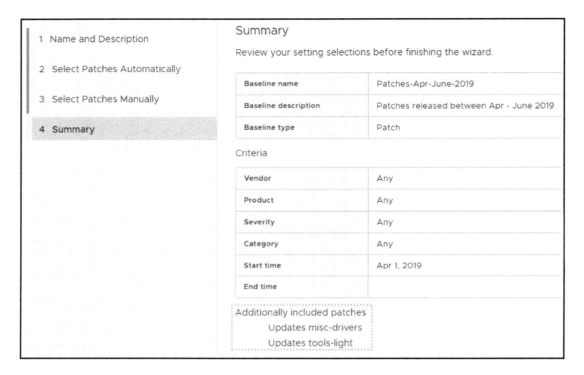

This completes the process of creating patch baselines.

How it works...

Creating a baseline is how you create a reference container for a set of patches that you would like to have installed on a host or a group of hosts. There are three different types of baselines:

- **Patch**: This will include security patches, bug fixes, enhancements, and other general patches.
- **Upgrade**: This will only include ESXi images, which will be used to upgrade the ESXi host to a new, updated version.
- **Extension**: This refers to the software updates that are pushed by the hardware vendor, which include hardware driver updates, updates that enable additional features, CIM providers, updates that will allow supportability, and updates that improve performance.

Creating Host Upgrade Baselines

In the previous recipe, we learned how to create patch baselines. Update Manager can also be used to upgrade ESXi hosts. This can be achieved by using upgrade baselines, which can then be applied to a common set of hosts.

Getting ready

Before you begin, you will need to import the ESXi ISO image that will be used to create the baseline. You can do this by going to the **ESXi images** tab of Update Manager:

The **IMPORT** option is used to browse and import the images into Update Manager. The files are imported into the `/storage/updatemgr/patch-store/host_upgrade_packages` directory on the vCSA.

How to do it...

The following steps will help you to create an upgraded baseline:

1. Connect to vCenter Server using the HTML5 client as an administrator.
2. Use the left-hand pane or the inventory **Menu** to navigate to **Update Manager**.
3. On the **Update Manager** screen, go to the **Baselines** tab and click **New** | **Baseline**.

4. On the **Create Baseline** wizard screen, supply a **Name** for the baseline and an optional **Description**, set the **Content** to **Upgrade**, and click **Next** to continue:

5. Select the desired ESXi image for the baseline and click **Next** to continue:

6. Review the settings in the **Summary** screen and click **Finish**.

This completes the process of creating host upgrade baselines.

How it works...

Since Update Manager is configured and operated from the vCenter layer, it can be used to upgrade ESXi hosts across different clusters. This means that you can create more than one upgrade baseline for use with the various hosts/clusters. These baselines, for self-evident reasons, are formed using different ESXi images. However, the important thing to keep in mind is that Update Manager cannot be used to create upgrade baselines that are older than its current major version. In our case, this means we cannot use Update Manager 6.7 to create ESXi 6.5 upgrade baselines. It would not allow you to import ESXi 6.5 images into the Update Manager cache.

Creating Baseline Groups

Host baseline groups are useful when you have to perform an upgrade and then install patches that were released at a later date than the host upgrade or an extension (for example, a driver upgrade) that will make the server hardware compatible with the newer upgrade.

Getting ready

Before you begin, you will need to have created the required upgrade baseline. Read the *Creating host upgrade baselines* recipe for instructions.

How to do it...

The following steps will help you to create baseline groups:

1. Connect to vCenter Server using the HTML5 client as an administrator.
2. Use the left-hand pane or the inventory **Menu** to navigate to **Update Manager**.
3. On the **Update Manager** screen, go to the **Baselines** tab and click **New** | **Baseline Groups**.
4. On the **Create Baseline Group** wizard screen, supply a **Name** for the baseline and an optional **Description**, and click **Next** to continue.
5. Select the desired upgrade baseline and click **Next** to continue:

6. Select the required **Patch Baselines** and click **Next** to continue:

7. Choose an extension baseline (if applicable) and click **Next** to continue.
8. Review the **Summary** and click **Finish**.

This completes the process of creating baseline groups.

How it works...

Baseline groups are used to team up upgrade baselines, along with additional patches that need to be installed post an upgrade. This is usually done to complete the upgrade and patching process in the same maintenance window. Extension baselines are for third-party software such as specific hardware drivers and CIM providers.

Configuring Update Manager's Remediation Settings

Unlike the previous versions, which allowed you to configure the Remediation Settings via the **Remediate** wizard, they are now configured as global settings for Update Manager. You don't necessarily need to change these settings.

How to do it...

The following steps will help you to configure the Remediation Settings:

1. Connect to vCenter Server using the HTML5 client as an administrator.
2. Use the left-hand pane or the inventory **Menu** to navigate to **Update Manager**.
3. On the **Update Manager** screen, navigate to **Settings | Remediation Settings | Hosts** and click **Edit**:
   - Specify what to do with the power state of the virtual machines on the host being remediated.
   - Configure the number of times the *enter maintenance mode* operation will be attempted and the delay between each retry.
   - Choose whether or not you wish to migrate powered-off and suspended VMs when the host is put into maintenance mode.
   - Choose to allow the installation of additional software on auto-deployed hosts:

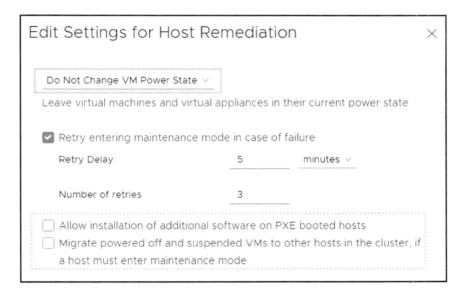

4. (Optional) Navigate to **Settings | Remediation Settings | VMs** and click **Edit and Configure VM Rollback**. By default, the snapshots are not deleted. You can change this behavior by specifying the number of hours the snapshots should be kept before being deleted.

This completes the process of configuring Update Manager's Remediation Settings.

How it works...

The host maintenance mode options can help you to reduce the downtime that's required to remediate an ESXi host by either choosing to power off or suspend the VMs running on it. Choosing to power off/suspend the VMs will cut down the time that would otherwise be required to VMotion the VMs off that host. However, keep in mind that we are gaining time at the expense of virtual machine downtime.

A host entering maintenance mode can fail at times. You can configure the number of retries vSphere Update Manager will attempt and the time interval between each retry. It is recommended that you choose to disable any removable devices connected to the VM, as this can prevent VMotion.

Patching/upgrading ESXi hosts using Update Manager

Earlier in this chapter, we learned how to create path baselines. A baseline is nothing but an accepted or test software/patch level for ESXi hosts in a vSphere infrastructure. Once we have baselines formed, we can use them to remediate ESXi hosts to the required patch level. Remediation refers to the process of installing the desired patches or upgrades on ESXi hosts to make them compliant with the baseline.

Getting ready

Before you begin, you will need to ensure that the following has been carried out:

- Create the necessary baselines. Read the *Creating patch baselines* and *Creating Host upgrade baselines* recipes for instructions.
- DRS should be enabled on the cluster. Update Manager will attempt to place the host into maintenance mode. Maintenance mode relies on DRS to migrate VMs with other hosts.
- What happens to the VMs on the host being put into maintenance mode by Update Manager can be controlled by using the Remediation Settings. Read the *Configuring Update Manager's Remediation Settings* recipe for more information.

How to do it...

The following steps will help you to remediate an ESXi host to the desired patch level:

1. The first step is to attach the desired baseline to the ESXi host or cluster. This is done from the **Updates** tab of the ESXi host. Select the ESXi host from the inventory and navigate to **Updates | Host Updates**. Then, click **ATTACH** to browse and select the desired baseline (patch or upgrade baseline):

2. Once the baseline has been attached, check the host/cluster for compliance. To do so, right-click on the host/cluster and navigate to **Update Manager | Check Compliance**:

3. If the host/cluster is **Non-compliant**, then you could choose to either **Stage** the patches or **Remediate** them:

4. If you click **Stage**, you will be presented with the **Stage Patches** window, which will list the patches in the baseline that will be staged. Click **Stage** to begin copying the patches to the ESXi host. You should see a **Stage patches to entity** task complete successfully in the **Recent Tasks** pane.

5. If you click **Remediate**, you will be prompted to accept the ELUA post, through which you will be presented with the **Remediate** window displaying the **Pre-check status**, patches that will be installed, and **Scheduling Options** and **Remediation Settings** (read-only). Read the *Configuring Update Manager's Remediation Settings* recipe for more information.

6. You should see a **Remediate entity** task completed successfully in the **Recent Tasks** pane.

This completes the process of patching or upgrading ESXi hosts using Update Manager.

How it works...

Attaching a baseline to an ESXi host or a cluster of ESXi hosts is a way to tell Update Manager about the patches that you would like to have installed on the selected hosts/cluster. Once a baseline/baseline group is attached to an entity, the entity needs to be scanned for compliance with the attached baseline. When you select a cluster to be scanned for compliance, it will scan all of the ESXi hosts in the cluster. Non-compliant hosts/clusters can be remediated. The remediation process will put the host in maintenance mode. By default, the VMs on the host will be migrated. If a cluster is chosen for remediation, then hosts in that cluster are remediated sequentially.

The remediation time is the cumulative time required to download and install patches on the ESXi server. VUM can download the patches to the ESXi server and perform remediation at a later date/time. This process is called **staging**. The staging process copies the patches to be installed onto the ESXi host. It is not required for the host to be in maintenance mode while the patches are being staged, thereby saving a considerable amount of downtime for the ESXi server. The VMs can still continue to run while the patches are being staged. Unlike remediation, staging cannot be scheduled. Once staging completes, remediation can be scheduled.

When you remediate a cluster, it is recommended that you disable the DPM and enable the EVC (if required). It is good practice to disable the high availability admission control and FT in order to increase the chances of the host entering maintenance mode successfully. You can also choose to migrate the powered off/suspended VMs to other hosts in the cluster so that if the remediated host fails to boot for some reason, then you are not left with VMs that need to be manually readded to the inventory.

Upgrading VMware Tools and virtual hardware using Update Manager

Update Manager can be used to orchestrate the upgrade of virtual machine hardware or VMware Tools to match the version that's available on the ESXi host. This method comes in handy when you have to perform activities on a large set of virtual machines.

Getting ready

Before you begin, it is important to understand that although virtual hardware upgrades do not require a reboot, the VMware Tools upgrade requires one.

 Upgrading VMware Tools on some Linux VMs may or may not require a reboot. Refer to *VMware KB#2147455* (`https://kb.vmware.com/s/article/2147455`) for more information.

It is also recommended to upgrade VMware Tools first so that it fully supports/is compatible with the new virtual hardware.

How to do it...

The following steps will help you to upgrade VMware Tools and virtual hardware using VUM:

1. Connect to vCenter Server using the HTML5 client as an administrator.
2. Select the desired host/cluster and navigate to its **Updates** tab.

3. Go to **VMware Tools**, select the VMs you want to upgrade, and click **Upgrade to Match Host**.

4. Reboot the VMs.

5. Go to **VM Hardware**, select the VMs you want to upgrade, and click **Upgrade to Match Host**.

This completes the process of orchestrating the upgrade of VMware Tools and virtual hardware using Update Manager. When orchestrating an upgrade of VMware Tools using Update Manager, it performs the upgrade immediately, regardless of the power state of the virtual machine.

Installing the Update Manager Download Service on Linux

Most vSphere environments do no expose vCenter Server to the internet. Since Update Manager runs as a service on the VCSA, it doesn't have access to the internet either. In such cases, we can configure what VMware calls an Update Manager Download Service on a Windows or Linux machine that has internet access to download patches.

In this recipe, we will learn how to install and configure the **Update Manager Download Service (UMDS)** on a Linux machine running Ubuntu 18.0.4.

Getting ready

UMDS can be installed on a supported 64-bit Windows or Linux machine. The machine should have access to the internet and allow vCenter to talk to it. Unlike the previous versions of UMDS (6.5 or earlier), you no longer need to install/prepare a database.

UMDS can be installed on any of the following supported operating systems, as of vCenter 6.7 Update 2:

- Ubuntu 14.0.4 or 18.04
- Red Hat Enterprise Linux 7.4 or 7.5
- For a list of supported Windows operating systems, please refer to *VMware KB 2091273* (https://kb.vmware.com/s/article/2091273)

The installer for UMDS is included in the installation ISO image for Windows and the appliance ISO for VCSA.

How to do it...

The following steps will help you to install and configure UMDS on a Linux machine running Ubuntu 18.0.4:

1. Map the VCSA installation ISO to the UMDS VM.
2. Mount the CD ROM device using the following command:

   ```
   # mount /dev/cdrom /media/cdrom
   ```

3. Copy the UMDS bundle from the /media/cdrom/umds directory to /tmp using the following command:

   ```
   # cp /media/cdrom/umds/VMware-UMDS-6.7.0-10164201.tar.gz /tmp
   ```

4. Extract the UMDS bundle using the following command:

   ```
   # cd /tmp
   # tar -zxvf  /tmp/VMware-UMDS-6.7.0-10164201.tar.gz
   ```

5. Run the following command to install UMDS:

   ```
   #  /tmp/vmware-umds-distrib/vmware-install.pl
   ```

6. Hit *Enter* to display the license agreement.
7. Use the *F* key a couple of times to reach the end of the EULA, type yes, and hit *Enter* to accept the license agreement.

8. Use the defaults for the following installation prompts to finish the installation:

This completes the process of installing UDMS on a Linux machine.

Configuring UMDS to download patches

Once UMDS has been installed on a Linux machine, it needs to be configured to download patches. Once configured correctly, the UMDS service can be used to download the patches to its local repository, either manually or periodically using a cron job. The local repository can be used as a shared repository for Update Manager with the help of a web server component. Read the *Configuring a web server on UMDS (Linux)* for more information.

Getting ready

Before you begin, you will need to install UMDS on a supported Linux machine. Read the *Installing the Update Manager Download Service on Linux* recipe for more information.

How to do it...

The following procedure will help you to configure UMDS so that it can download patches:

1. SSH into the Linux machine running UMDS.
2. Run the `vmware-umds -G` command to review the current configuration:

```
root@umds:/tmp# /usr/local/vmware-umds/bin/vmware-umds -G
Configured URLs
URL Type Removable URL
HOST      NO
HOST      NO          https://hostupdate.vmware.com/software/VUM/PRODUCTION/main/vmw-depot-index.xml

Patch store location  : /var/lib/vmware-umds
Export store location :
Proxy Server          : Not configured

Host patch content download: enabled
Host Versions for which patch content will be downloaded:
embeddedEsx-6.5.0-INTL
embeddedEsx-6.6.1-INTL
embeddedEsx-6.6.2-INTL
embeddedEsx-6.6.3-INTL
embeddedEsx-6.7.0-INTL
embeddedEsx-6.0.0-INTL

root@umds:/tmp#
```

3. Now, you can choose to disable patch downloads for specific host versions, for instance, vSphere 6.0, by using the `vmware-umds -S -d embdeddedEsx-6.0.0` command:

```
root@umds:/tmp# /usr/local/vmware-umds/bin/vmware-umds -S -d embeddedEsx-6.0.0
Setting up UMDS configuration
Host update downloads for platform embeddedEsx-6.0.0: Disabled
root@umds:/tmp# /usr/local/vmware-umds/bin/vmware-umds -G
Configured URLs
URL Type Removable URL
HOST     NO
HOST     NO         https://hostupdate.vmware.com/software/VUM/PRODUCTION/main/vmw-depot-index.xml

Patch store location  : /var/lib/vmware-umds
Export store location :
Proxy Server          : Not configured

Host patch content download: enabled
Host Versions for which patch content will be downloaded:
embeddedEsx-6.5.0-INTL       vSphere 6.0 has
embeddedEsx-6.6.1-INTL       now been
embeddedEsx-6.6.2-INTL       removed from
embeddedEsx-6.6.3-INTL       the list
embeddedEsx-6.7.0-INTL

root@umds:/tmp#
```

4. You can choose to configure a proxy for patch downloads by using the `vmware-umds -p host:port` command:

```
root@umds:/# /usr/local/vmware-umds/bin/vmware-umds -S -p "192.168.78.101:8888"
Setting up UMDS configuration
Proxy server: 192.168.78.101 : 8888
root@umds:/#
```

5. Once configured, you should be able to download the patches by issuing the `vmware-umds -D` command:

```
root@umds:/# /usr/local/vmware-umds/bin/vmware-umds -D
Starting download of updates ...
INFO -   Executing download job {48562512}, url=https://hostupdate.vmware.com/software/VUM/PRODUCTION/main/vmw-depot-index.xml
INFO -   curl_easy_perform() succeeded - url: https://hostupdate.vmware.com/software/VUM/PRODUCTION/main/vmw-depot-index.xml
INFO -   Validation passed for file downloaded from: https://hostupdate.vmware.com/software/VUM/PRODUCTION/main/vmw-depot-index.xml
INFO -   Removing existing dest file:/tmp/vciuMoom9
INFO -   Download job {48562512} finished, bytes downloaded = 605
INFO -   vendor index contains 1 vendors.
INFO -   Executing download job {48573280}, url=https://hostupdate.vmware.com/software/VUM/PRODUCTION/main/esx/vmw/vmw-esx-index.xml
INFO -   curl_easy_perform() succeeded - url: https://hostupdate.vmware.com/software/VUM/PRODUCTION/main/esx/vmw/vmw-esx-index.xml
INFO -   Validation passed for file downloaded from: https://hostupdate.vmware.com/software/VUM/PRODUCTION/main/esx/vmw/vmw-esx-index.xml
INFO -   Removing existing dest file:/tmp/vciJSxAYg
INFO -   Download job {48573280} finished, bytes downloaded = 2894
INFO -   Metadata index contains 6 platforms.
WARN -   Skipping download for vmw-ESXi-5.0.0-metadata.zip because platform embeddedEsx-5.0.0-INTL is disabled for downloads in the current configuration
WARN -   Skipping download for vmw-ESXi-5.1.0-metadata.zip because platform embeddedEsx-5.1.0-INTL is disabled for downloads in the current configuration
WARN -   Skipping download for vmw-ESXi-5.5.0-metadata.zip because platform embeddedEsx-5.5.0-INTL is disabled for downloads in the current configuration
WARN -   Skipping download for vmw-ESXi-6.0.0-metadata.zip because platform embeddedEsx-6.0.0-INTL is disabled for downloads in the current configuration
```

6. (Optional) You can choose to configure a cron job of the desired frequency to download the patches. The following screenshot shows an example of a weekly cron job:

```
root@umds:/# cd /etc/cron.
cron.d/         cron.daily/    cron.hourly/   cron.monthly/ cron.weekly/
root@umds:/# cd /etc/cron.weekly/
root@umds:/etc/cron.weekly# touch umds-path-download
root@umds:/etc/cron.weekly# chmod 755 umds-path-download
root@umds:/etc/cron.weekly#
root@umds:/etc/cron.weekly# nano umds-path-download
root@umds:/etc/cron.weekly# cat umds-path-download
#!/bin/sh
/usr/local/vmware-umds/bin/vmware-umds -D
root@umds:/etc/cron.weekly#
```

This completes the process of configuring the UMDS so that it can download patches.

How it works...

Once configured correctly, the UMDS service can be used to download the patches to its local repository, either manually or periodically using a cron job. The local repository can be used as a shared repository for Update Manager with the help of a web server component. Read the *Configuring a web server on UMDS (Linux)* recipe for more information.

Configuring a Web Server on UMDS (Linux)

Once we have UMDS installed and configured to download patches, the next step is to configure a web server component on the UMDS server so that it can be used as a shared repository with Update Manager.

Getting ready

Before you configure the web server component, it is essential that you install and configure UMDS. Read the *Installing the Update Manager Download Service on Linux* and *Configuring UMDS to download patches* recipes for more information.

How to do it...

The following steps will help you to configure a web server component on the UMDS server:

1. SSH to the UMDS server as root.
2. Install a web server on the server. In this case, we will be installing NGINX using the `apt-get install nginx` command.
3. In order to allow the web server component to access the files in the local UDMS patch store, you need to change the permission on the patch store directory using the following command:

   ```
   # chmod -R 755 /var/lib/vmware-umds
   ```

4. Create a separate site configuration using the default template:

   ```
   # cp /etc/nginx/sites-available/default /etc/nginx/sites-available/umds-site
   ```

5. Edit the site configuration file, `umds-site`, as shown in the following screenshot, to allow access to the file's local UMDS patch store, that is, `/var/lib/vmware-umds`:

```
# Default server configuration
#
server {
        listen 80 default_server;
        listen [::]:80 default_server;

        # SSL configuration
        #
        # listen 443 ssl default_server;
        # listen [::]:443 ssl default_server;
        #
        # Note: You should disable gzip for SSL traffic.
        # See: https://bugs.debian.org/773332
        #
        # Read up on ssl_ciphers to ensure a secure configuration.
        # See: https://bugs.debian.org/765782
        #
        # Self signed certs generated by the ssl-cert package
        # Don't use them in a production server!
        #
        # include snippets/snakeoil.conf;

        root /var/lib/vmware-umds;          ◀······●A

        # Add index.php to the list if you are using PHP
        index index.html index.htm;

        server_name localhost umds umds.vdescribed.lab;   ◀······●B

        location / {
                # First attempt to serve request as file, then
                # as directory, then fall back to displaying a 404.
                try_files $uri $uri/ =404;
                autoindex on;           ◀···············●C
        }
```

6. Delete the default site configuration file:

   ```
   # rm /etc/nginx/sites-enabled/default
   ```

7. Enable a site using the umds-site configuration file by creating a symbolic link
   to it in the /etc/ngnix/sites-enabled/ directory:

   ```
   # ln -s /etc/nginx/sites-available/umds-site /etc/nginx/sites-enabled/
   ```

8. Restart the web service to apply these changes:

   ```
   # service nginx restart
   ```

9. You should now be able to access files on the UMDS server using the `http://umds.vdescribed.lab` URL:

This completes the process of installing and configuring a web server component on the UMDS server.

How it works...

Once you have the UMDS server and the web server component configured correctly, Update Manager can now be told to use the repository on the UMDS server.

Use the web client to navigate to the Update Manager home page and then go to **Settings** | **Patch Setup** | **Change Download Source Type**:

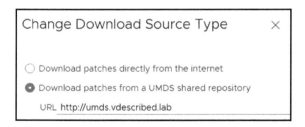

Once done, Update Manager will start sourcing patches from the UMDS server.

15
Securing vSphere Using SSL Certificates

Digital certificates have been around for a long time and are used to secure communications over networks. There are different types of digital certificates, such as **Secure Sockets Layer** (**SSL**), which is used to encrypt and decrypt communication in order to prevent man-in-the-middle attacks. The other types include *software signing*, which is a method to ensure that you are not downloading malicious software or code off the internet, and *DigitalID*, which is used to identify a person or a client who's connecting to a secure network. For example, a VPN uses client certificates to authenticate the connection source to the routers on the destination network.

VMware uses SSL certificates to encrypt network communication to and from its components. All vSphere nodes—vCenter, PSC, and ESXi—use SSL certificates to secure communication between them and their external clients. The following components make up the vSphere Certificate infrastructure:

- **VMware Certificate Authority** (**VMCA**)
- **VMware Endpoint Certificate Store** (**VECS**)
- **VM Directory** (**VMDIR**)

VMCA is an internal CA that is included as one of the components of the **Platform Services Controller** (**PSC**). By default, VMCA acts as the *root CA* for all vSphere components. During installation, VMCA creates a root CA certificate and endpoint (Machine SSL) and Solution User Certificates for each management node (vCenter/PSC). The use of VMCA allows for easier regeneration/revocation of certificates that are issued to the vSphere components. VMCA can also be configured to act as a *subordinate* (*intermediary*) to an Enterprise/Public CA (PKI).

VECS is a certificate repository that's maintained in each management node (PSC or vCenter) to store certificates and keys locally. The use of VECS removes the need to re-register components post replacing their certificates. Although VECS can have an unlimited number of key stores (in theory), by default, VMware uses the following essential ones:

- **Machine SSL Certificates Store (MACHINE_SSL_CERT)**: Machine SSL certificates are used by SSL endpoints on each node. These endpoints include *Reverse Proxy Service* and VMDIR.

 All of the services that run on a management node are assembled behind the reverse proxy and use the Machine SSL Certificate that's seen by the reverse proxy service to expose their endpoints.

- **Trusted Root Certificates Store**: TRUSTED_ROOTS.
- **Certificate Revocation List**: TRUSTED_ROOT_CRLS.
- **Solution User Certificates**:
  - `machine`: This is different to Machine SSL and is only used by the component manager, license, and logging services.
  - `vsphere-webclient`: This is used by the vSphere-client service and performance charts service to authenticate to SSO.
  - `vpxd`: This is used by `vpxd` to authenticate to SSO.
  - `vpxd-extension`: This is used by all other services, such as the auto-deploy and inventory services.
- **BACKUP_STORE**: Used by VMCA to store a copy of the most recent certificate configuration.
- **Virtual Volumes (SMS)**: Used by Virtual Volumes.

 Running the `/usr/lib/vmware-vmafd/bin/vecs-cli store list` command should list all of the key stores on the node.

Although VMCA uses VECS to store the certificates it generates, VECS is managed independently and run as a VMAFD() component. This means that, regardless of whether or not VMCA is used to issue certificates, VECS is mandatory so that it can store them. VECS also exports every certificate it stores to VMDIR, which, in turn, replicates the information with other VMDIRs to the same SSO domain.

Solution User Certificates services that run off a management node (PSC/vCenter) register themselves with **Single Sign-On** (**SSO**) as solution users. Therefore, the Solution User Certificates are used to authenticate the services to SSO. Each solutions' users encapsulates multiple services.

VMDIR is an LDAP-based directory service that runs as PSC components that store information such as Identity Sources, SSO Users/Groups, Policies, and Certificates.

 It is important to keep in mind that the SSO internal certificates are neither issued/managed by VMCA nor stored in the VECS. VMware does not recommend replacing the SSO certificates.

In this chapter, we will cover the following recipes:

- Using VMCA as a Subordinate or Intermediary CA
- Certificate management using the Hybrid approach
- Renewing ESXI certificates
- Trusting root certificates to stop browser security warnings

Using VMCA as a Subordinate or Intermediary CA

Most businesses already have an Enterprise PKI or a Public PKI they trust. VMware allows you to configure vCenter in order to leverage certificates from such PKIs. This is achieved by configuring VMCA as an Intermediary CA or Subordinate CA to your Enterprise CA or **Public Key Infrastructure** (**PKI**).

 Read the following Wikipedia article on PKI to gain a basic understanding: `https://en.wikipedia.org/wiki/Public_key_infrastructure`.

One of the benefits of doing so is to reduce the management overhead in the renewal of the Machine SSL and Solution Users Certificates. Once a subordinate, VMCA can issues certificates on behalf of the Enterprise CA. The following diagram depicts the approach of using VCMA as a subordinate authority:

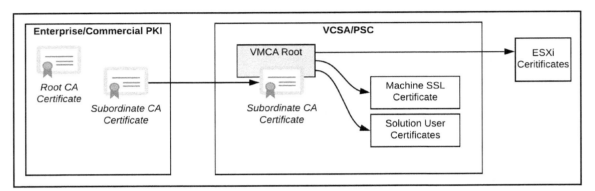

Although using VCMA as a subordinate CA is an option, VMware does not recommend doing so. Use the Hybrid approach for enhanced security.

Getting ready

Before you begin, do the following:

- You will need access to your PKI's key request portal.
- Ensure that you have a snapshot created on the vCenter Server before replacing the certificates.
- Since the certificate manager is used to perform this activity, you will need SSH access to vCenter Server.
- You will also need an SCP file transfer utility such as WinSCP.

How to do it...

The following steps will help you to make VCMA act as an intermediary for issuing trusted certificates in your environment:

1. SSH (putty) into the VCSA as root.
2. Change the default shell to bash to allow file transfers using WinSCP.
3. Make a temporary directory to store the certificate requests and certificates:

   ```
   # mkdir /tmp/certs
   ```

4. Start the certificate manager utility, `/usr/lib/vmware-vmca/bin/certificate-manager`, and use option **2. Replace VMCA Root certificate with Custom Signing Certificate and replace all Certificates**:

```
root@bkvc01 [ ~ ]# mkdir /tmp/certs
root@bkvc01 [ ~ ]#
root@bkvc01 [ ~ ]# /usr/lib/vmware-vmca/bin/certificate-manager

              |      *** Welcome to the vSphere 6.7 Certificate Manager  ***      |
              |                                                                    |
              |                       -- Select Operation --                      |
              |                                                                    |
              |      1. Replace Machine SSL certificate with Custom Certificate    |
              |                                                                    |
              |      2. Replace VMCA Root certificate with Custom Signing          |
              |         Certificate and replace all Certificates                   |
              |                                                                    |
              |      3. Replace Machine SSL certificate with VMCA Certificate      |
              |                                                                    |
              |      4. Regenerate a new VMCA Root Certificate and                 |
              |         replace all certificates                                   |
              |                                                                    |
              |      5. Replace Solution user certificates with                    |
              |         Custom Certificate                                         |
              |                                                                    |
              |      6. Replace Solution user certificates with VMCA certificates  |
              |                                                                    |
              |      7. Revert last performed operation by re-publishing old       |
              |         certificates                                               |
              |                                                                    |
              |      8. Reset all Certificates                                     |
Note : Use Ctrl-D to exit.
Option[1 to 8]:
```

5. Use option **1. Generate Certificate signing Request(s) and Key(s) for VMCA Root Signing Certificate** to the CSRs and the key. Here is a list of essential prompts:

- **Enter proper value for 'Name' [Previous value: CA]**: FQDN/host name of the node
- **Enter proper value for 'Hostname'**: FQDN of the node
- **Enter proper value for VMCA 'Name'**: FQDN of the node

```
Note : Use Ctrl-D to exit.
Option[1 to 8]: 2
Do you wish to generate all certificates using configuration file : Option[Y/N] ? : Y

Please provide valid SSO and VC privileged user credential to perform certificate operations.
Enter username [Administrator@vsphere.local]:
Enter password:

Please configure certool.cfg with proper values before proceeding to next step.

Press Enter key to skip optional parameters or use Default value.

Enter proper value for 'Country' [Default value : US] : AU

Enter proper value for 'Name' [Default value : CA] : bkvc01

Enter proper value for 'Organization' [Default value : VMware] : vDescribed

Enter proper value for 'OrgUnit' [Default value : VMware Engineering] : Lab

Enter proper value for 'State' [Default value : California] : NSW

Enter proper value for 'Locality' [Default value : Palo Alto] : Sydney

Enter proper value for 'IPAddress' (Provide comma separated values for multiple IP addresses) [optional] :

Enter proper value for 'Email' [Default value : email@acme.com] :

Enter proper value for 'Hostname' (Provide comma separated values for multiple Hostname entries) [Enter valid Fully Qualif
ied Domain Name(FQDN), For Example : example.domain.com] : bkvc01.vdescribed.lab

Enter proper value for VMCA 'Name' :bkvc01.vdescribed.lab
          1. Generate Certificate Signing Request(s) and Key(s) for VMCA Root Signing certificate

          2. Import custom certificate(s) and key(s) to replace existing VMCA Root Signing certificate

Option [1 or 2]: 1

Please provide a directory location to write the CSR(s) and PrivateKey(s) to
Output directory path: /tmp/certs
2019-07-14T02:11:00.559Z  Running command: ['/usr/lib/vmware-vmca/bin/certool', '--genkey', '--privkey', '/tmp/certs/vmca_
issued_key.key', '--pubkey', '/tmp/pubkey.pub']
2019-07-14T02:11:00.803Z  Done running command
2019-07-14T02:11:00.804Z  Running command: ['/usr/lib/vmware-vmca/bin/certool', '--gencacsr', '--privkey', '/tmp/certs/vmc
a_issued_key.key', '--pubkey', '/tmp/pubkey.pub', '--config', '/var/tmp/vmware/certool.cfg', '--csrfile', '/tmp/certs/vmca
_issued_csr.csr']
2019-07-14T02:11:01.000Z  Done running command

CSR generated at: /tmp/certs/vmca_issued_csr.csr
          1. Continue to importing Custom certificate(s) and key(s) for VMCA Root Signing certificate

          2. Exit certificate-manager

Option [1 or 2]:
```

Speech bubble: *That is the name of VMCA. The default is CA*

Speech bubble: *Location where .csr and .key will be exported to.*

6. Do not exit the certificate-manager or close the SSH session yet.

7. Start another SSH session on the VCSA and verify the /tmp/certs directory. It will contain a .csr and a .key file. Use WinSCP to copy the file onto your desktop or jumpbox:

```
root@bkvc01 [ ~ ]# cd /tmp/certs
root@bkvc01 [ /tmp/certs ]# ls -l
total 8
-rw-r--r-- 1 root root 1179 Jul 14 02:11 vmca_issued_csr.csr
-rw-r--r-- 1 root root 1707 Jul 14 02:11 vmca_issued_key.key
root@bkvc01 [ /tmp/certs ]#
```

8. Connect to your PKI certificate server portal and download the CA root certificate.

9. Generate a new certificate from your PKI using the vmca_issued_csr.csr CSR.

10. Create a CSR chain by combining the root CA certificate and the newly generated certificate in the following order:

```
-----BEGIN CERTIFICATE-----
Newly generated certificate
-----END CERTIFICATE-----
-----BEGIN CERTIFICATE-----
RootCA Certficate
-----END CERTIFICATE-----
```

11. Copy the CSR chain certificate into the VCSA's /tmp/certs directory using WinSCP:

```
root@bkvc01 [ /tmp/certs ]# ls -l
total 12
-rw-r--r-- 1 root root 3350 Jul 14 02:17 bkvc01_chain.cer
-rw-r--r-- 1 root root 1179 Jul 14 02:11 vmca_issued_csr.csr
-rw-r--r-- 1 root root 1707 Jul 14 02:11 vmca_issued_key.key
root@bkvc01 [ /tmp/certs ]#
```

12. Continue with the utility and select **Continue to importing Custom certificate(s) and key(s) for VMCA Root Signing Certificate**. Provide full paths to the new certificate and key files:

```
CSR generated at: /tmp/certs/vmca_issued_csr.csr
        1. Continue to importing Custom certificate(s) and key(s) for VMCA Root Signing certificate

        2. Exit certificate-manager

Option [1 or 2]: 1

Please provide valid custom certificate for Root.
File : /tmp/certs/bkvc01_chain.cer

Please provide valid custom key for Root.
File : /tmp/certs/vmca_issued_key.key

You are going to replace Root Certificate with custom certificate and regenerate all other certificates
Continue operation : Option[Y/N] ? : Y
Get site nameCompleted [Replacing Machine SSL Cert...]
default-site
Lookup all services
Get service default-site:43ce587f-5ced-443b-8e24-c00a286d0ad0
Update service default-site:43ce587f-5ced-443b-8e24-c00a286d0ad0; spec: /tmp/svcspec_xrjk3712
Get service default-site:c4f54de5-96ae-40a7-8228-4ad0e8c76cb5
Update service default-site:c4f54de5-96ae-40a7-8228-4ad0e8c76cb5; spec: /tmp/svcspec_3q08sh4s
```

13. Once the operation is complete, it will indicate the same and automatically exit the certificate-manager tool:

```
Get service 6e33671f-9c59-46f2-963d-f4fdd08b51d2
Don't update service 6e33671f-9c59-46f2-963d-f4fdd08b51d2
Updated 32 service(s)
Status : 100% Completed [All tasks completed successfully]

root@bkvc01 [ ~ ]#
```

This completes the process of replacing vCenter/PSC certificates by making the VCMA a subordinate certificate authority.

How it works...

During this process, the root CA certificate that was created during the installation is replaced with the trusted intermediate CA certificate. It also replaces the Machine SSL and the Solution User Certificates using the full certificate chain, including your Enterprise CA's trust rooted certificate and VMCA as the subordinate. When you verify the certificate, it shows the full chain:

Here, `vdescribed-AD01-CA` is the Enterprise CA and `bkvc01` is the name of the VMCA's CA. Refer to *step 5* of the *How to do it...* section, where you change the default name of the CA to `bkvc01`. It is not mandatory to change the default name, though.

In the case of external PSC deployments, do the following:

1. The procedure outlined in the *How to do it...* section should be performed on the PSC. Then, restart the services on each vCenter node.
2. Then, use certificate-manager and replace the Machine SSL using option **3**.
3. Finally, replace the Solution User Certificates using option **6**.

From here on out, you can use the web client's certificate management GUI to renew the certificates.

Certificate management using the Hybrid approach

One of the risks involved in making a VMCA the subordinate CA is the fact that anyone with access to the PSC can regenerate Machine SSL certificates for the PSC(s) and vCenter Server(s). In other words, VMCA completely relies on the operating system it is running on, such as Windows/PhotonOS, to secure the key stores. Anyone with root access to the node that's running VMCA can easily read the certificate authorities' root certificate.

Therefore, VMware allows for a much more secure approach, which is commonly referred to as the Hybrid method. In this approach, the Machine SSL of vCenter and PSC are replaced with custom certificates from the Enterprise CA. VCMA is only used to issue certificates for the solution users and ESXi hosts.

The following diagram depicts the Hybrid approach:

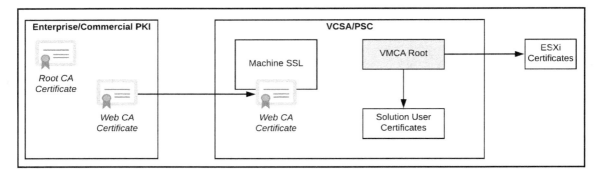

The Hybrid approach is the VMware-recommended method if you use an Enterprise or Public PKI.

Getting ready

Before you begin, do the following:

- You will need access to your PKI's key request portal.
- Ensure that you have a snapshot created on vCenter Server before replacing the certificates.
- Since the certificate manager is used to perform this activity, you will need SSH access to vCenter Server.
- You will also need an SCP file transfer utility such as WinSCP.

How to do it...

The following steps will help you to replace the certificates using the Hybrid approach:

1. SHH (putty) into the VCSA as root.
2. Change the default shell to bash to allow file transfers using WinSCP.
3. Make a temporary directory to store the certificate requests and the certificates themselves:

   ```
   # mkdir /tmp/certs
   ```

4. Start the certificate manager utility ,/usr/lib/vmware-
   vmca/bin/certificate-manager, and select option **1. Replace Machine SSL
   certificate with Custom Certificate**:

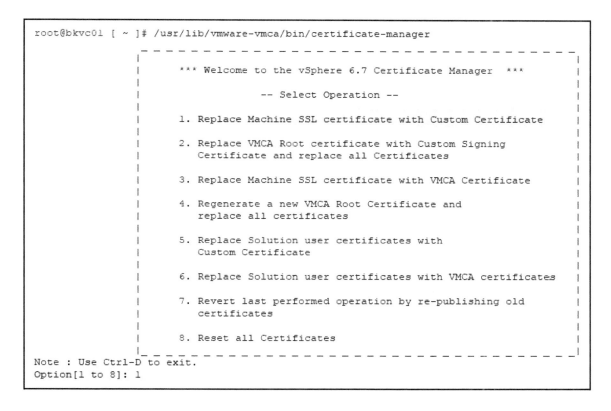

```
root@bkvc01 [ ~ ]# /usr/lib/vmware-vmca/bin/certificate-manager
 _ _ _ _ _ _ _ _ _ _ _ _ _ _ _ _ _ _ _ _ _ _ _ _ _ _ _ _ _ _ _ _
|                                                                |
|         *** Welcome to the vSphere 6.7 Certificate Manager  ***|
|                                                                |
|                     -- Select Operation --                     |
|                                                                |
|      1. Replace Machine SSL certificate with Custom Certificate|
|                                                                |
|      2. Replace VMCA Root certificate with Custom Signing      |
|         Certificate and replace all Certificates               |
|                                                                |
|      3. Replace Machine SSL certificate with VMCA Certificate  |
|                                                                |
|      4. Regenerate a new VMCA Root Certificate and             |
|         replace all certificates                               |
|                                                                |
|      5. Replace Solution user certificates with                |
|         Custom Certificate                                     |
|                                                                |
|      6. Replace Solution user certificates with VMCA certificates|
|                                                                |
|      7. Revert last performed operation by re-publishing old   |
|         certificates                                           |
|                                                                |
|      8. Reset all Certificates                                 |
|_ _ _ _ _ _ _ _ _ _ _ _ _ _ _ _ _ _ _ _ _ _ _ _ _ _ _ _ _ _ _ _|
Note : Use Ctrl-D to exit.
Option[1 to 8]: 1
```

5. On the next screen, select option **1. Generate Certificate Signing Request(s) and Key(s) for Machine SSL certificate**. Work through the prompts and specify an output directory for the `.key` and `.csr` files. In this case, it is `/tmp/certs`. Here is a list of essential prompts:

- **Enter proper value for Name [Previous value: CA]:** FQDN/host name of the node
- **Enter proper value for 'Hostname':** FQDN of the node
- **Enter proper value for 'VMCA Name':** FQDN of the node

```
Note : Use Ctrl-D to exit.
Option[1 to 8]: 1

Please provide valid SSO and VC privileged user credential to perform certificate operations.
Enter username [Administrator@vsphere.local]:
Enter password:
        1. Generate Certificate Signing Request(s) and Key(s) for Machine SSL certificate

        2. Import custom certificate(s) and key(s) to replace existing Machine SSL certificate

Option [1 or 2]: 1

Please provide a directory location to write the CSR(s) and PrivateKey(s) to:
Output directory path: /tmp/certs
certool.cfg file exists, Do you wish to reconfigure : Option[Y/N] ? : Y

Press Enter key to skip optional parameters or use Previous value.

Enter proper value for 'Country' [Previous value : AU] :

Enter proper value for 'Name' [Previous value : bkvc01] :

Enter proper value for 'Organization' [Previous value : vDescribed] :

Enter proper value for 'OrgUnit' [Previous value : Book] :

Enter proper value for 'State' [Previous value : NSW] :

Enter proper value for 'Locality' [Previous value : Sydney] :

Enter proper value for 'IPAddress' (Provide comma separated values for multiple IP addresses) [optional] :

Enter proper value for 'Email' [Previous value : email@acme.com] :

Enter proper value for 'Hostname' (Provide comma separated values for multiple Hostname entries) [Enter valid Fully Qualified Dc
main Name(FQDN), For Example : example.domain.com] : bkvc01.vdescribed.lab

Enter proper value for VMCA 'Name' :bkvc01.vdescribed.lab
2019-07-20T06:58:06.896Z  Running command: ['/usr/lib/vmware-vmca/bin/certool', '--genkey', '--privkey', '/tmp/certs/vmca_issued
_key.key', '--pubkey', '/tmp/pubkey.pub']
2019-07-20T06:58:07.030Z  Done running command
2019-07-20T06:58:07.031Z  Running command: ['/usr/lib/vmware-vmca/bin/certool', '--gencsr', '--privkey', '/tmp/certs/vmca_issued
_key.key', '--pubkey', '/tmp/pubkey.pub', '--config', '/var/tmp/vmware/certool.cfg', '--csrfile', '/tmp/certs/vmca_issued_csr.cs
r']
2019-07-20T06:58:07.114Z  Done running command

CSR generated at: /tmp/certs/vmca_issued_csr.csr
        1. Continue to importing Custom certificate(s) and key(s) for Machine SSL certificate

        2. Exit certificate-manager
```

6. You can choose to exit the certificate-manager at this stage.

7. Start another SSH session on the VCSA and verify the /tmp/certs directory. This will contain a .csr and a .key file.

8. Use WinSCP to copy the file onto your desktop or jumpbox.

9. Connect to your PKI certificate server portal and download the CA root certificate.

10. Generate a new certificate from your PKI using the vmca_issued_csr.csr CSR.

11. Create a CSR chain by combining the root CA certificate and the newly generated certificate in the following order:

```
-----BEGIN CERTIFICATE-----
Newly generated certificate
-----END CERTIFICATE-----
-----BEGIN CERTIFICATE-----
RootCA Certficate
-----END CERTIFICATE-----
```

12. Copy the CSR chain certificate and RootCA certificate to the VCSA's /tmp/certs directory using WinSCP:

```
root@bkvc01 [ /tmp/certs ]# ls -l
total 16
-rw-r--r-- 1 root root 1282 Jul 20 06:07 EntRootCA.cer
-rw-r--r-- 1 root root 3328 Jul 20 06:20 vcenter_machine_ssl_chain.cer
-rw-r--r-- 1 root root 1126 Jul 20 06:58 vmca_issued_csr.csr
-rw-r--r-- 1 root root 1703 Jul 20 06:58 vmca_issued_key.key
root@bkvc01 [ /tmp/certs ]#
```

13. Start the certificate-manager again and select option **1. Replace Machine SSL certificate with Custom Certificate** and then option **2. Import custom certificate(s) and key(s) for Machine SSL Certificate**. Provide full paths to the new certificate, root CA certificate, and key files:

```
Please provide valid SSO and VC privileged user credential to perform certificate operations.
Enter username [Administrator@vsphere.local]:
Enter password:
        1. Generate Certificate Signing Request(s) and Key(s) for Machine SSL certificate

        2. Import custom certificate(s) and key(s) to replace existing Machine SSL certificate

Option [1 or 2]: 2

Please provide valid custom certificate for Machine SSL.
File : /tmp/certs/vcenter_machine_ssl_chain.cer

Please provide valid custom key for Machine SSL.
File : /tmp/certs/vmca_issued_key.key

Please provide the signing certificate of the Machine SSL certificate
File : /tmp/certs/EntRootCA.cer

You are going to replace Machine SSL cert using custom cert
Continue operation : Option[Y/N] ? : Y
Command Output: /tmp/certs/vcenter_machine_ssl_chain.cer: OK

Get site nameCompleted [Replacing Machine SSL Cert...]
default-site
Lookup all services
Get service default-site:43ce587f-5ced-443b-8e24-c00a286d0ad0
Update service default-site:43ce587f-5ced-443b-8e24-c00a286d0ad0; spec: /tmp/svcspec_tsbpcilz
Get service default-site:c4f54de5-96ae-40a7-8228-4ad0e8c76cb5
Update service default-site:c4f54de5-96ae-40a7-8228-4ad0e8c76cb5; spec: /tmp/svcspec_txcqor82
Get service default-site:75b6c495-29ac-4bf9-b0f4-b1615f51344e
Update service default-site:75b6c495-29ac-4bf9-b0f4-b1615f51344e; spec: /tmp/svcspec_hlmmoclk
Get service b1543bd1-ae41-4c50-af11-50d6cf54f76e
Update service b1543bd1-ae41-4c50-af11-50d6cf54f76e; spec: /tmp/svcspec_4347_vq7
Get service 37ab8322-3ea4-4c70-afff-f04ee6ffebba
Update service 37ab8322-3ea4-4c70-afff-f04ee6ffebba; spec: /tmp/svcspec_dowh7yaf
Get service 3786b7b1-1adb-4700-8c7b-d03978028ceb
Update service 3786b7b1-1adb-4700-8c7b-d03978028ceb; spec: /tmp/svcspec_82c4i54j
Get service 14102409-1db0-45e8-895b-ee6c14c709ff
```

14. Once the operation is complete, it will indicate the same and automatically exit the certificate-manager tool:

```
Get service 48fa0eba-7599-4963-b81c-b00b04adf64f
Don't update service 48fa0eba-7599-4963-b81c-b00b04adf64f
Get service 6e33671f-9c59-46f2-963d-f4fdd08b51d2
Don't update service 6e33671f-9c59-46f2-963d-f4fdd08b51d2
Updated 32 service(s)
Status : 100% Completed [All tasks completed successfully]

root@bkvc01 [ ~ ]#
```

This completes the process of replacing the vCenter/PSC Machine SSL certificates to allow for a Hybrid approach.

How it works...

In the Hybrid approach, VCMA works independently of the Enterprise PKI. The Machine SSL certificate of each management node (VCSA/PSC) is replaced with a Web Certificate from the Enterprise or Public PKI.

Since VMCA is not configured as a subordinate of the Enterprise CA, it cannot issue CA chain certificates. It can only be used to issue/manage the certificates of solution users and ESXi hosts.

If you check the certificate for the web client connection, it will be marked as secure. The certification path will show you that the certificate is a child of the root CA:

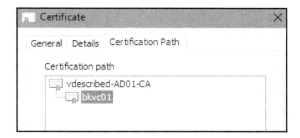

Renewing ESXi certificates

As we mentioned at the start of this chapter, ESXi nodes also use SSL certificates to secure communication between them and external clients. ESXi will have an autogenerated Machine SSL certificate assigned to it during the first boot post-installation. However, when an ESXi is added to vCenter Server, it is assigned a new self-signed certificate by the VMCA. VMCA issued certificates can be renewed via the web client GUI.

You can also assign custom certificates to an ESXi host, but this is a tedious certificate replacement process as it has to be manually performed on each host.

> The ESXi certificates are not stored in VECS; they are stored locally on each ESXi host in the `/etc/vmware/ssl` directory.

In this recipe, we will learn how to renew VMCA issued ESXi certificates.

How to do it...

The following steps will help you to renew ESXi certificates with VMCA issued certificates:

1. Connect to vCenter Server using the HTML5 Client.
2. Use the key combination *Ctrl + Alt + 2* to switch to the **Hosts and Clusters** view.
3. This is an optional step to select the vCenter service you want to use to manage the host. Then, navigate to **Configure | Advanced Settings**.
4. This is an optional step to **Edit Advanced vCenter Settings** and modify the certificate configuration values:

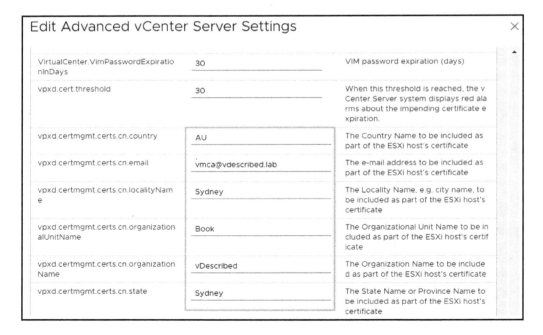

5. Right-click on the desired ESXi host and navigate to **Certificates** | **Renew Certificate**:

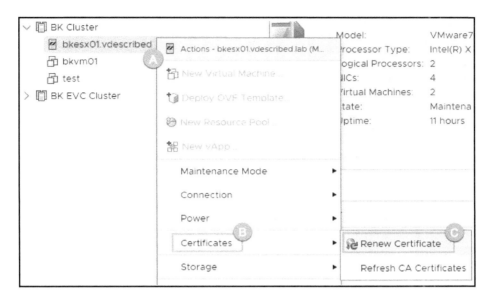

Renew Certificate option

6. You will be prompted to confirm the operation. Click **Yes** to do so:

7. You should see a **Refresh the subject certificate on the host** task completed successfully in the **Recent Tasks** pane.

8. Restart the management services on the host by issuing the /usr/sbin/services.sh restart command.

9. The host's **Configure** | **System** | **Certificate** section should now display the new certificate's details:

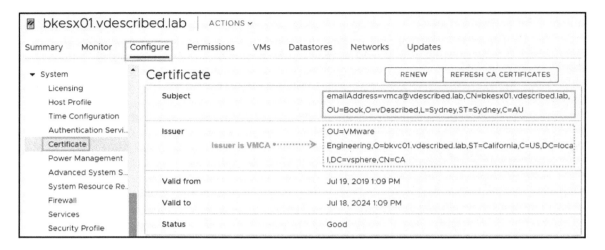

This completes the process of renewing VMCA issued ESXi certificates.

You can generate self-signed certificates directly from the ESXi host by running the /sbin/generate-certificates command.

Trusting root certificates to stop browser security warnings

The root certificates that correspond to the issuing certificate authority, whether it be VMCA or an Enterprise/Commercial PKI, should be trusted by the local computer/domain to get rid of the certificate warning displayed by the browser.

Most common browsers use the Windows Certificate Store, but some browsers, such as Firefox, maintain their own certificate store.

Getting ready

Before you begin, download or procure the root CA certificate from the PKI.

In order to download the VMCA default root certificate, connect to the node running VMCA (PSC/vCenter) by using the `https://FQDN` URL of vCenter. Then, click **Download trusted root CA certificates**:

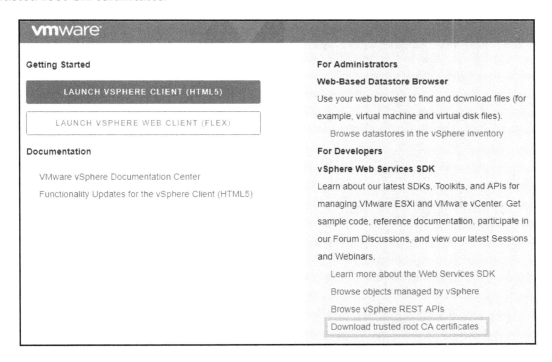

How to do it...

The following steps will help you to trust a root CA certificate to remove browser certificate warnings:

1. On a Windows machine, go to **Start** | **Run** and type MMC. Then, click **OK**.
2. On the **Console**, go to **File** | **Add/Remove Snap-in.**
3. Select **Certificate** from the left-hand pane and click **Add**.
4. Select to use the **Computer Account** and click **Finish**.
5. Select **Local computer**, click **Finish**, and then click **OK**.
6. Expand **Certificates** and go to **Trusted Root Certificate Authorities** | **Certificates.**
7. Right-click on **Certificates** | **All Tasks** | **Import...**:

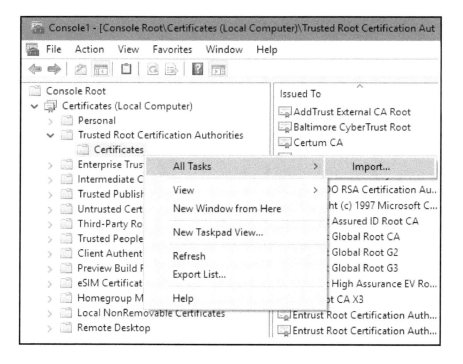

Start Certificate Import Wizard

8. Click **Next** on the **Certificate Import Wizard**.

9. Browse and select the Root CA certificate (`.cer`) file and click **Next** to continue:

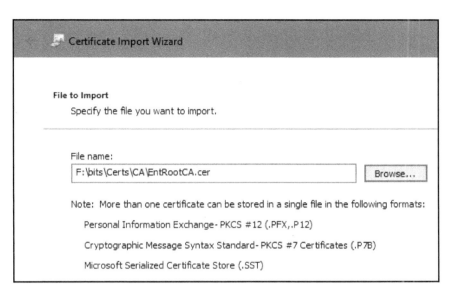

10. Choose to **Place all certificates** in the **Trusted Root Certificate Authorities** store and click **Next**:

11. Review the summary and click **Finish**.

12. A message indicating that **The import was successful** should be displayed. Click **OK**.

13. Once done, the root certificate should be listed in the certificates store:

Certum CA	Certum CA	11/06/2027	Server Authenticati...	Certum
Entrust Root Certification Auth...	Entrust Root Certification Authority	28/11/2026	Server Authenticati...	Entrust
Baltimore CyberTrust Root	Baltimore CyberTrust Root	13/05/2025	Server Authenticati...	DigiCert Baltimore ...
vdescribed-AD01-CA	vdescribed-AD01-CA	13/07/2024	<All>	<None>
Security Communication Root...	Security Communication RootCA1	30/09/2023	Server Authenticati...	SECOM Trust Syste...
GlobalSign	GlobalSign	15/12/2021	Server Authenticati...	Google Trust Servic...
DST Root CA X3	DST Root CA X3	1/10/2021	Secure Email, Serve...	DST Root CA X3

14. Now, close all of the browser sessions and reconnect to the vSphere Web/HTML5 client. You should no longer receive the certificate warning.

This completes the process of trusting root CA certificates to remove browser security warnings when connecting to vCenter Server.

How it works...

Once the root CA certificate of the PKI has been trusted, any connection to an endpoint using a certificate issued by the same authority, whether it be a web CA certificate or a subordinate CA certificate, will be considered secure by the web browser, as shown in the following screenshot:

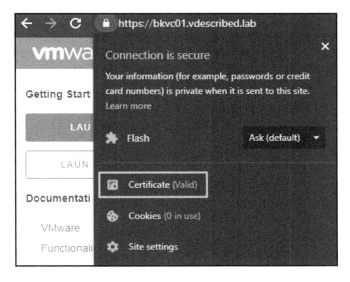

Browser Security Check

Since you are trusting the root certificate, there is no need to repeat this procedure every time you renew certificates; that is, unless the new certificates are procured from a different PKI or the PKI revokes the current root certificate.

16
Monitoring the vSphere Infrastructure

Any infrastructure, once deployed, needs to be monitored for any performance changes during its life cycle. Continuously monitoring a vSphere infrastructure aids in further optimization so that you can meet service-level agreements and reduce operational costs. There are several methods and tools available, such as **vRealize Operations Manager (vROPS)** which, unlike other monitoring tools, does what VMware calls **predictive analysis**. It learns what is normal from an environment over time, provides recommendations, and allows for capacity planning. More information about vROPS can be found at `https://www.vmware.com/au/products/vrealize-operations.html`.

Performance monitoring is a larger topic and cannot be confined to a single chapter. This chapter primarily introduces you to the most commonly used monitoring tools: esxtop, vscsiStats, and vCenter's Performance Charts.

In this chapter, we will be covering the following recipe:

- Using esxtop to monitor performance
- Exporting/importing esxtop configurations
- Running esxtop in batch mode
- Gathering VM I/O statistics using vscsiStats
- Using vCenter Performance Charts

Using esxtop to monitor performance

The **esxtop** command-line utility can be used to monitor the CPU, memory, storage, and network performance metrics on an ESXi host. The default output of this tool can be further customized to display the information you need.

For anyone who is familiar with Linux operating systems, this shouldn't be something completely new. Linux uses a command-line performance monitoring tool called **top**. It is used to view real-time CPU, memory, storage, and network statistics on a Linux machine.

The esxtop tool has two operating modes – interactive (default) mode and batch mode. In interactive mode, the screen output of the tool can be changed based on what or how much information you would like to view. In batch mode, you can collect and save the performance data in a file.

Getting ready

To run esxtop, you will need access to the CLI of the ESXi host. The CLI can be accessed on the host's console via an IPMI interface (such as Dell's DRAC or HP's ILO), or by connecting to the server using an SSH client.

How to do it...

The following steps will familiarize you with running esxtop and switching between different modes:

1. Connect to the console of the ESXi host using any of the methods that were mentioned in the *Getting ready* section of this recipe.
2. Once you are at the CLI, type un `esxtop` and hit *Enter* so that the tool brings up its interactive mode. The statistics view will default to CPU:

```
10:14:22am up  5:07, 527 worlds, 2 VMs, 2 vCPUs; CPU load average: 0.94, 0.93, 0.94
PCPU USED(%):  99   99 AVG:  99
PCPU UTIL(%):  99   99 AVG:  99

      ID       GID NAME              NWLD  %USED  %RUN  %SYS  %WAIT %VMWAIT   %RDY  %IDLE %OVRLP  %CSTP %MLMTD %SWPWT
   24534     24534 bkvm01               9  99.34 98.25  0.00  800.34    0.00   1.83   0.00   0.13   0.00   0.00   0.00
   26460     26460 test                 9  95.40 96.42  0.00  800.54    0.00   3.66   0.00   0.14   0.00   0.00   0.00
   27907     27907 esxtop.2104322       1   3.22  3.32  0.00   96.74       -   0.03   0.00   0.00   0.00   0.00   0.00
    6301      6301 hostd.2098535       25   0.74  0.74  0.00 2499.43       -   0.48   0.00   0.00   0.00   0.00   0.00
       1         1 system             160   0.52  0.91  0.00 15788.70      - 200.00   0.00   0.06   0.00   0.00   0.00
   10399     10399 vpxa.2099102        36   0.15  0.14  0.00 3600.00       -   0.82   0.00   0.00   0.00   0.00   0.00
   10592     10592 lwsmd.2099156       12   0.14  0.15  0.00 1199.00       -   1.89   0.00   0.00   0.00   0.00   0.00
    4776      4776 ioFilterVPServe      2   0.07  0.07  0.00  199.95       -   0.01   0.00   0.00   0.00   0.00   0.00
   11241     11241 vmtoolsd.209927      2   0.05  0.04  0.00  200.00       -   0.01   0.00   0.00   0.00   0.00   0.00
    2171      2171 net-lacp.209766      3   0.02  0.02  0.00  299.94       -   0.07   0.00   0.00   0.00   0.00   0.00
   15145     15145 sshd.2100166         1   0.02  0.02  0.00  100.00       -   0.02   0.00   0.00   0.00   0.00   0.00
    6002      6002 hostdCgiServer.     12   0.02  0.02  0.00 1200.00       -   0.01   0.00   0.00   0.00   0.00   0.00
       8         8 helper             152   0.01  0.01  0.00 15199.45      -   0.00   0.00   0.00   0.00   0.00   0.00
    6454      6454 rhttpproxy.2098     18   0.00  0.00  0.00 1800.00       -   0.00   0.00   0.00   0.00   0.00   0.00
    5104      5104 swapobjd.209837      1   0.00  0.00  0.00  100.00       -   0.00   0.00   0.00   0.00   0.00   0.00
    6591      6591 sdrsInjector.20      1   0.00  0.00  0.00  100.00       -   0.00   0.00   0.00   0.00   0.00   0.00
      10        10 drivers             12   0.00  0.00  0.00 1199.96       -   0.01   0.00   0.00   0.00   0.00   0.00
    9863      9863 nscd.2099029         6   0.00  0.00  0.00  600.00       -   0.00   0.00   0.00   0.00   0.00   0.00
    2780      2780 busybox.2098061      1   0.00  0.00  0.00  100.00       -   0.00   0.00   0.00   0.00   0.00   0.00
    6727      6727 storageRM.20986      1   0.00  0.00  0.00  100.00       -   0.00   0.00   0.00   0.00   0.00   0.00
      11        11 ft                   4   0.00  0.00  0.00  399.98       -   0.01   0.00   0.00   0.00   0.00   0.00
      12        12 vmotion              1   0.00  0.00  0.00  100.00       -   0.00   0.00   0.00   0.00   0.00   0.00
```

3. You can cycle between different resource statistics modes using the following table:

Key	Resource Statistics Mode (with a default set of columns)
c	CPU statistics
m	Memory statistics
d	Storage adapter statistics
u	Storage device(LUN) utilization statistics
n	Network utilization statistics
v	VM-specific storage statistics
V	VM-specific compute, network, and storage statistics
i	Interrupt vector information
p	CPU Power utilization statistics

Although the keystrokes outlined in the preceding table allow you to switch between different modes, each mode can be further expanded and customized so that you can dive into a level of detail that you would need to understand its performance, as well as to troubleshoot issues.

How it works...

The information that's displayed in interactive mode is refreshed at regular 5-second intervals. This can be modified by hitting the s key while in interactive mode, specifying the interval in seconds, and hitting *Enter* to make the change take effect, as shown in the following screenshot:

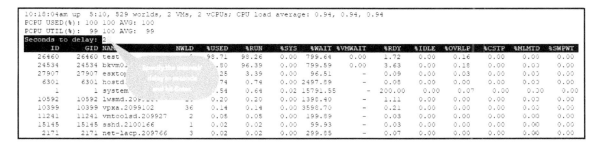

esxtop Interactive Mode.

The esxtop output can be further customized in terms of the metrics and counters that are displayed on the screen. Once you have launched esxtop, while in any metric view, hit the *F* key to bring up the field customization view.

Here, you can choose to include or not include a field/column by hitting the alphabet key listed next to it. The fields that have been chosen for the display are marked with an asterisk (*). Once you have made the necessary selections, just hit *Enter* to exit the field customization view and return to the metrics view with the customized field view, as shown in the following screenshot:

```
Current Field order: ABcDEFghij

 * A:   ID = Id
 * B:   GID = Group Id
   C:   LWID = Leader World Id (World Group Id)
 * D:   NAME = Name
 * E:   NWLD = Num Members
 * F:   %STATE TIMES = CPU State Times
   G:   EVENT COUNTS/s = CPU Event Counts
   H:   CPU ALLOC = CPU Allocations
   I:   SUMMARY STATS = CPU Summary Stats
   J:   POWER STATS = CPU Power Stats

Toggle fields with a-j, any other key to return:
```

Exporting/importing esxtop configurations

All the output customization that is done during interactive mode is lost the moment you exit the tool. However, you do have the option of exporting the output configuration to a file and reimporting the configuration to avoid spending time customizing the columnar output again.

Getting ready

You will need access to the CLI of the ESXi host. The CLI can be accessed on the host's console via an IPMI interface (such as Dell's DRAC or HP's ILO), or by connecting to the server using an SSH client.

How to do it...

The following steps can be used to export and then import an esxtop configuration:

1. To export the esxtop configuration to a file, launch esxtop, customize the output as required, and use an uppercase *W* to specify a directory patch to save the configuration file. Then, hit *Enter*:

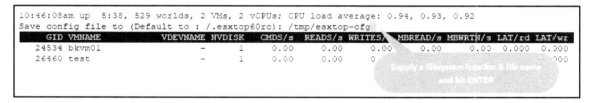

```
10:46:08am up  5:38, 529 worlds, 2 VMs, 2 vCPUs; CPU load average: 0.94, 0.93, 0.92
Save config file to (Default to : /.esxtop60rc): /tmp/esxtop-cfg
    GID VMNAME            VDEVNAME NVDISK   CMDS/s  READS/s WRITES/ MBREAD/s MBWRTN/s LAT/rd LAT/wr
  24534 bkvm01                  -       1     0.00     0.00    0.00     0.00     0.00  0.000  0.000
  26460 test                    -       1     0.00     0.00    0                                000
```

Saving esxtop configuration

2. Now, we can use the *exported* configuration file again to *import customizations* during the launch of the tool. The syntax is `"esxtop -c <filename>"`. An example of this is `# esxtop -c /tmp/esxtop-cfg`.

How it works...

The file that's created is a plain text file and will list all the column/field keystrokes that are stored inside it. These can be used to launch esxtop without us having to customize the screen output again:

```
[root@bkesx01:/tmp] esxtop
[root@bkesx01:/tmp] ls
esxtop-cfg            lwidentity.join.log  probe.session
[root@bkesx01:/tmp] cat esxtop-cfg
ABcDEFghij
aBcDefgHijKLmnOpq
ABCdEfGhijkl
ABcdeFGhIjklmnop
aBCDEfghIJKl
AbcDEFGHIJKLMNopq
ABCDeF
ABCDef
ABCd
5v
[root@bkesx01:/tmp]
```

Keep in mind that the default location is /.esxtop60rc. If you hit *Enter* without specifying the location and name of the new file, the changes will be written to the esxtop50rc file. Thenceforth, every time you launch esxtop, it will start with the custom output.

Running esxtop in batch mode

Unlike interactive mode, *batch mode* will let you issue a command to collect all or some of the statistics for a period of time and at the desired interval. This is particularly handy when you want to monitor the performance of an ESXi host for a certain period of time.

Getting ready

You will need access to the CLI of the ESXi host. The CLI can be accessed on the host's console via an IPMI interface (such as Dell's DRAC or HP's ILO), or by connecting to the server using an SSH client.

You need to plan the number of performance snapshots that you want to gather and the interval between each snapshot.

How to do it...

The following steps will help you run esxtop in batch mode:

1. SSH into the ESXi host as root.
2. Use the following command syntax to run esxtop in batch mode:

   esxtop -b -a -d <delay> **-n** <iterations> > export filename

   The following is an example of using the preceding command:

   esxtop -b -a -d 10 -n 50 > /tmp/perf_statistics.csv

3. Once exported, the comma-separated values can be viewed in any MS Excel file or can even be imported into tools such as **Windows Performance Monitor (PerfMon)** for analysis.

The following table lists the command switches that are used in the syntax:

Switch	Effect
-a	This will gather all esxtop statistics.
-d	This inserts a delay (in seconds) between every performance snapshot.
-n	This is used to specify the number of snapshot iterations that have to be run.

This completes the process of running esxtop in batch mode.

Once the statistics have been exported, the `.csv` file can be viewed using Microsoft Excel or a spreadsheet application. It can also be imported into PerfMon for analysis.

How it works...

Using batch mode essentially lets you collect statistics for a period of time, which is specified in terms of a number of iterations and delays:

Statistics Collection Duration = (Number of iterations) x (Delay in seconds)

The example that's used in the *How to do it...* section runs esxtop for 50 iterations with a delay for 10 seconds, which equates to data being collected over a period of *50 x 10 = 500 seconds*.

Gathering VM I/O statistics using vscsiStats

Unlike esxtop, which collects real-time data, the vscsiStats tool is used to gather the I/O statistics of a VM at a per-virtual-disk (VMDK) level. It can collect statistics such as the number of outstanding I/Os, size of the I/Os, and seek distance and latency. These statistics can be used in workload characterization. Understanding the characteristics of a workload will aid you in assigning the correct storage resources for virtual machines. For instance, if you have different datastores categorized into different storage tiers, then having a clear understanding of the I/O characteristics will facilitate the efficient placement of VMs.

 The whitepaper, *Storage Workload Characterization and Consolidation in Virtualized Environments*, is a very interesting read on the study that was conducted. You can find it at `https://communities.vmware.com/docs/DOC-10104`.

Getting ready

You will need access to the ESXi CLI via the console or SSH. Also, make note of the **World IDs** corresponding to the VMs you would like to fetch the statistics for. The `esxcli vm process list` command will list all the running VMs, along with their World IDs:

```
[root@bkesx01:~] esxcli vm process list
bkvm01
    World ID: 2101475
    Process ID: 0
    VMX Cartel ID: 2101474
    UUID: 42 3a db 15 de 10 f0 de-a3 d1 8e 15 1e 88 31 46
    Display Name: bkvm01
    Config File: /vmfs/volumes/5c35bf45-267aea32-7894-0050568837fe/bkvm01/bkvm01.vmx

test
    World ID: 2101619
    Process ID: 0
    VMX Cartel ID: 2101514
    UUID: 42 3a 92 0a d0 3d 00 fd-ed 95 67 a4 6d c9 31 d7
    Display Name: test
    Config File: /vmfs/volumes/5c35bf45-267aea32-7894-0050568837fe/test/test.vmx
[root@bkesx01:~]
```

How to do it...

The following steps will help you fetch the I/O statistics that correspond to a VM:

1. Find the `worldGroupID` that corresponds to the VM. This is achieved by issuing the `vscsiStats -l` command:

```
[root@bkesx01:~] vscsiStats -l
Virtual Machine worldGroupID: 2101474, Virtual Machine Display Name: bkvm01, Virtual Machine Config File:
 /vmfs/volumes/5c35bf45-267aea32-7894-0050568837fe/bkvm01/bkvm01.vmx, {
   Virtual SCSI Disk handleID: 8203 (scsi0:0)
}
Virtual Machine worldGroupID: 2101514, Virtual Machine Display Name: test, Virtual Machine Config File: /
vmfs/volumes/5c35bf45-267aea32-7894-0050568837fe/test/test.vmx, {
   Virtual SCSI Disk handleID: 8202 (scsi0:0)
}
[root@bkesx01:~]
```

Now, this can be a large list if you have a lot of VMs running on the host. If that is the case, then there are several ways to filter the list. One of them would be to send the output of the command to a file and then find the VM in it by using its display name.

2. Once you have the VM's `worldGroupID`, the next step will be to fetch the statistics. The following command syntax can be used for this:

   vscsiStats -s -w <worldGroupID of the virtual machine>

   The following is an example of using the preceding command:

   vscsiStats -s -w 2101474

   This will start a collection against every disk (vmdk or rdm) associated with the VM. The collection will continue to run for 30 minutes from the time it was started, that is, unless you choose to stop it by using the vscsiStats -x command:

   vscsiStats -x -w 2101474

   The following screenshot shows an example of the commands being executed on an ESXi host:

```
[root@bkesx01:~]
[root@bkesx01:~] vscsiStats -s -w 2101474  ◄········● Start Collection
vscsiStats: Starting Vscsi stats collection for worldGroup 2101474, handleID 8233 (scsi0:0)
Success.
[root@bkesx01:~] vscsiStats -x -w 2101474  ◄········● Stop Collection
vscsiStats: Stopping all Vscsi stats collection for worldGroup 2101474, handleID 8235 (scsi0:0)
Success.
[root@bkesx01:~]
```

This completes the process of collecting the I/O statistics of a virtual machine.

How it works...

Once the collection process is completed or stopped, you can view the data that was gathered by the collection based on the histogram type you need.

The following table lists the histogram types that are available:

Histogram Type	Description
all	All statistics
ioLength	Size of the I/O
seekDistance	Logical blocks the disk head must move before a read/write operation can be performed
outstandingIOs	Number of I/O operations queued
latency	I/O latency
Interarrival	The time gap between the VM disk commands (in microseconds)

The following command syntax can be used to generate histograms:

- **Syntax**: vscsiStats -w <*worldGroupID*> --printhistos <*histogram type*> -c <*name of the output .csv file*>
- **Example**: vscsiStats -w 2101474 --printhistos outstandingIOs -c /tmp/OutstandingIO.csv

The CSV file can then be imported into MS Excel or other similar tools for a better presentation of the data that's been collected.

Using vCenter Performance Charts

You can use vCenter Performance Charts to provide a graphical insight into the performance metrics. Supported metrics include CPU, cluster service, datastore, disk, memory, network, power, storage adapter, storage path, system, virtual flash, and vSphere replication.

Getting ready

You will need to be able to access vCenter with a user account that has permission to view and modify the performance charts.

How to do it...

The following steps will provide you with a very high-level workflow of using vCenter Performance Charts:

1. Log in to the vCenter Server using the HTML5 client.
2. Select the desired ESXi host from the cluster and navigate to **Monitor** | **Performance** | **Advanced** or **Overview**.

 Performance charts can be pulled against a vCenter instance, a data center, a cluster, an ESXi host, or a VM. The **Overview** pane shows the past day's performance. The **Advanced view** displays real-time data.

3. By default, the chart presents you with real-time CPU statistics. You can switch between different resource metrics using the dropdown box at the top right-hand corner of the chart:

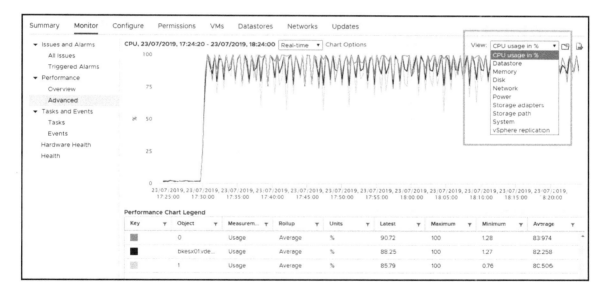

4. Although the real-time metrics are displayed by default, you can customize the charts so that the metrics, timespan, chart type, and the counters are included. Click on **Chart Options** to do so:

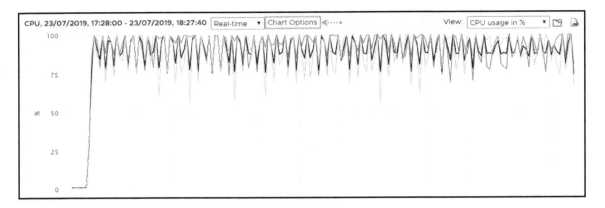

This completes a high-level overview of how to use vCenter Performance Charts.

How it works...

vCenter Performance Charts collect data using collection intervals.

vCenter uses four default intervals: a **day**, a **week**, a **month**, and a **year**. A **collection interval** defines the amount of time the performance data has to be stored in vCenter's database. Only the data for the collection intervals is saved in the database. In other words, real-time performance data will not be saved.

Every collection interval has a corresponding collection frequency. For example, the default collection interval frequencies are 5 minutes for a day, 30 minutes for a week, 2 hours for a month, and 1 day for a year.

vCenter performance charts support three different chart types—**Line Graph**, **Stacked Graph**, and **Stacked Graph per VM**:

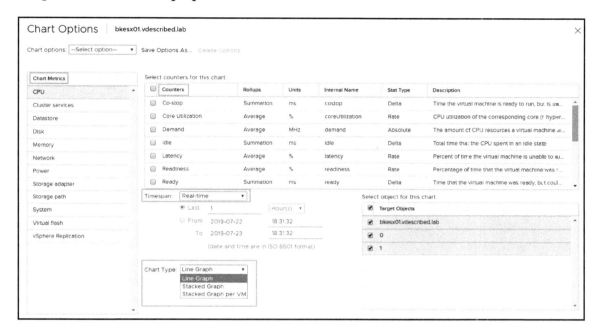

For more information on how to use vCenter Performance Charts, read the *About vSphere Monitoring and Performance* section of the following documentation: `https://docs.vmware.com/en/VMware-vSphere/6.7/com.vmware.vsphere.monitoring.doc/GUID-A8B06BE0-E5FC-435C-B12F-A31618B21E2C.html`.

Other Books You May Enjoy

If you enjoyed this book, you may be interested in these other books by Packt:

Mastering VMware vSphere 6.7 - Second Edition
Andrea Mauro, Karel Novak, Paolo Valsecchi, Martin Gavanda

ISBN: 978-178961-337-7

- Explore the immense functionality of vSphere 6.7
- Design, manage and administer a virtualization environment
- Get tips for the VCP6-DCV and VCIX6-DCV exams
- Understand how to implement different migration techniques across different environments
- Explore vSphere 6.7s powerful capabilities for patching, upgrading and managing the configuration of virtual environments.
- Understand core vSphere components
- Master resource management, disaster recovery, troubleshooting, monitoring and security

VMware vSphere 6.7 Data Center Design Cookbook - Third Edition
Mike B. Brown, Hersey Cartwright

ISBN: 978-1-78980-151-4

- Identify key factors related to a vSphere design
- Mitigate security risks and meet compliance requirements in a vSphere design
- Create a vSphere conceptual design by identifying technical and business requirements
- Design for performance, availability, recoverability, manageability, and security
- Map the logical resource design into the physical vSphere design
- Create professional vSphere design documentation

Leave a review - let other readers know what you think

Please share your thoughts on this book with others by leaving a review on the site that you bought it from. If you purchased the book from Amazon, please leave us an honest review on this book's Amazon page. This is vital so that other potential readers can see and use your unbiased opinion to make purchasing decisions, we can understand what our customers think about our products, and our authors can see your feedback on the title that they have worked with Packt to create. It will only take a few minutes of your time, but is valuable to other potential customers, our authors, and Packt. Thank you!

Index

T

www.ingramcontent.com/pod-product-compliance
Lightning Source LLC
LaVergne TN
LVHW081507050326
832903LV00025B/1406

Mastering Python

Machine Learning, Data Structures, Django, Object Oriented Programming and Software Engineering

(Including Programming Interview Questions) [2nd Edition]

Published by Newstone Publishing

ISBN 978-1-989726-01-3 (Paperback)

Table of Contents

Introduction

Welcome to my guide to learning Python. Unlike some guides that give you just the basics that you need to get started, my aim is to teach you everything you need to know about using Python including what you can use it for. Python is a diverse language and is the foundation of much of what we use in the world today. Most data applications, many websites, machine learning, are all powered by Python and you'll be pleased to learn that it really isn't difficult to learn. I have divided this book into five sections to make it easier for you:

- Part 1 – Data Structures and Algorithms
- Part 2 – Machine Learning
- Part 3 – Django
- Part 4 – ArcGIS Programming
- Part 5 – Software Development and Testing

Each part is comprehensive and complex; work through the sections one at a time and ensure that you understand it thoroughly before you move on to the next one. Below, is an overview of each part:

Part 1 – Data Structures and Algorithms

If you want to be successful building data applications that work, you need to have a good working knowledge of Python data structures along with algorithms that give those structures life. With this understanding, the secrets that lie within data can be unlocked. This is a skill that is becoming incredibly important in a world that is saturated with data, such a vast amount of data that we simply don't have the ability to analyze it all. What we do have are the tools, and in the first part of this guide, you will learn about the Python data structures and the algorithms, along with the basics of Python programming. Some of the algorithms we will look at are those that give us the solutions to common data analysis problems, such as searching data, sorting it, extracting statistics and more. You will learn about complex data structures and how to create stacks, lists, and queues. You will learn how to sort algorithms using techniques, such as insertion sort and bubble sort. You will learn the common structures and some of the techniques required to preprocess data, to model it, and transform it. You will learn how your code should be paganized for efficiency, manageability, and readability. And you will learn how you can build components that are easily understandable that can be used in multiple applications and can easily be debugged.

Part 2 – Machine Learning

We use machine learning more in our daily lives now than we ever have before and most of us don't realize it. In brief, machine learning is a subset of artificial intelligence, of using algorithms to improve how the machines learn autonomously. We do this by providing information and data in several formats, notably real-world interactions and observations. In short, we are teaching computers to think and act, to make decisions as humans do.

Most of Part Two will cover how machine learning works. We will talk about how the data should be processed so that the algorithms can make informed decisions and how to choose the correct algorithm for the problem we need to solve. We'll cover the why as well, such as why correct measurements are important, why one algorithm might work better than another in a certain scenario and so on.

This is the tip of the iceberg as far as machine learning goes and research is ongoing. Hopefully, by the end of this section, you will have enough information at your fingertips to continue as quickly and as painlessly as possible.

Part 3 – Django

This part looks at Django, the most popular framework for web development. With Django, it is possible to build top-quality web apps and maintain them with the least amount of fuss. Django is an exciting development and it takes the repetitiveness out of web development leaving you to concentrate on the fun side of creating a website. It gives you shortcuts for some of the tasks you do more frequently in programming and provides you with clear problem-solving conventions, all while staying as far out of the way as it can.

In this section, while I can't make you into a Django expert, I can tell you how it all works and walk you through building an application, the easiest way to learn the concepts behind it along with the skills you need.

Part 4 – ArcGIS Programming

ArcGIS is geographical software provided by ESRI, an industry leader that allows geospatial data to be analyzed and presented. The fact that Python has been integrated into ArcGIS means that the arcpy module is now one of the most important tools for anyone studying Geographical Information Systems (GIS). ArcPY has proven very powerful in geospatial analysis, especially to improve productivity. From basic scripts to the most advanced methods and properties from arcpy, the speed of any GIS workflow, as well as its repeatability, all seem set to vastly improve.

In this part of the guide, I will take you through basic scripts and the tools for advanced scripts. I will focus primarily on scripts for geospatial analysis with a look at how to automate cartographic output.

By the end of this section, you will have learned to create modules that you can reuse, add repeatable analyses in ArcToolBox as a scripting tool, and automatically export maps. You will also see just how efficient ArcGIS and arcpy are together, how one professional can have the power of an entire GIS team.

Part 5 – Software Development and Testing

In Part Five, the last part of the book, we take a look mainly at testing in Python. Testing is a requisite part of Python programming, particularly to build software and web apps. We will look at Test-Driven Development (TDT), Behavior-Driven Development (BDD), the Principles of Automated Testing and what the purpose is. We will look at the difference between unit and integration testing, how tests should be prioritized, and the testing of DSLs. We finish by looking at Python Mocking, a way of replacing bits of the system and making your unit tests far more efficient.

The Python programming language has led to more people learning to appreciate computer programming and what can be achieved with it. It is a fun language; it is concise in its problem descriptions and it makes learning easy.

We start the guide with an in-depth look at the language; you do not need to have any prior experience with Python.

The Zen of Python

Taken from https/python.org

"Beautiful is better than ugly.

Explicit is better than implicit.

Simple is better than complex.

Complex is better than complicated.

Flat is better than nested.

Sparse is better than dense.

Readability counts.

Special cases aren't special enough to break the rules.

Although practicality beats purity.

Errors should never pass silently.

Unless explicitly silenced.

In the face of ambiguity, refuse the temptation to guess.

There should be one-- and preferably only one --obvious way to do it.

Although that way may not be obvious at first unless you're Dutch.

Now is better than never.

Although never is often better than *right* now.

If the implementation is hard to explain, it's a bad idea.

If the implementation is easy to explain, it may be a good idea.

Namespaces are one honking great idea -- let's do more of those!"

Setting Up Your Environment

Before you can even start thinking about anything in this guide, you should set up your environment so there are no interruptions later. We'll start with Python itself.

You will need Python 2.7 or earlier; it's best to go for 3.6 if you can – the later the version, the more chance you have of everything being compatible.

Linux/Mac OS

You should already have Python installed on your computer; to check, open a terminal and type python 3 at the command prompt. You will see immediately if it is installed because you will see a version number.

Windows

You will need to download Python to your computer; go to https://www.python.org/downloads and download the latest version (3, not 2). Once the download has finished, open your computer's downloads folder and double-click the python.msi file and the installer will run.

Now, by default, the executable file for Python does NOT get added to the statement for Windows PATH – you need to add it, but this is simple. Wait for the installer screen to load and then check the box that says "Add Python 3.x to PATH" before you hit the Install button. Click Install and wait; when it has finished, open a command window and type python – you should see confirmation of the version you installed. If it doesn't show up, reboot your computer and try again. Once you see the confirmation, there is one last thing to do – close Python and then go to the command prompt in the command window – type the following:

python -m pip install -U pip

You will now see a message that tells you pip is up-to-date or you will see a message telling you that the latest version is being downloaded – the old version will be uninstalled first.

25

Pip is the package manager for Python and is what you will use to install the packages you need. Next, we 'll install a virtual environment. It's best to work inside a virtual environment so that you don't inadvertently write something that can change the variables and dependencies on which other software on your computer depend. The virtual environment wraps up environment variables and dependencies that your new software uses into one file system that is kept separate from anything else running on your computer.

To install the Python virtual environment, open your terminal or command prompt and type the following:

pip install virtualenv

You should now see a message in the window telling you that virtualenv is now installed.

This sets you up with Python; as we go through the guide, I will tell you, at the start of each section, what other packages you need to install.

Chapter 1: An Overview of Data Structures and Algorithms

Python is the chosen programming language for many different data tasks and there is a good reason for that. It is an easy programming language to learn and the addition of intuitive structures means that it is one of the most straightforward languages for a whole range of different data tasks. Python is not just for scripting; it is a fully featured object-oriented programming language (OOP).

One of the most useful features of Python is the fact that it has many built-in data structures and algorithms. Because it is object-based, creating custom data objects is relatively simple. We're going to be looking at the internal Python libraries, some external libraries, and we will be learning how to use first principles to build data objects.

I am assuming that you have some knowledge of Python but, just in case you need a refresher, this first section will go over the basics. If you still need a refresher, take a look at the tutorials at https://docs.python.org.

In this section, we will be:

- Looking at and learning about data structures and algorithms
- Learning the fundamental data types and what they do
- Looking into the object-oriented side of Python

Data Structures and Algorithms

Data Structures and Algorithms are perhaps the most basic of all computing concepts because they are the building blocks that we use to build software. Understanding these concepts is vital to software design and, for that, you will need to learn the following:

- How data inside a data structure is manipulated by algorithms
- How data is organized in memory
- The performance characteristic of certain data structures

Some of this will be addressed in Part Two when we discuss machine learning but we will be looking at the basics of Python from several perspectives, first and foremost from the perspective of the algorithms and data structures. We also need to make sure that we have the mathematical tools we need to understand the basic computer science concepts. For this, we need an understanding of mathematics, but, by developing a few guiding principles, understanding the key principles won't require anything more than high-school math.

Evaluation is also vital. To measure the performance of an algorithm, you must understand how the increases in the size of the data affect data operations. With real-world applications or large datasets, we must ensure that the data structures and the algorithms are working efficiently.

To understand a little about algorithmic thinking, we'll look at a quick real-world example. Let's say that we are in a marketplace that is not familiar to us. We have been asked to buy a specific list of items. Assume that the market has been randomly laid out and that each of the vendors will sell a random subset of the items, and some of these might just be on our list. What we want to do is minimize how long we are there, so we would start with an algorithm like this:

- Does the first vendor sell any of the items I want, and do they cost less than the predicted cost?
- If yes, buy the items and remove them from the list. If no, proceed to the next vendor.
- If there are no more vendors, we're finished.

Repeat for every vendor.

This is, in programming terms, nothing more than an iterator; it has a decision and it has an action. If this were to be implemented, we would need to define the item list that we have and the items that each vendor sells, and this is done through data structures. We would need to find the best way to match the items in each of the lists and we need a little logic to determine whether to buy or not.

We can see several things here. First, the cost calculation is prediction-based. We have no idea of the average cost. If we go with an underprediction we will leave the market with items left to buy so we need a way to go back to the vendor that has the lowest cost.

We also need an understanding of the time needed to compare the items on the list with what each vendor sells – either our list will increase or the number of items sold by a vendor will increase. The time it takes to search will depend on in what order we search and the data structure shapes. Clearly, it would be better to have the list structured in such a way that it matches the order of the vendors, thus cutting down the search time.

Still with me? Good, because next, we need to think about the effect if we were to change our purchase condition so that we bought at the lowest price and at the price that is just under the average. This makes the problem entirely different; instead of visiting the vendors in sequence, we need to go through the market once and then order the list as to the vendors we need to visit.

Clearly, there is more to turning a real-world problem into a programming language. As we go through the market, for example, we expand our knowledge of product costs so the variable we have for the predicted average price will improve; by the time we get to the end of the market, we can look at our whole strategy and review it. Adding in conditions like data structure shape, the variability of prices, backtrack cost, and so on, help us to work out the best solution.

Python for Data

Python very helpfully contains a number of built-in structures including dictionaries, lists, and sets and we can use these to build customized objects. There are also libraries, like collections and a math object; these let us create structures that are a bit more advanced and we can perform calculations on them. Lastly, there are external libraries, like those in the SciPy packages and it is these that let us do some of the more advanced data tasks that pertain to machine learning. However, while these external libraries are useful, there are penalties to pay in terms of performance compared to ground-up customized objects. If we can learn to code the objects, they can be targeted at particular tasks and this will make them far more efficient.

Chapter 2: Python Variables and Expressions

There are two associated tasks involved in translating real-world problems into those that an algorithm can solve. First, the variables must be selected and second, we need the expressions that are related to the variables. A variable is a label that is attached to an object. They are neither the object nor are they the object containers. Variables do not contain objects; they are pointers to objects. Look at this code:

a=[2, 4, 6]

b=a

a.append(8)

print(b)

[2, 4, 6, 8]

A variable has been created and this references a list object. Another variable is created, and this references the same object. When an element is appended, we see that both a and b reflect the change.

Python is known as a dynamically-typed language. We can bind a variable name to different types and values during execution; each of the values is of a specific type, perhaps an integer or a string but the name that references the value will not have a particular type. What this means is whenever a variable is initialized in Python, there is no need to declare a type. The object that a variable points to can also change type.

Variable Scope

One of the most important things to understand is the rules of scope surrounding a variable in a function. New local namespaces are created whenever a function is executed. These namespaces represent environments in which you will find the names of each parameter and each variable that the function assigned. When a function is called the namespace needs to be resolved and, to do this, the Python interpreter will search the function; if it can't find a match, it will then search the module in which the function is defined – this is the global namespace. If the name is still not there, the built-in namespace is searched and, if this doesn't work, the interpreter will raise a NameError exception. Look at this code:

```
a=20; b=30
def my_function():
    global a
    a=21; b=31
my_function()
print(a) #prints 21
print(b) #prints 30
```

We have defined a pair of global variables and the interpreter needs to be told that, within the function, we are using the global keyword to refer to a global variable. When the variable gets changed to 11 the global scope will reflect the changes. However, where the variable called b is set to 21, it is actually a local variable and, if we make any changes within the function, there is no reflection of them in the global scope. If you run that function and print that variable, you would see that b keeps its global value.

Iteration and Flow Control

All Python programs are made up of sequences of statements. Each statement is executed in order until all are done. All the statements have an equal status, regardless of whether they are function definitions, variable assignments, module imports or class definitions. None of the statement types have a priority that is higher than another and any statement can be placed anywhere within the program. Program exaction flow can be controlled in two ways – using loops and using conditional statements.

The conditional statements are:

- if
- else
- elif

Generally, a series of the if and elif statements end with an else statement:

```
x='two'
if x==1:
   print('False')
elif x==2:
  print('True')
else:
   print('Another value')
#prints 'Another value'
```

Did you spot the == operator? We use that to test for equal values and, if they are equal, it will return True, and False if otherwise. Also note that when x is set as a string, the return will not be a type error as you would expect; instead, it will be *something else*.

Loops are the other way of controlling program flow and we create this using two more statements:

- while
- for

Look at this example:

```
x=0
while x < 3: print (x); x += 1
```

0

1

2

Chapter 3: Overview of Data Types And Objects

Built into Python are no less than 12 data types including four that are numeric:

- int
- float
- complex
- bool

There are four that are sequence types:

- str
- list
- tuple
- range

A mapping type called dict and two of type set are also included. You may also create your own user-defined objects like classes or functions. First, we'll look at lists and strings and move onto the rest of the data types later.

Every Python data type is an object, as are functions, classes, modules, and pretty much anything else in Python – and that includes string and integer literals. Each Python object has its own type, identity, and value. For example, when you write *greeting = "hello world"* you are creating an instance. This instance is a string object that has an identity of *greet* and a value of *"hello world"*. The object identity is a reference to where the object is located in memory. The object type, otherwise known as its class, is a description of the internal representation of the object along with any operations and methods supported by it. When an object instance has been created, you cannot change either the type or the identity.

There is a function built into Python called id() and this can be used to find an object's identity. It will return an integer that identifies it, and this may refer to the location in memory – do not rely on this though. We can also compare objects in several ways:

if a== b: #a and b have identical values
if a is b: # if a and b are identical object types
if type(a) is type(b): # a and b are identical types

Before we go any further, we need to distinguish between objects that are mutable and immutable. With a mutable object, like a list, you can change their values using methods like append() or insert(). With an immutable object, like a string, you cannot change the values. When their methods are run, a value is returned; there is no change to the value of any underlying object. However, you can use the returned value – simply use it as a function argument or assign it to a variable.

Strings

A string is a sequence object that is immutable. Each character is representative of one element in that sequence. Operations are performed on the objects using methods. Because a string is immutable, the instances are not changed; each method will do nothing more than return a value. We can store this value as a variable or we can pass it to a method or a function as an argument. Below are the most common string methods along with a description:

s.count(substring, [start, end])

Will count the number of substrings that have optional start and end parameters

s.expandtabs([tabsize])

Will replace any tab with a space

s.find(substring, [start, end])

Will return the index of the first substring; -1 is returned if the substring can't be found

s.isalnum()

Will return True if every character is alphanumeric; False if not

s.isalpha()

Will return True if every character is alphabetic; False if not

s.isdigit()

Will return True if every character is a digit; False if not

s.join(t)

Will join together the strings in the given sequence (t, in this case)

s.lower()

Will convert the string to be lowercase

s.replace(old, new [maxreplace])

Will replace a substring (old) with another (new)

s.strip([characters])

Will remove any optional characters or whitespace

s.split([separator], [maxsplit])

Will split a string that is separated with an optional separator or whitespace and will return a list

Like every type of sequence, a string has support for both indexing and slicing. We use the index s[i] to retrieve a given character from the string and we can use s[i:j] to get a slice from the string – i and j indicate the start point and the end point of the slice. We can add a stride to get an extended slice s[i:j:stride]. Let's make this a little clearer with a piece of code:

greet = 'hello world'
print(greet[1])

Running this code will return:

[e]

print(greet [0:8])

Running this code will return:

'hello wo'

print(greet [0:8:2])

Running this code will return:

'hlow'

print(greet [0::2])

Running this code will return:

'hlowrd'

Example 1 and 2 are easy; we asked for and got the character located at the first index and the initial 7 letters from the string. Example 3 includes a stride of 2 which gives us every 2nd character while, in the last example, we left out the end index; the slice we got was every 2nd character from the whole string.

Any variable, expression or operator can be used for the index so long as it has an integer for the value:

print(greet [1+2])

Running this code will return:

'l'

print(greet[len(greet)-1])

Running this code will return:

'd'

As we know, strings are immutable so one of the most common questions is, how do we do operations like inserting a value? Instead of changing the string, we must come up with other ways of building new objects that give us the results we need. For example, let's say that we wanted to add a word to the greeting; we would assign variables like this:

print(greet[:5] + ' wonderful ' + greet[5:])

Running this code will return:

'hello wonderful world'

We split the string using the slice operator and we did this at index 5. The + operator is used to concatenate the strings. The string contents are never interpreted by Python as numbers. If we needed to do a math operation on a string, we would have to convert the string to type numeric:

x='3'; y = '2'
print(x + y) #concatenation

Running this code will return:

'32'

print(int(x) + int (y)) #addition

Running this code will return:

5

Lists

The list is the most common data structure and is used the most often because they can be made up of any data type. A list, like a string, is indexed using integers that begin with a zero. Below are the common list methods and a description of each:

list(s)

Will return a list of the given sequence (s)

s.append(x)

Will append the element called x to s (at the end)

s.extend(x)

Will append the list called x to s

s.count(x)

Will count how many times x is in s

s.index(x, [start], [stop])

Will return the index that is the smallest and may include an optional start, stop index

s.insert(i,e)

Will insert x at the given index (i)

s.pop(i)

Will return the element called i and take it out of the list

s.remove(x)

Will take x out of s

s.reverse()

Will reverse the order of s

s.sort(key,[reverse])

Will sort s using reverse and optional key

When we work with any list or any container object, we must understand what mechanism Python employs to copy them. Python will only create a real copy if it has no alternative. When a variable value is assigned to another variable, both of them will go to the same location in memory. We only get a new memory slot if a variable is changed. This has consequences for lists and other mutable compound objects. Look at this code:

```
x=1; y=2; z=3
list1 =[x, y, z]
list2 = list1
list2[1] = 4
print(list1)
```

Running this code will return:

```
[1, 4, 3]
```

The variables called list1 and list2 both point to the same memory slot; when the y variable is changed to 4, the y variable that list1 points to is changed as it is the same variable.

One other important thing about lists is that you can have nested structures in them. This means they can contain other lists, like this:

```
items = [ ["rice", 2.4, 8], ["flour", 1.8, 5], ["corn", 4.7, 6] ]
```

The brackets operator is used to access the values in the lists and, because the list is mutable, they are copied where they are. The next code example shows you how to update an element using this fact. We are going to raise the flour price by 20%:

```
items[1][1] = items [1][1] * 1.2
print(items[1][1])
```

Running this code will return:

2.16

We can also use list comprehensions to create a list from some expressions. We write one expression into the list and create a list:

```
l= [2, 4, 8, 16]
print([i**3 for i in l])
```

Running this code will return:

[8, 64, 512, 4096]

List comprehensions are flexible. Look at the next code; it is showing two ways that you can do a function composition applying one function to another. The code will print 2 lists that represent the compositions of f1 and f2, using a for loop and then a list comprehension to calculate them:

```
def f1(x): return x*2
def f2(x): return x*4

lst = []
for i in range(16):
    lst.append(f1(f2(i)))

print(lst)

print([f1(x) for x in range(64) if x in [f2(j) for j in range(16)]])
```

The first output line comes from the construct of the for loop while the second comes from the expression for the list comprehension.

We can also use a list comprehension to provide a more compact replication of the action of the nested loops. Each element is multiplied with each other within the list:

```
list1= [[1, 2, 3], [4, 5, 6]]
print([i * j for i in list1[0] for j in list1[1]])
```

Running this code will return:

[4, 5, 6, 8, 10, 12, 15, 18]

Lastly, list comprehensions can also be used together with objects to build other structures. The last code example shows a list of words created along with the word count:

```
words = 'here is a sentence'.split()
print([[word, len(word) ] for word in words])
```

Running this code will return:

[['here', 4], ['is', 2], ['a', 1], ['sentence', 8]]

As we continue, you will see that lists are a fundamental basis for a wide range of data structures. They are versatile, very easy to create, and we can use them to build highly complex and specialized data structures.

First-Class Objects – Functions

It isn't just the data types in Python that are treated as objects; both classes and functions are too, and they come under the heading of 'first-class' objects. They can be manipulated the same as any of the data types built-in. The definition of a first-class object is:

- That creation takes place at runtime
- That they are assigned in a data structure or as a variable
- That they are passed to functions as arguments
- That they are returned as a function result

The term, 'first-class object' is somewhat a misnomer because it gives the impression that there is some kind of hierarchy but, in Python, every object is first-class.

Look at the following function definition to see how this works:

```
def greeting(language):
```

```
  if language== 'eng':
    return 'hello world'
  if language  == 'fr':
    return 'Bonjour le monde'
 else: return 'language not supported'
```

Because any user-defined function is an object, we can add it into another object, like a list:

```
l=[greeting('eng'), greeting('fr'), greeting('ger')]
print(l[1])
```

Running this code will return:

' Bonjour le monde'

We can also use a function as an argument for another function. Look at this example:

```
def callf(f) :
  lang='eng'
  return  (f(lang))
```

```
print(callf(greeting))
```

Running this code will return:

'hello world'

In this code, callf() has a function as an argument; the language variable is then set to 'eng' and the function is called and takes the language variable as its argument. It's easy to see how this could be useful, especially if we wanted to build a program that would return given sentences in different languages, a language application program perhaps. Here we have a place to set up the language and alongside the greeting, we could have other functions that would return other sentences. By having a single point where the language is set, the rest of the logic in the program is ignored. If we wanted a different language, we would just set the language variable and leave everything else alone.

Higher-Order Functions

If a function takes a function as an argument or it returns a function, it is known as a higher-order function. There are two of these built into Python 3 – map() and filter(). In earlier Python versions, these functions would have returned lists, but in Python 3 we get an iterator. This makes them highly efficient. With the map() function, we can easily transform items into iterable objects. Look at this example of a neat and efficient way of carrying out an operation on a sequence. Note that we use the lambda function (anonymous):

lst=[1,2,3,4]

print(list(map(lambda x: x**3, lst)))

Running this code will return:

[1, 8, 27, 64]

In much the same way, the filter() function can be used for filtering list items:

print(list(filter((lambda x: x<3), lst)))

Running this code will return:

[1, 2]

The map() and the filter() functions both do exactly the same as what we can achieve with a list comprehension. In fact, there is little difference in terms of performance with the exception of using the built-in functions without using lambda provides a slight advantage over list comprehensions. In spite of this, list comprehensions are the preferred way of doing things as they can be read much easier.

The functional style of Python means that we can easily create higher-order functions. In the next example, we pass len to the sort function as the key, allowing us to sort a word list by word length:

words=str.split('The longest word in this sentence')
print(sorted(words, key=len))

Running this code will return:

['in', 'The', 'this', 'longest', 'sentence']

Let's have a look at another example, this time for case-insensitive sorting:

```
sl=['A', 'b', 'a', 'C', 'c']
sl.sort(key=str.lower)
print(sl)
```

Running this code will return:

['A', 'a', 'b', 'C', 'c']

```
sl.sort()
```

```
print(sl)
```

Running this code will return:

['A', 'C', 'a', 'b', 'c']

There is a difference between the method list.sort() and the built-in function sorted; list.sort() is a method of the object called list and it is used to sort an instance of a list without actually copying it. It will change the target object and the return will be None. One of the more important Python conventions is that methods or functions that can change an object will return None, and as such makes it clear that there haven't been any new objects created and that the object was changed.

On the other hand, the built-in function called sorted will return a brand-new list. It will take iterable objects as arguments but a list will always be returned. Both functions can take up to two optional arguments (keyword) as key.

A very easy way to sort complex structures is by using the element index to sort with lambda, like this:

items.sort(key=lambda item: item[1])

print(items)

Running this code will return:

[['flour', 1.8, 5], ['rice', 2.4, 8], ['corn', 4.7, 6]]

We sorted all the items in price order.

Recursive Functions

Recursion is a basic computer science concept and in Python, there is an easy way to implement recursive functions. All we do is call the function inside the body of the function. However, if we just use a recursive function, we run the risk of it turning into an infinite loop. To stop this, we require a minimum of one argument that will test for a terminating case that will finish the recursion. This is known as the "base case".

It is worth remembering that recursion is not the same as iteration. Although both revolve around repetition, an iteration will loop through an operation sequence whereas recursion will call a function repeatedly. Both can only end with a selection statement. In technical terms, recursion is actually a version of iteration called "tail iteration". It is nearly always possible for a recursive function to be converted to an iterative function and vice versa.

The next code will show the difference between the two. Both functions will print the numbers in between low and high – the first function uses iteration while the second uses recursion:

```
def iterTest(low, high):
    while low <= high:
        print (low)
        low=low+1

def recurTest(low, high):
    if low <= high:
        print(low)
        recurTest(low+1, high)
```

Note that in iterTest, we have used a while statement for testing the condition, then the print method is called, and the low value incremented. In recurTest, an if statement is used to test the condition, the print method called, and the low variable is incremented in the argument. Generally, iteration is far more efficient, but recursive functions tend to be easier to read and to write. Recursive functions are also good to manipulate data structures that are recursive, like trees and linked lists.

Generators and Co-Routines

Functions that return sequences of results rather than a single result can also be created and we do this with the yield statement. We call these functions 'generators' and, in Python you will see that there are some generator functions already built-in. These provide us with an easy and efficient way of creating iterators and they are a useful replacement for lists that are long and unworkable. Generators yield items; they don't build lists.

Have a look at the code example; this shows you why generators are a better option than creating lists:

```
# the running time of the list is compared to the generator
import time
# an iterator containing odd numbers between the letters n and m is created
by the generator function
def oddGen(n, m):
    while n < m:
        yield n
        n += 2
#a list of odd numbers from n to m is built
def oddLst(n,m):
    lst=[]
    while n<m:
        lst.append(n)
        n +=2
    return lst
#the length of time taken for a sum to be performed on an iterator
t1=time.time()
sum(oddGen(1,1000000))
print("Time to sum an iterator: %f" % (time.time() - t1))
```

```
#the length of time taken to build a list and sum it
t1=time.time()
sum(oddLst(1,1000000))
print("Time to build and sum a list: %f" % (time.time() - t1))
```

As you can see, it takes quite a bit longer to build a list for this calculation. The significant improvement in performance using a generator comes from the values being generated on demand instead of saving the list in memory. The calculation can start before the elements have all been generated and they will only be generated as and when they are required.

In the last example, the sum method is loading the numbers into memory when they are required for the calculation. This is done by the generator object; it calls the _next_() special method repeatedly. A generator is not able to return any value aside from None.

Usually, a generator object is used in a for loop. For example, the oddGen generator function that we generated in the last code can be used to print odd integers from 1 to 10:

```
for i in oddGen(1,10):print(i)
```

A generator expression can also be created. These use the exact same syntax as a list comprehension with the exception that we replace the square brackets with a set of parentheses. These create generator objects, not lists. The object will not create any data until it is demanded. What this means is that there is no support for sequence methods, such as insert() and append() but we can use the list() function to convert a generator to a list:

```
lst1= [1, 2, 3, 4]

gen1 = (10**i for i in lst1)

print(gen1)
```

Running this code will return:

```
<generator object <genexpr> at 0x000001B981504C50>
```

```
for x in gen1: print(x)
```

10

100

1000

10000

Chapter 4: Classes - Object Programming

We can use classes to create all kinds of objects and they are a central point of OOP. Classes define sets of attributes that may be shared over all instances of the class. A typical class is a set of properties, variables, and functions.

OOP is somewhat compelling because it gives us a good basis for thinking about the core functionality of any program that we write. Because we can organize those programs around data and objects and not logic and actions, we have a strong but flexible way of building algorithms, particularly complex ones. Of course, we still have the logic and the actions, but because we have them embodied in objects, we have a method of encapsulating the functionality so that we can change objects in highly specific ways. Because of this, our code is less prone to errors, we can extend it and maintain it much easier, and we can model real-world objects.

We create a class in python by using the class statement; this results in a shared attributes set being defined and this is associated with a class instance collection. Classes usually have several methods, computed properties, and class variables. It needs to be understood that, when you define a class, you do not create any class instances. For an instance to be created, you must assign a variable to the class. Inside the body of the class are several statements that will execute during the definition. The functions that are defined in the class are known as instance methods; they are used to apply operations to the instance of the class and this is done by an instance of the class being passed as the initial argument. By convention, the argument is known as self, but any legal identifier can be used for it. Look at an example:

```python
class Employee(object):
    numEmployee = 0
    def __init__(self, name, rate):
        self.owed = 0
        self.name = name
        self.rate=rate
        Employee.numEmployee += 1

    def __del__(self):
```

Employee.numEmployee -= 1

def hours(self, numHours):
    *self.owed += numHours * self.rate*
    return("%.2f hours worked" % numHours)

def pay(self):
    self.owed = 0
    return("payed %s " % self.name)

A class variable, like numEmployee, will share its values with all the class instances. In the example, we used numEmployee to count how many employee instances there are. Note: the class called Employee will implement the special methods calls _init_ and _del_ and we'll talk more about those shortly. First, let's look at an example to create an instance of the Employee object, how to run the methods, and how to return the class and the instance variables:

emp1=Employee("Jill", 15.50)
emp2=Employee("Jack", 15.50)
print(Employee.numEmployee)

Running this code will return:

2

print(emp1.hours(20))

Running this code will return:

'20.00 hours worked'

print(emp1.owed)

Running this code will return:

print(emp1.pay())

Running this code will return:

'paid Jill '

Methods: Special

The function called dir(object) can be used to get the attributes list for a specified object. If a method starts with an underscore and ends with one, it is called a special method. With one exception, a special method tends to be called by the interpreter and not the programmer: let's say that you use the + operator; what you are doing is calling _add_(). For example, instead of my_object_len_(), we could use len(my_object). It is a good deal faster using len() on string objects because the returned value is representative of the size of the object in memory. The exception mentioned earlier is the method called _init_. This is the only method that a programmer can call in a program and it is used for invoking the superclass initializer in the class definitions. One thing that must be made clear is that you should NOT use the double underscore for objects that you create because it could cause a conflict, either now or in the future, with the special methods built into Python.

However, there may come a time when you want special methods implemented into custom objects; you would do this if you wanted the object to have some of the built-in type behaviors. In the next code, we are going to create a class that will implement the method called _repr_. This method is used to create string representations of the object and this is good for the purpose of an inspection:

```
class my_class():
   def __init__(self, greet):
      self.greet = greet
   def __repr__(self):
      return 'a custom object (%r)' % (self.greet)
```

When an instance of that object is created and inspected, the custom string representation is present. Note that the %r format placeholder is used so the object's standard representation is returned. This is classed as best practice and is very useful because the object called greet is surrounded by quotation marks, indicating that is it a string:

```
a=my_class("gday")
print(a)
```

Running this code will return:

a custom object ('gday')

Inheritance

We can also create a class that will modify how an existing class behaves using inheritance. To do this, the inherited class is passed inside the class definition as an argument. We tend to use this when we want the behavior of an existing method to be modified. An example:

```
class specialEmployee(Employee):
    def hours(self, numHours):
        self.owed += numHours * self.rate * 2
        return("%.2f hours worked" % numHours)
```

Note that one instance of the class specialEmployee is exactly the same as an Employee instance with the exception of the change to the hours() method.

If we want to define a new class variable using a subclass, the _init_() method must be defined by the subclass, like this:

```
class specialEmployee(Employee):
    def __init__(self,name,rate, bonus):
        Employee.__init__(self, name, rate) #the base classes are called
        self.bonus = bonus

    def hours(self, numHours):
```

```
    self.owed += numHours * self.rate + self.bonus
    return("%.2f hours worked" % numHours)
```

The methods in the base class are not invoked automatically and, as such, the derived class must call them. Class membership can be tested if we use the isinstance(obj1, obj2) function built into Python. If obj1 belongs to the obj2 class or any class that has been derived from it, this function returns True.

It tends to be assumed that all methods in a class definition will operate on the class instance. This is not required, but there are some other method types – class methods and static methods. Static methods are ordinary functions that are defined inside a class; they do not do any operation on instances and we use the class decorator called @staticmethod to define them. A static method is not able to access any instance attributes so they tend to be used more as a convenient way of grouping together the utility functions.

Within a class definition, it is assumed that all methods operate on the instance, but this is not a requirement. There are, however, other types of methods: **static methods** and **class methods**. A static method is just an ordinary function that just happens to be defined in a class. It does not perform any operations on the instance and it is defined using the @staticmethod class decorator. Static methods cannot access the attributes of an instance, so their most common usage is as a convenience to group utility functions together.

A class method, on the other hand, performs operations on the class in much the same way that class variables are associated with the class and not the class instances. We use the decorator called @classmethod to define them and the differentiation between the two methods is that, in this one, the class gets passed as the initial argument. By convention, this has a name of cls.

```
class Aexp(object):
    base=2
    @classmethod
    def exp(cls,x):
        return(cls.base**x)
```

class Bexp(Aexp):
    base=3

The class called Bexp will inherit from the class called Aexp and the base class variable is changed to 3. The exp() method from the parent class is run like this:

BxSqr = Bexp()
print(BxSqr.exp(3))

Running this code will return:

27

There are a few reasons why a class method could be useful. For example, subclasses will inherit the same features that the parent class has and that means it can potentially break an inherited method. The class method can be used as a way of defining the methods that need to be run.

Data Encapsulation and Properties

Unless it is specified otherwise, methods and attributes can all be accessed without any restrictions. What this means is anything that has been defined inside the base class can be accessed from the derived class. When OOP applications are built, it can cause a few problems, especially if the internal implementation of the object is wanted to be hidden. This leads to conflicts in the namespace between the objects that were defined inside a derived class and the base class. To stop this happening, where we have defined private attributes in a method, that method has the double underscore, for example, __privateMethod(). This name would be changed automatically to _Classname__privateMethod() to stop the conflicts with the base class defined methods. This doesn't actually hide the private attributes; instead, it just stops the name conflicts.

The recommendation is that the private attributes should be used when a class property for defining attributes that are mutable are used. Properties are attributes that, when called, compute the value instead of returning a value that has been stored. As an example, we could do the following to redefine the property called exp():

```
class Bexp(Aexp):
    __base=3
    def __exp(self):
        return(x**cls.base)
```

Next, we are going to look at the data structures built into Python.

Chapter 5: Python Structures and Data Types

We'll start by looking at data types in some detail. The two that we have already used are str() and list(), the string and the list. In Python, you will often want to represent your data using specialized objects and, as well as the data types built into Python, there are some internal modules that provide the tools to correct common problems with data structures. First, we'll look at the common expressions and operations used for all data types.

Operations and Expressions

There are quite a few common operations; for example, the truth value operators can be used for just about all data types and objects. The values below are those that Python considers as False values:

- The data type 'None'
- False
- Any float, integer or complex zero
- Empty sequences or mapping
- Any instance of a class defined by a user that defines a _bool_() or _len_() method that returns False or zero

Python considers any other value to be True.

Booleans

Boolean operations return one of two values – True or False. They are in priority order, therefore, if there are two or more in one expression, the highest priority Boolean operation will happen first. Below are all three of the Boolean operators in order of priority, with the operator and an example.

not x

If x is False, this returns True; False is returned otherwise

x and y

If x and y are both True, this returns True; False is returned otherwise

x or y

if x or y is True, this returns True; False is returned otherwise

When they evaluate expressions, the 'and' and 'or' operators use something called short-circuiting. With this, Python evaluates an operator only if it is required. For example, let's say that x is True; in the expression, 'x or y', y isn't evaluated because it is obvious the expression is True. With the expression, 'x and y', where x is false, the Python interpreter will evaluate x, return a value of False, and ignore y.

Comparison and Arithmetic Operators

There are four basic arithmetic operators (as well as a few others):

- Addition (+)
- Subtraction (-)
- Multiplication (*)
- Division (/)

The other arithmetic operators are the //, which provides an integer quotient (3//2 will return 1, for example), **, which is the exponent operator and %, the modulus operator, returning the remainder of a division. The comparison operators, which are (<, <=, >, >=, == and!=) all work with numbers, lists, strings, and any collection object and, provided the given condition holds, they will return True. For a collection object, the operators make a comparison of how many elements there are and ==, which is the equivalence operator, will check to see if each of the objects is structurally equivalent and that each element has an identical value, return True if they are, False if otherwise.

Membership Operators, Identity and Logical Operations

The membership operators are 'in' and 'not in' and they are used to test for variables in given sequences; for example, x in y will return True should the variable x be in y. The identity operator, 'is', compares the identity of objects. For example, the next code snippet demonstrates object identity and contrast equivalence:

x =[1,2,3]; y=[1, 2, 3]

print(x == y) #equivalence

Running this code will return:

True

print(x is y) # object identity

Running this code will return:

False

x = y #assignment

print(x is y)

Running this code will return:

True

Built-In Data Types

The data types built into Python can be separated into three categories: Numeric, Sequence, and Mapping. There is also the object called 'None', which is representative of a Null or when there is no value. Do not forget, objects like files, classes, and exceptions are also considered as types, but we won't be discussing those here.

Every single Python value has a data type, but unlike other computer programming languages, Python does not require explicit declaration of a variable type because Python internally tracks the types. The following shows the built-in data types with the category, name and description:

Category	Name	Description
None	None	Null Object
Numeric	int	Integer
	float	Floating point number
	complex	Complex number
	bool	Boolean
Sequences	str	Character string
	list	Lists arbitrary objects
	tuple	Groups arbitrary
Objects	range	Creates ramges of integers
Mapping	dict	Ditionary containing key-value pairs
	set	Mutable collection of unordered, unique items
	frozenset	Immutable set

None

The type None is an immutable type and it has a single value of 'None'. It is used as a representation of no value and is returned by any object that doesn't explicitly return a value and in Boolean expressions, will evaluate as False. None tends to be used as a default value for optional arguments so that the function can determine whether a value has been passed by the caller or not.

Numeric

With the exception of the bool, all of the numeric types are signed and are immutable. The Booleans will return one of two values – True or False – and these are mapped, respectively, to 0 and 1. The int is used to represent whole numbers of an unlimited range while floats are represented by the double precision machine representation. Two floating point numbers represent the complex numbers, and these are assigned through the j operator signifying the 'imaginary' bit of a complex number, like this:

a = 2+3j

Accessing the real part and the imaginary part are done through a.real and a.imag respectively.

Sequences

A sequence is an ordered set containing objects indexed by integers that are non-negative. Tuples and lists are sequences containing arbitrary objects while a string is a character sequence. Tuple, string, and range objects are immutable. Every sequence type has some operations in common; index and slice operators apply to all sequences. For any immutable type, an operation will return a value; it will NOT change the value.

The following methods are common to all sequences:

len(s)

how many elements are in (s)

min(s, [,default=obj, key=func])

minimum value found in (s) – alphabetically if a string

max(s, [,default=obj, key=func])

maximum value found in (s) – alphabetically if a string

sum(s,[,start=0])

sum of all elements – if (s) isn't numeric, TypeError is returned

all(s)

if all elements in (s) are True, True is returned – they cannot be 0, Null or False

any(s)

Checks to see if any of the items in (s) are True

Sequences also all support these operations:

s + r

concatenation of two sequences of the same type

s * n

will make n copies of s (where n is an int)

v1, v2..., vn = s

unpacks n variables from s to v1, v2, etc.

s[i]

Indexing – this returns element i from s

s[i:j:stride]

Slicing – will return elements from i to j with an optional stride

x in s

if element x is in s, this will return True

x not in s

if element x is not in s, this will return True

Tuples

A tuple is an immutable sequence that contains arbitrary objects and are indexed by ints that are greater than zero. A tuple is hashable, meaning we can sort lists of tuples and they can also be used as dictionary keys. In syntax, a tuple is a sequence of values, each separated by a comma. Common practice has then enclosed in a set of parentheses:

tpl= ('a', 'b', 'c')

A trailing comma must be used when a tuple is created with just one element:

t = ('a',)

If you omit the trailing comma, the interpreter would see this as a string.

We can also use the built-in tuple() function to create a tuple. Without an argument, we get an empty tuple; if the argument was a sequence, a tuple of elements of the given sequence would be created.

Most of the operators, like those for indexing and slicing, work the same way on a tuple as they do on a list. However, the immutability of a tuple means that attempting to modify a tuple element will return a TypeError. We can use the ==, < and > operators to compare tuples the same as any other sequence.

One of the most important uses of a tuple is to assign multiple variables in one hit by putting a tuple on the left side of an assignment:

l=('one', 'two')
x, y = l # x and y are assigned respectively to 'one' and 'two'

We could use multiple assignments for swapping tuple values, like this:

x, y = y, x # x = 'two' and y = 'one'

If the number of values on either side of the assignment is not the same, we will get a ValueError.

Dictionaries

A dictionary is an arbitrary collection of objects that are indexed by immutable objects, such as strings or numbers. However, while a dictionary is mutable, its index keys must be immutable. Below is a list of the dictionary methods and what they do:

len(d)

tells us how many items are in (d)

d.clear()

will remove all items from (d)

d.copy()

will make a shallow copy of (d)

d.fromkeys(s [,value])

will return a dictionary that has keys from the sequence (s) and values all set to value

d.get(k [,v])

will return d[k] if it is found; otherwise v is returned or, if v is not given, None is returned

d.items()

will return a sequence of the key:value pairs from (d)

d.keys()

will return a sequence of the keys in (d)

d.pop(k [,default])

will return d[k] and take it out of (d). if d[k] cannot be found, the default is returned or KeyError raised

d.popitem()

will remove a random key:value pair from (d) and then return it as a tuple

d.setdefault(k [,v])

d[k] is returned; if not found, v is returned and d[k] is set to v

d.update(b)

all objects from b to d are added

d.values()

a sequence of the values in (d) are returned

Dictionaries are the only built-in mapping type in Python and they are much like the associative arrays or hash tables in other languages. We can think of it as a mapping from a key set to a value set. We use the syntax {key:value} to create them; the following example shows a dictionary that maps words to numbers being created:

d ={'one': 1, 'two': 2, 'three': 3 } # a dictionary is created

Keys and values can be added like this:

d['four']=4 # an item is added

Or we can do the following to update multiple values:

d.update({'five': 5, 'six': 6}) # multiple items are added

When d is inspected, we see the following:

print(d)

Running this code will return:

{'five' : 5, 'four' : 4, one' : 1, 'six' : 6, 'three' : 3, 'two' : 2}

And we can use the in operator for testing for a value occurrence, like this:

print('five' in d)

Running this code will return:

True

Be aware that the in operator doesn't work the same way for lists and dictionaries. With a list, we have a linear relationship between the time taken to locate an element and to list size. By this, we mean the bigger a list is, the time taken to find the element will grow linearly. In contrast, when we use the in operator on a dictionary, a hashing algorithm is used. This makes the time increase in looking up elements pretty much independent to the dictionary size.

When the key:value pairs are printed from the dictionary, they are done so in no specific order. Because we are using specified keys for looking up the values, this isn't an issue; it would be if we used a sequence of ordered integers, as we do with lists and strings.

Sorting Dictionaries

We can easily do a sort on the values or the keys of a dictionary, like this:

print(sorted(list(d))) # sorts keys

Running this code will return:

['five', 'four', 'one', 'six', 'three', 'two']

print(sorted(list(d.values()))) # sorts values

Running this code will return:

[1, 2, 3, 4, 5]

Line one of this code does the sorting in alphabetical order while the next one does it in integer value order. The method called sorted() has two interesting optional arguments – reverse and key. The key is nothing at all to do with the dictionary keys; it is a way to pass the sort algorithm a function that determines the sort order. Here's an example where we use a special method called __getitem__ to sort the keys as per the values in dictionary:

print(sorted (list(d), key = d.__getitem__))

['one', 'two', 'three', 'four', 'five', 'six']

What we have done here is, for each key in d, the corresponding value has been used to sort. The values can also be sorted as per the sorted order of the keys in the dictionary. However, because a dictionary does not contain any method that will return a key using its value, it becomes a little tricky to use the optional key argument. Another way of doing this would be to use list comprehension as in the next example:

print([value for (key, value) in sorted(d.items())])

Running this code will return:

[5, 4, 1, 6, 3, 2]

There is also an optional reverse argument in the sorted() method and, as expected, it does exactly what it says on the tin – reverses the sorted list order. An example:

print(sorted(list(d), key = d.__getitem__, reverse=True))

Running this code will return:

['six', 'five', 'four', 'three', 'two' 'one']

Look at the following dictionary. We have the keys written as English words and the values as French words. What we want to do is put the values into the right numerical order.

d2 ={'one':'uno', 'two':'deux', 'three':'trois', 'four': 'quatre', 'five': 'cinq', 'six':'six'}

When this dictionary is printed, it won't print in the right order, not as it is. The reason for this is both the values and the keys are strings, so we don't have any proper context to put them in numerical order. To do this, we must go back to the first dictionary we made; the words need to be mapped to the numerals so that English to French dictionary can be placed in order:

print(sorted(d2, key=d.__getitem__))

Running this code will return:

['one', 'two', 'three', 'four', 'five', 'six']

We've used the values from our first dictionary called d to sort the keys in the second dictionary called d2. Because the keys are the same in both of the dictionaries, we can make use of list comprehension to sort the English to French dictionary values.

print([d2[i] for i in sorted(d2, key=d.__getitem__)])

Running this code will return:

['uno', 'deux', 'trois', 'quatre', 'cinq', 'six']

We can, if we want, define a custom method for the key argument used in the sorted() method. In the next example, a function is defined to return the final letter in a string:

def corder(string):

  return(string[len(string)-1])

Now we can use this as the key to the sorted() function so that each element can be sorted by its final letter:

print(sorted(d2.values(), key=corder))

['quatre', 'uno', 'cinq', 'trois', 'six', 'deux']

Using Dictionaries for Text Analysis

One of the most common uses for a dictionary is to count the occurrences of similar items in a sequence, for example, how many times words appear in a specified body of text. The next piece of code will create a dictionary where each of the words in the given text is used as keys and the value of each key is how many times that word occurs. We are using nested loops here, a common loop in Python, to go through each line in the file using an outer loop with the dictionary keys in the inner loop.

```
def wordcount(fname):
  try:
    fhand=open(fname)
  except:
    print('File cannot be opened')
    exit()

  count= dict()
  for line in fhand:
    words = line.split()
    for word in words:
      if word not in count:
        count[word] = 1
      else:
        count[word] += 1
  return(count)
```

What will result will be a dictionary containing one element for each of the unique words within the file.

Sets

A Python set is an unordered collection containing unique items. While sets are mutable, meaning that we can add items to them and remove items, each item must itself be immutable. One important thing about sets is that you cannot have any duplicate items in them. We usually use sets to do mathematical operations, like union, intersection, complement, and difference.

Unlike a sequence type, a set type doesn't provide any slicing or indexing operations. The values do not have any keys associated with them as the dictionaries do. Python contains two types of sets – mutable set and immutable frozenset. Each type of set is created the same way with a set of curly braces containing values each separated by a comma. An empty set using the curly braces cannot be created though as a={} will create a dictionary! Empty sets are created by using a=set() or a=frozenset().

Below are the methods and the operations for sets:

len(s)

will return how many elements are in (s)

s.copy()

will return a shallow copy of (s)

s.difference(t)

will return a set containing the items in (s) but not (t)

s.intersection(t)

will return a set containing the items in both (s) and (t)

s.isdisjoint(t)

will return True if there are no common items between (s) and (t)

s.issubset(t)

will return True if the contents of (s) are in (t)

s.issuperset(t)

will return True if the contents of (t) are in (s)

s.symmetric_difference

will return a set of the items from (s) or (t) but not those in both

s.union(t)

will return a set containing the items in (s) or (t)

The parameter of (t) may be any object in Python that will support iteration and any method that is available to the objects set and frozenset. Be aware, if you need to use an operator version of these methods, you must set the arguments – the methods themselves will accept any type that is iterable. Below are the operator versions of the methods:

Operator Methods:

s.difference(t)

s − t − t2 - ...

s.issubset(t)

s<=t

s<(t(s!=t)

s.issuperset(t)

s>=t

s>t(s!=t)

s.symmetric_difference(t)

s^t

s.union(t)

s | t1 | t2 | ...

For the mutable set objects, there are some extra methods:

s.add(item)

will add the item to (s) – if the item is already there, nothing will happen

s.clear()

all items are removed from (s)

s.difference_update(t)

will remove items in (s) that are also in (t)

s.discard(item)

will remove the specified item from (s)

s.intersection_update(t)

will remove items from (s) that do not appear in the intersection of (s) and (t)

s.pop()

will return and remove a given arbitrary item from (s)

s.remove(item)

will remove the specified item from (s)

s.symmetric_difference_update(t)

will remove items from (S) that cannot be found in the symmetric difference of (s) and (t)

s.update(t)

will add the items from iterable (t) to (s)

The next example will show you a couple of set operations and the results:

s1={'ab', 3, 4, (5, 6)}
s2={'ab', 7, (7, 6)}
print(s1-s2) # identical to s1.difference (s2)

Running this code will return:

{(5, 6), 3, 4}

print(s1.intersection(s2))

Running this code will return:

{'ab'}

print(s1.union(s2))

Running this code will return:

{ 'ab', 3, 4, 7, (5, 6), (7, 6)}

The set object is not bothered if its members are of different types; they just have to all be immutable. If you were to try using mutable objects, like a list or a dictionary, in your set, an unhashable type error will be thrown. All hashable types have got a hash value that remains the same through the entire lifecycle of the instance and all of the built-in immutable types are of a hashable type. The built-in mutable types are not of a hashable type so cannot be included in sets as elements or as dictionary keys.

Note, when the s1 and the s2 union is printed, there is just one 'ab' value. Remember, sets do not include any duplicates. As well as the built-in methods, there are several other operations that can be performed on a set. For example, if you wanted to test a set for membership, you would do the following:

print('ab' in s1)

Running this code will return:

True

print('ab' not in s1)

Running this code will return:

False

Looping through the elements of a set would look like this:

for element in s1: print(element)

(5, 6)

ab

3

4

Immutable Sets

As mentioned earlier, Python has an immutable set type known as frozenset. It works much the same as set does but with one difference – you cannot use any operation or method that can change values, such as the clear() or add() methods. Immutability can be quite useful in a number of ways. For example, a normal set is mutable, which means it is not hashable and that, in turn, means that it cannot be a member of another set. On the other hand, frozenset can be a member of another set because it is immutable. Plus, this immutability of frozenset means that it can be used as a dictionary key, like this:

fs1 = frozenset(s1)

fs2 = frozenset(s2)

print({fs1: 'fs1', fs2: 'fs2'})

Running this code will return:

{ frozenset({(5, 6), 3, 4, 'ab'}): 'fs1', frozenset({(7, 6), 'ab', 7}); 'fs2'}

<u>Modules for Algorithms and Data Structures</u>

As well as these built-in types, Python has a few modules that can be used for extending those built-in functions and types. Much of the time, the modules may be more efficient and may offer advantages in programming terms that let us make our code simpler.

Up to now, we have examined the built-in types for dictionaries, lists, sets, and strings. These are often termed as ADTs or abstract data types and may be considered to be mathematical specifications for the operations that may be performed on the data. Their behavior is what defines them, not their implementation. Besides the ADTs we already looked at, there are a few Python libraries that include extensions for the built-in datatypes and we'll be looking at these next.

Collections

The module called collections contains alternatives for these data types, high-performance specialized alternatives, in addition to a utility function for the creation of named tuples. Below are the datatypes, the operations, and what they do:

namedtuple()

will create a tuple subclass with the given fields

deque

provides lists that have fast appends and that pop at either end

ChainMap

a class much like a dictionary that creates a single view showing multiple mappings

Counter

a dictionary subclass used for counting the hashable objects

OrderedDict

a dictionary subclass that will remember the order of entries

defaultdict

a dictionary subclass that will call a function that can supply the missing values

- UserDict
- UserList
- UserString

These datatypes are used as wrappers for the base class that underlies each one. We don't tend to use these very much now but subclass the base classes instead. They can, however, be used for accessing the underlying objects as attributes.

Deques

A deque (pronounced deck) is a double-ended queue. These objects are similar to lists with support for appends that are thread-safe and memory-efficient. A deque is mutable and has support for some of the list operations, like indexing. You can assign a deque by index, but you cannot slice one directly. For example, if you tried dq[1:2], you would get a Type Error; there is a way to do it though and we'll look at that later.

The biggest advantage of using a deque and not a list is that it is much faster to insert an item at the start of a deque than it is as the start of a list. That said, it isn't always faster to insert items at the end of a deque. All deques are thread-safe and we can serialize them using a module called pickle.

Perhaps one of the most useful ways to use a deque is for the population and consummation of items. Population and consummation of deque items happen sequentially from each end.

from collections import deque

dq = deque('abc') #the deque is created

dq.append('d') #value 'd' is added on the right

dq.appendleft('z') # value 'z' is added on the left

dq.extend('efg') # multiple items are added on the right

dq.extendleft('yxw') # multiple items are added on the left

print(dq)

Running this code will return:

deque(['w', 'x', 'y', 'z', 'a', 'b', 'c', 'd', 'e', 'f', 'g'])

To consume items in our deque, we can use the pop() and popleft() methods:

print(dq.pop()) #item on the right is returned and removed

Running this code will return:

'g'

print(dq.popleft()) # item on the left is returned and removed

Running this code will return:

'w'

print(dq)

Running this code will return:

deque(['x', 'y', 'z', 'a', 'b', 'c', 'd', 'e', 'f'])

We also have a method called rotate(n) which moves and rotates any item of n steps right for positive n integer values and left for negative n integer values, with positive integers used for the argument:

dq.rotate(2) #all the items are moved 2 steps to the right

print(dq)

Running this code will return:

deque(['e', 'f', 'x', 'y', 'z', 'a', 'b', 'c', 'd'])

dq.rotate(-2) # all the items are moved 2 steps to the left

print(dq)

Running this code will return:

deque(['x', 'y', 'z', 'a', 'b', 'c', 'd', 'e', 'f'])

We can also use these pop() and rotate() methods to delete elements too. The way to return a slice as a list is this:

print(dq)

Running this code will return:

deque(['x', 'y', 'z', 'a', 'b', 'c', 'd', 'e', 'f'])

import itertools

print(list(itertools.islice(dq, 3, 9)))

Running this code will return:

['a', 'b', 'c', 'd', 'e', 'f']

The itertools.islice() method is the same as a slice on a list, but instead of the argument being a list, it is an iterable and selected values are returned as a list, using start and stop indices.

One of the more useful deque features is that a maxlen parameter is supported as optional and used for restricting the deque size. This is ideal for circular buffers, a type of data structure which is fixed in size and is connected end-to-end. These tend to be used when data streams are to be buffered. Here is an example:

```
dq2=deque([],maxlen=3)
for i in range(6):
    dq2.append(i)
    print(dq2)
```

We have populated from the right and consumed from the left. As soon as the buffer has been filled, the older values are consumed, and new values come in from the right.

ChainMaps

The class called collections. chainmap was not added to Python until v3.2. It is used to link several dictionaries or mappings together so that they are, to all intents and purposes, a single object. There is also a new_child() method, a maps attribute, and a parents property. The mappings for the ChainMaps object are stored in lists and we use the maps[i] attribute to access them by retrieving the ith dictionary. Note: although a dictionary is unordered, the dictionaries in the ChainMap are in order.

We can use ChainMap in applications where multiple dictionaries contain data that is related. The application that is doing the consuming wants data in terms of priority, for example, a key found in two dictionaries is given the priority if it happens at the start of the underlying list. A typical use for ChainMap is to simulate nested contexts, for example, where you have several configuration settings that override one another.

This example shows one possible ChainMap use:

```
from collections import ChainMap

defaults={'theme':'Default', 'language':'eng', 'showIndex':True,
'showFooter':True}
```

cm=ChainMap(defaults) # ChainMap with default configuration created

cm2 =cm.new_child({'theme':'bluesky'}) # new ChainMap with a child for overriding the parent is created

print(cm2['theme']) # overridden theme is returned

Running this code will return:

'bluesky'

print(cm2.pop('theme')) # value for the child theme is returned and removed

Running this code will return:

'bluesky'

print(cm2['theme']) # default theme is returned

Running this code will return:

'Default'

Using a ChainMap instead of a dictionary has the advantage that we can hang on to values set previously. When you add a child context, it will override the values for the same key but will not take it out of the data structure. This can prove useful when we need a record of changes kept allowing us to go back to a previous setting very easily.

We can give the map() method the appropriate index to retrieve any value from any of the dictionaries and change the value. The index will represent a dictionary contained in the ChainMap. We can also retrieve parent or default settings with the parents() method.

Counter Objects

Counters are subclasses of dictionaries where each of the keys in the dictionary is a hashable object and the value associated with the key is an integer count. We can initialize a counter in three ways:

First, we can pass the counter to a sequence object, a tuple of format {object=value, ...}, or to a dictionary that has key:value pairs:

cm2.maps[0] ={'theme':'desert', 'showIndex': False} # root context that is identical to new_child is added

print(cm2['showIndex']) # overridden showIndex value is returned

Running this code will return:

False

print(cm2.parents) # returns defaults

Running this code will return:

ChainMap({'theme': 'Default', 'language': 'eng', showIndex': True, 'showFooter': True, })

Empty counter objects can also be created and then populated. This is done by passing an iterable or dictionary to the update() method:

from collections import Counter

print(Counter('anysequence'))

Running this code will return:

Counter({'a': 1, 'c': 1, 'e': 3, 'n;: 2, 'q': 1, 's': 1, 'u': 1, 'y': 1})

Note the update() adds counts; it doesn't replace them with a new value. When the counter has been populated, the stored values can be accessed the same as for a dictionary.

The biggest difference between the dictionary and counter object is that the latter will return a zero count for a missing item, where a dictionary will raise a key error.

It is possible to create iterators from Counter objects by using the elements() method. An iterator will be returned where any counts lower than 1 are not included and there is no guarantee of order. Below is an example of some updates being done, an iterator being created from the Counter elements, and the leys alphabetically sorted using sorted():

ct = Counter('anysequence')

for item in ct:

   print('%s : %d' % (item, ct[item]))

a : 1

n : 2

y : 1

s : 1

e : 3

q : 1

u : 1

c : 1

We can also use two more Counter methods – most_common(), which takes an integer argument which will determine how many of the common elements to return as a list of tuples in (key, value) format, and subtract(). The subtract()

method works in the same way as update except it subtracts values rather than adding them.

Ordered Dictionaries

The most important thing to remember about ordered dictionaries is that they will remember the order of insertion. When they are iterated over, the values are returned in the order in which they were inserted. By contrast, a normal dictionary has an arbitrary order. When we want to test if two dictionaries are equal, the equality will only be based on the keys and values. However, with OrderedDict, the order of insertion is also taken into account. If we were to run a test for equality between a pair of OrderedDicts that have the same keys and values but with different orders of insertion, the return would be False.

In the same way, if we use the update() method to add in values from a list, OrderedDict will keep the same order that the list has. This order is what is returned when we iterate over the values:

print(ct.most_common())

Running this code will return:

[('e', 3), ('n', 2), ('u', 1), ('c', 1), ('y', 1), ('s', 1), ('a', 1), ('q', 1)]

ct.subtract({'a':2})

print(ct)

Running this code will return:

Counter({'e': 3, 'n': 2, 'u': 1, 'c': 1, 'y': 1, 's': 1, 'q': 1, 'a': -1})

OrderedDict is often used together with sorted() to create sorted dictionaries. We can use the lambda function to sort the values and the following example is a numerical expression to sort the integer values:

from collections import OrderedDict

```
od1 = OrderedDict()

od1['one'] = 1

od1['two'] = 2

od2 = OrderedDict()

od2['two'] = 2

od2['one'] = 1

print(od1 == od2)
```

Running this code will return:

False

Defaultdict

Defaultdict is a dict subclass sharing operations and methods. Defaultdict is a convenient way of initializing dictionaries. If you try accessing a key that is not in the dictionary with dict, Python throws a KeyError. Defaultdict will override the __missing__(key) method and will create default_factory, a new instance variable. Instead of throwing errors, defaultdict will run the function, which will be supplied as the argument to default_factory and will generate a value. One of the easiest uses for defaultdict is to add item counts in the dictionary by setting the default_factory to int:

```
kvs = [('three', 3), ('four', 4), ('five', 5), ('six', 6)]

od1.update(kvs)

for k, v in od1.items(): print(k,v)
```

Running this code will return:

one 1

two 2

three 3

four 4

five 5

six 6

If we were to do this with a normal dictionary, a KeyError would be raised when we attempted to put the first key in. The int supplied as the dict argument is the int() function that returns only a zero. We could create a custom function to determine the values in the dictionary, such as the following one that returns True if the argument supplied is a primary color (red, blue or green); False is returned if not:

```
def isprimary(c):
    if (c == 'red') or (c == 'blue') or (c == 'green'):
        return True
    else:
        return False
```

Named Tuples

namedtuple() will return an object much like a tuple with fields that can be accessed through named indexes and through normal tuple integer indexes. This makes our code somewhat more readable and self-documenting. This is useful when we have an application with lots of tuples and we need to keep track of what each one is representing; namedtuple() will inherit its methods from and is backward compatible with tuple.

We pass the field names to namedtuple() as values separated by whitespace or commas, or they can be passed as a string sequence. Each field name is one string and they may be any Python identifier that is legal and does not start with an underscore or a digit.

namedtuple() can take two Boolean arguments, both optional – verbose and rename. Setting verbose=True will result in the class definition being printed when built. Setting rename=True will result in positional arguments being used to replace invalid field names. If we try to use def as the field name, normally an error would be generated, but because rename=True, the interpreter will let it pass. However, if you try to look def up, a syntax error is thrown because def is actually one of the reserved keywords. The field name is illegal, and it is replaced by a new name created by an underscore added to the positional value.

As well as the tuple methods inherited, namedtuple() will also define three of its own methods - _make(), _replace() and _asdict(). The underscore is used to stop conflict with field names. Below is an example of _make() and the method will take an argument of an iterable and convert it to a named tuple object:

from collections import namedtuple

space = namedtuple('space', 'x y z')

s1 = space(x = 2.0, y = 4.0, z = 10)

*print(s1.x * s1.y * s1.z)   #calculates volume*

Running this code will return:

80.0

_asdict() will return an OrderedDict, mapping the field names to index keys and the values to dictionary values. An example:

from collections import namedtuple

space = namedtuple('space', 'x y z')

s1 = space(x = 2.0, y = 4.0, z = 10)

*print(s1.x * s1.y * s1.z)   #calculates volume*

Running this code will return:

File "<ipython-input-79-75c7c11b4596>", line 1

    sl.def

∧

SyntaxError: invalid syntax

print(s1._1)

Running this code will return:

4

Lastly, _replace() will return a new tuple instance with the specified values replaced:

s1 = [4, 5, 6]

print(space._make(s1))

Running this code will return:

Space(x=4, y=5, z=6)

Arrays

The module, array, will define an array datatype that is much like the list datatype with one constraint – the array contents must be a single type of the representation that underlies it – this is determined by the machine architecture or C implementation.

Array types are determined when they are created and are indicated by one of these codes:

Code	C-Type	Python Type
'b'	signed char	int
'B'	unsigned char	int
'u'	Py_UNICODE	Unicode character
'h'	signed short	int
'H'	unsigned short	int
'i'	signed int	int
'I'	unsigned int	int
'l'	signed long	int
'L'	unsigned long	int
'q'	signed long	int
'Q'	unsigned long	int
'f'	float	float
'd'	double	float

Array objects have support for these methods and attributes:

a.typecode

typecode character for creating the array

a.itemsize

byte size of items that are stored in the array

a.append(x)

appends the item (x) to the array end

a.buffer_info()

returns length and memory location of the buffer used for storing the array

a.byteswap()

swaps the byte order for each item. Used when writing to a file or machine that has a different byte order

a.count(x)

returns how many times x appears

a.extend(b)

will append any iterable to the end of the array

a.frombytes(s)

will append string items as a machine value array

a.fromfile(f, n)

will read n items from a file object as machine values,   appending them to a. An EOFError is raised if n has fewer items than n

a.fromlist(l)

will append from list l

a.fromunicode(s)

will use an Unicode string to extend a. Array a has to be type u or ValueError will be raised

index(x)

will return the first smallest index item

a.insert(i, x)

will insert the item before the specified index

a.pop([i])

will remove and return items with the specified index but, if none specified, the last item will be defaulted

a.remove(x)

will remove the first occurrence of the specified item

a.reverse()

reverses the item order

a.tobytes()

will convert the array into machine values and return the byte representation

a.tofile(f)

will write all items to the file object as machine values

a.tolist()

will convert the array into a list

a.tounicode()

will convert the array to a Unicode string; array type must be 'of U' type or ValueError will be raised

Array objects also support all the usual sequence operations like concatenation, slicing, indexing and multiplication.

It is more efficient to use arrays instead of lists to store data of identical types. The next code will show you an integer array containing digits from 0 to 1 million minus 1 along with an identical list. To store a million integers in an array will use about 45% of the memory an equivalent list would use:

print(s1._1)

Running this code will return:

4

print(s1._asdict())

Running this code will return:

OrderedDict([('x', 3). ('_1', 4), ('z', 5)])

To save space when dealing with big datasets and a limit on memory size, in-place operations are done on arrays and copies only created when necessary. Typically, we would use enumerate when an operation is performed on each element; the next example shows 1 being added to each array item:

print(s1._replace(x = 7, z = 9))

Running this code will return:

Space2(x=7, _1=4, z=9)

In the next part, we look at basic algorithm theory and design techniques.

Chapter 6: The Principles of Algorithm Design

Algorithms are all-important; they are the very foundation of computers and computer science. Your computer may be constructed of hardware items, but without algorithms, it's all a waste of space. The Turing Machine is the theoretical foundation of all algorithms and this was established many years before we even thought about implementing a machine like that using digital logic circuits. The Turing Machine is a model that can translate a set of given inputs into outputs, working to a set of pre-defined rules, much like today's Machine Learning.

Algorithms affect our lives in more ways than we realize. Take page ranking on search engines for example. These are based on algorithms and these allow anyone to search quickly through huge amounts of information. This, in turn, hastens the rate at which new research can be done, new discoveries can be found, and with which innovative technologies can be developed.

Studying algorithms is also essential because it makes us think about problems in specific ways. Our mental abilities sharpen, and we can improve our problem-solving abilities by learning to find and isolate the core components of a problem and define the relationship between them.

In its simplest form, an algorithm is nothing more than a list of instructions to be carried out in sequence. Think of it, in Python terms, as a linear form of do x, then do y, and then do z. However, we can change things and make these algorithms do more by adding if-else statements. By doing that, the direction the action takes then depends on conditions being met, and then we add operations, while statements, for statements, and iteration. To expand our algorithm a bit more, we add recursion which often provides the same result that iteration does even though they are very different. Recursive functions apply the function to inputs that get progressively smaller. The input of one recursive step is the output of the previous one.

Paradigms of Algorithm Design

There are three main paradigms to algorithm design:

- Divide and Conquer
- Greedy
- Dynamic programming

Let's take these one at a time. Divide and conquer is self-explanatory – the problem is broken down into small subproblems and the results of each one combined into an overall solution. This has to be one of the most common techniques to solve problems and is perhaps the most common approach to the design of algorithms.

Greedy algorithms involve optimizing and combining. In short, it means to take the shortest path to the most useful solution for local problems, all the while hoping that somewhere it will all lead to the global solution.

Dynamic programming is most useful when the subproblems start to overlap. This is not the same as the divide and conquers paradigm. Instead of breaking the problem down into individual subproblems, intermediate solutions get cached and then used in a later operation. It does use recursion like divide and conquers but, with dynamic programming, we compare the results at different times. This provides a boost in terms of performance for some types of problems; it can be quicker to retrieve a previous result than it is to go through recalculating it.

Backtracking and Recursion

Recursion is incredibly useful in terms of divide and conquer but it can be hard to see exactly what is going on; each of the recursive calls spins off another recursive call. There are two types of cases at the heart of a recursive function:

- Base case – this tells recursion when it should terminate
- Recursive case – this calls the function the case is in

The calculation of factorials is one of the simplest examples of a problem that results in a recursive solution. The factorial algorithm is responsible for defining 2 cases:

- the base case where n is equal to zero
- the recursive case where n is more than zero. Here is an example of an implementation:

```
def factorial(n):
    #test for a base case
    if n==0:
        return 1
    # a calculation and a recursive call are made
    f= n*factorial(n-1)
    print(f)
    return(f)


factorial(4)
```

When this code is printed, we get 1, 2, 6, 24. For 24 to be calculated, we need the parent call and four recursive calls. On each of the recursions, a copy is made of the method variables and it is stored in memory. When the method has returned, that copy is removed.

It isn't always going to be clear whether iteration or recursion is the best result for a problem. Both repeat sets of operations and both work well with divide and conquer. Iteration keeps on going until the problem has been solved and recursion breaks it down into ever smaller chunks combining the results from each one. Iteration does tend to be better for programmers because control tends to remain local to the loop; with recursion, you get a closer representation to factorials and other like mathematical concepts. Recursive calls are stored in the memory; iterations aren't. All of this leads to trade-offs between memory use and processor cycles, so determination may come down to whether your task is memory or processor intensive.

Backtracking

Backtracking is a type of recursion that tends to be used more for problems like the traversal of tree structures. In these problems, each node presents us with several options and we need to choose one of them. Doing that leads to more options; dependent on the options chosen throughout, we either reach a dead end or a goal state. If the former, we need to backtrack to an earlier node and go down a different route. Backtracking is also a kind of divide and conquers method when we need to do exhaustive searches. More importantly, when we backtrack, we prune off the branches that don't provide any results. Look at this example of backtracking; a recursive approach has been used to generate all the permutations that are possible for a given strength of a given length:

def bitStr(n, s):

if n == 1: return s

return [digit + bits for digit in bitStr(1,s)for bits in bitStr(n - 1,s)]

print (bitStr(3,'abc'))

Notice that we have two recursive calls and a 'double list' compression. This results in all the elements of the first sequence being concatenated recursively with the return when n=1. Each of the string elements was generated in the recursive call that came before.

Divide and Conquer - Long Multiplication

Recursion isn't just a clever little trick, but to understand what it can do, we need to compare it to approaches like iteration and we need to be able to understand when to use it for a faster algorithm. In primary math, we all learned an iterative algorithm used for the multiplication of a pair of large numbers. That algorithm was long multiplication involving iterative multiplication and carrying, followed by shifting and addition.

What we want to do is work out whether this procedure really is all that efficient for the multiplication of the numbers. When you multiply two numbers each four digits long, it takes no less than 16 multiplication operations. This method of algorithm analysis, in terms of how many computational primitives are needed, is vital because it provides us with a way of understanding what the relationship is between the time taken to do the computation and the input size to the computation. What we really want to know is, what will happen when the input is massive? We call this topic asymptomatic analysis, otherwise known as time complexity, and it is important when studying algorithms; we will talk about it quite a bit through the course of this section of the book.

A Recursive Approach

As far as long multiplication goes, there is a better way; several algorithms exist for the more efficient operation of multiplying large numbers. The Karatsuba algorithm is one of the best-known long multiplication alternatives and it dates back to 1962. This algorithm takes a very different approach instead of iterative multiplication of single digits, it does recursive multiplication on inputs that progressively get smaller. A recursive program will call itself on each small subset of the parent input.

To build an algorithm, we need to take a large number and decompose it into smaller numbers. The easiest way is to split it into two – one half with important digits and one with less important digits. For example, a number with 4 digits of 2345 would become 2 sets of numbers, each with 2 digits, 23 and 45.

Let's take 2 n digit numbers and write a general decomposition for them. The numbers are x and y and m is a positive integer with a lower value than n:

$x = 10^m a + b$

$y = 10^m c + d$

We can now write the x and y multiplication problem like this:

$(10^m a + b)(10^m c + d)$

If we were to expand it and gather in like terms, we would get this:

$10^m ac + 10^{2m}(ad + bc) + bd$

A more convenient way of writing it would be:

$10^{2m} z_2 + 10^m z_1 + z_0$

Where:

$z_2 = ac; z_1 = ad + bc; z_0 = bd$

This does suggest that we are using recursion to multiply the numbers because the process involves multiplication. More specifically, ac, ad, bc, and bd all have smaller numbers than the input making it not inconceivable that the same operation could be applied as a partial solution to the bigger problem. So far, the algorithm has four recursive steps (all multiplication) and it is not yet clear whether this would be more efficient than traditional long multiplication.

So far, we have looked at nothing more than what mathematicians have known for years. However, the Karatsuba algorithm goes a step further and observes that we only really need to know three of the quantities to solve the equation. Those quantities are $z_2=ac$; $z_1=ad + bc$ and $z_0=bd$. We only need to know what the values of a, b, c, and d are in as much as they make a contribution to the overall sum and the products required to calculate z_2, z_1, and z_0. This brings about the possibility that we could reduce how many recursive steps are needed and, as it turns out, we can do that.

Because ac and bd have already been reduced to their simplest form, we can't really take these calculations out. What we can do is this:

$(a+b)(c+d)=ac+bd+ad+bc$

When ac and bd, calculated previously, are taken away, we are left with the quantity that we need – (ad + bc):

$ac+bd+ad+bc-ac-bc=ad+bc$

What this shows is that it is perfectly possible to compute ad+bc without having to compute the individual quantities separately. Below is the Karatsuba algorithm in a Python implementation:

```
from math import log10, ceil
def karatsuba(x,y):

    # The base case for recursion
    if x < 10 or y < 10:
        return x*y

    #sets n, which is the number of digits in the highest input number
```

```
n = max(int(log10(x)+1), int(log10(y)+1))

# rounds up n/2
n_2 = int(ceil(n / 2.0))
#adds 1 if n is uneven
n = n if n % 2 == 0 else n + 1

#splits the input numbers
a, b = divmod(x, 10**n_2)
c, d = divmod(y, 10**n_2)

#applies the three recursive steps
ac = karatsuba(a,c)
bd = karatsuba(b,d)
ad_bc = karatsuba((a+b),(c+d)) - ac - bd

#performs the multiplication
return (((10**n)*ac) + bd + ((10**n_2)*(ad_bc)))
```

Just to satisfy ourselves that this really works, there is a test function we can run:

```
import random
def test():
    for i in range(1000):
        x = random.randint(1,10**5)
        y = random.randint(1,10**5)
        expected = x * y
        result = karatsuba(x, y)
        if result != expected:
            return("failed")
    return('ok')
```

Runtime Analysis

By now, it should be clear that one of the more important sides of algorithm design is gauging how efficient it is in terms of time, or how many operations, and memory. The analysis of the number of operations is called Runtime Analysis. There are several ways to run this and the most obvious is nothing more than a measurement of the time taken for the algorithm to finish. There are problems with this approach; how long it takes depends on what hardware it is run, for a start. Another way, independent of the platform, is to count how many operations it takes, but this also causes problems in that we don't have any definitive way of quantifying operations. This would depend on the programming language used, the style of coding, and how we opt to count the operations. However, we could use this way if we were to combine it with an expectation that the runtime increases as the input size increases and it does it in a specific way. In other words, that there is a relationship mathematically between the input size (n) and the time the algorithm takes to run. There are three principles that guide this, and their importance will become clear as we go on. First, the principles:

- Making no assumptions about the input data giving us a worst-case analysis
- Ignoring or suppressing lower order terms and constant factors – with larger inputs, the higher-order terms will be dominant
- Focus only on those problems with the large inputs.

The first one is very useful because it provides us with an upper bound that is tight – the algorithm is guaranteed to fail. The second is just about ignoring anything that doesn't contribute majorly to the runtime making work easier and letting us focus on what impacts performance more.

With the Karatsuba algorithm, the square of the input size increased, and so did the number of operations used for multiplication. With a four-digit number, we use 16 operations and with an eight-digit number, we need 64. However, we're not so interested in how an algorithm with small n values behaves so we ignore the factors that only increase linearly or lowly. At the higher n values, the operations that increase fast as n is increased will be the dominant ones.

We'll talk briefly about the merge-sort algorithm here because it is useful to learn about performance at runtime. This is one of the classic algorithms from more than 60 years ago and it is still used today in some of the highly popular sorting libraries. Merge-sort is recursive and uses divide and conquer, which, as you know, means breaking a problem down, sorting the parts recursively, and putting the results together. Merge-sort is an obvious demonstration of this algorithm design paradigm.

Merge-sort has just three steps:

1. Sorts the left side of the input array recursively
2. Sorts the right side of the input array recursively
3. Merges the sorted arrays into one

One typical use is to sort numbers into numerical order. Merge-sort will divide the list in two and work on each side in parallel. Here is the Python code for the algorithm:

```
def mergeSort(A):
    #base case if the input array is one or zero just return.
    if len(A) > 1:
        # splitting input array
        print('splitting ', A )
        mid = len(A)//2
        left = A[:mid]
        right = A[mid:]
        #recursive calls to mergeSort for left and right subarrays
        mergeSort(left)
        mergeSort(right)
        #initializes pointers for left (i) right (j) and output array (k)
        # 3 initialization operations
        i = j = k = 0
        #Traverse and merges the sorted arrays
        while i <len(left) and j<len(right):
            # if left < right comparison operation
            if left[i] < right[j]:
                # if left < right Assignment operation
                A[k]=left[i]
                i=i+1
```

```
    else:
        #if right <= left assignment
        A[k]= right[j]
        j=j+1
      k=k+1

    while i<len(left):
        #Assignment operation
        A[k]=left[i]
        i=i+1
        k=k+1

    while j<len(right):
        #Assignment operation
        A[k]=right[j]
        j=j+1
        k=k+1
  print('merging ', A)
  return(A)
```

The easiest way to determine the running time performance is to start by mapping the recursive calls onto a tree structure with each tree node being a call that works on an ever smaller subprogram. Each time we invoke merge-sort, we get two recursive calls, so we can use a binary tree to represent this, with each child node getting an input subset. To work out the time the algorithm takes to finish relative to n, we start by working out how much work there is and how many operations are on each tree level.

Keeping our focus on the runtime analysis, on the first level we have two $n/2$ subproblems; level two gives us four, and so on. So, when does the recursion get to its base case? Simply, when the array is one or zero. To get to a number that is nearly one, we take the number of recursive levels and divide n by 2 that many times. This is the definition of log2 and, as the first recursive level is 0, the number of levels is $\log_2 n+1$.

Let's refine the definitions. Up to now, we have used n to represent the number of elements in an input, referring to how many elements are in the first recursive level, or the length of the first input. What we need to do is be able to know the difference between the initial input length and the input length at each recursive level. For this, we use m i.e. m_j for the input length at recursive level j.

Using recursion trees for algorithm analysis has the advantage of being able to know what is done at each recursive level. Defining the work is the number of operations in relation to the input size. We must measure the performance of an algorithm in a way that is independent of the platform although runtime will depend on the hardware. It is important to count how many operations there are because this is our metric related directly to the performance of our algorithm.

Generally, because we get two recursive calls each time merge-sort is invoked, each level has double the number of calls of the previous one. At the same time, each call is working on an input that is half the size of its parent. To work out how many operations there are, we must know how many operations are used by one merge of two sub-arrays. Look at the Python code above. After the first two recursive calls, we can count the operations – three assignments followed by three while loops. The first loop has an if-else statement and within each is a comparison and an assignment – two operations. This is counted as a set and there is only one set in an if-else, so this set was carried out m times. The last two while loops each have an assignment operation, making for a total of 4m+3 operations for each merge-sort recursion.

Because m has to be at least 1, the number of operations has an upper bound of 7m. This is not an exact science; it all depends on how the operations are counted. We haven't included any increment or housekeeping operations as we are only interested in the runtime growth rate related to n at the high n values.

All this may seem a bit daunting because every call from a recursive call spins off to even more recursive calls and things look as if they exponentially explode. What makes this manageable is as the recursive calls double, the subproblem size halves. These cancel each other out very nicely as we will demonstrate.

To work out the max number of the operations on each tree level, the number of subproblems are multiplied by the number of operations in each of those subproblems, like this:

$2^jx7(n/2^j)=7n$

What we see here is 2^j cancels out how the number of operations there are on each level independently of the level, giving us an upper bound to work with. In our example, it is 7n. This number includes the operations that each recursive call performs on that level only, not on any other. From this, as we get a doubling of the recursive calls for each level, and this is counter-balanced by the subproblem input size halving on each level.

If we wanted to know how many operations there were for one complete merge-sort, we would take the number of operations per level and multiply that by the total number of levels, like this:

$7n(\log_2n+ 1)$

Expanding that gives us:

$7n\log_2n+7$

The key to take from this is that the relationship between input size and running time has a logarithmic component and, if you remember your high-school math, logarithm functions flatten off fast. As x, an input variable, increases in size, so y, the output variable, will increase by progressively smaller amounts.

Asymptotic Analysis

Runtime performance of an algorithm can be characterized in one of three ways:

- Worst-case – using an input that is slow to perform
- Best case – using an input that gives us the best results
- Average case – assuming the input is random

To calculate each one, we must know what the lower and upper bounds are. We looked at using mathematical expressions to represent runtime using multiplication and addition operators. For asymptotic analysis, we need two expressions, one for the best and one for the worst-case.

Big O Notation

The "O" stands for order and denotes that the growth rates are defined as orders of functions. We could say that a function, T(n), is a big O of F(n) and this is defined like this:

T(n)=O(F(n)) if there are constants, n_o, and C in a way that:

T(n) ■ C(F(n)) for all n ■ n_o

The function of the input size n is g(n) and this is based on all large enough values of n, g(n) being upper bound by a constant multiple of f(n). What we want to do is find the smallest growth rate equal to less than f(n). We are only interested in the higher n values; the variable, n, represents the threshold – below that, we're not interested in the growth rate. T(n) is the function that represents F(n), the tight upper bound.

The notation that reads f(n) = O(g(n)) is telling us that O(g(n)) is a set of functions, within which are all the functions with smaller or equal growth rates than f(n). Below, are the common growth rates from low to high. These are sometimes called a function time complexity:

Complexity	Class Name	Operation Examples
O(1)	Constant	get item, set item, append
O(log n)	Logarithmic	find an element in an array that is sorted
O(n)	Linear	insert, copy, iteration, delete
nLogn	Linear-logarithmic	merge-sort, sorting lists
n^2	Quadratic	nested loops, finding the shortest path between nodes
n^3	Cubic	Matrix multiplication
2_n	Exponential	backtracking

Complexity Classes

Normally, we would be looking for the total running time of several basic operations, but it seems that we can take simple operations and combine their complexity classes to determine the class of combined operations that are somewhat more complex. The goal is to look at the combined statements in a method or a function to find the time complexity of executing multiple operations. The easiest way of combining complexity classes is to add them and this happens when the operations are sequential.

Let's say that we have a pair of operations that insert an element in a list and then proceed to sort the list. When the item is inserted, it happens in $O(n)$ time while sorting happens in $O(nlogn)$ time. The time complexity can be written as $O(n + nlogn)$. However, because we are focusing only on the high order term, we can work with just $O(nlogn)$.

Let's then assume that we use a while loop to repeat an operation; we would take the complexity class and multiply it by how many times the operation is done. For example, an operation that has a time complexity of $O(f(n))$ is repeated $O(n)$ times; both complexities are multiplied as follows:

$O(f(n) * O(n) = O(nf(n))$

Let's assume that a function called f(...) has $O(n^2)$ as a time complexity and it is executed in a while loop n times, like this:

for i n range(n):
  f(...)

This loop then has a time complexity of $O(n^2) * O(n) = O(n * n^2) = O(n^3)$. All we have done is multiply the operation's time complexity by the number of times that operation was executed. A loop's running time is no more than the combined running time of all the statements in the loop multiplied by the iterations. Assuming both loops will run n times, a single nested loop runs in n^2 time. For example:

```
for i in range(0,n):
    for j in range(0,n)
        #statements
```

Each of these statements is a constant (c) that is executed nn times. The running time can thus be expressed as; $cn\ n + cn^2 = O(n2)$

For all consecutive statements in a nested loop, the time complexity for each of the statements is added and then multiplied by the iterations of the statement. For example:

```
n = 500    #c0
#executes n times
for i in range(0,n):
    print(i)   #c1
#executes n times
for i in range(0,n):
    #executes n times
    for j in range(0,n):
        print(j)   #c2
```

We can write this as $c_0 + c_1 n + cn2 = O(n2)$.

Amortized Analysis

Sometimes we are not bothered so much about the time complexity of an individual operation; sometimes we want to know what the average running time is of a sequence of operations. This is called amortized analysis and, as you will see later, it is not the same as the average case analysis because it doesn't assume anything about the data distribution of any input values. What it does do is take the change in state of the data structures into account. For example, sorting a list should make finding operations faster in the future. The amortized analysis considers the change in the state because the sequence of operations is analyzed; it doesn't just aggregate single operations.

What amortized analysis does is determines the upper bound on runtime and it does this by imposing each operation in a sequence with an artificial cost. Each of these costs is then combined. This takes consideration of the fact that the initial expense of an operation can then make future operations much cheaper.

When there are multiple small operations that are expensive, like sorting, and multiple options that are cheaper, like lookups, using worst-case analysis can give us pessimistic results. This is because worst-case assumes that each of the lookups should compare every element until a match is found.

Up to now, we have assumed that we have random input data and we only looked at how the input size affects the runtime. There are two more common algorithm analyses we can look at:

- Average Case Analysis
- Benchmarking

Average case analysis takes some assumptions about the relative frequency of the different input values and determines the average running time. Benchmarking is when a previously agreed set of inputs is used to measure performance.

Both approaches rely on some domain knowledge. For a start, we would need to know what the expected or the typical datasets are. Ultimately, we will be trying to improve the performance by finetuning to an application setting that is highly specific.

A straightforward benchmarking approach would be to time how long the algorithm takes to finish given different input sizes. This is entirely dependent on what hardware the algorithm is run on; the faster the processor, the better the result. However, the relative growth rates that come with the increases in the input rates will retain the characteristics of the algorithm and not the platform they run on.

Let's look at an easy nested loop example. The time complexity is $O(n^2)$ because each n iteration in the external loop is matched by the same in the inner loop. In our example, we have one statement that is executed in the inner loop:

```
def nest(n):
    for i in range(n):
        for j in range(n):
            i+j
```

Next, you can see the test function required to run the nest function with n values that increase. With each iteration, we can calculate the time taken for the function to complete using the function called timeit.timeit. In this example, the function takes no less than three arguments – a string representation of the function being timed, an int parameter that indicates how many times the main statement is executed, and a setup function used for importing the nest function. All we want to know is how long, in relation to the size of the input, the nest function takes to complete. All we need to do is call that nest function one time for each iteration. The test function below will return a list of the runtimes calculated for each n value:

```
import timeit
def test2(n):
    ls=[]
    for n in range(n):
        t=timeit.timeit("nest(" + str(n) +")", setup="from __main__ import nest", number = 1)
        ls.append(t)
    return ls
```

We now run the test2 function and the results would be shown on a graph with an n^2 function scaled appropriately for comparison:

```
import matplotlib.pyplot as plt
n=1000
plt.plot(test2(n))
plt.plot([x*x/10000000 for x in range(n)])
plt.show()
```

This provides us with a result that we expect. Do keep in mind that this is representative of the algorithm performance and the way the software and hardware behave. Performance will always be subject to things like processor, constraints on memory, running processes, clock speed, and more.

Next, we will be looking at pointer structures, like linked lists.

Chapter 7: Lists and Pointer Structures

If you are familiar with Python, you are familiar with lists. Lists are powerful and they are convenient. Normally, when you want things stored in a list you would use the built-in Python list implementation, but for the purposes of this section, we are going to look at how a list works. As you will see, there is more than one type of list.

While the list implementation in Python is powerful and can be used for multiple use cases, we are going to be more stringent in the way we define a list. One concept that is vital to lists is the node.

One thing we are going to be covering is pointers so let's be reminded what a pointer is. Imagine that we are selling a house. We don't have much time, so we get an agent to find buyers for us. How do we do this? We give the agent the address of the house and directions; that is passed to prospective buyers. We might write this down several times and each time, each piece of paper we write on is called a pointer.

It is much the same in Python. Assuming we have some large resolution images that we want to pass among several functions. The images are kept in one place in memory and a variable is created for each image. Instead of passing the image to each function, we pass them a small variable instead that points to the image.

We don't directly manipulate a pointer in Python as we do in other languages and this has led to many people believing they are not used. As an example, look that the following assignment written in the Python interactive shell:

> >> *s = set()*

Normally we would say that s is a variable of the set type, so s is a set. However, this isn't quite true. In fact, s is a reference to a set. The constructor for the set will create a set in the memory and then returns the location of the start of the set and this is what s stores.

Arrays

Arrays are sequential lists of data. A sequence means that each of the elements is stored immediately one after the other in memory. If we have a large array and we have little memory, it may not be possible to store the array in memory.

There is an upside; arrays are fast. Because the elements are sequential, there isn't any need to search in different locations. This can be vital when we are making a choice between using a list or an array in our applications.

Pointer Structures

Unlike an array, a pointer structure is a list of items that may be spread across memory. This is because each of the items has at least one link to another structure item. The type of these links will depend on the structure type; if it was linked lists, then the links would be to the next structure item, and even the previous one. With a tree, there are sibling links and parent-child links. In a tile game where hexes are used to build a game map, each of the nodes will contain links to adjacent cells.

Pointer structures are beneficial in that sequential storage space is not required and they can begin quite small and arbitrarily grow as more nodes are added to the structure. This does come with a cost; with an integer list, each node will take the space of an integer and an extra integer to store the pointer besides the node.

Nodes

The concept of a node is at the heart of a list and some other data structures. Before we move on, let's consider an idea. We'll start with some strings:

>>> a = "eggs"
>>> b = "ham"
>>> c = "spam"

We have three variables. Each one is given a unique name, a type of its own, and a value. We don't have any way to say that these three variables are related to one another. This is where nodes come in. A node is a type of container that contains data as well as at least one link to another node; that link is a pointer.

One of the simplest types of nodes is one that has one link to the following node.

Knowing what we now know about pointers, however, it's clear that this isn't true – the string isn't stored inside the node; a pointer to the string is. As such, all we need for this kind of node is a pair of memory addresses as storage. The node data attributes are the pointers to the strings of ham and eggs.

Finding an Endpoint

So, we have three nodes, one with eggs, one with ham, and one with spam. The egg node is pointing to the ham node and this, in turn, is pointing to the spam node, which points ... where? Because spam is the final element, the next member of the list must have a value that makes it clear. By having the final element point nowhere that is made clear and, in Python, we will denote nothing by using the value of None. The last node's next point will point to None indicating that it is the final node in the node chain.

This is a simple implementation that demonstrates what we have discussed:

```
class Node:
    def __init__(self, data=None):
        self.data = data
        self.next = None
```

We have initialized the pointer called next to None. What this means is that, unless Next's value is changed, that node will be the endpoint. This means that we cannot forget to correctly terminate the list.

Other things can be added to the node class as wanted; all we need to do is ensure that we keep the distinction between data and node in mind. If our node has customer data in it, we need a Customer class to store the data.

We can also implement the _str_ method to call the same method of the contained object when the node object is passed for printing.

```
def __str__(self):
    return str(data)
```

Other Node Types

We have looked at a simple node type, one that points the next node, but we may require something a bit more complex and other node types can be created. Suppose we want to move from A to B and B to A simultaneously. To do that, we would add a next pointer and a previous pointer. The first and the last nodes would point to None showing that the boundary of the list endpoint has been reached. The previous pointer has no predecessor and the next pointer has no successor.

If we had a tile-based game and we were trying to create tiles for it, we wouldn't use previous or next; we would probably use north, east, south, and west. There are other pointer types, but the principle is that the tiles at the map's end will point to None.

Singly Linked Lists

Singly linked lists are lists that have just one pointer between successive nodes. Traversal is only possible in one direction – we may go from the first to the last node, but we can't go from the last to the first. We can implement a simple singly linked list by using the previously created node class:

```
>>> n1 = Node('eggs')
>>> n2 = Node('ham')
>>> n3 = Node('spam')
```

Net, the nodes are linked to form a chain:

```
>>> n1.next = n2
>>> n2.next = n3
```

Traversal of the list would look something like the following. The variable called current is set to the first list item:

```
current = n1
while current:
    print(current.data)
    current = current.next
```

The current element is printed in the loop after the current is set to point to the next successive list element. We continue to do this until the end of the list is reached but there are some problems with this kind of simplistic implementation:

- It takes far too much manual programming work
- It is prone to errors
- The inner list workings are exposed to the programmer

We will be looking at these in the next sections.

Singly Linked List Class

A list is clearly different from a node in terms of concept, so we will begin by creating a simple class that will contain our list. We start with a constructor; this has a reference to the initial node in the list and, because this list is empty to start with, the reference is set to None.

```
class SinglyLinkedList:
    def __init__(self):
        self.tail = None
```

Append Operation

First, items need to be appended to the list. The append operation sometimes is called the insert operation and we can use it to hide the Node class. In all truthfulness, anyone using the list class should never need to interact with Node objects because they are for internal use only.

The append() may look like this, to begin with:

```
class SinglyLinkedList:
    def __init__(self):
        self.tail = None
    def append(self, data):
        # Encapsulate the data in a Node
        node = Node(data)

        if self.tail == None:
            self.tail = node
        else:
            current = self.tail
            while current.next:
                current = current.next
            current.next = node
```

The data is encapsulated in a node and now has the attribute of the next pointer. Now we will look to see if any other nodes exist in the list – we look to see if self.tail points to any Node. If not, the new node is made into the first node. If there is another node, we traverse the list through to the last node looking for an insertion point and the next pointer for the final node is updated to the new node.

Now some items can be appended:

```
>>> words = SinglyLinkedList()
>>> words.append('egg')
>>> words.append('ham')
>>> words.append('spam')
```

List traversal is much the same as before and we get the initial list element from the list:

```
>>> current = words.tail
>>> while current:
        print(current.data)
        current = current.next
```

A Faster Way to Append

The previous append method has a large problem attached to it; finding the insertion point involves traversal of the entire list. If there are few items in the list, this isn't so much of an issue but when you need thousands of items added, the append operations will get progressively slower. We can fix this by storing a reference to both the first and last nodes in the list. By doing this, a new node can be appended quickly to the end. The worst-case analysis of the append running time is reduced from O(n) to O(1). What we need to do is ensure that the previous final node is pointing to the new one that is to be appended. The new code will look like this:

```
class SinglyLinkedList:
    def __init__(self):
        self.head = None
        self.tail = None

    def append(self, data):
        node = Node(data)
        if self.head:
            self.head.next = node
            self.head = node
        else:
            self.tail = node
            self.head = node
```

Note the convention we are using. We use self.head as the point at which new nodes are appended and self-tail points to the first list node.

Obtaining the List Size

We want to be able to count the nodes to determine the size of the list. One way would be to traverse the whole list with a counter increasing as we do so:

```
def size(self):
    count = 0
    current = self.tail
    while current:
        count += 1
        current = current.next
    return count
```

This does work, but using list traversal can be quite expensive and we shouldn't do it unless we have to. So, we will rewrite the method instead. A size member is added to the class called SinglyLinkedList and it is initialized in the constructor to 1. Then the size is incremented in the append method by 1:

```
class SinglyLinkedList:
    def __init__(self):
        self.head = None
        self.tail = None
        self.size = 0
    def append(self, data):
        node = Node(data)
        if self.head:
            self.head.next = node
            self.head = node
        else:
            self.tail = node
            self.head = node
        self.size += 1
    def size(self):
        count = 0
        current = self.tail
        while current:
            count += 1
            current = current.next
        return count
```

Now we are reading only the node object's size attribute rather than using loops to count the nodes. This means the worst-case running time is reduced from O(n) to O(1).

Improve the List Traversal

Notice when we traverse the list, there is still a point at which we are exposed to node and to determine the contents of the node we need node.data and getting to the next one requires node.next. Earlier, we said that the user should not interact with the Node objects and this is achievable through a method that will return a generator, like this:

```
def iter(self):
    current = self.tail
    while current:
        val = current.data
        current = current.next
        yield val
```

List traversal is now easier and looks better. We can forget about there being anything called a Node outside the list:

```
for word in words.iter():
    print(word)
```

Note, because the method called iter() gives us the node's data member, the client code or user need not worry about it.

Deleting Nodes

Node deletion is one of the more common operations to perform on a list. This might seem to be very simple, but we must first decide how we are going to choose the node for deletion. Will we use an index number, or will we opt for the data contained in the node? For our example, we will go with the latter.

When the node we want to delete is in between two others, the previous node must be directly linked to the successor of the following node. Simply, the node for deletion is removed from the chain. The delete() method implementation may look something like this:

```
def delete(self, data):
    current = self.tail
    prev = self.tail
    while current:
        if current.data == data:
            if current == self.tail:
                self.tail = current.next
            else:
                prev.next = current.next
            self.size -= 1
            return
        prev = current
        current = current.next
```

The time taken to delete the node should be O(n).

List Search

Sometimes, we might want to see if a list contains a specific item and this is easy to implement because we can use our previously created iter() method. Each iteration over the loop looks at the current data for a match to the data being looked for. If one is found, we get True; if not, we get False.

```
def search(self, data):
    for node in self.iter():
        if data == node:
            return True
    return False
```

Clearing Lists

It is also very easy to clear a list quickly by clearing the head and tail pointers; this is done by setting them to None:

```
def clear(self):
    """ Clear the entire list. """
```

self.tail = None
self.head = None

In one hit, all the nodes at the tail and head pointers are orphaned and this has a knock-on effect of all the nodes in between being orphaned too.

Doubly Linked Lists

We know what a singly linked list is all about and what operations we can perform on it. Now we turn to doubly linked lists. These are similar to the singly linked list in that we still use the idea of stringing nodes together. In the singly linked list, there is a single link between successive nodes; in the doubly linked list, there are two pointers – one to the next and one to the last node. Because there are two pointers, doubly linked lists now have additional capabilities.

They can be traversed in either direction. Nodes can refer to previous nodes where needed without having to use a variable to track the node. And, because we have access to the last and next nodes immediately, it is much easier to delete a node.

Doubly Linked List Nodes

In the Python code for creating the class to capture what the linked list node is, we include the three instance variables in the initializing method: prev, next, and data. When a node is created, those variables are set to None by default:

class Node(object):

   def __init__(self, data=None, next=None, prev=None):

     self.data = data

     self.next = next

     self.prev = prev

Inside the prev variable is a reference to the last node; next holds the reference to the net node.

We still need a class that will capture the data on which the functions are operating:

class DoublyLinkedList(object):

   def __init__(self):

     self.head = None

     self.tail = None

     self.count = 0

To enhance the size method, the instance variable called count is set to 0; tail and head point to the tail and head of the list when we start adding nodes into the list. Contrary to the singly linked list, we will be using a new convention whereby self.tail will point the newest node and self.head points to the first node.

A doubly linked list must also provide the functions that will:

- Insert a node
- Return the list size
- Delete a node

We'll be looking at the code that does this and we'll start with the append operation.

Append Operation

When the append operation is happening, we must check that head is None. If it is, the list is empty, and head should be set to point the newly created node. The tail should also point, through the head, to the new node. By the end of the following code, head and tail should both point to the same node:

def append(self, data):

   """ Append an item to the list. """

```
new_node = Node(data, None, None)
if self.head is None:
    self.head = new_node
    self.tail = self.head
else:
    new_node.prev = self.tail
    self.tail.next = new_node
    self.tail = new_node


    self.count += 1
```

The else section will only be executed if the list isn't empty and the previous variable of the new node is set to the list tail:

new_node.prev = self.tail

The next pointer of the tail is set to the newly created node:

self.tail.next = new_node

Finally, the tail pointer is updated and it points to the newly created node:

self.tail = new_node

Because the append operation raises the node number by one, we must increase the counter by the same:

self.count += 1

Delete Operation

Contrary to the singly linked list where the previous node needed to be tracked whenever the entire list was traversed, with the doubly linked list, that entire step is avoided by using the previous pointer. The algorithm to remove a node from the doubly linked list will go through four scenarios before completing the deletion. They are:

- When the search item is not found
- When the search item is at the start of the list
- When the search item is at the tail
- When the search item is in the middle of the list

The node for removal is identified by the data variable of the node matching the search data that was passed to the method. When a matching node is located and removed, the variable called node_deleted gets set as True; anything else would result in False:

def delete(self, data):

   current = self.head

   node_deleted = False

...

The current variable in the delete method point to self.head of the list and a set of if...else statements will then look through the different bits to the list to find the node that has the given data. First, the head node is searched. Because current points to tail, if current is returned as None, it will be assumed that there are no nodes to be searched:

if current is None:

   node_deleted = False

However, if current has got the data being searched for, self.head will be set so it points to the current next node. There is now no node behind head so self.head.prev is set as None:

```
elif current.data == data:

    self.head = current.next

    self.head.prev = None

    node_deleted = True
```

We would do something similar if the node for deletion were at the end of the list. The third statement looks for that possibility:

```
elif self.tail.data == data:

    self.tail = self.tail.prev

    self.tail.next = None

    node_deleted = True
```

Finally, the algorithm will loop through the node list and, if a matching node is located, the previous node of current is connected to the next node of current. After that, the next node of current will be connected to the previous node:

```
else:

    while current:

        if current.data == data:

            current.prev.next = current.next

            current.next.prev = current.prev

            node_deleted = True

        current = current.next
```

The variable called node_delete then is checked after the if-else statements have all been evaluated. If the variable were changed by any of those statements, it would mean the node had been deleted and the count variable is decremented by 1:

if node_deleted:

  self.count -= 1

List Search

The search algorithm is much like that for the singly linked list. The internal iter() method is called to return the data from all the nodes and, as the data is looped through, it is matched against the data that went into the method called contain. If a match is found, True is returned; if not, False is returned:

def contain(self, data):

  for node_data in self.iter():

    if data == node_data:

      return True

    return False

The doubly linked list has a running time for the append operation of O(1) and O(n) for delete.

Circular Lists

Circular lists are special types of linked list and they are lists that have the endpoints connected. In other words, the last node points to the first node. Circular lists may be based on singly linked and doubly linked lists; with the latter, the first node must also point to the last.

We're going to look at a singly linked circular list and is a straightforward implementation once you understand the basic concept. The node class we created for the singly linked lists can be reused; in fact, we can reuse much of the SinglyLinkedList class. What we will focus on are the methods where the implementation differs from a standard singly linked list.

Appending an Element

When an element is appended to a circular list, the new node must point back to the tail. We can see this in the next code. There is also an extra line above the singly linked implementation:

```
def append(self, data):
    node = Node(data)
    if self.head:
        self.head.next = node
        self.head = node
    else:
        self.head = node
        self.tail = node
    self.head.next = self.tail
    self.size += 1
```

Element Deletion

You might think the same applies as that of the append method and that the head must point to the tail. Doing that would give us this implementation:

```
def delete(self, data):
    current = self.tail
    prev = self.tail
    while current:
        if current.data == data:
            if current == self.tail:
```

```
    self.tail = current.next

    self.head.next = self.tail

  else:

    prev.next = current.next

  self.size -= 1

  return

prev = current

current = current.next
```

We only need to change one line; when the tail node is removed, we must ensure that we update the head node to point to the newly created tail node.

However, we have a problem. With a circular list, we have to wait for current to become None before we can loop and that isn't going to happen. If an existing node is deleted this would never be seen, but if we try to delete a node that is nonexistent we will have created an infinite loop.

So, we need another way of controlling our while loop. We can't check to see if current has got to head because the last node would never be checked. We can, however, use prev because it is one node behind current. There is a special case – in the initial loop iteration both current and prev point to the tail node. We need to make sure that the node is running here because the one-node list needs to be considered. Our delete method should now look like this:

```
def delete(self, data):

  current = self.tail

  prev = self.tail

  while prev == current or prev!= self.head:

    if current.data == data:
```

```
    if current == self.tail:

        self.tail = current.next

        self.head.next = self.tail

    else:

        prev.next = current.next

        self.size -= 1

        return

    prev = current

    current = current.next
```

Iteration Through Circular Lists

The iter() method doesn't need modifying as it will work just fine for the circular list. However, an exit condition needs to be added when the circular list is iterated through, otherwise, the program gets caught in a loop. We could do this with a counter variable:

```
words = CircularList()


words.append('eggs')

words.append('ham')

words.append('spam')


counter = 0

for word in words.iter():

    print(word)
```

```
counter += 1

if counter > 1000:

    break
```

When 1000 elements have been printed, the loop can be broken out of.

Next, we are going to be examining two more data structures that we implement using a list – queues and stacks.

Chapter 8: Stacks

In this section, we will continue building on what we learned to create special implementations of lists. We will continue to use linear structures; we will consider more complex structures later. We are going to look at:

- Implementations of stacks and queues
- Some of the applications stacks and queues are used for

<u>Stacks</u>

Stacks are data structures that look, in a real-world sense, like a stack of plates. When we wash one it goes on the top. When we need one, we take it from the top. The last added is the first removed and that makes a stack a LIFO structure, which means Last In, First Out.

Stacks do two main operations – pop and push. When you add an element to the top it gets pushed to the stack; when you remove an element, it is popped out. Another operation that is occasionally used on stacks is peek, which allows a glimpse at an element without needing to pop it out of the stack.

Stacks can be used for many things and one of the more common uses is to track the return address throughout a function call. Look at this next program:

def b():

  print('b')

def a():

  b()

a()

print("done")

As the program executes, when it gets to the a() call, the address of the next instruction is pushed to the stack and then it jumps to a(). In a(), we call b(), but before that happens, we push the return address to the stack. Once it is in b() and the function is complete, that address is popped from the stack and we go right back to a(). When a() is finished, we pop the return address off the stack and go back to the print statement.

The actual use of a stack is to pass data from one function to another. Look at the following function call that might be in our code somewhere:

somefunc(14, 'eggs', 'ham', 'spam')

So, 14, eggs, ham, and spam are all going to be pushed, one at a time, onto the stack. When the function is jumped into, the a, b, c, and d values get popped from the stack. Spam pops first and gets assigned to d; ham is assigned to c, and so on:

def somefunc(a, b, c, d):

   print("function executed")

Stack Implementation

Now, we'll look at how a stack is implemented in Python. The first step is to create a node class, as we did with lists:

class Node:

  def __init__(self, data=None):

    self.data = data

    self.next = None

You should be able to do this in your sleep by now – nodes hold data together with a reference that points to the next list item. We are implementing a stack this time, but the principle remains the same – nodes are linked together.

The stack class begins in much the same way as a singly linked list. We must know what the node is at the top of the list and we also need to track how many nodes are in the stack; that means we need these fields in our class:

class Stack:

  def __init__(self):

    self.top = None

    self.size = 0

The Push Operation

We add elements to the top of a stack using the push operation, which is implemented in this way:

  def push(self, data):

    node = Node(data)

    if self.top:

      node.next = self.top

      self.top = node

    else:

      self.top = node

    self.size += 1

If, after we create a new node, there is no existing one, self.top points to the new one. This is guaranteed by the else part of the if-else statement. Where we already have an existing stack, self.top would be moved so it pointed to the new node. The next pointer of the new node must point to the node that was originally on the top of the stack.

The POP Operation

To remove the top element off the stack, we use the pop operation. At the same time, the top element needs to be returned as well. If there are no other elements the stack can be made to return None:

```
def pop(self):
    if self.top:
        data = self.top.data
        self.size -= 1
        if self.top.next:
            self.top = self.top.next
        else:
            self.top = None
        return data
    else:
        return None
```

What we need to pay special attention to here is the inner if statement. If the next attribute of the top node points to another node, the top of the stack now must also point to the same node.

The Peek Operation

As we mentioned earlier, there is another operation sometimes used on stacks, and that is the peek operation. This returns to the top without removing an element from the stack, thus allowing us to see the top element without making any changes to the stack. This operation is very simple; if there is an element at the top, its data is returned; if not, None is returned and the rest of peeks behavior will be the same as pop:

```python
def peek(self):
    if self.top:
        return self.top.data
    else:
        return None
```

A Bracket-Matching Application

To learn how the stack implementation we built can be used, we will write a function that verifies whether a statement that has brackets of some description is a balanced statement. By that, we mean that the opening brackets should have a matched closing bracket and that there is the same number of opening and closing brackets. The function will also check that a pair of brackets is contained inside another:

```python
def check_brackets(statement):
    stack = Stack()
    for ch in statement:
        if ch in ('{', '[', '('):
            stack.push(ch)
        if ch in ('}', ']', ')'):
            last = stack.pop()
            if last is '{' and ch is '}':
                continue
            elif last is '[' and ch is ']':
                continue
            elif last is '(' and ch is ')':
```

```
                continue
        else:
                return False
    if stack.size > 0:
        return False
    else:
        return True
```

Our little function will parse each of the characters contained in the statement. If it finds an open bracket, it is pushed to the stack. If it gets a closing bracket, it will pop the top element from the stack and compare it to see if it has a matching bracket. If not, False is returned and parsing continues. Once the end of the statement is reached, one last check is needed. If there is nothing in the stack, everything is good and True can be returned. If the stack isn't empty, False is returned because we have an opening bracket that is not matched by a closing bracket.

The following code can be used to test the application:

```
s1 = (
    "{(foo)(bar)}[hello](((this)is)a)test",
    "{(foo)(bar)}[hello](((this)is)atest",
    "{(foo)(bar)}[hello](((this)is)a)test))"
)

for s in s1:
    m = check_brackets(s)
    print("{}: {}".format(s, m))
```

The only statements that should match are the first three.

True

False

True

This code works just fine. The push operation and the pop operation of the structure both attract o(1), The data structure is used for the implementation of a number of different functionalities in the real world. For example, the forward and back buttons in a web browser, redo and undo features in word processing programs, and so on, are all forms of stack.

Chapter 9: Queues

Queues are another type of special list. This is not much different from a standard queue, one that you could be part of in the real world. Anyone who has stood in a queue at a fast food place or at an airport, or anywhere, they know how queues work.

Queues are a very basic and important concept to understand because many of the Python data structures are built on one.

A queue works like this – the first person to join will be seen to first if everything is equal. This is where FIFO comes in – First In, First Out. In any queue, the person or item at the front is served first and the only time that a person or an item leaves the queue is when they have been served, at the front. Strictly, it is considered illegal to join a queue at the front. A queue participant must join at the very end; it doesn't matter what length the queue is, joining at the end is the only accepted and legal way to join a queue.

As humans, the queues that we join do not, in any way, conform to these rules. There may be people who decide to drop out of the queue or have someone standing in their place while they do something else. We cannot model the dynamics of a real queue but being able to abstract a queue and its behavior is what helps us solve multiple computing challenges.

We'll be looking at several queue implementations, but they will all be based on the same concept of FIFO. The operation that adds an element will be called enqueue and the operation that removes an element will be called dequeue. Whenever an element is enqueued, the size or length of that queue increases by one and when one is removed, the size is decreased by one. As a way of demonstrating those two important operations, the details below shows what happens when elements are added and removed from a queue:

Queue Op	Size	Contents	Results
Queue()	0	[]	creation of queue object
Enqueue "Simon"	1	['simon']	Simon added to the queue
Enqueue "Billy"	2	['simon', 'billy']	Billy added to the queue
Size()	2	['simon', 'billy']	Number of queue items returned
Dequeue()	1	['simon']	Billy dequeued and returned
Dequeue()	0	[]	Simon dequeued and returned

List-Based Queues

To put all that we have talked about into a code, we'll use the list class in Python to implement a simple queue. We will encapsulate all the queue operations inside the class called ListQueue:

class ListQueue:

  def __init__(self):

    self.items = []

    self.size = 0

The initialization method, __init__ is where we set the instance variable for items to []. This means when the queue is created, it is empty. The queue size has been set to zero and enqueue and dequeue are the two interesting methods we will look at now.

Enqueue Operation

Enqueue() takes the insert method from the list class and inserts data or items at the front of the queue:

  def enqueue(self, data):

    self.items.insert(0, data)

    self.size += 1

Note that insertions are implemented at the end of the queue. The first position of any array or list is index 0, but using a Python list to implement a queue in our code, index 0 of the array is the only place where we can insert a new element. Insert() moves the existing element up a position and then puts the new data at index 0 in the space that has been created.

To ensure that our queue reflects this new element, we increase the size by one:

self.size += 1

Dequeue Operation

We use the dequeue() operation to take items out of the queue. This will capture the point at which the first customer to join the queue is served:

def dequeue(self):

data = self.items.pop()

self.size -= 1

return data

The List class in Python has a pop() method which does the following:

- Removes the final item from the list
- Returns the item removed back to the code or the user responsible for calling it.

When the last list item is popped, it is saved in the variable called data and, the data is returned in the final line of the method.

Stack-Based Queue

A different queue implementation is a pair of stacks. Again, we use the list class to simulate the stack:

class Queue:

def __init__(self):

self.inbound_stack = []

self.outbound_stack = []

The queue class sets the instance variables to empty lists when initialization happens. These two stacks will help with the implementation of the queue and, in this case, our stacks are just lists that we can call pop() and push() on.

Elements that have been added to the queue are stored in inbound_stack and this is all that can happen on this stack, nothing else.

Enqueue Operation

We use enqueue() to add an element to the queue:

def enqueue(self, data):

self.inbound_stack.append(data)

This is a simple method that will receive only the data that is required to be appended to the queue. The data then gets passed to inbound_stack in the queue class, to the append() method. That append() method also mimics the push() operation, which puts the elements to the top. Enqueuing data on the inbound_stack is done like this:

queue = Queue()

queue.enqueue(5)

queue.enqueue(6)

queue.enqueue(7)

print(queue.inbound_stack)

Dequeue Operation

Dequeue() is slightly more complex than enqueue(). When an element is added to the queue it goes straight to the inbound_stack and instead of taking elements from that stack, we go to the outbound_stack and an element can only be deleted through that outbound_stack():

```
def dequeue(self):

    if not self.outbound_stack:

        while self.inbound_stack:

            self.outbound_stack.append(self.inbound_stack.pop())

        return self.outbound_stack.pop()
```

First, the if statement will check to see if there is anything in outbound_stack. If there is something in it, the element at the start of the queue is removed like this:

return self.outbound_stack.pop()

If outbound_stack is empty, all the inbound_stack elements are moved over to outbound_stack and then the front element gets popped:

while self.inbound_stack:

  self.outbound_stack.append(self.inbound_stack.pop())

And the code will continue to be executed. The while loop will go on for as long as the inbound_stack contains elements. The self.inbound_stack.pop() statement will take the newest element added to inbound_stack and pop the data to the method call self.outbound_stack.append().

To start with, the inbound_stack had the elements of 5, 6, and 7 and after the while loop is executed the final line of dequeue() will return a result of 5 after the outbound_stack pop operation.

return self.outbound_stack.pop()

The outbound_stack now has just two elements in it 6, and 7.

When the next dequeue operation gets called, the while loop doesn't execute because outbound_stack does not contain any elements; this causes failure of the outer if statement. The pop()operation will be called immediately so that the element waiting for the longest in the queue is returned.

Below is a typical code used for running this kind of queue implementation:

queue = Queue()

queue.enqueue(5)

queue.enqueue(6)

queue.enqueue(7)

print(queue.inbound_stack)

queue.dequeue()

print(queue.inbound_stack)

print(queue.outbound_stack)

queue.dequeue()

print(queue.outbound_stack)

This code adds some elements into the queue and then prints all the elements contained in the queue. We call the dequeue() method and then we see a change to the element numbers when the queue gets printed again.

Node-Based Queues

It provides a great understanding of queues when Python lists are used for implementation. It is possible to implement our own data structure by making use of what we learned about pointer structures.

We can use doubly linked lists to implement queues and the deletion and insertion operations will both have a time complexity of O(1). The node class definition remains exactly the same as that as Node when we looked at the doubly linked lists and we can use this list as a queue, provided it follows the rules of FIFO for data-access.

The Queue Class

The queue class looks much like the doubly linked list class:

class Queue:

   def __init__(self):

     self.head = None

     self.tail = None

     self.count = 0

As soon as a queue class instance is created, the self.head and self.tail pointers will be set to None and the instance variable called count is maintained and set to 0 so the nodes in Queue can be counted.

Enqueue Operation

Again, we add the elements to the Queue object using enqueue(); in this case the elements are the nodes:

   def enqueue(self, data):

     new_node = Node(data, None, None)

     if self.head is None:

       self.head = new_node

       self.tail = self.head

     else:

       new_node.prev = self.tail

       self.tail.next = new_node

       self.tail = new_node

     self.count += 1

We already explained this code in doubly linked lists for the append operation – it is the same code. A node is created for the data that has been passed to the enqueue method and it is appended to the end of the queue; it will point self.head and self.tail to the new node only if we have an empty queue. And self.count +=1 increases the total element count.

Dequeue Operation

The dequeue() method is the other method to make a doubly linked list act as a queue; it is the method used to remove the first node in the queue. Removing the first element that is pointed to by self.head requires an if statement:

```
def dequeue(self):

    current = self.head

    if self.count == 1:

        self.count -= 1

        self.head = None

        self.tail = None

    elif self.count > 1:

        self.head = self.head.next

        self.head.prev = None

        self.count -= 1
```

Initialization of current is done by pointing it to self.head. If self.count is set as 1 there is a single node in the list and in the entire queue. To remove that node we set the variables of self.head and self.tail to None. If there are several nodes the head pointer will be moved to point at the next node of self.head.

Once the if statement has been run, the method will return the node that head pointed to. We decrement self.count by one in whichever way the execution path for the if statement flows.

Using these methods, we now have a queue that is heavily based on a doubly linked list.

In the next chapter, we will look at trees including major operations and the spheres in which the data structure is applied.

Chapter 10: Trees

Trees are a type of hierarchical data structure. When we looked at the lists, the stacks and queues, the items followed one another, but in a tree, we have a parent-child relationship between the items. To visualize a tree, imagine a real tree, growing in the ground. Now turn it upside down so the roots are at the top. Trees are drawn from the top down, so you would start with the root node at the top. The root node is from where all other nodes descend.

Trees can be used for all manner of things - searches and parsing expressions for starters. Some document types may be represented by trees too, like HTML and XLM. In this section, we will be looking at tree definitions and terms, binary trees, binary search trees, and tree traversal.

Tree Traversal

Here are some of the terms that surround trees:

- **Node -** a structure that holds data.
- **Root Node** – the node that all other nodes descend from.
- **Sub-Tree** – a tree that has nodes descending from the root node of another tree.
- **Degree** – how many sub-trees are from a node. A tree with one node has a 0 degree while a tree with two nodes would have a degree of 2.
- **Leaf Node** – a 0-degree node.
- **Edge** – the connection between a pair of nodes. On occasion, an edge may connect one node to itself, creating what looks like a loop.
- **Parent** – a node that has connecting nodes in the same tree.
- **Child** – a node connected to the parent node.
- **Sibling** – all the nodes that are connected to the same parent.
- **Level** – the number of connections that come from the root node to a given node.
- **Height** – how many levels are in the tree.
- **Depth** – how many edges there are from the root to the given node.

Tree Nodes

As in the other data structures that we have come across, a tree is constructed of nodes, but the difference is these nodes must each contain information relevant to the parent-child relationship. We'll start by using Python to build a binary tree node class:

class Node:

  def __init__(self, data):

    self.data = data

    self.right_child = None

    self.left_child = None

Nodes are containers that hold data and reference other nodes. Because this is a binary tree, the references go to the right and left children. Let's create some nodes and test the class:

n1 = Node("root node")

n2 = Node("left child node")

n3 = Node("right child node")

n4 = Node("left grandchild node")

The next step is connecting the nodes to one another. The root node is n1 and the children are n2 and n3. Then n4 is connected to n2 as the left child so that when the left sub-tree is traversed, we get some iterations:

n1.left_child = n2

n1.right_child = n3

n2.left_child = n4

Now the structure of the tree is set, and we can traverse the left sub-tree, print the mode, and move down to the next node (left). This continues until the left sub-tree has been traversed.

current = n1

while current:

   print(current.data)

   current = current.left_child

This needs a lot of client code work because the tree structure needs to be manually built.

Binary Trees

Binary trees consist of nodes that each have no more than two children. It is a common type of tree and it is what we will use to construct a Python binary search tree (BST) implementation. Each child is either the right or the left of the parent node and because the parent is also a node, each of the nodes refers to a left and right node even if they are not in existence.

There are no rules how elements are arranged in regular binary trees; it just needs to satisfy the condition that there are no more than two children per parent node.

Binary Search Trees (BST)

A BST is a special binary tree, one that is, in structural terms, a binary tree. In functional terms, nodes are stored in a way that the tree can be efficiently searched. BSTs do have a structure. For a node that has a value, all nodes from the left sub-tree are equal to or less than the value of the node. Right sub-tree nodes are greater than the value of the parent node.

Implementing BST

Let's start implementing a BST that holds a reference to the BST root node:

```
class Tree:

    def __init__(self):

        self.root_node = None
```

That simple piece of code maintains the tree's state so let's look at the fundamental operations.

BST Operations

To have a BST that is useful, there are two operations needed – insert and remove. Both operations must abide by the rule that they maintain the principle that provides the BST structure. Before we look at those two operations, there are some other operations that will help to understand them better.

Finding Min and Max Nodes

The BST structure makes it very easy to find the min and max nodes. To find the min, we traverse from the tree root and whenever we get to a sub-tree, we go to the left node. To find the max, we do the opposite and go the right node of each sub-tree. This also applies to find the min and max of a sub-tree. The method to return the min node is:

```
    def find_min(self):

        current = self.root_node

        while current.left_child:

            current = current.left_child


        return current
```

The while loop will carry on to obtain the left node until the final left node points at None. It really is very simple; to return the max node, current_left_child would be replaced with current_right_child. To find the min or max of a BST, it takes O(h) – h = the tree height.

Inserting Nodes

The insert operation is important as it is what allows data to be added as nodes. In our first implementation, we added the nodes manually but now we are going to give the tree the job of storing its own data. To make it possible to search, nodes need to be stored in certain ways. For each node, the left child will have data that is less than the node value while the right child's data will be greater than the parent.

We will create another BST, this time one of integers, beginning with the data 5. We need to create a node whose data attribute is set to 5. Then, we add another node with a value of 3 which will be compared with the root node. Because 5 is more than 3, it will be placed into the left sub-tree of the node 5.

This trees fully satisfies the BST rule of all left sub-tree nodes being less than the parent node.

Adding another node with a value of 7 requires starting from the root node of 5 and comparing the values. As 7 is greater than 5, the new node will go to the right of the root.

What would happen if the node we wanted to add was equal in value to a node that already exists? We would add it on the left and keep that rule maintained through the structure.

If a node has a child in the place where the new node is to be placed, we must traverse down the tree and attach it elsewhere.

Now we will add a further node with a value of 1 and, starting at the top again, we compare 5 and 1. As 1 is lower than 5, we look at the left node for 5, which has a value of 3. The comparison reveals that 1 is less than 3 and so we move to the level below and left of 3. There isn't a node, so we can create one with 1 as a value and then associate it with the left node of node 3.

So far, we have considered only the nodes that have numbers or integers as values. For the numbers, we have clearly defined ideas of lesser or greater than. A string comparison would be alphabetical so that wouldn't cause any issues either, but if you had custom data types that you wanted to store in a BST, you would need to ensure that the class had support for ordering.

Let's create the function that allows us to add nodes to the BST in the form of data; it starts with the declaration:

def insert(self, data):

We already know that the data must be encapsulated inside the node so that we can hide the node class from our client code or user who only needs to concentrate on the tree.

node = Node(data)

The first thing to check for is whether there is a root node; if not, since a tree must have a root node, the new node will become that root:

if self.root_node is None:

self.root_node = node

else:

As we traverse down the tree, we must track the node we are currently working on along with the parent node and we always use the variable called current to do this:

current = self.root_node

parent = None

while True:

parent = current

Now we perform the comparison. We need to see if the data in our new node is less than that of the current node before checking to see if the current node has got a left child. If not, the new node is inserted there or, if it does, we keep moving:

if node.data < current.data:

> *current = current.left_child*
>
> *if current is None:*
>
> > *parent.left_child = node*
> >
> > *return*

Lastly, we look for the case for greater than or equal to. If there is no right child with the current node, the new node is inserted there; otherwise, we need to keep moving and looking for another point:

> *else:*
>
> > *current = current.right_child*
> >
> > *if current is None:*
> >
> > > *parent.right_child = node*
> > >
> > > *return*

Inserting nodes into BSTs will take O(h) – h = tree height.

Deleting Nodes

Removal of nodes is another very important operation and there are three possible scenarios that we need to take into account when we do it. The node for deletion may not have any children, it may have one child, or it may have two. No children is definitely the easiest to deal with; all we do is detach the node from the parent.

If we want to remove a node that has a single child, the parent must point to the child of the node for removal. It is important to preserve the parent-child relationship which is why we need to take note of the way in which the two are connected. The child node for the parent node that was deleted will be stored and then the parent node of the deleted one is connected to the stored child node.

Things get more complicated when there are two children connected to the parent node. We can't, for example, replace the node with the 9 value with that of 6 or 13 so we need to find the next largest descendent; in our case, this would be 12. To get to 12, we go to the right side of 9 and then we go left to the node at the outermost left. 12 is known as the "in-order successor" of 9 and step two is representative of the moves needed to find the max node in the sub-tree.

So, 9 is replaced with 12 and 12 is removed. By doing this, we are left with an earlier form of removal; 12 doesn't have any children so the first rule of removal will apply.

The node class has no parent reference and that means we need a helper method to find the node and return it with its parent. This is much the same as the search() method:

```
def get_node_with_parent(self, data):

    parent = None

    current = self.root_node

    if current is None:

        return (parent, None)

    while True:

        if current.data == data:

            return (parent, current)

        elif current.data > data:

            parent = current

            current = current.left_child

        else:

            parent = current
```

```
        current = current.right_child


    return (parent, current)
```

The difference is, before the current variable can be updated in the loop, the parent is stored using parent=current. The removal of the node starts with the code below:

```
def remove(self, data):

    parent, node = self.get_node_with_parent(data)


    if parent is None and node is None:

        return False


    # Get children count

    children_count = 0


    if node.left_child and node.right_child:

        children_count = 2

    elif (node.left_child is None) and (node.right_child is None):

        children_count = 0

    else:

        children_count = 1
```

The parent is passed to parent and the node we found is passed to node, using parent, node = self.get_node_with_parent.data. As always, we need to know how many children there are in the node for deletion and that is why we use the if statement.

After we do this, we must start handling the conditions that govern the deletion of a node. The first bit of the if statement handles the situation where there are no children:

> *if children_count == 0:*
>
>> *if parent:*
>>
>>> *if parent.right_child is node:*
>>>
>>>> *parent.right_child = None*
>>>
>>> *else:*
>>>
>>>> *parent.left_child = None*
>>
>> *else:*
>>
>>> *self.root_node = None*

When the BST has just one node, we can use if.parent.

Where the node for deletion has a single child, the elif bit of the statement will do this:

> *elif children_count == 1:*
>
>> *next_node = None*
>>
>> *if node.left_child:*
>>
>>> *next_node = node.left_child*
>>
>> *else:*
>>
>>> *next_node = node.right_child*

```
        if parent:

            if parent.left_child is node:

                parent.left_child = next_node

            else:

                parent.right_child = next_node

        else:

            self.root_node = next_node
```

We use next_node to track the position of the single node that the node for removal points to; we can then make the connection between parent.left_child or parent.right_child to the next_node.

The last thing we do is handle a condition when the node for deletion has two children:

```
    ...
    else:

        parent_of_leftmost_node = node

        leftmost_node = node.right_child

        while leftmost_node.left_child:

            parent_of_leftmost_node = leftmost_node

            leftmost_node = leftmost_node.left_child


        node.data = leftmost_node.data
```

We move over to the right-hand node using leftmost_node = node.right_child to find the 'in order successor'. So long as a left node exists, leftmost_node.left_child is always going to return True and the while loop will continue running. When we reach the leftmost node, it will either have a right child or it will be a leaf node, which means there are no children.

The node that is to be removed is updated with the in-order successor value using node.data = leftmost_node.data:

if parent_of_leftmost_node.left_child == leftmost_node:

parent_of_leftmost_node.left_child = leftmost_node.right_child

else:

parent_of_leftmost_node.right_child = leftmost_node.right_child

This statement lets us attach the leftmost node parent to any child node. What is on the right of the = remains unchanged – this is because the in-order successor is only able to have a right child.

The remove() operation will take O(h) – height = tree height.

Searching a Tree

Because the insert method will organize the data specifically, we use the same kind of procedure to find data. In the following implementation, if the data is found, we will return it; if not, None will be returned:

def search(self, data):

Our search must start at the root node:

current = self.root_node

while True:

If we passed a leaf node, the tree will not have the data and None is returned to the user:

if current is None:

return None

If we found the data, it will be returned:

```
elif current.data is data:
    return data
```

Going by the rules of data storage in the BST, if the data we want to find is less than the current node, we traverse the left of the tree:

```
elif current.data > data:
    current = current.left_child
```

We have one option left; if the data is more than that in the current node, we traverse the right of the tree:

```
else:
    current = current.right_child
```

We can now write the code to test the BST. The tree is created, a few numbers inserted and then we run a search for numbers within the range. Those that exist will be printed:

```
tree = Tree()

tree.insert(5)

tree.insert(2)

tree.insert(7)

tree.insert(9)

tree.insert(1)


for i in range(1, 10):
    found = tree.search(i)
```

print("{}: {}".format(i, found))

We can traverse the nodes in a tree in one of two ways – breadth-first or depth-first. These traversal modes are for all trees in general, not just BSTs.

Depth-First Traversal

In this mode, an edge or branch is followed to its very limit before it recoils and continues transversal upwards. We will make use of a recursive approach for this traversal.

Depth-first traversal takes three separate forms:

- In-Order
- Pre-Order
- Post-Order

We'll look at all three in turn.

In-Order Traversal with Infix Notation

Most people are used to using this form of arithmetic expression because this is how the schools teach us. We insert an operator (infix notation) in between the operands, for example, 5 + 9. Where needed, we can create more complex expressions using parentheses, for example, (5 + 9) * (8 − 4).

In this traversal mode, the left sub-tree would be visited first, then the parent, and then the right sub-tree. The recursive function that we use for returning in-order node listings is like this:

```
def inorder(self, root_node):

    current = root_node

    if current is None:

        return

    self.inorder(current.left_child)

    print(current.data)
```

self.inorder(current.right_child)

To visit the node, we print it and then we make two recursive calls using current.left_child and current.right_child.

Pre-Order Traversal with Prefix Notation

We commonly refer to prefix notation as Polish notation; the operator is placed before the operands, for example, + 5 9. Because there is none of the ambiguity surrounding the precedence, we don't need to use any parentheses - * + 5 9 − 8 4.

Traversing a tree in pre-order mode involves visiting the node, the left sub-tree, then the parent and the right sub-tree, in that particular order.

The recursive function used in this type of traversal would look like this:

def preorder(self, root_node):

   current = root_node

   if current is None:

     return

   print(current.data)

   self.preorder(current.left_child)

   self.preorder(current.right_child)

Pay special attention to what order the recursive call is made in.

Post-Order Traversal with Postfix Notation

Postfix notation, better known as Reverse Polish Notation, will put the operands first and then the operator, for example, 5 9 +. As we saw with Polish notation, operator precedence is not in any doubt, so we can dispense with the parentheses, for example, 5 9 + 8 4 - *.

The order of traversal is left sub-tree, right sub-tree and then the node.

The method for the post-order traversal is:

```
def postorder(self, root_node):

    current = root_node

    if current is None:

        return

    self.postorder(current.left_child)

    self.postorder(current.right_child)


    print(current.data)
```

Breadth-First Traversal

Breadth-first traversal begins at the root and goes to the node from one tree level to the other. Let's say that the level 1 node is 4; we can visit this by printing the value. Then we go to all the nodes on the next level, in this case, 2 and 8. Lastly, on level three, we go to the nodes called 1, 3, 5, and 10. The output would be 4, 2, 8, 1, 3, 5, 10.

We use a queue data structure to do this type of traversal. We first push the root node into a queue. The node that is at the start of the queue is dequeued and printed or stored. The left then right nodes get added in that order and, because we do not have an empty queue, we continue with the process.

If we do a dry run of this algorithm, root node 4 gets enqueued then dequeued and then accessed. As 2 and 8 are the left and the right nodes, they are enqueued; 2 is dequeued so it can be accessed. The left and right nodes of 2, which are 1 and 3, then get enqueued. The first node in the queue is 8 which will be dequeued and accessed, followed by the enqueueing of the left node and right nodes. This process will carry on until the queue has been emptied.

The algorithm is:

```python
from collections import deque

class Tree:

    def breadth_first_traversal(self):

        list_of_nodes = []

        traversal_queue = deque([self.root_node])
```

The root node is enqueued and a list of the visited nodes kept stored in list_of_nodes. The queue is maintained using the dequeue class:

```python
        while len(traversal_queue) > 0:

            node = traversal_queue.popleft()

            list_of_nodes.append(node.data)


            if node.left_child:

                traversal_queue.append(node.left_child)


            if node.right_child:

                traversal_queue.append(node.right_child)

        return list_of_nodes
```

If there are more elements in traversal_queue than zero, the loop body will be executed. The first node in the queue is popped off and is then appended to the list_of_nodes. The first of the if statements enqueue the left child of the node should that left node exist. The next if statement repeats that for the right child and the last statement will return the list_of_nodes.

Parsing Reverse Polish Expressions

The next tree we will build is one written in postfix notation and we will calculate the result. The implementation will be kept simple; we are going to grow this tree by using a number of smaller trees, so we only need to implement the tree node:

class TreeNode:

   def __init__(self, data=None):

     self.data = data

     self.right = None

     self.left = None

We will use a stack to build our tree and it will be clear why shortly. For now, we will create a relevant arithmetic expression and set the stack up:

expr = "4 5 + 5 3 - *".split()

stack = Stack()

Because Python has sensible defaults, the split() method will split, by default on whitespace. The result will be that expr ends up as a list that has values of 4, 5, +, 5, 3, -, *.

Each of the elements in expr will be one of two things – an operand or an operator. If it is an operand, it is embedded in a tree node and pushed to the stack. If it is an operator, it is embedded in a tree node and then the two operands that go with it are popped to the left and right children of the node.

The code to build this tree is:

for term in expr:

   if term in "+-*/":

     node = TreeNode(term)

```
    node.right = stack.pop()

    node.left = stack.pop()

  else:

    node = TreeNode(int(term))

  stack.push(node)
```

The conversion is performed from string to int where operands are concerned. In the end, there should be just one element in the stack and that is what holds the entire tree.

Now, we might want to evaluate this expression, so we use this function to help us:

```
def calc(node):

  if node.data is "+":

    return calc(node.left) + calc(node.right)

  elif node.data is "-":

    return calc(node.left) - calc(node.right)

  elif node.data is "*":

    return calc(node.left) * calc(node.right)

  elif node.data is "/":

    return calc(node.left) / calc(node.right)

  else:

    return node.data
```

This is a simple function. A node is passed in; if it has an operand, the value of it is returned. If it has an operator, the operation represented by that operator is performed on the children of the node. However, one or both of those children may also contain an operator or operand so we need to call the function called calc() recursively on the child nodes. Keep in mind that all the children of all of the nodes are also nodes.

Now, the root node is popped off and passed to calc() and the calculation result is:

root = stack.pop()

result = calc(root)

print(result)

We should get a result of 18 = (4 + 5) * (5 − 3).

Balancing a Tree

We said earlier that, provided all the nodes get inserted in a sequential order, the tree acts like a list with each node having one child. Normally, we want the tree height as small as possible, so we make sure each row is filled. We call this 'balancing'.

There are several types of self-balancing tree, like AA trees, red-black trees, and scapegoat trees and each of these balances the tree every time an operation is performed to modify the tree, operations like delete and insert.

Then there are some external algorithms that also balance trees and the benefit of using these is that we don't need to balance every time we do an operation; instead, the balancing is left until it really needs to be done.

Heaps

It's time to introduce a type of data structure called a heap. This is a tree specialization in which all the nodes are in a specific order. Heaps are divided in two – min and max. In the min heap, the parent nodes must be the same as or less than both children and the root node will hold the lowest value. By contrast, in a max heap, the parent nodes are the same as or greater than the children, so the root node holds the greatest value.

Next, we move on to graphs and other algorithms.

Chapter 11: Graphs and Other Algorithms

Graphs are a concept that descends from a branch of math called graph theory and they are used to solve all sorts of computing problems. A graph has less structure than the other data structures we looked at and traversal is somewhat more unconventional.

By the time this section is done you will:

- Understand what a graph is
- Understand the different types of graph and their constituents
- Know how to represent and traverse a graph
- Understand priority queues and how to implement them
- Be able to determine what the ith smallest element is in a list

Graphs

A graph is nothing more than a set of vertices and the edges that form the connections between those vertices. More formally, graphs G are ordered pairs of sets of vertices V and a set of edges E. The formal notation is G = (V, E). The following are some graph definitions:

- **Vertex or Node** – a point in a graph normally represented by a dot.
- **Edge** – the connection between a pair of vertices.
- **Loop** – when a node edge is an incident on itself, it forms a loop.
- **Degree of a Vertex** – the number of vertices incident on a specific vertex.
- **Adjacency** – the connection between nodes and their neighbors.
- **Path** – vertices sequence where an edge connects each adjacent pair.

Direct and Undirected Graphs

Classification of graphs is based on whether they are directed or undirected. The undirected graph edges are represented as lines between nodes. We are not given any extra information regarding the relationship between those nodes; all we know is that they are connected.

With a directed graph, as well as connecting the nodes, the edges also provide orientation which means the edges are drawn as lines with arrows that point to the direction in which the edges connect the nodes.

Weighted Graphs

Weighted graphs provide the edges with a bit more information; this may be a numerical value that has a meaning. For example, let's say that we want to go from A to D. There are several ways to do it; we could go straight there, we can pass through B, C or both. The information associated with each of the edges tells us how long the journey will take to the next node. The journey AD could require us to walk or ride a bicycle; B and C may be indicative of train stations; when we get to B, we would need to change trains to go on to C. Lastly, CD might indicate a short walk between the two points.

In the example we use, AD and ABCD are two separate paths and a path is nothing more than a sequence of edges that must be passed through between the nodes. We could say that going AD takes 40 minutes while going ABCD takes just 25 minutes. If time is your only concern, then the second path is your best bet, even having to change trains.

The sheer fact that these edges may be directed, along with the extra information they hold is quite interesting. In the data structures we looked at earlier, the lines that were drawn between the nodes were nothing more than connectors; even when arrows were used for pointing to a node, we could easily represent that in our node class using parent OR child, or next OR previous. With a graph, it is sensible to see both the nodes and the edges as objects; like a node and edge have the additional information needed to follow a path.

Graph Representation

We can interpret a graph in two fundamental forms – an adjacency matrix and an adjacency list. We'll start with the list.

Adjacency List

We can present a graph using a simple list; the list indices are representative of the vertices or nodes of the graph. At every index, we store the vertex's adjacent nodes. However, lists can be restrictive because we have no way of using the vertex labels directly. A dictionary is far more suitable, and we could use these statements to represent a graph:

graph = dict()

graph['A'] = ['B', 'C']

graph['B'] = ['E','A']

graph['C'] = ['A', 'B', 'E','F']

graph['E'] = ['B', 'C']

graph['F'] = ['C']

Now we can see that vertex A has two adjacent vertices, B and C while F only has one neighbor, C.

Adjacency Matrix

The adjacency matrix is another way of representing a graph. Matrices are 2D arrays and the idea is for the cells to be represented with either a 0 or a 1, depending on whether an edge connects two vertices. To create the adjacency matrix, we use a sorted list containing graph keys:

matrix_elements = sorted(graph.keys())

cols = rows = len(matrix_elements)

The matrix dimensions are provided by the length of the keys and those dimensions are stored in cols and rows; the values in these are equal:

adjacency_matrix = [[0 for x in range(rows)] for y in range(cols)]

edges_list = []

Next, an array of cols by rows is set up, filled with zeros. The variable called edges_list stores the tuples that make up the graph edges. An example of this would be the edge between A and B – this would be stored as (A, B).

A nested for loop is used for filling the multidimensional array:

for key in matrix_elements:

  for neighbor in graph[key]:

    edges_list.append((key,neighbor))

We use graph[key] to obtain the neighbors of a given vertex and this key together with neighbor is used for creating the tuple that edges_list stores. The iteration will output the following:

```
>>> [('A', 'B'), ('A', 'C'), ('B', 'E'), ('B', 'A'), ('C', 'A'),
    ('C', 'B'), ('C', 'E'), ('C', 'F'), ('E', 'B'), ('E', 'C'),
    ('F', 'C')]
```

What we need to do now is complete the multidimensional array and we do this with a 1 marking an edge using this code line:

adjacency_matrix[index_of_first_vertex][index_of_second_vertex] = 1:

for edge in edges_list:

  index_of_first_vertex = matrix_elements.index(edge[0])

  index_of_second_vertex = matrix_elements.index(edge[1])

  adjacency_matrix[index_of_first_vertex][index_of_second_vertex] = 1

The rows and cols in the array called matrix_elements run from A to E, indices 0 to 5. The tuples list is iterated through using a for loop and the index() method used for obtaining the corresponding index where the edge will be stored.

The adjacency matrix will look like this:

```
>>>
[0, 1, 1, 0, 0]
[1, 0, 0, 1, 0]
[1, 1, 0, 1, 1]
```

[0, 1, 1, 0, 0]
[0, 0, 1, 0, 0]

The 0 at col 1, row 1 represents the fact that there is no edge in between A and A, whereas the 1 at col 2, row 3 indicates that C and B do have an edge between them.

Traversing Graphs

Because a graph doesn't really have an ordered structure, traversal is a little more involved. Normally, traversal requires us to track the vertices or the nodes we already visited as well as those which haven't been visited. One strategy which is common is to follow a path to a dead end, back up, and go back until another path is found. It is also possible to move from one node to another iteratively as a way of traversing some or all the graph. We'll be looking at two graph traversal algorithms – breadth-first and depth-first.

Breadth-First

The breadth-first algorithm begins at one node, choosing it as the root, and then going to the neighboring nodes; it then moves to the neighbors on the next graph level and so on. An example of an adjacency list for a graph would be:

graph = dict()

graph['A'] = ['B', 'G', 'D']

graph['B'] = ['A', 'F', 'E']

graph['C'] = ['F', 'H']

graph['D'] = ['F', 'A']

graph['E'] = ['B', 'G']

graph['F'] = ['B', 'D', 'C']

graph['G'] = ['A', 'E']

graph['H'] = ['C']

To use breadth-first traversal, we use a queue. A list is created for storing the nodes that are visited throughout the traversal. We will begin, as an example, from the node called A.

A is added to the queue and to the list of nodes visited. A while loop would then be used to start graph traversal. In that loop, A is dequeued. The adjacent nodes of B, G, and D, as yet unvisited, are sorted into alphabetical order and added to the queue, in the order of B, D, G. They also are put in the list of visited nodes. The while loop iterates once more because we do not have an empty queue and that means we are not finished with the traversal.

B gets dequeued; it has three adjacent nodes – A, F, E. We already visited A, so only E and F are added to the queue in alphabetical order. E and F are also added to the visited nodes list. At this point, the queue holds D, G, E, F, while the visited node list holds A, B, D, G, E, F.

D is the next to be added to the queue, but it can be dequeued straightaway because we already visited all the adjacent nodes. G is also enqueued and then dequeued for the same reason. F is the only node left in the queue.

F is dequeued and we can see that of all the nodes adjacent to F, only C remains unvisited. C is enqueued; it has two nodes adjacent to it – F, H. We already visited F so we enqueue H and add it to the list of the nodes visited.

Lastly, the while loop will iterate leading to H being dequeued. C is the only adjacent node and that has been visited; the queue is empty, the while loop breaks.

The Python code for the breadth-first search algorithm is:

from collections import deque

def breadth_first_search(graph, root):

  visited_vertices = list()

  graph_queue = deque([root])

visited_vertices.append(root)

node = root

while len(graph_queue) > 0:

  node = graph_queue.popleft()

  adj_nodes = graph[node]

  remaining_elements = set(adj_nodes).difference(set(visited_vertices))

  if len(remaining_elements) > 0:

    for elem in sorted(remaining_elements):

      visited_vertices.append(elem)

      graph_queue.append(elem)

  return visited_vertices

If we used the Worst-Case Scenario, each of the nodes would be traversed and the time complexity would be $O(|V| + |E|) - V$ = vertices and E = Edges.

Depth-First

As the name indicates, the depth-first algorithm traverses a given path by depth before it traverses the breadth. Because of this, the child nodes are seen before the sibling nodes. This algorithm works well on finite graphs and a stack is required to maintain the algorithm state:

def depth_first_search(graph, root):

  visited_vertices = list()

```
graph_stack = list()


graph_stack.append(root)

node = root
```

The depth-first algorithm starts by creating a list to which all the visited nodes are stored. To help with traversal, we use graph_stack and, for the sake of continuity, our stack is a normal Python list. The root node is passed along with the adjacency matrix and graph.root is passed to the stack. The first node that is on our stack is held in node=root.

```
def depth_first_search(graph, root):

    visited_vertices = list()

    graph_stack = list()


    graph_stack.append(root)

    node = root

    while len(graph_stack) > 0:


        if node not in visited_vertices:

            visited_vertices.append(node)


        adj_nodes = graph[node]


        if set(adj_nodes).issubset(set(visited_vertices)):
```

```
    graph_stack.pop()
  if len(graph_stack) > 0:
    node = graph_stack[-1]
    continue
  else:
    remaining_elements = set(adj_nodes).difference(set(visited_vertices))



  first_adj_node = sorted(remaining_elements)[0]
  graph_stack.append(first_adj_node)
  node = first_adj_node
  return visited_vertices
```

The while loop body is executed so long as the stack isn't empty. If node is not included in the visited nodes list, we add it in. To collect all the nodes adjacent to node, we use adj_nodes=graph[node]; if they have all been visited, that node is popped from the stack and node is set to graph_stack[-1] – this is the first node of the stack. The continue statement goes back to the start of the test condition in the while loop.

If some of the adjacent nodes have not been visited, we need to get them and we do this by comparing adj_nodes and visited_vertices with:

remaining_elements=set(adj_nodes).difference(set(visited_vertices)) statement to find the difference. The first item that appears in sorted(remaining_elements) is assigned to first_adj_nodes and is pushed to the stack; the top of the stack then is pointed to the node.

When the while loop is in existence, visited_vertices is returned.

An example of an adjacency list of a graph would be as follows:

graph = dict()

graph['A'] = ['B', 'S']

graph['B'] = ['A']

graph['S'] = ['A','G','C']

graph['D'] = ['C']

graph['G'] = ['S','F','H']

graph['H'] = ['G','E']

graph['E'] = ['C','H']

graph['F'] = ['C','G']

graph['C'] = ['D','S','E','F']

The beginning node is A which is pushed to the stack and then added to the list called visited_vertices. Doing this marks the node as visited. A Python list is used to implement graph_stack. The stack has one element, A, whose adjacent nodes are examined – these are B and S. To test whether they have been visited or not, the if statement is used:

   if set(adj_nodes).issubset(set(visited_vertices)):

     graph_stack.pop()

     if len(graph_stack) > 0:

       node = graph_stack[-1]

     continue

The top of the stack is popped off if all the nodes have been visited, but if graph_stack isn't empty, the node at the top of the stack is assigned to node and the while loop starts another iteration. If all of the nodes present in adj_nodes are a subset of visited_vertices, then set(adj_nodes).issubset(set(visited_vertices)) evaluates True. If we see a failure of the if statement, there are still some nodes that are to be visited and we can get a list of those nodes by using:

remaining_elements=set(adj_nodes).difference(set(visited_vertices)).

The list of nodes would be accessed in alphabetical order:

first_adj_node = sorted(remaining_elements)[0]

graph_stack.append(first_adj_node)

node = first_adj_node

The remaining_elements is sorted, and the first node is returned to adj_node. The returned node is appended to graph_stack, thus pushing it onto the stack and is assigned to node to prepare it for access.

When the while loop iterates again, the node is added to the visited nodes list and the only adjacent node has already been visited. The node is popped off the stack leaving the adjacent node on the stack. This is returned and examined to see if all adjacent nodes have been visited; if it has one that hasn't been visited, this is pushed to the stack and we start over.

Depth-first algorithm searches tend to be used in applications to find connected components, solving maze problems, finding graph bridges and so on.

More Useful Graph Methods

Mostly, a path is wanted that is between a pair of nodes, but sometimes, all the paths between them may be wanted to be discovered. One method that is useful would be to find the shortest path and with an unweighted graph, that path would be the one with the least amount of edges between the nodes. With a weighted graph, we might need to calculate the total weight passing through the whole set of edges.

Another situation may require finding either the shortest or the longest path. The customer waiting times are 4, 30, 2 and 1 so the average waiting time is (4+34+36+37)/4, resulting in 27.75. However, let's say that the order of service is changed so that those waiting the least amount of time are served first; that gives us a new average waiting time. To calculate it, we now do this (1+3+7+37)/4 and this gives a new waiting time of 12, which is much better. There is clearly some merit in serving those who have waited the least amount of time first. The method of using priority to choose the next item or perhaps some other criterion is on which priority queues are based.

Heaps are data structures used to satisfy the heap property; this property states that parent and child nodes require a certain relationship and the property needs to apply through the entire heap. With a min heap, that relationship is the parent must always be less than or the same as the child, so the root node must be the lowest. In a max heap, it's the opposite; the parent is higher than or the same as the child and, as such, the root node is the largest.

The heap is a type of binary tree, but we are going to use a list to represent the tree. We can do this because a complete binary tree may be stored in a heap. A complete binary tree is a tree in which each row of the tree must be entirely filled before the next tree can be started.

We are going to make things easier; the first item in our list at index 0 is going to be left empty. Then the tree nodes will be placed into the list from left to right, top to bottom. We'll start by looking at an implementation of a min heap; it won't be too hard to reverse the logic to get a max heap:

class Heap:

   def __init__(self):

      self.heap = [0]

      self.size = 0

The heap list is initialized with a zero, which represents the first element. A variable is created to hold the heap size; this isn't normally necessary because we can easily determine a list size, but we would need to keep reducing it by one, so it is easier to use a separate variable.

Inserting

It is a very simple job to insert an item; the new element is added to the end of the list and the heap is incremented by the size of one. However, after each element has been inserted, the new element may need to be floated up. To do this, we need a helper method named float. This is how it is meant to work. We want to insert a value into our heap. When the new element has been slotted in it is compared with its parent. We divide the index value of the new element by its actual value to give us the index of the parent. The element at that index is higher in value than the new element so they are swapped. The new element moves up a level and this will continue until we get to the top of the heap. The following shows an implementation of this:

```
def float(self, k):
```

We continue to loop until we get to the root node; this allows us to keep floating the element upwards until it gets as high as it needs to be. Because integer division is used, once we drop below 2, the loop breaks out:

```
while k // 2 > 0:
```

Next, parent and child are compared and, if the parent is greater than the child, the two values are swapped:

```
if self.heap[k] < self.heap[k//2]:

    self.heap[k], self.heap[k//2] = self.heap[k//2], self.heap[k]
```

Lastly, we move up the tree:

```
k //= 2
```

Using this method, we can ensure that the elements are properly ordered; all that's left to do is call it from the insert method:

```
def insert(self, item):

  self.heap.append(item)

  self.size += 1
```

self.float(self.size)

The final line in the insert method is calling the float() method so the heap can be reorganized as needed.

POP

As with insert, the pop() method is simple. The root node is removed and the heap size is decremented by one. However, when the root has been popped off, a new root node is required. We'll make this simple; the final item in our list is made into the root – we move it to the start. However, that means the lowest value may not now be the root, so we need to do the opposite of float and allow the root to sink as needed.

Let's see how this works. When the root node is popped off, we have a rootless heap. We can't have this; if we move a child up, the whole tree will need to be rebalanced somehow, so we'll do something very different instead. We will take the final element of the list and move it up to take the position of the root node.

In the very likely event that this is not the lowest value in the heap, we need to sink it and first we need to work out where to sink it. The two children are compared to ensure that the one with the lowest element floats up as the root sinks.

For argument's sake, we'll say that the child on the right has the lowest value so we now compare the new root with this value. The node jumps down and we must now compare it with the lower of the children. We only have one child here so there aren't any issues and there is no need to swap. If there is just one row then that's it, all done. We can now implement the sink() method, but before we do, we must work out to which child the parent node is to be compared. We can do that like this:

def minindex(self, k):

If we wind up going past the end of the list, the index of the left child is returned:

*if k * 2 + 1 > self.size:*

> *return k * 2*

Otherwise, the index of the lesser child is returned:

> *elif self.heap[k*2] < self.heap[k*2+1]:*
>
> > *return k * 2*
>
> *else:*
>
> > *return k * 2 + 1*

Now the sink() function can be created:

> *def sink(self, k):*

Like we did before, we use a while loop so that the element can be sunk as low as needed:

> *while k * 2 <= self.size:*

Next, we need to determine which child to compare against – left or right. This is where minindex() function comes in:

> *mi = self.minindex(k)*

As with float(), the parent and child are compared to see where the swap needs to happen:

> *if self.heap[k] > self.heap[mi]:*
>
> > *self.heap[k], self.heap[mi] = self.heap[mi], self.heap[k]*

And we also need to ensure that we don't get stuck in the loop, so we move down the tree:

> *k = mi*

The last thing to do is implement pop(). This is easy because the sink() method does most of the hard work:

> *def pop(self):*

```
    item = self.heap[1]

    self.heap[1] = self.heap[self.size]

    self.size -= 1

    self.heap.pop()

    self.sink(1)

    return item
```

Testing the Heap

Next, we need a piece of code that will test our heap. We create the heap and we insert some data into it:

```
h = Heap()

for i in (4, 8, 7, 2, 9, 10, 5, 1, 3, 6):

    h.insert(i)
```

The heap list can be printed so we can see the order the elements are in. If this were redrawn in a tree structure, it would be evident that it meets all the properties needed for a heap:

```
    print(h.heap)
```

Now we pop the items off individually. The items will be sorted from low to high. Notice after each of the pops, the heap list will change. As we go through this, draw this using pen and paper, as a tree after each of the pops to gain a better understanding of the way sink() works:

```
for i in range(10):

    n = h.pop()

    print(n)

    print(h.heap)
```

Once our min heap works as it should and you have a good understanding of the way it works, try to reverse the logic and implement a max heap.

For the last part of this section, we will concentrate more on algorithms, as this will lead us to Part 2, Machine Learning.

Chapter 12: Sorting Algorithms

When data is collected, it needs to be sorted and, for that, we have a selection of sorting algorithms:

- Bubble
- Insertion
- Selection
- Quick
- Heap

We will consider the asymptotic behavior of these algorithms as we work with them. Some can be developed easily but may not perform very well, while others that require a bit more work to develop may perform impressively. We'll start at the top and work our way down the list.

Bubble Sort

Bubble sorting is a relatively simple idea; with a list that is unordered, the adjacent elements are compared, and with each comparison, they are placed in order of magnitude – just two elements at a time. The entire algorithm relies on a swap procedure.

We will start with a list that has just two elements – 5 at index 0, and 2 at index 1. To sort this, the two elements are swapped so 2 is now at index 0 and 5 is at index 1. To swap them, a temporary storage area is required.

Implementing the bubble sort algorithm begins with swap(). Element 5 is copied to temp, a temporary storage location. Element 2 then is moved so it occupies index 0 and 5 is then removed from temp and placed at index 1. The result is the elements have been swapped and the list is now sorted in order.

The code below swaps the elements in unordered_list[j] with unordered_list[j+1] if they are in the wrong order:

temp = unordered_list[j]

unordered_list[j] = unordered_list[j+1]

unordered_list[j+1] = temp

Now we know how to swap an array with two elements, it isn't too difficult to do this on an entire list. We'll use the swap operation to sort a double-nested loop. The inner loop is:

for j in range(iteration_number):

  if unordered_list[j] > unordered_list[j+1]:

    temp = unordered_list[j]

    unordered_list[j] = unordered_list[j+1]

    unordered_list[j+1] = temp

When we use the bubble sort algorithm it is important to know how many swaps are needed. For example, with an array of [3, 2, 1], no more than two swaps are needed, equal to the list length minus 1 – iteration_number=len(unordered_list)-1. We need to subtract 1 because it will tell us the greatest number of iterations that will need to run. If we swap the adjacent elements twice, we get the largest number occupying the last index. To ensure that we don't get any unnecessary swaps for elements that are already ordered correctly, we use the if statement. The inner for loop will only allow adjacent elements to be swapped twice in the list we are using.

However, when the for loop runs for the first time, it doesn't entirely sort the list. How many times do we need to swap for this to happen? That depends on how big the list is and to make the swapping process happen as it should, we use an outer loop. To sort our list, we need 4 comparisons so the inner and the outer loops must run len(unordered_list)-1 times to sort all the elements:

iteration_number = len(unordered_list)-1

for i in range(iteration_number):

  for j in range(iteration_number):

    if unordered_list[j] > unordered_list[j+1]:

temp = unordered_list[j]

unordered_list[j] = unordered_list[j+1]

unordered_list[j+1] = temp

We use this principle regardless of how many elements are in a list.

Bubble sort is not the most efficient of algorithms, showing a time complexity of $O(n2)$ and it shouldn't be used on large lists. For small lists, it is fine.

Insertion Sort

We can use the principle of swapping elements for sorting to implement the next algorithm, insertion sort. With this algorithm, we start by assuming that part of the list is sorted while the remainder isn't. We can move through the part that isn't sorted choosing one element at a time. That element is used to go through the sorted part of the list and place it in the correct position so that the sorted part stays in a sorted order. To make it simpler:

Index   **Element**

Index	Element
0	5
1	1
2	100
3	2
4	10

The algorithm begins with a for loop that goes between index 1 and index 4. We are beginning at 1 because we have assumed that the sub-array at 0 has already been executed.

At the start of the loop execution we have:

for index in range(1, len(unsorted_list)):

    search_index = index

    insert_value = unsorted_list[index]

When the for loop starts an iteration, the unsorted_list[index] element is stored in the variable called insert_value. Later, when the right position has been found in the sorted part we store insert_value at that location:

for index in range(1, len(unsorted_list)):

   search_index = index

   insert_value = unsorted_list[index]

   while search_index > 0 and unsorted_list[search_index-1] >

     insert_value :

    unsorted_list[search_index] = unsorted_list[search_index-1]

    search_index -= 1

   unsorted_list[search_index] = insert_value

We use search_index to give the while loop information on where to find the element to insert into the list in the sorted part. The while loop will traverse through the list backward and it is guided by a pair of conditions. The first one is that if search_index=0, there are a greater number of elements in the sorted part of the list. Second, to make the while loop run unsorted_list[search_index-1] needs to be greater than insert_value. The unsorted_list array will do one of two things:

1. It will point to the element that comes just ahead of unsorted_list[search_index] before the first execution of the while loop
2. It will point to one of the elements just before unsorted_list[search_index-1] after the first execution of the while loop.

In our example, because 5>1, the while loop is executed. In the while loop body, the element from unsorted_index[search_index-1] stored at unsorted_list[search_index] and search_index -=1 moves the traversal of the list backward until it has a value of 0.

We now have a list of 5, 5, 100, 2, 10.

Once the while loop has exited, we can now use the last position of search_index, in our case it is 0, to help us know where insert_value needs to be inserted.

When the for loop does its second iteration, search_index has 2 as its value; this is the index of the third element array. Now we can begin to compare left, toward the 0 index; 100 is compared to 5; because 100>5, the while loop is not executed; 100 replaces itself because the variable of search_index wasn't decremented and that means unsorted_list[search_index]=insert_value has no effect whatsoever.

When search_index points to index 3, 2 is compared with 100 and 100 is moved to where 2 was stored; 2 then is compared with 5, which is moved to where 100 was originally stored. Now the while loop breaks and 2 is stored at index 1. The array is partially sorted holding the values [1, 2, 5, 100, 10].

For the list to be sorted entirely, the last step will happen one more time.

This algorithm is one of the more stable because it doesn't make any changes to the relative order of those elements with equal keys. It also doesn't require any more memory than what the list consumes because the swapping of values is done in place.

The worst-case value is $O(n^2)$ while best case value is $O(n)$.

Selection Sort

Selection sort is another popular algorithm; it is one of the simplest to understand but it isn't efficient, having asymptotic values for both best and worst-case of $O(n^2)$. Selection sort starts by locating the smallest element in the given array and then interchanges it with data from another array index, for example, index [0]. That operation is repeated but this time the smallest element in the remains of the list is interchanged with index [1] data. Let's look at our list with index numbers:

[Number 5 22 65 10]

[Index 0 1 2 3]

Beginning at index 0, we look through the list for the smallest item between index1 and the last index with a value in it. When that element is found, it is swapped with the value at index 0 and this is repeated until the list is in a sorted order.

The process of searching for the list's smallest element is incremental. Elements 2 and 5 are compared and 2 is chosen as the smaller; the elements are swapped. Afterward, our array looks like:

[Number 2 5 65 10]

Remaining at index 0, 2 is compared with 6 and because 65 is the bigger number, they are not swapped; 2 is then compared with 10 and again, there is no swap. Once we have compared all the elements we know the smallest element is at index 0.

We start a new comparison, this time beginning at index 1 and the entire process is repeated. The following code is used to implement the selection sort algorithm. The function argument is a list of items, unsorted, that we want to be sorted into ascending order:

def selection_sort(unsorted_list):

  size_of_list = len(unsorted_list)

  for i in range(size_of_list):

   for j in range(i+1, size_of_list):

    if unsorted_list[j] < unsorted_list[i]:

     temp = unsorted_list[i]

> *unsorted_list[i] = unsorted_list[j]*
>
> *unsorted_list[j] = temp*

An outer for loop starts the process iterating through the list called size_of_list. It will do several iterations and because that list is passed to the range() method, the result is a sequence of 0 to size_of_list-1.

The inner loop will then iterate through the list, making any swaps needed whenever it encounters an element whose value is below that to which the element unsorted_list[i] points. Note that the inner loop starts from i+1 and goes up to size_of_list-1. The inner loop begins searching for the smallest element at i+1 using the j index.

Quick Sort

This algorithm comes under the class of algorithms called Divide and Conquer. The problems are chopped down into smaller problems (divide) that are easier to solve (conquer). In our case, the unsorted array we have would be broken down into smaller sub-arrays, each of which has been partly sorted, until each element is in its correct position, and resulting in the list becoming sorted.

List Partitioning

Before our list can be divided, it must be partitioned. This is the fundamental heart of this algorithm. Partitioning the array requires selecting a pivot and all the array elements will be compared with that pivot. When the partitioning process has ended, all the elements less than the pivot will be on the left side of it and those larger will be on the right of the pivot.

Selecting the Pivot

To keep things simple, we will use the first array element as our pivot. A selection like this will show a degradation of performance particularly when the list is already sorted. And it doesn't make things any better if we randomly select the last or the middle array element either. Later, we will look at a much better way of doing this but, for now, we'll stay with the first element.

Before we look at the code, we'll have a quick look through using an algorithm to sort the list. You need to understand partitioning, so we'll look at that first.

The following is a list of integers. We will partition this list using the function that is below it:

[43, 3, 20, 89, 4, 77]

def partition(unsorted_array, first_index, last_index):

  pivot = unsorted_array[first_index]

  pivot_index = first_index

  index_of_last_element = last_index

  less_than_pivot_index = index_of_last_element

  greater_than_pivot_index = first_index + 1
  ...

The parameters of the function are the list that needs partitioning; the first and last indexes. The pivot value is stored in the variable called pivot and the related index is in pivot_index. Note that we do not use unsorted_array[0] because when we call that unsorted parameter with part of an array, index 0 may not point to the very first index. The index of the element next to the pivot, first_index+1, is marking where the last element is, and this is where the search starts for the array element that is bigger than the pivot –
greater_than_pivot_index = first_index+1

The last list element is marked by less_than_pivot_index = index_of_last_element and this is where the search for the element with a lower value than the pivot begins.

  while True:

while unsorted_array[greater_than_pivot_index] < pivot and

   greater_than_pivot_index < last_index:

   greater_than_pivot_index += 1

while unsorted_array[less_than_pivot_index] > pivot and

   less_than_pivot_index >= first_index:

   less_than_pivot_index -= 1

The first of the inner loops moves to the right by one index until it arrives at index 2. This is because the value of index 2 is more than 43. Now, the first while loop will break out and will not continue. At each of the while loop test conditions, greater_than_pivot_index+=3 will only be evaluated if the test condition in the while loop is True. The search for the element that is larger than the pivot will now move to the next element to the right.

The second of the inner while loops will move to the left, one index at a time, until it gets to index 5 which has a value of 20, lower than 43. Now, neither of the while loops can be executed anymore.

if greater_than_pivot_index < less_than_pivot_index:

   temp = unsorted_array[greater_than_pivot_index]

   unsorted_array[greater_than_pivot_index] =
unsorted_array[less_than_pivot_index]

   unsorted_array[less_than_pivot_index] = temp

else:

  break

It should be clear that greater_than_pivot_index < less_than_pivot_index and, because of that, the if statement body will swap the elements at those indexes.

The infinite loop is broken by the else condition whenever greater_than_pivot_index is more than less_than_pivot_index. What this means is that the two have crossed each other.

The break statement executes when less_than_pivot_index = 3 and greater_than_pivot_index = 4.

When we come out of the while loop, the element at unsorted_array[less_than_pivot_index] is interchanged with the element at less_than_pivot_index which is then returned as the pivot index.

unsorted_array[pivot_index]=unsorted_array[less_than_pivot_index]

unsorted_array[less_than_pivot_index]=pivot

return less_than_pivot_index

To recap – when we called the quick sort function the first time, it was partitioned around the index 0 element. After the partition function was returned, we had an array of [4, 3, 20, 43, 89, 77]. It is clear the elements on the right of 43 are greater while those on the left are smaller – the partitioning has finished.

Using 43 with an index 3 as the split point, the two sub-arrays of [4, 3,20] and [89, 77] are sorted recursively using the same process as above.

The main quick sort function has a body of:

def quick_sort(unsorted_array, first, last):

  if last - first <= 0:

    return

  else:

    partition_point = partition(unsorted_array, first, last)

    quick_sort(unsorted_array, first, partition_point-1)

    quick_sort(unsorted_array, partition_point+1, last)

The quick sort function is quite easy and has no more than half a dozen code lines. The partition function does the heavy work. When we call the partition method, the partition point will be returned, and this is the point where all the elements to the left of the pivot in unsorted_array are lower than the pivot and those on the right are greater.

When the unsorted_array state is printed right after the partition, we can see how that partition happens:

Output:
[43, 3, 20, 89, 4, 77]
[4, 3, 20, 43, 89, 77]
[3, 4, 20, 43, 89, 77]
[3, 4, 20, 43, 77, 89]
[3, 4, 20, 43, 77, 89]

Going back a step, the first sub-array following the first partition needs to be sorted. When greater_than_pivot_index is at index 2 and index 1 is where less_than_pivot_index is, the sub-array of [4, 3, 20] will stop partitioning. Now the markers have crossed over. At this stage, greater_than_pivot_index is more than less_than_pivot_index so the while loop will stop. Pivot 4 is changed with 3 and the partition point is returned as index 1.

The worst-case complexity of the quick sort algorithm is O(n²) but it is very efficient for sorting large arrays.

Heap Sort

Earlier, we looked at implementing a binary heap structure. In that implementation, we ensured that the order of the heap property was maintained after the removal or addition of an element by using the sink() and helper() methods. We can also use this data structure to implement another algorithm called heap sort. Let's start by using the following to create a simple heap:

h = Heap()

unsorted_list = [4, 8, 7, 2, 9, 10, 5, 1, 3, 6]

for i in unsorted_list:

  h.insert(i)

print("Unsorted list: {}".format(unsorted_list))

The heap, h, has been created and the elements from unsorted_list have been inserted into it. After each insert method call, the order of the heap property is restored by the float method, called afterward. Once the loop has terminated, element 4 will be at the top of the heap.

We have 10 elements in the heap; if the pop() method is called 10 times on h, the heap object and the popped elements are stored, it will result in a sorted list. After each pop() the heap will be adjusted to maintain the order property.

Below is the heap_sort method:

class Heap:
  ...
    def heap_sort(self):

    sorted_list = []

    for node in range(self.size):

      n = self.pop()

      sorted_list.append(n)

    return sorted_list

The pop method called self_size is called several times by the for loop and sorted_list will have the sorted list of elements once the loop has terminated. The insert() method is called n times and, with the float() method it will have a worst-case runtime of o(n log n), the same as the pop() method.

Next, we will be looking at design and classification of algorithms.

Chapter 13: Algorithm Design and Classification

We've looked at some algorithms, now it's time to go back a step and look at the design and classification of algorithms. As you get more experienced with Python programming you will start to see certain patterns much easier. And, as with any skilled trade, you need some principles and techniques to guide you. Where algorithms are concerned, there are plenty of techniques and principles in design and if you want to go on to harder problems, you need to understand these techniques and principles and gain a working knowledge of them.

We'll be looking at how algorithms are classified and some of the other techniques for design. The aim here is to give you an idea of how wide the algorithm expanse is, not to make you into a professional algorithm designer.

Classification of Algorithms

There are several algorithm classification schemes based on what the algorithm is to achieve. We have looked at a few algorithms and one question asked is whether they all share the same form. If they do, how are they similar and what characteristics do they share as the basis. If they don't share the same form, can they be sorted into groups of classes? We will look at both issues in the coming section.

Classification by Implementation

When a series of processes or steps are translated into an algorithm that works, there are several forms that it can take:

Recursion

Recursive algorithms call themselves until a specified condition has been met. Some problems can be expressed much easier through the implementation of their solution via recursion. Other types of recursive algorithms include:

- Single recursion
- Multiple recursion
- Indirect recursion

- Anonymous recursion
- Generative recursion

By contrast, iterative algorithms use a repetitive construct to come up with a solution. This might be nothing more than a basic while loop or some other type of loop. We also tend to think of iterative solutions more than we do recursive implementations.

Logical

One way of implementing an algorithm is to express it as a controlled logical deduction. The logical component of the algorithm contains the axioms that the computation will need while the control component determines how the deduction is applied. The expression for this is algorithm = logic + control and this is the basis of this programming paradigm. The algorithm meaning is determined by the logical component while the control component affects only the algorithm efficiency. This efficiency can be improved without any modification to the logic just by making improvements to the control components.

Serial or Parallel

On most computers, the model of RAM will assume that the instructions are given one at a time for the computation. Serial algorithms also go by the name of sequential and they tend to be executed in sequence. Execution will go from the start to the finish with no other executions.

To process multiple instructions simultaneously, we require a different technique or model. The parallel algorithm can do multiple operations at once. The PRAM model, for example, uses multiple processors sharing a global memory. These processors can do several logical and arithmetic operations at the same time or in parallel and this is what allows several instructions to be executed at the same time.

Parallel or distributed algorithms will divide the problem into smaller subproblems among all the processors for the collection of results. You can effectively parallelize some of the sorting algorithms and some iterative algorithms can be generally parallelized.

Deterministic vs Nondeterministic

A deterministic algorithm produces an identical output every time it runs with an identical input. Some problems are far too complex in the way their solutions are designed that it can be a bit challenging to express that solution deterministically. The nondeterministic algorithm can change the execution order or change one or more of the internal subprocesses and this results in a change to the end result whenever the algorithm runs. For example, if an algorithm uses the probabilistic value, the outputs will be different for each successive execution, and dependent on a random number that is generated and its value.

Classification by Complexity

Determining algorithm complexity means trying to determine the amount of memory or space and time used during the entire computation or execution.

Complexity Curves

Consider that we have a problem that is of magnitude n. To work out the time complexity, it is denoted with T(n). The value may come under any of the following:

- $O(1)$
- $O(\log n)$
- $O(n)$
- $O(n \log (n))$
- $O(n^2)$
- $O(n^3)$
- $O(2^n)$

Depending on how many steps the algorithm performs, the time complexity may be affected, or it may not. $O(n)$ will capture the algorithm's growth rate.

Let's take a more practical example. How do we get to the conclusion that the quick sort algorithm works faster than the bubble sort algorithm? Or perhaps more generally, how can we measure algorithm efficiency against one another? The way to do that is to look at the Big O of multiple algorithms to see what their efficiencies are. This is how we get the growth rate or measure of time and this is what charts the way the algorithm behaves as n grows. Taking the runtime list, sorting it from best to worse is given as:

- $O(1)$
- $O(\log n)$
- $O(n)$
- $O(n \log n)$
- $O(n^2)$
- $O(n^3)$
- $O(2^n)$

Classification by Design

We are going to look now at the algorithm categories based on the way various algorithms are designed to solve problems. Any problem could have any number of different solutions. When we analyze the solution algorithms we can see that some of them will implement specific patterns or techniques and it is these that we will talk about briefly now.

Divide and Conquer

This is a recap because we have already talked about divide and conquer problem-solving. We know that the problems are broken down into smaller ones and all the solutions are combined in a way that the overall solution is the one that matches the original problem.

Recursion tends to be used mostly for dividing the problem and some of the algorithms that make use of the technique include binary search, quick sort, and merge-sort.

Dynamic Programming

This is like the previous technique. In divide and conquer, the subproblems must be all be solved before the result may be used on larger problems, but in dynamic programming, the solution is not computed to a subproblem already encountered; instead remembering techniques are used so that the computation is not repeated.

Greedy Algorithms

For some problems, it is not easy to determine the best solution. So, to make up for this, we turn to greedy algorithms, an approach that selects the nearest solution from a group of options that is closest to getting a solution.

The guiding rule for a greedy algorithm is that the solution selected is the one that will yield the highest benefit and carry on doing that in the hopes that the perfect solution may be reached. The technique has a goal of finding the "global optimal final solution" and it does this by making a series of choices that are locally optimal. These choices appear to lead toward the solution, but many of the choices are suboptimal, which means a bad asymptotic time complexity.

Complexity Classes

The problems that algorithms attempt to solve all fall inside a difficulty range in which the solution is found. We're going to look at 4 complexity classes:

- N
- NP
- NP-Complete
- NP-Hard Problems

P vs NP

The speedy advent of the computer system has hastened the speed at which some tasks are performed. Generally, a computer is good at perfecting calculations and any problem that may be divided into a set of computations. However, this isn't always true because there are some problem classes that take far too long to make even a decent guess, let alone solve the problem.

As far as computer science is concerned, the problem classes that a computer may solve in polynomial time using a sequence of logical steps are called P-Types – P means polynomial. These are quite easy to find solutions.

However, there is also another problem class that is hard to find a solution. We use the term "hard problem" to describe the increase in difficulty of a problem when attempting to find a solution. However, there is a good point – although these problems do have a high difficulty growth rate, it is perfectly possible to work out whether a given solution will solve that problem within polynomial time. These are known as NP-Type problems with NP meaning nondeterministic polynomial time.

We can use the Traveling Salesman problem to demonstrate the NP-Type of problem. The statement says: given n cities in this country, find the shortest route that goes between them all providing a cost-effective solution. When there are few cities, it doesn't take long to solve the problem; however, when the number of cities goes to 3 digits, it can take an awfully long time.

Many computer systems use RSA encryption algorithms and the strength and security come from it being based on a problem of integer factoring and that is an NP-Type problem.

It isn't easy to find the prime factors of any prime number made up of multiple digits. When you multiply two large prime numbers, you can only have a large non-prime number with a pair of large prime factors. Many algorithms take their strength from the factorization of that number.

P-Type problems are all subsets of the NP-Type problems and this means that, if a problem is solvable within polynomial time, it is also verifiable in polynomial time. But does P=NP? This question looks into whether a problem that is verifiable in polynomial time is solvable in polynomial time. More specifically, if they are equal it means that any problem that is solvable by attempting several solutions is solvable without having to attempt ALL possible solutions and this creates a shortcut proof. When discovered, that proof will have some serious consequences for the fields of mathematics, game theory, and cryptography, among many others.

NP-Hard/NP-Complete

A problem is classified as NP-Hard if all other NP problems are reducible or mapped to polynomial time. The problem is classified as NP-Complete if it is primarily NP-Hard and can also be in NP class.

Implementations, Tools, and Applications

While you can learn the theory of an algorithm, you will never truly understand it unless your use real-life applications. So, we are going to look at some of the algorithms and data structures that play a part in shaping the world in which we live.

One of the biggest benefits of the current time is the sheer amount of data – phone numbers, email addresses, image documents, text documents, all of these contain vast amounts of data. In this data, we can find some valuable information that gives the data a more important status, but getting this information out of the raw data requires the use of processes, data structures, and algorithms that are specialized.

We think of machine learning here because it makes use of many algorithms that will analyze the chances of certain variables and predict them. Using a numerical basis to analyze data still leaves a lot of information in the raw data. Visually presenting the data helps us to understand the data and gain a few insights. We will be looking in-depth at machine learning in the next part of this book, but we will look briefly at it now.

Tools

To go any further with machine learning, as you will learn later, you need several packages to preprocess the date and visually represent it. In brief, you will need the following packages installed in a virtual environment like pip:

% pip install numpy
% pip install scikit-learn
% pip install matplotlib
% pip install pandas
% pip install textblob

You may need to install other modules specific to your platform for these packages as well so be sure to install all relevant dependencies:

- **NumPy** – a library that contains functions for operating on matrices and n-dimensional arrays
- **Scikit-learn** – an advanced machine learning module that has several algorithms for regression, classification, and clustering, among others
- **Matplotlib** – a plotting library that uses NumPy to plot charts
- **Panda** – a library for dealing with data analysis and manipulation

Data Preprocessing

Real-world data collection is full of huge challenges and the raw data is overrun with issues. Because of this, we need to come up with ways of sanitizing data so it can be further used.

Why do we need to process the raw data? Simply because of the risk of human error. Data-entry offers huge chances for human error in data collection and even the technical and technological methods are not left out. Inaccurate device reading, bad gadgetry, and even environmental factors play a part in introducing errors in data.

You may also find that the data has become inconsistent with other records that have been collected and collated over time. Duplication of entries and records that are not complete dictate that we must treat data in such a way that we pull out the jewels hidden in the data, as well as getting past heaps of data that just isn't relevant.

Cleaning the data means that we can remove the irrelevant data which is called noise. If data is found to be incomplete, more sensible estimates can be used to replace it. And where we have inconsistent data, we must detect it and correct it.

Let's look at how NumPy and Pandas can be used for preprocessing data.

Missing Data

Data collection is awfully time-consuming and tedious and because of this, we shouldn't discard data too easily once we have collected it. There may be attributes or fields missing from a dataset, but it is still useful. We can use any one of multiple methods for filling in the missing data and one of these is to manually supply the data, use the mean dataset value, or use a global constant. Which one we choose will be based on the sensitivity and the context for which the data is being used.

Have a look at this data:

import numpy as np

import pandas

data = pandas.DataFrame([

   [4., 45., 984.],

   [np.NAN, np.NAN, 5.],

   [94., 23., 55.],

])

The data elements of data[1][0] and data[2][1] have np.NAN values, which tells us they do not have a value. If we don't want the np.NAN values in a dataset, we can set them to a constant figure. So let's do that; we'll set them to 0.1:

print(data.fillna(0.1))

The state of the data now becomes:

```
   0     1     2
0  4.0  45.0  984.0
1  0.1  0.1   5.0
2  94.0 23.0  55.0
```

If we wanted to apply mean values, we would do this:

print(data.fillna(data.mean()))

Each column's mean value is calculated and then inserted in the parts where the np.NAN values are:

```
   0    1     2
0  4.0  45.0  984.0
1  49.0 34.0    5.0
2  94.0 23.0   55.0
```

For column 0, we obtained the mean value through (4 + 94)/2 and the result of 49.0 is stored in data[1][0]. We do something similar for the other columns.

Feature Scaling

In a data frame, the columns are the features while the rows are observations or records. Have a look at this data matrix; we are referencing the data in subsections so do note it carefully:

```
[[ 58.   1.  43.]
 [ 10. 200.  65.]
 [ 20.  75.   7.]]
```

Feature 1 contains the data values of 58, 10, 20 and its values are clearly between 10 and 58. In feature 2, that date is between 1 and 200. If we gave this data to a machine learning algorithm we would get inconsistent results so we should scale our data into a specific range so the results are consistent.

Looking closely, we can see that each column is based around mean values that are different, so we need to align these features around mean values that are similar. A benefit of this is to give the learning parts of the machine learning a boost and we have a module called scikit that contains many scaling algorithms for us to use.

Min-Max Scalar

This form of data normalization takes the means and the standard deviations and boxes the data into one range between given min and max values. Mostly, the range will be 0 to 1, which is the default, but there are other ranges:

scaled_values = preprocessing.MinMaxScaler(feature_range=(0,1))

results = scaled_values.fit(data).transform(data)

print(results)

We can create a MinMaxScaler instance with a range of [0, 1] and then we pass it to the variable called scaled_values. We call the fit function to do the calculations to change the dataset internally. The transform function will do the operation on the dataset and the value is returned to results:

```
[[ 1.         0.         0.62068966]
 [ 0.         1.         1.        ]
 [ 0.20833333 0.3718593  0.        ]]
```

As we can see, the data has all been normalized and is now between the range 0 and 1; we can now apply this to the machine learning algorithm.

Standard Scalar

In the initial dataset, the features have mean values of 29.3, 92 and 38 respectively. To make them all have zero means and a unit variance, we use the standard scalar algorithm:

stand_scalar = preprocessing.StandardScaler().fit(data)

results = stand_scalar.transform(data)

print(results)

Note that we pass data to the fit method of the object that was returned from the instantiation of the class called StandardScaler. The transform method will act on all the data element and the output is returned to results:

```
[[ 1.38637564 -1.10805456  0.19519899]
 [-0.93499753  1.31505377  1.11542277]
 [-0.45137812 -0.2069992  -1.31062176]]
```

On examination of those results, we can see that the features are now distributed evenly.

Binarizing the Data

If we wanted to binarize a specified feature set, we need to use a threshold. If any of the values in a specified dataset is more than the threshold, 1 will replace that value. If it is less, it is replaced like this:

results = preprocessing.Binarizer(50.0).fit(data).transform(data)

print(results)

We create a Binarizer instance using the argument of 50.0. This is the threshold that is used in the algorithm:

```
[[ 1.  0.  0.]
 [ 0.  1.  1.]
 [ 0.  1.  0.]]
```

All the data values less than 50 have 0 and the opposite is also true; greater than will have 1 in their stead.

Machine Learning

Machine learning is classed as a "subfield of artificial intelligence". We already know that the creation of a machine that really can think is highly unlikely, but we can give a machine the models and the data by which it can learn to make a good judgment. Machine learning is focused on the creation of autonomous systems that can make decisions with very little or no intervention by a human hand.

To teach the machine what to do, the data must come from the real world. For example, if we wanted to work out which emails are spam and which are not, we would need to give the machine several examples of each. Once we have this data, we run it through the algorithms that make use of statistics and probability to find structures and patterns. Done properly, the algorithm alone will learn the ability to analyze and correctly categorize the emails and this is just one example of what a 'trained' machine can do. And that leads us neatly to the end of this part and on to Part 2 – Machine Learning.

Chapter 14: Machine Learning with Python

Thanks is given to tutorialspoint.com for the code in this section.

Python is a high-level but easy-to-use computer programming language and these days it is the language used the most for data science and for the design of algorithms for machine learning. This section is an overview of machine learning and the use of the required libraries – NumPy, SciPy, Pandas, and Matplotlib - in developing algorithms for solving real-world problems.

This will also be a practical tutorial so make sure you have everything installed that you need. The theory about machine learning is one thing, but the only real way to learn it is to get your hands dirty. We will show you how to set the required packages up and then we will delve into the most important concepts of machine learning, such as data analysis, preprocessing, extracting features, data visualization, regressing classification, and clustering along with performance evaluation.

We will be learning several projects that will teach you some of the machine learning functionalities and techniques, such as classification of news topics, detection of spam in emails, predicting, online ad clickthrough and more. First, a look at the history of machine learning.

A Brief History

We have reached a time when the lines between science fiction and science fact are becoming more and more blurred. We still have a long way to go but every day draws us ever closer to what is known widely as artificial intelligence.

Machine learning is one of the subsets of artificial intelligence in which algorithms are used to help computers learn autonomously from supplied information and datasets. A computer does not need to be programmed; instead, it can be taught to change and to improve those algorithms for the best result, all by itself.

These days, those machine learning algorithms are what enable computers and humans to communicate, autonomous cars, and much more. In time, machine learning will have a huge impact on most industries and this is just one reason why all management teams should learn at least the fundamentals of machine learning, what it's all about, and what it can do. Below is a brief timeline of events and the most important milestones in the history of machine learning:

- **1950** – Alan Turing comes up with the Turing Test to see if a computer can pass a test to fool a human into believing that the computer is also human.
- **1952** – The very first program was written for computer learning by Arthur Samuel. It was a game of Checkers – the IBM computer it was written on learned to get better every time it played by studying the moves that led to a winning game and then using those moves in its own games.
- **1957** – The very first neural network was designed for computers by Frank Rosenblatt. This was the perception, designed to simulate the human brain thought processes.
- **1967** – The algorithm called 'nearest neighbor' was written. This allowed the computer to begin using the basic recognition of patterns, allowing for shortest routes to be planned.
- **1979** – The 'Stanford Cart' was invented by Stanford University students, a cart that could get around obstacles by itself.
- **1981** – The Explanation-Based Learning concept was introduced by Gerald Dejong. The concept demonstrates a computer analyzing training data and then creating a rule by which it learns to discard data that it isn't important.
- **1985** – NetTalk is invented by Terry Sejnowski, a program that learns word pronunciation the way a baby learns.
- **1990s** – Machine learning work moves to a data-driven approach rather than knowledge-driven and scientists start to create programs for the analysis of large data amounts by computers and allows them to learn from the results.
- **1997** – Deep Blue from IBM beats the world chess champion at his own game.
- **2006** – The term, 'Deep Learning' is coined by Geoffrey Hinton. This term explains and covers new types of algorithms that allow a computer to see and distinguish between text and objects in videos and images.

- **2010** – Microsoft Kinect is released with the ability to track human features (20 of them) at a fast rate of 30 times per second so that humans can use gestures and movements as methods of interaction with the computer.
- **2011** – Watson by IBM beats human players at the game of Jeopardy.
- **2011** – We saw the development of Google Brain; it has a deep neural network that allows it to learn how to discover new objects and categorize them in a way similar to a cat.
- **2012** – A machine learning algorithm is developed by Google X Lab to browse through YouTube videos autonomously, identifying all videos with cats in them.
- **2014** – A software algorithm called DeepFace is developed by Facebook to look at photos and recognize/verify individuals in the same way as a human being does.
- **2015** – Amazon comes up with its own platform for machine learning.
- **2015** – The Distributed Machine Learning Toolkit is created by Microsoft to enable machine learning problems to be efficiently distributed across several computers at once.
- **2015** – An open letter is signed by more than 3000 AI and Robotics researchers warning of the dangers of autonomous weaponry that choose targets and engage with them with no human assistance. The letter is endorsed by Steve Wozniak, Elon Musk, Stephen Hawking and others.
- **2016** – Google's AI algorithm plays a professional Go player and beats them. This is the most complex board game in the world, much harder than Chess. The algorithm is called AlphaGo, developed by DeepMind (Google) and it won five out of five games in the competition.

So, is there any proof that we are getting ever closer to artificial intelligence? There are scientists that believe computers can never think the way humans do and that it is entirely wrong to compare algorithms and computational analysis to the way the human mind thinks. That said, the ability of a computer to see, to understand, and to interact with the real world is becoming more and more real, and the more data we produce, the more the abilities of computers will grow in processing that data, analyzing it, and learning from it.

Chapter 15: The Concepts of Machine Learning

Now we will look at the machine learning with Python concepts. With machine learning, we program the systems so that they learn by experience and they improve. By learning, we mean the recognition of input data, understanding it, and making informed decisions based on it. What is difficult to comprehend are all the possible decisions based on all the possible inputs and, to create solutions, we develop algorithms. These algorithms take specific data and build knowledge from that and from past experiences. They do this through the application of the principles of probability, statistical science, logic, reinforcement learning, mathematical optimization, and control theory.

Applications of Machine Learning Algorithms

Machine learning algorithms are used in many different applications, such as:

- Data mining

- Expert systems

- Forecasting such as stock market trends, weather

- Games

- Language processing

- Pattern recognition

- Robotics

- Vision processing

Steps Involved in Machine Learning

A machine learning project will involve these steps:

- Definition of a Problem

- Preparation of the Data

- Evaluation of the Algorithms

- Improving the Results

- Presentation of the Results

The very best way to understand machine learning is to follow a Python project from start to finish and cover the most important steps:

- Load the data

- Summarize the data

- Evaluate the algorithms

- Make predictions

This will produce a method that is replicable, which means it can be used on multiple datasets. Extra data can be added to improve the results even further.

Setting Up the Environment

Although we covered installing Python earlier, we need to look into how to install the required packages and libraries.

Installation

Installing Python can be done in two ways – the method we looked at earlier was installing directly from the Python website, or you can install a Python distribution called Anaconda. With the first method, once you have installed Python, use the following commands to install the packages:

$pip install numpy

$pip install matplotlib

$pip install pandas

$pip install seaborn

The second method, using Anaconda includes Jupyter Notebook already built-in – this is an interactive environment for Python – and it also includes the packages that you need already built-in. We download Anaconda from Continuum Analytics – it will take up to 20 minutes to do as Anaconda contains Python, the packages, a built-in code editor, and other files.

Now you can open Anaconda Navigator and go into Spyder IDE or Jupyter. Once you are in, type the following commands to import the packages:

import numpy

import matplotlib

Next, check to see if the installation has been successful by typing this command at the command line:

$ python

Python 3.6.3 |Anaconda custom (32-bit)| (default, 'system data and time')

[GCC 7.2.0] on (operating system)

The required libraries can be imported, and their versions printed:

>>>import numpy

>>>print numpy.__version__

x.xx.xx(version number)

>>> import matplotlib

>>> print (matplotlib.__version__)

x.x.x(version)

>> import pandas

>>> print (pandas.__version__)

x.xx.x(version)

>>> import seaborn

>>> print (seaborn.__version__)

x.x.x(version number)

Types of Learning

Machine learning is a type of automated learning that has little to no intervention by humans. The purpose is to explore data and to construct algorithms that are able to learn from old data and make predictions on new data. The input data is training data, and this is what represents the experience; the output is the expertise, normally a separate algorithm that performs some kind of task. Input data can be in many formats – text, numerical, visual, audio, or multimedia. The output that corresponds to the input can be a float (floating point number), an integer or an image of some description.

The Learning Concepts

Machine learning is the process of taking experience and turning it into knowledge or expertise. We can classify learning into three broad categories, each based on the learning data nature and the interaction between the environment and the learner:

- Supervised Learning

- Unsupervised Learning

- Semi-supervised Learning

In the same way, machine algorithms can also be categorized in four ways:

- Supervised learning algorithm

- Unsupervised learning algorithm

- Semi-supervised learning algorithm

- Reinforcement learning algorithm

Supervised and unsupervised are the two most common ones and they are the ones we will discuss now.

Supervised Learning

Supervised learning is the commonly used method for real-world applications, like speech or facial recognition, sales forecasts and more. We can classify supervised learning as two distinct types – regression and classification.

- Regression trains on data and predicts responses that are of a continuous value   type, like the prediction of real-estate prices.

- Classification tries to find the right class label, for example, analysis of positive or negative sentiment, the distinction between male and female, between malignant and benign tumors, unsecured or secured loans, and so on.

With supervised learning, all the data is complete with a description, a label, the targets or the output desired; the goal of it is to find the generalized rule that will map the inputs to the outputs. We call this kind of data labeled data and the rule that has been learned is then used to label the new data with outputs that are unknown.

Supervised learning is building a model that is based on data samples with labels. For example, if we wanted a system that estimated house or land prices based on certain features, we would need to create the database with the features in it and then label it. The algorithm needs to be taught what features correspond to which prices and, based on the data it gets, it learns how to make the price calculation using the input features values.

With supervised learning, we are dealing with a computer system that takes available training data and learns a function from it. The algorithm analyzes the data producing a function that can then be used for new examples. Types of supervised learning algorithms include neural networks, logistic regression, Naïve Bayes, and support vector machines while common supervised learning examples include labeling web pages as per the content they have, voice recognition, facial recognition, and learning to classify an email as spam or not spam.

Unsupervised Learning

We use unsupervised learning to detect oddities, to put customers with like behaviors together in groups for sales campaigns, detect outliers like defective equipment or fraud, and so on. It is the complete opposite of the supervised learning and none of the data is labeled.

When the training data have no labels and no descriptions, and just a few indications, it is down to the coder or down to the algorithm to work out what the structure is to the underlying data. The algorithm needs to find the patterns hidden in the data or work out how the data should be described. We call this data unlabeled.

Let's assume that we have several data points and we want them classified into a number of groups. At this stage, we probably don't know what the classification criterion is, so the unsupervised algorithm will attempt to classify the data into a given number of groups using the optimum way.

These are incredibly powerful algorithms for the analysis of data and for finding any trends or patterns in that data. They are used mostly for clustering similar inputs into groups in a logical way. Some of the common unsupervised algorithms include hierarchical clustering, random forests, and K-Means among others.

Semi-supervised Learning

If we have a dataset with some labeled and some unlabeled data, we call it semi-supervised learning. This algorithm uses the unlabeled data to train on and the labeled data to test on. It tends to be used where it is too expensive in computational terms to get a dataset that is fully labeled while labeling a smaller subset is a good deal more practical. For example, we sometimes need experts who are highly skilled to label some images, perhaps remote sensing images, and a lot of field experiments to find oil in a specific place; the acquisition of unlabeled data is quite easy by comparison.

Reinforcement Learning

With reinforcement learning, the data will provide feedback so that the system can adjust itself dynamically to achieve a specific objective. The system will evaluate its own performance based on that feedback and it will react accordingly. Some of the best-known uses for reinforcement learning are AlphaGo, which we mentioned earlier and the self-drive cars.

The Purpose of Machine Learning

We know that machine learning is a subset of Artificial Intelligence (AI) because the ability to take experience and turn into expertise or to see a pattern in a bunch of complex data is human or animal-level intelligence. As a science field, machine learning shares a number of concepts with disciplines, such as information theory, statistics, optimization, and game theory. Its objective as an IT subfield is to program a machine so that it can learn.

However, it must be realized that machine learning is not just about building a duplication of human or animal intelligent behavior; machine learning can also be used for the detection of patterns that are way beyond the scope of both animal and human perception.

Preprocessing, Analysis, and Visualization of Data

The real world is full of raw data that is not in a fit state for a machine learning algorithm to process. It must be preprocessed before being fed into the algorithms and so we will look at how this is done, the techniques used in preprocessing with Python.

Data Preprocessing

This is going to be a practical section; open any file with an extension of.py in your text editor and add this code to the file:

import numpy as np

from sklearn import preprocessing

We have imported two packages so now we need to create a little sample data and add the following line to the file:

input_data = np.array([[3, -1.5, 3, -6.4], [0, 3, -1.3, 4.1], [1, 2.3, -2.9, -4.3]])

Now we can do some operations on the data:

Techniques for Preprocessing

There are a number of techniques that we can use for preprocessing data:

Mean Removal

Mean removal takes the mean out of each feature, centering it on zero. Mean removal is helpful in removing the bias out of the features. This code may be used:

data_standardized = preprocessing.scale(input_data)

print("\nMean = ", data_standardized.mean(axis = 0))

print("Std deviation = ", data_standardized.std(axis = 0))

On your terminal, run this command:

$ *python (name of file).py*

You should see an output like this:

Mean = [5.55111512e-17 -3.70074342e-17 0.00000000e+00 -1.85037171e-17]

Std deviation = [1. 1. 1. 1.]

Note that mean is pretty much zero while the standard deviation = 1.

Scaling

All the features in the data point have a value and that can range between randomized values. Because of that, we should scale those values so that specified rules are matched. You can use this code:

data_scaler = preprocessing.MinMaxScaler(feature_range = (0, 1))

data_scaled = data_scaler.fit_transform(input_data)

print("\nMin max scaled data = ", data_scaled)

If you run this code you should see something like this:

Min-max scaled data = [[1. 0. 1. 0.]

[0. 1. 0.27118644 1.]

[0.33333333 0.84444444 0. 0.2]

]

All values have now been scaled so they fall in the given range.

Normalization

Normalization is about adjusting the feature vector values so they can be measures on a common scale. In our example, we adjust those values to sum up to 1. Add this code to your new.py file:

data_normalized = preprocessing.normalize(input_data, norm = 'l1')

print("\nL1 normalized data = ", data_normalized)

Run the code and you should see:

L1 normalized data = [[0.21582734 -0.10791367 0.21582734 -0.46043165]

[0. 0.35714286 -0.1547619 0.48809524]

[0.0952381 0.21904762 -0.27619048 -0.40952381]

]

We use normalization for ensuring that boosting of the data points cannot happen – this is possible because of their features.

Binarization

Binarization is used for the conversion of a numerical feature vector so it becomes a Boolean vector. This code is for binarization:

*data_binarized =
preprocessing.Binarizer(threshold=1.4).transform(input_data)*

print("\nBinarized data =", data_binarized)

Running the code should give you this:

Binarized data = [[1. 0. 1. 0.]

[0. 1. 0. 1.]

[0. 1. 0. 0.]

]

Binarization is very useful when we have some knowledge about the data upfront.

One-Hot Encoding

You may find that your numerical values are few and far between and scattered and it may also be that these values do not need to be stored. In this situation, the one-hot encoding technique is useful. Let's say that we have k distinct values; one-hot encoding transforms the vector into a k-dimensional vector – one of the values is a 1 and all the others are 0.

This code can be used for one-hot encoding:

encoder = preprocessing.OneHotEncoder()

encoder.fit([[0, 2, 1, 12],

> *[1, 3, 5, 3],*

> *[2, 3, 2, 12],*

> *[1, 2, 4, 3]*

])

encoded_vector = encoder.transform([[2, 3, 5, 3]]).toarray()

print("\nEncoded vector =", encoded_vector)

Running the code should give you something along these lines:

Encoded vector = [[0. 0. 1. 0. 1. 0. 0. 0. 1. 1. 0.]]

Using that example, we will look at the third feature in every one of the feature vectors. The values we are interested in are 1, 5, 2, 4. These are four entirely separate values, giving the one-hot encoded vector a length of 4. Now let's say that we want the value of 5 encoded; the vector will be [0, 1, 0, 0]. We can only have one value 1 and as the second element has that value, it indicates that 5 is the value as per our string of four values.

Label Encoding

With supervised learning, we tend to see a range of different labels and these labels may be words or numbers. If they are the latter, the algorithm can use them directly. However, mostly these labels must be readable, so they tend to be words.

Label encoding is about changing those word labels so they are numbers that the algorithm can understand and perform operations on them. Let's look into how label encoding is done.

Make a new file in Python and input the following to import our preprocessing package:

from sklearn import preprocessing

label_encoder = preprocessing.LabelEncoder()

input_classes = ['opel', 'suzuki', 'opel', 'bmw', 'suzuki', 'mercedes']

label_encoder.fit(input_classes)

print("\nClass mapping:")

for i, item in enumerate(label_encoder.classes_): print(item, '-->', i)

Run the code:

Class mapping:

mercedes --> 0

suzuki --> 1

opel --> 2

bmw --> 3

As you can see in the output, the words in the file have changed to numbers with 0-indexing. Now, whenever we have a set of labels that we need to deal with, we can do the following to transform them:

labels = ['bmw', 'suzuki', 'opel']

label_encoder.fit(labels)

encoded_labels = label_encoder.transform(labels)

print("\nLabels =", labels)

print("Encoded labels =", list(encoded_labels))

Run the code:

Labels = ['bmw', 'suzuki', 'opel']

Encoded labels = [3, 1, 2]

This is far more efficient than maintaining the mapping manually between the words and the numbers. If you want to doublecheck the mapping, transform the numbers back to words like this:

encoded_labels = [3, 2, 0, 2, 1]

decoded_labels = label_encoder.inverse_transform(encoded_labels)

print("\nEncoded labels =", encoded_labels)

print("Decoded labels =", list(decoded_labels))

Run the code:

Encoded labels = [3, 2, 0, 2, 1]

Decoded labels = ['bmw', 'opel', 'mercedes', 'opel', 'suzuki']

You can see from the output that the mapping has been perfectly preserved.

Data Analysis

In this section, we will look at data analysis using Python.

Loading the Dataset

The dataset can be directly loaded from the UCI Machine Learning Repository. We are going to use pandas to do this and to explore the data using both data visualization and descriptive statistics. Look at this code and note that we have given specific names for each of the columns when the data is loaded. We are loading the pima_indians.csv from the repository:

import pandas

data = 'pima_indians.csv'

names = ['Pregnancies', 'Glucose', 'BloodPressure', 'SkinThickness', 'Insulin', 'Outcome']

dataset = pandas.read_csv(data, names = names)

When this code is run, the dataset will load, and the data can be analyzed.

Summarizing our Dataset

We can summarize the data as follows:

- We can check the dataset dimensions.

- We can list all the data.

- We can see a statistical summary of every attribute.

- We can break the data down by the class variables.

Dataset Dimensions

The command below can be used for checking the number of rows (instances) and columns (attributes) in the data with the property of shape:

print(dataset.shape)

In the code, using the imported pima_indians.csv, we have 769 rows and 6 columns:

(769, 6)

Listing All the Data

We can see all the data summarized:

print(dataset.head(20))

The command above will print the specified number of data rows, in our example, 20:

No.	Pregnancies	Glucose	BloodPressure	Skin Thickness	Insulin	Outcome
1	6	148	72	35	0	1
2	1	85	66	29	0	0
3	8	183	64	0	0	1
4	1	89	66	23	94	0
5	0	137	40	35	168	1
6	5	116	74	0	0	0
7	3	78	50	32	88	1
8	10	115	0	0	0	0
9	2	197	70	45	543	1
10	8	125	96	0	0	1
11	4	110	92	0	0	0
12	10	168	74	0	0	1
13	10	139	80	0	0	0
14	1	189	60	23	846	1
15	5	166	72	19	175	1
16	7	100	0	0	0	1
17	0	118	84	47	230	1
18	7	107	74	0	0	1
19	1	103	30	38	83	0

Viewing Statistical Summary

The statistical summary of every attribute will include four attributes – count, unique, top, freq – and the can be seen with this command:

print(dataset.describe())

You should see an output of this:

	Pregnancies	Glucose	Blood Pressure	Skin Thickness	Insulin	Outcome
count	769	769	769	769	769	769
unique	18	137	48	52	187	3
top	1	100	70	0	0	0
freq	135	17	57	227	374	500

Breaking the Data Down Via Class Variable

We can also examine how many rows belong to each of the different outcomes as absolute count with this command:

print(dataset.groupby('Outcome').size())

The outcome will be:

Outcome

0   500

1   268

Outcome   1

dtype: int64

Data Visualization

We can use two plot types to visualize our data:

- Univariate for understanding each of the attributes

- Multivariate for understanding the relationship between the attributes

Univariate Plots

A univariate plot is a plot of an individual variable. Let's assume that all the input variables are of a numeric type. We want to create a 'box and whisker' plot of each one. The code below is importing the infamous iris dataset:

import pandas

import matplotlib.pyplot as plt

data = 'iris_df.csv'

names = ['sepal-length', 'sepal-width', 'petal-length', 'petal-width', 'class']

dataset = pandas.read_csv(data, names=names)

dataset.plot(kind='box', subplots=True, layout=(2,2), sharex=False, sharey=False)

plt.show()

Box and Whisker Plots

The code below can be used for creating a histogram for each of the input variables; this will give us some idea of their distribution:

#histograms

dataset.hist()

plt().show()

Looking at the output, it is clear that a couple of the variables are of a Gaussian distribution. These plots are helpful to give us a clue of the algorithms that can be used in the program we are working on:

Multivariate Plots

A multivariate plot is useful to see the way the variables interact:

Scatter Plot Matrix

The scatterplot shows every attribute pair. These are very useful to see where there may be a structured relationship between the input variables:

from pandas.plotting import scatter_matrix

scatter_matrix(dataset)

plt.show()

In the output we would see a diagonal group of some of the attribute pairs and this is indicative of a high-level of correlation and a relationship that is predictable.

Training and Test Data

These are two of the most important of all the machine learning concepts and we'll be looking at both test and training data in this section.

Training Data

What the algorithm observes in the training data is what it uses to learn. Under supervised learning, every observation is made up of an output variable and at least one input variable.

Test Data

Test data is an observation set that is used to evaluate model performance using a set of given metrics. One important thing is that none of the training set observations are included in the test data set. If there is any training data it won't be easy to determine if the algorithm has just memorized the training set or has learned generalization.

If a program can generalize well it can perform tasks very effectively with new data. By contrast, if a program memorizes the data through the learning of a model that is complex it may be able to predict the training set response variable values with accuracy but it won't be able to predict any response variable values for new data examples. The term applied to memorization of the data is "overfitting" and when a program memorizes the observations won't do a very good job at its task because it may end up memorizing structures or relations that are nothing more than noise or pure coincidence. One of the biggest problems faced by machine learning algorithms is trying to balance generalization (underfitting) and memorization (overfitting). In some cases, to cut the risk of overfitting, regularization is applied to the model.

There is another observation set called the "hold-out" or "validation" set that may be required on occasion. This observation set is used for tuning hyperparameters, which are a type of variable that controls the way the algorithm learns the model. The test set is still used to evaluate the model, providing a performance estimation for the real-world but the validation set performance shouldn't be used for real-world performance because the model is tuned only to the validation data. Commonly, a supervised observation set is split into three – test, training, and validation. There are no specific requirements for the partition sizes; it will depend on what data is available and how much there is of it. The most common partition sizes are at least 50% of data to training, 25% to test and the rest to validation.

Some of the training sets may have no more than a couple of hundred observations while others may have several million, even billions; the reasons behind these massive training sets are reduced storage costs, smartphones packed with different sensors, more options for network connections, and a change in attitude toward data and user privacy.

That said, every machine learning algorithm will follow one axiom – GIGO. This stands of Garbage in, Garbage Out. An example: Two students have an examination due. One studies from a large book that is somewhat confusing with a lot of errors while the second studies the same subject in a short book that is very well-written. Who will score higher? Neither. They will both score approximately the same. Likewise, an algorithm that has been trained on a dataset that is large with a lot of noise, data that hasn't been labeled correctly, or that is irrelevant will perform no better than the algorithm that is trained on the smaller dataset that better represents real-world problems.

Most of the supervised training sets are either prepared by a semi-automated process or manually. In some domains, the cost of creating large supervised datasets is too high, but thankfully, Scikit-learn contains a number of built-in datasets, which leaves you free to experiment with different models.

In the development phases, especially when there is little training data, we use "cross-validation" for the purpose of training and validating algorithms on the data. With cross-validation, we partition the training set and then train the algorithm using all partitions except for one. That final partition is used to test the algorithm. We then rotate all the partitions multiple times, training and evaluating the algorithm on all data in turn.

Let's consider that our dataset has been partitioned into five equal-sized subsets. Those subsets are given labels of A, B, C, D, and E. To start with, partitions B to E are used for training and A for testing. On the next go around, we use partitions A, C, D, E for training and B for testing. The partitions are rotated for each partition until the algorithm has been trained and tested on every partition. With cross-validation, we obtain better accuracy in the performance estimate than we do when we use a single partition for testing.

Variance and Bias Performance Measures

There are quite a few metrics that may be used to effectively measure how a model learns task performance. Where supervised learning is concerned, there are many different performance metrics for prediction error measurements. There are two things that could cause prediction error in a model – variance and bias. Let's say that we have far too many data training sets. Each is unique but each represents the population equally. If you have a high-bias model, the errors for any given input will be similar no matter which training set is used because the model's assumptions are biased about the relationship the training data demonstrates over the proper relationship. By contrast, a high-variance model produces errors that are different for a given input depending entirely on the training set used. High-bias models are not flexible but high-variance models can be over-flexible to the point where even the noise in a training set is modeled. In other words, a high-variance model may overfit the data while high-bias models may underfit.

In an ideal scenario, a model would have low-variance and low-bias but any efforts made to reduce one inevitably results in the other one increasing. The terms for this is the "bias-variance trade-off". With unsupervised learning, there is no error signal that can be measured. Instead, the performance metrics are used to measure some of the data structure attributes but most of the performance measures can only be used to work out specific task types.

The performance measures used to evaluate the machine learning systems should be representative of the costs of real-word errors. This may look trivial but the next example will demonstrate using a performance measure that is generally right for a given task but is not right for the specific application of that task.

Accuracy, Precision, Recall

Think about a classification task; the machine learning system is observing different tumors and its goal is to predict whether they are malignant or benign. One of the obvious measures of the program performance is accuracy, i.e. correctly classified instances as a fraction. However, while the accuracy is a performance measurement, what it doesn't do is distinguish between the benign tumors incorrectly classified as malignant and vice versa, the malignant tumors wrongly classified as benign. There may be similar or identical costs incurred on all the error types in some applications, but with this specific task, failure to correctly identify the tumors that are malignant is a far worse error than incorrectly classifying a benign tumor as being malignant.

The possible predictions can be measured in a way that provides us with different perspectives of the classifier's performance. When a tumor is correctly classified as malignant, we have a "true-positive" prediction, but when a benign tumor is classified as malignant we have a "false-positive" prediction. By the same token, an incorrect classification of a benign tumor is a "false-negative" and a correct classification of a benign tumor is a "true-negative". All four of those outcomes can be used to calculate a number of performance measures, such as precision, accuracy, recall and more.

We use this formula to calculate accuracy:

$$ACC = (TP + TN)/(TP + TN + FP + FN)$$

In this formula:

- TP = how many true positives there are
- TN = how many true negatives there are
- FP = how many false positives there are
- FN = how many false negatives there are

For precision, we are calculating the fraction of correctly classified malignant tumors and we use the following formula:

$$PREC = TP/(TP + FP)$$

For recall, we calculate the fraction of identified malignant tumors and, for that, we use this formula:

$$R = TP/(TP + FN)$$

In our example, precision is being used as a way to measure the fraction of correctly predicted malignant tumors while recall is used to measure the fraction of detected malignant tumors. Both these measures together may show that a classifier with great accuracy may not detect many of the tumors that are malignant. A classifier that never predicts a malignant tumor would show a high accuracy level if the vast majority of the tumors are benign. Another classifier with low-accuracy and high-recall would probably be better for the problem because it can and will detect the bulk of the tumors that are malignant.

Before we move on, let's look briefly at the machine learning techniques.

Classification

This technique uses known, existing data to determine how new data will be classified into categories that are already in existence. When the system classifies a set of data it will do the following:

- A learning algorithm is used to prepare a brand-new data model
- That model is tested
- Later, it will be used for examining new data and determining what its class should be.

Classification is also sometimes termed as categorization and, in a classification task, the model learns to look at the dependent input and output variables and predict a discrete value for each one using the independent variables. Put simply, the program needs to predict the class that is the most probable label, class, or category for new data. It is a supervised learning form and is widely used by email providers to classify email as spam or not spam.

Naïve Bayes Classifier

One of the more common classification techniques is the Naïve Bayes Classifier, a very simple technique for the construction of classifiers. It is not a single training algorithm; it is a group and it is used to construct models that will classify instance in problems using the data available to it.

One of the more important features of this classifier is that it only needs a little data to estimate what the necessary parameters are for the classification.

Regression

With regression, the program will predict values for response variables or continuous output using the explanatory variables or the input.

Recommendation

One of the more popular methods is called recommendation; this will make use of user information to provide us with close recommendations. This is a method that tends to be used by Amazon and Google to show users a list of recommended items or websites based on their previous choices. This is done by a recommender engine that works behind the scenes for this purpose to capture the behavior of users. This is also how Facebook sends you recommendations and suggestions for friends.

Clustering

A cluster is a group of observations that are related and one of the most common of the unsupervised learning tasks is to look through training data to find the clusters. Clustering may also be defined as a process of taking a given collection and ordering the items inside it based on features that are similar.

We often use the clustering technique to explore datasets. For example, if the dataset were a set of book reviews, clustering would look for groups of negative and positive reviews. However, it does not have the capacity to label those clusters only that, through one or more clusters, the groups are similar in some way.

There are two main types of clustering – flat and hierarchical. Flat clustering will create flat cluster sets that do not have a clear structure but can relate clusters to one another. Hierarchical clustering, on the other hand, will create cluster hierarchies which are then given an output that provides even more information than the flat clustering. You do not need to specify how many clusters there are before but it is a less efficient method than flat clustering is.

Clustering Algorithms

Clustering algorithms are required for any given date to be clustered and there are two commonly used clustering algorithms – canopy and K-Means. Canopy is unsupervised and it is a pre-clustering algorithm that is generally used as a K-Means or Hierarchical preprocessing step. We use it for speeding up the clustering operations done on the big datasets where the size may dictate that it isn't possible to use any other algorithm.

K-Means is also important; the K is representing how many divisions there will be in the clustering data, for example, if k=3 in the algorithm then the data is divided by that algorithm into three clusters. A vector in space is used to represent each of the objects and, to start with, the algorithm will randomly choose the k points and treat them as centers – all the objects closest to a given center will be clustered. Vector files are required as the k-means input so we need to create them before we can use the k-means algorithm.

Machine Learning Algorithms

These are the most common machine learning algorithms, all of which can be used on any real-world problem:

- Decision Tree

- Dimensionality Reduction Algorithms

- Gradient Boosting algorithms such as XGBoost, GBM, Catboost, and LightGBM

- K-Means

- KNN

- Linear Regression
- Logistic Regression

- Naïve Bayes

- Random Forest

- SVM

We will now look at each one in more detail.

Linear Regression

We use linear regression algorithms for the estimation of real-world values that are based on one or more continuous variables. Those values could be house prices, sales calls, the total number of sales, and so on. Linear regression is used to create a relationship between both independent and dependent variables and it does this by finding the best line and fitting it. We call this line the "regression line" and the linear equation that represents it is Y= a *X + b. The breakdown of this equation is:

- Y is the 'dependent' variable
- a is the slope
- X is the 'independent' variable
- b is the intercept

We take the distance between the regression lines and the data points, square the result and minimize the sum to derive a and b.

Perhaps the best way to understand linear regression is to look at an example. Let's say we have a class of students and we arrange them in ascending order of their weight. We can visualize the students and use a combination of an analysis of build and height (parameters); we arrange them in order as per these parameters by determining that both build and height directly correlate to weight through a relationship that looks much like the equation from earlier.

Linear Regression Types

There are two main types of linear regression – simple and multiple. The characteristic of a simple linear regression is a single variable that is independent while linear multiple regression has at least one, usually more of these independent variables. When we are looking for the best fit line we can fit curvilinear or polynomial regression.

The following code works:

import matplotlib.pyplot as plt

plt.scatter(X, Y)

*yfit = [a + b * xi for xi in X]*

plt.plot(X, yfit)

How to Build a Linear Regressor

Regression is the estimation of the relationship that exists between the input data and the output data, which is continuously valued. The data tends to be in the format of real numbers; we want to try to estimate what underlying function controls the input to output mapping.

The following is an example of the input to output mapping:

1 --> 2

4 --> 8

5.2 --> 10.4

9.3 --> 18.6

As a way of estimating what the relationship is between the inputs and the outputs, we can look at the pattern. We can see, quite easily in this case, that the output is equal to twice the value of the input; in this scenario, f(x) = 2x would be the transformation.

With linear regression, we estimate what the function is by a linear combination of all the input values. The example above has a single instance each of an input and output variable. The goal of this algorithm is the extraction of the correct model that creates a relationship between the input and output variables. The aim is to take the real output and the output that was predicted, determine the differences between them, sum the result, and minimize it using a linear function. We call this the "ordinary least squares" method. You could, possibly correctly, assume that a curvy line would fit better but this isn't allowed in linear regression. One of the benefits of linear regression is its lack of complexity and, while you may find non-linear regression models that are far more accurate, they will also be a lot slower. With linear regressions, the algorithm attempts to find an approximation of the input data points with a straight, not curvy, line.

We'll now look at how to use Python for building a linear regression model.

We'll start by assuming that we have a data file. It has a name of data_singlevar.txt. In this file are lines separated by commas; the input value is the first element, and the corresponding output value is the second element. We will use the following as our input argument:

Assuming that we have the best fit line for the set of data points, it is:

y = a + b * x

In this:

- b = (sum(xi * yi) - n * xbar * ybar) / sum((xi - xbar)^2)

- a = ybar - b * xbar

We can use this code:

 # sample points

X = [0, 6, 11, 14, 22]

Y = [1, 7, 12, 15, 21]

 # solve for a and b

def best_fit(X, Y):

  xbar = sum(X)/len(X)

  ybar = sum(Y)/len(Y)

  n = len(X) # or len(Y)

  *numer = sum([xi*yi for xi,yi in zip(X, Y)]) - n * xbar * ybar*

  *denum = sum([xi**2 for xi in X]) - n * xbar**2*

```python
    b = numer / denum
    a = ybar - b * xbar


    print('best fit line:\ny = {:.2f} + {:.2f}x'.format(a, b))


    return a, b


# solution
a, b = best_fit(X, Y)
#best fit line:
#y = 0.80 + 0.92x


# plot points and fit line
import matplotlib.pyplot as plt
plt.scatter(X, Y)
yfit = [a + b * xi for xi in X]
plt.plot(X, yfit)
plt.show()
```

best fit line:

y = 1.48 + 0.92x

Coefficients, variance score and the residual squares sum can be calculated with this program:

```
import matplotlib.pyplot as plt

import numpy as np

from sklearn import datasets, linear_model

from sklearn.metrics import mean_squared_error, r2_score

# Load the diabetes dataset

diabetes = datasets.load_diabetes()

# Use only one feature

diabetes_X = diabetes.data[:, np.newaxis, 2]

# Split the data into training/testing sets

diabetes_X_train = diabetes_X[:-30]

diabetes_X_test = diabetes_X[-30:]


# Split the targets into training/testing sets

diabetes_y_train = diabetes.target[:-30]

diabetes_y_test = diabetes.target[-30:]

# Create linear regression object

regr = linear_model.LinearRegression()

# Train the model using the training sets

regr.fit(diabetes_X_train, diabetes_y_train)
```

 # Make predictions using the testing set

diabetes_y_pred = regr.predict(diabetes_X_test)

 # The coefficients

print('Coefficients: \n', regr.coef_)

 # The mean squared error

print("Mean squared error: %.2f"

    % mean_squared_error(diabetes_y_test, diabetes_y_pred))

 # Explained variance score: 1 is perfect prediction

print('Variance score: %.2f' % r2_score(diabetes_y_test, diabetes_y_pred))

 # Plot outputs

plt.scatter(diabetes_X_test, diabetes_y_test, color = 'black')

plt.plot(diabetes_X_test, diabetes_y_pred, color = 'blue', linewidth = 3)

plt.xticks(())

plt.yticks(())

plt.show()

And, when that code is run, the result is an output along these lines:

Automatically created module for IPython interactive environment

('Coefficients: \n', array([941.43097333]))

Mean squared error: 3035.06

Variance score: 0.41

Logistic Regression

This technique has been "borrowed" from the field of statistics and is the commonly used method for the binary classification tasks, i.e. those tasks that have two class values. Logistic regression is not, as you might think, a regression algorithm; rather it is one of the classification algorithms and it is used to estimate discrete values based on the specified independent variable set. The algorithm is used to predict the probability that an event will occur, and this is done by taking a logit function and fitting data to it, hence the alternative name of "logit regression". Because it is used for binary tasks and because it predicts probabilities, the output values will always be between 0 and 1.

Understanding logistic regression is best done with an example. Let's assume that we have a puzzle that needs solving and it has just two possible outcomes – it has a solution, or it doesn't. Now let's assume that we have several puzzles that we can use to test a student to see what are his or her best subjects. If that student were given, for example, a trigonometry puzzle to solve, there could be an 80% chance of them solving it, but with a geography puzzle, there may only be 20% chance. Logistic regression helps here. As with mathematics, we use a linear combination of the variables (predictor) to express the outcome's log odds:

odds = p/ (1-p) = probability of event occurrence / probability of not event occurrence

$\ln(\text{odds}) = \ln(p/(1-p))$; ln is the logarithm to the base 'e'.

$\text{logit}(p) = \ln(p/(1-p)) = b_0 + b_1 X_1 + b_2 X_2 + b_3 X_3 \ldots + b_k X_k$

As p contains the probability that the interest characteristic is present, it will pick the parameters that will improve the likelihood that the sample values are observed rather than those that reduce the squared errors sum, as happens with ordinary regression.

These points are useful to learn for logistic regression:

- Logistic regression is like ordinary regression in that it has the objective of finding the values of those coefficients that are used to weight each of the input variables.
- Logistic regression is not like linear regression in that the output prediction is located using a logistic function, which is non-linear.
- The logistic function is sometimes called the "s-function" because it looks like a large S and it can change any given value to the 0 to 1 range. This means that we can give the logistic function's output a rule that says it must assign a value of 0 and 1 and then predict the class values.
- A logistic regression model learns in such a way that its predictions can be used as probabilities for specified data instances that belong to one of two classes – 0 or 1. This is helpful for tasks where more reasoning is required for a prediction to be made.
- As with linear regression, the logistic regression works much better when output variable attributes that are unrelated are removed along with any similar attributes.

With the next code, you can see how a plot is developed for logistic regression using a synthetic dataset that has been classified into 0 or 1 values, making use of logistic curve:

import numpy as np

import matplotlib.pyplot as plt

from sklearn import linear_model

 # This is the test set, it's a straight line with some Gaussian noise

xmin, xmax = -10, 10

n_samples = 100

np.random.seed(0)

```
X = np.random.normal(size = n_samples)

y = (X > 0).astype(np.float)

X[X > 0] *= 4

X +=.3 * np.random.normal(size = n_samples)

X = X[:, np.newaxis]


# run the classifier

clf = linear_model.LogisticRegression(C=1e5)

clf.fit(X, y)


# and plot the result

plt.figure(1, figsize = (4, 3))

plt.clf()

plt.scatter(X.ravel(), y, color='black', zorder=20)

X_test = np.linspace(-10, 10, 300)

def model(x): return 1 / (1 + np.exp(-x))

loss = model(X_test * clf.coef_ + clf.intercept_).ravel()

plt.plot(X_test, loss, color='blue', linewidth=3)

ols = linear_model.LinearRegression()

ols.fit(X, y)

plt.plot(X_test, ols.coef_ * X_test + ols.intercept_, linewidth=1)
```

plt.axhline(.5, color='.5')

plt.ylabel('y')

plt.xlabel('X')

plt.xticks(range(-10, 10))

plt.yticks([0, 0.5, 1])

plt.ylim(-.25, 1.25)

plt.xlim(-4, 10)

plt.legend(('Logistic Regression Model', 'Linear Regression Model'),

loc="lower right", fontsize='small')

plt.show()

Decision Tree Algorithm

A decision tree is a supervised learning algorithm that is commonly used in classification problems. It will work for two variable types – continuous dependent and discrete. This algorithm divides the population into at least two sets, based on the attributes that are the most significant, so that the sets are as distinct as they can be.

Decision trees are common in machine learning and they cover regression and classification. With decision analysis, the decision tree will represent both the decision and the decision-making explicitly and visually, using a decision model that looks something like a tree.

Decision trees are upside down trees, with the branches below and the root at the very top. The tree will divide into branches or edges depending on a given condition or internal node; where a branch end does not divide anymore, it is called the decision or leaf.

An example would be the passengers on the Titanic. We have a dataset that contains all the passengers and we want to predict whether a given passenger survives the disaster or not. We could use three attributes or features from the dataset – the age, the sex and the sibsp (number of children or spouse) and the decision tree will use those features to predict whether they died or not.

Some examples will show that the population is divided into groups and classified using several attributes to determine "whether they do this or not". Several techniques are used to divide the population including entropy, Chi-square, Information Gain, and Gini, to name a few. One of the best ways to understand a decision tree and the way it works is to play a game called Jezzball. This is a classic Microsoft game whereby you are in a room where the walls move; your goal is to create new walls to clear the maximum area without the balls. Each time the room is divided by a new wall, you are, in effect, creating two separate populations in the same area. Decision trees work in much the same way; the population is divided into groups that are as different as they possibly can be.

As a final example, have a look at this code and the output:

```
#Starting implementation

import pandas as pd

import matplotlib.pyplot as plt

import numpy as np

import seaborn as sns

# matplotlib inline

from sklearn import tree

df = pd.read_csv("iris_df.csv")

df.columns = ["X1", "X2", "X3","X4", "Y"]

df.head()
```

#implementation

from sklearn.cross_validation import train_test_split

decision = tree.DecisionTreeClassifier(criterion="gini")

X = df.values[:, 0:4]

Y = df.values[:, 4]

trainX, testX, trainY, testY = train_test_split(X, Y, test_size = 0.3)

decision.fit(trainX, trainY)

print("Accuracy: \n", decision.score(testX, testY))

#Visualization

from sklearn.externals.six import StringIO

from IPython.display import Image

import pydotplus as pydot

dot_data = StringIO()

tree.export_graphviz(decision, out_file=dot_data)

graph = pydot.graph_from_dot_data(dot_data.getvalue())

Image(graph.create_png())

The output is:

Accuracy:

0.955555555556

Support Vector Machines

A support vector machine is often coined as an SVM and it is one of the best-known of the supervised algorithms for classification; the SVM is used to separate different data categories. The SVM is classified through optimization of the line so that in each of the data groups the closest point is the furthest away from the other groups. By default, the vector is linear and is visualized as such. However, it can also be non-linear provided the type of the kernel is changed so it is no longer Gaussian, or linear.

SVM is a method of classification where each of the data items is plotted as a point in n-dimensional space – n= the number of features – and the value from each of the features is also the value of a specific coordinate. For example, let's say that we have two features for an individual – hair length and height. Both variables should both be plotted in 2D space first; each of the points will have a pair of coordinates which are called Support Vectors.

A line is found that will divide the data into two groups of data, each classified differently, and it is this line that determines that the distance from each group's closest point is also the furthest away. This line is called the "black line" because the closest points are the furthest from that line. The line is the classifier, and depending on the where and how the test data is divided either side of the line, the new data can then be classified:

from sklearn import svm

df = pd.read_csv('iris_df.csv')

df.columns = ['X4', 'X3', 'X1', 'X2', 'Y']

df = df.drop(['X4', 'X3'], 1)

df.head()

from sklearn.cross_validation import train_test_split

support = svm.SVC()

```
X = df.values[:, 0:2]

Y = df.values[:, 2]

trainX, testX, trainY, testY = train_test_split( X, Y, test_size = 0.3)

sns.set_context('notebook', font_scale=1.1)

sns.set_style('ticks')

sns.lmplot('X1','X2', scatter=True, fit_reg=False, data=df, hue='Y')

plt.ylabel('X2')

plt.xlabel('X1')
```

If you were to execute this code, you would get an output of:

Text(0.5,27.256,'X1')

Naïve Bayes Algorithm

The Naïve Bayes algorithm has its basis in the Bayes theorem, assuming that we have independent predictor variables. Simply put, the Naïve Bayes classifier will make the assumption that, although a specific feature may be present in a class, it is not related in any way to any of the other features that are present.

An example would be a fruit; if it is round, colored orange, and has a diameter of around 3 inches, it is classified as an orange. Even if those three features depended either on one another or on other features, the Naïve Bayes classifier sees that all the characteristics contribute independently of one another to the probability of the fruit being an orange.

It is very easy to create a Naïve Bayesian model and it is of huge usefulness where large datasets are concerned. Aside from being one of the simplest, the Naïve Bayes algorithm has been shown to vastly outperform some of the most advanced methods of classification.

The Bayes theorem provides a method to calculate the posterior probability, which is P(c|x) from P(c), P(x) and P(x|c). The equation is P(c/x) = P(x/c)P(c)/P(x). Breaking the equation down:

- P(c|x) is the target attribute's posterior probability
- P(c) is the class's prior probability

- P(x|c) is the likelihood – the probability of the given class's predictor

- P(x) is the predictor's prior probability

The following example will explain this better:

Let's assume that we have a training dataset called weather; the target variable that corresponds to it is called Play. We want to classify whether a player can or can't play based on the weather conditions. To do this, we need to follow these steps:

1. The dataset needs to be converted into a frequency table.

2. A Likelihood table needs to be created – to do this, find the probabilities of Playing – 0.64 and Overcast = 0.29.

3. A Naïve Bayesian may now be used to calculate what each class's posterior probability is and the prediction outcome will be the class that has the highest posterior probability.

The problem is this – if the weather is sunny, will the players play?

To solve that problem, we use the method we talked of earlier, so it would look like this:

P(Yes | Sunny) = P(Sunny | Yes) * P(Yes) / P (Sunny)

In our example, P (Sunny |Yes) = 3/9 = 0.33, P(Sunny) = 5/14 = 0.36, P(Yes) = 9/14 = 0.64

So, P (Yes | Sunny) = 0.33 * 0.64 / 0.36 = 0.60, because this has the highest probability.

The Naïve Bayes algorithm makes use of a similar method to predict probabilities of classes that are based on different attributes. We tend to use this algorithm more for text classification and where we have a task that has several classes.

You can see one example of an implementation of Naïve Bayes below:

```
import csv

import random

import math


def loadCsv(filename):

    lines = csv.reader(open(filename, "rb"))

    dataset = list(lines)

    for i in range(len(dataset)):

        dataset[i] = [float(x) for x in dataset[i]]

    return dataset


def splitDataset(dataset, splitRatio):

    trainSize = int(len(dataset) * splitRatio)

    trainSet = []

    copy = list(dataset)

    while len(trainSet) < trainSize:

        index = random.randrange(len(copy))
```

```python
        trainSet.append(copy.pop(index))
    return [trainSet, copy]


def separateByClass(dataset):
    separated = {}
    for i in range(len(dataset)):
        vector = dataset[i]
        if (vector[-1] not in separated):
            separated[vector[-1]] = []
        separated[vector[-1]].append(vector)
    return separated


def mean(numbers):
    return sum(numbers)/float(len(numbers))


def stdev(numbers):
    avg = mean(numbers)
    variance = sum([pow(x-avg,2) for x in numbers])/float(len(numbers)-1)
    return math.sqrt(variance)


def summarize(dataset):
```

```
summaries = [(mean(attribute), stdev(attribute)) for attribute in
zip(*dataset)]


def summarizeByClass(dataset):

  separated = separateByClass(dataset)

  summaries = {}

  for classValue, instances in separated.iteritems():

    summaries[classValue] = summarize(instances)

  return summaries


def calculateProbability(x, mean, stdev):

  exponent = math.exp(-(math.pow(x-mean,2)/(2*math.pow(stdev,2))))

  return (1 / (math.sqrt(2*math.pi) * stdev)) * exponent


def calculateClassProbabilities(summaries, inputVector):

  probabilities = {}

  for classValue, classSummaries in summaries.iteritems():

    probabilities[classValue] = 1

    for i in range(len(classSummaries)):

      mean, stdev = classSummaries[i]

      x = inputVector[i]
```

```
        probabilities[classValue] *= calculateProbability(x, mean, stdev)
    return probabilities


def predict(summaries, inputVector):
    probabilities = calculateClassProbabilities(summaries, inputVector)
    bestLabel, bestProb = None, -1
    for classValue, probability in probabilities.iteritems():
        if bestLabel is None or probability > bestProb:
            bestProb = probability
            bestLabel = classValue
    return bestLabel


def getPredictions(summaries, testSet):
    predictions = []
    for i in range(len(testSet)):
        result = predict(summaries, testSet[i])
        predictions.append(result)
    return predictions
def getAccuracy(testSet, predictions):
    correct = 0
    for i in range(len(testSet)):
```

```python
        if testSet[i][-1] == predictions[i]:

            correct += 1

    return (correct/float(len(testSet))) * 100.0


def main():

    filename = 'pima-indians-diabetes.data.csv'

    splitRatio = 0.67

    dataset = loadCsv(filename)

    trainingSet, testSet = splitDataset(dataset, splitRatio)

    print('Split {0} rows into train = {1} and test = {2}
rows').format(len(dataset), len(trainingSet), len(testSet))

    # prepare model

    summaries = summarizeByClass(trainingSet)

    # test model

    predictions = getPredictions(summaries, testSet)

    accuracy = getAccuracy(testSet, predictions)

    print('Accuracy: {0}%').format(accuracy)
main()
```

Running this long code provides this output:

Split 1372 rows into train = 919 and test = 453 rows

Accuracy: 83.6644591611%

K-Nearest Neighbors

K-Nearest Neighbors, usually shorted to KNN, is one of the supervised classification algorithms. It is one of the simpler ones used for storing all the available cases and then for classifying the new cases using a K-nearest majority vote. The class is assigned the case that is commonest among KNN and this is measured using a distance function.

Distance functions fall into 4 categories – Minkowski, Euclidean, Hamming, and Manhattan. Hamming is used for variables that are categorical and the others are for functions that are continuous. So, if K = 1, the case will be assigned to the class of the nearest neighbor. Sometimes it can be a challenge to choose K will you are carrying out KNN modeling.

KNN examines the different centroids and will use a function, normally Euclidean, to compare the distance. Those results are then analyzed, and each point is assigned to the group – this is to ensure it is optimally placed with all its nearest points.

KNN can be used for regression and for classification problems but it tends to be more used in the latter; KNN is also easy to map to real-life. Before you select KNN, note the following:

- In computational terms, KNN is expensive
- You should normalize variables otherwise the higher-range variables may bias it
- Before you choose KNN, work on the pre-processing stage first, like removing noise, etc.

The following piece of code will show you how KNN works:

#Importing Libraries

from sklearn.neighbors import KNeighborsClassifier

```
#Assumed you have, X (predictor) and Y (target) for training data set and
x_test(predictor) of test_dataset

# Create KNeighbors classifier object model

KNeighborsClassifier(n_neighbors=6) # default value for n_neighbors is 5

# Train the model using the training sets and check score

model.fit(X, y)

#Predict Output

predicted= model.predict(x_test)

from sklearn.neighbors import KNeighborsClassifier

df = pd.read_csv('iris_df.csv')

df.columns = ['X1', 'X2', 'X3', 'X4', 'Y']

df = df.drop(['X4', 'X3'], 1)

df.head()

sns.set_context('notebook', font_scale=1.1)

sns.set_style('ticks')

sns.lmplot('X1','X2', scatter=True, fit_reg=False, data=df, hue='Y')

plt.ylabel('X2')

plt.xlabel('X1')

from sklearn.cross_validation import train_test_split

neighbors = KNeighborsClassifier(n_neighbors=5)

X = df.values[:, 0:2]
```

Y = df.values[:, 2]

trainX, testX, trainY, testY = train_test_split(X, Y, test_size = 0.3)

neighbors.fit(trainX, trainY)

print('Accuracy: \n', neighbors.score(testX, testY))

pred = neighbors.predict(testX)

The output from this code is:

('Accuracy: \n', 0.75555555555555554)

K-Means

K-Means is an unsupervised algorithm used to deal with clustering problems. The K-Means procedure is a very simple way of classifying a provided data set through a specific number of k-clusters. The data points within a cluster are homogenous, and to peer groups, they are heterogenous.

How K-Means Forms a Cluster

K-Means follows the steps below to form a cluster:

1. It first chooses centroids – a k number of points for each of the clusters.
2. Each of the data points will form a cluster with the centroids nearest to it – k-clusters.
3. K-Means will then locate the centroid of each of the clusters. It bases this on members of existing clusters. We have got new centroids.

Because our centroids are new, steps 2 and 3 must be repeated to find the closest distance from the centroids for each of the data points. An association must be made with new k-clusters and the process must be repeated until there is convergence, i.e. the centroids no longer change.

Determining the Value of K

Each cluster in K-Means has a centroid. The sum of the square of the difference between the data points and the centroid in the cluster is equal to the sum of the cluster's square value. When the sums of all the square values for all the clusters are added together, we get the total within the sum of the square value for the clustering solution.

As the cluster number rises, the value will continue to decrease; however, if you plot that result, you will see a sharp decrease in the sum of the squared distance up to a given k-value and then it will decrease more slowly after. This is how we find the optimum cluster number.

Look at this code:

```
import numpy as np

import matplotlib.pyplot as plt

from matplotlib import style

style.use("ggplot")

from sklearn.cluster import KMeans

x = [1, 5, 1.5, 8, 1, 9]

y = [2, 8, 1.8, 8, 0.6, 11]


plt.scatter(x,y)

plt.show()

X = np.array([ [1, 2],

        [5, 8],

        [1.5, 1.8],
```

```
        [8, 8],

        [1, 0.6],

        [9, 11]])

kmeans = KMeans(n_clusters=2)

kmeans.fit(X)

centroids = kmeans.cluster_centers_

labels = kmeans.labels_

print(centroids)

print(labels)

colors = ["g.","r.","c.","y."]


for i in range(len(X)):

    print("coordinate:",X[i], "label:", labels[i])

    plt.plot(X[i][0], X[i][1], colors[labels[i]], markersize = 10)

plt.scatter(centroids[:, 0],centroids[:, 1], marker = "x", s=150, linewidths = 5, zorder = 10)

plt.show()
```

Running this code provides the following output:

[[1.16666667 1.46666667] [7.33333333 9.]]

[0 1 0 1 0 1]

('coordinate:', array([1., 2.]), 'label:', 0)

('coordinate:', array([5., 8.]), 'label:', 1)

('coordinate:', array([1.5, 1.8]), 'label:', 0)

('coordinate:', array([8., 8.]), 'label:', 1)

('coordinate:', array([1., 0.6]), 'label:', 0)

('coordinate:', array([9., 11.]), 'label:', 1)

Try this code to help you understand better:

from sklearn.cluster import KMeans

df = pd.read_csv('iris_df.csv')

df.columns = ['X1', 'X2', 'X3', 'X4', 'Y']

df = df.drop(['X4', 'X3'], 1)

df.head()

from sklearn.cross_validation import train_test_split

kmeans = KMeans(n_clusters = 3)

X = df.values[:, 0:2]

kmeans.fit(X)

df['Pred'] = kmeans.predict(X)

df.head()

sns.set_context('notebook', font_scale = 1.1)

sns.set_style('ticks')

sns.lmplot('X1','X2', scatter = True, fit_reg = False, data = df, hue = 'Pred')

And the output of this is:

<seaborn.axisgrid.FacetGrid at 0x107ad6a0>

Random Forest

Random Forest is one of the more popular of the supervised ensemble algorithms. By "ensemble", we mean that it uses a group of "weak" learners and getting them to work together to form a predictor that is stronger. In the Random Forest, the weak learners are decision trees that are randomly implemented and brought together to form the forest.

Look at this code:

from sklearn.ensemble import RandomForestClassifier

df = pd.read_csv('iris_df.csv')

df.columns = ['X1', 'X2', 'X3', 'X4', 'Y']

df.head()

from sklearn.cross_validation import train_test_split

forest = RandomForestClassifier()

X = df.values[:, 0:4]

Y = df.values[:, 4]

trainX, testX, trainY, testY = train_test_split(X, Y, test_size = 0.3)

forest.fit(trainX, trainY)

print('Accuracy: \n', forest.score(testX, testY))

pred = forest.predict(testX)

The output is:

('Accuracy: \n', 1.0)

Ensemble methods have the goal to combine predictions from multiple base estimators that have been built using a specified learning algorithm and the idea is to improve generalization over one estimator.

Inside the module called sklearn.ensemble, there are 2 averaging algorithms that have their basis in random decision trees – the method called Extra-Trees and the algorithm called RandomForest. Both are classified as 'perturb and combine' techniques designed specifically for trees. What this means is that a diverse classifier set is created by pushing randomness into the construction of the classifier. The ensemble prediction is the average prediction of all the individual classifiers.

Each forest classifier must be fitted with 2 arrays:

- A dense or a sparse array X of size [n_samples, n_features]

- A Y of size array [n_samples]

These arrays hold the class labels, or target values, for all the training samples, as in the next code:

from sklearn.ensemble import RandomForestClassifier

X = [[0, 0], [1, 1]]

Y = [0, 1]

clf = RandomForestClassifier(n_estimators = 10)

clf = clf.fit(X, Y)

Like a decision tree, forests will extend to problems that are multi-output, for example, Y is an array of size [n_samples, n_outputs]. In scikit-learn, classifiers are combined through an average of probabilistic prediction, rather than each of the classifiers voting for one class.

Random Forest is a trademark that describes a decision tree ensemble. Each collection of these decision trees is called a "forest", and for a new object to be classified on attributes, each of the trees will provide a classification and the tree will 'vote' for that class. The forest will choose the classification that earns the most votes.

Each of the trees in the forest is planted and then grown like this:

- If there are N number of cases contained in the training set, a random sample of N cases will be taking but replaced. This sample will become the training set required for the tree to grow.

- If the tree has M number of input variables, m<<M number will be specified in such a way that, at each tree node, random m variables are selected from M and the node is split based on the best split of m. The m value will remain constant throughout the growth of the forest.

- Each of the trees will be grown as large as possible and no pruning will happen.

Dimensionality Reduction Algorithm

Another of the commonly used unsupervised learning tasks is dimensionality reduction. Some problems can have hundreds of thousands, even up to millions of explanatory or input variables and these are computationally expensive. Not only that, if some of those variables are full of noise or bear no relevance to the underlying relationship, the generalization ability of the program could be diminished significantly.

We use dimensionality reduction to find those input variables that will cause the biggest changes in the response or output variable. We can also use dimensionality reduction for visualization of the data. Regression problems can be easily visualized, such as those that predict property prices from the size and plot the property size on the x-axis with the price plotted on the y-axis of the graph. In much the same way, we can easily visualize the same problem of price regression when we add in another explanatory variable. We could, for example, plot how many rooms are in the property on the z-axis. However, when we have a problem that has thousands of these input variables, it isn't possible to visualize it.

With dimensionality reduction, we can reduce impossibly large sets of these explanatory variables to more manageable sets of input variables that will hold on to the most information they possibly can.

The one-dimensionality algorithm that is very useful for data analysis is PCA. With this, we can reduce how many computations are needed in a model when we have thousands of input variables, all different. Because PCA is unsupervised, the user will still be required to analyze all the results and ensure that around 95% of the behavior from the original dataset is maintained.

This can be better understood by the following code:

```
from sklearn import decomposition

df = pd.read_csv('iris_df.csv')

df.columns = ['X1', 'X2', 'X3', 'X4', 'Y']

df.head()

from sklearn import decomposition

pca = decomposition.PCA()

fa = decomposition.FactorAnalysis()

X = df.values[:, 0:4]

Y = df.values[:, 4]

train, test = train_test_split(X,test_size = 0.3)

train_reduced = pca.fit_transform(train)

test_reduced = pca.transform(test)

print(pca.n_components_)
```

This code will output the following:

In the last decade, we have seen an aggressive rise in the capture of data at all possible points and levels. Not only are we seeing research organizations, governmental agencies and corporations producing new sources of data, they are also capturing extremely detailed data at multiple stages and points.

For example, we see e-commerce businesses capturing more and more customer data, such as browsing preferences, demographics, purchase history, dislikes, likes, and more as a way of giving more personalized attention to their customers. The available data may have many thousands of different features and it is challenging to try reducing that data while keeping most of the information. This is where dimensionality reduction can really help.

Boosting Algorithms

Boosting algorithms are a family of algorithms that are able to change a weak learner into a strong one. We can understand this better by looking at the problem of identifying spam emails. The first step is identifying whether an email is spam by using this criterion:

- An email contains just one advertising image – this is spam
- An email has only got links – this is spam
- The body of the email consists of a sentence similar to "you have a won a cash prize of $xxx" – this is spam
- An email is from an official domain that you are a member of and you know it to be real – this is not spam
- The email comes from a source that you know, such as a friend or family member – this is not spam

What we have done here is define a number of rules that initially classify an email as being spam or not spam. However, each individual rule is not strong enough to classify the emails and, as such, the rules are weak learners.

To change a weak learner to a strong one, the predictions from each of the weak learners are combined through methods such as:

- Using an average or weighted average
- Consider a prediction that has a much higher vote than the others

For example, let's say that we have 7 of these weak learners defined. Of these, 5 have been voted as spam and 2 are not spam. By default, an email is considered as spam because the highest vote is for 'spam'.

How It Works

Boosting algorithms will combine a weak or a base learner to form one strong rule. We are going to look at how weak rules may be identified by boosting.

To find weak rules, the ML or base-learning algorithms are applied with different distributions. Every time one of these base-learning algorithms is applied, we have a brand-new weak prediction rule. Iteration processes are used by this multiple times and, after several iterations, the boosting algorithm will combine all the weak rules into one strong one.

These steps should be followed to find the correct distribution for each of the rounds:

1. The base learner will take every distribution and assign each one with an equal weight.
2. If the initial base-learning algorithm causes a prediction error, a higher weight is paid to those observations that have a prediction error.

Step 2 needs to be iterated repeatedly until we reach the limit of the base-learning algorithm or we attain higher accuracy, whichever comes first. Lastly, the outputs from the weak learners are combined and a strong learner is produced and this will, in time, improve the model's predictive powers. Boosting algorithms focus more on the examples that have not been classified properly or because of weak rules, they have a much higher level of errors.

Boosting Algorithm Types

There are three main boosting algorithms:

- XGBoost
- Gradient Tree Boosting
- Adaptive Boosting – AdaBoost

We are going to discuss in more detail the two most common ones, Gradient and AdaBoost.

AdaBoost

AdaBoost will use different weighted data for fitting sequences of weak learners. The first thing it does is predict the original set of data and provide each observation with an equal weight. If the first learner produces wrong predictions, higher weights are applied to the incorrectly predicted observations. Because this is an iterative process, the learners will continue to be added until a given limit either in the accuracy or in the model number is reached.

With AdaBoost, decision stamps are used most of the time but the base learner can be any type of machine learning algorithm provided it will accept weights on the data in the training set. AdaBoost can be used for regression and classification and the following Python code may be used:

#for classification

from sklearn.ensemble import AdaBoostClassifier

#for regression

from sklearn.ensemble import AdaBoostRegressor

from sklearn.tree import DecisionTreeClassifier

dt = DecisionTreeClassifier()

clf = AdaBoostClassifier(n_estimators=100, base_estimator=dt,learning_rate=1)

#The base estimator is a decision tree but you can use any machine learning learner provided it will take sample weights.

clf.fit(x_train,y_train)

Tuning Parameters

The parameters for optimal algorithm performance can be tuned and the key parameters to be tuned are:

- **n_estimators** – Used for controlling how many weak learners are used.

- **learning_rate** – Used for controlling what contribution is made by the weak learners when they are combined at the end. There will be a trade-off between n_estimators and learning_rate.

- **base_estimators** – These are used to help in specifying the different machine learning algorithms.

The base learner parameters can be tuned to optimize their performance as well.

Gradient Boosting

With gradient boosting, a lot of models are sequentially trained. Each new one will minimize the loss function of the entire system using gradient descent: y = ax + b + e (e indicates the error term). The learning method will fit the new models consecutively to provide a response variable estimate that is far more accurate.

The idea is to construct some new base learners which can then be correlated optimally with the loss function negative gradient, relevant to the entire ensemble. The sklearn library in Python has Gradient Tree Boosting (GBRT) a boosting generalization to loss functions that are arbitrarily differentiable. We can use GBRT for classification and regression and the following code may be used:

#for classification

from sklearn.ensemble import GradientBoostingClassifier

#for regression

from sklearn.ensemble import GradientBoostingRegressor

clf = GradientBoostingClassifier(n_estimators = 100, learning_rate = 1.0, max_depth = 1)

clf.fit(X_train, y_train)

The terms we used here are:

- **n_estimators** – To control the weak learner numbers.

- **learning_rate** – To control what contribution the weak learners make to the final combination; again, there is a trade-off between n_estimators and learning_rate.

- **max_depth** – The maximum depth to which the individual estimators (regression) will go and this will limit how many nodes are in a tree. This parameter is tuned to get the best performance; the best value will depend on what interaction there is between the input variables.

You can also tune the loss function for a much better performance.

Applications for Python Machine Learning

Machine learning and Artificial Intelligence are everywhere we go. There's a good chance that you already use them in your day-to-day life and are not even aware of it. With machine learning, devices, software, and computers all perform using cognition that is very much like that of the human brain.

Some of the more common applications of machine learning that have proved successful include programs for detecting and decoding handwriting, voice, facial and speech recognition programs, programs for detecting spam email, weather forecasts, stock predictions, and more. We'll look at some of these in more detail to finish this section of the book.

Virtual Personal Assistants

Most of us use these now – Google Now, Siri, and Alexa are just 3 examples of VPAs, used to help us search out information when we ask them to by voice. All you need to do is activate the assistant and ask it a question. To answer, the assistant application will look for the correct information, look at previous queries you may have made and will also look at other sources to get the right answer. You can also use a virtual personal assistant to do things like set an alarm or to set reminders.

Analysis and Prediction of Traffic Congestion

Something many of us use is GPS navigation and these monitor your location, your velocity and then use them to build a current traffic map, to help prevent traffic congestion. This kind of machine learning is helpful to estimate areas where congestion is common based on earlier records.

Automated Video Surveillance

Most video surveillance is AI-powered, using machine learning technology to detect crimes and prevent them before they happen. These systems will track suspicious behavior and notify human attendants by alert giving them the chance to help prevent crime and accidents.

Social Media

Perhaps the most well-known use of machine learning is social media like Facebook. It constantly monitors your search patterns, your friends, interests, where you work or live, and so on, to provide you with a list of recommendations for friends. Twitter does the same, as do many of the other social media sites.

Face Recognition

When you upload an image of you and a friend, sites like Facebook will recognize that friend immediately. Facial recognition is also used in many security technologies and the core technology behind the Computer Vision techniques of extracting information from videos and images is machine learning.

Filtering Email Spam and Malware

Machine learning is used a great deal to detect spam and malware. The databases that hold the relevant information are constantly being updated for more efficient detection.

Customer Support Online

Many websites offer customer support in the form of an online chat where you chat with a computer in most cases. These are called chatbots and they will extract information from your query and from the website to get the right answer for you. As time goes by, the chatbots will learn a better understanding of your queries and will become more efficient to provide the best answer. All of this is made possible using machine learning algorithms.

Refining Search ENGINE Results

Most search engines will make use of machine learning to provide better results for users. Whenever a search request is made, the algorithms will watch the responses from the searchers. Depending on these results, those algorithms will work to improve the results.

Recommendations for Products

When you make a purchase online or you search for a specific product, you will often receive emails offering similar products or adverts about the product you searched for or your purchases. Based on your previous online behavior, the online company will send you recommendations for other products.

Online Fraud Detection

Lastly, machine learning is used to track financial fraud online. PayPal uses machine learning to stop money laundering for example; they use a toolkit that will help them to compare transactions in the millions making distinctions between illegal and legal transactions between parties.

That concludes machine learning with Python. It is by no means an exhaustive discussion because the subject is simply too large and too complex to discuss in such a short space, but I hope I have been able to give you an overview. Next, we look at Python and Django.

Chapter 16: Python and Django

<u>An Introduction to Django</u>

When the internet first came about, every web page would be written by hand and updates to websites would have meant editing the HTML by redoing each page individually. It didn't take long to realize that this kind of approach was never going to work. To fix this, hackers at the National Center for Supercomputing Applications (NCSA) allowed external programs to spawn from the server and these could generate the HTML dynamically. Thus, Common Gateway Interface (CGI) was born, and it changed the face of the internet forever.

However, CGI wasn't without its problems, mostly in the need for repetitive coding. So PHP was designed to fix those problems, fast becoming the most used tool for website creation. But again, PHP had its problems – bad code, insecure, and more. This is why new web frameworks were developed, the ones we use today. These new frameworks have brought about an increase in ambition with web developers being expected to do much more as each day passes and that's where Django steps into the picture.

A Brief History of Django

Django came to life in 2003 when Simon Williamson and Adrian Holovaty, web programmers for the Lawrence Journal-World newspaper, started using Python to build applications. Because the nature of news websites means they needed to be built and updated fast, Adrian and Simon built a web development framework that saved time allowing them to build applications that could be maintained under hard deadlines.

In 2005, the team opted to release their framework to the public as an open-source framework naming it after Django Reinhardt, a jazz guitarist. Because it was first built to service news sites, Django has a number of features that make it ideal for so-called "content sites", like Craigslist and Amazon, websites that offer dynamic information driven by databases, as well as being effective to build other types of website.

It's also important to note that, because Django rose from real-world code, it has a focus on real-world problems, those faced by the developers when they developed the framework and those being faced now; that is what makes Django dynamic, constantly updated to be improved. The idea of Django is to save developers time, ensure maintainable applications can be built, and to perform effectively even when heavily loaded.

Django allows developers to build websites that are deep and dynamic in a very short time. It takes the hard work out of developing leaving users to focus on the fun and taking away the repetitive parts of the job. Because of this, Django can provide high-level abstractions of the most common patterns in web development, shortcuts for programming jobs done frequently, and very clear conventions on solving problems. While providing all this, Django does its best not to get in the way leaving you to do as much work outside the framework scope as you want. Django is about making web development fun and easy. Over the course of this section, we will look at the basics of installing and using the framework.

Installing Django

To get going with Django, you need to know how to install it and you need to understand the Model-View-Controller (MVC) design pattern. The latter is very important for those who are new to computer programming or who have previously used a programming language that doesn't make a clear separation between the logic and the data behind the website to the way it is shown on screen.

The philosophy behind Django is called 'loose coupling' and this is also the philosophy that underlies MVC. We'll go into more detail about this later because an understanding of MVC means a better understanding of Django. First though, let's install some software.

There are three steps to doing this:

- Install Python – you should already have this
- Install a PVE – Python Virtual Environment
- Install Django

These installation instructions are aimed at Windows users; for Mac and Linux users it is best to go directly to the Django website for full installation instructions. Windows users should also consider using Visual Studio Code Editor. Microsoft provides this free of charge as a way of providing support to both Python and Django programmers.

Creating Your Project Directory

Before we get started, we need a project directory. This can be saved anywhere on your desktop or laptop although you should really create it within your user directory – this will avoid any issues with permissions later. For now, we'll use the My Documents folder.

1. Create a new folder in My Documents and call it mysite_project
2. Open a command window on your computer (Press the Windows and X buttons on your keyboard and choose Command Window or PowerShell, depending on which version of Windows you are running).
3. We need to create a virtual environment so, at the command prompt, type in the following command (don't forget to replace *your name* with the name of your user directory:

C:\Users*your name*\OneDrive\Documents\mysite_project> virtualenv env_mysite

You should see something like this:

Using base prefix 'c:\\users*your name*\\appdata\\local\\programs\\python\\python36-32'

New python executable in C:\Users*your name*\OneDrive\Documents\mysite_project\env_mysite\Scripts\python.exe

Installing setuptools, pip, wheel...done.

4. Once that is done open the project directory in Windows Explorer to see what has been created. You should see a folder named \env_mysite – open this folder and the following should be in it:

\Include

\Lib

\Scripts

pip-selfcheck.json

Inside \Lib, virtualenv has created a separate installation of Python allowing you to work on the project without any effect on the rest of your computer software.

5. The next step is to activate the virtual environment before you use it. Go back to the command window and type the following at the prompt:

env_mysite\scripts\activate

The activate script from the \scripts folder will run and you should see this at the command prompt:

(env_mysite) C:\Users*your name*\OneDrive\Documents\mysite_project>

6. Next, we must install Django. To do this, go to your command prompt once more and type:

pip install django==2.0

This tells pip to install Django and you should see the following output:

(env_mysite) C:\Users*your name*\OneDrive\Documents\mysite_project> pip install django==2.0

Collecting django==2.0

Using cached Django-2.0-py2.py3-none-any.whl

Collecting pytz (from django==1.11)

Using cached pytz-2018.2-py2.py3-none-any.whl

Installing collected packages: pytz, django

Successfully installed django-2.0 pytz-2018.2

At the time of writing, v2.0 is the latest Django version; if it has moved on by the time you read this, make sure you install the latest version. Now you can test to see if the installation worked; at the virtual environment command prompt, type python and press enter. If the installation worked, the Django module can be imported, and you will see this:

(env_mysite) C:\Users*your name*\OneDrive\Documents\mysite_project> python

Python 3.6.1 (v3.6.1:69c0db5, Aug 14 2018, 17:54:52) [MSC v.1900 32 bit (Intel)] on win32

Type "help", "copyright", "credits" or "license" for more information.

>>> import django

>>> django.get_version()

'2.0'

>>>

Starting Your New Project

Now that everything is installed, we can create a new project – this is just a collection of the settings needed for a new instance of Django. If you have never used Django before, you will need to do a little bit of setting up first. Some code needs to be auto-generated to establish your project and this code has the settings needed for the Django instance – Django options, database configurations, and the settings specific to the application. You should still be using your virtual environment for this and you should be in the mysite_project directory.

Go to the command line in your virtual environment and type:

django-admin startproject mysite

This will create a directory called mysite inside the project directory and will also provide the files needed for a very basic Django website that is fully functioning.

Note

Do NOT name any projects the same as any of the built-in Django or Python components. For example, do not use the name Django as it will cause conflict with Django and do not use the name 'test' as it will cause conflict with a package built-in to Python.

Let's see what startproject did:

mysite/

manage.py

mysite/

__init__.py

settings.py

urls.py

wsgi.py

These are the files that were created by startproject. Here's what each one does:

- **mysite/ -** outer - this is the root directory and is nothing more than a project container. Can be renamed as anything.

- **manage.py** – command line utility for interaction with the Django project
- **mysite/** - inner – Python package for the project and is the name used for importing anything in the project.
- **mysite/ __init__.py** – empty file informing Python that the directory should be seen as a Python package.
- **mysite/settings.py** – settings and configuration for the project
- **mysite/urls.py** – URL declarations for the project, a table of contents if you like
- **mysite/wsgi.py** – entry-point for web servers that are WSGI-compatible to serve the Django project

Setting Up the Database

By default, there are several applications in Django already and some of these will use at least one, usually more, database table. Because of this, we must create the tables in a database before they can be used. To do this, we go into the mysite folder that we just created by typing cd mysite at the command prompt and then type this command:

python manage.py migrate

This command will create an SQLite database and the required tables as per the settings file that the startproject command created. If everything goes as it should, you will see something like this:

 (env_mysite) C:\Users*your name*\OneDrive\Documents\mysite_project\mysite>python manage.py migrate

Operations to perform:

Apply all migrations: admin, auth, contenttypes, sessions

Running migrations:

Applying contenttypes.0001_initial... OK

Applying auth.0001_initial... OK

Applying admin.0001_initial... OK

Normally, this would not be something that a beginner should attempt, but Django makes life very easy by installing SQLite and configuring it for you.

Development Server

Now we should make sure that the project works so if needed, go to the outer mysite directory at the command prompt and then run these commands:

python manage.py runserver

You should see the following output:

Performing system checks...

System check identified no issues (0 silenced).

August 14, 2018 - 16:48:29

Django version 1.11, using settings 'mysite.settings'

Starting development server at http://127.0.0.1:8000/

Quit the server with CTRL-BREAK.

What we have done is started the development server for Django. This is a lightweight server that has been written in Python. It was included in Django to allow for rapid development without the need to configure production servers until you need them.

Do NOT use this server in a production environment as it is purely for development. Now that it is up and running, open your web browser and go to http://127.0.0.1:8000 and you will be taken to a page that says, "Welcome to Django".

You will find that the server will reload the Python code automatically as required for each request. There is no need to restart for any changes to the code to take effect but some things, such as adding files, will require a manual restart.

That is it for installation, time to look at MVC.

<u>MVC – Model-View-Controller Design Pattern</u>

This concept is almost as old as the hills but since the development of the internet, it has grown significantly since it is the best way of designing applications based on client-server. Pick any good web framework and you'll find it has been built using this concept and it is one that you will find very easy to understand:

- **M (Model)** – data model or representation. This is not the data, merely an interface to it and it will let you pull the data out of the database without needing to know the intricacies of that database. The model will provide you with an abstraction layer, so it can be used with more than one database.
- **V (View)** – this is what you see, the model presentation layer. On a computer, the view is what is displayed in a browser for web applications as the user interface in a desktop application. You will also get an interface used for collection of user input.
- **C (Controller)** – this will control the way the information flows between the first two components – M and V. Logic programmed into it is used to determine what information should come from the database through the model and what gets passed on to the view. It will also take the user information from view and will implement business logic, by modifying the data via the model, changing the view or doing both.

It starts getting a bit difficult because there are some very different interpretations about what goes on at each layer, but you don't need to worry about this. All you need to understand at this stage is how the MVC design pattern is implemented by Django and how closely it follows that pattern. However, despite this, Django does insert its own logic into the implementation.

The framework handles the 'C' part of MVC and a lot of the exciting stuff in Django takes place in the models, templates, and views – for this reason, you will often see Django called an MTV pattern and, in this:

- **M** is Model – this is the data-access layer and it holds everything relating to the data – how it is accessed, validated, the behaviors the data has and any relationships that exist between data.
- **T** is Template – this is the presentation layer and it holds all decisions related to presentation, such as how information is displayed on web pages or some other document.
- **V** is View – this is the business logic layer and it holds the logic that is responsible for accessing the model and deferring to the right template. It is something like a bridge that joins the models and the templates.

You now have Django and everything else you need installed, your development server is up and running so it's time to start looking into Django. We will start with Django views and the basics of using Django to serve a web page.

Views and URL-Confs

In this part, you will begin to learn how to create web pages in Django, in particular, dynamic web pages. We will start with the Hello World, the example that all programming languages use as their first one. What we want to do is create a web page that says "Hello World" on it. If you were not using a framework, all you would do is type the text "Hello World" in a text file, save it as hello.html, and then upload it into a web server directory. What you provide are two key pieces of information – the contents of the web page and the URL.

Your First View

With Django, you still provide that same information but differently – you use a View function for the webpage contents and a URLconf to specify the URL. Let's get down to business and write the view function.

Go to the inner mysite directory that you created earlier and, inside it, create a new file named views.py – this is where your views will be stored. Ensure that the file is saved in the inner mysite directory – it mustn't go in the directory that has manage.py in it because it won't work.

In that file, type in the following code – this is the whole view function for "Hello World", including the import statements:

from django.http import HttpResponse

def hello(request):

  return HttpResponse("Hello world")

It's quite an easy piece of code. We started by importing the class called HttpResponse from the module called django.http. This class is going to be used later in the code. Next, a function is defined, called hello. This is our view function and, like all view functions, it will take one or more parameters – in Django, these are called requests. This request is an object and in it is all the information pertaining to the web request that triggered off the view. It is an instance of a class called django.HttpRequest.

We're not going to do anything with this request, but regardless of that, it has to be the first view parameter. Note that it doesn't matter what the view name is. Django doesn't require a specific naming convention to recognize it; we've called it hello purely because it indicates what the view is about.

The function does nothing more than finding an HttpResponse object that was instantiated with the "Hello World" text and return it. Later we'll look at how Django finds the function, but for now, all you need to understand is that a view is nothing more than a function with an initial parameter of HttpRequest that returns an HttpResponse instance. A Python function must do both to be considered a Django view.

Your First URLconf

If you were to run python manage.py runserver at this stage, you would still be faced with the message "Welcome to Django". You won't see "Hello World" anywhere on the page and this is because we haven't yet told mysiteproject that there is a hello view. What we need to do is explicitly tell Django that this view is to be activated at a specific URL. To do this, we need to use a URLconf.

What is a URLconf? Think of it as being a contents table for your website. It is nothing more than a mapping between the URLs and the relevant view functions. It is the way in which we tell Django that we want a specific code called for a specific URL. In the last section, django-admin startproject was executed, a URLconf was automatically created, a file called urls.py. The default URLconf looks like this:

from django.conf.urls import url

from django.contrib import admin

urlpatterns = [

* url(r'^admin/', admin.site.urls),*

]

In line 1, we are importing two functions. These come from django.conf.urls and include, which lets you add a Python import path that leads to a second URLconf module and url, which makes use of a regular expression to match the pattern of the URL to a Django module.

Next, we call admin, a function in the module called django.contrib. The include function will call this so that the URLs for the admin site can be loaded. Last, urlpatterns is simply a list of the instances of url().

The important thing here is urlpatterns, a variable that Django wants to see in the module called URLconf. It is responsible for defining the mapping from the URL to the handling code. Adding a URL and a view to URLconf is a simple matter of adding a mapping from a URL pattern to a view function.

This is how we pull in our hello view:

```
from django.conf.urls import url

from django.contrib import admin


from mysite.views import hello


urlpatterns = [

    url(r'^admin/', admin.site.urls),

    url(r'^hello/$', hello),

]
```

Note that there are two changes:

First, the hello view was imported from the module, mysite/views.py. in the import syntax for Python, this reads as mysite.views. Secondly, url(r'^hello/$', hello), was added to urlpatterns. We call this line a URLpattern and the url() function is telling Django how the URL you configure should be handled. The initial argument is the pattern-matcher string while the second is view function needed for the pattern.

Note the 'r' at the start of the regular expression. This tells Python that it is dealing with a raw string, i.e. backslashes should not be interpreted by the contents. In a normal string, a backslash is used to escape a special character, for example, \n – a string of one character with a newline. When it is turned into a raw string, the backslash escape is not applied so r'\n' will become a string of two characters, with a newline and a literal backslash. Best practice with Django regular expressions is to use raw strings to avoid the collision that occurs between regular expression backslashes and the way that Python uses the backslash.

What we just did was told Django that the hello view function should handle any requests to the /hello/ URL. As it might not be obvious, we'll just take a bit of time to discuss this syntax. We want the /hello/ URL matched but the pattern doesn't look quite as it should and here's why:

Django takes the slash away from the start of all incoming URLs before URLpattern is checked. What this means it that URLpattern will not have that first slash in /hello/. Although this doesn't look intuitive, it does make things much simpler, especially when URL-confs are included inside other URLconfs.

Second, there is a caret and a dollar sign in the pattern. Both are characters that have special meanings in regular expressions. The caret is denoting that the pattern must match the beginning of the string and the dollar sign is denoting that the pattern must match the end. In short, if we had specified ^hello/ and not used a dollar sign, any of the URLs that begin with /hello/ would match while using hello/$, without the caret would cause a match with any URL that ended with hello/. The only way to make sure an exact match is found is to use both ^ and $.

One other thing of note: the hello view function has been passed as an object without the function being called. This is one of the best things about Python; a function is a first-class object that means they can be passed around the same way as any variable.

Open your Python virtual environment and run python manage.py runserver and this will detect any changes to your code automatically and will reload it as required. This means there is no need to restart the server when you make a change. Because the server is running at http://127.0.0.1:8000/, open your browser and then open http://127.0.0.1:8000/hello/ - you should now see Hello World on the webpage.

Regular Expressions

Often termed as a regex, a regular expression is a neat way to specify a pattern within the text. In practice, you will likely only use a small selection of the regex symbols, the most common of which are shown below:

. (dot)

Match with any single character

\d

Match with any single digit

[A-Z]

Match with any of the characters between uppercase A and Z

[a-z]

Match with any of the characters between lowercase a and z

[A-Za-z]

Match with any of the characters between a and z but case-sensitive

+

Match at least one of the last expression. i.e. \d+ will match at least one digit

[^/]+

Match at least one character up to but not including the forward slash

?

Match Zero or one of the last expression. i.e. \d? will match at least zero digits

*

Match Zero or more of the last expression. i.e. \d* will match at least zero digits

{1,3}

Match one to three of the last expression. i.e. \d{1, 3} will match up to three digits

Django Request Processing

Before we move on, let's see how requests are processed by Django. What is Django doing to show you the Hello World message when you visit the URL? It all begins with the file called Settings. When python manage.py runserver is run, the script will search in the inner mysite directory for a file with the name of settings.py. This file has the configuration for the project and each one is in uppercase i.e. DATABASES, TEMPLATES, etc.

ROOT_URLCONF.ROOT_URLCONF is the most important because it is telling Django the name of the Python module required as the URLconf. Think back to when settings.py and urls.py were create by django-admin startproject; settings.py contained a setting for ROOT_URLCONF that pointed to urls.py. Open settings.py and you should see this:

ROOT_URLCONF = 'mysite.urls'

This directly corresponds to a file named mysite/urls.py and, when a request is received for a specific URL, Django will load the URLconf to which ROOT_URLCONF points. It will then go through each URLpattern in the URLconf to find a match to the requested URL. When a match is found, the view function for the pattern is called and the first parameter passed to it is an

HttpRequest object. And, as you know, view functions must return HttpResponses. Once this is done, Django will convert that object into a web response containing the webpage content.

Dynamic Content – Second View

Now we'll look at the second view, dynamic content. The view for Hello World was helpful in showing how Django works but it isn't a dynamic webpage. Why? Because the content never changes. Whenever you go to /hello/ the same thing will be displayed.

For the second view, we'll create a webpage that shows the current time and date, a little more dynamic. This is quite simple because no databases are needed and no user input – it is the output from the internal clock in the server.

This view must do two things – determine the date and time and return that value in an HttpResponse. Python already has a datetime module for calculation of dates so look at this demo using the interactive interpreter in Python:

C:\Users*your name*>python

Python 3.6.1 (v3.6.1:69c0db5, Aug 14, 2018, 17:54:52) [MSC v.1900 32 bit (Intel)] on win32

Type "help", "copyright", "credits" or "license" for more information.

>>> *import datetime*

>>> *now = datetime.datetime.now()*

>>> *now*

datetime.datetime(2017, 5, 20, 14, 32, 25, 412665)

>>> *print (now)*

2017-05-20 14:32:25.412665

```
>>>
```

That is easy enough and Django didn't get involved at all; it is nothing more than Python code. For a Django view that shows the updated time and date, we need the datetime.datetime.now() statement hooked into the view and an HttpResponse returned. The updated views.py will look like this:

from django.http import HttpResponse

import datetime

def hello(request):

  return HttpResponse("Hello world")

def current_datetime(request):

  now = datetime.datetime.now()

  html = "<html><body>It is now %s.</body></html>" % now

  return HttpResponse(html)

What we have done is added an import datetime at the top so the dates can be calculated. The function called current.datetime will determine the date and time and store the datetime.datetime object as a local variable.

In line 2, we use the built-in format-string capability from Python to construct the HTML response. % inside the string is a placeholder and % at the end is saying that the % in the preceding string should be replaced with the current value of the variable called now. That variable is nothing more than a datetime.datetime object; it isn't a string but the use of the % converts it into a string representation and the result of this is an HTML string.

Lastly, an HttpResponse object is returned by view and this contains the response. After this has been added to views.py, the URLpattern is added, informing Django of the URL that should handle the view; like this:

from django.conf.urls import url

from django.contrib import admin

from mysite.views import hello, current_datetime

urlpatterns = [

   url(r'^admin/', admin.site.urls),

   url(r'^hello/$', hello),

   url(r'^time/$', current_datetime),

]

Again, two changes have been made. First, the function called current.datetime has been imported at the start and second, most important, a URLpattern that maps URL/time/ to the new view has been added.

Loose Coupling and URLconfs

Now would be a good time to look at one of the underlying philosophies of both URLconfs and Django – loose coupling. In basic terms, loose coupling is a developmental approach that supports the interchangeability of pieces. If we loosely couple two bits of code, a change made to one piece will not affect the other or, if it does, it will be minor.

The URLconfs in Django is a good example; in a web application built with Django, the URL definitions and their view functions are loosely coupled. This means that the URL decision for a function and the function implementation are in two different places.

For example: the current_datetime view we are using. If we need to make a change to the URL, i.e. from /time/ to /current-time/, we would change URLconf and the view would not be affected. In the same way, if we needed to make a change to the view function, perhaps change the logic, the URL would not be affected.

In the following example, the current_datetime is at two different URLs:

urlpatterns = [

  url(r'^admin/', admin.site.urls),

  url(r'^hello/$', hello),

  url(r'^time/$', current_datetime),

  url(r'^another-time-page/$', current_datetime),

]

Dynamic URLs – Third View

Back to our current_datetime view, the page contents are dynamic, but the URL called /time/ is static. Most of the time, the URL will have parameters that have a direct influence on the page output. What we want to do is create another view that shows the current date and the time but offset by several hours. Our goal is to make our site in a way that page/time/plus 1/ will show us the date and time an hour ahead, page /time/ plus 2/ is two hours ahead and so on.

A beginner would likely write new view functions for each of the offsets and this would give us a URLconf that looks like this:

urlpatterns = [

  url(r'^time/$', current_datetime),

url(r'^time/plus/1/$', one_hour_ahead),

url(r'^time/plus/2/$', two_hours_ahead),

url(r'^time/plus/3/$', three_hours_ahead),

]

The flaws here should be evident. Not only would we be creating view functions that are redundant, we also have an application that has been limited to just the hour ranges that have been defined. What we want to do is allow the application to handle any offset and the key to this is using wildcard URLpatterns. We know that a URLpattern is just a regular expression, so we can use one of the expression symbols we mentioned earlier, and that is d+ and this matches at least one digit:

urlpatterns = [

    #...

    url(r'^time/plus/\d+/$', hours_ahead),

    #...

]

The new pattern will match any URL that starts /time/ plus/. We will set a limit of 99 hours; to do this, we allow only one or two-digit numbers to be matched. The regex syntax for that is \d{1, 2}:

url(r'^time/plus/\d{1,2}/$', hours_ahead),

Now that we've designated a wildcard for the URL, we need a way of passing that wildcard data to the view function so that we can use a single view function for any arbitrary hour offset. We do this by placing parentheses around the data in the URLpattern that we want to save. In the case of our example, we want to save whatever number was entered in the URL, so let's put parentheses around the \d{1,2},
like this:

url(r'^time/plus/(\d{1,2})/$', hours_ahead),

If you're familiar with regular expressions, you'll be right at home here; we're using parentheses to *capture* data from the matched text. The final URLconf including our previous two views, looks like this:

from django.conf.urls import include, url

from django.contrib import admin

from mysite.views import hello, current_datetime, hours_ahead

urlpatterns = [

   url(r'^admin/', admin.site.urls),

   url(r'^hello/$', hello),

   url(r'^time/$', current_datetime),

   url(r'^time/plus/(\d{1,2})/$', hours_ahead),

]

You could, if you already have experience at programming, decide to use a query string parameter along the lines of /time/plus?hours=3 and the hours parameter will designate the hours in the query string that comes after '?'. This is possible, but Django likes its URLs to be smooth and beautiful.

A better way is to use the URL of /time/plus/3/ and is a good deal cleaner and infinitely more readable. Nice clean URLs are a good characteristic of a good web application and Django makes it much easier to use good URLs.

We can now write our view called hours_ahead. It is much like current_datetime but it has an additional argument and that is the number of offset hours:

```python
from django.http import Http404, HttpResponse

import datetime


def hours_ahead(request, offset):
    try:
        offset = int(offset)
    except ValueError:
        raise Http404()
    dt = datetime.datetime.now() + datetime.timedelta(hours=offset)
    html = "<html><body>In %s hour(s), it will be  %s.</body></html>" % (offset, dt)
    return HttpResponse(html)
```

In the hours_ahead view function, we have two parameters:

- request – this is an HttpRequest object
- offset – this is the string that the parentheses inside URLpattern captures.

The variable has been named as offset, but you can name it what you want so long as it stays within the conventions of naming Python identifiers. The name is irrelevant; what is important is that, after request, this is the second argument.

In the function, the very first thing to do is call, on offset, int(). This will change the Unicode value to an integer. If you were to call this on a value that may not be converted, you will get a ValueError. You might be wondering how this could happen given that our regular expression will only capture digits, and as a result, the offset can only ever be a string of digits. In theory, it can't happen but there is always the chance that the view function may be called another way. Therefore, make it part of your best practice to check for ValueErrors and only implement a view function in such a way that no assumptions are made about the parameters – loose coupling!

The next line is where the current date and time are calculated, and the right number of hours added. We saw the datetime.datetime.now() function in current_datetimeview but the concept with the new one is that date and time arithmetic can be performed with an object called datetime.timedelta, with a datetime.datetime object added to it. The result is then stored in the dt variable. We can also see why int() was called on offset – datetime.timedelta requires that an integer is used for the hours parameter.

Next, the HTML output of the view function is constructed using the format-string capability from Python with a pair of values. Note that there is a pair of % symbols.

Lastly, the HTML HttpResponse is returned.

Now you can start your Django development server again and go to:

http://127.0.0.1:8000/time/plus/3/ to see if it works. Also try:

 http://127.0.0.1:8000/time/plus/17/ and
http://127.0.0.1:8000/time/plus/72/.

Last, go to http://127.0.0.1:8000/time/plus/100/ to make sure that the URLconf pattern will only take numbers of one or two digits – you should see a "Page Not Found" error.

Up to now, our view functions have been written into the Python code using hard-code HTML. In reality, this doesn't happen. Django has a very powerful yet simple template engine that lets you keep the page design separate from the code so let's look at that now.

Django Templates

Although we used hardcoding to show you views in practice, it isn't really a good idea because, if you need to make a change to your page design, you need to change the code. It would be incredibly convenient if we could change the design without changing the code and we can do that by using the template system in Django.

Django templates are text strings used to keep presentation and data separate. Templates will define placeholders, along with basic logic for regulating presentation. What you must understand is that a Django template is NOT Python code embedded in HTML.

Let's look at a very simple example. This template has a description of an HTML page that is used for thanking someone when they place an order:

<html>

<head>

  <title>Ordering notice</title>

</head>

<body>

  <h1>Ordering notice</h1>

  <p>Dear {{ person_name }},</p>

  <p>Thank you for placing an order with {{ company }}. It will ship on {{ s

hip_date|date:"F j, Y" }}.</p>

  <p>Here are the items you've ordered:</p>

  <ul>

    {% for item in item_list %}

<li>{{ item }}</li>{% endfor %}

</ul>

{% if ordered_warranty %}

<p>Your warranty information is included in the packaging.</p>

{% else %}

<p>

You didn't order a warranty, so when things go wrong, you are on your own.

</p>

{% endif %}

*<p>Sincerely,
{{ company }}</p>*

</body>

</html>

This is HTML with template tags and variables. If a text is inside a pair of braces (), it is a variable. If text is inside curly braces with % signs, {%}, it is a template tag which is used for telling the system what it should do.

In this example, we have a for tag and an if tag. For tags work like Python for statements providing the ability to loop through each sequence item while the if tag works like an if statement. In our case, it checks to see if a given value will evaluate True. If yes, the template shows everything between a set of specified brackets; if not, different information is shown.

We also have a filter, an easy way to change a variable's format. In this template, in {{ ship_date|date:"F j, Y" }}, we pass the variable called ship_date to the date filter and provide that the filter with the argument of "F, j, Y". the dates are formatted as specified by the arguments and the pipe filter, |, is used to attach filters.

Every Django template can access a number of built-in filters and tags and we'll be talking briefly about some of these.

Using the Template System

We can configure any Django project with one or more templates and Django has a backend for its own templates called the Django Template Language (DTL). Before we move on, we'll look into DTL just to see how it works. First, we'll look at the easiest way to use the template system inside Python code and that is to provide a string as the raw template code to create the template object.

First, the object render() method is called using specified variables. This is called context. A rendered template is returned as a string and all variables and tags are evaluated as per this context. If we used the custom Python shell in Django of python manage.py shell, it would look like this:

>>> from django import template

>>> t = template.Template('My name is {{ name }}.')

>>> c = template.Context({'name': 'Paul'})

>>> print (t.render(c))

My name is Paul.

>>> c = template.Context({'name': 'Michael'})

>>> print (t.render(c))

My name is Michael.

Creating Template Objects

Direct instantiation is the best way to create a template object. The class called Template is in the module called django.template and one argument is taken by the constructor. That argument is the raw code. Open python manage.py shell from your mysite project directory and input the following:

>>> from django.template import Template

>>> t = Template('My name is {{ name }}.')

>>> print (t)

You should see this:

<django.template.base.Template object at 0x030396B0>

Ignore the number at the end; it will change every time and is nothing more than Python's way of identifying the template object.

When the object is created, the template system will compile the raw code so it is an optimized form ready to be rendered. If there are any syntax errors in the code, you will get a TemplateSyntaxError exception:

>>> from django.template import Template

>>> t = Template('{% notatag %}')

Traceback (most recent call last):

File "", line 1, in?

...

django.template.exceptions.TemplateSyntaxError: Invalid block tag on line 1: 'notatag'.

Did you forget to register or load this tag?

"block tag" is referring to {% notatag %}. Both "block tag" and "template tag" are the same and the error could have been raised for any one of these reasons:

- The tags are invalid
- Valid tags have invalid arguments

- The filters are invalid
- Valid filters have invalid arguments
- The template syntax is invalid
- Tags are left unclosed

Template Rendering

Data can be passed to a template object by providing it with a context, and this is nothing more than a set of variable names and the values that go with them. These are used to populate the variables of the template and a way of evaluating the tags. The context class is used to represent a context and this is found in the module called django.template. The constructor will take a single optional argument, a dictionary that maps the variable names to their values. The render() method is called with a context that tells it to fill up the template:

>>> from Django.template import Context, Template

>>> t = Template('My name is {{ name }}.')

>>> c = Context({'name': 'Stephen'})

>>> t.render(c)

'My name is Stephen.'

Dictionaries and Contexts

Python dictionaries are a map between keys and values of variables. Contexts are similar but have more functionality. A variable name must start with an uppercase or lowercase letter and may have letters, dots, underscores, and digits. They are also case-sensitive. Look at this example of the compilation and rendering of a template:

>>> from django.template import Template, Context

>>> raw_template = """"<p>Dear {{ person_name }},</p>

...

... *<p> Thank you for placing an order with {{ company }}. It will*

... *ship on {{ ship_date|date:"F j, Y" }}.</p>*

...

... *{% if ordered_warranty %}*

... *<p>Your warranty information is included in the packaging.</p>*

... *{% else %}*

... *<p> You didn't order a warranty, so when things go wrong, you are on your own.</p>*

... *{% endif %}*

...

... *<p>Sincerely,
{{ company }}</p>"""*

>>> t = Template(raw_template)

>>> import datetime

>>> c = Context({'person_name': 'Billy Bunter',

... *'company': 'Outdoor Equipment',*

... *'ship_date': datetime.date(2017, 7, 2),*

... *'ordered_warranty': False})*

>>> t.render(c)

"<p>Dear Billy Bunter,</p>\n\n<p>Thank you for placing an order with Outdoor Equipment. It\

will \nship on July 2,2017.</p>\n\n\n<p>You didn't order a warranty, so when\

things go wrong\nyou're on your own.</p>\n\n\n<p>Sincerely,<br\

/>Outdoor Equipment</p>"

First, the Template and the Context classes are imported from the django.template module. The raw text is saved into the raw_template variable. Note the use of triple quotes for the string – this is because it goes over several lines.

We pass raw_template to the class constructor for Template to create an object, t. The datetime module is imported from the standard library in Python – it will be needed for the next statement.

A Context object, c, is then created and the constructor will take a dictionary which will map the names of the variables to the values.

Lastly, the render() method is called on the template object and passed to context. The rendered template is returned.

That is the basics of the template system in Django – write your template string, create the template object, create the Context, call render().

Multiple Contexts on One Template

It is perfectly possible to render several contexts through one template object like this:

>>> *from django.template import Template, Context*

>>> *t = Template('Hello, {{ name }}')*

>>> *print (t.render(Context({'name': 'John'})))*

Hello, John

>>> *print (t.render(Context({'name': 'Julie'})))*

Hello, Julie

>>> *print (t.render(Context({'name': 'Pat'})))*

Hello, Pat

Looking Up Context Variables

So far, we have only passed the contexts simple variables, strings and one example of datetime.date. However, the Django template system can easily handle data structures that are more complex, like dictionaries, lists, and custom objects. The key is in the dot character and this can be used for accessing attributes, keys, methods or object indices. We can see how this works better with some examples. First, accessing dictionary values by key:

>>> *from django.template import Template, Context*

>>> *person = {'name': 'Sally', 'age': '43'}*

>>> *t = Template('{{ person.name }} is {{ person.age }} years old.')*

>>> *c = Context({'person': person})*

>>> *t.render(c)*

'Sally is 43 years old.'

In the same way, a dot lets you gain access to object attributes. The datetime.date object has three attributes – year, month, day. Here's how to access them:

>>> *from django.template import Template, Context*

>>> *import datetime*

>>> *d = datetime.date(2018, 8, 14)*

>>> *d.year*

2018

>>> *d.month*

8

>>> d.day

14

>>> t = Template('The month is {{ date.month }} and the year is {{ date.year }}.')

>>> c = Context({'date': d})

>>> t.render(c)

'The month is 8 and the year is 2018.'

We can also use a dot to refer to an object method. For example, each string in Python contains the upper() and isdigit() methods and these can be called like this:

>>> from django.template import Template, Context

>>> t = Template('{{ var }} -- {{ var.upper }} -- {{ var.isdigit }}')

>>> t.render(Context({'var': 'hello'}))

'hello -- HELLO -- False'

>>> t.render(Context({'var': '123'}))

'123 -- 123 -- True'

Lastly, accessing list indices:

>>> from django.template import Template, Context

>>> t = Template('Item 2 is {{ items.2 }}.')

>>> c = Context({'items': ['apples', 'bananas', 'carrots']})

>>> t.render(c)

'Item 2 is carrots.'

Note – negative indices cause a TemplateSyntaxError.

Python List Indices

If you are new to programming, it is worth keeping in mind that all Python lists have zero-based indices. What this means is that the index starts at 0, item 2 is at index 1, item 3 is at index 2 and so on.

We can summarize a dot lookup in this way – when the Django template system comes across a dot in the name of the variable, it will attempt the lookups in this order:

- Dictionary
- Attribute
- Method call
- List Index

The system will go through the lookups and will make use of the first one it comes across that works. We call this "short-circuit" logic. All dot lookups may be nested and there is no real limit on how many levels deep this nesting can go. For example, the next code makes use of {{ person.name.upper }} – this is a dictionary lookup of (person['name'] followed by a method call of (upper()):

>>> *from django.template import Template, Context*

>>> *person = {'name': 'Sally', 'age': '43'}*

>>> *t = Template('{{ person.name.upper }} is {{ person.age }} years old.')*

>>> *c = Context({'person': person})*

>>> *t.render(c)*

'SALLY is 43 years old.'

Method Call Behavior

A method call is a little bit more complex in behavior than all the other types of lookup so you need to keep some things in mind:

During the method lookup, if an exception is raised by the method, that exception is propagated. The only exception is if an attribute of silent_variable_failure is attached to the exception and this has a value of True. If this attribute is attached, the variable is rendered as a value of the string_if_valid config option of the engine and this is by default, an empty string. Look at this example:

```
>>> t = Template("My name is {{ person.first_name }}.")

>>> class PersonClass3:

...     def first_name(self):

...         raise AssertionError("foo")

>>> p = PersonClass3()

>>> t.render(Context({"person": p}))

Traceback (most recent call last):

...

AssertionError: foo


>>> class SilentAssertionError(Exception):

...     silent_variable_failure = True

>>> class PersonClass4:

...     def first_name(self):
```

...   raise SilentAssertionError

>>> p = PersonClass4()

>>> t.render(Context({"person": p}))

'My name is.'

Method calls only work if there are no required arguments to the method. If there aren't any, the system moves on to the next type of lookup. By its design, Django will limit, intentionally, how much logic processing is made available in the template, so it isn't possible to pass an argument to any method call that has been accessed from within a template. Data must be calculated in a view and passed for display to the template.

Some methods will have side-effects and it would not be good practice to let the template system have access to them, not to mention it being a potential security risk. Let's say that you have an object called BankAccount and it has a method called delete(). If a template were to have, for example, {{ account.delete }}, in which account is an object of BankAccount, when the template has been rendered, the object is deleted. To stop this from happening, the function attribute of alters_data should be set on the method:

def delete(self):

  # Delete the account

  delete.alters_data = True

If any method has been marked like this, it will not be executed by the template system. Carrying on from the example, if {{ account.delete }} is included in a template, and alters_date=True is set on the delete() method, that delete() method won't get executed when template rendering happens; instead the variable is replaced by the engine with string_if_valid.

Note. The delete() and save() methods that are generated dynamically on the Django model objects will automatically have alters_data=true set.

Invalid Variable Handling

In general, if a variable is not in existence, the string_if_valid config option value of the engine is inserted by the template system – by default, this is an empty string. An example is:

>>> from django.template import Template, Context

>>> t = Template('Your name is {{ name }}.')

>>> t.render(Context())

'Your name is.'

>>> t.render(Context({'var': 'hello'}))

'Your name is.'

>>> t.render(Context({'NAME': 'hello'}))

'Your name is.'

>>> t.render(Context({'Name': 'hello'}))

'Your name is.'

This is far better behavior than it is to raise an exception because it is designed to be more resilient where human error is concerned. In our case, every lookup failed because the names of the variables were named wrong or has the wrong case. In the real world, it is not acceptable for websites to be inaccessible because of nothing more than a syntax error in the template.

Template Tags and Filters

We already mentioned that templates come with built-in filters and tags. We're going to look the more common ones in this section.

Tags

if/else

The tag, {% if %} will carry out variable evaluation and the variable evaluates True, i.e. it is in existence, it is not empty, it does not have a value that is a false Boolean, and everything that falls between {% if%} and {% endif %} will be displayed. An example of this is:

{% if today_is_weekend %}

   <p>Welcome to the weekend!</p>

{% endif %}

A tag of {% else %} is optional:

{% if today_is_weekend %}

   <p>Welcome to the weekend!</p>

{% else %}

   <p>Get back to work.</p>

{% endif %}

Every {% if %} must be closed with {% endif %}; if it isn't, a TemplateSyntaxError is thrown by Django.

The if tags are also able to take at least one {% elif %} clause:

{% if athlete_list %}

   <p>Number of athletes: {{ athlete_list|length }}</p>

{% elif athlete_in_locker_room_list %}

   <p>Athletes should be out of the locker room soon!</p>

{% elif...

...

{% else %}

   <p>No athletes.</p>

{% endif %}

The {% if %}tag will take 'and', 'or' or 'not' for the purpose of testing several variables or even for the negation of a specified variable. For example:

{% if athlete_list and coach_list %}

   <p>Both athletes and coaches are available.</p>

{% endif %}

{% if not athlete_list %}

   <p>There are no athletes.</p>

{% endif %}

{% if athlete_list or coach_list %}

   <p>There are some athletes or some coaches.</p>

{% endif %}

{% if not athlete_list or coach_list %}

   <p>There are no athletes or there are some coaches.</p>

{% endif %}

{% if athlete_list and not coach_list %}

   <p>There are some athletes and absolutely no coaches.</p>

{% endif %}

It is perfectly allowable to use both 'and' clauses and 'or' clauses in the same tag; just remember that 'and' is higher in precedence than 'or'. For example:

{% if athlete_list and coach_list or cheerleader_list %}

Would be interpreted as:

if (athlete_list and coach_list) or cheerleader_list

It is also worth noting that using parentheses in an 'if' tag is not valid syntax. If parentheses are required to indicate what the preference is, nested if tags should be used. You will also find that there is no support for using parentheses for the control of operation order. Again, if you think that you need the parentheses, think about performing the logic external to the template and then pass the result as a dedicated variable, or you could just use nested tags.

You can use the same logical operator several times but combining different operators is not allowed. This is a valid example:

{% if athlete_list or coach_list or parent_list or teacher_list %}

{% if %} will also take in / not in to test whether specified values are or are not inside the given container; is / is not can also be used to test whether two separate entities are, in fact, the same object. For example:

{% if "bc" in "abcdef" %}

This will appear because "bc" is a substring of the string "abcdef"

{% endif %}

{% if user not in users %}

If there is a list called users, this appears if list is not a list element:

{% endif %}

{% if somevar is True %}

This will only appear if somevar evaluates True

{% endif %}

{% if somevar is not None %}

This will only appear if somevar is not None

{% endif %}

for

You can use the {% for %} to loop over the items in a sequence. As we see in the syntax of the for statement in Python, for X in Y and Y is the sequence to be looped over, while X is the variable name used for a specified loop cycle. For every loop, the template system renders anything that shows up between {% for %} and {% endfor%}. For example, the following code could be used for displaying a list of the athletes, given a variable called athlete_list:

<ul>

  {% for athlete in athlete_list %}

  <li>{{ athlete.name }}</li>

{% endfor %}

</ul>

If you want to loop back over the list in reverse order, the tag would need to be 'reversed', like this:

{% for athlete in athlete_list reversed %}

...

{% endfor %}

{% for %} tags can also be nested:

{% for athlete in athlete_list %}

<h1>{{ athlete.name }}</h1>

<ul>

{% for sport in athlete.sports_played %}

<li>{{ sport }}</li>

{% endfor %}

</ul>

{% endfor %}

If you have a list of lists that you need to loop over, the values of each sublist can be unpacked into separate variables. For example, if you have a list of (x, y) coordinates or points in the context, the following code could be used for outputting the list of points:

{% for x, y in points %}

<p>There is a point at {{ x }},{{ y }}</p>

{% endfor %}

You will also find this useful if you have a dictionary and you need to access the items in it. For example, if you have dictionary data in the context, you could use the following to display the dictionary keys and values:

{% for key, value in data.items %}

{{ key }}: {{ value }}

{% endfor %}

One of the most common patterns is to look at the list size before it is looped over and if the list is empty, outputting special text:

{% if athlete_list %}

{% for athlete in athlete_list %}

<p>{{ athlete.name }}</p>

{% endfor %}

{% else %}

<p>There are no athletes. Only computer programmers.</p>

{% endif %}

Because this is such a common pattern, the for tag provides support for an optional {% empty %} clause; this clause will allow you to define what the output should be in the event of an empty list. The next example is the equivalent of the last one:

{% for athlete in athlete_list %}

<p>{{ athlete.name }}</p>

{% empty %}

<p>There are no athletes. Only computer programmers.</p>

{% endfor %}

Breaking out of a loop before it is finished is not supported. If you want to do this, the variable being looped over must be changed so that it only has the values that are to be looped over. In a similar way, there is not a built-in support to continue statements that tell the loop processor to go to the loop front straightaway.

With every {% for %} loop, you automatically gain access to forloop, which is a template variable. This has some attributes that provide information about the loop progress. We always set the forloop.counter to an integer that is representative of how many times a loop has been entered into. It is one-indexed so, when the loop is gone through the first time, forloop.counter is set to 1. Look at this example:

{% for item in todo_list %}

<p>{{ forloop.counter }}: {{ item }}</p>

{%endfor %}

The forloop.counter() is much like forloopcounter with one exception – it is zero-indexed rather than one-indexed and has a value of 0 on the first loop. We always set forloop.revcounter as an integer that represents how many items are left in the loop. When the loop is gone through the first time, forloop.revcounter is set to the number of the items in the sequence being looped over. On the last loop, it is set as 1.

The forloop.revcounter0 is similar to forloop.revcounter with the exception that it is a zero-index. On the first lop, it is set as the number of the sequence elements minus 1, and on the last loop, it is set as 0.

The forloop.first is a Boolean value. It is set as True on the first loop and this is very convenient where special-casing is concerned:

{% for object in objects %}

```
{% if forloop.first %}

    <li class="first">

{% else %}

    <li>

{% endif %}

{{ object }}</li>

{% endfor %}
```

The forloop.last is another Boolean value that has been set as True if the loop is the last one. This is commonly used to place a pipe character in between a links list:

```
{% for link in links %}

    {{ link }}{% if not forloop.last %} | {% endif %}

{% endfor %}
```

The output of this might look something like:

Link1 | Link2 | Link3 | Link4

This is also used for inserting commas in between words in lists:

```
<p>Favorite places:</p>

{% for p in places %}

    {{ p }}{% if not forloop.last %}, {% endif %}

{% endfor %}
```

The forloop.parentloop is referencing the parent loop's forloop object where you have nested loops. An example:

```
{% for country in countries %}

  <table>

    {% for city in country.city_list %}

    <tr>

      <td>Country #{{ forloop.parentloop.counter }}</td>

      <td>City #{{ forloop.counter }}</td>

      <td>{{ city }}</td>

    </tr>

    {% endfor %}

  </table>

  {% endfor %}
```

Comments

As it in in Python or in HTML, DTL allows comments and these are designated using {# #}:

```
{# This would be a comment #}
```

The comment is ignored by the interpreter and won't be output on template rendering. However, you cannot use this syntax if you have a comment that goes over several lines; this is for single line comments only. This limitation provides improvement to the performance of template parsing.

In the next template, the output that is rendered looks identical to the template – the comment tag isn't parsed as a comment:

```
This is a {# this is not

a comment #}
```

test.

Where multi-line comments are required, you need to use the template tag of {% comment %}, in this way:

{% comment %}

This is now a

multi-line comment.

{% endcomment %}

Comment tags can optionally have notes that explain why a specific piece of code may have been commented out:

{% comment "This is an optional note" %}

...

{% endcomment %}

You cannot nest comment tags.

Filters

A template filter is nothing more than an easy way to change variable values before they are displayed. They make use of the pipe character in this way:

{{ name|lower }}

This shows the name variable value after it goes through the lower filter – this changes the text to lowercase. We can chain filters, i.e., we can use them together in such a way that the output of the first filter is applied to the second and so on. The following example converts the first list element to uppercase:

{{ my_list|first|upper }}

Some filters can take an argument, and this will follow a colon and must be inside a set of double quotes. An example:

{{ bio|truncatewords:"20" }}

This shows the first 20 words of the variable called bio.

Now we look at some of the more important filters:

- **addslashes** – puts a backslash in front of another backslash, double quote or single quote, and is useful for when you want to escape a string.
- **date** – this formats dates or datetime objects as per a given format-string in the parameter.
- **length** – will return the value length. In the case of a list, this would be the number of list elements, and for a string, it would return the number of string characters.

Templates in Views

We learned how to use the template system, now it's time to use that to create a view.

Earlier, we used the view called current_datetime, found in mysite.views. It looks like this:

from django.http import HttpResponse

import datetime

def current_datetime(request):

  now = datetime.datetime.now()

  html = "<html><body>It is now %s</body></html>" % now

  return HttpResponse(html)

We're going to change this, so it uses the template system in Django. You might think that the way to do that would be like this:

from django.template import Template, Context

from django.http import HttpResponse

import datetime

def current_datetime(request):

  now = datetime.datetime.now()

  t = Template("<html><body>It is now {{ current_date }}.</body></html>")

  html = t.render(Context({'current_date': now}))

  return HttpResponse(html)

Yes, that would make use of the template system, but it doesn't go anywhere near solving the problems we discussed. The template is still in Python code, so we cannot have true data and presentation separation. We can fix that by placing our template into a new file and that is where the view will load from. The first thing you should do is save the template on your filesystem and then read the contents of it using the file-opening functionality built-in to Python. That would look something like this, assuming, of course, that we used the path file\users\djangouser\templates\mytemplate.html:

from django.template import Template, Context

from django.http import HttpResponse

import datetime

```python
def current_datetime(request):

    now = datetime.datetime.now()

    # Simple way of using templates from the filesystem.

    # This is BAD because it doesn't account for missing files!

    fp = open('\\users\\djangouser\\templates\\mytemplate.html')

    t = Template(fp.read())

    fp.close()


    html = t.render(Context({'current_date': now}))

    return HttpResponse(html)
```

This isn't a very nice approach though and here's why:

- It doesn't deal with the missing file case. If mytemplate.html cannot be read or doesn't exist, open() call will throw up an IOError exception.
- Your template location is hardcoded. If you did this for all the view functions, all you would achieve would be template location duplication, not to mention sore hands from that typing!
- There is a load of boilerplate code; really, you don't need to be writing continuous open(), fp.read() and fp.close() calls every time you want to load a template.

Solving these problems requires the use of template loading and directories.

Template Loading

In Django, there is a very powerful and convenient API that loads the templates from the filesystem. This to get rid of the redundancy in the templates and the loading calls. To use the API, you need to let the framework know where your templates are being stored. You should store your templates in the settings file – settings.py, which was discussed earlier when ROOT_URLCONF was introduced. So, open settings.py and look for the TEMPLATES setting. This is nothing more than a configuration list, one configuration for each engine:

```
TEMPLATES = [

    {

        'BACKEND': 'django.template.backends.django.DjangoTemplates',

        'DIRS': [],

        'APP_DIRS': True,

        'OPTIONS': {

            #... some options here...

        },

    },

]
```

A dotted Python path, BACKEND leads to the template engine class and this implements the backend API for the Django templates. The backends built-in are:

django.template.backends.django.DjangoTemplates, and

django.template.backends.jinja2.Jinja2.

Most engines will load a template from a file and, because of this, each engine's top-level configuration has three settings that are common:

- DIRS – this defines the directory list where the engine searches for template source files and this is done in search order.

- APP_DIRS – this indicates if the engine should be looking inside the installed applications for the templates. By convention, is APP_DIR is set as True, DjangoTemplates will search for \templatessubdirectory inside each INSTALLED_APPS. This way, even if DIRS is empty, the template engine can still find the application templates.
- OPTIONS – this is where the settings specific to the backend are stored.

Template Directories

By default, DIRS is just an empty list. You need to let the mechanism to load templates in Django know where to find the templates, so choose a directory for your templates and then add it to DIRS, in this way:

'DIRS': [

'/home/html/templates/site',

'/home/html/templates/default',

],

There are a couple of things you need to be aware of:

Unless your program is going to be simple,with no applications, it is better to leave DIRS empty. APP_DIRS is configured to True by the settings file; instead, set up a subdirectory called "Templates" in your own Django application.

If you wanted a master template set at the project root, for example, mysite\templates, you would need to set DIRS like this:

'DIRS': [os.path.join(BASE_DIR, 'templates')],

You do not need to name your templates directory as "Templates". Django doesn't restrict any of the names you use but it makes things just a little easier for you if you can stick to a naming convention. If you want a directory other than the default one selected, you will need to specify that directory, but ensure that both the directory and the templates saved in it can be read by the user account that the web server is running.

If you are using Windows, you need to make sure the letter that indicates the drive is specified along with forward and to backslashes, like this:

'DIRS':

[

'C:/www/django/templates',

]

We haven't created any Django app yet, so we'll see how template loading works using a very easy configuration. The first thing to do is set DIRS to this path, as per the above example:

[os.path.join(BASE_DIR,'templates')]

Check your settings file; it should look something like this:

TEMPLATES = [

　{

　　'BACKEND': 'django.template.backends.django.DjangoTemplates',

　　'DIRS': [os.path.join(BASE_DIR,'templates')],

　　'APP_DIRS': True,

　　'OPTIONS': {

　　　#...

Now that DIRS has been set, you need to create a directory for your templates and this is done in the root \mysite folder. When you have done that, you should see something like the following as your folder structure:

\mysite_project

　\mysite

\mysite

\templates

manage.py

Next, you need to change your view code so that the Django functionality to load templates is used; this eliminates the need to hard-code the paths. Going back to the current_datetime view you've been working on, you can change it like this:

#mysite\mysite\views.py

from django.template.loader import get_template

from django.http import HttpResponse

import datetime

def current_datetime(request):

  now = datetime.datetime.now()

  t = get_template('current_datetime.html')

  html = t.render({'current_date': now})

  return HttpResponse(html)

In general, a Django template-loader will be used and not the template API we used previously. For this current example, we are going to use the function called django.template.loader.get_template() instead of going to the filesystem to manually load the template. The function called get_template) will take the name of a template as the argument; it will then work out where the template is on the filesystem, open it, and will return a Template object that has been compiled.

Note that there is a difference between the render() method we are using here and the one we used previously. Until now, we have called django.template.Template.render and this needs a context object passed to it. The one we are using now, get_template(), will return a Django template that is backend-dependent. This comes from django.template.backends.base.Template; here, the render() method can only take a dictionary object and not a Context.

The template we are using in this example is called current_datetime.html but don't make the mistake of thinking that the.html extension is anything special. Your templates can have an extension so long as it makes sense for the application you are building; you can even leave off the extensions altogether if you want.

To find out where the template is on the filesystem, get_template, look at these in order:

- If you are using the DTL and APP_DIRS has been set to True then get_template will look in the current application for a /templates directory.
- If the template can't be found in the current application, get_template() will take the template name that you have passed and combine it with the template directories in DIRS and it will go through each in order until the required template is found. For example, if you set the first DIRS entry to /home/django/mysite/templates, then the get_template() call will look for a template called /home/django/mysite/templates/current_datetime.html
- If a template can't be found with the provided name, a TemplateDoesNotExist exception is raised.

If you want to know what one of these template exceptions looks like, go to your Django project directory and run python manage.py runserver. From your browser, open the website that is being used to activate the current_datetime view – in our case, this is http://127.0.0.1:8000/time. Assuming that you have your DEBUG mode set as True and you don't have a template called current_datetime.html, you will see an error page showing the TemplateDoesNotExist error.

This is quite like the error page we looked at earlier but this one has an extra bit of information for debugging purposes – a section for "Template-loader postmortem". This tells us the templates that Django attempted to load and why each of them failed. For example, it could be that the file didn't exist. This is valuable information for when you want to debug loading errors with the templates.

To fix the problem we have with a missing template, we need to use the following code to create a current_datetime.html file:

 # \mysite_project\mysite\templates\current_datetime.html

<html>

  <body>

    It is now {{ current_date }}

  </body>

</html>

It is now {{ current_date }}.

Save this to your \mysite\templates directory and then refresh your web page. The page should now show up as fully rendered.

Shortcut - render()

We have looked at loading the templates, filling Contexts, and returning HttpResponse objects using the results from the rendered templates. Next, we looked at using get_template() rather than going down the route of hard-coding each template and its path. The thing is, the developers of Django had already seen that this was going to be one of the most common uses, so they created a

333

shortcut that would do everything with just one code line. That shortcut is render() and it resides in the module called django.shortcuts.

You will use render() most of the time, instead of loading each template and then manually creating the Context and the HttpResponse objects. However, you should learn the entire process and remember it because it will be handy when you have non-standard uses to fulfill.

Using render(), this is what our current_datetime example now looks like:

from django.shortcuts import render

import datetime

def current_datetime(request):

   now = datetime.datetime.now()

   return render(request, 'current_datetime.html', {'current_date': now})

Now doesn't that look neater! Let's look at what changed.

There is now no need for HttpResponse, Template, get_template() or Context to be imported. Instead, django.shortcuts.render is what is imported and we retain the import datetime.

Inside the function called current_datetime, now still needs to be calculated but the call to render() takes care of loading the templates, creating the context, rendering the templates, and creating HttpResponse. And, as render() will still return an HttpResponse object, that value can be returned in the view.

The request is render() and is the first argument, while the second argument is the name of the template that is to be used. If there is a third argument, it would be the dictionary that is to be used for Context creation in the template. If there is no third argument, an empty dictionary is used instead.

Template Tags – Include

Now we know how the loading mechanism works for templates, we can look at a template tag, built-in that will take full advantage of that mechanism. That tag is called {% include %}.

This tag will let you add the contents from another template and the tag's argument must be the name of that additional template. That name may be a variable or it may be a quoted hard-coded string – it can be in single quotes or double so long as the opening and closing quotes match.

If you are ever using the same code in more than one template, you should always consider using the {% include %} tag to get rid of the duplicate content. The next two examples have the contents of the template called nav.html. They are both the same; one shows single quotes, the other double quotes.

Duplicated content:

{% include 'nav.html' %}

{% include "nav.html" %}

This example has the nav.html contents:

{% include 'includes/nav.html' %}

This has the contents of the template named in the variable of template_name:

{% include template_name %}

{% include %} supports relative paths:

{% include './nav.html' %}

{% include '../nav_base.html' %}

As it was in get_template(), the template file name is determined in one of two ways:

- If APPS_DIR is set to True, the path is added to the current Django application, in the directory called \templates.
- The DIRS template directory is added to the specified template name. All the templates get evaluated using the context of the including template.

The following is an example of these templates:

 # mypage.html

<html>

<body>

  {% include "includes/nav.html" %}

  <h1>{{ title }}</h1>

</body>

</html>

 # includes/nav.html

  You are in: {{ current_section }}

If mypage.html is rendered with a context that contains current_section, the variable is made available inside the "included" template.

If a template with the specified name is not found in the {$ include} tag, Django will then do one of these things:

- Provided DEBUG is set as True, the TemplateDoesNotExist error will be thrown

- Provided DEBUG is set as False, the tag will silently fail and nothing will be shown.

Included templates do not share a state; each is a rendering process in its own right, and independent from the others. A block is evaluated before it will be included, and this means that, if a template has blocks that come from another template, it will have blocks that have been evaluated already and have been rendered, rather than blocks that could potentially be overridden by a template that has extending abilities.

Template Inheritance

So far, the templates we used have been minute snippets of HTML but, out in the real world you will be creating whole pages of HTML with Django's template system. This leads to a problem common in web development – how do we reduce redundancy and duplication of common areas on pages across a website, perhaps like navigation across the entire site?

One of the classic ways to solve a problem like this is to make use of server-side includes. These are directives that may be embedded in the HTML pages including one page in another and Django has support for that, using the {% include %} tag we discussed earlier.

However, there is a better way of doing this in Django and that is to use a very nice strategy known as Template Inheritance. What this is, in basic terms, is a strategy that provides you with the ability to build a kind of skeleton template as the base. This base has all the common bits of the website and it will define blocks that can be overridden by child templates. As an example, we'll create a template that is somewhat more complete for the current_datetime view and we do this by editing the html file we created earlier:

```
<!DOCTYPE HTML PUBLIC "-//W3C//DTD HTML 4.01//EN">


<html lang="en">
```

```html
<head>

  <title>The current time</title>

</head>

<body>

  <h1>My helpful timestamp site</h1>

  <p>It is now {{ current_date }}.</p>

  <hr>

  <p>Thanks for visiting my site.</p>

</body>

</html>
```

All that looks OK but what would happen if we wanted a template created for another view, let's say for the hours_ahead view that we created a while before? If we wanted, once again, to create a full HTML template that is fully valid, we can do this:

```html
<!DOCTYPE HTML PUBLIC "-//W3C//DTD HTML 4.01//EN">

<html lang="en">

<head>

  <title>Future time</title>

</head>

<body>

  <h1>My helpful timestamp site</h1>

  <p>
```

In {{ hour_offset }} hour(s), it will be {{ next_time }}.

</p>

<hr>

<p>Thanks for visiting my site.</p>

</body>

</html>

It's clear that a great deal of HTML has just been duplicated! What would happen if we had a typical website, one that had a couple of style sheets, a navigation bar, a bit of JavaScript? What would happen is we would be placing a lot of HTML in each of the templates of HTML that is redundant.

Using server-side include will factor the common parts of the templates out and put them into individual template snippets. These then get added to each of the templates. For example, you put the top part of the template into a file that you name header.html:

<!DOCTYPE HTML PUBLIC "-//W3C//DTD HTML 4.01//EN">

<html lang="en">

<head>

And the bottom part of the template in a file named footer.html:

<hr>

<p>Thanks for visiting my site.</p>

</body>

</html>

Using this kind of strategy, it's easy to deal with footers and headers; it is not so easy for the rest of the page. In our example, we have a title on both pages but it's quite a long title and it won't go into header.html – the title is different on each page. If <h1> were included in the header, the title would need to be included and that would eliminate our ability to do per page customization.

With the inheritance system in Django, we can fix these problems easily. Think of it as being a version of the server-side include from the inside out. Rather than defining the common snippets, we define those that are a bit different.

First, the base template is defined. This is the page skeleton that will be filled in later by the child templates. Look at this skeleton template as the example we are currently using:

```
<!DOCTYPE HTML PUBLIC "-//W3C//DTD HTML 4.01//EN">

<html lang="en">

<head>

   <title>{% block title %}{% endblock %}</title>

</head>

<body>

   <h1>My helpful timestamp site</h1>

   {% block content %}{% endblock %}


   {% block footer %}

   <hr>

   <p>Thanks for visiting my site.</p>

   {% endblock %}

</body>
```

</html>

We will name this template base.html; it defines a very simple skeleton document in HTML and we can use this for every page on our website. The child templates will add to, override, or leave the block contents alone. Now, we save this template as base.html in our template directory.

The template tag we use here is one you haven't been introduced to yet – {% block %}. This tag will inform the template engine that the specified parts of the template may be overridden by a child template.

Now that we have our new base template, we can make some changes to the current_datetime.html template we are already using:

{% extends "base.html" %}

{% block title %}The current time{% endblock %}

{% block content %}

   <p>It is now {{ current_date }}.</p>

{% endblock %}

Let's also make a new template for hours_ahead, the view we created earlier. Change hours_ahead so it will make use of the template system rather than hard-code HTML. It should look like this:

{% extends "base.html" %}

{% block title %}Future time{% endblock %}

{% block content %}

<p>

   In {{ hour_offset }} hour(s), it will be {{ next_time }}.

</p>

{% endblock %}

This is much nicer. Each of the templates has just the code that is unique to it and there is no need for any redundancy. If we need to make a change that is site-wide, all we do is change the base.html template and every other template will reflect those changes.

So, here's how this all works. When the current_datetime.html template is loaded, the {% extends %} tag gets seen by the template engine as a child template. Immediately, the engine will load base.html, which is the parent template. The template engine will now notice that there are three of the { block %} tags inside base.html and it replaces them with the child template contents. A title was defined in {$ block title %} and this will be used alongside the {% block content %}.

Note: the footer block is not defined by the child block; the parent template value is used by the template system instead. It is worth noting that, where there is a {% block %} tag inside a parent template, the content in it will always be used as something to fall back on.

The template context is not affected by inheritance. So, any of the templates that are inside the inheritance tree will be able to gain access to each of the template variables from within Context. There is no limit to how much inheritance we can use and one of the most common of using it is by the three-level approach described below:

1. A base.html template is created to hold the fundamental feel and look of the website. This is the parts of the site that really don't change much, if at all.
2. Next, a base_SECTION.html template is created for each of the sections on the website. These templates will extend the base.html template and will all include styles and design that are specific to the template.
3. Last, an individual template is created for each page type, like a Gallery page, Forum page, etc. These will extend the templates for each related section.

Taking this route means that code reuse is maximized and adding items to shared parts of the website is much easier.

Read and learn the following guidelines for template inheritance:

- If {% extends %} is used inside a template, it must be the first tag; if it isn't, the inheritance will not work.
- The more of the {% block %} tags used in a base template, the better it is. Remember that a child template is not required to define all the parent blocks; this means that reasonable defaults may be filled in for some blocks and only those needed for the child templates may be defined. More hooks are always better than too few.
- If you are duplicating your code in multiple templates, you should consider using a {% block %} t house than code in a parent template.
- Use {% block super %} to get the block content out of the parent template. This variable is "magic" and it provides us with the parent template's rendered text. This is incredibly useful if we want the parent block contents added to and not overridden.
- You cannot define several {% block %} tags that have identical names inside the same template. This is because block tags work both ways, which means they don't just give us something to fill, it also tells us what content to use in filling the parent hole. If two of the block tags had similar or the same names in one template, the parent would not know from which of the blocks to take the content.
- The name of the template that is passed to {% extends %} uses the same method as get_template() does for loading purposes. That is to say, the name is appended to the DIRS setting – the Django app's \templates folder.
- Most of the time, a string is used as the {% extends %} argument, but it can be a variable as well – you won't always know what name the parent template has until its runtime.

Now that we know how the template system works, we can move on. Most of the websites we see today are driven by databases which means relational databases are used to store the website contents. This means that we get a much cleaner data/logic separation. Next, we are going to look at what Django provides us with for database interaction.

Django Models

Earlier, we explained how to use Django to build a dynamic website – the views and the URLconfs. Views, as you know, are responsible for doing some logic and returning responses and, in one example we used, the logic we did was to calculate what the current time and date were.

In a web app of today, this logic will often require database interaction, and in the background, this means connecting to a database server, getting some information out of it, and then showing that information on a webpage. The website might also give users a way to populate the database for themselves.

Many of the more complex sites provide some combination of both; Amazon, for example, is one of the best examples of a website driven by a database. Each of the product pages on Amazon is nothing more than a query to the website's database of products, formatted in HTML; when a customer posts a review, it will go straight into the database that holds the customer reviews.

Django is a great tool to create these websites that are database-driven because it has everything you need to use Python to perform a database query. In this chapter, we are going to look at this functionality a bit closer. To use the Django database layer, you don't need to have much knowledge of SQL or relational databases, but it does help. That is beyond this book's scope, but you should continue to read because everything will be kept as simple as possible.

Dumbing Down Database Queries in Views

Earlier, we talked about a 'dumb' way of producing an output in a view – simply hardcode your text into the view. Now we are going to look at a 'dumb' way of getting the data out of a database that is in a view. It really is quite simple – an SQL query is executed, using any library from Python, and then we take the results and we do something with them. On our view, we are connecting to a MySQL database using the MySQLdb library. We get some records out of it and then we put into a display template to be displayed as the contents of a webpage.

from django.shortcuts import render

import MySQLdb

def book_list(request):

   db = MySQLdb.connect(user='me', db='mydb', passwd='secret', host='localhost')

   cursor = db.cursor()

   cursor.execute('SELECT name FROM books ORDER BY name')

   names = [row[0] for row in cursor.fetchall()]

   db.close()

   return render(request, 'book_list.html', {'names': names})

This does work but you should have immediately spotted what the problems are:

- First, the connection parameters to the database have been hardcoded. In an ideal world, the Django configuration would be used to store these.
- Second, there is a lot of boilerplate code here; the connection is created, a cursor is created, a statement is executed, and the connection is closed. Really, what we want to do is specify that results that we are after.
- This code is tying us into using MySQL. If we wanted to change later to PostgreSQL, it would mean having to write a lot of the code again. Ideally, we would be using an abstracted database server; this way, changes to the server could be done in one place.

Of course, there is a solution to all of this and it's the Django database layer.

The Configuration of the Database

Keeping all that in mind, we'll start to look at this database layer. First of all, we'll look at the configuration that was put into settings.py when the application as created:

DATABASES = {

  'default': {

    'ENGINE': 'django.db.backends.sqlite3',

    'NAME': os.path.join(BASE_DIR, 'db.sqlite3'),

  }

}

This is quite simple; ENGINE is determining the database engine that will be used. In our case, we will leave it as the django.db.backends.sqlite3 default. NAME is informing Django what name your database goes under.

Because we have used SQLite, a filesystem path was created by startproject leading to the database file.

That's all we need to do for the setup.

Our First App

Now we know the connection works, we can start creating an app in Django. This is just some code that includes views and models, all living in one package. We will review the terminology used because this is where some new users tend to get stuck. Earlier, we created a project but how does a project differ from an app? The answer to that lies in configuration versus code.

Projects are instances of a set of specified Django apps and their configurations. Technically, all we require from a project is that it gives us a settings file. This should define the information that relates to the database connection, the apps installed, the DIRS, and more.

Apps are sets of the functionality that usually includes the views and the models, all in one package. Django has a number of built-in apps and one thing about apps that is key is that they are portable and can be reused across several projects.

As far as rules go for fitting our Django code in, there are few to worry about. If it's just a simple website that we are building we can get away with one app while a complex website that has multiple parts all unrelated may need to be split into different apps; this will allow us to reuse each one in the future, as and where it is needed.

Really, we don't even need to create any apps. We've already seen that we can create a views.py file, add a few view functions, and then point URLconf to the functions. However, there is one thing to be aware of; if we use the database layer in Django, we must create Django apps. Models can only live in apps. So to write the models, we must first create the app.

Inside mysite project directory, let's start creating a books app by typing this command:

python manage.py startapp books

We won't get any output from this but we will get a new directory in the mysite directory; it's called books and we can see what the contents should be by looking at the tree below:

\mysite_project

  \books

    \migrations

    __init__.py

    admin.py

    apps.py

    models.py

tests.py

views.py

\mysite

\templates

manage.py

All the views and the models that we need for the app are in these files. For example, open views.py and models.py in our text editor. We will see that both have nothing in them bar comments and, in models.py, an import. This is our blank piece of paper, ready for our new Django app.

Defining the Django Models

A model is a description of the data that is represented by the code in our database. It is basically the layout of the data, the SQL CREATE TABLE, but in Python, not SQL and it has more in it than just definitions of database columns.

Models are used by Django to execute behind-the-scenes SQL code, turning it into Python data structures that represent the database table rows. Models are also used as a way of representing concepts that SQL may not be able to handle because they are high-level. You might, if you have some familiarity with databases, be wondering why we would bother to use Python for defining data models when we have SQL. Well, there are several reasons why Django works as it does:

- Introspection is not perfect, and it needs overhead. So that Django can provide data-access APIs that are convenient, it must know what the database layout is, and this is done in one of two ways. First, we could use Python to describe the data explicitly and, second, the database could be introspected at runtime in order to determine the data models. Introspection puts in a layer of overhead that is not acceptable and may not be accurate; because of this it was determined by the Django developers that the best option was the first.

- Python is more fun and, if you can keep everything within Python, it cuts down on how often your brain needs to switch contexts. Productivity is much higher if you stay in one programming environment for as long as you can whereas flicking between languages can be disruptive.
- If you can store your data models as code then it is much easier for models to be kept under version control and changes can be better tracked that are made to the data layout.
- SQL limits what level of metadata can be kept regarding a data layout. Most of the database systems have no special data type for URL or email representation, for example, whereas a Django model does. High-level data types offer one main advantage – more productivity and code that can be reused.
- SQL is not consistent across all database platforms. If a web application is being distributed, it is better to use a Python module that defines the layout of the data than it is to use a lot of separate SQL CREATE TABLE statements.

There is a drawback; there is every possibility that the Python code can lose sync with the database contents. When the Django model is changed in any way, the exact same changes must be made in the database, so they remain consistent.

Our First Model

We'll use the layout of the book, author and publisher for this, simply because the relationship between all three is well-known. We will follow these assumptions:

- Every author has a first and last name and also an email address.
- Every book has a title and it has a publication date. There may also be a many-to-many relationship, i.e. more than one author and a one-to-many relationship, i.e. one publisher.
- Every publisher has a name and an address, a country, and their own website

The very first step we take in the Django database layout is expressing it in Python. Open the models.py file and input the following:

```python
from django.db import models


class Publisher(models.Model):
    name = models.CharField(max_length=30)

    address = models.CharField(max_length=50)

    city = models.CharField(max_length=60)

    state_province = models.CharField(max_length=30)

    country = models.CharField(max_length=50)

    website = models.URLField()


class Author(models.Model):
    first_name = models.CharField(max_length=30)

    last_name = models.CharField(max_length=40)

    email = models.EmailField()


class Book(models.Model):
    title = models.CharField(max_length=100)

    authors = models.ManyToManyField(Author)

    publisher = models.ForeignKey(Publisher)

    publication_date = models.DateField()
```

Let's look at the code. Notice that a Python class represents each of the models and that class is a django.db.models.Model subclass. Models is the parent class, and this has everything needed to ensure the objects can interact with a database leaving the models responsible only for the definition of their fields, using neat syntax.

This really is all we need to write to have data-access. Each of the models will correspond to one database table with each model attribute corresponding to a column in the table. The name of the attribute corresponds to the name of the column and the field type will correspond to the column type. For example, the model called Publisher is the equivalent of this table, assuming the syntax of the PostgreSQL CREATE TABLE:

CREATE TABLE "books_publisher" (

　"id" serial NOT NULL PRIMARY KEY,

　"name" varchar(30) NOT NULL,

　"address" varchar(50) NOT NULL,

　"city" varchar(60) NOT NULL,

　"state_province" varchar(30) NOT NULL,

　"country" varchar(50) NOT NULL,

　"website" varchar(200) NOT NULL

);

Django is able to automatically generate the CREATE TABLE statement. There is one exception to the rule of one class to one database and that is the many-to-many relationships. In the example that we are using, Book has a field called Authors and this is a ManyToManyField which designates a book as having one or more authors, but the database table called Book does not have a column called Authors. Instead, another table is created by Django and this one is a many-to-many joint table. This takes care of the books to authors mapping.

Lastly, we did not explicitly define primary keys for any model. Unless you tell Django otherwise, it will give each model a primary key field of an auto-incremental integer. This field is called id and each model in Django must have a primary key for "single column".

Installing Our Model

The code is written and now we need to come up with the database tables. To do this, we first need to activate our models in the project. We add our books app to settings file in the installed apps list. The settings.py file can be edited again and then we can look for the setting for INSTALLED_APPS. This informs Django of the apps that are activated for any given project and it will look like this by default:

INSTALLED_APPS = [

'django.contrib.admin',

'django.contrib.auth',

'django.contrib.contenttypes',

'django.contrib.sessions',

'django.contrib.messages',

'django.contrib.staticfiles',

]

For the "books" app to be registered, the following should be added to INSTALLED_APPS – books.apps.BooksConfig – the settings file should now look like this:

INSTALLED_APPS = [

'books.apps.BooksConfig',

'django.contrib.admin',

'django.contrib.auth',

'django.contrib.contenttypes',

'django.contrib.sessions',

'django.contrib.messages',

'django.contrib.staticfiles',

]

A full Python path represents every app inside INSTALLED_APPS. This is a dotted path of packages that end in the app package. In our case, the path leads to the BooksConfig class created by Django in apps.py.

The Django app has now been activated so we can get on with creating the database table. First, the models need to be validated and we do that with this code:

python manage.py check

This will run the system check framework in Django and this is a series of static checks used to validate every project in Django. If everything is OK, a message will appear saying 'System check identified no issues (0 silenced). If you don't see that message, you need to check that the model code was typed incorrectly.

If you have valid models, the following code can be run to let Django know that a few changes have been made to the models – in our case, we have a new one:

python manage.py makemigrations books

The output should look a bit like this:

Migrations for 'books':

  0001_initial.py:

   - Create model Author

- Create model Book

- Create model Publisher

- Add field publisher to book

A migration is how Django stores any changes made to the models and, by extension, the database schema; they are just files. In our example, if we look in our books app inside the folder called \migrations, there should be a file named 0001_inital.py. With the migrate command, the newest migration file is used to automatically update the schema. First, though, we need to see what SQL gets run by the migration. The command of sqlmigrate will return the SQL of each migration name:

python manage.py sqlmigrate books 0001

Now you should see something like this:

BEGIN;

CREATE TABLE "books_author" (

   "id" integer NOT NULL PRIMARY KEY AUTOINCREMENT,

   "first_name" varchar(30) NOT NULL,

   "last_name" varchar(40) NOT NULL,

   "email" varchar(254) NOT NULL

);

CREATE TABLE "books_book" (

   "id" integer NOT NULL PRIMARY KEY AUTOINCREMENT,

   "title" varchar(100) NOT NULL,

```
    "publication_date" date NOT NULL
);
CREATE TABLE "books_book_authors" (
    "id" integer NOT NULL PRIMARY KEY AUTOINCREMENT,
    "book_id" integer NOT NULL REFERENCES "books_book" ("id"),
    "author_id" integer NOT NULL REFERENCES "books_author" ("id"),
    UNIQUE ("book_id", "author_id")
);
CREATE TABLE "books_publisher" (
    "id" integer NOT NULL PRIMARY KEY AUTOINCREMENT,
    "name" varchar(30) NOT NULL,
    "address" varchar(50) NOT NULL,
    "city" varchar(60) NOT NULL,
    "state_province" varchar(30) NOT NULL,
    "country" varchar(50) NOT NULL,
    "website" varchar(200) NOT NULL
);
CREATE TABLE "books_book__new" (
    "id" integer NOT NULL PRIMARY KEY AUTOINCREMENT,
    "title" varchar(100) NOT NULL,
    "publication_date" date NOT NULL,
```

```
    "publisher_id" integer NOT NULL REFERENCES
    "books_publisher" ("id")
);


INSERT INTO "books_book__new" ("id", "publisher_id", "title",
"publication_date") SELECT "id", NULL, "title", "publication_date" FROM
"books_book";


DROP TABLE "books_book";


ALTER TABLE "books_book__new" RENAME TO "books_book";


CREATE INDEX "books_book_2604cbea" ON "books_book" ("publisher_id");


COMMIT;
```

Note

We get our table names by putting the app name, which is books, together with the model name in lowercase.

For each table, Django automatically adds primary keys, and these are called idfields. '_id' is appended by Django to the name given to the foreign key field.

A REFERENCES statement is used to make the key relationship explicit.

Each CREATE TABLE statement is specifically made for the database. Field types that are specific to the database like serial in Postgre SQL, auto_increment in MySQL or SQLite's integer primary key, are automatically handled, as is the double or single quoting that happens with the names of the columns.

The command, sqlmigrate, doesn't create a table, nor does it interact with the database; what it does is print the output so that we see what is executed by SQL Django if requested. This SQL could be copied and pasted to the database client but there is a better way of doing this – using the migrate command:

python manage.py migrate

Run the above command and you should see an output like this:

Operations to perform:

Apply all migrations: admin, auth, books, contenttypes, sessions

Running migrations:

Applying books.0001_initial... OK

Should we end up with a load more migrations, this will be because the initial migrations weren't run earlier. When we migrate for the first time, Django creates every system table needed by Django for the apps that are built-in.

Basic Data-Access

Django provides us with a Python API for working with our models and we can try this out – go to your virtual environment and run python manage.py shell; input the following:

>>> from books.models import Publisher

>>> p1 = Publisher(name='Apress', address='2855 Telegraph Avenue',

...   city='Berkeley', state_province='CA', country='U.S.A.',

```
...      website='http://www.apress.com/')
>>> p1.save()
>>> p2 = Publisher(name="O'Reilly", address='10 Fawcett St.',
...      city='Cambridge', state_province='MA', country='U.S.A.',
...      website='http://www.oreilly.com/')
>>> p2.save()
>>> publisher_list = Publisher.objects.all()
>>> publisher_list
```

<QuerySet [<Publisher: Publisher object>, <Publisher: Publisher object>]>

This actually does quite a lot:

First, the model class called Publisher is imported. This allows us to interact with the publisher's database table.

Next, a Publisher object is created; this is done through instantiation providing each field with values.

The object is saved into the database by calling the save() method of the object. In the background, an SQL INSERT statement is being executed by Django.

We use the Publisher.objects attribute to get the publishers out of the database and we use Publisher.objects.all() to get a list from the database of the Publisher objects. Again, Django is working behind the scenes, executing an SQL SELECT statement.

In case this example didn't make it clear: when we use the Django model API to create an object, Django won't save that object not the database until the save() method has been called:

```
p1 = Publisher(...)
```

 # Right now, p1 has not been saved to the database.

p1.save()

 # It has now.

If we wanted to take just one step to create and save an object in the database, we would need to use the method called objects.create(). The following example uses the above example but with the new method:

>>> p1 = Publisher.objects.create(name='Apress',

...   address='2855 Telegraph Avenue',

...   city='Berkeley', state_province='CA', country='U.S.A.',

...   website='http://www.apress.com/')

>>> p2 = Publisher.objects.create(name="O'Reilly",

...   address='10 Fawcett St.', city='Cambridge',

...   state_province='MA', country='U.S.A.',

...   website='http://www.oreilly.com/')

>>> publisher_list = Publisher.objects.all()

>>> publisher_list

<QuerySet [<Publisher: Publisher object>, <Publisher: Publisher object>]>

Model String Representations

When the publisher list was printed, the output we got was not very helpful and made it very hard to distinguish the Publisher objects from one another. It should have looked like this:

<QuerySet [<Publisher: Publisher object>, <Publisher: Publisher object>]>

This is easily solved: all we do is add another method to the Publisher class – the __str__() method. All __str__() methods let Python know how to show an object representation in a format readable by the human eye. If you add a __str__) method to our three models, we can see how this works:

```
from django.db import models


class Publisher(models.Model):

    name = models.CharField(max_length=30)

    address = models.CharField(max_length=50)

    city = models.CharField(max_length=60)

    state_province = models.CharField(max_length=30)

    country = models.CharField(max_length=50)

    website = models.URLField()


    def __str__(self):

        return self.name


class Author(models.Model):

    first_name = models.CharField(max_length=30)

    last_name = models.CharField(max_length=40)

    email = models.EmailField()
```

```
def __str__(self):
    return u'%s %s' % (self.first_name, self.last_name)


class Book(models.Model):
    title = models.CharField(max_length=100)
    authors = models.ManyToManyField(Author)
    publisher = models.ForeignKey(Publisher)
    publication_date = models.DateField()


    def __str__(self):
        return self.title
```

The __str__() method does whatever is necessary to return a readable object representation:

- The __str__() methods added to Book and Publisher return the title and the name of each object
- The __str__() method added to Author is a little more involved. It will add the first_name field to the last_name field with a space between the two.

__str__() methods have just one requirement – that a string object is returned. If a string object is not returned and we get an integer instead, and a TypeError is raised by Python.

When we add a __str__() method, for the changes to happen, we need to come out of the Python shell and go back into it through python manage.py shell. Now this is a much better output:

```
>>> from books.models import Publisher
```

```
>>> publisher_list = Publisher.objects.all()
```

```
>>> publisher_list
```

```
<QuerySet [<Publisher: Apress>, <Publisher: O'Reilly>]>
```

For the sake of convenience when we use the interactive interpreter, we ensure a ___str___() method is defined for all models. This is also helpful to Django because it uses the ___str___() output in multiple laces when it has objects to be displayed.

Lastly, using ___str___() is also one of the best ways to give a model new behaviors. Django models don't only define the layout of the database table for an object; they also define the functionalities that the object does, one of which is ___str___().

Inserting Data and Updating It

We do this by inserting a database row which requires us to use keyword arguments to create a model instance, like this:

```
>>> p = Publisher(name='GNW Independent Publishing',
...         address='123 Some Street',
...         city='Hamilton',
...         state_province='NSW',
...         country='AUSTRALIA',
...         website='http://djangobook.com/')
```

This instantiation method does not do anything to anything to the database; until save() is called, the record will not be saved:

```
>>> p.save()
```

This is translated roughly into the following for SQL:

INSERT INTO books_publisher

  (name, address, city, state_province, country, website)

VALUES

  ('GNW Independent Publishing', '123 Some Street', 'Hamilton', 'NSW',

   'Australia', 'http://djangobook.com/');

The Publisher model is using a primary key id that auto-increments so the first save() call will do an additional thing – it will work out what the primary key value is for the record and, on the instance, is set to idattribute:

>>> p.id

3   # this will depend on what your data is

Any further save() calls will save that record and will not create a new one, i.e. an SQL UPDATE statement is performed rather than INSERT:

>>> p.name = 'GNW Independent Publishing'

>>> p.save()

This translates roughly into the following for SQL:

UPDATE books_publisher SET

  name = 'GNW Independent Publishing',

  address='123 Some Street',

  city='Hamilton',

  state_province='NSW',

  country='AUSTRALIA',

website='http://djangobook.com/')

WHERE id = 3;

All fields are updated, not just those we made changes to. Depending on what the application is, we could end up with a race condition. Later we look at how to update several objects in a single statement to execute the following query which is a little different:

UPDATE books_publisher SET

   name = 'GNW Independent Publishing'

WHERE id=3;

Selecting the Objects

While it is important to know how to create a database record and update it, there is a good chance that most of the web apps that you will be building will likely query objects that already exist rather than creating new objects. We know how to get all the records in any specified model:

>>> *Publisher.objects.all()*

<QuerySet [<Publisher: Apress>, <Publisher: O'Reilly>, <Publisher: GNW Independent Publishing>]>

In SQL this would be:

SELECT id, name, address, city, state_province, country, website

FROM books_publisher;

Note that SELECT * is not used by Django when data is being looked up. Rather, all the fields are explicitly listed. This is in the design – there are circumstances where SELECT * is quite a lot slower and, if you read and understood the Zen of Python at the start of the book, you will have picked up that field listing follows one specific principle – "Explicit is better than implicit".

Let's break down the Publisher.objects.all() line:

First is the Publisher model. Whenever we have data we want to look up, we need the model that relates to that data.

Second is the objects attribute, known as a manager. A manager is used to look after the table-level data operations including the most important one, data lookup. Every model has an objects manager given to it automatically and these are used when we need to look up any model instance.

Last we use the all() method, an objects manager method that will, in a QuerySet, return every row in a database. A QuerySet is an object used to represent a given set of database rows.

Pretty much any database lookup will follow this pattern – methods are called on the manager that goes with the model we are querying.

Filtering the Data

It isn't very often that everything in a database will be selected at once; mostly, just a subset of the data will be wanted. There is a method in the Django API called filter() that lets filter which data is wanted:

>>> Publisher.objects.filter(name='Apress')

<QuerySet [<Publisher: Apress>]>

The filter() method will take keyword arguments that are subsequently translated into the right SQL WHERE clauses. The above example would look like this:

SELECT id, name, address, city, state_province, country, website

FROM books_publisher

WHERE name = 'Apress';

The filter() method can take several arguments at once, helping to narrow the requirements down even more:

>>> Publisher.objects.filter(country="U.S.A.",

state_province="CA")

<QuerySet [<Publisher: Apress>]>

Again these arguments are translated, this time in SQL AND clauses so the above example would look like this:

SELECT id, name, address, city, state_province, country, website

FROM books_publisher

WHERE country = 'U.S.A.'

AND state_province = 'CA';

By default, the SQL = operator is used by the lookups for exact matches:

>>> Publisher.objects.filter(name__contains="press")

<QuerySet [<Publisher: Apress>]>

In between name and contains, we have a double underscore, and this is used in both Django and Python to indicate a bit of magic. In this case, the __contain bit of this code is translated to an SQL LIKE statement, like this:

SELECT id, name, address, city, state_province, country, website

FROM books_publisher

WHERE name LIKE '%press%';

Other lookup types include icontains, which translates to LIKE (Case-insensitive), startswith, endswith, and range, which translates to SQL BETWEEN.

Retrieving a Single Object

All the filter() examples we used above returned the same – a QuerySet, which may be treated as a list. However, sometimes it might be better to retrieve just one object rather than a QuerySet and that is what we use the get() method for:

>>> Publisher.objects.get(name="Apress")

<Publisher: Apress>

Instead of getting a QuerySet, only one object is returned and, as such, a query that results in several objects will end up with an exception being raised:

>>> Publisher.objects.get(country="U.S.A.")

Traceback (most recent call last):

...

books.models.MultipleObjectsReturned: get() returned more than one Publisher - it returned 2!

And, if the query doesn't return any objects at all, that will also raise an exception:

>>> Publisher.objects.get(name="Penguin")

Traceback (most recent call last):

...

books.models.DoesNotExist: Publisher matching query does not exist.

The exception called DoesNotExist is an attribute of the class belonging to the model – Publisher.DoesNotExist. The following needs to be done in your applications to catch those exceptions:

try:

* p = Publisher.objects.get(name='Apress')*

except Publisher.DoesNotExist:

  print ("Apress isn't in the database yet.")

else:

  print ("Apress is in the database.")

Ordering the Data

As you get to grips with the examples we used so far, you might start to notice that the objects are returned in what seems to be a random order. No, you are not seeing things. Up to now, the database has not been told how the results should be ordered so the data is given back in an order that the database chooses. When you build your applications, you will most likely want your results ordered using a specific value, say, numerically or alphabetically. We do this using the method called order_by():

>>> Publisher.objects.order_by("name")

<QuerySet [<Publisher: Apress>, <Publisher: GNW Independent Publishing>, <Publisher: O'Reilly>]>

This looks much like the all() example we used earlier but now SQL has a specific order:

SELECT id, name, address, city, state_province, country, website

FROM books_publisher

ORDER BY name;

You can use whatever field you want to order by:

>>> Publisher.objects.order_by("address")

<QuerySet [<Publisher: O'Reilly>, <Publisher: GNW Independent Publishing>, <Publisher: Apress>]>

>>> *Publisher.objects.order_by("state_province")*

<QuerySet [<Publisher: Apress>, <Publisher: O'Reilly>, <Publisher: GNW Independent Publishing>]>

If you want to order using multiple fields, multiple arguments are required:

>>> *Publisher.objects.order_by("state_province", "address")*

<QuerySet [<Publisher: Apress>, <Publisher: O'Reilly>, <Publisher: GNW Independent Publishing>]>

And you can also do reverse ordering by adding a minus character (-) to the start of the field name:

>>> *Publisher.objects.order_by("-name")*

<QuerySet [<Publisher: O'Reilly>, <Publisher: GNW Independent Publishing>, <Publisher: Apress>]>

All that said, while the flexibility is great, it can get quite repetitive to keep using order_by(). Mostly, you are going to have a specific field that you want used for ordering and, in cases like this, Django allows you to specify default ordering within the model:

```
class Publisher(models.Model):

    name = models.CharField(max_length=30)

    address = models.CharField(max_length=50)

    city = models.CharField(max_length=60)

    state_province = models.CharField(max_length=30)

    country = models.CharField(max_length=50)

    website = models.URLField()
```

```
def __str__(self):

    return self.name


class Meta:

    ordering = ['name']
```

We've looked at a new concept called the Meta class. This class is embedded in the definition of the Publisher class and it can be used on whatever model you want to specify any options that are specific to the model. There are several Meta options, but we are only interested in the ordering option here. When we use it, we are telling Django that, unless order_by() specifies an explicit order, the name field is used to order the Publisher objects by whenever the database API is used to retrieve them.

Chaining Your Lookups

We looked at filtering and ordering data but, on many occasions, you will want to do both. This entails chaining the lookups, like this:

```
>>> Publisher.objects.filter(country="U.S.A.").order_by("-name")

<QuerySet [<Publisher: O'Reilly>, <Publisher: Apress>]>
```

The SQL translation is to SQL WHERE and SQL ORDER BY:

```
SELECT id, name, address, city, state_province, country, website

FROM books_publisher

WHERE country = 'U.S.A'

ORDER BY name DESC;
```

Slicing the Data

What if you only wanted to look up a set number of the database rows? You could have a database that is full of publishers, thousands of them, but you only want to display the first one. Django allows for QuerySets to be treated as lists and this means you can use the standard syntax in Python for list slicing:

>>> Publisher.objects.order_by('name')[0]

<Publisher: Apress>

This is translated to something like:

SELECT id, name, address, city, state_province, country, website

FROM books_publisher

ORDER BY name

LIMIT 1;

In much the same way, a specified subset of the data can be retrieved with the standard syntax for range-slicing in Python:

>>> Publisher.objects.order_by('name')[0:2]

Two objects are returned which translate to something like:

SELECT id, name, address, city, state_province, country, website

FROM books_publisher

ORDER BY name

OFFSET 0 LIMIT 2;

Note – there is no support for negative slicing:

>>> Publisher.objects.order_by('name')[-1]

Traceback (most recent call last):

...

AssertionError: Negative indexing is not supported.

We can get around this quite easily; all we do is make a change to the order_by statement:

>>> Publisher.objects.order_by('-name')[0]

Updating Several Objects in a Single Statement

Earlier, we discussed the save() method to update the columns in a database row. Depending on what the application does, we might only want some of the columns updated. For example, let's assume that we want the Apress Publisher to change from the name Apress to Apress publishing. If we used save(), it would look like this:

>>> p = Publisher.objects.get(name='Apress')

>>> p.name = 'Apress Publishing'

>>> p.save()

A rough translation of that would be:

SELECT id, name, address, city, state_province, country, website

FROM books_publisher

WHERE name = 'Apress';

UPDATE books_publisher SET

   name = 'Apress Publishing',

   address = '2855 Telegraph Ave.',

city = 'Berkeley',

state_province = 'CA',

country = 'U.S.A.',

website = 'http://www.apress.com'

WHERE id = 1;

In this example, we are assuming that the publisher id of Apress is 1. The save() method sets the values for all columns, not just that of the name column. If our environment causes the other database columns to change because of another process, the smart thing to do is to only change the column we need to change. We use the update() method for this on the QuerySet objects:

>>> Publisher.objects.filter(id=1).update(name='Apress Publishing')

The SQL translation here is much more efficient and has no chance of race conditions:

UPDATE books_publisher

SET name = 'Apress Publishing'

WHERE id = 1;

This method will work on all QuerySets and this gives us the means to edit bulk records. Let's say that we want to changer U.S.A. to USA in each record in Publisher:

>>> Publisher.objects.all().update(country='USA')

3

The return value of the update() method is an integer that represents the number of records changed. In our example, it was 3.

Deleting an Object

If we want an object deleted from the database, we call the delete() method for that object:

>>> p = Publisher.objects.get(name="O'Reilly")

>>> p.delete()

(1, {'books.Publisher': 1})

>>> Publisher.objects.all()

<QuerySet [<Publisher: Apress>, <Publisher: GNW Independent Publishing>]>

Note Django's return value when an object is deleted. First, the total number of affected records is listed – in our case, it's one). Then a dictionary lists the models that are affected, and the number of records deleted out of each table.

Objects can be bulk deleted too. Simply take the result of a QuerySet and call delete() on it. This is much like the update() method from before:

>>> Publisher.objects.filter(country='USA').delete()

(1, {'books.Publisher': 1})

>>> Publisher.objects.all().delete()

(1, {'books.Publisher': 1})

>>> Publisher.objects.all()

<QuerySet []>

Be very careful when you delete data. Django has a failsafe in place to stop you accidentally deleting the entire contents of a table – explicit use of all() if you want everything deleted. The following example would NOT work:

>>> Publisher.objects.delete()

Traceback (most recent call last):

 File "", line 1, in

AttributeError: 'Manager' object has no attribute 'delete'

But, if you use the all() method, it will work:

>>> Publisher.objects.all().delete()

If we only want a subset of the data deleted, all() does not need to be used:

>>> Publisher.objects.filter(country='USA').delete()

We should now be able to write a basic application that is based on a database. When we have defined the models, the database must be populated with data. We could have some legacy data, or we might be relying on our website users to supply the data for us – we'll need a form for that. Sometimes we might need to manually input data, and, for this, it would be very helpful if we had an interface that we could use for the entry and management of the data. That leads us to the admin interface in Django.

Django Admin Site

Most of today's websites have an admin interface as an integral part of their infrastructure. The admin interface is web-based and can only be used by a trusted admin of the website. It is where site content is added, edited, and deleted. Think of a WordPress blog, for example; the interface where the content is added is the admin interface. If you built a website for a client, the admin interface is the way in which they update their website, and so on.

Admin interfaces do have one problem though – they are incredibly boring to build. Web development is meant to be fun and wasting time on boring jobs simply isn't fun. You need to display forms, handle them, authenticate site users, validate all input, and more. Not only is it boring work, but it is also very repetitive.

So, what does Django do? It does everything for us. Admin interfaces are solved problems in Django, so we are going to take a look at the Django admin site, how it works and what we can do with it.

How to Use the Django Admin Site

Earlier you ran django-admin startproject mysite and when you did that the default admin site was created by Django and configured. All that is left for you to do is create the superuser (admin user) and then you can gain access to your admin site.

Open the virtual environment for your project and run this command:

(env_mysite) C:\...\mysite_project\mysite> python manage.py createsuperuser

Type in the username you want to use and hit the Enter key – in our case, we are using admin as the username:

Username: admin

Next, type in the email address you want to use:

Email address: admin@example.com

Lastly, you will be asked to put your password in, and then re-enter it to confirm. You will need a secure password, even for the purpose of testing.

Django will run a test on your password strength; if it is too simple or too common you won't be able to use it. This is somewhat irritating when you are testing but you can be safe in the knowledge that Django will not let you use a weak or stupid password to break through the security that it crafts very carefully.

Password: **********

Password (again): *********

Superuser created successfully.

Start the Development Server

The latest version of Django activates the admin site by default so the next step is to run the development server and have a look around. We start the server like this:

(env_mysite) C:\...\mysite_project\mysite> python manage.py runserver

Next, go to your web browser and type in your local domain – you want the admin section so you would type something like http://127.0.0.1:8000/admin/. The login screen should open. Translation is activated by default so you may see the screen in your language, although this is dependent on what your browser settings are and whether Django can translate your particular language.

Enter the Admin Site

Log in using the superuser account you just created. The admin index page will load and there should be two types of content that you can edit – Users and Groups. These come from django.contrib.auth, which is Django's authentication framework. The Django admin site has been designed with non-technical users in mind, so it should be relatively easy to use. However, the following is a walk-through of the basics.

Each data type within the admin site has two things – a change list and a form for editing. The change list is where you can see all the database objects while the editing form is where you add records, change them or delete them. To bring up the users change list page, go to the "Users" row and click on "Change".

The page will show you all the database users; if you are following our example, you should only see a single user for now but when you add more, the options for sort, filter, and search will become far more useful.

To get the options for filtering, look to the right side of the page; for sort, click on any column header, and the search facility is at the top giving you the option to use the username as a search filter. Click on the name of the user you created earlier, and the edit form will load. Here, you change the user's attributes, such as name and permissions. Note you will not see the password – raw passwords are not stored by Django, so you can never retrieve one – instead, you must change it.

One more thing you need to note is that fields that have different types are given different widgets. For example, the fields for data and time are given controls for a calendar, while a Boolean field will be given checkboxes, and character fields are given simple fields for inputting text.

To delete records, simply click on the Delete button on the edit form for the record – the button is at the bottom left of the page. From there, you go to a confirmation page which, where necessary, will also show you a list of the record's dependent objects which will also be deleted. For example, deleting a publisher would mean any books related to that publisher would be also deleted.

To add a record, go to the relevant column on the home page and click on Add. You will be given an empty edit page; just fill it in with the relevant details. Input validation is handled by the admin interface; if you were to leave a required field empty or input a date in an invalid format, you get an error when you attempt to save the record.

When you want to edit an object, you see a History link in the window; whenever you make any change through the interface, it is logged and you can click on the History link to see this log.

How it Works

So how does it all work behind the scenes?

It's really quite easy; at server startup when Django loads, the admin.autodiscover() function is run. This will iterate over INSTALLED_APPS looking for the admin.py file in each of your installed apps. If it finds it, the code in the file is executed and this will happen for every app the file is found in.

The admin site displays the edit/change interface for any model that has been registered explicitly with admin.site.register(_ in the admin.py file of the app. The django.contrib.auth app has an admin.py file of its own and this is why you can see Users and Groups.

Other than that, the admin site is a Django application. It has models, it has templates and views, and it has URLpatterns. It can be added into your own application; simply hook it into URLconf in the same way your views are hooked. The templates can be inspected, as can the URLpatterns, and the views by going into django/contrib/admin in your Django codebase. Don't change anything though, you could cause a lot of problems.

Adding Models to The Django Admin Site

There is one very important thing we have not looked at yet, and that is adding models to the admin site. We want to do this so that we can use this interface to add objects, change, or delete objects in our database tables. We'll continue with the example we have been using all through this section. In mysite_project\mysite\books, look in startapp – there should now be an admin.py file. If there isn't, just make one and input this code:

from django.contrib import admin

from.models import Publisher, Author, Book

admin.site.register(Publisher)

admin.site.register(Author)

admin.site.register(Book)

This is telling Django that an interface is required for each of the models. You can now go back to the admin home page by going to http://127.0.0.1:8000/admin/ - there should be a section for Books that has links in it for Authors, Publishers, and Book. If you don't see the changes; stop the server and restart it.

What you have now is an admin interface that is functional for each of the models.

Now take a bit of time out to play around with it; add some records, change them, delete them, and see how it all works.

One thing to mention is the way the Django admin site handles many-to-many relationships and foreign keys. Both can be seen in the model called Book. Just to remind you, this is the book model:

class Book(models.Model):

  title = models.CharField(max_length=100)

  authors = models.ManyToManyField(Author)

  publisher = models.ForeignKey(Publisher)

  publication_date = models.DateField()

  def __str__(self):

   return self.title

On the Add Book page, which you will find at http://127.0.0.1:8000/admin/books/book/add/, you will see a select box this represents the ForeignKey (the publisher); a multiple-select box is used to represent the ManyToMany field (the authors). Both the fields have a green plus icon beside them allowing you to easily add records that are related.

Click the plus next to Publisher, for example, and a window will load allowing a publisher to be added. Once the new publisher has been created, the form for Add Book is updated with the details.

Making a Field Optional

After you've been getting to know the site for a while, you will notice that there is one glaring limitation – every field on the edit form must be completed. Most of the time you are likely to want some of the fields to be optional. Let's assume that we want the email field for the Author model to an optional one, i.e. a blank string can be allowed. In reality, you may not have this information for every author so, to specify this field as an optional one, we need to edit the model. Go to mysite/books/models.py, open the Author model and, for the email field, add blank=True:

class Author(models.Model):

  first_name = models.CharField(max_length=30)

  last_name = models.CharField(max_length=40)

  email = models.EmailField(blank=True)

What we've done here is told Django that we will allow a blank value for the email addresses; by default, every field is set as blank=False, meaning that we can't have any blank values.

Something quite interesting is going on – up to this point, leaving the ___str___() method aside, all the models have been used as database table definitions, in essence, a Python expression of the SQL CREATE TABLE statement. By putting blank=true, we are now moving our model away from just a simple table definition.

The model class is beginning to get a little richer in terms of the information, what the Author objects are, and what they are able to do. A VARCHAR column represents the email field in our database, but the email field is also, as far as contexts like the admin site go, an optional field.

Now, once you have completed the above code, reload the edit form for "Add Author" and you will see that the email field label is no longer in bold, which tells you it is no longer a requirement. Authors can now be added to the database without the need to provide an email address for each one.

Making the Date and Numeric Fields Optional

One of the more common mistakes that relate to blank=true surrounds the numeric and date fields. SQL has its own unique way to specify a blank value and that is by using a value known as NULL. This may be used to mean "invalid" or "unknown" or anything else that may be specific to the application. The NULL value in SQL is not the same as an empty string in the same way that the NONE object in Python is not the same as an empty string.

What all this means is that a character field may have both an empty string value and a NULL value. this can cause no end of confusion and to help avoid this, the CREATE TABLE statements that are generated automatically in Django add to each of the column definitions an explicit NOT NULL. The example below shows the statement generated for the Author model:

```
CREATE TABLE "books_author" (

    "id" serial NOT NULL PRIMARY KEY,

    "first_name" varchar(30) NOT NULL,

    "last_name" varchar(40) NOT NULL,

    "email" varchar(75) NOT NULL

);
```

Most of the time, this kind of behavior will be the best thing for your application and will save you from headaches surrounding inconsistent data, not to mention working very well with everything else in Django. That includes the admin site which uses an empty string rather than the NULL value when a field is left blank.

However, there is an exception as far as the column types that don't consider an empty string to be valid – this includes numbers, times and dates. If you were to try putting an empty string into an integer or date column, you will more than likely get an error, depending on the database – PostgreSQL will definitely throw up an exception while MySQL may or may not.

In our case, the only way we can specify empty values is to use NULL. With a Django model, NULL is specified by doing something similar to what we did earlier, this time giving a field a value of null=True. That was all rather a long way of saying that when you want blank values to be accepted in date or numeric fields, you must use blank=true as well as null=True.

Let's edit the Book model so that publication_date will accept a blank value. The new code should look like this:

class Book(models.Model):

  title = models.CharField(max_length=100)

  authors = models.ManyToManyField(Author)

  publisher = models.ForeignKey(Publisher)

  publication_date = models.DateField(blank=True, null=True)

Adding blank=True is quite a bit easier than it is to add null=True simply because the latter will change the database semantics. What it does is change the CREATE TABLE statement so that NOT NULL is removed from publication_date. A database update is needed to complete this.

For several reasons, Django will not make database schema changes automatic – it is down to you to execute python manage.py migrate when a change is made. Going back to our admin site, the edit form for "Add Book" should now allow the publication date field to stay blank.

Customizing the Field Labels

On each of the edit forms on the admin site, it is the name of the model field that generates the field labels and the algorithm is one of the simplest – Django takes the underscores away and inserts spaces in their place and then makes the character a capital letter, i.e. the publication_date field in the Book model has a label of "Publication date".

That said, a field name won't always lead to a nice label for the corresponding admin field which will mean you may need to do some customization on occasion. To do this, you need to specify verbose_name in the right field. For example, to change the Author.emailfield so it reads "e-mail", we would do this:

```
class Author(models.Model):

    first_name = models.CharField(max_length=30)

    last_name = models.CharField(max_length=40)

    email = models.EmailField(blank=True, verbose_name ='e-mail')
```

When you have done this, the server must be reloaded, and the new label can be seen on the edit form for Author. Do NOT make the first letter of verbose_name a capital unless it is one that should always be a capital. Django will put capital letters where and when needed and the exact value for verbose_name will be used somewhere else where capitalization is not required.

Custom ModelAdmin Classes

So far, we have only made model-level changes – null=True, blank=True, and verbose_name. None of these are admin-level – they are all a basic part of our model and may be used by admin but are not admin-specific.

Going past those, the admin site has quite a few options that allow you to customize the way the admin site operates for any given model. You can find these options inside the ModelAdmin classes, each containing the configuration for the given model in a given instance of the admin site.

Customizing the Change Lists and Forms

Let's look into customizing admin by specifying which fields are to be shown on the Author model change list. By default, the __str__() result is shown on the change list for each of the objects. Earlier, the __str__() method was defined for Author objects so it showed both the first and last names together:

```
class Author(models.Model):

    first_name = models.CharField(max_length=30)

    last_name = models.CharField(max_length=40)

    email = models.EmailField(blank=True, verbose_name ='e-mail')
```

def __str__(self):

   return u'%s %s' % (self.first_name, self.last_name)

The result of this is that the Author object change list will now show both the first and last names together.

This, however can be improved by putting a few extra fields on our change list display. For example, what if we add the email addresses for each author to the display? Plus, it would be quite nice if we could sort by both first and last name.

We can do this by giving our Author model a ModelAdmin class, the key to admin customization. One of the fundamental uses is to specify which fields are to be shown on the change list and we do all of this by editing admin.py:

from django.contrib import admin

from.models import Publisher, Author, Book

class AuthorAdmin(admin.ModelAdmin):

   list_display = ('first_name', 'last_name', 'email')

admin.site.register(Publisher)

admin.site.register(Author, AuthorAdmin)

admin.site.register(Book)

What we did is create the AuthorAdmin class put django.contrib.admin.ModelAdmin as a subclass and is home to a custom configuration for a given admin model. All we did was specify a single customization, which was list_display. This has been set in order that a field named tuple will show on the change list. Obviously, the field names must already exist within the model.

Next, we changed admin.site.register() so that AuthorAdmin is after Author. This function will take a second argument, optional, of a ModelAdmin subclass. If a second argument hasn't been specified, the default options for admin are used by Django.

Once that is done, we can reload the page and should now see three columns titles First Name, Last Name, E-Mail Address. Each column can also be sorted – just click the header on the column you want to be sorted.

Next, we want a search bar added so we give AuthorAdmin a search_fields, like this:

class AuthorAdmin(admin.ModelAdmin):

   list_display = ('first_name', 'last_name', 'email')

   search_fields = ('first_name', 'last_name')

Reload the page and a search bar will be at the top. What we did was tell the change list for admin that we want a search bar that we can use to search both the first_name and the last_name fields. This is not case-sensitive, and both fields will be searched. If you wanted to search for a string of "bar", you would find the results would be an author that has the last name of Hobarson and one with the first name of Barney.

Now we want some date filters added to the change list for Book model:

from django.contrib import admin

from.models import Publisher, Author, Book

class AuthorAdmin(admin.ModelAdmin):

   list_display = ('first_name', 'last_name', 'email')

```
    search_fields = ('first_name', 'last_name')


class BookAdmin(admin.ModelAdmin):

    list_display = ('title', 'publisher', 'publication_date')

    list_filter = ('publication_date',)


admin.site.register(Publisher)

admin.site.register(Author, AuthorAdmin)

admin.site.register(Book, BookAdmin)
```

This is a different option set that we are dealing with, so a new ModelAdminClass has been created called BookAdmin. First, a list_display was defined so the change list looks better. Second, a list_filter was used and set the tuple of fields that will be used for creating filters on the right-hand side of the change list. As far as date fields are concerned, shortcuts are provided by Django, so the list can be filtered by four options:

- Today
- Past 7 days
- This month
- This year

We can also use list_filter on other types of field, not only DateField and the filters will appear if there are two or more values. We can also use the date filters by using the admin option of date_hierarchy, in this way:

```
class BookAdmin(admin.ModelAdmin):

    list_display = ('title', 'publisher','publication_date')
```

```
    list_filter = ('publication_date',)

    date_hierarchy = 'publication_date'
```

Once all this is done, we now have a change list that shows a navigation bar for dates; the drop-down starts with all the years that are available, then the months and then the days.

Be aware that date_hierarchy does not take tuples, only strings because the hierarchy is made from a single date field. Lastly, the default order is changed so that, on the change list, the books are ordered in descending order by date of publication.

The default setting is for the change list to order all the objects as per the ordering of their model in the Meta class, but we didn't specify this, so we have undefined ordering:

```
class BookAdmin(admin.ModelAdmin):

    list_display = ('title', 'publisher','publication_date')

    list_filter = ('publication_date',)

    date_hierarchy = 'publication_date'

    ordering = ('-publication_date',)
```

The above ordering option will work the exact same way as the Meta ordering with the exception that only the first field name is used. If we want the order to be in descending order, we pass a tuple of field names or a list and put a minus sign on the relevant field.

Reload the page and you will see all your changes. The header for Publication date now displays an arrow that tells you the way the records have been sorted.

Although we only covered a few of the list option changes, these are the main ones and will give you the tools needed to produce an incredibly powerful interface that is for data editing in just a line or two of simple code.

Customizing the Edit Forms

In the same way that we can customize the change list, we can also customize the edit form. First, let's change the order of the fields. The default order will correspond to how they are in the model but that can be changed by going to the ModelAdmin subclass and using the fields option, like this:

class BookAdmin(admin.ModelAdmin):

  list_display = ('title', 'publisher', 'publication_date')

  list_filter = ('publication_date',)

  date_hierarchy = 'publication_date'

  ordering = ('-publication_date',)

  fields = ('title', 'authors', 'publisher', 'publication_date')

Once you have done this, the Books edit form will now use the new order for the fields. It looks better to have the author name follow the title of the book, but the order of the files will depend entirely on data-entry workflow. Every form is going to be different.

Something else that we can do with the fields option is make it impossible to edit some fields. All you do is leave out the relevant fields. We could consider doing this if we only trust the admin users to edit specific parts of the data or if external processes change some fields.

In the book database, for example, the publication_date field could be hidden so it can't be edited:

class BookAdmin(admin.ModelAdmin):

  list_display = ('title', 'publisher','publication_date')

  list_filter = ('publication_date',)

  date_hierarchy = 'publication_date'

```
ordering = ('-publication_date',)

fields = ('title', 'authors', 'publisher')
```

The result is that the books edit form no longer lets us specify the date of publication. In some cases, this would be quite useful; perhaps an editor doesn't want their authors pushing publication dates back, a hypothetical example. When the incomplete form is used to add new books, publication_date is set as None by Django, so it is important to ensure that null=True has been added to the field.

One more customization to the edit form that is quite common relates to the many-to-many fields. Multiple-select boxes are used to represent each of the ManyToMany fields but these boxes are not easy to use. If we need multiple items selected, the CTRL or CMD key must be held down on the keyboard first.

Although the text is added to explain this, when we have lots of options to choose from it all gets a bit awkward to use. The solution provided by the admin site is called filter_horizontal so let's put this into BookAdmin to see what happens>

```
class BookAdmin(admin.ModelAdmin):

  list_display = ('title', 'publisher','publication_date')

  list_filter = ('publication_date',)

  date_hierarchy = 'publication_date'

  ordering = ('-publication_date',)

  filter_horizontal = ('authors',)
```

Reload the form and the section for Authors now has a nice JS interface that allows for dynamic searching of the options and the ability to move an author from the Available Authors section to Chosen Authors – this works the other way too.

It is recommended that filter_horizontal be used for ManyToMany fields that contain 10 or more items. It is a good deal easier than a multiple-select box and, if we wanted to use filter_horizontal in multiple fields, we just ensure that the tuple contains each of the field names.

Support for filter_vertical is also there in the ModelAdmin class and this works the same way as filter_horizontal but with the boxes being stacked vertically. Which one we choose is down to personal requirements.

Neither of these options works on ForeignKey fields, only on ManyToMany. The select boxes are used by default for ForeignKey field but we won't always want every object to show up in the drop-down menu. Let's assume that our book database now contains thousands of different publishers; our form for "Add Books" is going to take quite a while to load because each publisher is displayed in the select box. There is a way to solve this and that is to use the raw_id_fields option:

class BookAdmin(admin.ModelAdmin):

   list_display = ('title', 'publisher','publication_date')

   list_filter = ('publication_date',)

   date_hierarchy = 'publication_date'

   ordering = ('-publication_date',)

   filter_horizontal = ('authors',)

   raw_id_fields = ('publisher',)

This should be set to a tuple of the ForeignKey field names which will be shown in admin in a text input box and not a select box. In this box goes the publisher's database ID and, because we humans tend not to memorize these IDs, we also get a handy magnifying glass that will bring up a window where we can choose the correct publisher.

Users, Groups and Permissions

Because you are a superuser, you get the tools to create objects, edit them and delete them. The site admin for Django uses a system of permissions that allow you to provide certain users access to the parts of the interface that they require and no more. These accounts are supposed to be generic so that they can be used elsewhere but, for our purposes, they'll be seen as admin user accounts.

Users and permissions may be edited in the same way as any other object is in the admin interface. A user object has a standard field – username, password, real name, and email but they also have another set of fields that allow you to define what that user can do.

First, we have three Boolean flags:

- **Active Flag** – this controls if the user is active or not; if set to off and the user attempts to log in, they will be denied access;
- **Staff Flag** – this control if the user is actually considered staff and is able to log in. The same system is used for public access sites, so this flag is intended to differentiate between public and admin users;
- **Superuser Flag** – this provides the user with total access, so they can add, delete or create an item within the interface. If set, all the regular permissions, or the lack thereof are ignored.

A normal admin use, i.e. an admin user who is not a superuser, is given access via a set of permissions assigned to them. Each of the objects that may be edited in the admin interface has three of these permissions: create, edit, and delete.

When a user is assigned permission, the user can only do what the permission allows. When a user is first created, no permissions are set so they must be provided; as an example, a user may be given permission to add a publisher or edit an existing one but not to delete any.

Permissions must be defined on a per-model basis, not per-object; the latter is very complicated and not within the scope of this book.

Note - more of a warning really. When you provide a user with the permission to edit users, they can also make changes to their permissions – it wouldn't take much for them to change themselves into a superuser! Lastly, users can be assigned to groups which provide the same permissions to a group of users.

So far, we have created some models and configured our interface to edit data. Now it is time to move on to the real part of web development – creating and processing forms.

Django Forms

HTML forms are a fundamental part of any interactive website. The search box for Google, the submission forms for a blog comment, right up to the incredibly complex interfaces for data-entry – everything is an HTML form. In this section we will look at how Django may be used to access user data submitted on a form, how to validate that data, and use it. We'll also look at Form object and HttpRequest objects.

Retrieving Data from Request Object

We talked briefly about HttpRequest object earlier, when we looked at the view functions but now we'll go into them in more detail. Remember that every view function will take, as its first parameter, a HttpRequest object, as we saw in the hello() view function:

from django.http import HttpResponse

def hello(request):

  return HttpResponse("Hello world")

An HttpRequest object has several methods and attributes that you should get to know so you know what can be done with them. These attributes may be used to gain information on the current request, for example the browser used for loading the Django-powered webpage, at the same time as the view function execution.

URL Information

Every HttpRequest object also contains some information about the URL that is currently being requested. Below is the different HttpRequest methods, their attributes, and an example:

request.path

entire path, without the domain but with the
        "/hello/" leading slash

request.get_host()

host or domain "127.0.0.1:8000"

request.get_full_path()

path and query string, if available
        "/hello/?print=true"

request.is_secure()

if HTTPS used for request, evaluates True; True or False, if otherwise, evaluates False

Rather than hard-coding an URL into your views, use the above attributes; the code will be far more flexible and reusable. A simple example is:

 # BAD!

```python
def current_url_view_bad(request):

    return HttpResponse("Welcome to the page at /current/")
```

```python
# GOOD

def current_url_view_good(request):

    return HttpResponse("Welcome to the page at %s"

% request.path)
```

Other Request Information

A Python dictionary called request.META is where the HTTP headers available for the specified request are found and that includes the IP address of the user, and the user-agent, usually the web browser name, and operating version. The list will depend entirely on what headers were sent by the user and those that are set by your web server. Some of the more common keys in the dictionary are:

- HTTP_REFERER – The referring URL, if there is one. Note that REFERER is misspelled – this is not a mistake on my behalf!
- HTTP_USER_AGENT – The user-agent string from the user's browser, if there is one.
- REMOTE_ADDR – Client's IP address, for example, 12.345.67.89. If there is more than one address, each will be separated by a comma.

If the user attempted to access a key that didn't exist, a KeyError exception would be thrown. This is because of request.META is nothing more than a basic dictionary. HTTP headers come via a user's browser and that means they are considered external data. Because of this they are not to be trusted and your application should be designed to fail if a header does not exist or is empty. To handle undefined keys, use get() or a try/except clause:

```python
# BAD!
def ua_display_bad(request):
    ua = request.META['HTTP_USER_AGENT']  # Might raise KeyError!
    return HttpResponse("Your browser is %s" % ua)


# GOOD (VERSION 1)
def ua_display_good1(request):
    try:
        ua = request.META['HTTP_USER_AGENT']
    except KeyError:
        ua = 'unknown'
    return HttpResponse("Your browser is %s" % ua)


# GOOD (VERSION 2)
def ua_display_good2(request):
    ua = request.META.get('HTTP_USER_AGENT', 'unknown')
    return HttpResponse("Your browser is %s" % ua)
```

Try to write a view that will show all of the data in request.META so that it can be seen and understood. That view might look like this:

```python
def display_meta(request):
    values = request.META
```

```
html = []

for k in sorted(values):

    html.append('<tr><td>%s</td><td>%s</td></tr>' % (k, values[k]))

return HttpResponse('<table>%s</table>' % '\n'.join(html))
```

Another excellent way of seeing what a request object contains is to look at the error pages thrown up by Django when the system is crashed. These pages contain quite a bit of useful information including the HTTP headers and any other request object.

Information Regarding Submitted Data

Aside from the metadata, an HttpRequest object has another two attributes that each have user-submitted information in them. Those attributes are: request.GET and request.POST. Both are dictionary-like, and provide access to the POST and GET data. POST data usually comes from an HTML form and the GET data comes from a form or from the page URL query string.

Being described as dictionary-like means that, although they are not dictionaries, they act like a standard Python dictionary. They both contain the methods get(), values(), and keys() within request.GET to iterate over the keys. The reason there is a distinction is that these two both have methods that can't be found in normal dictionaries.

Django Form-Handling – a Simple Example

Carrying on with our examples of books, we'll now create a view that will allow a user to search through the book database using titles. In general, development of a form is in two parts – the interface (HTML) and the backend code that will process the data. The first bit is easy; we set up a view that will show a search-form. We already have views.py in our \books folder so we'll open it and add a new view:

\books\views.py

from django.shortcuts import render

def search_form(request):

  return render(request, 'books/search_form.html')

Next, the template needs to be created, but before that, we are going to need some new folders. The APP_DIRS in settings should be set to True; if it isn't, we'll change it now. This will force Django to look for a \templates folder in all our apps.

In our books app folder, we'll make a new \template folder and then, inside that, we'll create another called books. The structure should look like books\templates\books. This new books folder is very important in terms of name spacing our existing templates. Django looks for a match in all our apps so having a namespace will ensure that the correct template is used if we have two of the same name.

The following is a search_form.HTML file; we'll create it and then save it in the new folder:

 # mysite_project\mysite\books\templates\books\search_form.html

<html>

<head>

  <title>Search</title>

</head>

<body>

<form action="/search/" method="get">

  <input type="text" name="q">

  <input type="submit" value="Search">

</form>

</body>

</html>

Next a URLconf must be created so that the new view can be found. In the books folder, we'll make a new urls.py file (this is not created by startapp) and then add this pattern to the new file:

 # mysite\books\urls.py

from django.conf.urls import url

from books import views

urlpatterns = [

  url(r'^search-form/$', views.search_form),

]

When Django makes a search for URL pattern, it only looks in the mysite\urls.py file. If we want it to search elsewhere we need to add the specific URL patterns so we'll make a change to urlpatterns:

 # mysite\urls.py

from django.conf.urls import include, url

urlpatterns = [

#...

  url(r'^', include('books.urls')),

]

The new pattern should go at the end of the existing urlpatterns list and the reason for this is that r'^'regex will send everything to the books.url file and we need to make sure there are no other matching patterns; then Django can look in books\urls.py for the match. We'll go to http://127.0.0.1:8000/search-form/ to see our new search interface.

If we submit that form; we should get a 404 error because the form is pointing to a path that has not been implemented. We can solve that with another view function:

 # books/urls.py

urlpatterns = [

  url(r'^search-form/$', views.search_form),

  url(r'^search/$', views.search),

]

 # books/views.py

```
from django.http import HttpResponse

#...

def search(request):

    if 'q' in request.GET:

        message = 'You searched for: %r' % request.GET['q']

    else:

        message = 'You submitted an empty form.'

    return HttpResponse(message)
```

All this will do is show the search term that was input, allowing us to ensure that Django gets the data in the proper way and so that we have an idea of the way the search terms flow throughout our system. A basic way of describing this is:

- A variable called q is defined by the HTML <form>. When submitted, q's value goes via the GET method to URL/search/
- The Django view responsible for handling URL/search/ will be able to access the value of q in request.GET

One thing of note is the explicit checking to ensure that q is in request.GET – as mentioned earlier, never put trust in anything submitted by a user. If this check was not included and an empty form was submitted, we would get a KeyError:

```
# BAD!

def bad_search(request):

    # The following line will raise KeyError if 'q' hasn't been submitted!
```

message = 'You searched for: %r' % request.GET['q']

return HttpResponse(message)

Query String Parameters

GET data is processed in a query string so that means request. GET can be used to access variables in query strings. You already know how to access the parameters in the query strings inside your views. POST data works in much the same way; you just use request.POST instead. So, what is the difference between the two?

GET should be used when form submission is nothing more than a request to 'get' some data. POST should be used when form submission will have an effect of some kind, i.e. sending an email, changing some data, or anything that goes beyond the display of the data. In our example, we used GET because our query is not making any changes to any of the data on the server.

Now we know that request.GET has been properly passed in, we can hook the search query into the database in views.py:

from django.http import HttpResponse

from django.shortcuts import render

from books.models import Book

def search(request):

  if 'q' in request.GET and request.GET['q']:

    q = request.GET['q']

    books = Book.objects.filter(title__icontains=q)

    return render(request, 'books/search_results.html',

{'books': books, 'query': q})

   else:

     return HttpResponse('Please submit a search term.')

A note or two or what we've done:

We checked that q existed in request.GET and we also checked that the value of request.Get['q'] is non-empty before it can be passed into the database query.

We are querying the book table using Book.objects,filter(title_icontains=q) to look for any book that has a title with the provided submission. icontains is a type of lookup that we can translate this statement as something along the lines of "get any books with a title containing q, not case-sensitive".

This is one of the easiest ways of searching for a book, but if we are searching on a large production database, icontains is not the best type of query to use as it isn't fast. A list of the book objects, called books, is passed to the template and, so the search-form works, we need to create a file called search_results.html:

 # \books\templates\books\search_results.html

<html>

  <head>

  <title>Book Search</title>

  </head>

  <body>

    <p>You searched for: {{ query }}</p>

    {% if books %}

```
<p>Found {{ books|length }} book{{ books|pluralize }}.</p>

<ul>

  {% for book in books %}

  <li>{{ book.title }}</li>

  {% endfor %}

</ul>

{% else %}

  <p>No books matched your search criteria.</p>

{% endif %}

</body>

</html>
```

Note that we use a pluralized template filter; an 's' is outputted where required based on how many books were found.

When we run the development server now and go to http://127.0.0.1:8000/search-from, we should get a useful result.

Improving Our Example

We looked at a simple example of form-handling, now we need to look at some of the problems and how we can fix them. First, the way our search() view handles empty queries is not very good; all it does is display a message that asks the user to submit a search term. This means the user has to hit their browser's back button. This is not professional and if we were ever to do something like that, we can be sure that we wouldn't have any Django privileges left!

The easiest thing to do is display the form again with an error – this would let us try *again straightaway and the best way of doing that is to render the template once more:*

from django.shortcuts import render

from django.http import HttpResponse

from books.models import Book

def search_form(request):

   return render(request, 'books/search_form.html')

def search(request):

   error = False

   if 'q' in request.GET:

     q = request.GET['q']

     if not q:

       error = True

     else:

       books = Book.objects.filter(title__icontains=q)

       return render(request, 'books/search_results.html', {'books': books, 'query': q})

   return render(request, 'books/search_form.html', {'error': error})

We've made some improvements to our search() method so that the search_form.html template can be rendered once more should the query be empty. Because an error message needs to be displayed in the template, a template variable needs to be passed. Now, search_form.html can be edited so it checks for an error variable:

```
<html>

<head>

  <title>Search</title>

</head>

<body>

  {% if error %}

    <p style="color: red;">Please submit a search term.</p>

  {% endif %}

  <form action="/search/" method="get">

    <input type="text" name="q">

    <input type="submit" value="Search">

  </form>

</body>

</html>
```

The template of search_form() that was in the original view can still be used because it doesn't pass the template an error and that means that the error message won't display.

Now that we have made the change, we have a better application, but it raises a question – do we really need a dedicated search_form()? As it is now, putting in a request to URL/search with no GET parameters, we will see an empty form that has an error on it. The search_form () view can be removed together with the URLpattern associated with it so long as search() is changed so the error message is hidden when a user goes to /search/ without using any GET parameters:

def search(request):

  error = False

  if 'q' in request.GET:

    q = request.GET['q']

    if not q:

      error = True

    else:

      books = Book.objects.filter(title__icontains=q)

      return render(request, 'books/search_results.html', {'books': books, 'query': q})

  return render(request, 'books/search_form.html', {'error': error})

In our newly updated view, when a user goes to/search/ without any GET parameters, they will be confronted with a search-form and no error message. If the form is submitted with an empty q value, the search-form is accompanied by the error message. Lastly, if a non-empty value is provided for q when the form is submitted, the search results will show up.

There is one final change that can be made to get rid of some of the redundancy. Now the two views have been rolled into one, together with the URLs, and we have /search/ handling the search_form and results displays, we don't need a URL hard-coded in the HTML form inside search_form.html:

<form action="/search/" method="get">

It can be changed to this:

<form action="" method="get">

action="" stands for "Submit the form to the same URL as the current page", and with this change, we will not need to remember that the action has to be changed as the search() view is hooked to another URL.

Django Form Validation

Right now, we still have quite a simple search example, especially where data validation is concerned. All we are doing is making sure we don't have an empty search query. Most HTML forms will have some kind of validation that is a little more complex than doing this. We've all been faced with error messages when we try to input data on a web form, such as:

"Please enter a valid phone number. 888 is not a valid area code"

"Please enter a valid email address. Xxx.com is not a valid provider"

And so on.

Let's make a change to our search() view to make it validate whether our search terms is equal to or less than 20 characters. How would we do that? Well, the easiest way to do it is to embed our logic in the view:

def search(request):

  error = False

  if 'q' in request.GET:

    q = request.GET['q']

    if not q:

      error = True

    elif len(q) > 20:

```
        error = True

    else:

        books = Book.objects.filter(title__icontains=q)

        return render(request, 'search_results.html', {'books': books, 'query': q})

    return render(request, 'search_form.html', {'error': error})
```

If we were to try submitting a query that was more than 20 characters now, we wouldn't be able to; instead, we would get an error message. At this stage, that message simply reads, "Please submit a search term". This needs to be changed:

```
<html>
<head>
  <title>Search</title>
</head>
<body>
  {% if error %}
    <p style="color: red;">
      Please submit a search term 20 characters or shorter.
    </p>
  {% endif %}

  <form action="/search/" method="get">
    <input type="text" name="q">
```

```
        <input type="submit" value="Search">

    </form>

</body>

</html>
```

This isn't very pretty! We have an error message that could be quite confusing because it comes up for anything including an empty submission. Why would we need to know about characters in an empty form? Error messages must always be specific, and they should never confuse the user. Our problem lies in the fact that we are only using a Boolean value for our error; what we should be using is a list containing various error strings. We could fix that like this:

```
def search(request):

    errors = []

    if 'q' in request.GET:

        q = request.GET['q']

        if not q:

            errors.append('Enter a search term.')

        elif len(q) > 20:

            errors.append('Please enter at most 20 characters.')

        else:

            books = Book.objects.filter(title__icontains=q)

            return render(request, 'search_results.html', {'books': books, 'query': q})

    return render(request, 'search_form.html', {'errors': errors})
```

Now we just need to make a small change to our search_form.html template to show that an errors list is being passed and not a Boolean value.

<html>

<head>

  <title>Search</title>

</head>

<body>

  {% if errors %}

    <ul>

      {% for error in errors %}

      <li>{{ error }}</li>

      {% endfor %}

    </ul>

  {% endif %}

  <form action="/search/" method="get">

    <input type="text" name="q">

    <input type="submit" value="Search">

  </form>

</body>

</html>

Making Contact Forms

We've iterated over our book form a few times now and we've made it a bit nicer than it was, but it is still really simple. It's just one field called 'q'. As forms become more and more complex, the above step must be repeated over and over for each of the form fields we are using, and this does nothing more than introduce a lot of unnecessary stuff and it increases the margin for human error. Luckily, Django is on our side and we have a high-level library built-in that will handle all the tasks related to forms and validation.

Our First Form Class

Django has a built-in form library called django.forms. This will handle many of the problems we have talked about so far so let's get straight into it and edit out contact form app using this framework. The main way of using it is to define a Form class for each of the HTML<forms> we have. At the moment, we have just one form, so we will only have one class. Convention dictates that we should keep our Form classes in a file called forms.py so we'll start by creating this in mysite\views.py with the following code:

```
# mysite_project\mysite\mysite\forms.py


from django import forms


class ContactForm(forms.Form):

    subject = forms.CharField()

    email = forms.EmailField(required=False)

    message = forms.CharField()
```

This is quite an intuitive code and it is much like the model syntax in Django. Each form field is represented by a Field class, the type of which will depend on the field. We are using EmailField and CharField as the Form class attributes.

These are required fields, by default so we have specified require=False to make the email field optional.

Over to our interactive interpreter and see what we can do with this class. First, it will display as HTML:

(env_mysite) C:\Users\...\mysite> python manage.py shell

>>> *from mysite.forms import ContactForm*

>>> *f = ContactForm()*

>>> *print(f)*

\<tr>\<th>\<label for="id_subject">Subject:\</label>\</th>\<td>\<input type="text" name="subject" required id="id_subject" />\</td>\</tr>

\<tr>\<th>\<label for="id_email">Email:\</label>\</th>\<td>\<input type="email" name="email" id="id_email" />\</td>\</tr>

\<tr>\<th>\<label for="id_message">Message:\</label>\</th>\<td>\<input type="text" name="message" required id="id_message" />\</td>\</tr>

A label is added to each of the fields by Django and the \<label> tags to make them more accessible. What we want is for the default behavior to be as optimal as it possibly can be. The output is, by default, an HTML \<table> but there are some other outputs built-in:

>>> *print(f.as_ul())*

\<li>\<label for="id_subject">Subject:\</label> \<input type="text" name="subject" required id="id_subject" />\</li>

\<li>\<label for="id_email">Email:\</label> \<input type="email" name="email" id="id_email" />\</li>

```html
<li><label for="id_message">Message:</label> <input type="text"
name="message" required id="id_message" /></li>
```

>>> *print(f.as_p())*

```html
<p><label for="id_subject">Subject:</label> <input type="text"
name="subject" required id="id_subject" /></p>

<p><label for="id_email">Email:</label> <input type="email" name="email"
id="id_email" /></p>

<p><label for="id_message">Message:</label> <input type="text"
name="message" required id="id_message" /></p>
```

Note that we have not included the opening or closing <table>, <form> or <url>
tags in the output; this allows us to add extra rows or any customizations we
want. The HTML can also be displayed for specific fields:

>>> *print(f['subject'])*

```html
<input type="text" name="subject" required id="id_subject" />
```

>>> *print f['message']*

```html
<input type="text" name="message" required id="id_message" />
```

Form objects can also validate data; to do this, we create a Form object and then
pass a dictionary of data to it. This dictionary will map the field names to the
data:

>>> *f = ContactForm({'subject': 'Hello', 'email': 'Paul@example.com',
'message': 'Nice site!'})*

When data has been associated with a Form instance, a 'bound' form has been
created:

>>> *f.is_bound*

True

To find out if data is valid you can call is_valid() on a bound form. In our example, a valid value was passed for each field so the whole Form is valid:

>>> f.is_valid()

True

If the email field is not passed, it will still be valid because required=False has been specified for the field:

>>> f = ContactForm({'subject': 'Hello', 'message': 'Nice site!'})

>>> f.is_valid()

True

But if the message or the subject is omitted, the Form won't be valid anymore:

>>> f = ContactForm({'subject': 'Hello'})

>>> f.is_valid()

False

>>> f = ContactForm({'subject': 'Hello', 'message': ''})

>>> f.is_valid()

False

You can go right down to retrieve messages that are specific to certain fields:

>>> f = ContactForm({'subject': 'Hello', 'message': ''})

>>> f['message'].errors

['This field is required.']

```
>>> f['subject'].errors
```

```
[]
```

```
>>> f['email'].errors
```

```
[]
```

Each of the bound Form instances will have an errors attribute; this will provide a dictionary that maps the field names to lists of error messages:

```
>>> f = ContactForm({'subject': 'Hello', 'message': ''})
```

```
>>> f.errors
```

```
{'message'`: ['This field is required.']}
```

Lastly, with a Form instance that has valid data, there is a cleaned_data attribute. This attribute is a dictionary containing the submitted data after it has been cleaned. The forms framework in Django will validate the data and then convert the values to the correct types in Python to clean it:

```
>>> f = ContactForm({'subject': 'Hello', 'email': 'Paul@example.com',
'message': 'Nice site!'})
```

```
>>> f.is_valid()
```

```
True
```

```
>>> f.cleaned_data
```

```
{'subject': 'Hello', 'email': 'Paul@example.com', 'message': 'Nice site!'}
```

Our example form will only take strings that have been cleaned up into string objects but, should we use a DateField or an IntegerField, the framework will still make sure that cleaned_data makes use of the correct datetime.data objects or integers for the relevant fields.

Tying Forms to Views

Our contact form isn't good at the moment because our users cannot see it. We need to make an update to mysite\views.py:

 # mysite_project\mysite\mysite\views.py


```
from django.http import Http404, HttpResponse, HttpResponseRedirect

from django.shortcuts import render

import datetime

from mysite.forms import ContactForm

from django.core.mail import send_mail, get_connection


#...


def contact(request):

    if request.method == 'POST':

        form = ContactForm(request.POST)

        if form.is_valid():

            cd = form.cleaned_data

            con = get_connection('django.core.mail.backends.console.EmailBackend')

            send_mail(
```

```
            cd['subject'],

            cd['message'],

            cd.get('email', 'noreply@example.com'),

            ['siteowner@example.com'],

            connection=con

        )

        return HttpResponseRedirect('/contact/thanks/')

    else:

        form = ContactForm()

    return render(request, 'contact_form.html', {'form': form})
```

The contact function has been added to our view to handle the form submission. With the function, we can see if POST method has been used to submit the request. If not, a blank form is displayed. We can also see if there is valid data on the form; to do this, call is_valid(). If the form does have valid data, the email is sent and the user is sent to another view - /contact/thanks/. If there is no valid data, the if block will jump to the last render() and the form goes to the browser.

There is no error handling in the view because the Form class does that for us. If there is no validation an error list is created by Django and then appended to the response.

Contact forms are not a lot of use if there is no way for the contact information to be sent to the site owner. One of the most common ways of doing this is by sending an email and Django has that ability built-in. The email functions are found in the module called django.core.mail and we imported this at the top of views.py. The send_mail() function is being used to send an email to a dummy account.

Send Emails in Development

We've used django.core.mail.get_connection() as a way to retrieve a mail connection to django.core.mail.backends.concole.EmailBackend(), which is a special backend for email. This is a useful backend in development because there is no need to set up email servers while developing applications in Django. The email output is sent by the console.EmailBackend to the console. This can be checked in the terminal window after the form is submitted.

Now, to display the contact form, we need to create a contact form and save it to mysite\templates\:

 # mysite_project\mysite\templates\contact_form.html

```
<html>

<head>

  <title>Contact us</title>

</head>

<body>

  <h1>Contact us</h1>


  {% if form.errors %}

    <p style="color: red;">

      Please correct the error{{ form.errors|pluralize }} below.

    </p>

  {% endif %}
```

```
<form action="" method="post" novalidate>

    <table>

        {{ form.as_table }}

    </table>

    {% csrf_token %}

    <input type="submit" value="Submit">

  </form>

</body>

</html>
```

Because this is a POST form, it can modify our data; so we need to consider something called Cross Site Request Forgeries. Once again Django comes to the rescue and provides us with a system that protects against this. All POST forms that target an internal URL should have the template tag of {% csrf_token %}.

There is something else in the <form> tag – a novalidate attribute. When HTML5 is used in newer browsers, particularly in Chrome, the browser will validate the fields automatically. The attribute is used to tell the browser it doesn't need to do this because we need Django to do it.

Lastly, urls.py needs to be changed so our contact form is displayed at /contact/:

```
#...

from mysite.views import hello, current_datetime, hours_ahead, contact


urlpatterns = [
```

```
#...

url(r'^contact/$', contact),

url(r'^', include('books.urls')),

]
```

We run this by loading the form, submitting with no fields completed. Then we submit it with an email address that isn't valid. Lastly, we submit it with completely valid data. When the final form is submitted, a Page Not Found error, not what we would expect. But there is a reason for this; we haven't yet created a URLconf or a view to redirect a user to /contact/thanks/. That is something that we can do.

Changing the Way Fields are Rendered

When this form is locally rendered, the message field is an <input type="text"> whereas we need it to be a <textarea>. This is easily sorted by setting the widget for the field:

```
from django import forms


class ContactForm(forms.Form):

    subject = forms.CharField()

    email = forms.EmailField(required=False)

    message = forms.CharField(widget=forms.Textarea)
```

The presentation logic for each of the fields is separated into sets of widgets by the forms framework. There is a default widget for each of the field types but that can be overridden or you can use custom widgets. Basically, the Field classes are representative of validation logic while the widgets are representative of presentation logic.

Set Maximum Length

One of the more common needs for validation is to see if a field is a specific size. We can do this by improving the ContactForm so the subject is limited to 100 characters. All we do is give the CharField a max_length like this:

from django import forms

class ContactForm(forms.Form):

   subject = forms.CharField(max_length=100)

   email = forms.EmailField(required=False)

   message = forms.CharField(widget=forms.Textarea)

There is also a min_length but this is optional.

Setting the Initial Value

We can improve this even more by giving the subject field an initial value. We'll make this say, "I love your site!" and we do it by using the argument whenever a Form instance is created:

def contact(request):

   #...

   else:

    form = ContactForm(

     initial={'subject': 'I love your site!'}

```
    )
```

return render(request, 'contact_form.html', {'form':form})

The subject field will now be displayed with the statement already there. Passing the initial data is not the same as passing the data that will bind the form. The main difference is with initial data the form is unbound, meaning there are no error messages.

Custom Validation Rules

Let's suppose that our feedback form has been launched and we are starting to see emails come in. There is a problem – some of the messages submitted only have a couple of words in them and this is not enough to make sense. We need a new policy for validation purposes – four or more words.

There are several ways to hook some custom data into Django for validation purposes; if we have a rule that is going to be constantly reused, we can use a custom type for the field. Usually, a custom validation tends to be a one-off thing though, and these can be tied into the Form class directly. We need our message field to have some extra validation, so the Form class is given a clean_ method:

from django import forms

class ContactForm(forms.Form):

  subject = forms.CharField(max_length=100)

  email = forms.EmailField(required=False)

  message = forms.CharField(widget=forms.Textarea)

```
def clean_message(self):

    message = self.cleaned_data['message']

    num_words = len(message.split())

    if num_words < 4:

        raise forms.ValidationError("Not enough words!")

    return message
```

The form system in Django will automatically look for methods with a name starting with clean_ and ending with a field name. If a method is found, it will be called during the validation. More specifically, clean_message() is called once the default logic validation has been called. Our field data has been processed partly so we can get it from self.cleaned.data.

We also don't need to be concerned about checking to see if a value exists and is a non-empty value because the default validator will do this for us. Perhaps naively, we use a len() and split() combination to count how many words there are; if there aren't enough, a forms.ValidationError is raised. The user will see the string from this exception as one of the error list items.

One thing that is incredibly important is that the cleaned field value is explicitly returned when the method ends so that we can modify our value inside the custom validation method we created. If we don't input the return statement, we will get a value of None returned and our original value gets lost.

Specifying the Labels

By default, the auto-generated form HTML labels are created by putting spaces where the underscores are and making the first letter a capital; the email field label would be "Email". This is the algorithm used by models in Django to calculate the verbose_name field values. In the same way as we did with the models, these labels can also be customized for specified fields. To do that, we use a label like this:

```
class ContactForm(forms.Form):

    subject = forms.CharField(max_length=100)

    email = forms.EmailField(required=False, label='Your e-mail address')

    message = forms.CharField(widget=forms.Textarea)
```

Form Design Customization

Right now, the contact_form.html template displays our form using {{form.as_table}} but we can use other methods to give us better control over our display. There is a very quick way to customize the presentation of our forms by using CSS. Our error lists could do with a bit of sprucing up and this is why the error list that is automatically generated uses <ul class+"errorlist"> - so they can be CSS-targeted. To make the errors more prominent, we'll add this CSS into contact_form.html in the <head></head> section:

```
<style type="text/css">

    ul.errorlist {

        margin: 0;

        padding: 0;

    }

.errorlist li {

        background-color: red;

        color: white;

        display: block;

        font-size: 1.2em;

        margin: 0 0 3px;
```

```
        padding: 4px 5px;

    }

</style>
```

It is convenient for us to have the HTML generated automatically for our forms but there will be times when we want the default rendering overridden. We can use {{ form.as_table }}, among others, as shortcuts while our application is being developed but pretty much everything that goes into displaying a form may be changed, usually in the template, and we will do this.

The widget for each field may be individually rendered by going into {{ form.fieldname }} inside the template and, if there are errors associated with fields, they can be accessed in form.fieldname.errors }}. Bearing this in mind, a custom template can now be constructed for the contact form using this code:

```
<html>

<head>

    <title>Contact us</title>

</head>

<body>

    <h1>Contact us</h1>


    {% if form.errors %}

        <p style="color: red;">

            Please correct the error{{ form.errors|pluralize }} below.

        </p>

    {% endif %}
```

```
<form action="" method="post">
    <div class="field">
        {{ form.subject.errors }}
        <label for="id_subject">Subject:</label>
        {{ form.subject }}
    </div>
    <div class="field">
        {{ form.email.errors }}
        <label for="id_email">Your e-mail address:</label>
        {{ form.email }}
    </div>
    <div class="field">
        {{ form.message.errors }}
        <label for="id_message">Message:</label>
        {{ form.message }}
    </div>
    {% csrf_token %}
    <input type="submit" value="Submit">
</form>
</body>
```

```
</html>
```

In this code, {{ form.message.errors }} is showing <ul class="errorlist"> if there are any errors and, if there aren't but the field is valid, there is a blank string. The same applies to all fields on the form.

The form.message.errors can also be treated as Boolean or it can be iterated over as a list. This is very useful when a field may have several errors associated with it. For example:

```
<div class="field{% if form.message.errors %} errors{% endif %}">

  {% if form.message.errors %}

    <ul>

    {% for error in form.message.errors %}

      <li><strong>{{ error }}</strong></li>

    {% endfor %}

    </ul>

  {% endif %}

  <label for="id_message">Message:</label>

  {{ form.message }}

</div>
```

Where validation errors are concerned, an errors class is added to the <div> and the list of errors that are associated with the field are displayed as unordered.

That is the end of this section and you have more than enough information to start building a basic Django application. In the next section we are going to move on to Python and ArcGIS.

Chapter 17: Python and ArcGIS Development

ArcGIS is a mapping and geographic system – Geographic Information System – that is used to create and use maps, to analyze data from the maps, to compile geographic data, to share the information discovered, to use maps in a variety of different applications, and manage the geographic information in databases.

The system provides users with the infrastructure needed to make the maps and the information on them available throughout the organization, across entire communities or on the internet. ArcGIS has the following software for Windows desktops:

•   ArcReader – to view and query maps that were created using another ArcGIS product

•   ArcGIS for Desktop Basic – used to be called ArcView, allows the viewing of spatial data, the creation of layered maps and basic analysis of spatial information

•   ArcGIS for Desktop Standard – used to be called ArcEditor and includes additional tools to manipulate geodatabases and shapefiles

•   ArcGIS for Desktop Advanced – used to be called ArcInfo, and includes data manipulation capabilities, analysis, and editing.

We will start by looking at how to set up an environment for ArcGIS.

Before we look into ArcGIS and how to use it, there is some information needed about Python and ArcGIS.

What You Need

Your computer will require a minimum of 2 GB RAM, be 32-bit or 64-bit configuration, Windows 7 as an absolute minimum, and Python. You will also need the latest version of ArcGIS. Python will be installed when you install ArcGIS.

Important Modules

Python modules are libraries that a script can call to add to its potential; they are built-in to Python or can be added later. Most get written in the Python language, but on occasion, they may be written using another programming language and then wrapped up in Python so they can be used in a Python script. Modules also make it possible for Python to use other programs. The modules you are going to need are:

ArcPY

This module has two purposes. First, it is a wrapper that helps you to interact with the tools in ArcGIS; ArcGIS then executes these in internal code format. Second ArcPY is a code base that allows better control of map production and geospatial analysis. ArcPY controls the ArcToolBox tools, even though they are not written in Python; it is ArcPY that allows us to use those tools.

We can also use ArcPY to control MXDs – ArcGIS Map Documents – and any object included in the MXD, such as images, legends, layers, titles, and the map view. ArcPY also contains a set of tools external to ArcToolBox, such as the incredibly powerful data cursors. These Data Analysis Cursors enable a much better interface with the GIS data.

Being able to have better geospatial analyses control helps to integrate the ArcGIS tools into a workflow that may have additional Python modules. Because Python is a glue language, ArcGIS is made more useful because there is no need to use special methods for geospatial data.

OS Module

This is in the standard Python library and is how Python gains access to the functionality in the operating system. One of the more common uses is using a method called os.path to divide file paths into directory paths or folders and base paths or files.

Another method called os.walk goes through a directory and then returns all the files found in folders, right down to the subfolders. When we carry out GIS analysis, the OS module will be continuously accessed.

SYS Module

This module is also in the standard library and it references the actual Python installation. In the sys module are several methods that will retrieve information about Python including the version number, and also about the script, as well as any parameters that have been given to it – this is done using sys.argv(). Another useful method in the sys module is sys.path used for appending the file path which means that any folder with a script may be referenced by any other script so that the functions in them can be imported to another script as needed.

XLRD and XLWT

These are used to read and write spreadsheets from Excel. They can extract the data from a legacy sheet and turn it into data that can be used for GIS analysis or when the geospatial analysis is finished they can write the results. Neither module is in the standard library but will be installed with ArcGIS and Python.

Built-in Functions

There are several of these that will be used, the main two being:

- **str** – string functions are used to convert data to string ints. The int (integer) function converts a float or string to an integer and, to avoid errors, a string that is passed to int has to be a number.
- **float** – float functions convert strings or ints into floats, and is similar to the int function.

Standard Library Modules

These modules need to be imported:

- **datetime** – used to retrieve date and time information and convert string format dates to Python dates
- **math** – used for high-level math functions that will be required from time to time, like calculation of a number's square or obtaining a Pi value
- **string** – used to manipulate strings

- **csv** – used to create files of comma-separated values and to edit them

That covers the basics, next we will start looking at configuring Python so it can be used with ArcGIS and how we use IDEs for script writing.

Configuring Python

In this part, we will be configuring Python and our computer systems so that they work to execute scripts written in Python. We will need to configure both environment and path variables so that our import statements work correctly and that a script runs when asked to. We'll look at Python folder structures and the ArcPY module in the folder structure for ArcGIS. Finally, we will look at IDEs, or Integrated Development Environments and how we use them to create and execute code.

What Are Python Scripts?

A Python script is nothing more than a text file that uses a formalized language to write commands. The file extension is.py and this is all that will allow us to tell it apart from other text files. We can use a text editor, like Notepad, to open these files.

Python scripts do not contain Python. If we don't use the Python interpreter, we cannot run the scripts and none of the commands contained in the scripts will be executed.

How Are Scripts Executed?

This is just as important to learn as it is to learn Python itself; if you take just a little time to set Python up properly, you can save yourself a great deal of time debugging and checking errors. Because Python is an interpretive language, scripts first need to be changed into bytecode and we'll be covering that later.

What is the Interpreter?

The interpreter is a program with the.exe extension which means it is executable. The Python Interpreter was written in the C language, much older than Python and used in languages that have more complex syntax. Any program that has been written in the C language, usually a text file to begin with, must first be changed to an executable file by a compiler. This program turns text commands into machine code for the creation of.exe programs. This is a laborious process, but it has the benefit of producing programs that can stand alone and do not require any dependencies to run. Conversely, Python will interpret the commands and execute them quickly, which makes it one of the best languages for scripting. However, those scripts cannot be executed until they go through the interpreter.

The Python interpreter will look at a Python script and will interpret the commands contained in it. When the script is run, the first thing that happens is the syntax is checked to ensure that it follows all the Python rules, such as indentation, and that the variables are named following convention. Provided it is a valid script, the commands will be converted to bytecode which can then be executed by a virtual machine that was written in the C language, the bytecode interpreter. This interpreter will then turn that bytecode into the right code for the machine being used. The script is then executed by the CPU. This is quite a complicated process which all takes place behind the scenes, giving Python an air of simplicity.

Where is the Python Interpreter?

This is a very important thing to learn and understand. Very often, Python will be downloaded from the official website and installed separately to ArcGIS. However, every version of ArcGIS needs a specific version of Python so when you download ArcGIS, Python is included. Your Python folder structure can be found on your C: drive unless you tell it to install elsewhere. The folder will be C:\Pythonxx (xx denoting the version of Python). In that folder is a folder named ArcGISxx.x (again, x denotes the version number and/or the operating system).

Inside this folder are more folders and python.exe along with an interpreter version called pythonw.exe which will execute scripts without terminal windows. Pythonw.exe, like python.exe, contains all the commands in Python and is usable for script execution.

Which Interpreter?

Generally, you should use pythonw.exe as the interpreter to execute your scripts as it does not bring up the terminal window. When you need to see your code outputs in a window or you want to test snippets of code, use python.exe. When you start this, you will see the interpreter console. Just under the header that tells you which version you have, you will see three chevrons (>>>) – this is the prompt where you enter your code, line by line, rather than entering an entire script. This is useful to test small amounts of code and help you understand Python syntax. ArcMap and ArcCatalog both contain a version of the interpreter called Python Window.

How Does My Computer Know Where to Find the Interpreter?

To understand this, you need admin access and a good idea of how Windows looks for programs. We need to go into the advanced system settings and change a variable to tell it where the interpreter is. Go into your computer's control panel and then into the option for Security/System. Click the option for Advanced System Settings and then on System Properties. At the bottom you will see a button that says Environment Variables – click this. At the bottom of the menu that loads, move through the window for System Variables until you see the Path variable. Click it and click Edit.

There are two components to the Path variable – the variable name or path and the value, which is several folders, each separated by a semicolon. This path is what Windows searches through to find the executables associated with a specific extension. You will add a path that has the interpreter in it – c:\Pythnxx\ArcGISxx.x – and this is added to the field for the variable value ensuring a semicolon is used to separate it. Click OK three times to exit out of the menu entirely. Now, your computer knows where that interpreter is and will search every folder listed in the path variable looking for the python executable file. You can test how your edit worked by opening a command window on your computer and typing in python. You should see the interpreter running. And you should see the header with the Python version and the three chevrons.

How to Make a Python Script Executable When Clicked On

The last thing to do to make a script run when clicked on, which will also allow them to run externally to ArcGIS, is to ensure that the files with the.py extension are properly associated with the interpreter. If this hasn't been done, the files will appear as a text file or as an unknown type.

Changing this is quite simple; choose your script and right-click it. Choose Open With and Choose Default Program. If you do not see python.exe or python.exe as a choice, go to the folder that houses them and choose one of them – the best one is pythonw.exe for script execution and python.exe to test code.

The IDE – Integrated Development Environment

In the Python interpreter is everything you need to execute or test a script. However, to write that script you need a text editor and there are two on a Windows PC – WordPad and Notepad. However, these are simplistic - they are OK for an emergency but they don't really have too much in the way of functionality to make long scripts or multiple scripts easier to write.

To correct that, the IDE has been developed. This is a series of programs and there is one for every computer language. In the IDE are functions like code assist, variable listing, and much more, to make them perfect for writing those scripts. We'll look at two of the best ones, all well-established within the different communities that surround Python:

IDLE

When you install Python, you get IDLE, an integrated IDE. To start it in Windows, find the ArcGIS folder on your computer. Inside the Python folder you will see IDLE as a choice – to start IDLE, select it. IDLE has an interactive interpreter built-in and can easily run full scripts. The GUI module built into Python is used to write IDLE so it is the same language as the one it will execute.

IDLE has another advantage over python.exe in that script outputs, including print statements, are sent straight to the interactive window in IDLE, and this doesn't disappear once the script has executed. IDLE also uses little memory.

There are disadvantages too; not much in the way of code assist, i.e. autocomplete, and not much in the way of organization in terms of logical projects. Every variable in a script cannot be located like in other IDEs and there is a limit to the number of scripts listed in the Recent Files menu – this is a bit of an obstruction when it comes to finding scripts that haven't been run for a while. IDLE isn't a bad IDE, it is ideal if there aren't any other options and it can be used to quickly test a snippet of code.

PythonWin

Python for Windows, or PythonWin, includes a number of useful modules and the IDE for using Python with Windows. Download the latest version of PythonWin and select the right version of the 32 module for your Python version. Run the.exe file and, if everything is correct, Python will be recognized in the registry by the installation GUI and it will then install itself.

In PythonWin, there is an interactive window where the user and the interpreter can interact. The user can also open scripts in PythonWin and there are some tiling commands to organize who the interpreter is and where the open scripts are displayed.

PythonWin has another advantage that IDLE doesn't have; it can show different parts of a script in the same window. If a script is too long, it is a nuisance to have to keep scrolling through it in order to edit it. In PythonWin, the top of the script can be pulled down to create another window which will show another part of the script. Another window can be opened to show all the variables and classes, which makes it far easier to go to a certain section of the script.

The PythonWin interactive window may also search through code statements that were previously entered. To do this, at the prompt (>>>), hold the CTRL key and use the arrow keys to go through each line until you find what you want.

Overall, PythonWin is a useful IDE used by most ArcGIS professionals. The only thing it can't do is organize scripts into logical projects or list the script variables.

There are lots of other IDEs for Python coding. It really is down to personal choice which to choose, the one that works best for you. You may find that you need to use different ones for different tasks so test several until you find the one or ones that you want.

Python Folder Structure

You will find much more than the interpreter in the folder structure. Inside the subfolders are several scripts, modules for C language and some digital link libraries. You won't use all the scripts all the time but every one of them works to make it possible to use Python for programming. The folder called site-packages is the most important one because that contains most of the modules that scripts will import.

Inside every one of the Python folders is another one called lib and inside the lib folder is the site-packages folder.

Using sys Module

Adding modules is done by using the sys module. It gives access to a vast number of system tools that are included in the interpreter. As we mentioned earlier, sys.path is an incredibly useful tool, one that can be modified to change where Python finds its modules without the need for administrative access.

When ArcGIS installs Python, the installer uses the functions in sys.path to add the ArcPY path which should look something like this:

C:\Program Files (x86)\ArcGIS\Desktopxx.x\arcpy.

You can test this by opening the interpreter or your IDE and inputting the following:

>>> import sys

>>> print sys.path

The output is as follows:

['', 'C:\\WINDOWS\\SYSTEM32\\python27.zip',

'C:\\Python27\\ArcGIS10.2\\Dlls', 'C:\\Python27\\ArcGIS10.2\\lib',

'C:\\Python27\\ArcGIS10.2\\lib\\plat-win',

'C:\\Python27\\ArcGIS10.2\\lib\\lib-tk',

'C:\\Python27\\ArcGIS10.2\\Lib\\site-packages\\pythonwin',

'C:\\Python27\\ArcGIS10.2', 'C:\\Python27\\ArcGIS10.2\\lib\\site-packages',

'C:\\Program Files (x86)\\ArcGIS\\Desktop10.2\\bin', 'C:\\Program Files (x86)\\ArcGIS\\Desktop10.2\\arcpy', 'C:\\Program Files

(x86)\\ArcGIS\\Desktop10.2\\ArcToolbox\\Scripts',

'C:\\Python27\\ArcGIS10.2\\lib\\site-packages\\win32',

'C:\\Python27\\ArcGIS10.2\\lib\\site-packages\\win32\\lib']

In the system path are the folders needed by ArcPY for the automation of ArcGIS. All the directories from the environment variable called PYTHONPATH, if that variable has already been created. This is not the same as the environment variable for the Windows path that we talked about earlier. Both variables work together helping Python to find the modules.

sys.path.append()

Because the function sys.path is a list, it can be appended or extended to add other file paths pointing to modules that can be imported. So that we don't need to change sys.path, we should copy the entire module into our site-packages folder. If you can't do this, there is another way; using sys.path.append():

>>> sys.path.append("C:\\Projects\\Requests")

>>> sys.path

['', 'C:\\WINDOWS\\SYSTEM32\\python27.zip',

 'C:\\Python27\\ArcGIS10.2\\Dells',

 'C:\\Python27\\ArcGIS10.2\\lib',

..'C:\\Python27\\ArcGIS10.2\\lib\\plat-win',

..'C:\\Python27\\ArcGIS10.2\\lib\\lib-tk',

..'C:\\Python27\\ArcGIS10.2\\Lib\\site-packages\\pythonwin',

..'C:\\Python27\\ArcGIS10.2',..'C:\\Python27\\ArcGIS10.2\\lib\\site-packages', 'C:\\Program

..Files (x86)\\ArcGIS\\Desktop10.2\\bin', 'C:\\Program Files

..(x86)\\ArcGIS\\Desktop10.2\\arcpy', 'C:\\Program Files

..(x86)\\ArcGIS\\Desktop10.2\\ArcToolbox\\Scripts',

..'C:\\Python27\\ArcGIS10.2\\lib\\site-packages\\win32',

..'C:\\Python27\\ArcGIS10.2\\lib\\site-packages\\win32\\lib',

..'C:\\Projects\\Requests']

When this method is used, the change is only a temporary one. If the change is to be permanent, go to System Properties and change the PYTHONPATH variable.

Once more important thing to note is if you want to import modules without making those changes or copying the module to site-packages, you must put the relevant module into the folder that contains the importing script. So long as the configuration is correct on the module, it will all work.

Programming in ArcGIS:

GIS analysts don't necessarily need to know how to program to do their jobs, but they can be sure that, if they can program in Python, they will go a lot further. That said, this isn't as easy as you might think if you have no clue where to start. Earlier we talked about what you would need to get started because GIS programming does begin with Python, even though it doesn't end there.

Python is a great language for both programming and scripting but, when it is combined with ArcGIS, Python scripting is great for task automation. For that reason, it is important to learn the basics of using Python and that includes the syntax, commands, data types, functionalities, loops and everything else that goes with it. You don't need to know Python inside out, much of it can be learned as you get to grips with ArcGIS. One more thing you should learn is how to get help files via the interpreter and how to list all the modules, functionalities and methods instead of having to keep going to the external files for help.

There are many free tutorials online to help you learn Python basics and they will all cover the same things – syntax, strings, data types, functions, etc., everything you need to learn. Python 3 is best for GIS users although the ArcGIS desktop does still use Python 2. If you already have ArcGIS desktop on your computer, Python has already been installed so you don't need to worry about getting the right version. Just go to the Windows taskbar and find the ArcGIS submenu. Click it and click on IDLE and the Python terminal will open with the command line. Here, you can write code and press Enter to execute that code.

Practice is also important. You can't just read something, do it once, and that's it; you will need to find free exercises online or in books and keep practicing them until you know what you are doing. Once you have the basics down then you can move onto Python scripting, know the difference between writing a script and running it, along with how to use the interactive interpreter. This won't really be covered in many of the free online courses, so you will need to do some searching – this is vital to learn though if you want to be a GIS analyst. Write a few scripts even if they are only simple ones and run them. Learn about commenting code – it will help you later.

You should use an Integrated Development Environment (IDE) for your scripts; this isn't complicated; it is just software, a code editor that lets you write code, run it, save it, and debug it. An IDE will color code depending on the elements, to help you pick up on errors much easier. You should also take time to look at some of the functionality built into Python, like the Math module in the standard library. Numbers are an important part of GIS and you might need to refresh what you learned at college. Python gives you the ability to work with object geometrics within a GIS so understanding what the library has to offer will be handy. You can access the online and offline Python documentation to help you with this, along with learning how to write data into new files, ensuring source paths are correctly written, the correct way to write SQL statements, about error messages, and about the 'try' and the 'except' blocks.

Python and ArcGIS

Once you have had some practice with Python, try using it in ArcGIS. One of the best ways to start is by using the Python window to learn the arcpy site package, which is a module collection that gives users access to some great features including the geoprocessing functions. ArcGIS Pro requires Python 3 and ArcMap requires Python 2. There is an interactive Help window in the Python window that will help you to write code. It allows you to specify a tool's parameter and provides for code autocompletion that can save you a great deal of time. This is one of the best ways to learn arcpy and it should really be your starting point; get some confidence with arcpy, use local GIS data to write a few standalone scripts and run them, and see what they do.

Use your best friend here – common sense. Spelling paths and filenames wrong is common and, yes, it will cause errors. Python scripts can be properly checked for errors by the IDE, but there may be those that get missed, such as incorrectly spelled names, commands, tools and paths. Another common mistake is to misuse capital letters, something to which Python is very sensitive. One way of controlling your script process is to allow it to 'print' messages, such as "print("geodatabase correctly created"). This way you can check the progress. If your script terminates error-free, go to ArcMap and run a visual of your results. If you don't see the output you expect to see, check your code again.

Again, there are plenty of tutorials and help online to get you acquainted with Python scripting and with arcpy. You can find plenty of detailed information about how it all works. Start at the bottom and work your way through the basics. Make use of the ArcGIS help section to get to know arcpy and then look for books that contain scripts, heavily annotated, and those that contain expertly created data that you can use to experiment.

Beyond Scripting

Once you have some experience, you might want to know where you should head next. Don't be too quick to start on other languages or other frameworks as a way of improving your code, such as using a list comprehension to refactor some of it. Instead, try finding new geospatial modules that can help improve your code; look at professional works, compare them, and look for code habits that you can you use.

This learning path is not going to be easy; it will take time and it will be iterative, i.e. you will be going between stages, back and forth continuously, learning something new every time. It is fun though, and it is surprising. The more you practice, you more you learn, and the easier it will get. Python is an excellent way of extending GIS with so many extra geospatial libraries at your disposal.

After you learn the basics of Python, of scripting and of ArcGIS, you can go in so many other directions. For example, you can use the ArcGIS Python API that ESRI has recently released enabling you to use Python and maps on the internet; this takes it beyond desktop use.

Why We Need GIS Automation

GIS, or Geographic Information Systems, are able to manipulate spatial datasets, as well as analyzing them. This is to solve problems of a geographic nature and GIS analysts will do all sorts of data operations to find the solution for a specific problem. Included in this are:

- Clipping
- Reprojection
- Merging
- Buffering
- Mosaicking
- Extraction of data subsets

There are many other operations of course, all of which are called geoprocessing in the ArcGIS software and tools are used to perform them.

Being successful in GIS analysis means that you need to be able to choose the right tools for the data operation. In ArcGIS, there is a toolbox metaphor for the organization of the tools suite; you choose the tools and make sure they run in the right order.

Let's say that part of your job is to choose the sites for a chain of restaurants. You could use one tool for the selection of the parcels of land on a major road; another one for parcels that are 0.25 acres or more, and so on. If you only had a small area to work with for your selection process, you would probably be better off doing the work manually.

However, assume that you need to do exactly the same kind of analyses but over multiple areas in the country. This is where automation comes in - when you need to use the same tool sequence for multiple areas. Automation brings a number of benefits to the table:

- It makes work much easier. Once a process has been automated, you won't need to do so much work to remember which tools you need or in which the order they need to be used.
- It makes work much faster. Computers can open tools and execute them in the right sequence much quicker than you can do it with a mouse.
- It provides a higher level of accuracy. Whenever a task is manually performed, there is always a margin for error. The more tasks and the more complex they are, not to mention the fatigue you will experience when you need to repeat a task over and over, will all increase the margin for error. Conversely, once you have configured an automated task, the computer will get on with the task at hand accurately and as many times as needed.

There are three ways that ArcGIS allows for automation of geoprocessing tasks. These options are all different, each requiring a different level of skill in producing an automated solution and in what each can address in the way of scenarios.

Option one involves using ModelBuilder to build a model. This program is interactive, allowing you to link a series of tools so that the output from one becomes the input to the next. ModelBuilder offers an excellent feature in that it can be used for the automation of complex workflows without needing to do any programming.

There are tasks that need more flexibility than ModelBuilder offers; for this, scripts are recommended. Scripts will generally execute a sequence of steps and you can opt to either run the tools one at a time or you can link them together. Conditional logic can be added to handle a case where the output from one operation will affect the tool that needs to be run next. Iteration can be included so that one action may be repeated over and again until a task is finished.

Scripting can be done using one of many different languages, but Python is the main one as it tends to be included with ArcGIS as standard.

The last option is to use ArcObjects to build an automation solution because it allows you to customize the interface, so it has the commands and tools needed for more focused work. These tools may be standard ArcGIS tools, or you can modify them, so they work as you need them to. We won't be touching on this option in this book; instead we will be concentrating on the scripting side and on ModelBuilder.

All the tools that Python and ModelBuilder are based on ArcObjects but, when you use Python scripting there is no requirement to learn the logic behind these tools; all you need to do is learn what the tools are and the order they need to be run to complete a specific task.

First, we will look at some of the concepts behind writing scripts and model building, starting with the ArcGIS toolbox and how they fit in with ModelBuilder. After that, we'll look at some Python basics and how the tools work in a script.

The ArcGIS Toolbox

The ArcGIS software is home to hundreds of different tools that can be used to manipulate and analyze GIS data. In the early days, ArcGIS did not have a graphical user interface (GUI) so commands were needed to access the tools.

These days, there is a sequence of toolboxes that you can point and click through via the ArcCatalog or you can go to ArcMap and use the Catalog window. You might have seen these toolboxes before, but we can take a look at them now:

Launch ArcMap

If you don't see the Catalog window, click Windows>Catalog. Pin this window, so it doesn't hide so you can see it whenever you need to.

In Catalog, go to Toolboxes and then System Toolboxes and continue to go through the ones you want to see. Notice that they have all been organized and are in toolboxes and in toolsets. You might find it faster to go to Geoprocessing>Search and look for the specific tool you want.

For the purposes of this, open Analysis Tools>Proximity and click the Buffer tool.

If you are familiar with ArcGIS tools, you might already have seen this tool. This time, I want you to pay close attention to how the user interface is constructed. In particular, you are seeing one dialog that has multiple fields. Each of the geoprocessing tools will have a requirement for inputs and outputs and you will see these indicated by a green dot. These are representative of the absolute minimum level of information needed for a tool to run. For Buffer, you need to supply a location for the input features, that is the features that are to be buffered, and you need to supply a buffer distance. Alongside that is the requirement to indicate a class location where the newly buffered features will go.

Some tools also have a set of optional parameters and these are modifiable if required. If these are not supplied, default values will be used to run the tool. As far as the Buffer tool goes, the optional parameters include:

- Side Type
- Dissolve Type
- End Type
- Dissolve Fields

Generally, the optional parameters will follow the required parameters.

Look for the Show Help button in the bottom-right corner of the Buffer tool and click it. Choose a parameter and click it to see an explanation appear in the window on the right. This is a great way of learning what parameters mean. For example, keeping the Help open, in the Buffer tool, click the input box called Side Type – it should say Full. Help will show you what the parameter means, and it will show you all the options – FULL, RIGHT, LEFT, OUTSIDE_ONLY.

If you require more help, you can go to the ArcGIS Desktop help documentation where you will find full explanations of each one, along with Python examples. To get the help pages you will need:

Open ArcGIS and click on Help>ArcGIS Desktop Help.

Click the tab for Contents and then click on Tools>Tool Reference. Each of the help topics has been placed in toolsets and toolboxes for your ease.

Continue to go through the table until you get to Analysis Toolbox. Click on Proximity Toolset and then on Buffer. Look through the topic; you will find plenty of information about the tool, what it does, how it should be used, and how the parameters should be supplied.

When you are happy, move on to the Code Sample section where you will find Python examples of how to run the tool automatically.

The ArcGIS Python Window

One of the best ways to introduce Python is to look at some code so we'll now run the Buffer tool in the ArcGIS Python window. In this window, you can run a series of commands without having to draw up a permanent script. What we will do this time is make some buffers of a distance of 15 miles around some cities:

Open ArcMap so you have an empty map.

Download the us_cities.shp dataset from Github and add it to the map.

Click the button for Python Window on the Standard toolbar and then drag the open window to the bottom or side of the screen – this will dock it.

Input the following code to the Python window (minus the >> prompt – that will already be there). Don't copy and paste it, type it in so you get used to doing it:

>>> import arcpy

>>> arcpy.Buffer_analysis("us_cities", "us_cities_buffered", "15 miles", "", "", "ALL")

Now zoom in and look at the buffers you just created. You don't need to have a full understanding of this at this stage but there are a few things to note:

The first line, import arcpy, informs the interpreter that you will need special functions and tools for scripting from ArcGIS. If you don't add this line of code, Python will not have any knowledge of ArcGIS, so you must remember to add this in on any code related to ArcGIS. Technically, when you are working within the ArcMap Python window, arcpy has already been imported so you won't need to do it, but you will need it in scripts written outside of this window.

The second line is what runs the tool. To run any tool in Python, all you need to do is input arcpy, followed by a dot and the name of the tool, i.e. arcpy.buffer, to run that tool. You also include an underscore and the toolbox name. This is required because there are tools that have the same names but are in different toolboxes, so you must specify which toolbox to look in.

All the parameters are separated with a comma and the entire list must be inside a set of parentheses. Again, this is a pattern that you need to get used to because it is required with all tools. We also added a few optional parameters; in places where we wanted the default values used, we left a set of empty quotes.

The big question is, how do you know what parameter structure or syntax to use? For the distance, do you input 15MILES, 15 Miles, '15Miles' or '15 Miles'? To find the answer to questions such as this you should go back to the help page we discussed earlier. All the topics in the reference section will show you command lines and structure examples. All optional parameters will be inside a set of braces, requisite parameters are not. From our example, you can see that we used '15 miles' as the distance – because a space is inserted between the words, it must be inside single quotes.

Did you spot that the Python Window offers a bit of help? It gives you several options for each parameter and we call this autocompletion. It's a helpful feature when you are a novice at running the tools and are not sure of the right way to type the parameters.

There are some notable differences between using a program like PythonWin to write your code and writing it in the Python Window. In the window, it is a simple matter to reference the map document layers using just their names; in any other program, you would need to specify the file path. As such, we could type something easy like "us_cities" rather than specifying the whole path. We could also come up with a new name for a new layer, "us_cities_buffered" and have it added by default to the map once the code was run. The lesson here is, if you use any program other than PythonWin, you need to use the full file path.

When the scripts are more complex, it is better to use an IDE and later we will look closer at the PythonWin IDE. For now, think back to when we talked about linking tools together in ModelBuilder to solve problems. Well, we can do this in Python too so, to give you a bit of grounding, we'll start off with a bit of work on the Python basics.

The Basics of Python and ArcGIS

We already know that the Python computer language is great for writing scripts to automate computer-related tasks. We also know that automation makes it easier and faster as well as far more accurate. The same applies to computer science, in particular GIS and, by learning Python, you will be a far better GIS analyst.

Because Python is what is known as a 'high-level' language, you can use it quite easily without needing to understand how a computer works. The syntax Python uses is quite simple to read, to write, and understand and you don't need much in the way of overheads to get up and running with a Python program.

We can use Python in ArcGIS for something called "coarse-grained" programming and what this means is that it is easy to use for geoprocessing tools, such as Buffer. You could, if you wanted to, use ArcObjects and some finer-grained programming but this takes time and, for the most part, is not necessary. It is far easier to call a tool using a Python script and a single code line.

There is an additional way to get help with the Python syntax, the language structure, for any individual tool:

Interactively run the tool using your input and output data and any parameters that are relevant to the tool.

Go to Geoprocessing>Results and find the tool.

Right-click it to run it.

Choose the option for Copy Python Snippet and then paste it into the Python window or PythonWin – you will be shown how the operation you ran would be coded.

How to Install PythonWin

Python comes with a built-in editor, a simple one called IDLE. However, we are going to be using PythonWin IDE. This is free and already has basic features for debugging built into it. We can get PythonWin from Source Forge but make sure you download the win32 version, and nothing else.

Once you have downloaded PythonWin, launch the file by right-clicking on it and choosing Run as Administrator.

The PythonWin wizard will start, click on Next to get the installation started. You will need to make your own PythonWin desktop shortcut as there isn't one automatically made.

Let's Explore PythonWin

Before we start, open up PythonWin; it will make it easier to follow as we work through the main bits of the program.

When you open PythonWin, the first thing that you will see is the Interactive Window with the >>> prompt. Type your code here and it will be executed and the result printed, if there is one. This window is an excellent place to begin practicing using Python and you will find it is very much the same as the ArcGIS Python window.

To start writing a script, choose File>New>Python Script. You will now see a blank page that is color-coded using the Courier font which is common in programming. You can also very easily track indentation and spacing, two important factors with Python.

On the standard toolbar, you will see many tools used to load your scripts, to run them, and save them. Two important buttons are the Undo and Redo buttons – these are a godsend to new programmers as they can get you out of trouble. The Run button is also important because it gives you the opportunity to run a script for testing purposes without having to go through Windows Explorer.

You will also see a toolbar called Debugging which allows you to find errors by checking your code one line at a time. If you can't see the toolbar, click on View>Toolbars>Debugging. This is another important toolbar and is perhaps the most important reason to use an IDE instead of another text editor.

Using ArcGIS

It is now time to move on to using ArcGIS. One of the most important parts of any GIS is the data that is representative of geographic feature location and the attributes that go with the features. This is what will take GIS way beyond simple mapping – being a GIS analyst involves adding new features and attributes, modifying existing ones, and deleting them from a GIS.

Aside from data maintenance, you will also need to understand querying data and selecting that which is important to the projects you are undertaking. You may even want to look into a dataset and query it to find specific records, perhaps those that match to particular criteria, and use only those records to calculate some stats.

It can become tiresome and time-consuming to do all these tasks, not to mention increasing the chances of errors when you do it all manually. Scripts are a much better, more efficient way of reading large data chunks, as well as being far more accurate. We already have lots of tools at our disposal to select data and manage it, all in the ArcToolbox and you can use any of these within your Python scripts. If you wanted to modify the records in a table individually, you can make use of some special objects in arcpy. These are called cursors and are used for individual record examination.

When you use scripts, you can also take advantage of a few advantages that you don't get when you enter data manually. Checks can be added into scripts to make sure that entered data conforms to a specified format. Steps can be linked together to provide a chain of selection logic; doing this in ArcMap would be incredibly time-consuming.

What we are going to look at is how to use Python to read GIS data and write it. We will begin by examining the creation of datasets and how to open them in a script. We'll move on to using cursor objects and tools for geoprocessing to read data and write it. We'll also be looking at rasters, even though these are mostly used for vector datasets.

Storing and Retrieving Data in ArcGIS

Before looking at ways to read attributes and modify them, it would serve you well to understand how ArcGIS stores the geographic datasets. This is important if you are to learn how to open a dataset in a script and, where necessary, how new datasets are created.

The Geodatabase

ESRI, the most powerful of all the mapping software on the market, has come up with a number of methods to store spatial data and one of the best ways is to use geodatabases. A geodatabase is a well-organized structure used for the storage of and definition of the relationships between two or more datasets. Which geodatabase you use will be dependent on the data you are using:

- **Personal** – these are small geodatabases, almost deprecated now, that are used for data storage on local systems. A Microsoft Access Database is used to hold the data, and provide limits on how much can be stored.
- **File** – these are one of the more recent methods for data storage on local systems. An ESRI-developed format is used to store the data and these can hold significantly more data than the personal ones can.
- **ArcSDE** – sometimes called Enterprise, these use a central server within an RDBMS (Relational Database Management System) to store the data. This could be SQL Server, PostgreSQL or Oracle, for example. These databases are very large, and they are designed to serve an enterprise with data. RDBMSs can be hard work in themselves so the ArcSDE was developed to act as the middleman, to help you configure datasets in ArcMap or ArcCatalog and read them without going anywhere near the relational database software.

If you have one vector dataset inside one of these geodatabases, it is known as a feature class. You can, if you want, organize these classes into feature datasets and your geodatabases may also be used to store raster datasets.

The Standalone Dataset

Geodatabases are vital to store and organize data long-term but, on occasion, you might want a standalone format to access the datasets from a local system. Perhaps the best standalone format for vector data is shapefile. A shapefile is made up of multiple files that all combine to store the geometrics and their attributes. Each file shares a root name but has a different extension. Each of the files can be zipped together and emailed or placed in a folder for easy downloading. In ArcMap and ArcCatalog, the shapefiles are a single file in the browsers. A quick note here – you will sometimes see a shapefile called a feature class; so when you see that term, consider that it could be referring to vector dataset that may also be used in ArcGIS.

There is another standalone dataset that is from the early ArcGIS days –
ArcInfo Coverage. In a similar way to the shapefile, this also has a number of
files that all work in combination. These are not so common now, but if you
work for an organization that has ArcInfo WorkStation and still uses it, you may
come across them.

You will often find a raster dataset stored as a standalone rather than being in a
geodatabase. A raster may be one file, or it may be several files, like the
shapefile.

Python Scripts and Paths

More often than not you will need to add dataset paths to scripts and it isn't
always easy to know the right syntax to specify the path – this is down to the
number of storage methods. How should the dataset path be specified? You
could come up against the same with shapefiles; even though they may have
better names, they do have at least three files that participate.

Perhaps the easiest and best way to find the required paths is to go to the
ArcCatalog dataset and browse through it and look in the Location toolbar for
the path.

The following example is a way that you could use the Python script to access
the feature class:

import arcpy

featureClass = "C:\\Data\\USA\\USA.gdb\\Cities"

desc = arcpy.Describe(featureClass)

spatialRef = desc.SpatialReference

print(spatialRef.Name)

Don't forget; backslashes are reserved Python characters, so you must choose
between using a forward slash - / - or a double backslash - \\ - when you write
the path. You could also use a raw string to write the path – this will allow

backslashes to be added along with other characters that have been reserved into the string, so long as you add an 'r' as a prefix to the quotation marks:

featureClass = r"C:\Data\USA\USA.gdb\Cities"

...

Workspaces

Workspaces are often used in a geoprocessing framework to denote which geodatabase or folder you are working in at the time. When a workspace is specified inside your script, there is no need to list the entire path for each individual dataset. When a tool is run, the geoprocessor will 'see' the name of the feature class and will assume that it lives in the specified workspace.

Where workspaces really come into their own is when they are used in batch processing, where one action is performed on multiple datasets within that workspace. For example, let's say that you wanted to clip every feature class in one folder to a county boundary. The proper workflow would be:

1. Definition of the workspace
2. Creation of the list of the workspace feature classes
3. Definition of the clip feature
4. Configuration of the loop that runs on each of the listed feature classes
5. The Clip tool is run in the loop.

Look at a piece of code that will clip each of the file geodatabase feature classes to the state boundary for Alabama, followed by the output, then going to another file geodatabase. Note – the lines of code that follow the import arcpy statement relate to the 5 steps listed above:

```
import arcpy


arcpy.env.workspace = "C:\\Data\\USA\\USA.gdb"

featureClassList = arcpy.ListFeatureClasses()

clipFeature = "C:\\Data\\Alabama\\Alabama.gdb\\StateBoundary"


for featureClass in featureClassList:

        arcpy.Clip_analysis(featureClass, clipFeature,
"C:\\Data\\Alabama\\Alabama.gdb\\" + featureClass)
```

In this example, the arcpy.ListFeatureClasses() method was the important part in the list creation. The method goes through a specified workspace, listing each of the contained feature classes – this is a Python list. Once this list has been created, a for loop may be configured to act on the individual items.

Note, also, that the workspace path was designated using the file geodatabase location, C:\\Data\\USA\\USA.gdb. If these were shapefiles you were working with, all you would need for the workspace is the path that leads to the containing folder.

If it were ArcSDE you were using, the path to the.sde file would be required; this file is created when you go into ArcCatalog to connect to ArcSDE and you will find the file inside the directory for your local profile. We won't be using ArcSDE for the purposes of this section, but you may come across it – remember the ArcCatalog location toolbar can be used to understand the ArcSDE dataset paths.

How to Read the Vector Attribute Data

You know now how a dataset is opened so we need to go a bit deeper and start looking at the data records. We will be looking at reading the data tables and searching them. These tables are where you will often find the feature attributes for the vectors, but sometimes, they can be standing alone.

First, we will look at writing the data to the tables, so copy the code I give you into some scripts, so you can practice. This will help you to learn what you need to do and how it all works. Practice is everything and trial and error is how you will learn.

Data Fields

Before we discuss accessing vector data, we need to take a look at how we store the data in the software. The vector features from any ArcGIS shapefile or feature class are always stored in tables, each having rows, which are the records, and columns, which are the fields.

Each field is used to store feature geometry and the information about the attributes. Each table will have two fields that cannot be deleted. One, usually with the name of Shape, is used to store the feature geometry information and included in this are the feature vertex coordinates, allowing drawing of each feature onto the screen. Geometry information is always in binary format and it would be unlikely to make any sense if you were to see it as is. However, arcpy provides objects that allow us to read geometrics and work with them.

The second field is named either FID or OBJECTID. It is an ID field for the object and it holds a unique identifier for each ArcGIS record that is used to track features. The ID is useful to avoid any confusion when you work with the data. On occasion, two or more records may share identical attributes; for example, San Francisco and Los Angeles may have the same State attribute called California but the ID field will never hold identical values for different records.

All the other fields will contain descriptive information about the feature attributes, normally stored in text or number format.

Discovering the Field Names

When a script is written, you must specify which field names you are reading or writing. You can use arcpy.ListFields() to gain access to the field names in a Python list.

 # Reads the fields in a feature class

import arcpy

featureClass = "C:\\Data\\USA\\USA.gdb\\Cities"

fieldList = arcpy.ListFields(featureClass)

 # Loop through each field in the list and print the name

for field in fieldList:

  print(field.name)

This code would give you a list of all the fields under the feature class called Cities; this is in a file geodatabase called USA.gdb. If you were to try running this in PythonWin, the output would be this:

>>> OBJECTID

Shape

UIDENT

POPCLASS

NAME

CAPITAL

STATEABB

COUNTRY

Note that the static fields we mentioned earlier are there – Shape, with its record geometry information, and OBJECTID, with the unique ID number for the individual records. We also have other fields, specifying NAME, STATE, CAPITAL, and more.

The fields are treated as objects by arcpy and this means that they have properties describing them. You can only read the field properties, you can change or delete them in any way using a Field object in your script. If, for some reason, you needed to change the precision and scale of any particular field, a new field would need to be added programmatically.

Reading Records

We've looked at a horizontal traversal of the table and what fields there are. Now we need to look at vertical traversal, i.e. going through the records up and down.

Cursors, contained in the arcpy module, are useful objects that make moving through each table record easier. These are not unique in ArcGIS; if you have ever used ArcObjects, you will have seen them before.

Because multiple versions of ArcGIS are still in use, we will look at the way cursors are used in both the older and newer versions of the software before we look at the changes that make cursor usage easier and require less code. For the most part, the code we use in this section will be for the newer versions with solutions for older versions too.

First, we will look at the search cursor. This cursor was designed to make data reading simple. We will begin with the early uses of this cursor that is used in the older ArcGIS versions; you will find this code a little more, shall we say, verbose, than newer versions but it does give you a great idea of how the search cursor is working. First, the workflow:

1. The search cursor is created using arcpy.SearchCursor() method, which will take multiple parameters for the specification of the dataset and, if required, the rows required for reading.
2. Next, SearchCursor.next() is called so the first row can be read.
3. We now need to take the values from the row we are on and do something with them.
4. SearchCursor.next() is called again so the first row may be read.
5. A loop is started; this will exit when we run out of rows to read.
6. Next, we take the values in the row we are on and do something with them.
7. Last, SearchCursor.next() is called to go to the following row; because a loop was created, you will go back to the last step if another row is there to read. If not the condition for the loop has not been met and it will terminate.

When you begin to look at cursors, try visualizing the attribute table showing an arrow that indicated the current row. When you create the cursor, the arrow will point to the line above the first row. When the next() method is called for the first time, that arrow will drop to the very first row and a reference to the row is returned. Whenever next() is called after this, the arrow will move down by one row until the final row is reached. At this point, calling next() will return a data type of None.

Look at this very easy example showing a search cursor reading a cities dataset and then printing each name:

 # Prints the name of each city in a feature class

import arcpy

featureClass = "C:\\Data\\USA\\USA.gdb\\Cities"

rows = arcpy.SearchCursor(featureClass)

row = rows.next()

while row:

  print row.NAME

  row = rows.next()

Note that the final five rows of this code relate to the workflow steps above. Cursors are not always easy to understand to start with, so we'll take a closer look at each line. Look at those lines again, this time commented so that you can understand what is going on:

 # Create the search cursor

rows = arcpy.SearchCursor(featureClass)

 # Call SearchCursor.next() to read the first row

row = rows.next()

 # Start a loop that will exit when there are no more rows available

while row:

  # Do something with the values in the current row

  print(row.NAME)

  # Call SearchCursor.next() to move on to the next row

row = rows.next()

Before we move on, there are a couple of important things to understand:

The 'while row' is a loop condition and is nothing more than a Boolean method to specify if a loop should carry on or stop. If there is a row object, the statement will return true and the loop will carry on; if there is no row object, false is returned and the loop will stop.

Field values may be read as row properties. Take row.NAME, for example; this provides a value in the field called NAME. If you had a field called POPULATION, you would use row.POPULATION to get the field value.

The names you see of 'row' and 'rows' are nothing more than variable names. They are representative of the ROW and SearchCursor objects and could, in effect, be named anything you wanted.

Look at another more complex example of the row values. In this script, we are trying to find what the average population of all counties within a given dataset. To do this, we must take the total population number and divide it by how many counties there are. The code example below is going to loop through each individual record and will make a running tally of what the population is and how many records have been counted. When all the records have been read, we only need to use a single division line to see the average:

 # Finds the average population in a counties dataset

import arcpy

featureClass = "C:\\Data\\Pennsylvania\\Counties.shp"

rows = arcpy.SearchCursor(featureClass)

```
row = rows.next()


average = 0

totalPopulation = 0

recordsCounted = 0


# Loop through each row and keep running total of the population

#  and records counted.


while row:

    totalPopulation += row.POP1990

    recordsCounted += 1

    row = rows.next()


average = totalPopulation / recordsCounted

print("Average population for a county is " + str(average))
```

This script example may be quite a bit longer than the one we first looked it, but the pattern is the same – a search cursor is created, it goes to row one, does something with it and then repeats this until all records are dealt with.

Reading Variable Values

In our last example, we used row.POP1990 to reference a record population where the name of the field is POP1990. This is one of the easier ways to obtain field values. But what if you were to get 2009 data from the POP2009 field but need to script run again? What if you have multiple scripts, all long ones, all referencing the POP field in the exact same way? What you would need to do is look through each script very carefully for the row called POP1990 and then give it a new name – row.POP2009. This will take forever and is highly prone to errors.

Scripts can be made much more versatile if you were to represent the names of the fields using variables. Variables, like populationField, can be declared as a way to reference the field name for population, be it POPULATION, POP2009, POP1990, or whatever it is called. Our interpreter will not be able to recognize row.populationField. Instead, Row.getValue() must be used and passed as a parameter to the variable.

The next script example uses a variable name as a way of obtaining each record's population. You will see that we have commented on the lines we changed from above with a comment starting ###. Note – the population Field variable has been created and we also have a method call to row.getValue(populationField) – this will get each of the record populations.

 # Finds the average population in a counties dataset

import arcpy

featureClass = "C:\\Data\\Pennsylvania\\Counties.shp"

This row below is new

populationField = "POP1990"

rows = arcpy.SearchCursor(featureClass)

row = rows.next()

```
average = 0

totalPopulation = 0

recordsCounted = 0


# Loop through each row and keep running total of the population

#  and records counted.


while row:
### This row below is new
    totalPopulation += row.getValue(populationField)

    recordsCounted += 1

    row = rows.next()


average = totalPopulation / recordsCounted

print("Average population for a county is " + str(average))
```

Updating this script would require only that populationField = "POP2009" is set near to the start of the script. This is a great deal easier and more efficient than looking for row.POP1990 manually through the entire script. However, there is more to this; you could take it to another level and let a user input any specific name for a field that they want to be added as an argument when the script is run.

Remember when we looked at arcpy.GetParameterAsText()? This lets a user supply the variable value and this technique may be used for the population field name and for the path for the feature class, making your script incredibly versatile and flexible. The code below does not have any numbers other than 0 or 1, hard-code path names nor field names, and this means that running the script could be done with any of the feature classes that contain any population field name without a need to change any code. You could, if you wanted, use similar code to look for the averages of any of the numeric fields.

```
# Finds the average population in a counties dataset


import arcpy


featureClass = arcpy.GetParameterAsText(0)

populationField = arcpy.GetParameterAsText(1)


rows = arcpy.SearchCursor(featureClass)

row = rows.next()


average = 0

totalPopulation = 0

recordsCounted = 0


# Loop through each row and keep running total of the population

#  and records counted.
```

```
while row:

    totalPopulation += row.getValue(populationField)

    recordsCounted += 1

    row = rows.next()


average = totalPopulation / recordsCounted

print("Average population for a county is " + str(average))
```

For Loops With Cursors

The examples we looked at so far use while loops together with the method called next() to move the cursor. It may, however, be much easier to use a for loop for iteration. This came into use with the later ArcGIS versions and the example below shows how we can modify the previous script so a for loop can be used. Note the syntax that we have used for row in rows:

```
# Finds the average population in a counties dataset


import arcpy


featureClass = "C:\\Data\\Pennsylvania\\Counties.shp"

populationField = "POP1990"


rows = arcpy.SearchCursor(featureClass)
```

```
average = 0

totalPopulation = 0

recordsCounted = 0


# Loop through each row and keep running total of the population

#  and records counted.


for row in rows:

    totalPopulation += row.getValue(populationField)

    recordsCounted += 1


average = totalPopulation / recordsCounted

print("Average population for a county is " + str(average))
```

We didn't even need to use the next() method in this script because the for loop implies that the script is going to iterate over every individual record. The declaration of the for loop declared the row object.

This is somewhat tighter in syntax than the while loop, but it is useful to see how the method called next() works. This is more important if you are working with early ArcGIS scripts or if you are using ArcObject cursors. Eventually, with practice, you will become used to traversing tables using a for loop and you will be unlikely to want to return to the while loops.

ArcPY Data-Access Module

In later versions of ArcGIS, that code example could be used for the search cursors or you could choose another route – a data-access module supplied by arcpy. Each of the functions has the arcpy.da prefix and they provide much faster and more efficient performance, as well as being far more robust in behavior when the cursor crashes or runs into errors.

The arcpy.da module will allow for the creation of cursor objects, much like arcpy, but the creation is a little bit different. Look at the next example very closely. The scenario from the previous code has been repeated, calculating a county's average population:

```
# Finds the average population in a counties dataset


import arcpy


featureClass = "C:\\Data\\Pennsylvania\\Counties.shp"

populationField = "POP1990"


average = 0

totalPopulation = 0

recordsCounted = 0


with arcpy.da.SearchCursor(featureClass, (populationField,)) as cursor:

    for row in cursor:

        totalPopulation += row[0]
```

recordsCounted += 1

average = totalPopulation / recordsCounted

print("Average population for a county is " + str(average))

Note that the structure of this script is basically the same as the last one but there are a couple of changes that are quite important. The first thing you should have noticed is that we used a with statement to create our cursor. Explaining this with statement is rather technical but the important thing to really understand is that the statement will let the cursor come out of the database in a graceful manner, regardless of whether it was successful or whether it crashes. This is one of the biggest problems with the cursors; if they do not get exited correctly, they may place a lock on the data and hold it there.

When you use a with statement, all the code that comes after it must be indented. Once the cursor has been created in that statement, a for loop must then be initiated to go over every individual row in your table. Extra indentation will be required for this.

The with statement has also created an object called SearchCursor and has made a declaration that the name will be cursor in any later code. When you use arcpy.da to create a search cursor, each will have different parameters for initialization than the search cursors created using arcpy. The main difference though, is that when arcpy.da is used for the creation of the cursors, you must supply a field name tuple; the cursor will return this tuple. Remember: tuples are data structures in Python that are similar to lists with the exception of a set of parentheses enclosing it and that there is no way of modifying the tuple contents.

When this tuple is supplied, the cursor's work is hastened because it no longer has any need to deal with a large number of fields that are in the dataset. In our previous script example, the tuple only has one field called populationField. Even though it has only the one item, that item must be followed by a comma, so it would look like (populationField,). If there were more than one item in the tuple, there must be a comma separating each item.

We also still have row objects in arcpy.da, the same as we do in arcpy but we no longer get the row values by using the method called getValue(). Instead, we take the field name from the tuple named when the object was created and use its index position. In the previous example, only one item was submitted within the tuple, we would use the populationField index position which, in our example is 0. Remember, we begin at 0 to count in Python, so row[0] would be used to obtain the populationField value for any specified row.

Using Attribute Queries to Retrieve Records

In our previous script examples, the SearchCursor object was used to read through individual dataset records. However, you can make your search cursor work a bit more specifically and ask it to retrieve only a subset of those records with attributes complying with specified criteria. For your information, the code snippet below shows you how to use arcpy.da to build the search cursor to work on all records in a specified dataset:

with arcpy.da.SearchCursor(featureClass,(populationField,)) as cursor:

If the search cursor is only to retrieve a subset of the dataset records based on specified criteria, an SQL expression should be supplied as an argument in the constructor used to create your SearchCursor. An example would be:

with arcpy.da.SearchCursor(featureClass, (populationField,), '"POP2009" > 150000') as cursor:

In this example, the SQL expression we use is 'POP2009">150000 and this will retrieve just the subset of records with a population from 2009 and more than 150000. SQL is a Structured Query Language and it is a specific syntax that we use when we want to query a database. If you have used ArcMap before and have ever filtered data using a Definition Query, then you will have a better understanding of what an SQL query is all about. If you are not familiar with SQL or queries, go to the Desktop Help in ArcGIS and read the help topic on Building Query Expressions, a simple overview of the SQL as far as ArcGIS is concerned.

In an SQL expression, you can use any combination of different criteria to ensure that you get the exact subset of data that you want. The only limit to your query is the data that you have available. For example, you could write an SQL query that helps you to find the States whose names begin with M, were made settlements after 1800, and that have a population of more than 150 people per square mile. That's pretty specific!

The SQL expression supplied to any search cursor will not be spatial queries, only for attribute queries. There would not be a way to use an SQL query to choose the records that are within the Canadian borders or to the north of the Arkansas River, for example, unless an attribute had been added and populated earlier to specify whether a condition is True. i.e. CANADIAN = True or REGION = 'Northern'. Later, we'll cover spatial queries using the geoprocessing tool Select By Location.

Once the subset has been retrieved, iteration through the records is done using a for loop:

with arcpy.da.SearchCursor(featureClass, (populationField,), '"POP200p" > 150000') as cursor:

  for row in cursor:

    print(str(row[0]))

Using Quotation Marks

When an SQL expression is used in the constructor for the SearchCursor, that expression must be in the format of a string. Things can get a little complicated where quotation marks are concerned. In SQL, double and single quotation marks are required in specific places but, because the expression is a string, the whole thing needs to be inside quotes. So how do we do this without running into utter confusion?

With Python, strings can be enclosed in either single or double quotes. Note from our previous example that the SQL expression was inside a set of single quotes and not double ones – '"POP2009">150000'. The reason for this was because, inside the SQL statement, the field name is surrounded by double quotes, so it is better to use the single quotes for the string. This not only makes reading the code easier; if you were to use two sets of double quote marks together, the Python interpreter would get in a muddle and would think that an empty string was being created. Using double quotes for the string is not an option in this case.

Things get a little more confusing when the SQL expression needs both single quotes and double quotes. An example of this would be if you were querying string variables. Let's suppose that, in your script, a user is allowed to enter a Parcel ID and you want to use a search cursor to find it. Some of the IDs have letters in them while others do not, so each Parcel ID would need to be treated as a string. The SQL expression could look something like this – "PARCEL" = 'B3994NRF'. The expression has double quote marks at the start and single ones at the end. So which ones do we use for the whole expression?

With this example, you can't use a single quote mark style for the whole expression. Instead, the expression needs to be broken down into separate strings. Look at this next example carefully:

ID = arcpy.GetParameterAsText(0)

whereClause = '"Parcel"' + " = '" + str(ID) + "'"

with arcpy.da.SearchCursor(featureClass, (parcelField,), whereClause) as cursor:

...

Note that we have split our SQL expression, the whereClause, into smaller chunks that don't mix up the quote styles. If a chunk has double quotes, like "Parcel", then it will be surrounded with single quotes. Vice versa, if a chunk has single quotes, like =', then double quotes are used to enclose it. In this type of case, it often helps if you add a temporary print statement into the code or if you check that the where clause has been properly constructed using debugging tools. You will also find it very helpful if you can concentrate on the + sign as the separator between each independent part of the string that you construct.

Field Delimiters

In those examples, we used double quotes to surround the field name. This is the right syntax for the two types of data we will use in this part – geodatabases and shapefiles. If, in the course of your daily work, you are using personal geodatabases, you will find that there are multiple delimiters for the field name. For other data types, or to give your script flexibility to take any data type, go to the ArcGIS Desktop Help and look up SQL reference with regards to query expressions.

Using Spatial Queries to Retrieve Records

Using an SQL expression in the search cursor will only ever be useful where attribute queries are concerned. As we mentioned earlier, they can't be used for spatial queries. You could, if you wanted, run a search cursor using an SQL expression on all the counties with the name "Lincoln", but if you wanted all those counties that included or touched on the Arkansas River, you would need to take a different approach. When you want a record subset, based on spatial criteria, you need to use the Select by Location geoprocessing tool.

For this, you need to have some knowledge about the way that ArcGIS works with selections and layers. Let's say that you are looking for all the States with a boundary touching on Oklahoma. Most of the time, there won't be any need to create new feature classes for the States. All you would need to do is maintain the records for those States in the computer memory while an attribute is updated. ArcGIS uses a concept known as feature layers as a way to represent feature class record sets in memory.

A tool called Make Feature layer is used to create a feature layer made up of all or some of the records from a specified feature class. An SQL expression may be applied when Make Feature Layer is run to use attributes to reduce the feature layer records. After that, the tool called Select Layer by Location may be used with spatial criteria to reduce the records even further.

To open a search cursor for Oklahoma and all the bordering states can be done in 4 steps:

1. Make Feature Layer is used to create a layer of all the US States; we will call this layer All States.
2. Make Feature Layer is then used to create a second layer, just Oklahoma this time. To do this, an SQL expression must be applied when the feature layer is made. We'll call this layer Selection State.
3. Select Layer by Location is used to reduce the All States layer from step 1 to the States that border Oklahoma, the Selection State layer from step 2.
4. A search cursor is opened on All States; this cursor has just Oklahoma and the bordering States in it because of the selection that we apply to All States. Remember; the feature layer is nothing more than a record set in memory. You could perhaps call it All States – as soon as a selection is applied, it would no longer have all the States in it.

Look at some example code that will apply to these 4 steps:

 # Selects all the states whose boundaries touch

 # a user-supplied state

import arcpy

 # Get the US States layer, state, and state name field

usaLayer = "D:\\Data\\USA\\USA.gdb\\Boundaries"

state = "Wyoming"

nameField = "NAME"

try:

  # Make a feature layer with all the US States

```
arcpy.MakeFeatureLayer_management(usaLayer, "AllStatesLayer")


# Make a feature layer containing only the state of interest

arcpy.MakeFeatureLayer_management(usaLayer,

        "SelectionStateLayer",

        "" + str(nameField) + " =' + """ + str(state) + """)



# Apply a selection to the US States layer

arcpy.SelectLayerByLocation_management("AllStatesLayer","BOUNDARY_T
OUCHES","SelectionStateLayer")



# Open a search cursor on the US States layer

with arcpy.da.SearchCursor("AllStatesLayer", (nameField,)) as cursor:

  for row in cursor:

    # Print the name of all the states in the selection

    print(row[0])


except:

  print(arcpy.GetMessages())
```

 # Clean up feature layers

arcpy.Delete_management("AllStatesLayer")

arcpy.Delete_management("SelectionStateLayer")

When you use SelectLayerByLocation, you have the option of several spatial operators. The example above uses the operator called "BOUNDARY_TOUCHES" but some of the other operators include "WITHIN A DISTANCE" (which could eliminate a buffering step), "INTERSECT", "CONTAINED_BY", and "CONTAIN" among others.

Did you spot that "row", the ROW object, only returns a single field, "NAME"? We use the index position from the field list to access this, and because we have just one field, the index is therefore 0. The syntax would be row[0]. When the search cursor has been opened on the specified records, any action you desire may then be performed. The code used above prints only the name of the State, but you will probably want to update the values of the attributes or summarize them. Later, we will look at how to write the values for these attributes.

Cleaning the Cursors and Feature Layers

To delete feature layers, we need to use the Delete tool. The reason for this is that a feature layer may lock and maintain that lock on the date and this would stop the data being used by any other application until your script has been executed and is finished. In theory, arcpy does a cleanup at the end of a script but it is best to delete the feature layers manually, just in case they get missed or a crash occurs. In the previous examples, we used an except block that would catch any crashes; the script would carry on and the Delete tool would be run.

A cursor may also lock data but there is no need for explicit deletion of these; the with statement will do the cleanup automatically and this is one of the main benefits of using the data-access module cursors.

Writing Data for Vector Attributes

In a similar way to use a cursor to read the data in vector attributes, we can also use them to write the data to them as well. There are two cursor types for this purpose:

- The update cursor will allow you to edit values from records that exist or deleting records.
- The insert cursor will insert a new record.

Update the Existing Records

The update cursor is used to edit the records that already exist inside a dataset and the steps to use this cursor would be:

We call arcpy.da.UpdateCursor() for the purpose of creating the update cursor. You may, if you want, pass an argument in the form of an SQL expression to the method – a good way to reduce the rows that need editing if you really don't want to edit every table row.

A for loop is used for iteration through all the rows individually

The field values are then modified for the row that needs to be updated

UpdateCursor.updateRow() is then called so the edit can be finished.

Field Value Modification

When UpdateCursor is created and used to iterate through the rows with the variable named row, the field values can be modified through assignments made using row[<field index to be changed>] = <new value>. An example would be row[1] = "Tania Williams".

There is one thing that you must note – the index inside the square brackets, [], used for determining which of the fields is to be modified, is provided with respect the fields tuple supplied at the creation of UpdateCursor. For example, if we were to use this command to create our cursor:

with arcpy.da.UpdateCursor(featureClass, ("Company name", "Owner")) as cursor:

row[0] would be referencing the Company Name field while row[1] is referencing the Owner field.

In the script example below, we are carrying out an operation to search and replace on a table of attributes. For example, let's say that your dataset is representative of local business and that includes banks. One bank has been taken over by another bank, so we need to search for all instances of the name of the old bank and replace them with the new bank name. Using this script, that task could be automatically performed:

#Simple search and replace script

import arcpy

 # Retrieve input parameters: the feature class, the field affected by

 # the search and replace, the search term, and the replace term.

fc = arcpy.GetParameterAsText(0)

affectedField = arcpy.GetParameterAsText(1)

oldValue = arcpy.GetParameterAsText(2)

newValue = arcpy.GetParameterAsText(3)

 # Create the SQL expression for the update cursor. Here this is

 # done on a separate line for readability.

queryString = "" + affectedField + "' = ' + """ + oldValue + """

 # Create the update cursor and update each row returned by the SQL expression

with arcpy.da.UpdateCursor(fc, (affectedField,), queryString) as cursor:

   for row in cursor:

     row[0] = newValue

     cursor.updateRow(row)

Note that we have a flexible script here, having all the parameters in text format. However, because of how the query string has been set up, the script can only be used on string variables. Note that we use quotes to enclose the old value, like "'" + oldValue + "'". We could have tried to handle other variable types, but this would have lengthened the example.

Again, one very important thing to understand is the tuple passed in when the update cursor is created. In our example, we have just one field affected which, for the sake of simplicity, we have called affectedField. In the tuple, it has a position of 0 on the index. As such, we use row[0] = newValue to set the value of the field. There is no requirement to clean up the cursor when the script ends because the with statement will do this.

On the final line, we have updateRow(...) and this is required to ensure that the row we modified is written back to the table of attributes. Note that we need to pass the variable row to updateRow(...) as a parameter.

Dataset Locking

We have mentioned before that ArcGIS will occasionally put a lock on a dataset so that there can be no conflict in editing between two or more users. If you have any reason to believe that a lock is causing problems with one of your datasets, perhaps by stopping you from viewing it or making you believe that all the rows in the dataset have been removed, the only way to remove the lock is to close PythonWin. You can also check to see if ArcMap or ArcCatalog are making use of that specific data in some way. This might be a possibility if you left a data edit session open, if you have the data in an open ArcCatalog Preview tab, or if the layer is within a table of contents within an MXD, or map document that is still open.

New Record Insertion

The Insert cursor is used for adding new records to a table and these are the steps you would take:

We use arcpy.da.InsertCursor() for the insert cursor creation.

InsertCursor.insertRow() is called and a new row may be added to the dataset.

Like we did with the cursor for search and update, the insert cursor can be used in conjunction with a with statement to avoid locking issues.

An insert cursor is a bit different to a search and update cursor in that an SQL expression cannot be used when the insert cursor is created. This does make a kind of sense because, with the insert cursor, all we are doing is inputting new records; it has no need to be aware of any existing records.

When we use InsertCursor.insertRow() to add a new row, the tuple of field values for the additional row must be delimited using commas. These values must be in an order that matches the order of the affected fields value supplied in the tuple when the cursor was created. For example, if you were to use the following to create your cursor:

arcpy.da.InsertCursor(featureClass, ("First name","Last name")) as cursor:

the new row would be added with the values of Simon for "First Name" and Bobbins for "Last Name" using this command:

cursor.insertRow(("Simon","Bobbins"))

The inner set of parentheses is required to convert the values to the tuple which is then passed to insertRow(). If you were, for example, to write cursor.insertRow("Simon", "Bobbins"), you would get an error.

The next script example is creating a new point in our dataset using an insert cursor; this point is then being assigned to an attribute which is a string description. We could, potentially, use this script behind an application that the public can use, perhaps one where a user would click on a web map and write a description of some kind of incident that the specified municipality needs to deal with, like a streetlight that is broken.

```
# Adds a point and an accompanying description
import arcpy
# Retrieve input parameters
inX = arcpy.GetParameterAsText(0)
inY = arcpy.GetParameterAsText(1)
inDescription = arcpy.GetParameterAsText(2)

# These parameters are hard-coded. User can't change them.
incidentsFC = "C:/Data/Yakima/Incidents.shp"
descriptionField = "DESCR"

# Make a tuple of fields to update
fieldsToUpdate = ("SHAPE@XY", descriptionField)
# Create the insert cursor
with arcpy.da.InsertCursor(incidentsFC, fieldsToUpdate) as cursor:
    # Insert the row providing a tuple of affected attributes
    cursor.insertRow(((float(inX),float(inY)), inDescription))
```

Read through this a couple of times and make sure that you understand how the following two things are being done in this code:

- The insert cursor created with a tuple of the affected fields and stored in the fieldsToUpdate variable.

- The row is inserted using insertRow() and variables that contain the new row's field values.

One thing that you should have spotted is that the "SHAPE@XY" string is being used as a way to specify our Shape field. You could, not unsurprisingly, expect this to be Shape, but with arcpy.da, we have a choice of tokens that we can use if the field needs to be specified in a particular way. For our example, we could just give the values for X and Y points with a tuple full of coordinates. The token called "SHAPE@XY" lets us do that. If you want to learn about the other tokens, check the InsertCursor help topic.

If we put it all together, we have a script in which a tuple of the affected fields is created – ("SHAPE@XY", "DESCR"). In line number 14, the descriptionField variable is used containing "DESCR", which is the second column name in element 2 of our tuple. Using a variable to store the column name allows for easy adoption of the script later, for example, where the column may be named differently. When we insert the two, the Simone order is used to provide the item values - cursor.insertRow(((float(inX), float(inY)), inDescription)). We pass a tuple as an argument to insertRow(); this tuple contains another one, (inX, inY) and this is the point coordinates for the floating point numbers for element 1 and the "DESCR" field text as element 2.

Working with Rasters

Up until now, our scripts have only been used to read vector datasets and to edit them. This mostly consists of going through record tables, reading values and then writing them to specific fields. With raster data, things are very different; we have just a series of cells and each one has a value. So, how do we use Python to access the raster data and manipulate it?

To be honest, it isn't likely that you will ever need to use your Python to go one cell at a time through a raster and that really isn't within the scope of this book. What you will do most often is use tools that have already been defined to read and manipulate the rasters. The tools have been carefully designed to do the cell by cell computation for you on a number of different raster types making your job much easier.

Most of the ArcGIS tools that you will use with a raster will be in one of two toolsets – the Data Management>Raster or the Spatial Analyst toolbox. We can use these tools to clip, reject, mosaick, and to reclassify a raster. They can also be used to calculate the slope, aspect, and hillside rasters from DEMs.

In the Spatial Analysis toolbox, there is also a set of tools that allow us to carry out map algebra on a raster. An important part of the GIS site selection is to be able to use map algebra to multiply or link rasters together. An example: you may be looking for a good location for a brand-new restaurant and 7 different criteria need to be met. If a Boolean raster could be created with 0 for unsuitable location and 1 for a suitable location, map algebra can be used to multiply the rasters and to determine which of the cells will meet all 7 criteria and be given a value of 1.

One part of map algebra that could be tricky is in the expression construction. This expression is a string which will lay out what is supposed to be done by the map algebra. In ArcGIS Desktop, there are a number of interfaces that can be used to construct an expression for a single run. What, though, would we do if we needed the analysis to be run multiple times or to be run on different types of dataset? Even using ModelBuilder, constructing an expression that is flexible into the tools for map algebra is going to be somewhat challenging. Using Python, the expression can be manipulated as much and as often as you want.

Let's consider an example. This will take the maximum and the minimum values for the elevation as parameters and, using those values, will then do some magic with map algebra. The expression will find those areas with a greater elevation than the smallest parameter and lower than the largest parameter. Any cell that will satisfy that expression will be provided with a value of 1 because they are suitable. If a cell doesn't meet the expression, it is given the value of 0 as being unsuitable.

What if we don't want to see these values of 0 all over our raster? The script below will eliminate them by running a tool called Reclassify. This has a remap table that is very simple and that states input values of 1 must stay as 1 and 0 is not included in the remap table so it will be given a new classification of NoData:

```
# This script takes a DEM, a minimum elevation,

#  and a maximum elevation. It outputs a new

#  raster showing only areas that fall between

#  the min and the max


import arcpy

from arcpy.sa import *

arcpy.env.overwriteOutput = True

arcpy.env.workspace = "C:/Data/Elevation"


# Get parameters of min and max elevations

inMin = arcpy.GetParameterAsText(0)

inMax = arcpy.GetParameterAsText(1)


arcpy.CheckOutExtension("Spatial")


# Perform the map algebra and make a temporary raster
```

inDem = Raster("foxlake")

tempRaster = (inDem > int(inMin)) & (inDem < int(inMax))

 # Set up remap table and call Reclassify, leaving all values not 1 as NODATA

remap = RemapValue([[1,1]])

remappedRaster = Reclassify(tempRaster, "Value", remap, "NODATA")

 # Save the reclassified raster to disk

remappedRaster.save("foxlake_recl")

arcpy.CheckInExtension("Spatial")

Make sure you go through that script example a few times until you have understood what is happening in every line and spot the following:

We have an intermediate raster – this isn't the final output – that you don't really want in there because it just clutters up the output directory. This is known as a tempRaster and, when the script is executed, you will see this in ArcGIS. When PythonWin is shut down, it will disappear.

There are < and > signs in the expression, alongside the & operator. The expression must be wrapped in parentheses so that the & operator does not get confused.

We have our input parameters using arcpy.GetParameterAsText() and, because of this, the input must be cast to an integer before any map algebra can be done. If inMin was used on its own, for example, '3000' would be seen by the software and it would be interpreted as a string. We need to use int(inMin) to do numerical comparisons; 3000 would then be seen as the number and not as the string of '3000',

We can use map algebra for several operations and math types on a raster; it isn't limited to using "less than" or "greater than". You could, if you wanted, find a raster cosine using map algebra.

If the license manager at your place of work puts a restriction on the number of users for the Spatial Analysis extension, the extension must be checked out and then checked back into the script – note the two calls in the script, arcpy.CheckOutExtension(), followed by arcpy.CheckInExtension(). You are not restricted to passing in the Spatial extension; there are others that can be used as method arguments too.

Our script isn't using arcpy to call the spatial functions. Rather, the functions are imported from arcpy.da import * directly – this is the spatial analyst module – and the functions are also called directly. Note that instead of arcpy.Reclassify(), we have directly called Reclassify().

Look in the Help topics for Remap classes to give you a better understanding of the way we created our remap table. When Reclassify is run, a remap table needs to be created describing how to reclassify old values to new values. The example we used is a very simple one; the help documentation will tell you about more complex remap tables.

GIS Analysis and Practical Python – Modules and Functions

We didn't look at functions yet and this is one of the most basic areas of Python programming that you need to know. In this section, we will look at the functions and the ways they can be used in longer Python scripts.

In a function, there will be just one bit of focused functionality inside a code piece that is reusable. The idea is that the function is written once and called wherever needed in the code. Groups of functions that are related can be placed into a module so they can then be used in multiple scripts. When they are used properly, a function will remove a lot of repetition in the code and the code will then become much more readable and shorter.

Functions are not special to Python; they can be found in many computer programming languages and each language will have its own unique way to define the function. With Python, the def statement is used for function definition and every line of the function that comes after the def statement must be indented. Here's an example of a function written to read a circle's radius and returns an approximation of the circle's area. If you remember your math from school, you will know that area = pi [3.14159..] multiplied by the radius squared [**2]:

>>> def findArea(radius):

...   area = 3.14159 * radius ** 2

...   return area

...

>>> findArea(3)

28.27431

Note that a function may take arguments or parameters, and when we call the function above, the circle radius is placed inside a set of parentheses. The function will return the circle's area – note that we have used something new here, only a return statement.

If you have a circle that has a 3-inch radius and you want the area of it, the function call could be findArea(3) with a return value of 28.27431, which would be in inches.

It isn't uncommon for returned values to be assigned to variables and then used later in the code. For example, the lines of code below could be input to the Interactive Window:

>>> aLargerCircle = findArea(4)

>>> *print(aLargerCircle)*

50.26544

For now, I want you to go to this link. This takes you to a website called pythontutor.com where we will use the visualization feature for code execution to call and execute the findArea(...) function from our example. A browser window will open and the code will be at the top-left of it. Click on the buttons that say Forward and Backward and you can go through the code while, at the same time, see what is stored in memory by Python at any one time, and is shown at the top-right.

The first time you click Forward, the function definition will be read in, followed by the creation of a function object that goes under findArea and is then is accessible globally.

Next, the call to findArea(4) is executed (line 5). A new variable is the result of this, being given the name of the only parameter in the function. That name is radius and it is assigned with a value of 4. This variable is local and can only be accessed from within the code that is inside the function body.

The execution will go straight to the code that starts in line 1 in the function definition.

For the next step, line 2 then is executed and a local variable called area created. This is assigned with the result from the computation done in line 2, taking the local variable value of 4 (the variable called radius).

Next, we go to line 3 where the return statement will set the value of the function return to the value of the area, the local variable. At this point, the value is 50.2654.

When Forward is clicked again, we go to line 5, where we called the function. Because we are going out of the function body execution, the two function local variables called area and radius are now removed. Where the function call was in line 5, we now have the return value instead; in our case, the value has been assigned to another global variable with a name of aLargerCircle. This will appear in memory.

In the last step, the value of 50.2564 that is assigned to that variable will be printed.

What is very important for you to understand is the structures for:

- Going from the function call in line 5 to the function definition code and back.

- The creation of the local variables for each parameter and all the variables that are defined in the body of the function and how they are then discarded when we get to the end of that body. All that remains from and is returned from the function execution is the return value.

- There is no requirement for a function to return a value. You might, for example, have a function with a parameter that is a text file path. That function will read line 1 and then print it to the Interactive Windows. Because all the logic for printing happens within a function, there will not be a return value.

- There is also no requirement for functions to take parameters. You might want to write a function to calculate or retrieve a static value.

Try inputting this in the Interactive Window:

>>> def getCurrentPresident():

...   return "Donald Trump"

...

>>> president = getCurrentPresident()

>>> print(president)

Donald Trump

The getCurrentPresident() function will not take any parameters supplied by the user. It has just one purpose and that is to return the current president's name – you cannot ask it to do anything but that.

Modules

When we place the logic for getCurrentPresident() into a function, what are we gaining by doing so? What was stopping us from defining a simple string of currentPresident and then setting it as =DonaldTrump? The main reason is code reusability.

Let's say we have 15 different scripts. Each works in its own way with the current President name. Eventually, that name is going to change, so this function could be placed into a module file. That file would then be referenced in each of your 15 scripts and, when a new President takes office the name changes and you won't need to open all the different scripts and modify them. Simply open the module, modify one file and all the rest will update automatically.

You should, by now, be familiar with the pattern we use for the import of the arcpy site package at the start of each script. Site-packages can be home to many modules and, in arcpy's case, these have some of the geoprocessing functions in them.

When using Python for GIS work, you will no doubt be writing functions that may be used in numerous script types. These could be used to convert coordinates between projections or to create polygons from coordinate lists. Any of these functions will fit nicely into modules so, if you ever find yourself wanting to make improvements to any of your code, use modules; make one change in the module and it will update everywhere.

Creating Modules

Creating a module requires the creation of a new script and this is done in PythonWin. The script must be saved with a.py extension but all you need in the script are some functions, not an entire script with all the logic in it. The example below shows what a module file might look like; it is just a simple one that has a single function. That function will use a coordinates list to add a points set to a features class.

 # Save this file with the extension of.py

```python
# The function below creates points from a list of coordinates
#  Example list: [[-113,23][-120,36][-116,-2]]


def createPoints(coordinateList, featureClass):

    # Import arcpy and create an insert cursor
    import arcpy


    with arcpy.da.InsertCursor(featureClass, ("SHAPE@",)) as rowInserter:


        # Loop through each coordinate in the list and make a point
        for coordinate in coordinateList:
            point = arcpy.Point(coordinate[0],coordinate[1])
            rowInserter.insertRow((point,))
```

The createPoints function could prove useful in several scripts so it fits into a module very nicely. Notice that we have point objects and insert cursors for our script to work with so arcpy is a requirement. It is also perfectly legal in Python to import a module or a site package inside another module.

You should also have noticed that we import arcpy inside the function this time, not at the start of the module like we have been doing. Performance is the reason for this; the module can be given additional functions later, functions that do not need arcpy. Really and truthfully, arcpy should only be imported when it is absolutely needed, for example if you call a function that needs it.

You will find that the arcpy site package can only be available in the scope of the function. If we were to call other functions from the module, they would not have access to arcpy. Scope is also applicable to any variable that has been created inside the function, like rowInserter for example. Scope is also subject to limits from loops in the function. The variable called point will only be valid in the for loop that is in the function and will not work anywhere else.

Using Modules

How can we use our practice module inside a script? Let's suppose that our module has been saved, by itself, with the name of practiceModule.py. The script below shows how to import that module:

 # This script is saved as add_my_points.py

 # Import the module containing a function we want to call

import practiceModule

 # Define point list and shapefile to edit

myWorldLocations = [[-123.9,47.0],[-118.2,34.1],[-112.7,40.2],[-63.2,-38.7]]

myWorldFeatureClass = "c:\\Data\\WorldPoints.shp"

 # Call the createPoints function from practiceModule

practiceModule.createPoints(myWorldLocations, myWorldFeatureClass)

This script is quite a simple one and is also easy to read. This is because we didn't need to add in all the logic normally required to create a point. Instead the function called createPoints does that for us inside the imported module.

Note, if we want a function called from within a module, the syntax to use is module.function().

Practice

Before we go on any further, it would be a good idea to get some practice in using PythonWin. You can do this by trying the functions listed below. I won't be providing the answers, just do your best with them. You can always look on the internet for help if you really are stuck:

1. Write a function that will return a square's perimeter with one side length provided.
2. Write a function that will take a parameter of a feature class path and will return a list of all the fields contained in that feature class. Have some practice at the function calls and in printing but you shouldn't try printing the list that is inside the function.
3. Write a function that will take two coordinates and will return the Euclidean distance between the two. You can supply these coordinates as parameters in the following format – (x1, y1, x2, y2). To make things a bit more challenging, you could make use of the Pythagorean formula of A**2 + B**2 = C**2 and try using negative coordinates.

The best way to practice is to place the functions in a module and then use another script to see if you can call them. Try using the debugger to go through your code and you should see that it will go between the module and the script when a function is called in the module.

Python Dictionaries

On occasion, when we are programming, we will have large data amounts that we want to be stored. This data will all belong within one variable. Earlier, we talked about lists, one way of storing the data, and so long as you have sufficient memory, you can store as much in a list as you want; using the append() method will let you store more.

There is another way, another type of data structure that lets you use one variable to store complex, large data amounts and it's called a dictionary. Lists are used to store elements in a sequence; access to those elements is dependent on their index position. With a dictionary, the elements are simple key-value pairs; the key part of the pair is used to retrieve the value par. Think of a real dictionary – you look up a meaning (the value) stored under a specific word (the key).

Dictionaries are very useful when mapping is required. In our example, we are mapping English words to their Spanish words; this shows you how to create dictionaries, although it is a very simple example:

>>> englishToSpanishDic = { "one": "uno", "two": "dos", "three": "tres", "four": "cuatro" }

Note the curly brackets; these are used for delimiting our dictionary in much the same way as the squared brackets do in a list. In this dictionary, we have 4, comma-separated, key-value pairs and a colon is used to separate the key and value in each pair. The key is on the left while the value is on the right.

This dictionary stored inside a variable called englishToSpanishDic may now be used to find the Spanish equivalent of an English number, for example:

>>> print(englishToSpanishDic["two"])

dos

If you want to retrieve a value from the dictionary, the variable name is used, followed with a pair of square brackets inside which is the key to the dictionary value. If the same notation is used on the left of our assignment operator, a new pair can be added into the dictionary.

>>> englishToSpanishDic["five"] = "cinco"

>>> print(englishToSpanishDic)

{'four': 'cuatro', 'three': 'tres', 'five': 'cinco', 'two': 'dos', 'one': 'uno'}

We added a new value to our dictionary, "cinco" and this, as you can see, is on the right-hand side of the assignment operator (=) and is stored under the key named "five". If there were already a value stored in "five", the new value would have overwritten it. Did you notice a change in the element order in our dictionary, specifically in the output? The order doesn't matter because we always use the key to access the related value in a dictionary. If we had lots of more pairs in the dictionary, we could use it as a simple translator that would replace each English word in a text with the Spanish equivalent from the dictionary. However, this would give us some strange translations!

Let's move on to something more complex with our dictionaries. This time, we will create an index of books; this index will have the page numbers where specified keywords can be found. We will begin with a completely empty dictionary and iterate, one page at a time, through a book. When we come across a word we consider should be in the index, the word and the page number is put in the dictionary.

We'll start by making a new dictionary, an empty one with the name of bookIndex. To do this, we will use the curly brackets notation, but the brackets will be empty:

>>> *bookIndex = {}*

>>> *print(bookIndex)*

{}

Now, we are going to imagine that we are working our way through a programming book and the first word we want to add is "function" and the first place it appears is on page 1. The page number is the value and it will be stored under the key within our dictionary. However, this is not the only place that this word will appear, so rather than single page numbers as the values, we will store lists that contain multiple page numbers. In our dictionary, we will add a list with a single element of 1 (the page number):

>>> *bookIndex["function"] = [1]*

>>> *print(bookIndex)*

{'function': [1]}

The next word we want to add is 'module' and we first see this word on page 2. We use the same method to add this to the dictionary:

>>> bookIndex["module"] = [2]

>>> print(bookIndex)

{'function': [1], 'module': [2]}

We now have two of our key-value pairs in the dictionary; for each key we have a list. At the moment, each list has just one value in it. Next, we see the word "function" again, on page 4 this time. The code we use to add this number to our "function" list is a little different because there is already a dictionary value in there and we don't want that value over-written. What we do is get the page number list we stored earlier and use the append() method to add the next number:

>>> pages = bookIndex["function"]

>>> pages.append(4)

>>> print(bookIndex)

{'function': [1, 4], 'module': [2]}

>>> print(bookIndex["function"])

[1, 4]

Note that we didn't need to put our list back after the new number was added. The list was stored in a variable called pages and both the dictionary and variable reference the very same list – this means that, when we make a change in the variable using the append() method, the same change is made in the dictionary.

Now we have 2 numbers in our list for "function" and just 1 for "module". You should now be able to see how we can use this process to enlarge our dictionary.

You might also be interested to know that a dictionary can be used together with a for loop. This is to iterate through our dictionary keys and we can use this code to print our dictionary:

>>> for k in bookIndex: # loop through the keys of the dictionary

...   print("keyword: " + k)   # print the key

...   print("pages: " + str(bookIndex[k])) # print the value

...

keyword: function

pages: [1, 4]

keyword: module

pages: [2]

When we added the second number, we made the decision that we needed to do it differently from when the first number was added. But how would this work in code? What we can do is use an if statement and the in operator to see if a value is already being stored in a dictionary key:

>>> keyword = "function"

>>> if keyword in bookIndex:

...   print("entry exists")

... else:

...   print("entry does not exist")

...

entry exists

Assuming the current word is stored in a variable called word, and the number that corresponds to it is stored in a variable called pageNo, the next code example would make its own decision on how new numbers should be added:

word = "module"

pageNo = 7

if word in bookIndex:

> *# entry for word already exists, so we just add page*
>
> *pages = bookIndex[word]*
>
> *pages.append(pageNo)*

else:

> *# no entry for word exists, so we add a new entry*
>
> *bookIndex[word] = [pageNo]*

If we could take the code to the next level, it would also look at whether the numbers list that the if block retrieves already has the new number in readiness for when a word appears twice or more on one page. Think about how this could be done – we won't be going into it here, but it will get your brain ticking over.

Using Python CSV Module to Read and Parse Text

If you really want to be effective at GIS programming, you need to learn manipulation of information that is text-based. We looked at reading data from native ArcGIS formats, like the feature classes, but more often or not, we would be collecting our GIS data in other formats, called 'raw' formats. These include CSV spreadsheets, text files containing coordinates, XML responses and so on.

When you are faced with files like this, you must know whether the GIS software you use already contains the tools that you need or a script that is able to read this data and convert it into a usable format. If you don't have that script or tool, you will have a little work to do in terms of programming to be able to read these files and work out what text you need. This is known as 'parsing'.

For example, take a web service that returns multiple XML lines listing the readings taken from a specific weather station. All you really need from the information are the weather station coordinates and the average annual temperature. To parse these lines, we need to write code that will go through each line and each tag within the XML and isolate the values that we want.

There are a few ways that we can approach parsing. Perhaps the most commonsense method is to determine whether any module exists in Python that will go through the text for you. That module would then need to convert the text into a workable object. We will be starting our journey by looking at the csv module in Python. This module will read values delimited by commas and convert those values to a list.

If there is no library or module that can do this for you, you will need to make use of the method Python provides to manipulate strings. Perhaps the commonly used method is string.split(); this will convert one long string into several small strings based on a specified delimiting character, like a comma or a space. When you need to write a parser, it isn't easy to determine every case that you might encounter. An example of this would be a value file that is separated by commas; it may also contain substrings that have naturally occurring commas, like an address or dates. In a case like this, it is nowhere near sufficient to use a delimiting comma to split a string; additional logic will be needed.

Magic numbers are another downside to parsing, especially when they are used to slice a given number of characters from a string, or to reference a specified column number from a spreadsheet, etc. If changes are made to a data structure, or we try to apply a script to data that is structured differently, we could end up making our code useless, having to 'operate' on it to fix it. If your code is read by others and numbers other than 1 (for counter incrementation) or a 0 (to start a series) appear, those others will want to know where the numbers came from and what they are referencing. With Python programming, any number that is not a 1 or a 0 is classed as a magic number and these should really be avoided wherever possible; if they can't, a comment is needed to explain what the number references.

There are so many different parsing situations that you may come across and we are going to look at the most general approach, which is going through a single module and an accompanying example.

The Python CSV Module

The CSV file, which stands for Comma-Separated-Value, is one of the more common of the formats for interchanging text data. You often find these with tabular data or with data transferring from spreadsheets. Every line in one of these files is representing a dataset row while the columns within the data are comma-separated. A CSV file will often start with a header that has a list of the names of all fields in the file.

Certain programs, like Excel, are designed to read and understand this structure and show all the values in a grid set out in rows and columns. When a CSV file is opened inside a text editor it may not look very pretty, but you should always be in the frame of mind that it is a grid. If we were in possession of a list containing the rows and a list containing the row values in the columns, we could use loops to extract the information we need, and this is where the CSV module in Python proves useful. The best way to learn the CSV module is to work through real examples. We are going to examine a situation where we can get information from a GPS track file using the CSV module.

GPS Track File – Parsing Example

In this example, we will be taking some text that is read from a GPS device. Each file line is representative of a reading from the unit as a user traveled a route. We will start by parsing the coordinates from each of the readings and will then move on to look at another example that demonstrates writing the track to a feature class of a polyline nature.

The file, gps_track.txt, looks a bit like what is shown below:

type,ident,lat,long,y_proj,x_proj,new_seg,display,color,altitude,depth,temp,time,model,filename,ltime

TRACK,ACTIVE LOG,40.78966141,-77.85948515,4627251.76270444,1779451.21349775,True,False,

255,358.228393554688,0,0,2008/06/11-14:08:30,eTrex Venture,,2008/06/11 09:08:30

TRACK,ACTIVE LOG,40.78963995,-77.85954952,4627248.40489401,1779446.18060893,False,False,

255,358.228393554688,0,0,2008/06/11-14:09:43,eTrex Venture,,2008/06/11 09:09:43

TRACK,ACTIVE LOG,40.78961849,-77.85957098,4627245.69008772,1779444.78476531,False,False,

255,357.747802734375,0,0,2008/06/11-14:09:44,eTrex Venture,,2008/06/11 09:09:44

TRACK,ACTIVE LOG,40.78953266,-77.85965681,4627234.83213242,1779439.20202706,False,False,

255,353.421875,0,0,2008/06/11-14:10:18,eTrex Venture,,2008/06/11 09:10:18

TRACK,ACTIVE LOG,40.78957558,-77.85972118,4627238.65402635,1779432.89982442,False,False,

255,356.786376953125,0,0,2008/06/11-14:11:57,eTrex Venture,,2008/06/11 09:11:57

TRACK,ACTIVE LOG,40.78968287,-77.85976410,4627249.97592111,1779427.14663093,False,False,

255,354.383178710938,0,0,2008/06/11-14:12:18,eTrex Venture,,2008/06/11 09:12:18

TRACK,ACTIVE LOG,40.78979015,-77.85961390,4627264.19055204,1779437.76243578,False,False,

255,351.499145507813,0,0,2008/06/11-14:12:50,eTrex Venture,,2008/06/11 09:12:50

etc....

The file begins with the header, telling us what the values in the readings mean. Every line thereafter is a reading and our goal is to come up with a list that has the X and Y coordinates from each of the readings. More specifically, our script must have the ability to read the file and print out text strings like this one:

[['-77.85948515', '40.78966141'], ['-77.85954952', '40.78963995'], ['-77.85957098', '40.78961849'], etc.]

The Approach

Before parsing any file, you should know exactly what you are going to do and how. It helps to split a task into smaller tasks; this is a piece of pseudocode showing our approach:

1. Open file
2. Read header
3. Loop through the header to find the lat and long index position values
4. Read the remaining lines one at a time
5. Find relevant values corresponding to lat and long
6. Write values to a Python list

Before you can do anything, the CSV module must be imported at the start of the script, exactly as you did with arcpy. There is no need for anything special to be imported, just type the following:

import csv

The script must open the file and, in Python, we have a method built-in – the open() method. The method parameters are the file path and how you want the file opened, i.e. read, write. In our example, we are using 'r' to open it in read-only mode. For write, you would use 'w':

gpsTrack = open("C:\\data\\Geog485\\gps_track.txt", "r")

There is no need for the file to have the.csv extension for the CSV module to read it; it can have the.txt suffix so long as the text is in a CSV pattern, columns separated by commas and carriage returns between the rows. When the file has been opened, a CSV reader object needs to be created like this:

csvReader = csv.reader(gpsTrack)

The CSV reader object is similar to a cursor in that the next() method may be used to move forward a line. However, a for loop can be used to iterate through the remaining lines.

Working Through the Rest of the File

We start with the header, a line that is very different from all other lines in the file. It provides the information we need about the names of the fields. Because of that, we need to look at this line somewhat differently from the others. The first thing we do is use the next() method to move the CSV reader to the start of the header:

header = csvReader.next()

This will return a list of each of the items in the header line. Remember; that header is quite a long string, so the CSV reader will chop it into a list, each containing a part that an index number will be used to reference. The delimiter is the default one, the comma. The first part of the header is "type.indent, lat, long" so header[0] has a value of 'type' while header[1] has a value of "indent".

The information we really want is the lat and long values, so we need to note where the lat and long columns are located in the file, i.e. their positions. Using the above logic, header[2] would be used for lat and header[3] would be used for long. What would happen if you had a file where the names of the fields were ordered differently? You would not be very certain that the column with an index of 2 was representing lat, for example.

Using the list.index() is the safest way of parsing; you would request the index position of a specific name for a field, in this way:

latIndex = header.index("lat")

lonIndex = header.index("long")

in our example, latIndex has 2 as a value while lonIndex has 3 but we also now have a piece of code with the flexibility to handle instances where columns are in different positions.

As far as the remaining lines in the file go, we can use a loop to read them. For our example, csvReader would be treated as an iterable list that contains the rest of the file lines. Each time the loop runs, it will take one row and turn it into a Python list containing values. The variable called latIndex is representing the index 2 value, while lonIndex represent the index 3 value. If we have a 2 we would have the latitude, a 3 would indicate longitude. When we have the new values, they can be added to a newly created list named coordList:

 # create an empty list

coordList = []

 # Loop through the lines in the file and get each coordinate

for row in csvReader:

   lat = row[latIndex]

   lon = row[lonIndex]

   coordList.append([lat,lon])

 # Print the coordinate list

print(coordList)

There are two main things to note with this code:

The list, coordList, has multiple mini lists inside one main list. Each mini list is a pair of coordinates that represent longitude (x) and latitude (y) for a single GPS reading.

The method called list.append() adds new elements to coordList. Again, we can append lists that are representing coordinate pairs using the list.append() method.

Below is the entire code for this example:

 # This script reads a GPS track in CSV format and

 # prints a list of coordinate pairs

import csv

 # Set up input and output variables for the script

gpsTrack = open("C:\\data\\Geog485\\gps_track.txt", "r")

 # Set up CSV reader and process the header

csvReader = csv.reader(gpsTrack)

header = csvReader.next()

latIndex = header.index("lat")

lonIndex = header.index("long")

```
# create an empty list

coordList = []


# Loop through the lines in the file and get each coordinate

for row in csvReader:

    lat = row[latIndex]

    lon = row[lonIndex]

    coordList.append([lat,lon])


# Print the coordinate list

print(coordList)
```

Script Applications

At this point, you may be wondering what you could possibly do with a coordinates list. Right now, we still only have raw data that cannot be properly read by a GIS. However, the fact that we have those coordinates in a Python list means that we can easily convert them to formats that can be read as feature class points or polyline vertices. We could send this list to a web service that could reverse geocode it, which means taking each point and locating the associated address. Those points could be placed onto a web map with Google Maps API or other similar programming tools. The applications really are quite endless when you get down to it.

To parse any text, you must first understand the methods for opening files and reading the text, the text structure, the modules that will work with your text, methods for manipulating strings, and so on. In the example we used earlier, a basic text file was parsed, and we extracted the information we wanted and the coordinates stored in a small GPS unit. The CSV module was used to break the readings down and locate the lat and long values. Next, we will look at how to take this information further with polygon datasets.

Geometry Writing

As information of a geographic nature is parsed from text files and other raw sources, you might be thinking about converting it into a format that your particular GIS can read. We will now be discussing how vector geometries are written to feature classes in ArcGIS. We'll use the same GPS text file, but we'll add in another step – we are going to write each of the coordinates to a shapefile of polyline format.

When we talked about insert cursors earlier, we got a bit of experience in how to write point geometry. In review, arcpy.Point() is used to create Point objects and the object is then used in the insertRow() tuple for the "SHAPE@" geometry field:

 # Create point

inPoint = arcpy.Point(-121.34, 47.1)

...

 # Create new row

cursor.insertRow((inPoint,))

Where polygon and polylines are concerned, several Point objects can be created and added to an Array object. That array is then used to make the Polygon or Polyline object. If you use Polygons you should get into the practice of making the start and end vertex the same if you can.

Take a look at the following code example. We are creating an empty array and then using Array.add() to add in 3 points. That array then is used to create the

Polyline object. The first parameter to be passed in with any polyline will be the array that has the polyline points. The second will be a spatial reference to the map coordinates – this must always be passed to make sure that your data is precise:

```
# Make a new empty array

array = arcpy.Array()


# Make some points

point1 = arcpy.Point(-121.34,47.1)

point2 = arcpy.Point(-121.29,47.32)

point3 = arcpy.Point(-121.31,47.02)


# Put the points in the array

array.add(point1)

array.add(point2)

array.add(point3)


# Make a polyline out of the now-complete array

polyline = arcpy.Polyline(array, spatialRef)
```

Normally, you wouldn't even consider the manual creation of points using coordinates that are hard-coded. In fact, you will more than likely capture the coordinates from another source or parse them from a file of some description.

Using a GPS Track to Create a Polyline

We're now going to look at how coordinates could be parsed from a text file created from GPS data, much like the one we looked at earlier. Our code is going to read all the GPS-captured points and add them into a single polyline. That polyline then is written to a polyline shapefile that already exists and is empty. That polyline is named tracklines.shp and contains a system of geographic coordinates. If you didn't have a shapefile already, you could create one using Create Feature Class in your script:

```
# This script will read a GPS track in CSV format and

#  writes geometries from the list of coordinate pairs

import csv

import arcpy


# Set up input and output variables for the script

gpsTrack = open("C:\\data\\Geog485\\gps_track.txt", "r")

polylineFC = "C:\\data\\Geog485\\tracklines.shp"

spatialRef = arcpy.Describe(polylineFC).spatialReference


# Set up CSV reader and process the header

csvReader = csv.reader(gpsTrack)

header = csvReader.next()

latIndex = header.index("lat")

lonIndex = header.index("long")
```

```python
# Create an empty array object
vertexArray = arcpy.Array()


# Loop through the lines in the file and get each coordinate
for row in csvReader:
    lat = row[latIndex]
    lon = row[lonIndex]


    # Make a point from the coordinate and add it to the array
    vertex = arcpy.Point(lon,lat)
    vertexArray.add(vertex)


# Write the array to the feature class as a polyline feature
with arcpy.da.InsertCursor(polylineFC, ("SHAPE@",)) as cursor:
    polyline = arcpy.Polyline(vertexArray, spatialRef)
    cursor.insertRow((polyline,))
```

This script starts the same way as our last one. The header line is parsed to work out what the lat and long coordinates are in the readings. However, we then created an array which holds the polyline points:

```python
vertexArray = arcpy.Array()
```

That is followed by a loop that will read every line one at a time; this will use the lat and long values to create the point object, and when the loop finishes, the point goes into the array.

for row in csvReader:

  lat = row[latIndex]

  lon = row[lonIndex]

  # Make a point from the coordinate and add it to the array

  vertex = arcpy.Point(lon,lat)

  vertexArray.add(vertex)

When every line is read, the loop will terminate and "SHAPE@" is used to create an insert cursor. This is the single element in the tuple that contains the affected fields. The Polyline object creation comes next and this becomes the one and only element in the tuple that is passed to insertRow():

 # Create an insert cursor

with arcpy.da.InsertCursor(polylineFC, ("SHAPE@",)) as cursor:

  # Place the array in a polyline and write it to the feature class

  polyline = arcpy.Polyline(vertexArray, spatialRef)

  cursor.insertRow((polyline,))

Remember; the cursor is going to put a lock on the dataset, so we don't create that cursor until it is really needed, in our case, when the loop is done.

A Look at Multiple Polylines

Let's assume, just for a bit of fun, that your GPS offers the option of marking start and end points for multiple routes. This isn't a practical example so just read along.

Note, in our GPS text file, we have an additional entry – new_seg:

type,ident,lat,long,y_proj,x_proj,new_seg,display,color,altitude,depth,temp,time,model,filename,ltime

This entry is actually a Boolean property and it is used to determine whether the reading will start on a new track. If we have new_seg=True, the current polyline would need to be written to the shapefile and we would need to create another one. Look at this next example and see how it is different from the last one we used – this is to handle several polylines:

```
# This script reads a GPS track in CSV format and

#  writes geometries from the list of coordinate pairs

#  Handles multiple polylines


# Function to add a polyline

def addPolyline(cursor, array, sr):

    polyline = arcpy.Polyline(array, sr)

    cursor.insertRow((polyline,))

    array.removeAll()


# Main script body

import csv
```

```python
import arcpy

# Set up input and output variables for the script
gpsTrack = open("C:\\data\\Geog485\\gps_track_multiple.txt", "r")
polylineFC = "C:\\data\\Geog485\\tracklines_sept25.shp"
spatialRef = arcpy.Describe(polylineFC).spatialReference

# Set up CSV reader and process the header
csvReader = csv.reader(gpsTrack)
header = csvReader.next()
latIndex = header.index("lat")
lonIndex = header.index("long")
newIndex = header.index("new_seg")

# Write the array to the feature class as a polyline feature
with arcpy.da.InsertCursor(polylineFC, ("SHAPE@",)) as cursor:

    # Create an empty array object
    vertexArray = arcpy.Array()

    # Loop through the lines in the file and get each coordinate
```

```
for row in csvReader:

    isNew = row[newIndex].upper()


    # If about to start a new line, add the completed line to the
    # feature class
    if isNew == "TRUE":
        if vertexArray.count > 0:
            addPolyline(cursor, vertexArray, spatialRef)


    # Get the lat/lon values of the current GPS reading
    lat = row[latIndex]
    lon = row[lonIndex]


    # Make a point from the coordinate and add it to the array
    vertex = arcpy.Point(lon,lat)
    vertexArray.add(vertex)


# Add the final polyline to the shapefile
addPolyline(cursor, vertexArray, spatialRef)
```

What you should have spotted first of all is that we have a function in the script. This is called addPolyline and it is, as you would expect, to add a new polyline to the feature class, given these 3 parameters:

- An insert cursor already exists

- An array

- A spatial reference – remember, we said this should be standard practice to keep your data precise.

This function reduces repeat code making the script easier to read:

 # Function to add a polyline

def addPolyline(cursor, array, sr):

  polyline = arcpy.Polyline(array, sr)

  cursor.insertRow((polyline,))

  array.removeAll()

It is absolutely fine to use arcpy in this function; this is because the script that it is in already imports arcpy. However, what you want to avoid is the use of variables that haven't been defined inside the function or haven't been passed in as an argument.

We call the function 2 times – one time in the loop, which is expected, and one time at the very end to ensure the polyline is properly added into the shapefile. This is where functions come into their own, reducing the need to keep repeating code.

As you go through the code line by line, how do you work out if a new track is started or not? First, there is another value in this script that you should be looking for:

  newIndex = header.index("new_seg")

The variable called newTrackIndex will tell us the line position that the Boolean property of new_seg holds. This property is what tells if a new polyline has been started and you might have spotted that later in the code we checked that:

isNew = row[newIndex].upper()

 # If about to start a new line, add the completed line to the

 # feature class

if isNew == "TRUE":

We used the upper() method to convert the string from lower to upper case; this means there isn't any need to worry about the way 'true' is written – it could be true, TRUE, or even True. But there is still one more situation that needs to be handled – the first file line. This should be saying 'true' but the current polyline cannot be added to the file at the moment for the simple reason that there isn't one. So, another check is carried out to ensure that the array contains more than 0 points before that array is written to our shapefile:

if vertexArray.count > 0:

    addPolyline(cursor, vertexArray, spatialRef)

This checks to ensure we have one or more points in the array and then we call addPolyline, passing the cursor and the array in.

We learned that geometrics can be written to the feature classes in ArcGIS through the geometry objects prebuilt into ArcGIS. It is common the create the Point objects, add them to an Array object and then use that object, together with a spatial reference, to create both Polygon and Polyline objects. An insert cursor then is used to assign the array geometry to the geometry field of the feature class, which is normally called "Shape".

You might now be asking yourself how a multi-part feature could be created, for example, the Hawaiian State which contains several islands, or how Polygon which has a 'hole' in it could be created? We need to learn some special rules for the order and nesting of Arrays and Points to create this kind of geometry. That takes us nicely to the next section.

Automation Using Scheduled Tasks and Batch Files

We have briefly talked about how beneficial it can be to use Python to automate your work. It's great to get multiple geoprocessing tools on the go in a row without having to go through the toolboxes manually. How can it be automatic when you have to open PythonWin, open a script, click the run button and so on? In the next section, we are going to take automation to the next level by looking at ways to have your scripts run automatically.

Python Scripts and Your OS

For the most part, we have used PythonWin to run our scripts, but you can run them through Windows. You might have tried, at some point, to run a script by double-clicking on a file with a.py extension. So long as Windows is aware that a.py extension is representing a script written in Python, and that the Python interpreter should be used to run that script, it will run straight away.

You may get a Windows message telling you that the operating system doesn't know what program needs to be used to open the file. Simply browse in the dialog box to the executable which will likely be found in C:\Pythonxx\ArcGISxx.x\Python.exe. Enable the option to "Always use the selected program to open this type of file" and then click OK. Windows will now know to use Python to run.py files.

When you click the.py file, you are telling Windows to run the script. Alternatively, you can use the Windows command line to give that command. All you need to do is type in the command and your wish will be done. We won't go into too much detail about the command line here. All we need to say is that you type cmd into the Windows search box to bring the window up and then type in the Python executable path, as above, followed by the path that leads to the script, as such:

C:\Pythonxx\ArcGISxx.x\Python.exe
C:\WCGIS\yourname\filename\Project1.py

If your script requires parameters, each of the arguments must be delimited using a space. The argument is the value supplied for the parameter of the script. Look at the following example; this is a command that will run one script that has two arguments. Both arguments are strings containing the pathname. Note, the single \ should be used in paths when command line arguments are provided – never use the single / or double \\ as you do with PythonWin:

C:\Pythonxx\ArcGISxx.x\Python.exe
C:\WCGIS\yourname\filename\Project2.py C:\WCGIS\yourname\filename\
C:\WCGIS\yourname\filename\CityBoundaries.shp

If execution is successful, you should only see a command prompt, and nothing else, unless your script is tasked with printing a message; in this case, the message should appear. If your script is tasked with the modification of data or files, you can check them to ensure that the script ran as it should.

The only other time you will see anything on the screen is if the script doesn't run as it should. Sometimes the messages are not helpful, other times they are more helpful than those you see in PythonWin and makes the command line good for debugging purposes.

Working with Batch Files

Why is it important to talk about the command line when we want to talk about automation? You still need to manually open that command window and type your commands in. Well, the good thing is you can also script commands. Several commands can be listed in a text file and these are called batch files. When you run the batch file, all the commands contained in it are run.

Look at the following simple batch file example. It runs the pair of scripts we just looked at. To create the file, you could copy the text from below into a new Notepad file, save it, and ensure you give it an extension of.bat. Keep in mind that we are now talking about command syntax, not Python.

@ECHO OFF

REM Runs both my project scripts

C:\Python27\ArcGIS10.3\Python.exe
C:\WCGIS\Geog485\Lesson1\Project1.py

ECHO Ran project 1

C:\Python27\ArcGIS10.3\Python.exe
C:\WCGIS\Geog485\Lesson2\Project2.py C:\WCGIS\Geog485\Lesson2
C:\WCGIS\Geog485\Lesson2\CityBoundaries.shp

ECHO Ran project 2

PAUSE

Have a look at these notes about this file, beginning from line 1:

We use @ECHO OFF to stop every file line from printing to the command line, the console or window when the file is run. This is standard, and you should get into the habit of adding this as your first line. The exception to this is if you need to see which line is being executed, perhaps if you are debugging.

Comments are added in a batch file using REM. This is the equivalent of the # in Python.

Commands are placed into a batch file using the syntax used on the command line.

ECHO will print to the console, which is useful to use when debugging, particularly when @ECHO OFF is used at the start to stop all lines printing.

PAUSE will give a prompt to "Press any key to continue". If this is not added at the end of the file, as soon as the file is executed, the console closes. Using PAUSE will allow you to see if an error message prints while the file is being run. When the file has been tested and is working as it should be, PAUSE can be removed.

In a batch file, you can have loops, variables, comments, even conditional logic. All of this is outside the scope of the book, but if you are likely to be writing multiple scripts and running them, it is worth taking the time to learn more about batch files.

Task Scheduling

We are not far off full automation here, but we still need to be able to open and run the batch file or script. Right now, we still need to use the command line, click the file, or somehow tell the OS it needs to run it. To get full automation here, we can use an OS utility like Task Scheduler in Windows.

Task Scheduler is a hidden gem in the System tools that you may have otherwise ignored. It isn't a difficult program and it lets you schedule batch files and scripts to run automatically as and when needed. This comes in very useful when you have tasks that need to run regularly enough that manual launching becomes time-consuming. What is even more useful is when the task is quite resource-tense; you can schedule it to run at the weekend or overnight.

Let's discuss a real-world situation where it is important to use Task Scheduler, or some other similar utility. Fast Web maps use map images that are already generated and are cached server-side, making it much quicker to load. Web Map admin uses ArcGIS Server will run a tool called Manage Map Server Cache Tiles to ensure the maps are made before the web map is deployed. Once the map has been deployed, the server will send the correct maps to the users as they look through the Web Map. Sound good so far?

At times, the Source data for a map is likely to change and that means the maps cached on the server-side will be out-of-date. They are only images and do not have the required ability to change as the data changes and that means the cache must be updated on a regular basis. Creating the cached maps takes time and a lot of CPU resources so Task Scheduler is used for this task. This would normally involve a script being written or maybe a batch file that will run the Manage Map Server Cache Tiles tool, along with other necessary tools, on a schedule that runs the script overnight or at a weekend when it is unlikely to have too much impact on Web map users.

Before we move on, let us have a look in Task Scheduler:

1. Open the Start menu in Windows and go to All Programs>Accessories>System Tools>Task Scheduler.
2. Click the button to Create a Basic Task – you will now go through a wizard which will help you set the task up. Don't worry about advanced options, these can be configured later.
3. Name your task something that you will remember and, if you want, add a description. Then you can click Next.
4. Choose the frequency with which the task should run. For now, choose Daily and click on Next.
5. Choose your start time and how often the task will recur and then click on Next.
6. Click Start a Program>Next.
7. Now you need to say which batch file or script is to be run. To do this, click on Browse and go to a script that you wrote; for now, choose one that has no arguments. Click on Next.
8. Review your task information and click on Finish.
9. You should now see that task in the Task Scheduler list. Highlight it and you will see the properties of the task or right-click on it and choose Properties if you need to set them.
10. Wait until your task is first scheduled to run or, if you are a little impatient, right-click and then choose Run. A console window will appear as the script runs and it will close when it has finished. If your script is a Python script and you want the console window to stay open, add something like lastline = raw_input(">") as the last line of that script. The script will stop until the Enter button is pressed. You can take this line out when you are used to the way the script runs so that open windows don't clog your screen up.

Running ArcGIS Toolbox Tools

Sometime down the line, you will be required to use a geoprocessing tool that is not familiar to you. You may never have heard of it, let alone run it from a script or GUI. Other times, you may be aware of the tool, but you may be a little rusty on using Python or you might have forgotten or not know how the parameters should be constructed.

Either way, we use the same approach. Look at these basic steps for running ArcGIS tools with Python:

1. Find the reference for the tool. As you already know, you can get the help topic for each tool by going to ArcGIS help and looking in the section for Geoprocessing tools. Open that topic, read it first, before doing anything else. Make sure you read the section entitled Usage right at the start to make sure you have the correct tool and that it is going to be used properly.

2. Look at the tool parameters. Under the Syntax section, you will see a list of the parameters accepted by the tool. Note which ones are necessary and which are optional and then determine which one will be supplied by your script.

3. When you write your script, you must create a new variable for each of the parameters being used. When you look at the syntax section, you will see a data type with each of the parameters. If you 'String' as a data type, the variable for that parameter must be a string variable.
On occasion, you will find that the data type does not translate very well into a variable. For example, the reference for the tool may say that you need a Feature Class variable and what this is saying is that script requires a string variable that has the path leading to the feature class in it. Another example would be the tool reference saying that a 'Long' data type is required, and this means that a numerical variable must be created, rather than a string for the parameter.

If you are in any doubt about creating the right variable for the data type, look in the Code Sample section of the tool reference. Look for the example script; it should show you the definition of a variable that you are struggling with. Use the patterns in that script and you should be just fine.

You will find that most tools come with great script examples; others may not be so good. If you are in any doubt, run a search on the internet and you should find what you are looking for.

4. Your next step is to run that tool and you will need error handling. Your script may be run in the Interactive Window without using any try blocks or except blocks to catch simple errors. If you don't see anything useful, add the blocks in and then add print arcpy.GetMessages() into the except block.

Map Documents

We have looked at the automation of geoprocessing tools, we looked at the update of GIS data and we looked at how to read text files. What we haven't discussed yet is working with map documents. There are several things that we can do with a map document, all perfectly suitable for automation:

- We can find text in a map/maps and replace it. For example, we could replace Copyright 2017 with Copyright 2018.
- We can repair layers that are using the wrong paths to reference a data source. For example, you may have been using a computer where the map data was in the C:\folder 1whereas now it is on a computer where it is stored in D:\data\folder 1.
- We can print data frame or map series.
- We can export maps to a PDF format and we can join them together, so we have a map book.
- We can make maps available on the ArcGIS server to other users.

Map documents tend to be in binary file format and this means they cannot be read or parsed too easily with the techniques we already looked at. Up until recent times, we had to use ArcObjects to automate any task on a map document, but ArcObjects isn't ideal for beginners and it needs a programming language that isn't Python. With the later version of ArcGIS, we got a Python module that helps us to automate common map document tasks.

ArcGIS Modules – arcpy.mapping

The arcpy.mapping module can be used with map documents in a script and one very important object in it is called MapDocument. This object will tell the script the map you want to work with. To get a MapDocument, a path needs to be referenced in this way:

mxd =
arcpy.mapping.MapDocument(r"c:\data\Arkansas\UtilityNetwork.mxd")

Note that we used r in this code line and this is to tell us that we have a string literal. What this means is that, if r is included just before a string, you can make use of Python reserved characters. An alternative to using a string path would be to use a variable that contains the path. This is more useful when you want to use a loop to iterate over the map documents contained in a folder or where the path was obtained previously in the script with something like arcpy.GetParameterAsText(). Using arcpy.mapping is convenient in the ArcMap Python window because there is no need to add the path leading to MXD. Instead, you can use the CURRENT keyword to retrieve a reference to the MXD that is already open:

mxd = arcpy.mapping.MapDocument("CURRENT")

As soon as you have your map document something must be done with it. Most of the arcpy.mapping functions will take any MapDocument object as one of their parameters. Let's look at a script and see what is happening; comments have been added to help:

 # Create a MapDocument object referencing the MXD you want to update

mxd = arcpy.mapping.MapDocument(r"C:\GIS\TownCenter_2015.mxd")

 # Loop through each text element in the map document

for textElement in arcpy.mapping.ListLayoutElements(mxd,
"TEXT_ELEMENT"):

   # Check if the text element contains the out-of-date text

if textElement.text == "GIS Services Division 2015":

   # If out-of-date text is found, replace it with the new text

   textElement.text = "GIS Services Division 2016"

 # Export the updated map to a PDF

arcpy.mapping.ExportToPDF(mxd, r"C:\GIS\TownCenterUpdate_2016.pdf")

 # Clean the MapDocument object by deleting it

del mxd

In line 1 the MapDocument object is used to reference C:\GIS\TownCener_2014.mxd. We then have 2 arcpy.mapping functions – ListLayoutElements with a MapDocument parameter and a TEXT_ELEMENT parameter which details the layout element type you want to be returned.

The return from this script is a Python list containing the TextElement objects that represent every one of the Map text elements. We use a for loop to look at every element to see its TextElement.text property. The TextElement.text property can be read, and it can also be written; if you wanted to add new text you would simply use the assignment operator (=) as you can see where it says textElement.text = "GIS Services Division 2016". We have used a simple ExportToPDF function which will take the MapDocument and the output path as its parameters

Learn arcpy.mapping

As with many things, the best way to learn arcpy.mapping is to use it. It is a very simple place to practice Python and is a good way to learn how the ArcMap

Python window works mainly because the results of any action can be seen immediately.

ArcGIS and Python Scripting Limitations

We've had a good look at the basics of Python programming and we have delved into Python automation of GIS functions with ArcGIS toolboxes. Scripting provides a great deal of power and you should, by now, be starting to see ways in which you can apply that outside this book. One very important thing we need to discuss is what you can't do with scripting and ArcGIS.

Within ArcGIS, Python interactive is somewhat limited to reading data, writing it, editing map document properties, and running the ArcGIS toolbox tools. While these tools may be useful for some things, they are kind of a 'black box'. This means that you put into them and you get things out of them without having any knowledge about what goes on inside; if you were even concerned about it. If you wanted a better level of control over the way your data is manipulated by ArcGIS you would need to look at using ArcObjects.

Consider ArcObjects to be the bricks and mortar of ArcGIS, a set of Lego bricks if you like. When you program with ArcObjects, you have a huge box of Lego bricks, all different sizes and shapes. By contrast, Python scripting could be thought as being more like a kit project; you have all the pieces needed to make construction easy, but you don't have the choice available that is in ArcObjects.

ArcObjects is incredibly challenging compared to Python scripting because you have so much more available to you in the way of objects and functions. Normally, a task written in a Python script would require many more code lines if it were written in ArcObjects. However, ArcObjects does give you a much greater degree of control over what goes on in the program. One small bit of functionality can be used without needing a tool or all the parameters that are attached to the tool.

Early ArcGIS Interface Customization

So far, we have done little in the way of customization with the ArcMap interface; we haven't added any toolbars, buttons, or anything else to help kick off our programs. All we have done is made a scripting tool and a toolbox. Scripting tools are very useful but sometimes we will want the functionality taken out of the toolbox and placed into a toolbar button in ArcMap. For example, you might want a button that launches a window containing labels, text boxes, and buttons that you make yourself.

With ArcGIS v10.0, you would need to use VBA (Visual Basic for Applications, C++, or one of the.NET languages to place custom programs or functionality straight into ArcMap. It might be a simple matter of putting some customized functionality into a button or you could go further and have an entire program open, one that you developed containing menus, options, forms and more. VBA, C++ and the.NET languages all have their own IDE where custom interfaces can be designed with buttons, boxes, labels and more.

New Functionality

To provide more functionality between a Python script and a user interface in ArcMap, ArcGIS v10.1 brought with it the concept of Python add-ins. These add-ins have the option of attaching Python logic to a small amount of ArcMap actions; perhaps to open a new document, zoom in on a map, click buttons on custom toolbars and so on. An example would be creating an add-in that adds a layer set automatically whenever a specific button on the toolbar is clicked.

Python add-ins provide a selection of elements for Python script front ends. These elements include menus, buttons, toolbars, boxes, file browsing, dialog boxes, and anything else you might expect to see on a user interface. You also have access to common events that you can respond to using your code. This would include a map being opened, the extent of the map changing, a change to the spatial reference, etc. In short, with add-ins, there are many more possibilities than with the earlier ArcGIS versions.

<u>ArcGIS and Machine Learning</u>

We talked about Machine Learning earlier in this book. ML, as it is known, refers to techniques and algorithms driven by data,that automate the processes of predicting, classifying, and clustering data. ML plays an important role in solving problems of a spatial nature, working in many different areas and applications, such as classifying images, detecting spatial patterns, including the problems of multivariate predictions.

As well as the traditional techniques for machine learning, ArcGIS contains a subset of spatial machine learning techniques. These methods, with an incorporation of geographic notations built into the computation, can help us toward a much deeper understanding. More often than not, the spatial component will take form as a density, shape, spatial distribution, contiguity, or proximity measure. Machine learning, both spatial and traditional, play a very important part in spatial problem-solving and, with ArcGIS, we get support in several ways.

ArcGIS Machine Learning Examples

Prediction

Prediction is all about estimating the unknown by using the known. With ArcGIS, there are several techniques for both interpolation and regression that can be used to perform prediction. Applications that this pertains to include home value estimation based on recent data for sales, home and related characteristics for the community, as well as the creation of a surface of air pollution-based n measurements taken from sensors.

ArcGIS Prediction Algorithms

Prediction algorithms in ArcGIS include:

- Areal Interpolation
- EBK Regression Prediction
- Empirical Bayesian Kriging
- Exploratory Regression
- Geographically Weighted Regression
- Ordinary Least Squares Regression

Classification

With classification, we have to determine the category that a specific object is to be assigned to and that is based on a set of training data. In ArcGIS, we have several classification methods at our disposal, all focused on data that is remotely sensed. With these tools we can analyze the values of pixels and configurations that are used to categorize pixels. Examples include identification of areas where the forest is being lost or the delineation of types of land use.

ArcGIS Classification Algorithms

Classification algorithms in ArcGIS include:

- Maximum Likelihood Classification
- Random Trees
- Support Vector Machine

Clustering

Clustering is focused on a group of observation that is based on similar locations or values. In ArcGIS, there is quite a choice of algorithms that will locate a cluster based on one or more locations, attributes or both. These methods can be used to analyze things like areas that have the most activity on social media following a natural disaster or using demographics and socioeconomic characteristics to analyze school districts.

ArcGIS Clustering Algorithms:

Clustering algorithms in ArcGIS include:

- Cluster and Outlier Analysis
- Density-Based Clustering
- Hot Spot Analysis
- Image Segmentation
- Multivariate Clustering
- Space Time Pattern Mining
- Spatially Constrained Multivariate Clustering

As well as all these techniques and methods, we can also use machine learning throughout the ArcGIS platform as a way of selecting defaults that are smart and data-driven for workflow automation, and for the optimization of the results. For example, PCA (Principle Component Analysis) is used by EBK

Regression Prediction to reduce dimensions to arrive at better predictions. Density-based clustering has an OPTICS method that uses machine learning to find cluster tolerances that are based on a reachability plot, and evidence accumulation is a technique used by the Spatially Constrained Multivariate Clustering algorithm to provide probabilities that are related to the results of clustering.

Integration

Machine learning is a very deep and broad field, one that is evolving all the time. ArcGIS is a platform that is both open and interoperable, allowing techniques and methods to be integrated through R-ArcGIS Bridge or the ArcGIS Python API. With this integration, ArcGIS users get the power of solving complex tasks through a combination of tools and machine learning packages, be it TensorFlow, Scikit-Learn, Microsoft AI, and so on, while gaining the benefit from spatial validation at the same time, not to mention being able to visualize the results in ArcGIS and geoenrichment.

Chapter 18: Software Development and Testing

One of the most important parts of Python that you should learn is test-driven development. This is all about creating tests that will test your code, test that it works as it should before you write the proper code. Only when you have run these tests, only when you are completely happy with the results, should you begin to write the real code that satisfies all the conditions in your tests. If you can do this, your code will have been carefully planned to give you the confidence to start refactoring later to enable you to catch errors and bugs as they arise.

Why is this so important?

Over time, software has scaled to the extent that it isn't possible for an entire team, let alone one person, to keep abreast of all the additions and changes and how those changes interact with one another and with the rest of the code. The best way, the only proven method to build software that is reliable, is automated testing. Most of the biggest developmental failures in major software can easily be tracked back to a real lack of testing.

To be fair, you can't possibly know whether your software works or not without testing it. Yes, you can test manually; you could type in some input, click a few buttons, but automated testing is the way forward. There are several different testing types, and rather than just picking one, you should use them all. For example, isolating one function from a program to test it is called unit testing while testing two or more functions together is called integration testing. With user interface testing, you are ensuring that everything is present and correct for user interaction with the software. And, if you are testing a large program, you would be considering the use of things like browser testing, database testing and load testing. The list goes on!

Testing in Python

The culture that surrounds software development in Python is very heavily into testing. Python is what we call a 'dynamically-typed' language which means, converse to static languages, testing is even more important. We'll start by looking at the Integration and the Unit tests.

Unit and Integration Tests

If this is your first time looking at testing, then welcome. You need to understand the importance of testing your code because applications that are not tested make it virtually impossible to make improvements to code and developers of these applications could end up quite paranoid, constantly wondering what will go wrong and when. If you automate the tests on your applications, you can change things safely and know whether your changes are correct or not.

By nature, a unit test is used to isolate and test small code units or single functions. This is done to make sure that the output is as you expect it to be. Many times, because external API calls will be needed or you may need to tap into a database, a unit test can be done on fake data, known as 'mocking' - we will discuss more of this later. When you test fake data, the tests can be much faster to run, but by the same token, they may not be quite so effective, not to mention be far more difficult to maintain. Because of this, for now we are not going to use mock tests; we are going to read to the database and write to it as we need to. Rest assured, you will learn about the mock tests later, just so you know what to expect.

Bear in mind that, when a test touches a database, technically it is called an "integration' test because we are not testing just one unit.

Let's Get Started

In most situations, it won't be easy to work out how and where to start with the testing so one way around this is to consider your application in terms of what it offers the end user. For example:

- An unregistered user must register and sign in before they can use the application.
- Once a user has registered with the application, they will receive a confirmation email – at this stage, they are an unconfirmed user.
- The user may log in to the application but they cannot access it – instead, they will be taken to a page that tells them they need to action the email confirmation first.

- When the user has actioned this confirmation, they will have access to the application; they can see the home page, any content on the application, modify their user details, and log out of the application.

For now, we are only going to write the tests we absolutely need to test these functions. Testing is not easy; rather than writing tests that cover everything, concentrate only on what is the most important. Added to coverage testing (more later on that) we can construct a pretty tough suite for testing purposes.

Setup

The first thing we need to do is activate the virtualenv (remember earlier in the book) and then set these environment variables:

$ export APP_SETTINGS="project.config.DevelopmentConfig"

$ export APP_MAIL_USERNAME="foo"

$ export APP_MAIL_PASSWORD="bar"

Now we can run the test suite:

$ python manage.py test

test_app_is_development (test_config.TestDevelopmentConfig)... ok

test_app_is_production (test_config.TestProductionConfig)... ok

test_app_is_testing (test_config.TestTestingConfig)... ok

Ran 3 tests in 0.003s

OK

All we are doing right now is testing our environment variables and the configuration – this should be the most straightforward part.

If we wanted to expand our test suite, we would begin with a structure that keeps everything organized in a neat order. We'll create a couple of test files, saving them in the directory called 'tests'. We'll call the files test_main.py and test_user.py and then add this code into each of the files:

import unittest

from flask.ext.login import current_user

from project.util import BaseTestCase

#

 # Tests go here

#

if __name__ == '__main__':

   unittest.main()

Part 1: The Main Blueprint

First, we go to https://github.com/realpython/flask-registration to download the necessary files for this project. We will need all the files for Handling Email Confirmation as this is what we will be testing:

https://github.com/realpython/flask-registration/tree/v1/project - click on User and download the code files there.

When we open a hypothetical folder called views.py, located in the main/project folder, and combine it with the workflow for the main user, we would see that we needed to test one thing: the main path, which is /, is requiring that a user is logged in to the application. As such, we would add this code to our test_main.py file we created earlier:

def test_main_route_requires_login(self):

  # Ensure the main route requires a logged in user.

  response = self.client.get('/', follow_redirects=True)

  self.assertTrue(response.status_code == 200)

  self.assertTemplateUsed('user/login.html')

We are making it clear that we have a response code of 200 and that the right template is in use. If we run the testing suite now, we should find that all the tests pass satisfactorily.

Part 2: User Blueprint

In this blueprint, we would find a lot more going on, so we need testing that is somewhat more intensive. What we want to do is test our views and, to do this, the test suite needs to be broken apart. First, we need to create 2 classes – these will ensure that the tests are divided logically.

Open the test_user.py file and add the following code:

class TestUserForms(BaseTestCase):

  pass

class TestUserViews(BaseTestCase):

  pass

Forms

If we have an application based on users logging in, the main concept is around the user registering. If we don't have this, the door is open to a whole heap of trouble. Everything must work exactly as it was designed. So, if we follow the workflow of the user, we would begin with the registration form and the following code should be placed into the class called TestUserForms() that we created with the last code:

```
def test_validate_success_register_form(self):

    # Ensure correct data validates.

    form = RegisterForm(

        email='new@test.test',

        password='example', confirm='example')

    self.assertTrue(form.validate())


def test_validate_invalid_password_format(self):

    # Ensure incorrect data does not validate.

    form = RegisterForm(

        email='new@test.test',

        password='example', confirm='')

    self.assertFalse(form.validate())


def test_validate_email_already_registered(self):

    # Ensure user can't register when a duplicate email is used
```

```
form = RegisterForm(

    email='test@user.com',

    password='just_a_test_user',

    confirm='just_a_test_user'

)

self.assertFalse(form.validate())
```

What these tests do is make sure that the form will do one of two things – pass validation or fail it and this is based entirely on what data is input. Let's look at the file called forms.py in Project/user as a comparison. In the test we performed previously, we registered the same user from the method called setUpClass() from the BaseTestCase that was in util.py.

While we are about the task of form testing, why not do the login form too:

```
def test_validate_success_login_form(self):

    # Ensure correct data validates.

    form = LoginForm(email='test@user.com', password='just_a_test_user')

    self.assertTrue(form.validate())


def test_validate_invalid_email_format(self):

    # Ensure invalid email format throws error.

    form = LoginForm(email='unknown', password='example')

    self.assertFalse(form.validate())
```

Lastly, we will test our form for changing the password:

```python
def test_validate_success_change_password_form(self):
    # Ensure correct data validates.
    form = ChangePasswordForm(password='update', confirm='update')
    self.assertTrue(form.validate())


def test_validate_invalid_change_password(self):
    # Ensure passwords must match.
    form = ChangePasswordForm(password='update', confirm='unknown')
    self.assertFalse(form.validate())


def test_validate_invalid_change_password_format(self):
    # Ensure invalid email format throws error.
    form = ChangePasswordForm(password='123', confirm='123')
    self.assertFalse(form.validate())
```

Ensure the correct imports are added:

```python
from project.user.forms import RegisterForm, \
    LoginForm, ChangePasswordForm
```

Now we can run the tests:

```
$ python manage.py test
test_app_is_development (test_config.TestDevelopmentConfig)... ok
test_app_is_production (test_config.TestProductionConfig)... ok
```

test_app_is_testing (test_config.TestTestingConfig)... ok

test_main_route_requires_login (test_main.TestMainViews)... ok

test_validate_email_already_registered (test_user.TestUserForms)... ok

test_validate_invalid_change_password (test_user.TestUserForms)... ok

test_validate_invalid_change_password_format (test_user.TestUserForms)...
ok

test_validate_invalid_email_format (test_user.TestUserForms)... ok

test_validate_invalid_password_format (test_user.TestUserForms)... ok

test_validate_success_change_password_form (test_user.TestUserForms)...
ok

test_validate_success_login_form (test_user.TestUserForms)... ok

test_validate_success_register_form (test_user.TestUserForms)... ok

----

Ran 12 tests in 1.656s

For these tests, all we did was instantiated our form and then the validate
function was called; this triggers the validation, and that includes any custom
validation, and the return is a Boolean that tells us whether the data in our form
is valid or otherwise. That's the forms done and dusted, we'll move on to testing
our views.

Views

Two very important parts of application security are logging in to the
application and viewing a profile, so these are things that need to be tested
properly:

login:

```python
def test_correct_login(self):
    # Ensure login behaves correctly with correct credentials.
    with self.client:
        response = self.client.post(
            '/login',
            data=dict(email="test@user.com", password="just_a_test_user"),
            follow_redirects=True
        )
        self.assertTrue(response.status_code == 200)
        self.assertTrue(current_user.email == "test@user.com")
        self.assertTrue(current_user.is_active())
        self.assertTrue(current_user.is_authenticated())
        self.assertTemplateUsed('main/index.html')


def test_incorrect_login(self):
    # Ensure login behaves correctly with incorrect credentials.
    with self.client:
        response = self.client.post(
            '/login',
            data=dict(email="not@correct.com", password="incorrect"),
```

```python
        follow_redirects=True
    )
    self.assertTrue(response.status_code == 200)
    self.assertIn(b'Invalid email and/or password.', response.data)
    self.assertFalse(current_user.is_active())
    self.assertFalse(current_user.is_authenticated())
    self.assertTemplateUsed('user/login.html')
```

profile:

```python
def test_profile_route_requires_login(self):
    # Ensure profile route requires logged in user.
    self.client.get('/profile', follow_redirects=True)
    self.assertTemplateUsed('user/login.html')
```

Add the required imports as well:

```python
from project import db
from project.models import User
```

register and resend_confirmation:

Before we write any tests for either the register view or the resend_confirmation view we look at the views file. Note that we are using send_email() from the file called email.py – this will send the user a confirmation email. Now, the question is this – should we send the email, or should we use mocking to fake it? Even if it is sent, we have no guarantee that it will arrive in the fake inbox without needing to use Selenium to load a real inbox in a web browser. We'll choose mocking for now:

confirm/<token>:

```
def test_confirm_token_route_requires_login(self):

    # Ensure confirm/<token> route requires logged in user.

    self.client.get('/confirm/blah', follow_redirects=True)

    self.assertTemplateUsed('user/login.html')
```

The same way as our last two views, the last bits of this one may well be mocked because we need a confirmation token to be generated. However, we could do this simply by going to the token.py file and using a function called generate_confirmation_token():

```
def test_confirm_token_route_valid_token(self):

    # Ensure user can confirm account with valid token.

    with self.client:

        self.client.post('/login', data=dict(

            email='test@user.com', password='just_a_test_user'

        ), follow_redirects=True)

        token = generate_confirmation_token('test@user.com')

        response = self.client.get('/confirm/'+token, follow_redirects=True)

        self.assertIn(b'You have confirmed your account. Thanks!', response.data)

        self.assertTemplateUsed('main/index.html')

        user = User.query.filter_by(email='test@user.com').first_or_404()

        self.assertIsInstance(user.confirmed_on, datetime.datetime)

        self.assertTrue(user.confirmed)
```

```python
def test_confirm_token_route_invalid_token(self):
    # Ensure user cannot confirm account with invalid token.
    token = generate_confirmation_token('test@test1.com')
    with self.client:
        self.client.post('/login', data=dict(
            email='test@user.com', password='just_a_test_user'
        ), follow_redirects=True)
        response = self.client.get('/confirm/'+token, follow_redirects=True)
        self.assertIn(
            b'The confirmation link is invalid or has expired.',
            response.data
        )
```

Add in our imports:

```python
import datetime
from project.token import generate_confirmation_token, confirm_token
```

And then we can run the tests – we should see one of them fail:

Ran 18 tests in 4.666s

FAILED (failures=1)

Why did our test fail? That's simple - there is an error in our view:

```python
@user_blueprint.route('/confirm/<token>')
@login_required
def confirm_email(token):
    try:
        email = confirm_token(token)
    except:
        flash('The confirmation link is invalid or has expired.', 'danger')
    user = User.query.filter_by(email=email).first_or_404()
    if user.confirmed:
        flash('Account already confirmed. Please login.', 'success')
    else:
        user.confirmed = True
        user.confirmed_on = datetime.datetime.now()
        db.session.add(user)
        db.session.commit()
        flash('You have confirmed your account. Thanks!', 'success')
    return redirect(url_for('main.home'))
```

What is this error? What went wrong?

Our flash call has not made our function exit. Because of this, the function goes to the if/else statement and the user would be confirmed regardless of whether the token was valid or not. This is an excellent reason that testing is so important:

The best thing we can do is write our function again:

```
@user_blueprint.route('/confirm/<token>')
@login_required
def confirm_email(token):
    if current_user.confirmed:
        flash('Account already confirmed. Please login.', 'success')
        return redirect(url_for('main.home'))
    email = confirm_token(token)
    user = User.query.filter_by(email=current_user.email).first_or_404()
    if user.email == email:
        user.confirmed = True
        user.confirmed_on = datetime.datetime.now()
        db.session.add(user)
        db.session.commit()
        flash('You have confirmed your account. Thanks!', 'success')
    else:
        flash('The confirmation link is invalid or has expired.', 'danger')
    return redirect(url_for('main.home'))
```

Run all those tests again and everything should pass.

So, what would happen if a generated token were to expire? We would write a test:

```python
def test_confirm_token_route_expired_token(self):
    # Ensure user cannot confirm account with expired token.
    user = User(email='test@test1.com', password='test1', confirmed=False)
    db.session.add(user)
    db.session.commit()
    token = generate_confirmation_token('test@test1.com')
    self.assertFalse(confirm_token(token, -1))
```

Now re-run the tests:

```
$ python manage.py test
```

test_app_is_development (test_config.TestDevelopmentConfig)... ok

test_app_is_production (test_config.TestProductionConfig)... ok

test_app_is_testing (test_config.TestTestingConfig)... ok

test_main_route_requires_login (test_main.TestMainViews)... ok

test_validate_email_already_registered (test_user.TestUserForms)... ok

test_validate_invalid_change_password (test_user.TestUserForms)... ok

test_validate_invalid_change_password_format (test_user.TestUserForms)... ok

test_validate_invalid_email_format (test_user.TestUserForms)... ok

test_validate_invalid_password_format (test_user.TestUserForms)... ok

test_validate_success_change_password_form (test_user.TestUserForms)... ok test_validate_success_login_form (test_user.TestUserForms)... ok

test_validate_success_register_form (test_user.TestUserForms)... ok

test_confirm_token_route_expired_token (test_user.TestUserViews)... ok

test_confirm_token_route_invalid_token (test_user.TestUserViews)... ok

test_confirm_token_route_requires_login (test_user.TestUserViews)... ok

test_confirm_token_route_valid_token (test_user.TestUserViews)... ok

test_correct_login (test_user.TestUserViews)... ok

test_incorrect_login (test_user.TestUserViews)... ok

test_profile_route_requires_login (test_user.TestUserViews)... ok

----

Ran 19 tests in 5.306s

OK

Behavior-Driven Development

Behavior-driven development is what lets us determine how our app behaves and it lets us drive the feature development. It does this by allowing us to add in new tests and to make those tests pass. By being very clear in our description of how our app will behave in multiple situations, we can have the peace of mind that the end product will do exactly what it was developed to do. By following the concepts of BDD, we can build our application up, one piece at a time, while maintaining a living document of the system; this is maintained naturally as the tests continue to pass. By the time this section is complete, you will:

- Have the ability to use the Flask framework to come up with a REST application
- Use the Lettuce library for writing acceptance/behavior tests
- Explain how your tests will be structured, using the syntax for Given, When, Then, And
- Execute your tests and debug them

What You Need

Before you begin, obviously you will need Python on your computer, but you will also need to find and download Lettuce library, Flask Framework, and Nosetests.

Your Project Structure

You are going to develop a RESTful application that will be able to handle the storage of user data as well as being able to retrieve it. To begin with, you will need a directory structure for your filesystem project. You will also need some empty files which will be added later down the line:

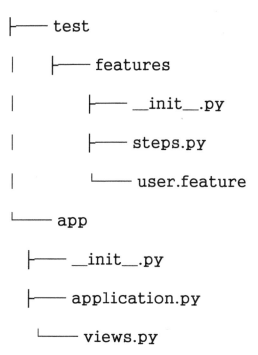

```
├── test
│   ├── features
│       ├── __init__.py
│       ├── steps.py
│       └── user.feature
└── app
    ├── __init__.py
    ├── application.py
    └── views.py
```

These files can be described as:

- __init__.py: marks the directory as a package in Python.

- steps.py: This is the code that the.feature file will execute.

- user.feature: A test that describes what the user endpoint functionality is in the application.

- application.py: The point at which the Flask app gets created and the server is started.

- views.py: This is the code that handles view registration and the response definition for the HTTP requests made to the view.

Creating a Flask Application

For this, you are going to create a web app built on Flask and, using the BDD approach, you will add features later. For now, you just need a basic app skeleton so go to the application.py file and add this code:

from flask import Flask

app = Flask(__name__)

if __name__ == "__main__":

  app.run()

All this code did was create the instance of Flask to begin the development server provided by Flask when the Python file is executed. Provided everything was installed as it should have been, you can open your command prompt, go to the project root and execute this command:

python app/application.py

If you see something like the following, the Flask app is running as it should be and you can continue:

$ python app/application.py

  * Running on http://127.0.0.1:5000/ (Press CTRL+C to quit)

Writing Your First BDD Test

Following BDD testing principles, you can begin by writing a test that provides a description of the basic functionality required in the app. As soon as you have the test in place and it is in failure, you will move on to writing the necessary code that will ensure the test passes.

The Feature File

Open the file called user.feature and add this as line 1:

Feature: Handle storing, retrieving and deleting customer details

All this first line is doing is documenting the functionality is covered by the situations in the file. So, add your first situation:

Situation: Retrieve a customer's details

Again, this is documenting the functionality this situation will test so now you need to add the body of the situation test:

Situation: Retrieve a customer's details

Given some users are in the system

When I retrieve the customer 'Jonathon01'

Then I should get a '200' response

And the following user details are returned:

| name |

| Jonathon Simpson |

This test is using a standard keyword set known as gherkin – Given, When, Then, And. The syntax is what gives your test its structure and it will usually follow this pattern:

- **Given** – initialization/setup of the test situation conditions. You could, for example, prime a few mocks so they return either an error response or a successful response. In the test detailed above, we are making sure that we have registered users so that the system can be queried.

- **When** – the action that is being tested, such as a GET request to the application endpoint.

- **Then** – the expectations you want from the test; you are, in the test above, for example, expecting to get a web app response of a 200 status code.

- **And** – lets you continue from the Then keyword. If the last statement started with the keyword When and the following line starts And, the And line is also going to be treated as a When.

There is one more important thing you need to note – the style the test is written in and the way that it reads. Your situations need to be as easy to read as possible and they must also be reusable. Anyone who reads them must be able to see exactly what this test is doing, what functionality is being tested and how it should behave. Your steps should be as reusable as they possibly can be, eliminating the need to keep rewriting code as well as maintaining consistency across the suite of tests.

You can now use Lettuce to execute the user.feature file and this is done from your project's root directory. This command is executed at the command prompt:

lettuce test/features

The output should be something like this:

```
$ lettuce test/features/
```

Feature: Handle storing, retrieving and deleting customer details #
test/features/user.feature:1

  Situation: Retrieve a customer's details   #
test/features/user.feature:3

    Given some users are in the system   #
test/features/user.feature:4

    When I retrieve the customer 'Jonathon01'   #
test/features/user.feature:5

    Then I should get a '200' response   #
test/features/user.feature:6

    And the following user details are returned: #
test/features/user.feature:7

   | name |

   | Jonathon Simpson |

1 feature (0 passed)

1 situation (0 passed)

4 steps (4 undefined, 0 passed)

Notice that the tests have failed but you should have expected no different; your
code has not yet been written so the feature file has nothing to execute. Define
the code for execution in steps and the Lettuce output does its best to put n the

right path by providing a steps outline – all you need to do is complete the steps in executable Python code. Consider each of the steps to be an execution instruction to Lettuce and those steps will be matched by Lettuce to the proper code for execution.

Steps Definition

Beneath the feature file are the steps; these are nothing more than code written in Python along with some regular expressions that will give Lettuce what it needs to match the feature file lines with the step for execution. To start with, you need the steps.py file and you will add these Lettuce library imports:

from lettuce import step, world, before

from nose.tools import assert_equals

What you need to note are the Lettuce imports. These are what allow the steps to be defined, and the values for the steps stored on the object called world. You also need to note that the nose test library imports will allow you to make better assertions in the tests.

You now need to add what Lettuce calls a hook. This will be a step called @before.all and it will execute the given code before every situation. This code block will be used to create an instance of the test client built into Flask and this will let you put requests into your application just as if you were a proper client. So, open the steps.py file and input this code, not forgetting the import statement near to the top:

from app.application import app

@before.all

def before_all():

  world.app = app.test_client()

Now we have our test client sorted out, we can go ahead with the definition of the first step, the line that starts with "Given".

from app.views import USERS

@step(u'Given some users are in the system')

def given_some_users_are_in_the_system(step):

  USERS.update({'Jonathon01': {'name': 'Jonathon Simpson'}})

What this step is doing is adding a section of test data to the dictionary that is in memory. For your purposes, this dictionary will act as if it were a real system database. Note that you are importing code out of the application – this must now be added. An in-memory data store called USERS will act as a real application database so, now, you can add the code for USERS to our views file:

USERS = {}

Now that you have this, the next step can be defined. This step will call the application with the intention of retrieving user details. The response from the call will be stored in the Lettuce-provided object called world. The world object gives you the ability to save your variables and these are then accessible across the steps – without this object, this couldn't be done or, if it could, your code would end up very messy. Open steps.py and add this code:

@step(u'When I retrieve the customer \'(.)\'")*

def when_i_retrieve_the_customer_group1(step, username):

  world.response = world.app.get('/user/{}'.format(username))

With this definition, have you spotted that a capture group is used within the regular expression? This is how variables are passed in and also allows you to reuse the steps that were discussed earlier. This makes your behavior tests far more flexible and significantly more powerful. When capture groups are used, they are passed automatically by Lettuce as arguments to the method – in your code, this is named username. There are no limits on the number of variables in your definition.

The next thing to do is add the initial assertion step. This is going to check the application response for a status code and this code needs to be added to the steps.py file:

@step(u'Then I should get a \'(.)\' response')*

def then_i_should_get_a_group1_response_group2(step, expected_status_code):

   assert_equals(world.response.status_code, int(expected_status_code))

You are using the assertion that you imported from the assert_equals library from nosetests. This will take two arguments and will check them against one another to see if they are equal. Again, you are placing the status code you expect to get into a variable using a capture group. On this occasion, you should have an integer as your variable, so the type may be converted before the status code the application returned is compared to it.

Lastly, you must have a step to check that the returned data from the application is as it was expected to be. This definition is an excellent example of why there is support in Lettuce to pass data tables into the definitions – this is perfect for this example because you may end up a with a lot of data and using a table ensures that you can easily read what you expect to see. Open steps.py and add this last step:

@step(u'And the following user details are returned:')

def and_the_following_user_details(step):

   assert_equals(step.hashes, [json.loads(world.response.data)])

As you can see, when a data table is passed in, you can use the step object stored under hashes to access it. This is nothing more than a list of the dictionaries for each table row. A JSON string will be returned, a dictionary listing the name key to the name of the user. As such, your assertion will load a string into a dictionary; that is, the string returned by the application and then it is wrapped in a list making it equal to what is expected.

Execution

Now you have the steps you need, together produces a description of the functionality you expect your application to have, it's now time to execute your test; it should fail. As before, open the command prompt and execute this code:

lettuce test/features

We should see the following when the test fails, as it should do:

$ lettuce test/features/

Feature: Handle storing, retrieving and deleting customer details # test/features/user.feature:1

  Situation: Retrieve a customer's details   # test/features/user.feature:3

    Given some users are in the system   # test/features/steps.py:17

    When I retrieve the customer 'Jonathon01'   # test/features/steps.py:22

    Then I should get a '200' response   # test/features/steps.py:27

    Traceback (most recent call last):

      [SNIPPET REMOVED FOR READABILITY]

    raise self.failureException(msg)

AssertionError: 404!= 200

And the following user details are returned: #
test/features/steps.py:32

  | name |

  | Jonathon Simpson |

1 feature (0 passed)

1 situation (0 passed)

4 steps (1 failed, 1 skipped, 2 passed)

List of failed situations:

  Situation: Retrieve a customer's details   #
test/features/user.feature:3

Right now, you have a 404 Not Found error response and this is because you do
not have the URL/user/<username> defined just yet; this is what the test wants
to access and it can't. To make this right, to ensure that the test passes and you
get what you expect, what was described in the behavior test, open views.py and
add this code:

GET = 'GET'

@app.route("/user/<username>", methods=[GET])

def access_users(username):

```
if request.method == GET:

    user_details = USERS.get(username)

    if user_details:

        return jsonify(user_details)

    else:

        return Response(status=404)
```

First, the new URL is registered in /user/<username> - the <> are telling Flask that it should capture whatever comes after the / and put it into a variable with the name of username. The method is then defined to handle requests to the URL; in this, a statement is made that the only requests that can be made to the URL are GET requests. Next, check to see if the received request is a GET request and, if yes, attempt to get the username details as provided by the data store called USERS. If you find those details, the response is a status code of 200 and a JSON string listing the details of the user; if no, you get a 404 Not Found error response.

Go to your command prompt, execute your tests once more and they will all pass:

```
$ lettuce test/features/
```

Feature: Handle storing, retrieving and deleting customer details # test/features/user.feature:1

  Situation: Retrieve a customer's details   # test/features/user.feature:3

    Given some users are in the system   # test/features/steps.py:17

When I retrieve the customer 'Jonathon01'   # test/features/steps.py:22

Then I should get a '200' response   # test/features/steps.py:27

And the following user details are returned: # test/features/steps.py:32

  | name |

  | Jonathon Simpson |

1 feature (1 passed)

1 situation (1 passed)

4 steps (4 passed)

You now have the exact functionality that your behavior test described, and you can go to another situation; repeat these steps for each situation to ensure they all pass. This is, as you might have guessed, a cycle of iteration.

Behavior-driven development is one of the best testing procedures to follow, no matter whether you are part of a large enterprise working on an application or a single developer working on a smaller application. With BDD, you can make sure that your code does exactly what you want it to do before you write the actual code. With BDD, you also have the benefit of gaining what is called "living documentation" that is updated as your tests are maintained and new functionalities are delivered.

Pytest

Pytest is one of the easiest testing tools to use because it offers simplicity. In this section, we will acquaint you with the basics of pytest and you can then go on to do your own homework and learn how to use it for complex testing purposes, a task that pytest is more than capable of doing.

What You Need

You will need Python 3 and a virtualenv which you will create now using the support built-in to Python 3. Open your command prompt and run these commands:

mkdir pytest_project

cd pytest_project

python3 -m venv pytest-env

You now have a virtual environment with the name of pytest-env and it has been saved to your current working directory.

Now you must activate the virtual environment like this:

source pytest-env/bin/activate

Provided you have an active virtualenv working, any packages will be installed there rather than the Python installation. Begin by installing pytest:

pip install pytest

Basic Usage of Pytest

You are going to start by building a simple test. Python will want to find any tests that are written in files that start test_ or finish _test.py. The file you are going to create will be named test_capitalize.py and it will contain a function by the name of capital_case. The argument to this function must be a string and the return should be a version of that string in capitals. Alongside this, you will be writing a test called test_capital_case to make sure your function does what you want it to do. The test function is prefixed with test_ because pytest will expect this:

 # test_capitalize.py

```
def capital_case(x):

    return x.capitalize()
```

```
def test_capital_case():

    assert capital_case('semaphore') == 'Semaphore'
```

The first thing you should notice is that a vanilla assert statement is used by pytest – you can remember these a lot easier and you will find them very easy to use.

Running the test is done with the pytest command:

pytest

You should see a pass for the test.

Now, if you were really up on Python and knew your code back to front, you would have spotted something. You could end up with a bug in this code because there is nothing in place to check whether the argument type is a string as it should be. So, if a number were passed in as the function argument, an exception would be raised.

How is this handled? You do it inside the function and you raise a custom exception that shows a user a nice error message. Let's see if you can capture it in the test:

```
# test_capitalize.py
```

```
import pytest
```

```
def test_capital_case():

    assert capital_case('semaphore') == 'Semaphore'


def test_raises_exception_on_non_string_arguments():

    with pytest.raises(TypeError):

        capital_case(9)
```

There is a big addition to this code – pytest.raises, which is a helper that will assert a TypeError is to be raised by the function should you have anything other than a string as the argument. Right now, running those tests should result in a fail with an error:

```
def capital_case(x):

    return x.capitalize()
```

E   AttributeError: 'int' object has no attribute 'capitalize'

You have already verified that this case has not been handled so you can do something about fixing it.

In the function called capital_case, you need to make sure that you have a string or, at the very least, a string subset as the argument before the capitalize function is called. If you don't have that string, a TypeError must be raised with your custom message:

```
# test_capitalize.py


def capital_case(x):

    if not isinstance(x, str):

        raise TypeError('Please provide a string argument')
```

return x.capitalize()

Now, when the tests are rerun, they should pass.

The first of your test functions uses the fixture called empty_wallet. This gives your test a wallet instance that has a 0 balance. The three tests that follow this are all given a wallet instance with equal balances of 20. And your last test is given the fixture called empty_wallet. This fixture is then used by your tests just as if the creation of the fixture had happened in the test function, just like before.

Now you can run your tests again and see if everything is working as it should be.

Using fixtures is a good way of reducing duplication of code. If you spot in any of your code a place where one piece of code is used over and over again in several tests, you could consider using a fixture.

Test Fixture Pointers

Look at a few pointers to use these text fixtures:

- Each of the tests is given a Wallet instance that is freshly initialized; they will never use an instance that has already been used elsewhere.

- Try, where you can, to give your fixtures docstrings. If you want to know what all the fixtures available are, run this command:

pytest --fixtures

Running this will give you a list of some of the pytest fixtures built into Python, as well as the custom fixtures that were created. You will see the docstrings as fixture descriptions:

- wallet – a wallet instance is returned with a value of 20 as the balance
- empty_wallet – a wallet instance is returned with a value of zero as the balance

Parametrized Test Functions

Now that you have run tests on the Wallet class method on an individual basis, you can move on and test several combinations of all the methods. This will answer some questions, like "If I start with a balance of 25, spend 15, add 75 and then add a further 50, what should my balance be?"

I'm sure you would agree that writing that as a test would not only be time-consuming, it would be somewhat tedious as well. That is where Python comes to the rescue with parametrized test functions.

If you wanted to capture something like the situation above, you would write your test like this:

```
# test_wallet.py


@pytest.mark.parametrize("earned,spent,expected", [

    (30, 10, 20),

    (20, 2, 18),

])
def test_transactions(earned, spent, expected):

    my_wallet = Wallet()

    my_wallet.add_cash(earned)

    my_wallet.spend_cash(spent)

    assert my_wallet.balance == expected
```

Using this test, you can test a number of different situations using just one function. The decorator called @pytest.mark.parametrize is used to specify the names of those arguments that the test function takes, along with the arguments that go with the names.

The test function that has the decorator then is run one time for each of the parameter sets. For example, the first time the test is run, there is an earned function with a value of 30, a spent parameter with a value of 10 and an expected parameter with a value of 20. On the second test, the second argument set is given to the parameters and then those parameters are used in the test function. This helps to capture your situation nicely:

- The wallet has an initial value of 0

- 30 cash units are added

- 10 cash units are spent

- The balance should now be 20

This is a nice way of testing multiple combinations without needing to write repetitive code.

Parametrized Test Functions and Test Fixtures Together

So that we can remove some of the repetitiveness from the tests, we can go even further and combine the parametrized test functions with the test fixtures. We can do this by taking the initialization code for the wallet out and putting in a test fixture, much like we *did earlier. The result will be:*

 # test_wallet.py

@pytest.fixture

def my_wallet():

   '''Returns a Wallet instance with a zero balance'''

   return Wallet()

```python
@pytest.mark.parametrize("earned,spent,expected", [

    (30, 10, 20),

    (20, 2, 18),

])

def test_transactions(my_wallet, earned, spent, expected):

    my_wallet.add_cash(earned)

    my_wallet.spend_cash(spent)

    assert my_wallet.balance == expected
```

A new fixture with a name of my_wallet is created; this is identical to the earlier empty_wallet fixture. A wallet instance is returned with a 0 balance and to use the parametrized functions and the test fixtures together, the fixture is included as the initial argument, with the parameters as the other arguments.

We then perform the transactions on the function-provided wallet instance.

Now it's time to turn our attention to what we talked about earlier – automated testing.

Automated Testing

If you want to write software that is reliable and that works, you need to learn about automated testing. There really is only so far that you can go with manual testing and, to be fair, testing manually is never going to be as thorough as a machine can do it. We won't go into details about individual testing techniques or tool; rather we will try to get you into the mindset of thinking of automated testing as something that can be applied regardless of the project you are doing. We will attempt to give you a foundation you can work with when you need to move away from developing software and into broad automated testing, whether you are a solo developer or working for an organization.

So, what are automated tests for? In the same way as your manual tests, automated tests are designed to test that your software does exactly what it is meant to do. Okay, so this is a pretty vague definition, but it is reflective of just how many ways there are to verify what your software is doing:

- We can call functions on known inputs and use assert to see if the result is what we expect;
- We can set up a dummy website and make sure that the pages work as they should, that basic operations are performed properly and that the systems behind the website work;
- We can chuck loads of random data and inputs at the system to see what, if anything, will make it crash;
- We can compare our program behavior against that of reference implementations that are known to be good to make sure they behave the same way.

Did you spot anything there? We didn't mention integration or unit testing once! Why? Because on almost every occasion, neither of those will be your end goal. With automated testing, we want tests that will run automatically, to test the entire system, doing whatever is necessary, to see that it all works. Unit tests and integration tests are just one small part of the whole picture, just one tiny consideration in the ways we approach testing. Let's discuss these a bit more.

Unit Tests vs Integration Tests

When we work on automated tests there are three main arguments that always come to light:

- Are we writing integration tests or unit tests?
- Should we write integration tests or unit tests?
- How are integration tests and unit tests meant to be defined?

We could go on ad infinitum about how many correct ways there are to tell the difference between an integration test and a unit test and every way is different. There are rules, such as:

- A unit test must be done wholly within one process
- A unit test may not execute code from any more than one file and all imports should be mocked
- A unit test is any test that doesn't cross over the boundary between the client and server.

There is a real lack of perspective here. The reality is, the point where the line is drawn is arbitrary. Every system, every piece of code that you write is, in fact, a unit that is an integration of multiple smaller units:

- Clusters integrate several virtual or physical machines
- A physical or virtual machine integrates several different processes
- A process integrates several subprocesses, such as workers, databases, etc.
- Subprocesses integrate several modules
- Modules or packages integrate several small modules
- A module integrates functions that are all individual
- A function uses simple arithmetic to integrate primitives, i.e. Ints

Everything is a unit that can be tested, and every unit is an integration of multiple other units. That is the way all software can be broken down, now and in the future.

Automated testing is done to make sure your software behaves as it should; that software will contain code at every one of those hierarchical levels mentioned above. And every single piece of that code must be tested and verified by you.

To keep things simple, if a piece of code is low in that hierarchy, such as a function that integrates primitives, we will call it a unit test and, if it is higher, like the cluster that integrates the machines, we will call it an integration test. This is purely for the purposes of this part of the book – please don't take it that this is what they really are!

The most important thing is that you are aware of how your code breaks down in terms of that hierarchy and that you can have automated tests at each and every level. However, there is a distinction in the properties that each type of test has:

Unit Tests	Integration Tests
Low hierarchy	High hierarchy
Speedy	Not so fast
Reliable	A little more unreliable
Not much setup needed	Loads of setup!
Not many dependencies	A lot of dependencies
Not many modes for failure	Many more failure modes
Failure messages are specific	Failure messages are generic

In short:

- A unit test will be faster because there is less code to run
- A unit test will be more reliable because less code means fewer failures that can't be determined
- Unit tests don't need much setting up because they don't have so many dependencies
- When a unit test fails, it tends to be more specific and have fewer causes; with an integration test, you may get broad, generic failures that are pretty meaningless and have multiple causes.

So, as a person who is going to start writing tests, what does all of this mean?

What it really means is, it is down to you as the writer to define the distinction between integration and unit tests. Much depends on what the tests are for. For example, if you are testing a website, it will define unit and integration tests differently from, let's say, an algorithm library and this, in turn, will have a different definition than a system designed for cluster deployment.

- An algorithm library sees the unit tests as those that run a single function on the smallest of inputs while it may see the integration tests as using several functions to build algorithms.

- A website may see the unit tests as any test that doesn't go near the HTTP API while an integration test would.
- A website may also see a unit test as being any test that doesn't load a browser while the integration tests would open a browser and use Selenium for server interaction through JavaScript.
- A system for cluster deployment may see a unit test as any test that does not result in the physical creation of a virtual machine and that would include those that use database access or the HTTP API, while an integration test would be seen as one that uses a staging environment to open a cluster.

While there may be differences in speed, reliability, and so on, at the end of the day, all the different systems will use tests that may be more or wholly unit or more or wholly integration. As such, it is down to you to draw that line and then build your test practices using that line. In short, there is no real classification of what a unit or an integration test is because there is too wide a range of projects for classification to mean anything.

Hierarchical Testing

Each separate bit of software is written in a hierarchical manner as individual units integrating multiple small units. It is possible, at every level of that hierarchy, for a programmer to do something wrong. Ideally, whatever mistakes are made would be caught by an automated test. So, don't take any notice of the restrictive rules that state only integration tests or only unit tests should be written:

- You can't write only integration tests because, although the theory suggests it will work, if only because the code higher up in the hierarchy will exercise the lower code, you would require many integration tests to exercise enough cases. For example, if you needed to check the behavior of one function with 8 primitive argument sets, you would end up setting the application process up and tearing it all down no less than 8 times, a huge waste of time and resources.
- You can't write only unit tests because, regardless of how much you test a function, it won't matter if the functions are combined wrongly by the

module or if each module is used wrongly by the application process. Having a suite of tests is a good idea if each test is fast but if it misses the bugs that come in at the higher levels, it's of no use.

What you need is a test structure that mirrors as closely as possible the way your software is structured. You need to be able to test every level of the hierarchy in relation to how much code is there and the likelihood of it being wrong. Only then can you have some safeguard against errors being introduced.

Prioritizing Your Tests

With the automated tests, there are two purposes to serve – ensuring that you don't already have broken code that couldn't be detected through manual tests, and, ensuring the code that works cannot break in the future. The broken code may be a result of an implementation that wasn't complete; the reasons why a code may break in the future would be down to mistakes through the evolution of the codebase.

As such, there is no sense in having a set of automated tests for any code that is working (not broken), code where it is not important if it breaks, or code that is more likely to be long gone before anyone has the chance to break it.

It is far more of an art than it is science to determine the amount of testing needed on a specific code or system, but you could use these guidelines to help you:

- If something is important, it must be tested heavily. For example, if you have a system of passwords and authentication, it needs heavy tests to make sure bad passwords cannot be used, whereas some of the other random logic may not need so much testing.
- If something isn't quite so important, you must decide whether it needs little testing or even no testing. If it doesn't matter if a small part of your website doesn't get uploaded for a day or two, you could even consider small manual tests rather than the expense of automated testing.
- If you have code that is being actively developed, it must be tested over and over but if your code is no longer being developed, it won't need so

much testing. If you have a piece of code that has not been touched for some time, if it wasn't broken then, it isn't likely to break now. You might want to run a small test to make sure it hasn't broken but you won't need to run the tests that stop it breaking in the future.

- If an API is not going to disappear, it will need more testing than an API that has a chance of disappearing. Focus your real efforts on the parts of your interface that are stable; leave the unstable code until later or leave it alone altogether. Together with the previous guideline, you will see that the code that needs the most testing is undergoing development, but its API is stable.

- If your code is complex in odd places, such as browser-server, inter-process, etc., ensure that this logic is tested regardless of how awkward it may be. Don't stick with testing the easy stuff and ignoring the rest; it matters not if each function is through tested if the glue that holds them together doesn't work.

Tests Are Just Code

Writing a test is no different from writing a piece of code. Your testing suite is just a little bit of software that makes sure the main software works correctly. As such, test code is to be treated in the same way as any other software:

- You should refactor common testing logic into helpers. If you have a bug in any of this test logic, it is far better to fix it in just one place than have to keep going through loads of code to fix it.

- Your test code must be up to the same standard that your normal code has been written in; correct naming, correct formatting, comments added in, properly organized code, inline-docs, the correct style of coding and convention.

- In order to maintain the quality of the code, your tests must be refactored. All code has the potential to get a little bit messed up and, as it gets bigger, it will get harder to handle. As such you must refactor regularly, so that things stay neat, organized and follow the DRY principles (Don't Repeat Yourself) and the same applies to your test code.

- You must have a test suite that is flexible and agile. If you are testing an API that changes, your tests must be written in a way that they too can change quickly. If some code is deleted, you should remove the corresponding test and, if you should rewrite a piece of code, you should be able to rewrite your tests accordingly. Using the correct fixtures, helpers, and abstractions will ensure that this becomes an easy job.

- And that leads to this – if those fixtures, abstractions and helpers themselves start to become complex, then they too must be tested, if only to a minimal level.

Not everyone is going to agree with all these; some may be of the opinion that tests are not the same as standard code. You may believe that it is better to have a type of copy and paste test code rather than using helpers and abstractions to follow the DRY principles. How you see things is entirely up to you but there is no denying one thing – when you write a test, you are writing computer code.

DRY Tests, Data-Driven

Because tests are just code, and code should always be DRY and must be factored so that we can only see the logic that is truly necessary; we also shouldn't have too much repetitive code. An example would be the definition of a test-helper that allows multiple test cases to be put through the testing suite to easily see which inputs are being tested. For example, look at this piece of test code:

// Sanity check the logic that runs when you press ENTER in the REPL and

// detects whether a set of input lines is...

//

// - Complete, and can be submitted without needing additional input

// - Incomplete, and thus needs additional lines of input from the user

def test1 = {

```scala
  val res = ammonite.interp.Parsers.split("{}")

  assert(res.isDefined)

}

def test2 = {

  val res = ammonite.interp.Parsers.split("foo.bar")

  assert(res.isDefined)

}

def test3 = {

  val res = ammonite.interp.Parsers.split("foo.bar // line comment")

  assert(res.isDefined)

}

def test4 = {

  val res = ammonite.interp.Parsers.split("foo.bar /* block comment */")

  assert(res.isDefined)

}

def test5 = {

  val res = ammonite.interp.Parsers.split(

    "val r = (1 until 1000).view.filter(n => n % 3 == 0 || n % 5 == 0).sum"

  )

  assert(res.isDefined)

}
```

```scala
def test6 = {

  val res = ammonite.interp.Parsers.split("{")

  assert(res.isEmpty)

}

def test7 = {

  val res = ammonite.interp.Parsers.split("foo.bar /* incomplete block
comment")

  assert(res.isEmpty)

}

def test8 = {

  val res = ammonite.interp.Parsers.split(

    "val r = (1 until 1000.view.filter(n => n % 3 == 0 || n % 5 == 0)"

  )

  assert(res.isEmpty)

}

def test9 = {

  val res = ammonite.interp.Parsers.split(

    "val r = (1 until 1000).view.filter(n => n % 3 == 0 || n % 5 == 0"

  )

  assert(res.isEmpty)

}
```

If you spotted, that piece of code is repeating itself continually; it should have been written like this:

```
// Sanity check the logic that runs when you press ENTER in the REPL and

// detects whether a set of input lines is...

//

// - Complete, and can be submitted without needing additional input

// - Incomplete, and thus needs additional lines of input from the user


def checkDefined(s: String) = {

  val res = ammonite.interp.Parsers.split(s)

  assert(res.isDefined)

}

def checkEmpty(s: String) = {

  val res = ammonite.interp.Parsers.split(s)

  assert(res.isEmpty)

}

def testDefined = {

  checkDefined("{}")

  checkDefined("foo.bar")

  checkDefined("foo.bar // line comment")

  checkDefined("foo.bar /* block comment */")
```

checkDefined("val r = (1 until 1000).view.filter(n => n % 3 == 0 || n % 5 == 0).sum")

}

def testEmpty = {

checkEmpty("{")

checkEmpty("foo.bar /* incomplete block comment")

checkEmpty("val r = (1 until 1000.view.filter(n => n % 3 == 0 || n % 5 == 0)")

checkEmpty("val r = (1 until 1000).view.filter(n => n % 3 == 0 || n % 5 == 0")

}

This kind of refactoring is normal, the kind that we would do on our code regardless of language. However, what it does is turns heavy repetitive code methods into something rather more elegant that follows DRY, allowing you to see instantly the inputs being tested and their output. You could do this in other ways, for example by defining the Empty cases within an array, the Defined cases within an array and then using asserts to loop over them:

def definedCases = Seq(

"{}",

"foo.bar",

"foo.bar // line comment",

"foo.bar /* block comment */",

"val r = (1 until 1000).view.filter(n => n % 3 == 0 || n % 5 == 0).sum"

)

```
for(s <- definedCases){

  val res = ammonite.interp.Parsers.split(s)

  assert(res.isDefined)

}


def emptyCases = Seq(

  "{",

  "foo.bar /* incomplete block comment",

  "val r = (1 until 1000.view.filter(n => n % 3 == 0 || n % 5 == 0)",

  "val r = (1 until 1000).view.filter(n => n % 3 == 0 || n % 5 == 0"

)


for(s <- emptyCases){

  val res = ammonite.interp.Parsers.split(s)

  assert(res.isEmpty)

}
```

Both of these result in the exact same goal and are joined by many other ways; the style you opt for is entirely up to you. You will hear phrases such as "data-driven", "table-driven", and others with respect to the tests, but the basics are the same – your test cases must be concise and you must be able to see the behavior at a glance. Normal techniques for refactoring are more than capable of helping you to do this without you needing to use any other tools or techniques; that is something you should go into only after you have mastered manual and automated testing.

DSL's for Testing

There are several DSL's (Domain Specific Languages) available to help you to write tests in different ways than how you normally write code. General purpose DSLs should be avoided where possible although they do give a whole new way of writing tests. Take this situation, for example:

Ernie wants to use an ATM to take some money out of his bank account.

Given that he is in possession of a valid Debit or Credit card.

He has an account balance of $150.

When he puts his card into the ATM

And withdraws $50

The ATM should return $50

Leaving him with a balance of $100

Now the outline of that situation would be:

A user takes money from an ATM

Given <Name> is in possession of a valid Debit or credit card

They have an account balance of <OriginalBalance>

They put their card into the ATM

And withdraw >WithdrawalAmount>

The ATM should return <WithdrawalAmount>

Leaving the user with a balance of <NewBalance>

An example of this would be:

| Name | OriginalBalance | WithdrawalAmount | NewBalance |

Ernie	150	50	100	
Simon	175	25	150	
Billy	1500	500	1000	

While other DSLs will allow you to write the code as you would write normal code:

```
"An empty Set" should "have size 0" in {

  assert(Set.empty.size == 0)

}


"A Set" can {
  "empty" should {
   "have size 0" in {

    assert(Set.empty.size == 0)

   }
   "produce NoSuchElementException when head is invoked" in {

    intercept[NoSuchElementException] {

     Set.empty.head

    }
   }
   "should be empty" ignore {

    assert(Set.empty.isEmpty)
```

```
      }

    }

  }
```

val result = 8

result should equal (3) // By default, calls left == right, except for arrays

result should be (3)   // Calls left == right, except for arrays

result should === (3) // By default, calls left == right, except for arrays

val one = 1

one should be < 7   // works for any T when an implicit Ordered[T] exists

one should be <= 7

one should be >= 0

result shouldEqual 3   // Alternate forms for equal and be

result shouldBe 3   // that don't require parentheses

As a rule, these DSLs are often not worth using because they do nothing more than make things more complex and provide indirection. Both make it somewhat more difficult to work out what, exactly, is being tested by a test. The easiest way is just to use your normal for loops, helper methods, and asserts to write your tests. And you also have frameworks like PyTest to fall back on:

$ cat test_foo.py

def test_simple():

```
    result = 8

    assert result == 3
```

```
$ py.test test_foo.py
```

```
================================= FAILURES
=================================

_____ test_simple
_____
```

```
    def test_simple():

        result = 8

        assert result == 3

        assert 8 == 3
```

```
test_foo.py:3: AssertionError
```

```
=========================== 1 failed in 0.03 seconds
===========================
```

Specialized DSLs

While the general DSLs may not be a good idea, there are specialized ones that are. MyPy, for example, has a specialized syntax for defining the input and the output of the test cases:

```
[case testNewSyntaxBasics]
```

```
# flags: --python-version 3.6

x: int

x = 5

y: int = 5


a: str

a = 5  # E: Incompatible types in assignment (expression has type "int",
variable has type "str")

b: str = 5  # E: Incompatible types in assignment (expression has type "int",
variable has type "str")


zzz: int

zzz: str  # E: Name 'zzz' already defined
```

The # E comments are nothing more than asserts; specific errors will be raised by the type checker at specific points when this file is checked.

Example Tests vs Bulk Tests

An example test is a test that takes your code through one example (in some cases, a few examples) using carefully placed asserts to make sure that the code does exactly what it should do. On the other hand, a bulk test is one that floods your code with loads of examples but not examining the behavior of each of the cases as thoroughly. All it really does is checks that your code isn't crashing and is behaving somewhat as it should.

As we saw with the unit and the integration testing, bulk and example tests are at opposite ends of a spectrum and most of the tests fall somewhere in between. For example, the DRY data tests we touched on earlier are in the middle somewhere because they covering multiple input data sets using just one check set.

Example Sets

An example test is exactly what most people think of as automated testing, especially those tests that make use of APIs in specific ways before checking results. One test like that is shown below, testing a trivial parser which will parse just one character:

```
import fastparse.all._

val parseA = P( "a" )


val Parsed.Success(value, successIndex) = parseA.parse("a")

assert(

  value == (),

  successIndex == 1

)


val failure = parseA.parse("b").asInstanceOf[Parsed.Failure]

assert(

  failure.lastParser == ("a": P0),

  failure.index == 0,

  failure.extra.traced.trace == """parseA:1:1 / "a":1:1..."b""""

)
```

As you see from this example, several steps are needed:

- The parser is defined.
- The parser is used for parsing strings that are different.
- The test checks to ensure that success or failure happens where it should.
- The test checks that what is in the success of failure are what is expected.

Example tests are an excellent form of good documentation. On most occasions, just from a couple of examples, you can see quite clearly what a module is doing and how it should be used. Example tests are also good to provide examples of success and failure cases, maybe those on which you already ran manual tests. What they cannot cover are the unexpected cases. You can use the DRY data-driven tests to cover multiple test cases for inputs and outputs but you will come up against a limit of what you can imagine in terms of examples and this is where we discuss bulk testing.

Bulk Tests

A bulk test is used to check a great deal more cases than manual testing alone can check. Instead of running one bit of code one time and seeing what it does, a bulk test will use hundreds, even thousands of outputs to run the code. This way, unexpected cases are covered, those you couldn't add into the example test or forgot about when you did the manual testing.

The nuts of bolts of bulk testing come down to this:

for i in range(0, 9999):

  for j in range(0, 9999):

    result = func(i, j)

    assert(sanity_check(result))

What we did here was to call func with an impressive 100,000,000 outputs. We used a sanity check function that has no idea of every output that could come from each of the inputs, but is able to check simple things like whether the output is negative or not. By the same token, we are also checking to see that func doesn't loop infinitely or throw exceptions on any input.

Bulk tests are used on such high input numbers that they are somewhat slower than example tests. Because of this, the cost of the tests is a good deal higher (more about this later) and that means they should be used carefully. However, when we are testing functionality with large input ranges, when it is hard to choose example tests manually to cover all the cases, bulk tests may well be worth it.

When we have such a large input set to deal with, we cannot define "correct" as being an expected output set of the same size. Instead, we define "correct" as the relationship that you expect as being true between the inputs and outputs, irrespective of the input.

Usually, we will do simple checks in bulk tests, checks that aren't quite as precise as those done in example tests. Running a file parser is not practical to do against a large dump to assert the many thousands of returned values will match exactly to a list of the values we expect. Errors are just as likely when your expected outputs are input as you are when writing the parser logic. However, there are some properties that, regardless of the values output by our program, will also be true. It is these properties that bulk tests are used for testing.

Quite apart from the large amount of data generated using the for loops, there is often quite a lot of useful, real-world data that you can use in your code. For example, a bulk test used to test a program that is designed to gain access to the source code in Python might look like this:

repos = [

  "dropbox/changes",

  "django/django",

```
    "mitsuhiko/flask",

    "zulip/zulip",

    "ansible/ansible",

    "kennethresitz/requests"

]

for repo in repos:

    clone_repo("https://github.com/" + repo)

    for file in os.walk(repo):

        if file.endswith(".py"):

            result = process_python_source(file)

            assert(sanity_check(result))
```

We know that bulk tests are not as fast as example tests; rather than milliseconds, they take seconds, and in some cases, minutes to run. Bulk tests are not quite as easy to read as an example test either; when you don't have many thousands of values being generated or you are not loading test inputs in the thousands from the internet, it won't always be very clear what inputs are cases and what ones are not very interesting.

Cost of Tests

We mentioned this earlier; testing does not come free. After all, they have to be written and, even after that, they will each impose some kind of cost on your testing suite. Each test you write will:

- Slow down your test suite
- Make your test suite less reliable

- Need to be maintained and must be updated as and when your code changes, it must be grepped through whenever you refactor your code, and so on.

You could parallelize the tests using many machines but, while this will speed up the testing, it will cost more in real-money terms, far more than running a test on one machine because each machine has a setup overhead.

If an automated test takes forever to run, isn't reliable, is far too difficult to keep maintained, then it may be considered as not being worth it. These tests can cause more harm than good, and shouldn't really be written; if they have been written they should be deleted.

Mocking

Mocking is a way of isolating certain bits of code that are under test conditions and replacing it with a 'dummy' piece of code. In this way, you can test how certain things are handled, like email responses, without actually receiving the emails in the application. Rather than calling the real implementation, the mock is called and assertions made about what is expected to happen.

The Benefits of Mocking

- Faster – Any test that runs fast is of benefit and this is especially true of functions that are resource-intensive. If you mocked that function it would reduce testing time by not using so many resources.

- No Bad Side-Effects – Let's say that you test a function that calls external APIs. You wouldn't want to make that API call in your tests because you would need to refactor your code whenever the API changed – mocking eliminates that need.

What You Need

Obviously you will need Python 3.x and a virtual environment. We'll set that up specifically for mocking so at your command prompt, type:

python3 -m venv mocking

And then run the following command to activate it:

source mocking/bin/activate

After that, create 2 files – main.py for the code and test.py for the tests

touch main.py test.py

Basic Mocking Usage

Let's imagine that we have a very simple class, something like:

class Calculator:

  def sum(self, a, b):

    return a + b

In this class, we are implementing a single method called sum. The 2 arguments this method takes are a and b, the numbers that are being added and the return should be a + b. So, we could build a very easy test case for this like this:

from unittest import TestCase

from main import Calculator

class TestCalculator(TestCase):

  def setUp(self):

    self.calc = Calculator()

```python
def test_sum(self):

    answer = self.calc.sum(2, 4)

    self.assertEqual(answer, 6)
```

To run this test, you would use this command:

```
python -m unittest
```

And your output should look like this:

```
.

----------------------------------------------------------------------

Ran 1 test in 0.003s

OK
```

Now that was fast but now think about what would happen if our code was more like this:

```python
import time


class Calculator:

    def sum(self, a, b):

        time.sleep(10) # long running process

        return a + b
```

Because we only have a simple example, we simulate a longer running time by using time.sleep(). We now get this output if we run it:

.

————

Ran 1 test in 10.003s

OK

Doing that has slowed things down considerably so its clear that calling the sum method whenever we run a test is not the best idea. In this situation we could use mocking – this would make the test faster and also eliminate the unwanted side-effects.

Now we will refactor this so that, when the test is run, rather than having to call sum, we call a mock sum with behavior that is properly defined:

from unittest import TestCase

from unittest.mock import patch

class TestCalculator(TestCase):

  @patch('main.Calculator.sum', return_value=9)

  def test_sum(self, sum):

    self.assertEqual(sum(2,3), 9)

We imported a called patch form unittest.mock. This puts a mock function in place of the real sum function and the mock function does what we want it to do. In our case, that mock will always return a 9. If we run this, we get:

.

————

Ran 1 test in 0.001s

OK

You might think this is somewhat counter-intuitive but remember what mocking is all about faking a part of the implementation to give you more flexibility.

Another Example

This time, we are going to make our API calls using a library called requests. To get this, type the following at the command prompt:

pip install requests

The code in main.py will look like this:

import requests

class Blog:

   def __init__(self, name):

      self.name = name

```python
    def posts(self):

        response = requests.get("https://jsonplaceholder.typicode.com/posts")


        return response.json()


    def __repr__(self):

        return '<Blog: {}>'.format(self.name)
```

We have defined a class called Blog and given it a method called Posts. When Posts is invoked on Blog, an API call is triggered to jsonplaceholder. What we want to do is mock the API call because it behaves unpredictably and ensures our test only makes sure that the Posts method of Blog will only return posts. To do that, all the posts methods in Blog need to be patched, like this:

```python
from unittest import TestCase

from unittest.mock import patch, Mock




class TestBlog(TestCase):

    @patch('main.Blog')

    def test_blog_posts(self, MockBlog):

        blog = MockBlog()
```

```
blog.posts.return_value = [

    {

        'userId': 1,

        'id': 1,

        'title': 'Test Title',

        'body': 'Far out in the uncharted backwaters of the unfashionable end
of the western spiral arm of the Galaxy\ lies a small unregarded yellow sun.'

    }

]


response = blog.posts()

self.assertIsNotNone(response)

self.assertIsInstance(response[0], dict)
```

As you can see, test_blog_posts has been given the @patch decorator. When this is used to decorate a function, the return is a mock of the method, class or function that was passed to @patch and this is then passed to the decorated function as an argument.

In our case, we called @patch with the main_blog target and a Mock is returned and passed as MockBlog to our test function. Note that any target passed into @patch must be importable from the environment from which we invoke @patch. The main import Blog form should be resolved without any errors.

It is also worth noting that MockBlog is actually the name of a variable that is representing the mock created – we can call it whatever we want. When we call blog.posts on the mock, we get a return of the JSON we defined. All tests should now pass:

.

Ran 1 test in 0.001s

OK

When we test a value that has been mocked rather than a real object, we can make additional assertions about the way the mock is used. For example, we could test the number of times the mock is called, which arguments were used and whether the mock even got called. We'll see some more examples next.

Other Assertions

Continuing with our example, there are some other assertions that we can make on our Mock object:

import main

from unittest import TestCase

from unittest.mock import patch

class TestBlog(TestCase):

  @patch('main.Blog')

  def test_blog_posts(self, MockBlog):

```python
blog = MockBlog()

blog.posts.return_value = [
    {
        'userId': 1,
        'id': 1,
        'title': 'Test Title',
        'body': 'Far out in the uncharted backwaters of the unfashionable end
of the western spiral arm of the Galaxy\ lies a small unregarded yellow sun.'
    }
]

response = blog.posts()
self.assertIsNotNone(response)
self.assertIsInstance(response[0], dict)

# Additional assertions
assert MockBlog is main.Blog # The mock is equivalent to the original

assert MockBlog.called # The mock wasP called
```

blog.posts.assert_called_with() # We called the posts method with no arguments

blog.posts.assert_called_once_with() # We called the posts method once with no arguments

 # blog.posts.assert_called_with(1, 2, 3) - This assertion is False and will fail since we called blog.posts with no arguments

blog.reset_mock() # Reset the mock object

blog.posts.assert_not_called() # After resetting, posts has not been called.

Remember, we said that the mock object will let us test the way it was used by looking at how it was called and the arguments that were passed, rather than just checking the return value.

We can also reset a mock object to a state whereby it hasn't yet been called. This proves useful when we need to make several calls on the mock and each one needs a fresh mock instance on which to run.

Side-Effects

Side-effects are what we want to happen when we call our mock function, commonly, exceptions being raised or another function being called. Let's go back to the sum function from earlier. What would happen if, rather than hard-coding our value for return, we decided we wanted a custom sum function to run instead? The custom function mocks time.sleep() out and leaves us with the sum function that we really want to test. All we do is add a newly defined side_effect to the test:

```python
from unittest import TestCase

from unittest.mock import patch


def mock_sum(a, b):
    # mock sum function without the long running time.sleep
    return a + b


class TestCalculator(TestCase):
    @patch('main.Calculator.sum', side_effect=mock_sum)
    def test_sum(self, sum):
        self.assertEqual(sum(2,3), 5)
        self.assertEqual(sum(7,3), 10)
```

The tests should now pass:

```
.
_____

_____


Ran 1 test in 0.001s


OK
```

This was just a basic look at mocking, enough to give you the idea of what it is all about. You can take this much further if you wish; there is plenty of information to be found on the internet.

Chapter 19: Python Interview Questions

Have you found the job you have long sought? A job in Python? Not sure how you are going to get through the interview? We have 25 of the top questions asked in Python interviews as well as the answers. Keep in mind that every interview is going to be different, as will a job's scope.

These questions are split into two parts – Basic interview questions and Advanced questions:

Basic Questions

These are the very basic questions that you can expect to be asked at any Python interview:

1. What is Python and what are some of its key features?

Python is an interpretive computer programming language, both object-oriented and interactive, and used for scripting. It is designed as the most readable computer language in the world. Its key features are:

- It is interpretive which means you do not need to compile the program before you run it; it is interpreted at runtime by the interpreter, unlike other languages like C.
- It is a dynamically-typed language and this means there is no need to define datatypes for the variables you declare, or anything else for that matter. For example, a variable called x=10 can be declared, followed by x="Hello World" and, providing there are no errors, the datatype will be defined as per the value.
- Python functions are first-class objects.
- Python may be used for many applications, cross-platform, including web applications, big data applications, scientific models, and a whole lot more.

2. What is the difference between Python Lists and Tuples?

The single biggest difference between them is that a list is mutable, while a tuple is immutable. This means once a tuple has been created, the value cannot be edited or changed in any way; in a list, the value may be edited. The main differences are:

Tuples	**Lists**
Tuples are sequences of objects, immutable datatypes, mutable	Lists are very versatile
Parentheses are used for tuple syntax syntax	Square brackets are used for list
Tuples are fixed in length	Lists may be variable in length

3. What Operator Types Does Python Use?

Python uses the following types of operators:

Arithmetic Operators:

- Addition operator (+) for adding values
- Subtraction operator (-) for subtracting the value on the right from the value on the left
- Multiplication operator (*) for multiplying values
- Division operator (/) for dividing the left value by the right value
- Modulus operator (%) for dividing the left operand by the right operand and returning the remainder
- Exponent operator (**) for performing exponential value calculations

Relational Operators:

- == - if a pair of values are equal, the condition is true
- != - if two operand values are not equal, the condition is true
- <> - if a pair of values do not equal one another, the condition is true
- > - if the operand on the left is greater than the operand on the right, the condition is true

- < - if the operand on the left is less than the operand on the right, the condition is true
- >= - if the operand on the left is equal to or greater than the operand on the right, the condition is true
- <= - if the operand on the left is equal to or less than the operand on the right, the condition is true

Assignment Operators:

- = - Add
- += - Add And
- -= - Subtract And
- *= - Multiply And
- /= - Divide And
- %- -Modulus And
- **= - Exponent And

4. What is the maximum length a Python Identifier can be?

There isn't any maximum length because a Python identifier may be any length.

What do we mean by Python Decorators?

Python decorators are used for the modification or injection of code into classes or functions. By using a decorator, we can log calls and we can check to see what permissions are there.

5. What is a Python Dictionary?

A Python Dictionary is a list of the datatypes built-in to Python.

6. What is Python Memory Management?

Memory management in Python is carried out using the private heap space. Every data structure and every object in Python can be found in a private heap.

7. In one sentence, explain Python.

Python is one of the most powerful and modern of the interpreted computer languages, containing exceptions, modules, objects, threads, and with a memory management property.

8. Explain Python Interpretation

Python interpretation is nothing more complicated than the source code being used to run Python.

9. Explain the Python rules for global and local variables.

A local variable is one that has been assigned a value within the function while a global variable is one that has been defined externally to the function. A local variable can only be accessed from inside the function while a global variable can be accessed externally.

10. How are global values shared in Python?

To share a global variable, a config file is created and the variable to be shared is stored inside it.

11. How are Keyword or Optional Parameters passed between functions in Python?

To pass parameters we use the * specifier and the ** specifier from the parameter list attached to the function.

Advanced Questions

Now we move onto some of the more advanced questions you may be asked during an interview.

1. What are the different Python sequence types?

These are strings, lists, Unicode strings, xrange objects, buffers, and tuples.

2. What is the Python Lambda Form?

We use the Lambda keyword to create small functions that are anonymous, random, and can be thrown away.

3. What is Pickling?

Pickle is one of the standard Python modules used to serialize and de-serialize object structures.

4. How do we copy Python objects?

We can use two methods to copy objects in Python – shallow copy, which is where a compound object is constructed and object references placed into it, and deep copy, where a compound object is constructed and object copies are recursively inserted.

5. are Strings converted to Numbers?

Python contains many functions that we can use to convert datatypes and to convert strings to numbers and you would use the int or float functions.

6. How do we use a Python Script to send an email?

By importing the module called smtplib, an SMTP client-session object may be defined to send email using a script.

7. What command do we use to exit out of the Help command prompt?

We use the command called 'quit'

8. What do the Python Methods of sub(), subn() and split() do?

Split() uses its own regex pattern to split a specified string into a list. Sub() will find every substring that contains a match to the regex pattern and replaces the string. Subn() is much like sub(); the new string is returned with all the other replacements.

9. How do we display text content of a file in reverse order?

The file must first be converted into a list; reversed() is then used to reverse that list.

10. are the ODBS Modules?

The Python OBDS modules are:

- PythonWin ODBC
- MxODBC
- Pyodbc

11. What are the append() and extend() Python methods for?

The append() method is to add elements at the end while extend() will add the elements from a different list to the end.

12. What is TKlner?

TKlner is one of the Python libraries, a tool used for GUI development.

13. What is the difference between Python and Java?

The main difference is that Python datatypes are dynamically-typed while Java's are statically typed.

Hopefully these questions will give you a good head start when you attend your hard-fought-for Python interview.

Conclusion

Well, we finally reached the end of this guide and a long one it was too. But don't be disappointed when I tell you that we only really covered the basics as far as each subject is concerned. The idea behind the guide was to give you an overview in terms of learning the Python programming language and what you can do with it.

In Part 1, we started by looking at the Python language, going in-depth into data structure and algorithms. These are the fundamentals of Python and we learned how the two combine to help with Machine Learning. We also looked at Python variables, control structures and lists, along with objects and conditional statements. Data types followed that along with some internal modules before we moved on to the design of algorithms. Data structures followed that, primarily linked lists, stacks and queues. More algorithms came next, showing us the first steps in making sense out of vast amounts of data. This moved us neatly on to the next part.

In Part 2, we looked at Machine Learning. We learned what machine learning is and what the different types are. We looked at Sci-kit learn, the best Python machine learning toolkit you could ever have. We looked at classification and training, including training errors, moving on to preprocessing of data, clustering and the conversion of noisy text into a meaningful vector that could be clustered. We also learned about debugging classifiers, feature extraction and how they impact the performance of a classifier and we looked at several different algorithms.

In Part 3, we discussed Django and learned what it is and how to use it. We covered model-view-controller patterns and views and URL-confs before moving onto dynamic content. We looked at web templates, forms, content and dictionaries and then moved to tags and filters. Throughout this section, we built our first website using Django, learning how it all goes together and works seamlessly in the process.

Next we discussed ArcGIS and we learned what GIS is and how arcpy works. We learned about script execution and the developmental environments needed to create these scripts. Then we moved onto using the ArcGIS ModelBuilder, how to use it to create analyses and export scripts; we learned more about autogenerated code, how to generalize it and how to add functions that we can reuse elsewhere. We learned about model cursors, cursor parameters, and how to use geometry objects in arcpy. We looked at turning scripts into a permanent script tool that can be shared, before moving onto arcpy.mapping. We also learned how to create functions that can be reused and modules. We ended the section with a look at common ArcGIS for arcpy Desktop Advanced extensions.

We then discussed some of the different methods of testing, something that is vital to the success of your code, software or app. We discussed why testing was important, what TDD and BDD are, along with DSLs. We talked about automated testing, what it is used for and the differences between unit and integration testing. Finally, we went over some examples of using Mocking in Python as a way of making your tests more efficient.

Python is a great language to learn and I would suggest that if any of the sections in this guide particularly interest you that you take the time to learn more. There are plenty of online resources, books, and tutorials that you can use to learn more.

Remember, no matter what it is, practice really does make perfect and if you can grasp the fundamentals of all these areas of Python, you will be light years ahead of most people on the planet.

References

https://djangobook.com/

https://docs.djangoproject.com

https://interactivepython.org

https://pythonschool.net

https://medium.com

https://mathworks.com

https://towardsdatasience.com

https://arcgis.com

https://esri.com

https://pro.arcgis.com

https://agiledata.org

https://news.codeacademy.com

https://code.likeagirl.com

https://github.com/PacktPublishing/Python-Data-Structures-and-Algorithms

https://smartbear.com

https://realpython.com

https://semaphoreci.com

https://fullstackpython.com

https://jacobian.org

https://blog.fugue.co

http://pythontutor.com

www.ingramcontent.com/pod-product-compliance
Lightning Source LLC
LaVergne TN
LVHW080109070326
832902LV00015B/2489